MW01284320

JACKSON SCHOOL PUBLICATIONS

IN INTERNATIONAL STUDIES

JACKSON SCHOOL PUBLICATIONS

IN INTERNATIONAL STUDIES

Senator Henry M. Jackson was convinced that the study of the history, cultures, political systems, and languages of the world's major regions was an essential prerequisite for wise decision making in international relations. In recognition of his deep commitment to higher education and advanced scholarship, this series of publications has been established through the generous support of the Henry M. Jackson Foundation, in cooperation with the Henry M. Jackson School of International Studies, and the University of Washington Press.

THE PRODUCTION OF

# Hindu-Muslim Violence

IN CONTEMPORARY INDIA

PAUL R. BRASS

UNIVERSITY OF WASHINGTON PRESS

Seattle and London

This publication was supported in part by the Jackson School
Publications Fund, established through the generous support of the
Henry M. Jackson Foundation and other donors, in cooperation with
the Henry M. Jackson School of International Studies
and the University of Washington Press.

Copyright © 2003 by the University of Washington Press
Designed by Pamela Canell
Printed in the United States of America

Library of Congress Cataloging-in-Publication Data
Brass, Paul R.
The production of Hindu-Muslim Violence in contemporary India /
Paul R. Brass.
p. cm. — (Jackson School publications in international studies)
Includes bibliographical references and index.
ISBN 0-295-98506-2 (alk. paper)
1. Communalism—India—Aligarh.
2. Riots—India—Aligarh.
3. Hindus—India—Aligarh.
4. Muslims—India—Aligarh.
I. Title. II. Series.
DS422.C64 B73 2003    954'.2—DC21    2002027192

The paper used in this publication is acid-free and recycled from 10 percent
post-consumer and at least 50 percent pre-consumer waste. It meets the minimum
requirements of American National Standard for Information Sciences—
Permanence of Paper for Printed Library Materials, ANSI z39.48–1984.♾♲

In memory of my teacher,

MYRON WEINER,

ever a source of inspiration,

ever a friend

# CONTENTS

# ABBREVIATIONS USED IN THIS BOOK

| | |
|---|---|
| ADM | additional district magistrate |
| AMU | Aligarh Muslim University |
| AMUSU | Aligarh Muslim University Students Union |
| BJP | Bharatiya Janata Party |
| BJS | Bharatiya Jan Sangh |
| BKD | Bharatiya Kranti Dal |
| BLD | Bharatiya Lok Dal |
| BSF | Border Security Force |
| BSP | Bahujan Samaj Party |
| CPI | Communist Party of India |
| CRPF | Central Reserve Police Force |
| DM | district magistrate |
| DSP | deputy superintendent of police |
| FIR | First Information Report |
| INC | Indian National Congress |
| ISI | Inter Services Intelligence |
| LA | Legislative Assembly |
| LS | Lok Sabha (Indian Parliament) |
| MLA | Member, Legislative Assembly |
| MP | Member of Parliament |

| | |
|---|---|
| PAC | Provincial Armed Constabulary |
| PUCL | People's Union for Civil Liberties |
| RPI | Republican Party of India |
| RSS | Rashtriya Swayamsevak Sangh |
| SO | station officer |
| SP | Samajwadi Party |
| SSP | senior superintendent of police |
| SUA | standard urban area |
| U.P. | Uttar Pradesh (United Provinces before Independence) |
| VHP | Vishwa Hindu Parishad |

# MAPS, FIGURES, AND TABLES

# PREFACE AND ACKNOWLEDGMENTS

This book follows upon my last two books on collective violence, *Riots and Pogroms* and *Theft of an Idol,* published in 1996 and 1997, respectively. Although temporally earlier than this book, many of the ideas contained in them were developed first in my work on riots in Aligarh. It was here, during my field work in 1983, that I first developed the notion of the "institutionalized riot system" as a central factor in the production of Hindu-Muslim violence.

I had originally intended to include my work on Hindu-Muslim riots in Aligarh in *Theft of an Idol,* but concluded that the material was too extensive to go alongside the other case studies in that volume. My next thought was to produce a book focusing specifically on Hindu-Muslim violence based on my research in several districts of Uttar Pradesh (U.P.), including especially Meerut and Kanpur, on which I have collected very considerable materials over the years, as in Aligarh. However, after looking over my interview data in Aligarh over thirty-eight years and digging into boxes of documentary material and election data that I had collected in the same period, I decided finally on a book in which the city of Aligarh, standing in for so many other cities and towns in India, would form the center. That decision has allowed me to do something that I believe is unprecedented in studies of collective violence, namely, to carry out a diachronic study at a single site, keeping my analysis sharply focused—so I hope the reader will agree—on the same set of questions and problems throughout. Although studies have been done of riot-prone cities (such as, for example, Detroit) that analyze each riot in succession, those I have looked at treat each riot as something new and different from its predecessor. Here, on the contrary, I have discovered continuity, extension, and development of what I intuitively felt in 1983 was an institutionalized system of riot production. I now feel that I have established my case in this book and that the findings herein can be generalized to other parts of India and to other times and places in the world.

I first visited Aligarh in the winter of 1961–62 to carry out field research for my Ph.D. dissertation on the Congress Party in Uttar Pradesh. That was a different time in many respects. Aligarh then was a relatively small town with a population around 185,000, now over half a million. The Congress was the dominant party in the district. Many of the prominent politicians I interviewed then are now gone. Although party politics then was not lacking in volatility, bitter conflict, and some violence, it appears relatively genteel in retrospect compared to the atmosphere of recent years. During the past twenty years, a new generation of militant Hindu politicians has risen to prominence; I have met most of the leading persons among them. I have also maintained and extended my contact with politicians from all other political parties and organizations in Aligarh, Hindu and Muslim alike, and with members of the faculty of the Aligarh Muslim University. In most of my visits to Aligarh, I have always also interviewed key members of the civilian administration and police, and many subordinate civilian and police officials as well.

Aligarh was very different in 1961–62 in many other respects as well. It was a relatively much quieter and more peaceful place in general, not only with respect to incidents of violence. Persons of prominence from the pre-Independence era were still present in those days, including not only most senior Congressmen, but men like the Nawab of Chhatari, former leader of the National Agriculturalist Party and later a member of the Muslim League, and A. M. Khwaja, a leading so-called nationalist Muslim, and others of similar aristocratic or landlord backgrounds. Upper-caste and upper-class persons dominated in all spheres of life, something that has changed considerably since then with the rise to self-assertion of the middle and lower castes in politics. Most of the senior politicians spoke good English then, fewer do so now. One could breathe the air everywhere in the absence of the internal combustion engine, which now pollutes the atmosphere even in this place far from any major industrial conurbation.

The Aligarh Muslim University (AMU) in the Civil Lines area of the city, like the whole area around it, was then a kind of oasis, a quiet, appealing, and peaceful place, though the AMU simmered internally with conflicts between so-called conservative/communal and progressive/Communist faculty. The AMU now has the appearance more of a fortification, surrounded with high walls in an effort to keep out rowdy, criminal, and other unfriendly elements from the campus. It is at the same time a place of internal turmoil, where confrontation and violence between groups of students, students and faculty,

faculty against each other, and students and faculty against the vice-chancellor have occurred repeatedly over the years.

I had selected Aligarh as one of five districts for my research in 1961–62 specifically for the purpose of analyzing how the Congress functioned in an environment of Hindu-Muslim tension. As if to demonstrate the validity of my selection of this district for that purpose, my visit, between December 25 and January 20, occurred between the riots of October 1961 and the General Elections of 1962, held in February. I returned to Aligarh again in September 1962 to continue the research on that district in the aftermath of the elections that were influenced decisively in the city by the riots that had occurred the previous October. I did not visit Aligarh again for seventeen years. Since then, I have visited the city and the district numerous times, for short trips during elections when I toured U.P. in connection with several election studies projects, for an extended research period in August 1983, and since then on several occasions when I have returned to India for research, conferences, and workshops. On more than a few occasions in those years, I arrived to find that another riot had recently occurred, or, as in 1990–91, I arrived just as the great riots of December 1991–January 1992 were coming to an end.

My experiences in this latter respect were mirrored in others of the districts that I have visited repeatedly during the past thirty-eight years. So, during these later years, I increasingly built in to my research visits to north India more focused and increasingly systematic questions, interviews, and data on the reasons for the recrudescence of Hindu-Muslim violence. I continued this practice during the writing of this manuscript in my most recent visits to Aligarh in November 1997 and March–April 1999.

I have presented earlier versions of aspects of my research on Hindu-Muslim violence in Aligarh at many universities, conferences, and workshops between 1987 and 2000, far too many to note here. It is more important that I note and acknowledge with appreciation colleagues and others who have assisted me in the final preparation of this rather complex manuscript. At the top of the list are two persons who read the entire manuscript in earlier versions. David Laitin read the first version when it was several hundred pages longer and still in preliminary form. Kanchan Chandra read a complete, but still imperfect, second draft. The comments of both were indispensable to me in making the revisions that preceded my submission of the manuscript for review by the University of Washington Press. Elizabeth Mann read several chapters of the earliest version of the manuscript and her comments also led me to make several changes. Walter Andersen and Richard Flathman gave me the benefit of their comments on particular chapters. The two anonymous reviewers for the press and Michael Duckworth, the acquisitions editor, will, I hope, also note that I have taken their criticisms and suggestions seriously. Of course, I am alone responsible for the arguments and points of view adopted as well as any errors that may be found herein.

Naresh Saxena facilitated my visits to Aligarh during the past twenty years. Kanchan Chandra and Violette Graff provided me with valuable maps of Aligarh that I had not been able to obtain. Iqbal A. Ansari and Asghar Ali Engineer cleared up in correspondence with me a few details on which I needed information. Several persons have accompanied me to Aligarh over the years to assist me in moving about the city and interpreting when necessary; they include Pallav Kumar, Gyan and Jayati Chaturvedi, Sumit Mehta, and Aftab Ahmad. Arup Singh has been unfailingly helpful to me during all my recent visits to India.

My past practice in citing interviews has been to provide simply the date and place of the interview. I have modified that practice somewhat in this manuscript. I have masked most of my sources for interviews. However, I no longer invariably promise my respondents confidentiality, and carry out the great majority of my interviews with a tape recorder plainly in view. Since so much of my material comprises direct quotes that lose part of their significance if the identity of the respondent is masked, I felt it important not to do so in such cases where no confidentiality was promised.

I have been engaged more or less continuously in the research and writing of this manuscript for the past four years, that is, since my teaching responsibilities at the University of Washington ended in June 1997. In that period, others also have been extremely helpful to me. They include Irene Joshi, since retired as the South Asia librarian at the University of Washington, and her successor in that position, Alan Grosenheider. Michael Shapiro has helped me from time to time in translating some lines from Hindi newspapers and from my tape-recorded interviews. Jere Bacharach, Director of the Jackson School of International Studies, University of Washington, made available a small grant from Rockefeller funds, which provided partial funding for the drawing of the maps included herein, prepared by Guirong Zhou. Fred Nick, director of the Center for Social Science Computation and Research at the University of Washington, and his staff, especially Dixielynn Gleason, have been a tremendous help to me on countless occasions with computer and software problems of all kinds, including recovery from a total and irretrievable crash of my previous computer ten minutes before the Seattle earthquake of February 28, 2001, that hit just as I was trying to plug my portable computer with the backups for this book into the wall under my table. Thanks to the portable computer, a few other backup disks, and Fred's help in deciding on the purchase of a new computer and getting me through the process of reestablishing my work on new software, this book is now presented here.

Susan Halon bore patiently my apparently unending absorption in the details and complexities involved in the construction of this book. She travelled with me to India and to Aligarh during my last two visits there and took all but three of the photographs included herein.

While this book was being written, my teacher, Myron Weiner, passed away on June 3, 1999. It was from him that I first learned the methods of field research that I have practiced during the past four decades. It was under his supervision that I carried out the first field research in Aligarh and the other districts of U.P. in 1961–62. He was himself then also in India, carrying out the research for his book on the Indian National Congress. He advised, helped, and encouraged me then and remained a source of inspiration and a friend to me for the rest of his life, even when my work went off in directions and with methods and modes of analysis different from his own. I think he would have liked this book and I dedicate it to him.

P.R.B.
Seattle, Washington
December 16, 2001

THE PRODUCTION OF

# Hindu-Muslim Violence

IN CONTEMPORARY INDIA

PART I

*Introduction*

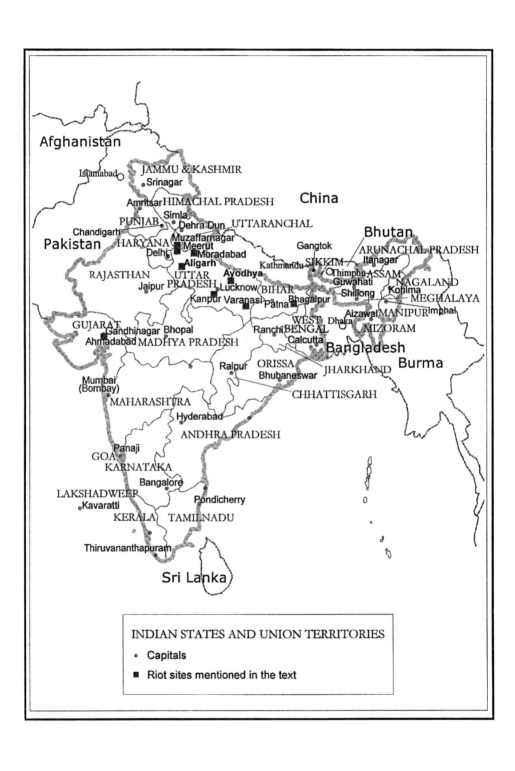

INDIAN STATES AND UNION TERRITORIES

∘ Capitals

■ Riot sites mentioned in the text

# 1 / Explaining Communal Violence

Among the many paradoxes and contradictions that must confront observers of India is the competing imagery of violence and non-violence, symbolized in two recurrent representations of that country. One is the image that has been flashed countless times during the past half-century in the media and the cinema of the bloody riots that occurred immediately before and after Independence as a consequence of the events associated with the simultaneous partition of the country into two new, mutually hostile sovereign states that immediately fought their first war and have since fought two more. The second image is that of the saintly Mahatma Gandhi traversing the country for decades proclaiming the message of nonviolence and devising strategies of nonviolent opposition to British rule that have since been adopted round the world by the weak to fight against exploitation and discrimination by the strong and privileged. The two images merge in Attenborough's film, *Gandhi*, when Gandhi appears in Noakhali in the province of Bengal during the pre-partition riots there to end the killing. He is shown lying on his bed, fasting to death against the violence, which is brought to an end as the repentant, weeping murderers deposit their weapons at his side.

Forty-five years after Independence, the world was presented with another image of India, that of violent mobs of Hindus descending upon the old, mainly Hindu religious town of Ayodhya to climb upon a five-hundred-year-old mosque to destroy it. This image was then followed by the pictures flashed round the world of Bombay in flames from the riots that followed after the destruction of the mosque a thousand miles away. Few people outside India, however, knew that similar riots also took place in cities and towns in large parts of the country, in which Muslims, having seen one of their mosques destroyed on BBC television or having otherwise learned of it, were now being

slaughtered, allegedly because they came out into the streets in shock and outrage and engaged in riotous behavior.

Even fewer people—indeed, only specialists—know that Hindu-Muslim
riots and anti-Muslim pogroms have been endemic in India since Independence.[1] They have occurred and recurred in many cities and towns throughout the country, but especially in the northern and western parts. Their
frequency and intensity have fluctuated from time to time and place to place,
but hardly a month passes in India in which a Hindu-Muslim riot does not
occur that is large enough to be noted in the press. But there are also many
such events on a smaller scale that occur much more frequently. Indeed, it
is likely that not a day passes without many instances of quarrels, fights, and
fracases between Hindus and Muslims in different places in India, many of
which carry the potential for conversion into large-scale riots in which arson,
looting, and killing may take place.

Neither in December 1992, nor on most of the occasions between Independence and 1992 in which so much destruction of people's lives, homes,
and property have occurred, have many saintly figures appeared to quell the
violence. In fact, both these images—of frenzied, murderous masses in India
and saintly figures moving about spreading their message of nonviolence as
a cure for their frenzy—are part of a grand discourse of violence that I hope
to undermine in this book. Riots are not explained by the spontaneous furies
of mad mobs nor are there any weeping murderers among them nor can they
normally be stopped by saints.

On the contrary, it is a principal argument of this book that the whole political order in post-Independence north India and many, if not most of its leading as well as local actors—more markedly so since the death of Nehru—have
become implicated in the persistence of Hindu-Muslim riots. These riots have
had concrete benefits for particular political organizations as well as larger
political uses. Hindu-Muslim opposition, tensions, and violence have provided the principal justification and the primary source of strength for the
political existence of some local political organizations in many cities and
towns in north India linked to a family of militant Hindu nationalist organizations whose core is an organization founded in 1925, known as the Rashtriya
Swayamsevak Sangh (RSS). Included in this family, generally called the *Sangh
Parivar,* are an array of organizations devoted to different tasks: mass mobilization, political organization, recruitment of students, women, and workers, and paramilitary training. The leading political organization in this family,
originally called the Jan Sangh, is now the Bharatiya Janata Party (BJP), currently (2001) the predominant party in India's governing coalition. All the

organizations in the RSS family of militant Hindu organizations adhere to a broader ideology of *Hindutva,* of Hindu nationalism that theoretically exists independently of Hindu-Muslim antagonisms, but in practice has thrived only when that opposition is explicitly or implicitly present.[2]

The benefits for the consolidation of Hindu communal sentiment behind the organizations of militant Hindu nationalism in the RSS family of organizations and the Shiv Sena in the western state of Maharashtra (which also adheres to an ideology of militant Hindu nationalism) have been great: they have served to bring these parties to power in numerous states in India outside the south and have at last brought them to power at the Center,[3] in New Delhi, as well. These formations have launched numerous Hindu-oriented campaigns since Independence in which the Muslims have been portrayed directly as obstacles to the achievement of national aspirations or have been clearly assumed to be the main obstacle. The two most massive such campaigns were the cow protection movement of the mid-1960s and the Ayodhya movement of the mid-1980s and early 1990s. In the former movement, there was no Muslim structure to stand as the centerpiece to be brought down, but, obviously, it was the Muslims of India, who slaughtered and ate beef, whose opposition was implied. The political context at that time, however, did not provide the same potential benefits for the RSS family of organizations as the context that existed in the 1980s during the Ayodhya movement.[4] For, after a brief resurgence in its strength after the assassination of Indira Gandhi in 1984 and the installation of her son, Rajiv Gandhi, as prime minister, the Indian National Congress, India's dominant ruling party since Independence, began a severe decline in its fortunes in U.P., the most important state in the country, which has since spread to most of the other Indian states as well.

The years 1988–89 were to mark the beginning of the end of Congress dominance in the state and the country. In a bitterly contested national election campaign centered around north Indian personalities, the Congress was defeated by a coalition of non-Congress parties in 1989. When that coalition itself disintegrated and new elections were held in 1991, the leader of the Congress, Rajiv Gandhi, was assassinated in the midst of the campaign; the Congress was nevertheless once again returned to power under Prime Minister P. V. Narasimha Rao, whose government lasted its full parliamentary term till 1996. While the Congress was weakening even during its last term in power after losing its popular leadership from the Nehru-Gandhi family, and while its rivals among the left parties were unable to consolidate their strength and emerge as a stable alternative governing force, the militant Hindu organizations, including the BJP, were gathering strength from the mass mobilizations associated with the Ayodhya movement.

The Ayodhya movement made explicit use of a Muslim structure, a mosque, which stood for a religion that militant Hindus—and many non-militant Hindus as well, for that matter—disdain as foreign, immoral, and evil. But, even more important, just five years short of the celebration of India's fiftieth year of independence from British rule, this mosque stood in the minds of its enemies as the mark of an earlier "slavery," as they called it, of Hindu subjection to Muslim rule. The movement also created martyrs, especially after the killing of sixteen Hindus in Ayodhya in 1990, who were then portrayed in a grossly exaggerated and fantastic manner as the latest in a long series of martyrs to the cause of the removal of the defiling mosque from its place in the Hindu town of Ayodhya on the allegedly sacred ground of the god, Ram. This movement was also accompanied throughout north India by deliberate provocations directed against Muslims, whose effect was certain to bring down violence upon them, as it did massively in many cities and towns in northern and western India between 1989 and 1993.[5] The movement also contributed significantly, along with other changes taking place in India at the time—particularly the controversy over reservation of places in public sector jobs for a large section of India's Hindus commonly referred to as "backward castes"—to a major transformation in the sources of strength of the BJP, to such an extent as to turn the BJP of the 1991 and 1996 elections in its northern India stronghold state of Uttar Pradesh (U.P.) into a virtually new and much stronger political formation than ever before.[6] It should be clear enough by now, therefore, how valuable Hindu-Muslim opposition, antagonism, and violence have been to the fortunes of the BJP.

But Hindu-Muslim riots in India obviously did not begin only with the Ayodhya movement. They have been a recurring feature of modern Indian politics for nearly a century. Moreover, there have been periods during which Hindu-Muslim rioting has occurred in what are commonly referred to as great "waves" or "chains." These periods include especially the years 1923–27, after the collapse of the noncooperation/Khilafat movement against British rule in India in which Hindu and Muslim political and religious organizations and groups worked together; 1946–48, when massive waves of rioting and massacres preceded, accompanied, and followed the partition of India and the consequent formation of the two successor states to the British Raj of India and Pakistan; and the succession of riots that occurred between 1989 and 1993 during the Ayodhya movement.

But it would be a mistake to confine our gaze only to these great waves of rioting, for there has never been a period in modern Indian history, most especially in the north, when Hindu-Muslim riots have not occurred. It is a crucial part of the argument to be developed and demonstrated in this volume that the maintenance of communal tensions, accompanied from time to time by lethal rioting at specific sites, is essential for the maintenance of militant Hindu nationalism, but also has uses for other political parties, organizations, and even the state and central governments. It is necessary, therefore, for a fuller understanding of the phenomenon of the persistence of Hindu-Muslim rioting and its manifestation from time to time in great waves, to examine as well its appearance in relatively quieter times and at sites where it is endemic.

My first question, therefore, is: why do Hindu-Muslim communal riots persist in India? Or, put another way, how have such riots become endemic in that country? Consider in this connection the available data on Hindu-Muslim riots for the period 1960–93.[7] Using a restrictive definition of riot-proneness, Varshney and Wilkinson have pointed out that the incidence of Hindu-Muslim communal riots in India is skewed towards urban India in general and towards 24 cities in particular. There are, therefore, only certain sites in which riots may be considered endemic. At the same time, while the incidence and timing of Hindu-Muslim riots vary from region to region and city to city, it is not incorrect to consider India as a whole a country in which Hindu-Muslim riots persist and are endemic. First of all, the number of such riots in the worst-hit cities account for only half the total incidents in the country. Second, even the worst-hit cities are scattered throughout a very large part of the country, in ten of its states. Third, from time to time, new sites that have either never before experienced large-scale Hindu-Muslim riots, or have not experienced them in several decades, have entered or reentered the lists.

Given the situation just described, a satisfactory explanation of the phenomenon of persistence must account both for the dispersion of rioting in India in time and space and for its concentration in particular sites. The explanation to be provided in this volume will attempt to encompass India as a whole through an analysis of the discursive framework of communalism that affects, however differentially, all parts of the country where Hindus and Muslims abide side by side. However, I will focus the detailed analysis of riot production on a single site, the town of Aligarh, where riots have persisted since Independence, and which stands as a choice exemplar of riot persistence for other reasons as well, especially because of the presence there of the Aligarh Muslim University (AMU). The Pakistan movement itself grew out of conditions in U.P., and the AMU was one of its storm centers. Consequently, in the minds of many Hindus, the AMU stands in for the Muslims of India, for Partition and the creation of Pakistan, and for so many of the ills that afflict Indian society. Without the presence of the AMU, the Jan Sangh, the BJP, and other local communal groups would have had greater difficulty in establishing a strong presence in this city.

A second question is: why do Hindu-Muslim riots ebb and flow, appearing now here, now there at different times? As noted above, Hindu-Muslim riots sometimes occur in what appear to be great waves that spread from town to town and region to region of the country, affecting a great number of sites either simultaneously or one after the other. Those great waves are usually associated with large-scale political movements that precede them. On the other hand, there has never been an extended period of time in India since Independence when Hindu-Muslim riots have not occurred in some town or other, apparently unrelated to any broader movement in a region or in the country as a whole. So, there is persistence as well as variation in the country as a whole and at particular sites.

A third question concerns how it happens that large-scale violent events, in which mostly Muslims are killed, mostly by the police, get classified in the press, by the authorities, and by the public as riots rather than pogroms. I have argued elsewhere that there are two types of struggles that take place when riots occur. The first is the violent conflict between riotous groups and between rioters and the police. The second is the rhetorical struggle that takes place afterwards to control the interpretation of the riot, determine its meaning, explain the violence.[8] It is at this stage that classification occurs. However, such classification is often automatic: often one explanation emerges dominantly, and sometimes a hegemonic consensus arises that lasts for a long time in the form of a master narrative that requires no knowledge of facts on the ground for its immediate acceptance.[9] Such a master narrative exists in India, comprising two key elements. First, riots in general are perceived as spontaneous occurrences that arise out of petty quarrels that become converted into mass frenzies through the spread of rumors that exaggerate the precipitating incident. Second, Hindu-Muslim riots in particular are said to arise from the prejudices and hostilities that exist between these two religious groups, such that there is a natural tendency to expand any quarrel between a Hindu and a Muslim into a riot. In order to prevent such conversions of quarrels into riots, it is commonly urged, peace committees and other forms of intercommunal cooperation need to be developed to combat them. It is in this way, almost automatically and without reflection or challenge, that trivial incidents involving Hindus and Muslims that precede large-scale riots are said to have been their cause. The automatic mechanism that produces such an explanation is based upon the deep-seated belief that popular passions are aroused as much by a preexisting history of communal antagonisms and a pervasive atmosphere of tension between Hindus and Muslims as by the actual or perceived circumstances surrounding the precipitating incident. It is my purpose in this volume to demonstrate that neither the prior history of communalism nor the immediate circumstances surrounding the so-called precipitating incident, nor the two alleged causes combined, provide a satisfactory explanation for the outbreak of large-scale Hindu-Muslim riots or anti-Muslim pogroms. On the contrary, the decisive factor is the action that takes place before the precipitating incidents and immediately thereafter, action that is often planned and organized and that fills the intermediate space and time between past history and immediate circumstance.

The fourth question asks: what interests are served and what power relations are maintained as a consequence of the wide acceptance of the reality of popular communal antagonisms and the inevitability of communal violence?

These four questions may be summed up in a nutshell as issues of persistence, differential incidence/timing, classification/meaning, and power. They are large questions that require diverse approaches. They raise issues of causality, function, and discourse. Issues of persistence and incidence/timing seem to require causal and/or functional analysis: why do riots persist, occur here and not there, occur now and not then? Whose interests are served by the occurrence, persistence, or disappearance of Hindu-Muslim riots? The struggle over meaning, explanations, and power relations requires attention to discourse. To what extent is there a communal discourse that accounts for the persistence of communal rioting over time by providing a framework of explanation and meaning, an ordering of relations between Hindus and Muslims, and an ordering of the respective relations of these two categorical groups to the state? Further, to what extent does such a discourse itself contribute to the persistence of the violence that it claims to explain? I will make use of methods appropriate to each type of analysis in an attempt to arrive at as full a picture as possible of the mechanisms that lead to the production of riots in India and of the dynamic processes that precede them, produce them, and explain them after their occurrence. The framework that unites the various themes and questions pursued herein is a theoretical formulation, a kind of ideal type, of the manner in which large-scale riots are produced in sites where riots are endemic, whether in Aligarh, other parts of India, or other parts of the world.

## THE DYNAMICS OF RIOT PRODUCTION

The primary approach taken in this volume to the dynamic process of riot production has some affinity with theories of collective action and social movements, developed most notably in the works of Tilly, Tarrow, McAdam and others of their colleagues.[10] That affinity as well as the differences were noted in part in *Theft of an Idol*,[11] but will be restated and elaborated briefly here. In agreement with this group of scholars, riots are conceived in this book as a form of collective action, one among a number of repertoires of collective action that developed in India primarily in the late nineteenth and twentieth centuries. As much, therefore, as the great movements of noncooperation and civil disobedience and a whole host of other nonviolent forms of agitation, demonstration, and protest, riots have become a common and even an anticipated form of collective action.

The term "anticipated" is used here in two senses. People expect riots to occur from time to time and in certain places in India without being able to predict exactly when and where they will occur, but they also anticipate and expect riots during particular types of mass mobilization. Euphemistic terms have even been developed for the latter, such as "direct action." A different rhetoric is also used during movements in which Hindu-Muslim violence is anticipated, an inflammatory rhetoric of hostility with scarcely-veiled encouragement to listeners to act out against the other community. Most commonly, the rhetoric is laced with words that encourage its members not to put up any longer with the attacks of the other but to *retaliate* against *their* aggression. There are also specific forms of action that are designed to provoke the other community into aggressive action, which is then met with a stronger retaliatory response. These forms include, especially, processions through neighborhoods inhabited primarily by persons from the other community, and the insistence by processionists that shopkeepers "down their shutters" and close their shops to honor whatever demand is being made during a demonstration. In the latter case, a demonstration ostensibly directed against the state or local administration may turn into a communal riot.

Consistent with the Tilly-Tarrow conceptualization of the development of social movements, every great wave of rioting in modern India has been preceded by new mobilizing tactics that become integrated into the new repertoire and promote violence. For example, between 1923 and 1927, the rioting was accompanied by competitive movements for the conversion and reconversion of Hindus and Muslims in many localities in India—again especially in the north and west—to the other religion. Also common at this time was the interference of political and religious organizations in religious processions organized by the other community, especially the opposition of Muslims to the Hindu Ram Lila processions that marched through localities in which Muslims were concentrated. In contrast, the great massacres of 1946 to 1948 were more directly linked to political actions and mobilizations around the demand for Pakistan.

The various forms of religious and political mobilization that were developed in these earlier waves of violence have persisted into the present, but they have been subordinated to more direct appeals to Hindu religious sentiment and solidarity that confront and directly offend Muslim religious sentiments. These have included *yatra*s ( journeys) from one Hindu religious site to another or from one emotionally charged nationalist site to another, of which the most famous was the *rath yatra*[12] of the BJP leader L. K. Advani in 1990 from the Hindu temple of Somnath in the western state of Gujarat to the Babri Mosque at Ayodhya. Although this *yatra* was aborted before it reached U.P., it gathered a massive following of Hindus and was accompanied by rioting in its wake at numerous sites through which it passed. Other actions associated with this movement included the carrying of bricks from all parts of India—and even from far-flung parts of the world where Hindus reside—to be consecrated and carried to Ayodhya to be used in the construction of the new temple to Ram at the site of the destroyed mosque; the carrying of the ashes of "martyrs" killed by the police at Ayodhya during the first assault on the mosque in 1990; and the travel of thousands of *kar sevak*s (volunteers) to Ayodhya to participate in the work of construction itself. In the localities of India, the passage of the *rath yatra* or the movement of *kar sevak*s was preceded or accompanied by "street corner meetings, the blowing of *shankh* (conch shell), clanging of *ghanta-gharial* (ringing of prayer bells and striking at a plate of alloyed metals), hoisting saffron flags in the daytime and *mashal*s (flaming torches) at night on terraces, and organizing *mashal jaloos* (processions bearing lighted torches)."[13] In the western state of Maharashtra, the Shiv Sena adopted the tactic of blocking the Bombay streets with *maha-aarti*s, that is, gatherings for mass Hindu worship, mimicking the similar street-blocking that had for long accompanied Muslim *namaz* (worship) at prayer times.

Although, therefore, Hindu-Muslim and other forms of collective violence in India are expected, anticipated, have a fairly stable set of forms of action that are fortified by new forms from time to time, and a distinct rhetorical form as well, they differ from the nonviolent forms in critical ways aside from the violence itself. However frequent and anticipated and however accompanied by new forms of mobilization that become integrated and legitimized in a repertoire of mobilizing acts, the riots that follow from them are illegitimate. Their illegitimacy, moreover, is acknowledged both by those who deplore the violence and by those who enact it. The authorities and the English-language press invariably condemn the violence that ensues after Hindu-Muslim riots, but the promoters of the violence also recognize its illegitimacy by claiming that the aggressor community was not aggressing, but was acting only in desperation in defense against the attacks of the other.

Another critical difference between these violent and nonviolent movements follows from the illegitimacy of the former.[14] Their violent manifestations appear spontaneous, undirected, unplanned—and even the most carefully planned and well-organized assaults on the other community are *designed* to appear so. Since such riotous violence is illegitimate and the elements of preplanning in it are disguised, the struggle that takes place afterwards to explain it—that is, to control its interpretation—is crucial. The most common explanation is that the violence was in fact an unplanned, spontaneous expression of the deep feelings of an aggrieved people, but there are many others that will be illustrated in this volume. Here I want to note mostly the multiple functions served by capturing the meaning of a Hindu-Muslim or any other intercommunal, interreligious, interethnic riot in a particular way. These include legitimizing illegitimate violence, concealing the extent of preplanning and organization that preceded it, and maintaining intact the persons, groups, and organizations most deeply implicated in the violence by preventing punishment of the principal perpetrators.

The illegitimate and hidden aspects of riotous violence have posed almost insurmountable obstacles to those who have set out to analyze them. Only one author, not an academic, has dared to engage in actual participant observation of riots.[15] Most who care to ascertain the "facts on the ground" appear after the riots to interview their victims. Within a few days, however, often even the victims, coached by lawyers, have prepared their accounts, been advised what to emphasize, who to name and blame, what to conceal. Most social science studies of riots in the West have not even been based on any direct or indirect observation of the events themselves, but on information derived from census and other "datasets." In this study, a variety of instruments and methods have been used to penetrate the dynamic processes of riot production in contemporary India, which will be discussed below.

Before doing so, however, I want to outline the specific structure and argument that will be used to organize the information and data collected.

*Phases in the Production of Riots*

The structure and argument to be developed in this volume depart from nearly all previous studies of collective violence by insisting that, in sites where riots of a particular type are endemic, they are a grisly form of dramatic production in which there are three phases: preparation/rehearsal, activation/enactment, and explanation/interpretation. In sites of endemic riot production, preparation and rehearsal are continuous activities. Activation or enactment of a large-scale riot takes place under particular circumstances, most notably in the case of competitive political systems in a context of intense political mobilization or electoral competition in which riots are precipitated as a device to consolidate the support of ethnic, religious, or other culturally marked groups by emphasizing the need for solidarity in face of the rival communal group. The third phase follows after the violence in a broader struggle within, but also outside, the local community to control the explanation or interpretation of the causes of the violence. In this phase, wider elements in society become involved, including journalists, politicians, social scientists, and public opinion generally. This third phase is marked by a process of blame displacement in which the social scientists themselves become implicated, a process that does not isolate effectively those most responsible for the production of violence, but diffuses blame widely, blurring responsibility, and thereby contributing to the perpetuation of violent productions in future.

In India, all this takes place within a discourse of Hindu-Muslim hostility. The second major theme of the book concerns the link between this discourse of Hindu-Muslim antagonism and the practice of violence enacted in what are called Hindu-Muslim riots. The third theme is that the practice of violence, especially in sites where riots are endemic, becomes embedded in what I call institutionalized riot systems. These systems of riot production are marked by two interrelated features: the existence of a multiplicity of roles, in which there is a specialized division of labor.

It is an essential part of the argument herein that the third phase in riot production, the interpretation phase—and the struggle for control over the explanation of riots that occurs during this phase—is as important as the production itself, as in any dramatic production. Finally, the keynote of this phase, suffusing it, is a process of blame displacement in which all are involved and whose end result is the diffusion of responsibility in such a way as to free all from blame and allow the principal perpetrators to go scot-free.

The explanation of riot production to be developed herein relegates all spontaneity theories of the causes of riots to the realm of blame displacement. It is the most common form of blame displacement, in fact. Such theories are at worst utterly false, at best—and invariably so—misleading.

Although the primary focus of the book, therefore, is on the dynamic process of riot production, that is, on *how* riots are produced rather than on *why* they happen, several causal explanations of Hindu-Muslim violence in India will nevertheless be examined. In the course of this examination, conventional social science techniques of correlation and regression will be used to uncover associations from which causal explanations are often inferred. For the rest of my analysis both of the functional utility of persisting riots to a multiplicity of social, economic, and political groups and of the struggle to control the meaning of riots, the principal sources will be interviews and personal observations carried out in India during field trips over the thirty-eight years from 1961 to 1999. Newspaper accounts of riots will also be used, though my experience with such accounts is that they are invariably deficient, sometimes utterly false, and altogether inadequate for serious social science research on the subject of collective violence. Public and confidential documents will also be used, but they are sparse on this subject and some potentially useful reports are inaccessible.

Before laying out the outline of this volume, I want to take up some methodological issues concerning causal analysis of collective violence and indicate how I will make use of causal explanations as well as alternative methods of functional analysis and the analysis of discursive formations in interpreting and understanding the incidence and dynamics of the production of riots and pogroms in contemporary India.

### EXPLANATION: CAUSE, FUNCTION, DISCOURSE

*Problems of Causal Analysis in the Comparative Study
of Forms of Collective Violence*

Virtually every scholar who has written about riots, pogroms, and other forms of collective violence seeks their causes, and not a few scholarly articles feature the word in their titles.[16] Many of those who seek causes also seek cures—as if dealing with an illness—or solutions, as if dealing with a social problem. Commissions of inquiry are often appointed after particularly serious riots or after a wave of riots. Their charge is invariably to determine the causes of the riot or riots in question. Their purpose is often different from the work of scholars. It is to assign responsibility, especially upon the state authorities and their agents, administrative officers, and police. In this case, riots are seen as problems for the authorities, disturbances of law and order in which their own competence and effectiveness in allowing riots to occur and in failing to control them when they do occur are judged. Such an approach introduces a secondary search for causes, namely, for the failure to control a riot in its early stages and allowing it to get out of hand.

Numerous problems have arisen in the literature that seeks causes for riots. One is that participants in riots often do not conform to expectations based on the imputed causes. For example, many participants in riots whose causes have been said to be poverty and unemployment turn out to be employed.[17] Such a finding raises another kind of causal issue, that of individual motivation for participation. But the two sets of findings, one based on ecological factors, the other on individual motivations, may conflict. In statistics, this is, of course, the problem of the ecological fallacy.

It will be argued throughout this volume that it is essential to the understanding of the dynamics of riot production that we separate explanations for riots seen as crowd behavior from explanations for individual behavior in riots. Yet, this is not an easy task, for the former usually take the form of justifications masquerading as explanations, while individual actions are normally hidden from view in the hubbub and furor during large-scale rioting, after which individual motivations are obscured by the public explanations, especially those offered by political persons.[18] Three solutions to this analytical problem are proposed here. The first is to note how a discourse of public good and evil becomes integrated into individual thought and behavior, thereby providing an internal motivation for the instigation of and participation in acts of violence. Second, I note throughout the volume the multiplicity of types of violent action that occur during large-scale rioting under the cover of the discourse of communalism, actions that cannot be explained or justified in terms of that discourse, but can easily be fit into more parsimonious explanations of individual pursuit of political advantage, profit, and vendetta. But it must at the same time be recognized that there can be no perfect separation between public explanations and private motivations, that the ecological fallacy is not merely a problem of methodology but a deliberate and often impenetrable form of political and public obfuscation. Third, all forms of deep psychological interpretation of individual motivations for participation in riotous activity will be eschewed as essentially futile; instead, the focus will be on the hidden face itself, what can be made visible behind the mask of discourse.

Another problem concerns the relationship between the immediate acts that precipitate riots and the "underlying causes" that make it possible for such acts to be followed by large-scale crowd violence. There is often a discrepancy here, as well, between imputed underlying causes and the immediate acts that precipitate an event classed as a riot. It is not, say some scholars, the pig in the mosque or some other insult to the religious beliefs of Muslims or Hindus that is responsible for riots in India, but the economic issues that lie behind these incidents; rivalry between Muslim and Hindu manufacturers and wholesalers in urban areas, disputes between Hindu and Muslim villagers over land.[19]

A critical problem in assessing the relationship "between underlying causes and immediate precipitants of racial disturbances" in the United States has been that the former are "relatively stable," whereas the latter "are random occurrences, the kind of events which occur daily in most communities and usually are disposed of routinely."[20] Spilerman found little or no connection or correlation between the standard list of underlying causes and the occurrence of black ghetto riots in the 1960s. Instead, he found that the strongest predictor variable was the size of the Negro population. He then asked the question, which is of central importance in this study as well, how one explains the escalation of random, routine occurrences that affected black-white relations in American cities into large-scale riots. His answer is the existence of racial consciousness among the black population that allows "bystanders to the conflict to interpret it in primarily racial terms," and to respond accordingly, a consciousness stimulated not by differences in the extent of unemployment, dilapidated housing conditions, and other economic disadvantages experienced by blacks, but by racial solidarity produced uniformly across the black population in the United States, primarily by means of television coverage of the problems confronting them throughout the country. In this study, it will be demonstrated that not television, but a pervasive discourse that emphasizes Hindu-Muslim differences and hostilities in India, provides the framework that allows the escalation of trivial incidents into major riots. But this process also is neither automatic nor spontaneous; it requires the presence of other factors that will be spelled out below, principally political-process factors that Spilerman does not discuss.

Social scientists and political scientists are divided among methodological individualists, that is, rational choice and game theorists, devotees of the case study method, and dataset enthusiasts. Between and within these alternative approaches, there are other divisions as well. In the search for causes, is it not necessary, say some, to consider places where riotous violence has not occurred as well as those where it has occurred? The question here is: why here and not there? What are the social, economic, and political differences between places where riots have occurred and places that have been free from riots? One method adopted to answer this kind of question is "paired comparison analysis," which can be done by using statistical data[21] or by historical narrative comparison.[22] Either way, the method is designed to pair two sites or two sets of sites that are as much alike as possible except in the one respect under consideration (the dependent variable), namely whether or not they have experienced incidents of collective violence.

Game theorists, notably Fearon and Laitin,[23] have sought to develop comprehensive theories of conflict, including interethnic conflict. Like the proponents of paired comparison, they have also challenged the validity for the development of a theory of interethnic violence of an exclusive focus on the situations that lead to violence, arguing that, in fact, interethnic cooperation rather than violence is the norm. What is required, they argue, is a theory that explains both why violence is so infrequent, given the numbers of potential conflicts in the world or any part of it, and why the norm sometimes breaks down. They have developed a model to explain both situations, derived from a theory of games, in which the crucial issue concerns the control of individual opportunism that threatens the relations between ethnic groups. They identify two mechanisms that are used for such control. The first, which they call the spiral equilibrium, controls individual opportunism through the fear based on knowledge that an infraction of interethnic relations will lead to mutual violence that will spiral out of control. The knowledge is sufficient most of the time to prevent such dangerous infractions, but when it is not, the violence that ensues is likely to be awful.

The second mechanism is "in-group policing" by which any member of one ethnic group who commits an infraction against a member of another ethnic group will be disciplined by his own group. Violence between ethnic groups ensues only when the intraethnic policing mechanisms fail. The authors are aware that their model leaves out many other critical factors, whose inclusion would require a further extension of it, but have provided examples of empirical situations to demonstrate its applicability. There will be occasion to refer later to examples that relate to their hypotheses in the discussions of riots in Aligarh. For the present, it is sufficient to note first that riots can follow from a breakdown of either equilibrium situation, but that the frequency of rioting and the type that has occurred in Aligarh since Independence falls primarily in the category of the spiral equilibrium that repeatedly breaks down. Second, as will be argued later, a different game is being played in Aligarh, a political game of brinkmanship whose purposes are not to maintain interethnic cooperation and prevent violence, but to keep always in readiness the mechanisms to bring group relations to the brink of conflict, and to let the violence loose at times considered advantageous to one side or the other or both.

Whatever the method in the literature on collective violence, the search for causes remains primary. I believe it is overemphasized and often misplaced, for the following reasons. First, for all the scientific pretensions of causal analysts, the search for causes cannot be separated from the values of the observer, whether politician, judicial enquiry commissioner, scholar, or journalist. It is obvious in the case of the politicians,[24] more subtle in the case of social scientists and historians, but it is nevertheless present amongst all, whether consciously or unconsciously, by design or in the implications of our findings. Indeed, all categories of persons just mentioned merged to produce probably the most famous riot inquiry of the twentieth century, the Kerner Commission Report on the racial disturbances in the 1960s in the United States: former politician Governor Kerner, acting as judicial commissioner, other politicians, and members of interest groups—racial, labor, and business—a team of social scientists, and, of course, all making use of newspaper reports as well as their own sources for their findings.[25]

Second, the search for causes easily turns from an expression of the values of the observer and his identification with those perceived as the victims of violence to the assignment of blame.[26] If the cause of riots is system strain,[27] structural conditions, or any general condition prevailing in society, then blame may be dispersed or dissolved or it may be directed towards the regime considered responsible for the strains. If it is perceived as poverty, inequality, unemployment, or discrimination, again, depending upon whether these in turn are considered aspects of a general social transformation or are seen as themselves caused by state policies, blame may be dispersed or concentrated on the regime. In the case of interethnic violence, cause and blame may be placed upon the prejudices of particular groups and their upbringing, their "family values," or upon objective conditions of economic interaction, competition, or perceived exploitation of one group by another. And so on.

All these forms of causal analysis are deficient, Keith argues, because of their adherence to a Humean model of probability that makes use of statements of the form "if $x$, then $y$," or, put more precisely, statements that most probably the phenomenon $y$ (in our case standing for riots) will follow whenever $x$ (the cause or causes) recurs in a social situation. This kind of focus ignores or downplays in particular three aspects of human action and struggle, namely, intentionality, process, and meaning.[28] In other words, first, it ignores or underplays the self-fulfilling and self-denying prophecies, the possibility that riots may be willed actions, concerted productions of thinking, acting people who may also decide to cancel a performance. Second, following from the first, it ignores the dynamic processes of riot production, being satisfied instead with explanations that focus on social, political, or economic conditions or on spontaneous crowd responses to stimuli such as rumors or atrocities perpetrated against ethnic compatriots by members of a rival ethnic group or police brutality against the former. Third, it ignores the constant struggle to control the meaning of riots after they occur, to represent them appropriately, which then feeds back into both common-sense and social-science causal explanations converted into cures. The primary focus in this volume will be on these three elements of riot production and representation, from out of which I will also seek to generate causal statements that are limited and cautious with regard to their truth claims. The causal statements that will be made herein, however, will not be of the "if . . . then" variety. It will not be said, for example, that, if the possibility for enhancing a party's electoral chances will be increased by a riot, there is a high probability that a riot will take place. It will be said only that large-scale riots are associated with intensified party/electoral competition in which the causal arrow points from riots to intensified competition rather than the reverse. It will also be inferred that the instigators of such riots have in mind such a result in which their side will be favored.[29]

Permeating all the forms and varieties of causal analysis applied to the study of collective violence—sometimes hidden, but often quite explicit—is a foundational substratum of opposition between those who attribute collective violence primarily to the prejudices, hostilities, aggressions, and propensities to violence of particular peoples, segments of them, or the populace in general, on the one hand, and those who argue to the contrary that one must look elsewhere for explanations of violence, not only to other underlying causes, but to the mechanisms for crowd mobilization. In its simplest form, the opposition is between those who perceive collective violence, especially that which takes the form of riots, as arising from the acting out spontaneously by mobs of feelings that pervade a population, on the one hand, and those who perceive mass mobilization as a difficult task at best that requires a degree of skill, planning, and organization on the part of specialists.

The problem with this dichotomization and indeed with most of the causal arguments concerning riots and other forms of collective violence is the neglect of the intermediate space in which riotous activity actually takes place, that space between popular sentiments and state action that is occupied not just by the social science category of "riot participants" gleaned from police reports but by those who organize and plan acts of violence, which include a whole range of specialists carrying out a variety of tasks. Indeed, the framing of the causal debate in the terms described above has served no purpose so much as obfuscating the operations of riot systems, the mechanisms of pogroms, and the organization of collective violence.[30]

There is a further question, moreover, that goes to the heart of the problem of causal reasoning in the contemporary social sciences and the uses to which it is put in the explanations for riots as well as the solutions offered to prevent, control, or suppress them. Caught up in the scientific pursuit of the causes of riots, all observers who have participated in that pursuit have either failed to see or paid insufficient attention to the fact that a fully satisfactory explanation will always remain elusive, and, further, that the very pursuit of causes is itself implicated in the political process. A full causal explanation of a complex event such as a large-scale riot can never be arrived at. Every attempt to do so must involve reduction and concentration on sets of manageable, observable "variables." But riots involve often many thousands of people who, despite the existence in today's world of widespread electronic devices of surveillance, seek anonymity in crowd action and to a high degree still succeed in doing so. A full explanation of a large-scale riot, pinpointing all the true causes, would involve some kind of exercise in repetition of the event in the manner of Jorge Luis Borges.[31] Social scientists seek to avoid this by reduction or by modelling, both processes that cannot fail, by the very methods of reduction and abstraction, from feeding into the interests and purposes of individuals, groups, governments, and societies that seek satisfying explanations.

With regard to the second statement, that the pursuit of causal explanations is implicated in the political process, I mean that this pursuit in itself constitutes a political struggle that occurs invariably after every riot, for the capturing of its meaning, for the establishment of a hegemonic consensus, which in turn will influence, even determine power relations in society thereafter—relations among groups, within groups, and between state and society. It is not only a question of control of policy decisions taken in the aftermath of riots to prevent their future occurrence, but of deciding what is the social problem of which riots are the outcome, who are the persons and groups to blame for their outbreak, and whether or not those persons and groups deserve blame and punishment or are to be seen as victims deserving immediate succor and future amelioration of their condition. It may also lead in some societies, including India, to definitions of groups as either loyal and patriotic citizens or antinational persons owing loyalties to a foreign power.

### Functional Analysis

The persistence of a system, a set of institutions, or practices such as collective violence may sometimes be better understood by a form of functional analysis used by Robert Merton in his classic study and explanation of the persistence of the political machine in American big-city politics. How, he asked, could an institution universally associated with corrupt and criminal practices for which no public figures had a good word to say and all respectable citizens condemned persist for a century in the great American democracy? He argued that there was no simple causal explanation, particularly no explanation that singled out some "powerful subgroups in the society" manipulating things from behind the scenes. On the contrary, he found that the machine performed necessary functions for society and served the needs of many groups.

Merton did not see his kind of functional analysis as a displacement of "causal interpretation," but as a supplement to it.[32] He did not say that the machine persisted *because* it fulfilled "*x, y,* and *z*" functions for particular individuals, groups, and society as a whole. He argued rather that it was simply not in the interest of any substantial or powerful social force in society to displace the machine, from which at the same time particular social, political, and institutional forces benefit. In that case, it would not necessarily follow that the machine would not persist if it failed to perform the stated functions, since it would still be the case that no powerful force would gain from its destruction.

I intend to make use of a kind of Mertonian functional analysis in my search for an explanation for the persistence of Hindu-Muslim riots and anti-Muslim pogroms in contemporary India. No societal functional necessity for the persistence of riots will be assumed nor will it be argued that there is any kind of "feedback loop," such that riots benefit certain groups, who then support directly or indirectly the persistence of riots. It is sufficient for my purposes simply to note that riots serve the interests of particular individuals, groups, organizations, and even society as a whole in concrete, useful ways that are beneficial to them. Further, I will adopt one of the more common uses of the term *function,* that of use or utility, and will speak of the functional utility of the persistence of Hindu-Muslim riots in India for a wide variety of interests, groups, institutions, and organizations, including ultimately the Indian state. Under these circumstances, it is not possible to produce a broad enough consensus in society to eliminate violent riots from Indian public life, just as it was not possible for a century to eliminate the machine from American public life.

## *Discourse*

Much of my recent work and a good part of the present volume are concerned with the question of the struggle for control of the meaning of riots in their aftermath. Although I will take up causal issues below, especially with regard to the association between riots and political competition, and I will also seek to demonstrate the functional utility of riots in India, I am especially concerned with the analysis of the explanations for the occurrence of riots given by ordinary people, politicians, the media, the police, and the civil authorities. These explanations will be treated "as representations," whose contruction and organization as well as "the types of function they serve"[33] need to be analyzed in and for themselves as part of the struggle of social and political forces in contemporary Indian society.

I intend to show also that a hegemonic discourse exists in Indian society, which I call the communal discourse, which provides a framework for explaining riotous violence. That framework allows Indian citizens, particularly its dominant castes and classes, to accept the persistence of such violence in their society without seeing it as a fundamental flaw in their democracy, their essential nonviolence, their acceptance of Indian cultural diversity, in short, their ideals. People claim to live according to ideals and become uncomfortable when the discrepancy between their ideals and the prevalent practices in their society is too stark. There are only a few ways of dealing with that kind of discrepancy. One is denial. Another is recognition followed by some form of social action in the direction of reform through political organization, social work, writing, cultural protest, resistance, nonviolent demonstration, or the taking up of arms. There is a third way that is the most prominent in all societies with recognized severe social problems, including India, namely, blame displacement. Blame displacement makes it possible to acknowledge the existence of evils such as riotous communal violence and pogroms by attributing violent practices to others or to natural human propensities that must be accepted by any realistic person as a part of life. It makes it possible, also, either to accept the violence as inevitable or to direct rhetoric or action towards one's favorite causes that may or may not have anything to do with the violence.

## THE STUDY OF RIOTS IN INDIA

### Argument among Historians

Historical analysis of Hindu-Muslim communal conflict, its causes and preconditions, has been highly contentious in character. Contemporary historians of India do not even agree on whether or not there existed before the nineteenth century anything that could be called Hindu or Muslim communal identities, and, a fortiori, on whether or not Hindu-Muslim conflict was endemic. On one side are those who argue that Hindu-Muslim consciousness and conflict are largely modern constructions, in which the British colonial rulers played a major role, either through deliberate "divide and rule" policies or through the ways in which they categorized, classified, and counted the various peoples of India.[34] Historians who accept this point of view also tend to see Hindu and/or Muslim communal consciousness or communalism as forms of ideology or discourse connected to class, group, and elite political interests. In this perspective, the creation or development of communal consciousness is an instrument of struggle, either against the British or between Hindus and Muslims for political advantage or supremacy. In the course of struggle, communal violence could be and often was the result of conflicts framed within a communal discourse.[35]

On the other side are historians who argue that there is more continuity between past and present, extending backward at least to the early eighteenth century and, in some arguments, into the earlier period of Mughal rule. In this view, interreligious strife and riots that resemble contemporary Hindu-Muslim conflict were present, even endemic, in premodern times.[36] Arguments concerning the causes of Hindu-Muslim violence flow logically from these distinctive views, with constructivists taking the position that communalism is a cover that hides a multiplicity of mainly political and economic causes, while those who emphasize continuities between past and present modes of conflict place greater weight on their religious significance and on the existence of strong communal identities that preceded them.

My argument in this volume and elsewhere has been on the constructivist side. Whatever similarities, continuities, and persisting idioms may be found before the nineteenth century, it would seem idle to overemphasize them. The consolidation of the heterogeneous Hindu and Muslim groupings on the subcontinent and the politicization of the differences between them are overwhelmingly a modern phenomenon deeply connected with the striving for control over the modern state apparatus, involving a claim to rightful inheritance on the part of Hindu and to self-determination on the part of Muslim leaders. In the course of the struggles for power that developed during British rule, intensified in the late nineteenth century, and culminated in the division of India in 1947, a discourse of Hindu-Muslim difference was created that has struck deep roots in both communities and acquired a partly self-sustaining momentum that at the same time continues to be fed by political competition. In the construction of this discourse, competing historiographies and historians have themselves played and continue to play substantial contesting roles.[37]

### Contemporary Social Science Studies

Most available social science methods have been applied to the study of riots in South Asia. Contemporary and historical case studies are by far the majority. Asghar Ali Engineer has been the most prolific writer on Hindu-Muslim riots in India since Independence.[38] In countless articles and numerous edited books, he has chronicled virtually every major riot and many smaller ones. Deeply committed to secular, universal values, he has blamed neither Hindus nor Muslims as communities for the carnage that has been inflicted upon the victims of communal riots. He has instead consistently pointed the finger at the politicians, on the one hand, and at forms of economic competition between Hindus and Muslims, on the other hand.

The incidents that precipitate riots in Engineer's view are sometimes secondary, sometimes primary, but they either hide or reveal the hands of politicians and political movements. Minor disputes are exploited by "petty-minded politicians" who do not shrink from the sacrifices in human lives that follow upon their exploitation of such disputes for their political advantage.[39] At times, political movements themselves are the cause of violence, as in the famous "Ramshila pujan processions" of militant Hindus carrying bricks to Ayodhya in the movement to bring down the Babri Mosque there and replace it with a temple to the god Ram. Riots followed in the wake of these processions in almost every part of the country.[40] For Engineer, therefore, the primary cause of communal riots in India is the pursuit of political advantage at any cost.

Beth Roy has produced an exceptional case study of a single Hindu-Muslim riot in a village in East Pakistan, now Bangladesh, that occurred soon after Independence and Partition. She has reconstructed the course of the riot from its beginnings in a trivial conflict to the full-scale confrontation that ultimately resulted. Although the way in which this riot developed and its relatively minor consequences in casualties and injuries appear almost quaint in comparison with the seriousness and brutality that accompany urban riots in contemporary South Asia, her case study nevertheless illuminates many aspects of the process of riot production that will be analyzed throughout this volume. Of particular interest is her analysis of how a trivial conflict between two villagers, one Hindu, the other Muslim, over an incident of one villager's cow eating the plants of the other developed into a politicized confrontation between Hindus and Muslims in the surrounding area. She argues further that the villagers did not act spontaneously, but deliberately, choosing to riot. Moreover, she has noted distinct stages in the development of this riot that, though different from my conceptualization of the phases of riot production, nevertheless are consistent with the view that riots are indeed deliberate productions.[41]

Paired comparison analysis has been done by Varshney. Varshney and Wilkinson[42] have pioneered in the creation of an extensive dataset for all riots noted in one of India's leading English-language newspapers between 1960 and 1993. Both authors in their separate and joint works have insisted that "To explain the causes of violence we must . . . move beyond explanations which ignore the many times and places where, though communal tension may exist, riots do not take place.[43]

Aside from the general problems that the method of paired comparison shares with causal theorizing in the social sciences, discussed earlier in this chapter, there are three additional problems specific to it. One is that it may lead to downplaying the significance of collective violence in those places where it does occur. This is clear enough in the case of Varshney's paired comparisons of specific sites and in the Varshney and Wilkinson comparisons of the incidence of riots by state and city in India. By localizing and regionalizing the sites of violence in India, they do not refine their gaze, but instead disperse it. In Varshney's case, it leads as well to a doubtful conclusion that civic engagement between Hindus and Muslims can prevent violence, when it is more likely that the creation of institutionalized riot systems overrides and displaces whatever forms of civic engagement and interethnic cooperation exist at specific sites. But neither alternative argument can be proved on the basis of such comparisons.[44]

The second problem is that such comparisons, by diverting one's gaze from the specific sites of institutionalized violence, fail to reveal the dynamic processes of riot production. They claim to tell us why riots occur here, not there, but they do not tell us how they happen. Until we know how they happen, the former question cannot be answered.

Third, the method of paired comparison as it has been generally used in practice suffers from a fundamental flaw of misidentification or inadequate specification of the actual sites of collective violence. The sites of riots are too often referred to as the cities in which they occur rather than the specific neighborhoods or street locations from which they originate or to which they are even sometimes confined. When, as in the United States, it has often been the case that the entire black ghetto has been affected by riot activity, there is some justification for using the cities as the named sites when what is actually meant is the black ghetto within those cities. However, it is never the case in either the United States or India that an entire city becomes a site of collective violence.[45] It is also rare that all parts of a city that share similar demographic features are affected equally or even at all. In such circumstances, the method of paired comparison by city or town is a kind of unnecessary and wasteful methodological flourish, for such comparison would be better done within the specific city or town, comparing instead the neighborhoods and streets that are affected with those that are not. In this volume, I specify as clearly and precisely as possible those localities that have been repeatedly, occasionally, or never affected by communal rioting. I demonstrate also that, while there are demographic, economic, and caste/communal differences that distinguish the populations in such localities, it is political activity, organization, and leadership that demarcate most clearly the riot-prone or riot-affected from the less affected localities.

Kakar has adopted a psychoanalytic, social-psychological approach to the study of riots in India, finding their source in mass persecutory fantasies.[46] Although his approach falls squarely in a primordialist interpretation of inter-communal relations and ethnic violence that I have consistently opposed in all my writings on ethnicity, nationalism, and collective violence, there are nevertheless some points of contact between his work and mine. Our approaches coincide insofar as we both, along with the leftist historians in India, agree that the "representations of collective pasts" and the way "collective memories are transmitted through generations" are of considerable importance in contributing to the persistence of communal violence in India. Kakar adds to this perspective the argument that these "representations of collective pasts" are psychic ones, not just intellectual ones.[47] They do not merely justify collective violence, they explain it.[48] I will have occasion to refer to several explanations from my interviews that suggest a form of psychic delusion on the part of those militant Hindus who speak from the vantage point of the communal discourse. Their statements do indeed suggest that they harbor persecutory fantasies. Moreover, these fantasies seem also to have become quite widespread among middle- and upper-class, upper-caste Hindus in northern India.

However, Kakar carries his psychic argument too far, into a kind of psychological essentialism. For example, he argues that "the Muslim butcher in his blood-flecked undervest and *lungi*, wielding a huge carving knife was . . . a figure of awe and dread for the Hindu child and of a fear-tinged repulsion for the adult."[49] But this fear that may conceivably afflict Hindu vegetarians can hardly extend to all "Hindus," since it is the same butcher who slaughters the goats that nonvegetarian Hindus love to eat. More important, it is difficult to accept Kakar's argument that it is "religious ultimacy," fed by "an arsenal of ideational and ritual symbols" on both sides of the communal divide that makes communal riots so much more "violent and . . . difficult to control" than other types of collective violence.[50] This is a form of objectification of religious difference that does not hold up in at least two respects. It does not differentiate communal violence from, say, the slaughter of landless Scheduled Castes by Hindu landlords in Bihar and South India, or even more atrocious forms of genocide in places such as Rwanda and Burundi or Cambodia, where religious conflict is not at issue. Second, neither the killers interviewed by Kakar nor those I have interviewed appear to me to be motivated by "an arsenal of ideational and ritual symbols."

Further, Kakar repeatedly writes of Hindu perceptions in general, seeing them as causes of the tension that leads to riots, as if riots simply follow from particular tensions, such as a Bihar government move "to raise the official status of Urdu" that, he argues, "was perceived by the Hindus as a step down the road of Muslim separatism which led to the Ranchi riots in 1967."[51] Kakar here not only presents "the Hindus" as an undifferentiated mass, but mistakes precipitants for causes.[52] Further, Kakar adopts the utterly misleading social-psychological approach, going back to Le Bon, that treats riotous crowds as an undifferentiated mass of individuals who adopt the identity of the crowd, losing their own in the process.[53]

This view of the crowd is all made up, pure conjecture that has been shattered by the personal participant observations of Bill Buford.[54] It is one of the principal arguments of this book that we cannot understand what happens in riots until we examine in detail the multiplicity of roles and persons involved in them and the justifications presented concerning them by their promoters and participants. The argument that individuals lose their identity in crowds belongs among those interpretations of riots that displace blame onto entire collectivities, who cannot be held responsible for their actions because they have lost any sense of what it is that they do as individuals. Kakar takes the argument even further towards the primordialist perspective by arguing that group identity in general "is *inherently* a carrier of aggression,"[55] thus placing the ultimate responsibility for communal violence in the irrational tendencies of the human psyche, in other words precisely nowhere.

Tambiah has included in his massive work on riots in South Asia case studies of Sikh violence in the Punjab and the anti-Sikh massacres in New Delhi in 1984, as well as the riots that accompanied and followed the destruction of the mosque at Ayodhya in 1992. His work and mine are in agreement, especially, on three aspects of collective violence in India: (1) the tendency for explanations of riots to be variously contextualized in a manner that suits the interests of political actors and others involved in the struggle to control the meaning of riots in their aftermath; (2) the routine rather than exceptional character of violence, making it, in effect, an aspect of the political process that is as predictable/unpredictable as other aspects; (3) the existence of a multiplicity of roles performed in the production of riots, a kind of division of labor that makes arguments concerning the spontaneity of riots suspect.[56]

## THE PRODUCTION OF HINDU-MUSLIM COMMUNAL VIOLENCE

The focus of this volume is on the production of Hindu-Muslim communal violence in post-Independence India and its relationship to the construction of the categories "Hindu" and "Muslim" in modern Indian history. In the course of my research, I have arrived at three conclusions concerning the persistence of Hindu-Muslim communal violence in the specific form called "riots." The first, based on my analysis of the available evidence marshalled in favor of various causal interpretations, is that no single causal explanation of Hindu-Muslim riots and anti-Muslim pogroms will suffice to explain all or even most instances of such collective violence in India. Nor could it be otherwise, given the vast differences from instance to instance in what are classified as riots in India, ranging from fights between small groups that lead to injuries with or without the death of one or more parties to vast conflagrations that occur in many areas of a large town or city leading to tens or even hundreds of deaths, large-scale arson, looting, and property destruction.

It is, in fact, rather a loose form of scientific analysis that would lump the latter with the former. It is also extremely dubious even to classify the larger events as a single instance of the phenomenon. An event described as a riot or pogrom that takes place more or less simultaneously in widely spread areas of a large town may or may not have been precipitated by a single incident, have spread to other areas by means of news, rumor, or "contagion," have been preplanned or spontaneous. In other words, such a large event as the Bombay riots of December 1992 or the Aligarh riots of 1990–91 may be one riot or many, each with its own precipitants, underlying enmities, and sets of interests involved.

Although, given these difficulties, no single cause of riots can possibly be adduced successfully, I have also found that there is at least a kernel of truth in all but the most bizarre explanations of riots. There is sufficient evidence, for example, that riots between Hindus and Muslims often occur where Hindu and Muslim areas are in close juxtaposition to each other, in nasty slums where landlords or businessmen of one or the other community seek to displace persons from the other community in order to acquire valuable real estate, and at times of intense political competition and mass mobilization when different political parties seek to mobilize the votes of one or the other of the two communities. But the mere presence of any one of these factors or any combination of them is neither necessary nor sufficient to produce large-scale riots. At the same time, it is also the case that many or all of these factors and others to be discussed in this book are present in all large-scale riots.

For many social scientists and historians, the obvious solution to the causal dilemma here is simply to resort to a multicausal explanation, either through the listing of all the factors discovered to have operated in one or more cases or through statistical methods of correlation and regression that will assign percentages of explanatory power to each of the active variables. But, as I will show in this volume, this also will not do. It will not do principally because, when one examines the actual dynamics of riots, one discovers that there are active, knowing subjects and organizations at work engaged in a continuous tending of the fires of communal divisions and animosities, who exercise by a combination of subtle means and confrontational tactics a form of control over the incidence and timing of riots. But their control is not total. Some of the pogroms that have occurred in India in recent history have been shown to have had a high degree of organization and preplanning, notably the anti-Sikh pogroms after the assassination of Indira Gandhi in 1984 and the Shiv Sena–organized pogrom against Muslims in Bombay in January 1993. Even in these cases, however, control is not total. So, while the production of many large-scale riots can be seen as deriving from the political interests and calculations of specific organizations, groups, and leaders, many other interests also then come into play whose actions at the multiplicity of sites in which violence occurs require secondary explanations.

It is the combination of "objective," underlying factors of demography, economics, and electoral competition with intentionality and direct human agency that makes causal explanation of riots in general so difficult. We can surely say that *Krystallnacht* in Germany was a preplanned, coordinated attack on carefully specified targets, namely, the Jews and their property and religious objects. But even this attack was designed to appear spontaneous, to fool outside observers. What makes riots and pogroms in India or the United States or nineteenth-century Russia so much more difficult to analyze and comprehend is that they combine objective and intentional factors, spontaneity and planning, chaos and organization. They are best conceived as dramatic productions in which the directors are not in complete control, the cast of characters varies—some of them being paid, some of them acting voluntarily for loot or fun—and many of the parts have been rehearsed, but others have not.

This then brings me to the second argument of this book, that, where riots are endemic, what I call "institutionalized riot systems" exist in which known persons and groups occupy specific roles in the rehearsal for and the production of communal riots. In such systems, a central role is played by what I call "conversion specialists," those whose task it is to decide when a trivial, everyday incident will be exaggerated and placed into the communal system of talk, the communal discourse, and allowed to escalate into communal violence.

The production of communal riots is very often a political one, frequently associated with intense interparty competition and mass political mobilization. This was true before Independence as well as after. This fact goes a long way also towards understanding Gandhi's emphasis on nonviolence as the basis for the mobilizations against British rule in India. Nonviolence may have been a religious principle for him as well as a political tactic of the weak against the strong, the relatively unarmed against the armed, but it also arose from his profound knowledge of Indian social and political life, from his own understanding of the violent mechanisms that could so easily be brought into play under the cover of the vast mass movements that he launched, which would undercut their purposes and direct local political energies to other targets. Moreover, there were other politicians already playing a different game of direct instigation of communal violence for other political purposes.

The institutionalized riot systems or networks that exist in riot-prone cities and towns comprise a multiplicity of roles that I have identified elsewhere.[57] A good part of this book will be devoted to showing how and when they come into operation. For now, it need only be noted that they include informants who carry messages to political group leaders of the occurrence of incidents that may affect the relations between Hindus and Muslims; propagandists who create messages to be conveyed to particular segments of society, to the press, to the general public; vernacular journalists who publish these messages in the form of "news," poster plasterers who place them on walls, rumor-mongers who transmit them by word of mouth; recruiters who collect crowds from colleges and universities and *goondas* (thugs) to kill, loot, and burn when the time is ripe.

But there are two roles that are crucial in the dynamics of riot production, designated herein by the terms "fire tender" and "conversion specialist." The fire tender keeps the embers of communal animosities alive by bringing to the notice of the politicians, the authorities, and the public situations that are known to be sensitive in the relations between Hindus and Muslims. These situations may be genuine or bogus, they may refer to incidents that actually happened naturally or that were created deliberately for the purpose of stoking communal passions.

The second role, that of the conversion specialist, is the pivotal one of turning a mere local incident or a public issue affecting the two communities into one with riot potential by inciting a crowd and giving a signal to the specialists in violence to let loose the violent action: stone throwing, stabbing, or arson. The conversion specialist is generally, if not always, a political person. He is part of the political group whose interests are to be served by the violence and may even be a leader in the group. He usually does not himself engage in violence, but instigates others to do so when the political context favors it.

The third and fourth arguments concern the issue of riot persistence. Since much if not all of the information to be presented in this book concerning the mechanisms of riot production is known to the leaders of the country, the journalists, the local authorities where riots occur, and to the literate and illiterate public, and is deplored by all, how is it that riots persist? The question is especially puzzling since the politicians and the authorities know where and when riots are likely, who the principal riot-mongers are, how to prevent riots and to control them when they break out. How is it that they do not do so always? In fact, how is it that they do so only irregularly?

The first answer to these questions refers primarily to large-scale riots and those that occur in waves. There is a clear association between such riots and waves of riots, on the one hand, and electoral competition and mass political mobilization. Not only is there an association, but the evidence to be presented below demonstrates that there is a direct causal link between riots and electoral/political competition, such that Hindu-Muslim riots are a product of actions designed to consolidate one community or the other or both at the local, regional, and national levels into a cohesive political bloc. Riots do in fact have that result. Riots precede elections and intensify political competition. Riots accompany political mobilizations around religious symbols and contribute to the strengthening of the movements, which in turn solidify communal solidarity in subsequent elections.

The second answer is functionalist: riots persist because they are functionally useful to a wide array of individuals, groups, parties, and the state authorities. In other words, this particular form of endemic, recurrent violence is a function of the unwillingness, failure, or lack of desire of such bodies and entities to take preventive measures, the effectiveness of which are well known whatever the imputed causes of particular incidents, which vary widely. Their functional utility is in turn heavily influenced by the political benefits that derive from them.

The third answer is that there exists in India a discourse of Hindu-Muslim communalism that has corrupted history, penetrated memory, and contributes in the present to the production and perpetuation of communal violence in the country. Large-scale riots involve considerable mass participation in their enactment as well as a commitment to the belief on the part of many people that they could not have been prevented by the actions of well-intentioned persons or governments. It involves a belief that they are in fact endemic to and a consequence of fundamental hostilities, prejudices, and passions in society. It is necessary here to say a few words about the origins of this discourse before proceeding further.

## THE DISCOURSE OF COMMUNALISM: HISTORY, MEMORY, AND COMMUNAL VIOLENCE IN POST-INDEPENDENCE INDIA

India is a country whose peoples live today under the signs of several great historical ruptures that are perceived as having disrupted the historial reality of the pre-existence of an Indian nation and prevented its full realization in political form: the prolonged rupture that is seen as the Muslim conquest of the subcontinent, the establishment of British rule in the eighteenth century, and the division of the country in 1947. Two of these events are associated in the minds of most Hindus and in the ideology of militant Hindu nationalism with the large Muslim population of the country. Despite the contrary attempts of secular nationalist leaders and historians, a divisive history of India has acquired a hegemonic place in the school textbooks and in the national mythology of the country which defines the millennially long arrival of both the religion of Islam and Muslim arms into the subcontinent as a foreign, Muslim conquest. Despite the fact that probably 95 percent of the Muslim population of the subcontinent is of indigenous origin, descendants of converts to Islam, Islam is considered in the history of the Hindu nation "as a foreign element."[58]

The millennium that saw the establishment of Islam and Muslim rulership is seen as one coherent period in Indian history, the period of the Muslim conquest that followed upon the classical Hindu period. Both periods are defined in communal-religious terms, the first as the "Hindu period"— though it encompasses the rise of other world as well as specifically Indian religions such as, respectively, Buddhism and Jainism—the second as the Muslim period.[59] The first period is described as the glorious age of imperial Hindu achievement in politics and culture, the second—despite its own glories of art and architecture, which are acknowledged—as a period of conquest, destruction, and consequent decay of Hindu civilization. The Hindu practices, customs, and superstitions that exist today are a consequence of that decay and, as many Hindu reformers of the nineteenth century argued, did not exist in the past. To revivify India and build a great, new, modern nation-state, it is necessary to "revive the true ideals of the past."[60]

This process of historical rectification also has been accompanied by a demonization of the Muslims as a separate people, a foreign body implanted in the heart of Hindu India, perpetually "warlike," who "believe it is their religious duty to kill infidels."[61] Muslims are also held responsible for the partition of the country because so many of their leaders remained aloof from the nationalist movement and ultimately fought for the creation of the separate independent state of Pakistan. The memory of the partition and the violence associated with it is ingrained in the minds of most Hindus and is kept alive by the constant tension in the relations between India and Pakistan. During the last decade, the "memory" of Muslim violence in Indian history has been kept vivid also by the militant Hindu demand to recapture and restore temples allegedly destroyed by Muslim conquerors and replaced by mosques, a movement that led to the destruction of the mosque at Ayodhya on December 6, 1992.

The periodization of Indian history that achieved ascendancy in Indian nationalism—not just militant Hindu nationalism—in the late nineteenth century was itself largely a product of British history-writing of the mid-nineteenth century that sought to place British rule within the long sweep of Indian history. Slightly refurbished by Indian nationalists, it emerged as the tripartite division of Indian history as a movement from "classical glory" to "medieval decline" under Muslim rule to a "modern renaissance"[62] of a new India which, in its secular version, encompassed Muslims, but in its Hindu nationalist version either did not or did so only grudgingly. In the latter version, as Chatterjee has put it in his discussion of one Bengali example, "a stereotypical figure of 'the Muslim'" emerged, "endowed with a 'national character': fanatical, bigoted, warlike, dissolute, and cruel."[63]

Although Muslim history and Muslim character in the Indian subcontinent were blackened and demonized in these ways and often were used to justify demands by Hindu nationalists in the nineteenth century for the British to rectify matters and restore to Hindus their rightful place in the new India emerging under colonial rule, ultimately the target of this historiography was the British, then the West in general, and finally the great powers, particularly the United States. India soon was perceived in the minds of Indian nationalists, when they gradually directed their aims towards the elimination of British rule, as a potential great power, the equal of the great powers of the West. It was a great, modern state that Indian nationalists, both secular and Hindu, sought to create after Independence.

In the pursuit of that goal, the Muslims of India came to be seen, particularly by Hindu nationalists, as an obstruction, along with Pakistan, whose very existence has, in the minds of such Hindu nationalists, been the principal post-Independence obstacle to India's achievement of its rightful place in a world dominated by great nation-states. This historical consciousness and teleology of Hindu nationalism has framed the modern discourse of Hindu-Muslim communalism and violence. The demographic distribution of the peoples of India and the landscape of the country have become populated with *lieux de mémoire*[64] that signify the violence done by Muslims to the Hindu body, the dangers of the Muslim populations that reside in the midst of Hindus in cities and towns, and Muslim institutions that teach Muslims to become traitors, all of which must be reformed, replaced, or extirpated before India can become whole, united, and powerful.

In the first category, signifiers of the violence done by Muslims to the Hindu body, are the mosques, said to number three thousand, that are alleged to have been built upon the ruins of Hindu temples destroyed by Muslim conquerors. In the second, signifying the dangers to the Hindu body in the present, are the concentrations of Muslim populations in cities and towns, described by militant Hindus as "mini-Pakistans." The leading example in the third category, signifying the traitors in the midst of the country, is the Aligarh Muslim University (AMU) located in the town of Aligarh in western Uttar Pradesh, ninety miles south-southeast of Delhi. The AMU was in fact one of the principal sites from which the ideology of Muslim separatism and then the Pakistan movement developed and spread in the late nineteenth and twentieth centuries.[65] It stands today in Aligarh on the outskirts of the city as a symbolic presence that signifies to militant Hindus the persistence into the present of Muslim separatist, communalist, and anti-Hindu designs, and justifies, along with the existence of "mini-Pakistans" in the center of the old city, violence against Muslims that is enacted in periodic outbursts of large-scale rioting. Aligarh has become, in fact, one of the principal sites of Hindu-Muslim violence in all of India since Independence up to the very recent past.

### PLAN OF THE VOLUME

I have selected Aligarh as the site of the present study and have chosen to focus on a single site for several reasons. First, as just indicated, it has been for more than a century, since the founding in 1875 of the Mohammadan Anglo-Oriental College that later became the AMU, a principal site of Hindu-Muslim tension. Second, numerous riots, large and small, have occurred in Aligarh both before and since Independence. In fact, since Independence, though there have been other cities and towns in India in which riots have been endemic and where some much larger riots and pogroms have occurred, it will be shown below that Aligarh stands close to the top, in some respects absolutely, in others relatively. In absolute terms, it has been second in the state of Uttar Pradesh (U.P.) in the number of known riots and deaths associated with them since Independence. Moreover, relative to its size, that is, by a crude measure of deaths per thousand persons, it stands close to the top in the country as well. Third, during thirty-eight years in which I have gone back and forth to Aligarh for research, I have heard here all the explanations for riots that are commonly given for riots everywhere else in the country: demographic, economic, and political. Finally, the city, as will be demonstrated later, is characterized by many of the features that characterize other riot-prone cities: notably, the relative size of the Hindu and Muslim populations and their juxtaposition in relation to each other, the existence of economic competition between segments of the two communities in particular trades and industries, and a history of intense electoral competition.

I have chosen to concentrate here on a single site rather than several sites for methodological reasons. First, although I have gathered considerable materials from several other sites of the same sort to be presented herein, and have published some of it elsewhere, I have concluded that studies from different sites of riots that have occurred in the same time period or at different times cannot explain their occurrence at a particular site at a particular time. For example, I have analyzed the post-Ayodhya riot in the metropolis of Kanpur in 1992.[66] An even worse riot occurred in Aligarh in 1990–91. Why did the Kanpur riot not occur the previous year, and why did no Aligarh riot occur in the following year? No form of ecological analysis can answer such a question. To answer that kind of question, diachronic rather than synchronic analysis is required. Second, concentration on a single city makes it possible to focus one's gaze more closely and intently at the specific localities in which riots have occurred within it, to determine what especially characterizes them. In other words, one achieves thereby a more fine-tuned look at riots than is possible when one classifies an entire city as riot-prone and seeks to compare it with other equally large units. Third, whereas much work has been done in attempting to explain "waves" of rioting, including many analyses that have claimed to have found a "contagion" effect in the spread of riots from one site to another in a short time period, I am not aware of any studies that have looked at rioting in a different way, namely, as a phenomenon endemic to a particular site or sites. While I remain alert in this volume to what is happening elsewhere when rioting does and does not occur in Aligarh, I am seeking an explanation for its persistence at this site, which can in turn be generalized as an explanation for recurring riots elsewhere as well. Fourth, during the thirty-eight years in which I have visited Aligarh, I have collected all the available election data for the city since Independence, down to the polling booth level, which I have converted into a large dataset that has made it possible for me to analyze precisely the relationship between riots and electoral competition.

Although Aligarh is a site of persistence, it is also a site of variation in two respects. First, even here, where Hindu-Muslim tensions seem to be always on the edge of violence in some parts of the city, there have been periods of relative relaxation. Those periods of abatement in rioting need to be explained as well as the numerous explosions. Of course, it is obvious that no society can live with continuous rioting, so there must be some break. If there is not, the situation is best described as a civil war. Since this is not the case in Aligarh, the absence of rioting in the town at certain times must be explained as well as its presence at others. It will be shown that presence and absence are explained by the same sets of factors.

Aligarh is a site of variation in another respect as well, namely, in the differential spatial incidence of rioting within the city when it does occur. Not all parts of the city are always affected by Hindu-Muslim riots and some have never been touched by it. For these reasons, it will be possible to demonstrate at this one urban site precisely in which localities rioting occurs, and to point out the differences between them and localities where rioting is not endemic, in ways that are not possible by the paired comparison method that selects entire cities as sites.

The rest of this volume is organized into five parts. Part II, consisting of four chapters, first presents a description of the general features of the demographic, caste, and communal composition of the city, then provides a detailed history of riots in Aligarh since Independence, with a separate chapter that focuses specifically on the great riots of December 1990 and January 1991, followed by a chapter that discusses the relative decline in riotous activity in the city during the following decade. Part III, consisting of two chapters, focuses on those factors in the social composition, distribution, and economic characteristics of the population that have commonly been considered conducive to Hindu-Muslim riots. Part IV, comprising five chapters, marshals evidence primarily from interviews and electoral data to demonstrate the close connection between riots and political competition. Part V contains three chapters that focus on the discourse of communalism and alternative contextualizations of riotous violence by politicians, police, and press. The conclusions concerning the persistence of riots and pogroms in Aligarh are provided in Part VI. A postscript has been added that brings the situation in Aligarh up to date as of the February 2002 elections. I have also included a discussion of the pogrom in the state of Gujarat that began at the end of February 2002 and continued until the end of March, with sporadic incidents of violence for weeks thereafter.

PART II

# Communal Riots
# in India and Aligarh

# 2 / Aligarh

## Politics, Population, and Social Organization

P arty politics, elections, and riots are political dramas of contestation involving simplification of complex realities. They reduce hetero-geneity and complexity in order to mobilize large enough numbers to form a party or movement, win an election, or confront a rival ethnic or religious group in riotous violence. This is especially so for competitive polit-ical systems in which election contests are decided by the first-past-the-post system in single-member, plurality constituencies, that is, where there is only one winner in a constituency in which the outcome is determined simply by who gets the largest number of votes. In the society of unparalleled hetero-geneity that is India, such simplification is both necessary for political suc-cess and difficult to achieve. Consolidation and mobilization of large ethnic groupings in violent conflict with each other is one of the methods that has been used in many parts of India, whose effect has been to create solid vot-ing blocs in succeeding elections.

Since the death of India's first prime minister, Jawaharlal Nehru, in 1964, and the decline of India's former ruling party, the Indian National Congress, along with the consensus that prevailed throughout Nehru's lifetime on the maintenance of a secular, composite nationalism, politics in India have oscil-lated between periods of fragmentation and consolidation, complexity and simplification. At the national level, repeated attempts have been made to articulate appeals and programs that would be effective in mobilizing large categories of voters across regions to encompass the country as a whole. These appeals have been both economic and cultural, including Indira Gandhi's pro-grams and policies designed to capture the votes of all the poor and disad-vantaged segments of society as well as the lowest castes (termed "Scheduled Castes") and minorities. The center and left opposition parties in north India countered with appeals to a huge segment of Indian society known as "backward castes," comprised primarily of middle agricultural and artisan casts encompassing a wide range of economic conditions and social status. In recent years, also, a new political formation has become politically important in north India, the Bahujan Samaj Party (BSP), claiming to speak for another "majority" *(bahujan)*, all the lowest and most deprived castes and classes of the country. Against both the Congress and the parties claiming to speak for caste categories and minorities have stood the Bharatiya Janata Party (BJP) and its associated organizations, claiming to speak on behalf of all the Hindus of India, north and south. In contrast, the parties opposed to the BJP have sought to amplify their own support bases among the backward and lower castes by seeking Muslim support; the Samajwadi (Socialist) Party (SP), the principal rival of the BJP in Uttar Pradesh (U.P.), has been particularly successful in doing so during the past decade.

Each of the regions of India has its own complexities. Indeed, the particularities of language, religious distributions, and regional cultures have been sufficient so far to prevent any reconsolidation of power at the Center behind a single new dominant party to replace the former hegemony of the Congress in the country as a whole. The BJP, presently (2001) the leading party in a central government coalition, has been the principal claimant for such a role.

India is so heterogeneous a country that complexity, and the consequent political need for simplication to overcome it, are evident not only in each region, but in every district, town, and village as well. Insofar as the huge state of U.P. is concerned (see frontispiece map), there have been four primary political formations in recent years, each of which has sought to consolidate large segments of the population. The formerly dominant Congress has declined to such an extent that it cannot be said any longer to be an effective political party in the state. The major political parties at present are the BJP, claiming to speak for all Hindus; the SP, which has its greatest strength among certain of the backward castes, particularly Yadavs; and the BSP, which has its greatest strength among the largest of the Scheduled Castes, the Chamars and Jatavs. None of these parties have been able to produce effective governing majorities in this state in recent years, either alone or in coalition. The ruling coalition in the state in 2001 was led by the BJP.

The same political formations have been important in the politics of Aligarh City, but Aligarh has been different in one important respect that foreshadowed the state's future. In 1962, twenty-five years before the disintegration of the Congress in the state as a whole, that party was defeated in the city in a critical election from which it never recovered. That victory was achieved by a consolidation and simplification of complexities through an alliance among the Muslims and Scheduled Castes, made possible by Muslim anger against the Congress after the communal riots of October 1962. As a consequence of that anger, Muslims joined with Scheduled Castes under the banner of a party called the Republican Party of India, then the leading party claiming to speak for the low castes. Since then, politics in Aligarh as well as in the state as a whole have oscillated between periods of consolidation and fragmentation. In Aligarh, in common with several other of the larger towns and cities in the state, consolidation has been associated with interreligious violence—indeed, as I will show, has followed upon communal rioting. When communal rioting has declined, the natural heterogeneity of the population has been reflected in increased fragmentation of voting and dispersion of votes among a larger number of political parties.

The purpose of this chapter is to lay out both the social heterogeneity of Aligarh's urban population as well as the simplified categories that are used in the census to encompass that heterogeneity. It has been noted by many historians and in my own earlier work that British census definitions of the population of India, imposed upon its diversity, were ultimately converted into social realities. One can witness the same process at work in contemporary census and political definitions of India's population, where political formations seek, in effect, to match in politics the consolidated numbers reflected in census categories. I will begin this discussion of complexity and simplification in Aligarh with the simplified religious and caste categories used in the census, after which I will show the very considerable heterogeneity that lies beneath those categories and that continues in peaceful times to be reflected in politics.

## RELIGION AND CASTE IN THE CENSUS OF ALIGARH

Census figures for the total population of Aligarh are available from 1901 to 1991,[1] during which period the population multiplied by nearly seven times from 72,084 to nearly half a million, or 480,520. The growth rate in both the municipality of Aligarh and in the census-defined standard urban area (SUA) surrounding it in the decade 1981–91 was huge, somewhat under 50 percent in the city and over 50 percent for the entire SUA, which includes a large number of villages. The population of the city has certainly passed the half-million mark during the last decade. However, some of this increase must be attributed to changes in the boundaries of the city through incorporation of outlying rural areas, including some previously unpopulated areas where new settlements have been established as well as some populated villages. The area incorporated within the city limits nearly tripled between 1941 and 1961, from just over 11 to nearly 32 square kilometers. Since then, the city area has increased by another two square kilometers, to 34.05 in 1991. It is believed by many Muslim and Hindu politicians in the city that the larger number of persons in the newly populated and incorporated areas comes from Muslims migrating from the villages of Aligarh District to the city, a matter that will be discussed further below (see Chapter 6).

For purposes of this book, the most important figures concern the religious and caste composition of the population. The census provides information—rather sporadically and incompletely—for three very broad caste/communal categories: Hindus, Muslims, and Scheduled Castes. Scheduled Castes are sometimes included in the Hindu population, sometimes not. Jains, Sikhs, Buddhists, and Christians have at times been lumped together in a general category designated "Hindus and others." Fortunately for our purposes, the numbers of these religious groups are quite small, although some are prominent in particular *mohalla*s (neighborhoods) of the city. Muslims, because of prejudices against them and political fears concerning their allegedly more rapid increase than Hindus, are sometimes undercounted both in census enumerations and in the preparation of voters' lists, another source of information on the Muslim population.[2]

Only four censuses provide a three-way division of the total population into Hindus, Muslims, and Scheduled Castes, those for 1951, 1971, 1981, and 1991 (Table 2.1). In 1951, Hindus comprised 54.17 percent of the city's population, Muslims 34.53 percent, and Scheduled Castes 9.99 percent. By 1991, however, the relative proportions of the three categories had changed considerably: they were 44.52 percent for Hindus, 37.41 percent for Muslims, and 16.51 percent for Scheduled Castes.

These figures are quite important for political reasons and calculations. Militant Hindus have claimed that the Muslim population has been increasing in the city through natural population growth and migration from the rural areas, thereby reducing the Hindus to a minority. While the figures now do show non–Scheduled Caste Hindus comprising less than a majority of the city's population, the result has been obtained not so much by a rapid increase in the Muslim population, which—despite a higher growth rate than that for Hindus—has increased in the census by less than 3 percentage points overall, but by a much greater increase in the Scheduled Caste population, which increased by 6.52 percentage points, or by 61 percent from 1951 to 1991. However, when the figures for Scheduled Castes are added to the non–Scheduled Caste Hindu population, they can be read as showing a continu-

TABLE 2.1 Population (in percentages) of Aligarh City
by religion and caste, 1951–91

| Year[a] | Hindus | Muslims | Scheduled Castes | Others |
|---|---|---|---|---|
| 1951 | 54.17 | 34.53 | 9.99 | 1.31 |
| 1971 | 50.34 | 33.08 | 14.44 | 2.14 |
| 1981 | 46.75 | 34.47 | 17.04 | 1.75 |
| 1991 | 44.52 | 37.41 | 16.51 | 1.55 |

[a] No figures available in 1961 for Hindus and Muslims; the percent Scheduled Caste in that year was 14.45.

ing Hindu majority in the city of above 60 percent. The political significance of these numbers lies in the fact that, when elections have been held in Aligarh City at times of tension between Hindus and Muslims, that is, in an atmosphere of communalization tending towards polarization, militant Hindu candidates have been likely to prevail. If, however, Scheduled Castes and Muslims combine, then no militant Hindu candidate can win the Aligarh Legislative Assembly seat. If a Scheduled Caste party or leader enters the fray, then the vote will be split at least three ways. All three of these outcomes—Hindu-Muslim polarization, Muslim–Scheduled Caste combination, and three-way division of the votes—have occurred at different times in the course of the electoral history of Aligarh from 1951 to 1998, as will be demonstrated in Part IV below.

Despite the fact that Muslims are sometimes undercounted, we get a clearer picture of Muslim population change in the city for the longer period from 1931 to 1991. The Muslim population stood at 42.85 percent in 1931, increased to 45.90 percent in 1941, then took a dramatic drop to 34.53 percent in 1951 in the aftermath of the mass migrations to Pakistan at the time of Partition in 1947 and after, which affected Aligarh profoundly. It is likely, considering the drop in the percentage of Muslims between 1941 and 1951, that somewhere around 13,000 to 16,000 Muslims left the city. The figure given during my first visit to Aligarh in 1961 was approximately 15,000 people, who left after the 1946 and 1950 riots.[3] After Prime Minister Nehru intervened to facilitate the return of Muslim emigrants who wanted to come back to India after the rioting ended, many did come back, but certainly the vast majority did not. In some localities, the communal character of the population changed radically during this period. According to Elizabeth Mann, one of the most riot-prone localities of the city, Manik Chauk, changed from a Muslim-majority *mohalla* to one "almost entirely inhabited by Hindus."[4]

In the intervening years, as already indicated, the Muslim population increased by less than three percentage points to reach 37.41 percent in 1991. It is generally believed that the Muslim population has increased still further during the past decade. As will be shown in Chapter 12, the dual increase in the Scheduled Caste and the Muslim population in the city limits has recently undermined the political base of the militant Hindu party, the BJP, in the politics of Aligarh, rendering its victory in the Aligarh City Legislative Assembly contests problematic.

CASTE, COMMUNITY, *BARADARI*

*Hindus and Others*

*Bania castes.* Census data on the distribution of Hindus and others by caste and community are not available. Among the Hindu castes, Vaishyas, also commonly called Banias, are generally considered to be the largest broad grouping, comprising around a fifth of the total population of the city and nearly 40 percent of the Hindu population. The two most prominent castes in this broad category in Aligarh are Barahsenis (also called Varshneys) and Agarwals. In Aligarh City, persons from both castes are primarily businessmen, shopkeepers, bankers, and industrialists.[5]

In Aligarh District and Aligarh subdivision (*tahsil* Koil), Agarwals have comprised the largest of the Bania castes, although in Aligarh City the Barahsenis are generally considered to be twice as numerous, accounting for 12 percent of the total population of the city compared to 6 percent for the Agarwals.[6] They are also "the most powerful group in the city—politically and economically," they "largely dominate trade and industry and have an elaborate group organization."[7] The mayor of the city, elected in 1995, was Ashutosh Varshney, a manufacturer and exporter of brass building hardware, handicrafts, and food products. The previous mayor, from 1989 to 1994, was O. P. Agarwal.

Before Independence, Agarwal cotton traders identified with the 1930 Congress boycott of British cloth, since they "had acquired much wealth by using locally produced cotton in ginning and pressing mills," while both Muslims and "the Baraseni [sic] wholesalers" did not participate in the boycott.[8] For some time after Independence, also, it was said that the Agarwals tended to be "pro-Congress,"[9] while the Barahsenis identified with militant Hindu nationalism and with the Jan Sangh and the BJP.

The local colleges in the city, whose faculty and students have provided leadership as well as mass support for political parties, rallies, and riotous activity, were also identified in 1962 with different Bania castes and different political identifications. Thus, the Maheshwaris, another Bania caste in the city, had their own college, the Maheshwari Inter-College, then managed by the Jan Sangh candidate for the Legislative Assembly seat in 1962. The Barahsenis had their own college also, the Barahseni Degree College, the manager of which at that time was also said to be a Jan Sanghi, while the D.S. (Dharma Samaj) College was "in the hands of the Congress."[10]

Politically, as late as 1980, Barahsenis and Agarwals were reported to have been divided, with the Agarwals declining to support the BJP candidate for the assembly election in that year. However, for the most part, as the communal polarization in the city has intensified after Independence, Barahsenis and Agarwals have been generally found on the same side politically, as members of the RSS,[11] as supporters of the BJP,[12] the Vishwa Hindu Parishad, and other RSS/BJP-affiliated organizations,[13] and as antagonists of the AMU.[14] In recent Aligarh elections, marked by polarized contests between Krishna Kumar Navman, a militant Hindu Barahseni politician from the *mohalla* of Manik Chauk, and a Muslim candidate, all Bania castes have voted overwhelmingly for Navman.[15] Nevertheless, there remains some sentiment among persons from the Agarwal community in favor of the Congress, one of whose members, Vivek Bansal, contested for the Aligarh Legislative Assembly constituency as the candidate of that party in 1993.[16]

*Brahmans.* After the Banias, the largest group of elite castes in the city is Brahman. Their proportion in the total population of the city has been estimated at approximately 8 percent. The Brahman population is widely distributed in the "predominantly Hindu localities," none in particular being identified as primarily Brahman.[17] Before Independence and for many years afterwards in U.P. and in Aligarh as well, Brahman castes provided both leadership and a relatively stable basis of support for the Congress, while at the same time contesting with other elite castes, particularly Thakurs,[18] for leadership predominance in both the district and city Congress organizations. Brahmans, for the most part, remained Congress supporters in Aligarh City as well as the rural areas of the district for many years after Independence. It was only in the 1980s, with the decline of the Congress in the state as a whole and with the rise of Hindu communal mobilization during the Ayodhya movement in the 1980s, that Brahmans, along with other high-caste Hindus such as Thakurs and Kayasthas, turned away from the Congress to join with the Banias in supporting the BJP.[19] However, Brahmans have never been prominent in Aligarh in the militant Hindu politics of the RSS and its affiliated organizations, including the Jan Sangh and the BJP.[20]

*Maithel Brahmans.* The Maithel Brahmans, who take the name of a high Brahman caste category from the north Bihar region of India,[21] are not accepted locally as such. They are an artisan caste, among whom those with the surname Sharma have been traditionally associated with carpenty. Maithels are described by Haqqi as an artisan caste "mostly engaged in the lock industry." They are said to constitute "one of the most cohesive and highly organized group[s]" in Aligarh, maintaining "an Intermediate College for the benefit of the community." Haqqi estimated the voting strength of this "lower rank" Brahman caste in 1971 at "between four to five thousand,"[22] so they would certainly number above five thousand today. They have large concentrations in some localities of Aligarh.

The Maithels do not always behave politically in the same manner as the other Brahman castes. One local politician remarked that, ordinarily, the Maithel and other Brahmans "are against each other," but in the case of a political/electoral contest between Brahmans and Thakurs, "they will join hands."[23] Moreover, in contemporary Aligarh politics, they have tended to vote, like upper-caste Hindus, for the BJP. All three of the Maithel Brahman municipal corporators were elected on the ticket of the BJP. At the same time, they identify themselves as backward castes and associate politically with other backward castes in local politics.

*Other Hindu castes.* Very little information is available on the other Hindu castes of Aligarh. Among the elite castes, the population of Kayasthas is estimated at around 4 percent of the electorate.[24] There are not many Rajputs (Thakurs) living in the city, but, like Rajputs everywhere in U.P., there are prominent persons from Rajput landowning families living in the city, who have some influence in local politics. Among the backward castes, the most important in the city numerically and politically are Yadavs, who support the SP, and Lodhs, Sainis, and Nais, who support the BJP.

### Scheduled Castes

Among the Scheduled Castes, the largest caste is Jatav, estimated at about 11 percent of the total population,[25] but comprising the overwhelming majority of the Scheduled Caste population in Aligarh City, as in the state as a whole. Jatavs in Aligarh have been an upwardly mobile caste for over a century; the caste's members having changed their preferred name from Chamars (traditionally leather workers) to Jatavs. Some converted to Sikhism and

Christianity in the pre-Independence years. Many in Aligarh, following the example of Dr. B. R. Ambedkar, who initiated this form of protest against Hindu caste discrimination in Maharashtra years before, adopted Buddhism in a mass conversion at the Achal Talab (see Figure 2.1), site of the central place of worship for Hindus in Aligarh, in 1957.[26] Although most Jatavs are manual laborers, some are "engaged in various types of professions and occupations including small-scale industries."[27]

Politically, the Scheduled Caste population, particularly its Jatav/Chamar segments, has played a critical role in several elections in Aligarh. Although in the state as a whole, Muslims and Scheduled Castes were part of the broad Congress coalition that underpinned that party's dominance in most of the post-Independence period up to the 1980s, as noted above, Jatavs in Aligarh broke early from the Congress to join with Muslims in administering the party's first major defeat in the city and the district. Since that time, Scheduled Castes have at times supported the Congress, at times opposition parties, and lately have concentrated their votes behind the BSP.[28] Despite fluctuations in Jatav voting behavior, there has been a consistent underlying basis of antagonism to parties such as the Congress and the BJP that have been dominated by upper castes, and a potential reservoir of support amongst the Jatavs for leaders or parties that speak on their behalf.

As in other parts of U.P., Scheduled Castes are divided politically. The lowest of the low castes, those whose traditional occupation is sweeping and scavenging, traditionally called Bhangis, but nowadays Balmikis, formerly supported the Congress.[29] They did not join with the Jatavs against the Congress in the 1960s[30] and in the 1990s have not supported the new Scheduled Caste party, the BSP, which they are said to consider a party "for the Jatav only, not for any other."[31] There are a number of other smaller groups of Scheduled Castes in the city, notably Koris (traditionally weavers), Dhobis (washermen), Dhuniyas (cotton carders), Aheriyas,[32] Kolis (foundry workers),[33] and Baghels. The bulk of the votes among these non-Jatav Scheduled Castes probably now goes to the BJP.[34]

Although Muslims and Jatavs among the Scheduled Castes have sometimes joined together electorally, it has also been reported, especially in recent years, that persons from some Scheduled Castes have participated in riots against Muslims. I was told that Scheduled Castes had "participated in a big way" in the 1990–91 riots in Aligarh, destroying and looting Muslim property, and had become "tools" in the hands of militant Hindus.[35] It was also charged that money was provided to lower castes by Krishna Kumar Navman for the purpose.[36] Persons from the Koli and Bhangi castes, particularly, were mentioned as hav-

FIG. 2.1. Achal Talab, 1999

ing engaged in "arson, looting, and stabbing,"[37] including working hand in hand with the police in singling out and stabbing and killing Muslims.[38]

## *Muslim* Baradaris

Although Islam does not recognize status or caste categories, Muslims in India are generally divided in fact into status and caste-like categories, called *baradaris* (brotherhoods) in Aligarh as well as elsewhere in the subcontinent. These *baradaris* are endogamous and are frequently associated "with a specific traditional occupation or lineage."[39] The *baradaris* also sometimes act as corporate groups, establishing mosques, shrines, and schools,[40] cooperating in economic activity, and taking political decisions on a group basis, influenced by "formal or informal leaders" who "establish liaison" between their *baradaris* and political parties.[41] Mann has argued for the importance of *baradaris*, which she characterizes as "the core unit of social organisation in the [old] City"[42] and which she claims have persisted as boundary-defining and identity-forming groups that are not necessarily all moving "towards a high Islamic tradition,"[43] nor, by implication, therefore, towards an overarching Muslim solidarity. Although she does not deny the "relevance of a corporate Muslim identity," she stresses the importance of "context" in determining the influence of *baradari,* on the one hand, and Islam, on the other.[44] Although there are other ways in which the Muslim populations of Aligarh and elsewhere have been classified,[45] for political purposes it is *baradaris*, on the one hand, and the Muslim community as a whole, on the other hand, that are most important.

Mann has identified twenty-four *baradaris* in Aligarh and listed them in hierarchical order based on her interviews between 1984 and 1986.[46] She has also identified some of the localities in which large concentrations of particular *baradaris* are found or where a particular *baradari* is prominent "in its internal affairs."[47] Table 2.2 lists those localities as well as others that Haqqi and others, including myself, have identified as being numerically dominated by or otherwise associated with particular Hindu castes and/or Muslim *baradaris*. There are no precise or reliable estimates of the size and relative numerical ranking of the Muslim *baradaris*. The most "prominent," socially, economically, and politically, in Mann's view[48] as well as in my own observations are the Qureshis, Ansaris, and Saifis. These three groups have undergone considerable social change and upward mobility in Aligarh and elsewhere and, like many Hindu castes, have adopted new names that do not carry the stigma associated with the older names.[49]

Qureshis are a quite numerous *baradari* that is commonly identified with the name Qasai, which in turn was traditionally identified with the occupation of butcher. However, the name Qasai, as well as the occupation associated with it, is rejected by virtually all Qureshis in the city, whose members have a multiplicity of occupations, including lock manufacturing, fruit and vegetable selling, transport, and manual labor.[50] The *baradari* as a whole has been upwardly mobile for some time; it has been undergoing "rapid economic growth," according to Mann.[51] Further, many of the most active and prominent Muslim politicians in the city come from this *baradari*. There are also Qureshis on the faculty of the AMU.

Haqqi characterizes the Qureshis as "the largest and most compact single unit among the Muslims." In 1978, he described the *baradari* as socially cohesive, but economically poor, with a low literacy rate and "negligible political influence," with a "voting strength of . . . a little over 5,000"[52] or approximately 5 percent of the electorate. Much has changed in the intervening years, as the members of this *baradari* have become more prominent in Aligarh public life and more politically influential.

Twelve *mohallas* have been identified in Table 2.2 in which Qureshis are the predominant *baradari,* and two in which they share predominance with Pathans. Pathans predominate in five *mohallas* and share dominance in three

TABLE 2.2. *Mohallas* in which particular castes/*baradaris*/sects are predominant

| Ward | Mohalla | Predominant caste/baradari/sect | Riot-hit/Crime-prone |
|------|---------|-------------------------------|---------------------|
| Kanwariganj | Sunet | Ansari | |
| Kanwariganj | Chandan Shaheed | Ansari | |
| Kanwariganj | Tila | Ansari | |
| Kanwariganj | Bani Israilan | Ansari | Riot-hit and crime-prone |
| Kanwariganj | Chira Ghachain | Ansari | |
| Achal Talab | Surendranagar | Bania/Thakur | |
| Shahpara | Sarai Ghosian | Ghosi | |
| Achal Talab | Gambhirpura | Maithel Brahman | |
| New Ward 33 | Jwalapuri | Maithel Brahman | |
| Achal Talab | Vishnu Puri | Maithel Brahman (Sharmas/Misras) | |
| Kanwariganj | Gali Hajjaman | Nai | |
| Jaiganj | Turkman Gate | Pathan | |
| Kanwariganj | Atishbazan | Pathan | Riot-hit and crime-prone |
| Turkman Gate | Turkman Gate | Pathan | Riot-hit and crime-prone |
| Turkman Gate | Usmanpara | Pathan | Sensitive and crime-prone, but not riot-hit |
| Turkman Gate | Ataiyan | Pathan | |
| Jaiganj | Sarai Pathanan | Pathan/Qureshi | |
| Turkman Gate | Delhi Darwaza | Pathan/Qureshi | Riot-hit and crime-prone |
| Kanwariganj | Tantanpara | Pathan/Saifi | Sensitive |
| Mamubhanja | Sarai Behram Beg | Qureshi | Riot-hit, but not crime-prone |
| Raghubirpuri | Sarai Rahman | Qureshi | Riot-hit, but not crime-prone |
| Mamubhanja | Phapala | Qureshi | |
| Shahpara | Qanungoyan | Qureshi | |
| Shahpara | Sarai Sultani | Qureshi | |
| Shahpara | Qazipara | Qureshi | |
| Shahpara | Sarai Bibi | Qureshi | |

TABLE 2.2. *(continued)*

| Ward | Mohalla | Predominant caste/baradari/sect | Riot-hit/ Crime-prone |
|---|---|---|---|
| Shahpara | Khaidora | Qureshi | Riot-hit and crime-prone |
| Jaiganj | Babri Mandi | Qureshi | |
| Jaiganj | Sarai Kale Khan | Qureshi | |
| Kanwariganj | Khaidora | Qureshi | Crime-prone |
| Turkman Gate | Sarai Mian | Qureshi | |
| Kanwariganj | Sheikhan | Sheikh/Saifi | Sensitive |
| Jaiganj | Syedwara | Shi'a | |
| Mamubhanja | Manik Chauk | Varshney (Barahseni) | Riot-hit |

others. Three of the five predominantly Pathan *mohallas* are considered communally sensitive, riot-hit, and/or crime-prone.[53] Four of the twelve Qureshi *mohallas* are also so classified. Two others in this category are *mohallas* in which Pathans share dominance with Qureshis and Saifis. Several of my interview respondents and some documentary sources as well claim that Qureshis are particularly active during riots, but this is a disputed matter that will be taken up at several places later in this book. Strangely, though the association in the table between riot-proneness and Pathan localities is even stronger than that with the Qureshis, I have not myself heard the Pathans mentioned as a *baradari* that is particularly active in riots.

The third numerous and important *baradari* is the Momin Ansars (Ansaris), who predominate in five *mohallas*, only one of which is classed as riot-hit and crime-prone. Ansaris in Aligarh today are mostly manufacturers and workers, according to Mann, but there are also prominent Ansaris in many walks of life, including at the AMU.[54]

In the pre-Independence era, Ansaris, the largest Muslim *baradari* in the whole of north India, were mostly pro-Congress, while the upper-status *baradaris* tended towards the Muslim League and ultimately towards the Pakistan movement. While members of some of the high-status *baradaris*, such as the Shamsi, left Aligarh for Pakistan after partition,[55] "the Ansaris of Aligarh largely remained in the city." Their continuing support for the Congress after Independence was rewarded by their recognition "as a backward group by the government," entitling them to receive "favourable terms for business loans and educational opportunities from state and government agencies," which in turn made it possible for many members of the *baradari* to rise on the economic and status ladders.[56]

The question of *baradari* versus a broader Muslim identity is of considerable political importance in Aligarh, as we will note throughout this volume, where it will be shown that *baradari* has sometimes undermined Muslim political solidarity, while at other times Muslim identity has consolidated and brought together all or virtually all *baradaris* on a common political platform. However, insofar as *baradari* members do recognize "a common sense of being a Muslim," I agree fully with Mann that this sense of unity "is not vested in a high Islamic tradition." There is, in her view, both an internalization of a sense of Islamic oneness (which, however, "does not stand up very well to external pressures") as well as an externalization that arises "through contrast, and at times even confrontation, with other religious communities."[57] As I will argue below, it arises in Aligarh primarily out of political contestation against the rise of militant Hinduism. In the absence of such direct contestation, the tendency among Muslims, as among Hindus, is to identify with the contradictory but "empirical reality of baradari and elites," rather than with "solidarity under a banner of Islam."[58]

Mann has provided a clear example of inter-*baradari* conflict in Aligarh, between the high-status Shamsi and the lower-status *baradaris*, led by the Ansaris, for control over the *dargah* (Muslim shrine) of Shah Jamal, a struggle over "both spiritual and financial" resources under the control of the *dargah,* as well as an assertion of status on the part of the Ansaris.[59] Such examples of inter-*baradari* conflict over the symbols and rituals of Islam challenge, in her view, the role of the latter in building Muslim solidarity. My own interviews provide evidence, also, of political divergence among *baradaris* in electoral contests, which will be noted in the analysis of electoral contests in Part IV. These examples of inter-*baradari* conflict support the argument that will be made below, that Muslim solidarity arises primarily as a consequence of political struggle with militant Hindus, that even then it is difficult to achieve, and that it is not at all religious sentiment that provides the catalyst for political solidarity.

### Caste, Community, and Political Influence

Varshney has noted that, if the figure of 21 percent is taken as an accurate estimate of the population of the trading castes in the city, and if one adds to this figure the known figures for Muslims and Scheduled Castes, then these

TABLE 2.3 Caste/community of members
of the Aligarh municipal corporation, 1995

| | | |
|---|---|---|
| Total Hindus and others | | 29 |
| Bania and other business castes | 11 | |
| Agarwal (5) | | |
| Varshney (4) | | |
| Khatri (1) | | |
| Sindhi (1) | | |
| Brahman castes | 7 | |
| High Brahman castes (4) | | |
| Maithel Brahmans (3) | | |
| Thakurs (Jadon) | 2 | |
| Backward castes | 8 | |
| Lodhi (4) | | |
| Saini (1) | | |
| Nais (2) | | |
| Other (1) | | |
| Jain | 1 | |
| Muslims | | 19 |
| Scheduled Castes | | 12 |
| TOTAL | | 60 |

three categories of the population comprise "about 70 per cent of the town population."[60] Although there has been a tendency in Aligarh politics for these three potential groups in the population to act as if they were politically solid blocks, I have noted above that there are multiple divisions among all three of these broad categories that also express themselves in politics from time to time. Both tendencies will be analyzed in detail in succeeding chapters. It is readily observable, however, from the distribution by caste and religion of the members of the Aligarh municipal corporation elected in 1995, that Varshney's calculations are precisely reflected therein (see Tables 2.3 and 2.4): the Bania castes taken together account for 18 percent of the seats, the Muslims for 32 percent, and the Scheduled Castes for 20 percent, amounting in all to 70 percent of the total.

Table 2.5, which gives the distribution by political identification of the castes and communities represented in the municipal corporation, also

TABLE 2.4. Caste/community of members (in percentages)
of the Aligarh municipal corporation, 1995

| | | |
|---|---:|---:|
| Hindus and others | | 48 |
| Bania and other business castes | 18 | |
| Brahman castes | 12 | |
| Thakurs | 3 | |
| Backward Castes | 13 | |
| Jain | 2 | |
| Muslims | | 32 |
| Scheduled Castes | | 20 |
| TOTAL | | 100 |

TABLE 2.5. Political identification of members of the Aligarh
municipal corporation by caste/community, 1995

| | Political Identification | | | |
|---|---|---|---|---|
| Caste/community | BJP | BSP | SP | Ind. |
| Hindus and others | 27 | 0 | 0 | 2 |
| Scheduled Castes | 5 | 6 | 0 | 1 |
| Muslims | 0 | 5 | 8 | 6 |
| TOTAL | 32 | 11 | 8 | 9 |

gives a sense of the relative importance of caste and communal solidarity/ division as a basis for political influence and control in Aligarh. In the 1995 municipal corporation, all but two Hindus (a Varshney and an Agarwal) affiliated with the BJP. The Scheduled Castes divided three ways: six with the BSP, five with the BJP, and one Independent. The five Scheduled Caste BJP members provided that party with majority control in the corporation. Among the three main caste/communal categories in the city, the Muslims were the most divided: six were independents, eight affiliated with the SP, and five with the BSP. As of 1995, therefore, one could say that political identifications in the municipal corporation were communalized to a degree, but not polarized. Non-Scheduled Caste Hindus and Muslims shared no political identification. "Hindus and others" (the latter including one Jain) were virtually completely unified across all caste and religious boundaries, but

Muslims were divided. Scheduled Castes constituted a divided swing force. It will be shown in succeeding chapters how politics in Aligarh City have fluctuated since Independence between poles of consolidation and fragmentation, communalization and internal division, polarization and depolarization, and how these fluctuations have been influenced by riotous violence.

# 3 / Hindu-Muslim Violence in India and Aligarh

THE INCIDENCE OF HINDU-MUSLIM RIOTS
AND THEIR CONSEQUENCES FOR THE MEMBERS
OF THE TWO COMMUNITIES

*Incidence and Basic Facts: 1950–95*

The annual reports of the Home Ministry of the government of India, whose responsibility includes reporting on the state of law and order in the country, including the incidence of communal riots, has failed to produce its annual reports for the past fifteen years, the most recent one available being for the year 1984–85. Those reports that were produced in earlier years have many defects, including absence of a definition of what constitutes a communal incident[1] and a failure to specify for most years the numbers of persons killed according to religious community as well as the numbers killed in communal clashes and those killed by the police. The latter types of figures certainly exist, but have been available even unofficially only for the years 1968 to 1980.

Official figures compiled from several sources, including the Home Ministry, calculate the total number of incidents of communal violence between 1954 and 1982 as 6,933, but provide no other details between 1954 and 1967 and after 1980. Between 1968 and 1980, the Home Ministry reported that there had been 3,949 communal incidents in which 530 Hindus, 1,598 Muslims, and 159 "other" persons and police personnel were killed.[2] The latter figures confirm, at least in the period for which such a breakdown by community is available, the often-stated fact that a disproportionate number of Muslims have been killed in communal riots. In some riots, the ratio of Muslims to Hindus killed has been very much higher. For example, during the

60

riots of September 1969 in the city of Ahmadabad, 512 persons were killed of whom 24 were Hindus, 430 Muslims, 58 "others" and unidentified;[3] the latter category is a rather grisly one since it suggests either burning of the murdered person's body beyond recognition, or mutilation. The official figures that are available as well as media and other reports concerning police treatment of Muslims during riots demonstrate clearly, also, that police arrest, fire upon, and kill disproportionately more Muslims than Hindus.[4] Moreover, concerning several major riots, commissions of inquiry have established that the police arrest innocent Muslims, kill them inside their homes, and enter mosques to shoot and kill Muslims as well.

Varshney and Wilkinson, using news reports from the *Times of India,* have compiled sets of figures on the numbers of riots—defined as communal incidents in which there was at least one death—for India as a whole and by state for the period 1960–93. Unfortunately, the figures have been published only in chart form; consequently, exact numbers for the entire period or for any part of it cannot be calculated. The trends, however, are quite clear from their charts. The number of Hindu-Muslim riots rose during the 1960s, reaching a peak in 1969, declined between 1971 and 1977, then began "an unambiguous and alarming increase during the years from 1978–93."[5]

Rioting and killings in the years between 1990 and 1993 reached peaks not seen since 1947. In these three years, there were two waves of riots across large parts of northern and western India, associated with the mass mobilizations and provocative and incendiary tactics used by two of the organizations in the RSS family, the Vishwa Hindu Parishad (VHP) and the BJP, to mobilize the Hindu community behind the demand to remove the Babri Mosque from its site in Ayodhya. This movement was also associated with the electoral strategy of the BJP to displace the Congress from power in the northern and western states and at the Center by consolidating the Hindu vote in its favor. Since the last wave of riots occurring in December 1992 and January 1993 in the aftermath of the destruction of the mosque, there has been a marked decline in the incidence of communal riots, but no exact figures are available at this writing.[6]

Among the fifteen largest states in the Indian Union, five ranked especially high in the incidence of Hindu-Muslim clashes involving fatalities; in rank order by number of such clashes, they were Gujarat, Maharashtra, Uttar Pradesh, Bihar, and Madhya Pradesh.[7] In Uttar Pradesh (U.P.), which is the focus of our inquiries here, Wilkinson identified 193 riots in the period between 1950 and 1993, in which 1,313 deaths occurred.[8] Varshney's figures for riot deaths in U.P. in riots in which there was at least one death in the period 1950–1993 show a sharp drop in the years after Partition, between 1950 and 1980, when the number of deaths in a single year never reached the level of 1950 (approximately 75 deaths). In many years during this period, there were no riots with fatalities. Although there were several years in which there were major riots with large numbers of fatalities, particularly 1961, 1968, 1971, 1972, and 1978, the peak year in this period was 1978, when fatalities rose to nearly 60. Between 1980 and 1992, however, the situation in the state changed dramatically. Successive new peaks of riot-produced fatalities were reached in 1980 (over 160 deaths), 1990 (over 180 deaths), and 1992 (over 200 deaths). In 1987, also, the number of deaths (above 140) surpassed the number in 1950. Moreover, the general level of such violent riots remained quite high during this second period, except in 1981 and between 1983 and 1985.[9]

The violence in U.P. has also been spread widely among a number of large and small cities and towns. Between 1960 and 1993, Wilkinson identified 24 cities and towns in India that he characterized as "riot-prone." Of the 24, six (25 percent) were located in U.P., the largest state in India, containing 16 percent of the population of the country as a whole. Fifty-nine of the 249 communal incidents, or 24 percent, occurred in these six towns, and 579, or 14 percent, of the total of 4,005 deaths. Within U.P., figures provided by Wilkinson for the longer period from 1950 to 1993 placed the town of Aligarh at the top; according to his dataset, there were 25 riots in this town in that period, in which 388 persons were killed.[10] However, his count of both Hindu-Muslim riots and of reported deaths is not accurate (see Table 3.1). The count I have compiled includes 18 riots and riotous periods, in 10 of which there were deaths in the period 1950–93, giving an estimated total death toll of 176; adding the pre-Independence and the 1994 and 1995 riots to the count gives a total of 23 riots, 14 with deaths totalling 195. If the other figures in the Wilkinson/Varshney dataset are accurate, Aligarh would stand second to the nearby district of Meerut, for which their reported death toll, 1950–95, is 265.[11] Even given the lower figures for Aligarh, it remains clear enough that the town is among the most riot-prone in the country. Moreover, although Aligarh is associated in the minds of most Hindus in north India with the name of Sayyid Ahmad Khan, the founder of the AMU and the Muslim League, and with the Muslim separatist movement that led to the creation of Pakistan, it is a matter of some surprise to note that in the entire period from 1900 to 1949, the number of riots and riot deaths was substantially lower; there were 4 Hindu-Muslim riots in Aligarh and 11 riot deaths in that period. Aligarh ranked eighth in the state in that period in the number of riots.[12] Aligarh's rise to promi-

TABLE 3.1. Riots and riot deaths in Aligarh City, 1925–95

| Date | Official or newspaper death toll |
|------|----------------------------------|
| September 22, 1925 | 6 |
| April 10–11, 1927 | 0 |
| November 3, 1937 | 1 |
| March 29, 1946 | 4 |
| Pre-Independence Total | 11 |
| March 3–4, 1950[a] | 5 |
| June 6, 1954 | 0 |
| September 14, 1956 | 0 |
| October 1–3, 1961[b] | 15 |
| 1966 (date not specified)[c] | 0 |
| 1969 (date not specified) | 0 |
| March 2, 1971[d] | 17 |
| June 1971[e] | 0 |
| June 1972[f] | 1 |
| October 3–5, 1974 | 0 |
| October–December 1978[g] | 28 |
| May 1979[h] | 5 |
| June 17, 1979[i] | 0 |
| August–November 1980[j] | 11 |
| October 1988[k] | 2 |
| November 10, 1989[l] | 0 |
| November 1990–January 1991[m] | 92 |
| December 1992 | Some, but no figure |
| March 10, 1995[n] | 8 |
| Post-Independence Total | 184 |
| GRAND TOTAL | 195 |

[a]Wilkinson's code sheet from the *Times of India* lists 4 dead in this riot; so does the *Free Press Journal,* March 6, 1950. My figure comes from the *Times of India* (Bombay edition), March 6, 1950; however, the headline of the article lists 7 dead while the text refers to 5 dead. There is clearly no consensus in the press on this matter. I have simply chosen the *Times of India* over the *Free Press Journal* to try to make the data source the same as that for Varshney-Wilkinson wherever possible. However, the Varshney-Wilkinson dataset lists 68 dead in this riot, which is certainly incorrect. Wilkinson has acknowledged in a personal communication that their total may have included Moradabad (a town in a different district) as well as Aligarh. So, there is a small discrepancy between my and the Varshney-Wilkinson data on what

TABLE 3.1 *(continued)*

the actual figure is in the *Times of India* as well as a very large one with regard to my figure and their dataset.

[b]I have two unpublished documents prepared by a former district magistrate, one of which, "Riots in Aligarh," gives the official figure of deaths in this riot as 13, while a second, "Muslims and the Aligarh Muslim University," gives the official death toll as 15, all Muslims. Since the latter document also notes that "unofficially the number [of deaths of Muslims] was believed around 40," I am using the larger figure as closer to the truth.

[c]References to a riot this year and in 1969 from "Riots in Aligarh."

[d]Source for figure in column 2: *Times of India* (New Delhi edition), March 31, 1971.

[e]Centre for Research in Rural and Industrial Development (CRRID), Chandigarh, "Communal Violence and its Impact on Development and National Integration," unpublished, undated, p. 35. However, I have not been able to find any press reports on this riot.

[f]Source for this riot and the single death is from "Riots in India." However, the date given for this riot in the report is August 1972, which is incorrect, so the reported death also may be erroneous.

[g]Source for figure in column 2: *Patriot*, November 26, 1978. This, of course, is an extended riotous period, not a single event or cluster of events.

[h]Source for figure in column 2: *Times of India*, May 12, 1979.

[i]Graff, "Religious Identities and Indian Politics," p. 72.

[j]As indicated in the discussion below of this series of riots, there is ambiguity in the press reports concerning whether or not the death toll, including two policemen, was actually 13.

[k]Source of figure in column 2: *Times of India*, October 9, 1988.

[l]The Wilkinson dataset lists 3 deaths in this riot, but I found no reported deaths in either the *Times of India* (New Delhi edition) or in a Hindi newspaper of which I have only copies of the relevant articles with no source or date.

[m]The Wilkinson dataset gives a figure of 240 deaths in this riot, but is certainly incorrect and is probably derived from a lumping together of riot deaths in other towns at the same time with those from Aligarh. The figure of 92 is the official death toll, which neither Muslim groups nor the People's Union for Civil Liberties ("Communal Riots in Aligarh, Dec. 1990–Jan. 1991," *PUCL Bulletin* [March, 1991]) accept. Muslim groups claim a documented list of 100 deaths for Muslims alone, whereas the PUCL estimates the total death toll for both Hindus and Muslims as between 125 and 150.

[n]The figure of 8 deaths is the official figure reported by the District Magistrate to Asghar Ali Engineer, "Aligarh Riots—An Unplanned Outburst," in *Towards Secular India* 1, no. 2 (April–June, 1995): 92. The last report that mentioned the number of deaths in the *Times of India* (New Delhi), March 12, 1995, gave a figure of 6 till that date. The discrepancy again reveals the dangers of relying on newspaper reports in such matters.

nence as one of the most riot-prone towns in the state and country, therefore, is a phenomenon of its post-Independence history.

From the point of view of persistence, there can be no doubt that Aligarh ranks close to the top in India in the number and seriousness of Hindu-Muslim riots since Independence. In Varshney's count, using four different criteria for riot-proneness in Indian cities and towns, the same five cities appear at the top by all four counts as well as by the total number of deaths in riots between 1950 and 1995: Bombay, Ahmadabad, Hyderabad, Meerut, and Aligarh. The four criteria are: minimum of 15 deaths in 3 riots over two five-year periods; minimum of 20 deaths in 4 riots over three five-year periods, minimum of 25 deaths in 5 riots over four five-year periods, and minimum of 50 deaths in 10 riots over five five-year periods.[13]

*Some Other Important Features of Hindu-Muslim Riots*

Deaths in Hindu-Muslim riots have three sources: "mob action," police killings, and "isolated incidents." "Mob action" may take the form of confrontations between gangs or crowds from different communities or segments of them, armed with sticks, knives, swords, occassionally bombs and small weapons, and kerosene. It often also involves armed gangs from one community seeking out defenseless persons or whole families in their homes, slashing and cutting up the male members and sometimes the female members, raping the latter, and burning all alive. A second source is police killings, which account for a large percentage of deaths in several major riots for which figures have been provided in inquiry commission reports, and which cannot be justified in terms of "crowd control." These killings are disproportionately of Muslims. Third, a good part of the killing takes the form of cold-blooded murder of individuals in "isolated incidents" rather than in killings arising from "mob frenzy." Such killings are often the precipitant or perhaps the starting signal for the production of a riot.

One further feature of riots deserves note. The government of India and the state governments do virtually nothing after a riot to prosecute and convict persons suspected of promoting or participating in riots. Occasionally, but less frequently in recent years, commissions of inquiry are appointed. If the final reports are not too damaging to the government of the day or to the political supporters of that government in the Hindu or Muslim communities, the report may be published. More often than not, there is a significant delay before publication. Some reports are never made public.[14] The consciences, if any, of the authorities are fully served by the payment to the survivors of riot victims a fixed sum of money—fixed in advance by law and in a published schedule—for the lives of the persons killed, thereby transforming riots into a ghastly, crude form of public relief, which in turn is abused by some members of the public, whose sons and brothers conveniently disappear from the slums after riots while other family members claim—and sometimes quarrel over—the death benefit.

HISTORY OF RIOTS

AND OTHER COMMUNAL INCIDENTS IN ALIGARH

*Problems in Riot Enumeration*

Both riot counting and the counting of deaths in riots are precarious exercises. They also carry an odor of callousness about them that must be avoided as far as possible, for they resemble nothing so much as body counts in contemporary insurrectionary warfare. Like such body counts, the numbers of riot deaths are suspect and contested by opposing sides.

There is first the matter of defining a riot. In Indian criminal law, a riot is "an assembly of five or more persons" engaged in unlawful activities directed against government institutions, the laws, persons, or property for the purpose of commiting "mischief or criminal trespass, or other offence."[15] Such a sweeping definition allows for much disputation in law concerning whether, when, and for what purposes an assembly is or is not "unlawful" and whether or not the persons assembled committed any of the prohibited acts. Further, although the case law on the subject refers to various incidents of rioting between Hindus and Muslims, there is no separate law defining communal riots. The definition of a riot as a communal or Hindu-Muslim riot, therefore, is a matter of public interpretation and labelling that takes place on the streets, in the media, in the legislatures, in cabinet meetings, and in the civilian and police administration.

There is, therefore, a double ambiguity built into riot counting that stems from the definition of riots in general and the absence of a definition of communal riots. This ambiguity is compounded when the variable of administrative action is considered. The latter enters the picture before the law when the local or state administration does or does not decide to be vigilant in preventing and/or controlling riots. The paradoxical result in this case is that riot figures may go up—and have in fact gone up—when the administration is most vigilant in enforcing the law against riots, including communal riots.

Still another complication arises when the numbers of persons involved in riots increases exponentially beyond the minimal five persons and when such activities extend to numerous and sometimes widely separated areas of a city or town. In such cases, the police may or may not count 50 riots, while the press and the politicians lump all or most incidents that occur within a particular time frame as one riot, communal or otherwise. In the Aligarh case, as will be shown below, this problem becomes extreme when riotous activity extends over weeks and months. It is a statistical artifice to count, for example, periods of riotous activity extending over three or four months, such as occurred in Aligarh in 1978 and 1980 (see Table 3.1), as one riot or two or three, when the number of incidents—some communal in nature, some not, some ambiguous—may be very high.

One might think that there would be no similar ambiguity in the counting of persons killed during a period of rioting. A death is not usually a matter of dispute, although the circumstances of the death may be. Nevertheless, every large-scale riot in India occasions dispute over the numbers of persons killed or injured. Members of the community targeted in riots always say that the number of deaths was higher than that officially noted, while persons from the other community say the figures were accurate. The local administration obviously has an interest in minimizing its failure to maintain law and order by undercounting. Rival parties in and out of office exaggerate or minimize the death counts to blame and embarrass each other or to decrease responsibility.

But, how can the counts be so disputable? There are grisly as well as some less grisly reasons for overcounting or undercounting. Bodies are burnt to ashes, thrown in canals, dumped in wells and sewers. As previously indicated, men may disappear during riots so that their families can make a claim for death payments from government. For all these and other reasons, both the counting of riots and the numbers killed and injured must be treated cautiously.

Although Aligarh ranks very high in the country in riot-proneness proportionately to population and in the number of deaths over the 50 years from 1946 to 1995, there has been, even here, considerable variation in the number of riots and the number of deaths that have occurred during them. Of the twenty riots classifiable as Hindu-Muslim, eleven led to deaths, distributed as follows: 1946–50, two riots with 9 deaths; 1951–55, no riots with deaths; 1956–60, no riots with deaths; 1961–65, one riot with 15 deaths; 1966–70, no riots with deaths; 1971–75, two riots with 18 deaths; 1976–80, numerous riots with 44 deaths; 1981–85, no riots with deaths; 1986–90 (terminating in January 1991), two riots with 94 deaths; 1991–95, two riots with more than 8 deaths. Since the number of communal riots in two of these periods cannot be counted accurately, extending as they did over several months in 1978, 1980, and 1990–91, they cannot be presented graphically. Therefore, the number of deaths in each period will have to stand—and reasonably so, for that matter—for variation in the intensity of riot activity in Aligarh (see Figure 3.1).

There are three aspects of riot variation to note from these figures and the accompanying chart. First, there was an initial decline in riot activity in Aligarh after the rioting that occurred before and after Partition, as elsewhere in the country. Second, there are four periods in which there were no riots

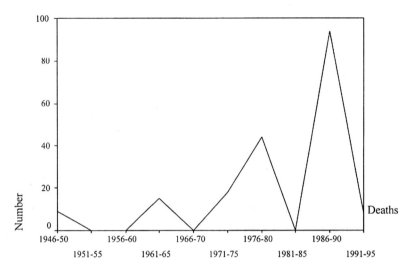

Five-Year Period

FIG. 3.1. Number of deaths in Hindu-Muslim riots
in Aligarh by five-year periods, 1946–95

in which deaths occurred. Third, however, over the entire period there has been a marked increase in the peaks of violence, with the number of deaths increasing sharply with each successive time of intense and murderous riot activity.

Intense rioting in Aligarh has at times deviated from the pattern in the rest of the country, at times mirrored it.[16] For example, there were no riots with deaths in Aligarh in 1966–70, when riot deaths in the country reached a peak not to be encountered again until the post-Ayodhya period. Similarly, although an unknown number of deaths occurred in December 1992 and an additional 8 deaths occurred in March 1995, the number was certainly small in comparison to other parts of the state and country, which were experiencing between 1991 and 1995 the worst five-year period in the history of post-Independence India, as well as in the state of U.P. On the other hand, the two five-year intervals from 1971 to 1980 were ones of intense riotous activity in Aligarh, partly mirrored in the state as a whole, but much less so in the country as a whole. Finally, there is one period marked by intensive riotous activity in Aligarh, in the state of U.P., and in the country as a whole, namely that of 1986–90, in which the movement to destroy the mosque in Ayodhya waxed. It is the case, therefore, that intense riotous activity in Aligarh must be explained partly in terms particular to the city and partly in relation to activities taking place simultaneously in the state and in the country as well as in Aligarh.

There is a further aspect of variation in Aligarh's history of riot production. If we count all riots in the post-Independence period, then it would appear to be the case that Aligarh is a site of persistence, of recurring riotous activities. That fact would be further confirmed by visits to particular riot-prone *mohallas* where, as the Centre for Research in Rural and Industrial Development study has noted, and I have personally experienced many times, there is a palpable sense of tension "in the air," evidenced by the existence of simmering local issues involving Hindus and Muslims on opposite sides and by the reactions to my very presence in such *mohallas*, especially when I have attempted to make inquiries on these local issues. Suffice it to say that I and my companions were always eager to leave such places without pursuing questions very far, as crowds, almost always Hindu crowds, began to form and persons began to appear wanting to know my business and eager to set me straight in no uncertain terms about my questions.

Yet, even given the situation just described in the most riot-prone areas of the city, there is variation in the very fact that some riots lead to killings, others do not; that some riots are prevented or controlled quickly by firm administrative action, others are not; and that, at times, riots occur when least expected and do not occur when most expected. In all these respects, the history of flux in riotous activity in Aligarh provides ample materials to consider the dynamics of riot production from all relevant angles. The remainder of this chapter will provide a detailed history, from information provided in official records, newspaper reports (mostly from the *Times of India*), a few secondary sources, and my own interviews, of all riots in which either deaths occurred or there are reports of violence and injuries from five or more sites in the city (see Table 3.1 and Appendix Table A.2) between 1925 and 1995, a seventy-year period.

In this overview, especially with regard to newspaper reports and government documents, the information that comes from these sources is predominantly of two types. The first consists of factual accounts of specific actions said to have precipitated the riots, occasionally including some background describing "rising tensions" that preceded the precipitating incidents, and accounts from day to day of particularly dramatic incidents involving clashes between Hindus and Muslims or between the police and rioters, all of this accompanied by daily body counts and counts of the injured. In the case of the larger riots, there also generally follows more or less extensive commentary from a variety of individuals, groups, political parties, the media itself, and other sources on their causes, which are predominantly exercises in blame displacement. In the largest riots, which occasion not only press reports but reports from visiting teams of human and civil rights organizations, we get glimpses of the dynamics of riot production that are otherwise hidden from view. My own interviews here and in the succeeding chapters of this volume are designed to enlarge to the extent possible the concealed and systematic aspects of riot production. Sometimes the reporting on riots also notes a connection between them and local and extralocal political circumstances. Some attention will also be paid to those circumstances in this chapter, but they will be given more detailed treatment in later chapters.

## Pre-Independence Riots

It is noteworthy, given the nationalist historiography concerning British policies of divide and rule and their responsibility for communal antagonisms and violence, that the number of riots in this town—and for that matter in the twenty towns in U.P. classified by Wilkinson as "riot-prone"—were greater in the forty-three years from 1950 to 1993 than in the 49 years from 1900 to 1949. The earlier period includes not only all the years of British rule in the twentieth century, but the years of pre- and post-Independence, post-Partition rioting in 1946–47.

Between 1923 and 1927, there were 88 riots classified as communal in the United Provinces (as U.P. was then known) "in which thirty-nine Hindus and forty-two Muhammadans were killed and one thousand five hundred and sixty-six Hindus and seven hundred and thirty-five Muhammadans were wounded."[17] Serious rioting was reported from several of the large cities and towns in U.P. in each of the five years between 1923 and 1927. These riots occurred during an intense period of competitive Hindu-Muslim political and religious mobilization accompanied by a great wave of rioting following upon the collapse of Hindu-Muslim cooperation during the combined non-cooperation/Khilafat movement of 1921–22. A riot occurred in Aligarh during this period on September 22, 1925. The Aligarh riot of 1925 was the major riot noted in that year in U.P. and was among the worst of "sixteen communal riots reported in 1925" in the country as a whole.[18] Indeed, it even drew the attention of the London *Times* in two notices on September 25 and 26.[19]

Although the London *Times* referred to this riot as having occurred in "the Moslem university city of Aligarh in connexion with a Hindu procession," it appears that the riot had nothing to do with the university itself, having occurred in the old city in the Madar Darwaza (Madar Gate) area (referred to as "Madho Dharwaza" in the report) and having in fact begun during a Ram Lila procession. The official death toll in this riot was 6, of whom 4 were Muslims, 2 Hindus.[20]

Information is also sparse concerning the second riot, which occurred on April 10–11, 1927. The press referred to its origins in a "fracas" arising out of "a private quarrel at the carriage stand" between two castes or *baradari*s over a contract for the stand awarded by the District Board. News of the fracas "spread in the city," and fighting was "free and fierce," but did not involve the university. Both "the official version" and the press version took the view that religious antagonism was not the "cause" of the riots.[21]

The third pre-Independence Aligarh riot occurred on November 3, 1937. It took place in an atmosphere of intensifying political competition in the province as a whole and in Aligarh between the Congress and the Muslim League and among Muslim groups as well, some of whom supported the former, others the latter political organization. Although another considerable wave of rioting occurred during the Hindu festival of Holi in U.P. in March 1938 at several sites, Aligarh was not affected at this time.[22]

In 1946–47, the Congress government in power on the eve of Independence paid special attention to "law and order in Aligarh district with particular reference to the Aligarh University." They specifically were concerned to prevent an "invasion of the City by the University students," and devised a "riot scheme" that provided "for guarding six main points on the railway line" (dividing the Civil Lines area where the university is located from the city; see Map 1) "through which the students are likely to enter the city." An entire "military police company" was to be posted "at three of these points."[23]

The last riot in this pre-Independence period occurred in Aligarh on March 29, 1946. At the end of March and in early April 1946 there were several riots in other western districts of U.P. as well, which were attributed in press reports directly to political conflicts between militant pro- and anti-Pakistan forces, namely, the Muslim League on one side and the RSS on the other. Although the origin of this series of riots was said to have been an incident in Aligarh on March 29, which then "had repercussions" in other western districts, the press reports of the time did not attribute the Aligarh incident itself to conflict between RSS and Muslim League activists. On the contrary, it was attributed to "student indiscipline," in the *Times of India* as well as in the Governor's Report found in confidential records since made available. According to both accounts, the riot began with an altercation between AMU students and the proprietor of a Hindu cloth shop, in which the students beat up the shopkeeper, after which "a full-blown riot ensued during which the whole grain market got burnt down."

The British governor clearly blamed the students for the precipitating incident, referring to them as "a bobbery lot," for fear of whom the "Hindus in the town always live in a kind of half panic." This riot occurred after several months of electioneering in the province and on the eve of the transfer of power in the province to the Congress, which had won a decisive victory. The governor noted that "the local authorities" had been charged with doing "nothing at all to control the students" and anticipated "vindictive" action on the part of the incoming chief minister, Pandit Govind Ballabh Pant, against both the local administration and the students, but hoped to have "forestalled him by ordering an immediate joint enquiry by the Commissioner and the local D.I.G. of Police."[24] The chief secretary's report dated four days later also blamed "student indiscipline" for the outbreak and provided a few additional details on the manner in which it spread.[25]

Although the precipitating incident appeared to have nothing to do with the preceding elections and political activity, the action of the AMU students immediately became an interparty and intercommunal issue. The chief secretary reported that "the condemnation of the Aligarh students for their indiscipline and hooliganism is being interpreted as a biased attempt to victimize Muslims in general and the League in particular."[26] Chief Minister Pant, in fact, wished to take action against the AMU by imposing "some sort of penalty on the University and to justify himself with his public,"[27] a desire that caused an internal dispute in the government between him and the British governor Wylie.[28]

Precise figures were provided for the numbers of persons killed and injured as well as for the duration of this riot. It was a one-day affair, but 4 persons were killed and 16 injured. These latter figures are important for comparison with later events in the town, for they constitute a kind of benchmark. The years between 1946 and 1948 are when the vast carnage associated with the partition of India occurred, when political leaders and organizations on both sides openly called for violence, revenge, and retaliation over the partition decision and over violent incidents attributed by one side to the other. The Pakistan movement itself grew out of conditions in U.P., and the AMU was one of its storm centers. Yet, in Aligarh City, the violence was contained to a day, the deaths to 4, and the injured to 16. All riotous events in Aligarh that have occurred since 1946 should be compared with this one that occurred in the midst of an extremely hostile and violent political and social environment when India was still under British rule.

The British governor remained concerned throughout the remainder of the year 1946 about the spread of communal violence in the province and about the partiality of the Congress government in dealing with it. Although Aligarh was not the worst site of violence in U.P. in this period,[29] the British were concerned with the intensification of political conflict between Congress and the Muslim League over the Pakistan demand; the formation of and recruitment to volunteer paramilitary forces established by the Muslim League, the RSS, and other militant groups; and, after August, the possibility that the Muslim League's "Direct Action" movement for the achievement of Pakistan, which was associated throughout north India with considerable violence—most famously in Calcutta in August 1946—would spread to the AMU campus. It was reported that, in June, the RSS was very actively organizing camps, offices, and branches in several districts, including Aligarh (though in another town than Aligarh City) and that the Muslim League was particularly active in three districts in the state, including Aligarh, in "the training of Muslim Guards," the Muslim League's paramilitary force.[30] It was, in fact, reported that the staff at the AMU was "in favour of 'direct action'" and that "it would be difficult to control the students if religious aspect is given to the 'direct action.'"[31]

For its part, the Congress government in the United Provinces set out in October to establish "Home Guards" in nine towns where violence had occurred between Hindus and Muslims. These Home Guards, the British governor thought—most likely correctly—were designed as a government-supported volunteer force to deal with any Muslim League–sponsored "Direct Action" in those towns. Aligarh was among the nine towns, with a force of 300 to be established.[32] In November, it was reported "from Aligarh . . . that the University hopes to send a batch of 100 students for relief work and the students are also collecting subscriptions."[33] This reference suggests that the orientation of the AMU students was outward to the broader areas of the province and the country where Hindu-Muslim riots were taking place. The British were concerned with the spread of what they perceived as a chain of riots that had begun with the Great Calcutta Killings of August to the riots in Noakhali where Hindus were the principal victims to the riots in Bihar where mostly Muslims were killed. Indeed, this same report noted that a secret meeting was held at the AMU campus, "attended by over 2,000 persons," at which one "A. T. Mustafa, Vice-President of the Muslim University Union in appealing to all students to take revenge for events in Bihar, stated that he had killed 10 persons with his own hand during the Calcutta riots." Further, it was noted that "at another meeting on November 10 the necessity for revenge was again stressed. Members of the staff and ex-members are taking part in these activities, the Khaksars under the leadership of Mr. Shamin, a lecturer in the Chemistry Department, being particularly active." The Khaksars were a Muslim paramilitary force whose purported aim was to defend Muslims from Hindu attacks in riots.

In the second half of November, the chief secretary's fortnightly report noted again the political activity at the AMU, where "there have been several meetings both of the students and the staff, at which very strong speeches were delivered against the Congress and the Hindus."[34] On the other side, the RSS was recruiting intensively in the district of Aligarh, where the chief secretary remarked that an attendance of 2,000 at the training camp in the district was the highest among 8 districts where such camps were held on the first of January 1947.[35]

It is evident, therefore, that the AMU, at this critical moment in the modern history of U.P. and the country, was seen by the incoming Congress government as a primary source of Muslim political organization and communal activity directed against the Congress and Hindus in general. That the AMU students were feared by the Hindu population in the town was also explicitly stated by the British governor. It is also clear from the disputes between the governor and the chief minister that the incoming Congress government was bent on action, considered vindictive by the governor, against Muslim organizations and institutions, including the AMU. Furthermore, Pandit Pant accused the police in Aligarh of partiality—obviously, in favor of Muslims—in the March riot in Aligarh, at a time when the police force in the state was 47 percent Muslim. It is also known that Pant took immediate steps to change this situation by various actions designed to reduce the Muslim component in the police force, which, by the end of his tenure, had fallen to approximately 5 percent. That position has not changed significantly since these early years of Congress rule in U.P.[36]

Several aspects of the riots in the pre-Independence period deserve particular notice in relation to the general issues raised earlier and to be discussed throughout the remainder of this volume. First, the waves of rioting as well as the particular incidents in Aligarh were placed by the authorities and the press in a dual context: one religious-communal, the other communal-political. The first form of contextualization referred to the riots as precipitated by controversies associated with the manifestation of religious zeal or playfulness that irritated the other community, in these cases particularly Muslim objections to Hindu Ram Lila processions or Holi pranksterism. The second form of contextualization was communal-political, relating Hindu-Muslim riots to the communal competition for power in the state and the country between the Congress and the Muslim League. Sometimes, both contextualizations were present. Thus, the first wave of riots between 1923 and 1927 followed upon the collapse of Hindu-Muslim political cooperation, but it also occurred simultaneously with a revival of Hindu-Muslim competitive religious proselytization. The second wave of rioting in 1937–38 occurred during a very critical period in pre-Independence political history, when the Congress came to power in U.P. and negotiations to share power with the Muslim League broke down, which many persons consider to have been a turning point on the road to partition of the country and the creation of Pakistan. The two years of Congress rule were marked by intense political competition between the Congress and the Muslim League, including the use of "direct action" methods that often led to riots, but riots also occurred sometimes during religious festivals such as Holi.

The simultaneity of religious and political activities at times of rioting has left room for differing interpretations of their sources: religious or political differences, spontaneous resentments, or politically inspired actions. The opposition between these two types of contextualization is, however, spurious. Religious observances in public spaces were highly politicized in the pre-Independence years and religious proselytization was politically as well as religiously motivated.

When we come to 1946, the political aspect of riot production is fully evident. It is now a manifestation of the communal conflict over the future of the subcontinent. Moreover, Aligarh provides at this moment a miniature crystallization of the subcontinental divide. The AMU is at the center of political activity, seen as the originating source of Muslim separatism, many of whose faculty and students became supporters, members, and leaders of the Muslim League. Moreover, the very division of the country as well as the problems that were to follow it were already symbolically present in Aligarh itself. The city was divided by the railway line between the Civil Lines and the old city. Forces massed on either side of the line, threatening to cross it, to invade the other side. Militant nationalist and separatist organizations and paramilitary formations were present and ready for confrontations. But so, too, were complications present, for on the city side of the line there remained a substantial Muslim population, the vast majority of whom would be left behind in Aligarh bereft of political leadership and organization, living side by side with the majority Hindu population, among whom a small militant Hindu segment was to build political support around the resentments of Hindus at the partition of the country for which the AMU stood as the symbol.

## From 1946 to 1961

Between 1946 and 1961, when I first visited Aligarh, there were three other riots, in one of which deaths occurred. The latter riot—much more serious than its predecessor in 1946—occurred over two days on March 3 and 4, 1950. The origin of this riot, like so many in the pre-Independence period as well, was attributed to a trivial incident during the Hindu festival of Holi, "when a Hindu boy threw coloured water on a passer-by," who, though the report does not say so, was obviously a Muslim. In the communal disturbances that followed, "five persons were killed and 40 injured" and "there were many cases of looting and arson."[37] It was reported, as in March 1938, that similar incidents followed by communal "disturbances" occurred during the Holi festival days in several other towns in western and central U.P., namely Moradabad, Pilibhit, Bareilly, and Shahjahanpur.[38]

Pars Ram remarked somewhat ambiguously in his *UNESCO Study of Social Tensions in Aligarh in 1950–51* that "the Hindu students' record in inflaming the Hindu-Muslim conflict to make it appear more violent" was "impressive." His study also referred to "the stopping of a passenger train," "the way-laying and the assaulting of stray Muslim pedestrians," "the assaulting of Muslims in their residential quarters," and "assaulting of a number of Muslim rickshaw pullers by Hindu students."[39] Despite the ambiguity concerning the extent of involvement of Hindu students in the actual violence perpetrated in this riot, it is clear that Pars Ram attributed some role in the actual assaults to Hindu students and that he saw Muslims assaulted at random as the victims in this riot.

A brief, quickly controlled riot occurred in Aligarh on June 6, 1954. The *Times of India* account attributed its origins to "a dispute between a hawker and customer" that "sparked communal disturbances," what Wilkinson codes as a "private quarrel."[40] No one was killed in this riot, though 8 people were injured.

The third reported riot in the 1950s occurred on September 14, 1956.[41] The sequence of events leading up to this riot illustrates the process by which external and local factors interact to produce communal confrontation and violence at particular sites. The symbolic pretext for rioting in Aligarh and elsewhere was provided by the publication by the Bharatiya Vidhya Bhavan[42] of a book called *Living Biographies of Religious Leaders,* written by an American, that contained some references to the Prophet Mohammad that were considered blasphemous by Muslims. The head of the Bharatiya Vidhya Bhavan, K. M. Munshi, was a figurehead president only, who happened also to be the governor of the state of U.P. Demonstrations took place in Aligarh the last week of August,[43] which were discussed in the U.P. Vidhan Sabha (Legislative Assembly) and reported in the press some days later. The students of AMU had taken out "a procession carrying an effigy of the U.P. Governor, beat the effigy with shoes [a great insult in India] and ultimately burnt it." In discussion in the Vidhan Sabha, it was alleged that "the processionists [had] shouted slogans like 'Hindustan Murdabad' [Death to India] and 'Pakistan Zindabad' [Long Live Pakistan]" and that "Pakistani agents were also behind the demonstrations."[44] The first allegation appears to have been generally accepted, the second was never proved. The attention given to these particular slogans immediately transformed the local incidents into an issue affecting Hindus and Muslims throughout the subcontinent as well as India-Pakistan relations. The charge that Pakistani agents were behind the events has been since Independence to the present day a recurring theme in speeches by Hindu politicians from both the Congress and the militant Hindu parties and in news reports whenever Hindu-Muslim confrontations and violence occur. These allegations were repeated in the press on numerous occasions during the month and were made again in the Lok Sabha by militant Hindus within the Congress.[45]

No violence was reported from Aligarh in this first week of September, but significant rioting, including deaths in some places, occurred in several other towns of U.P. during the month, as well as in Bhopal, Jabalpur, and Nagpur in Madhya Pradesh, and in the East Pakistan capital of Dhaka.[46] The riots in all these cities and towns appeared to follow a common pattern of processions and counterdemonstrations: Muslim processions protesting the Bharatiya Vidhya Bhavan book—including in some places ritual burning of the Hindu religious text, the *Bhagavad Gita,* and attacks on idols of the Hindu god, Ganesh, whose festival was being celebrated in various parts of north India during this period[47]—followed by Hindu counterprocessions or demonstrations, often ending in arson and riotous violence. One Muslim religious organization normally allied with the Indian National Congress, the Jamaat-ul-Ulama, was reported to have "telegraphically urged its district units to take part in the protest meetings and demonstrations." The Urdu vernacular press also contributed to the inflammatory situation "by publishing the offending contents of the impugned book in screaming headlines."[48] The English-language press, however, acting with restraint, never published the passages from the book that had perturbed Muslims.

Insofar as Aligarh is concerned, the principal riotous incidents occurred in connection with militant Hindu counterprocessions and demonstrations on September 14. The processions, which were organized within the various predominantly Hindu- and RSS-dominated degree colleges of the town, were "taken out from one college to another," and demands were made for "'stern action' against the Aligarh University authorities and students" for having taken out or allowed their protest processions. When the procession approached the Moti Masjid (a mosque near Phul Chauraha), "it was reported to have been attacked with stones and brickbats."[49] A few cases of arson were reported in several localities and there were some injuries as a result of the stone throwing, but no deaths occurred. It is noteworthy that these processions followed a week after the Muslim student processions, that they were well organized, and that they set out deliberately through areas known to have been sites of Hindu-Muslim confrontations in the past. It is obvious, therefore, that the processions were deliberately provocative, that they were not spontaneous, and that violence was a probable if not predictable and desired result.

Within the university itself, its retiring vice-chancellor, Zakir Hussain— a "nationalist Muslim" who had been opposed to the Pakistan demand— later to become president of India, made a farewell speech in which he condemned the actions of the AMU students in very strong terms. He went even to the extent of saying that the AMU deserved criticism for its "past history," and that students should not react against such criticism.[50] However, a few days later, he issued a statement criticizing press reports on his farewell speech that suggested he was giving "the impression that the university was a hot-bed of anti-national feelings and anti-social activities." On the contrary, he insisted that generally the AMU students were well behaved and that, although their behavior in connection with their protests against the offending book and the governor was "reprehensible," there was nothing communal about it.[51]

The incidents in Aligarh and in other towns where processions, demonstrations, and riots occurred were framed within a broad national context that extended beyond either the precipitating issue of a religious insult to the Muslims of India or the local contexts in which rioting occurred. Pandit Pant, now home minister of the government of India, referred to "the old tendencies of the Muslim League" reappearing among Muslims that could only "disturb the communal amity prevailing in the country," balanced by criticisms of those Hindus who wished to establish a "Hindu Raj" in the country. Pandit Pant reminded the country that a major reorganization of the internal boundaries of India was about to take place in the form of the linguistic reorganization of states and remarked that, in this context, every citizen should remember that he was an Indian first rather than a member of a particular region, state, or community; otherwise, the Indian state itself might be weakened. A disruption of "communal amity" was said to have the even more grave implications of harming the "prestige and respect" that India was believed to hold in the world. Finally, Pandit Pant used this occasion to claim that India was a better protector of Muslim interests, not only in South Asia, but in the broader Muslim world, where, at this very time, India had come to the support of Egypt in the Suez Canal crisis, whilst Pakistan, then an American ally, had not.[52]

The president of the militant Hindu organization, the All-India Hindu Mahasabha, also used this occasion to condemn the "agitation against the book" published by the Bharatiya Vidhya Bhavan and called for "firm action" against the "trouble-makers." He described the Muslim protests as a "planned attack by anti-national elements in the country" and, in a refrain that was to be repeated and to gather force decades later, called for an end to the government's "policy of appeasement" of Muslims that could threaten even "the security of India."[53]

Several features of this sequence of events and rioting in Aligarh and elsewhere are notable. The initial protests and demonstrations were begun by Muslim organizations, and Muslim university students comprised the main, if not the only participants in them. The protests were initially against an offense to Islamic religious faith. Further, the Muslim protests provided an occasion for responses from Hindu students and militant Hindu organizations that led to violence. It is essential to understanding the dynamics of riot production, however, to note that the counterdemonstrations in Aligarh were separately generated from within the city, that they constituted provocative behavior in city *mohallas* with heavy concentrations of Muslims. That is, it was not a case of a direct confrontation between two protesting groups, but of separately organized incidents. Further, the Hindu counterdemonstrations and attacks on Muslims produced symbolic countermoves in the allegation that Muslims had insulted a Hindu religious text, the *Gita,* and in the shifting of focus to the AMU as a grand symbol of antinational sentiments. Yet a further broadening of the context occurred in the statements made by political leaders that both Muslim and Hindu communalist groups were threatening the communal harmony of the country and, thereby, the country's future and its prestige in the world.

But what, then, was behind this wave of demonstrations, counterdemonstrations, and rioting that broadened out from a few sentences in a book published by a centrally funded educational foundation that certainly had no intention of insulting Indian Muslims? There are particular, local answers to this question as well as more general ones. We cannot know without detailed knowledge of each case in which rioting occurred why it occurred in some places and not others. Many cities and towns in U.P. and Madhya Pradesh were affected, but the demonstrations and riotous violence occurred at specific sites in each such city. We know that there are two areas from which politically charged demonstrations in Aligarh are generated: the AMU and the *mohallas* in the city where the local degree colleges are located. They stand in polar opposition to each other, but the actions in this case were separate. In later riots, we will see militant Hindu activists and rioters moving directly to the university area to attack Muslims, Muslim property, and Muslim institutions, but even later it is not always the case. What is constant is the existence of the AMU as a symbolic presence, providing a fund of Hindu enmity for political mobilization and violent acting out that takes place at sites of Muslim concentration, though the Muslim population at those sites has nothing to do with the AMU or its history.

Finally, there is the question of the relationship between these riots in 1956 and the general elections that were to follow in five months. This was a time of Congress dominance in Aligarh, U.P., and nearly all of India. The militant Hindu parties were not yet a major threat to Congress supremacy. Yet, any consolidation of either Muslim or Hindu sentiment that could be directed against the Congress could threaten its ascendance. The general secretary of the Congress drew attention to the possible electoral purpose behind the demonstrations and rioting in a speech in which he called upon party workers to combat "communal forces." He remarked, "Both Hindu and Muslim communal parties and organisations are trying to fan the flames and create riots mainly for sordid political motives in connection with the forthcoming general elections."[54] The Congress at this time was presenting itself as a secular force maintaining a fragile peace between dangerous Hindu and Muslim communal forces, whose actions allegedly threatened the unity of the country, but more certainly threatened Congress preeminence. Insofar as Aligarh is concerned, Congress dominance remained undisturbed in the 1957 elections. It was to take the far more serious and deadly riots of October 1961 to overthrow it.

### The Riots of October 1961

The riots of October 1961 began with a scuffle among Hindu and Muslim students at the AMU in the aftermath of Students Union elections, which had been fought wholly on communal lines.[55] Rumors spread to the town that a

Hindu student had been killed in the university. Large mobs from the town, mostly students from the Hindu colleges, massed, burned some shops in the University market areas, and attacked some university employees. Rioting then spread to the town. In the notorious Manik Chauk *mohalla*—which will feature again and again in our accounts—a Hindu businessman used a mob of students to raid the houses of a Muslim with whom he had a property dispute, as well as other Muslim houses. The police were present, but stood by without interfering, even though this incident alone led to the deaths of 7 Muslims and the injury of 21. Altogether, by official reckoning, 15 Muslims were killed, but the true number is believed to be around 40; no Hindus were killed. Police allegedly colluded with the Hindu students, deliberately denied protection to Muslims, and, it is confirmed, entered the AMU hostels, beat up Muslim students, and looted their belongings. Curfew was maintained in the town for two weeks. Muslim conservatives on the faculty of the university, where there was an ongoing struggle for primacy between so-called communalists and so-called Communists, entered the 1962 general elections thereafter, joined forces with the opposition to the ruling Congress, and helped administer a major defeat to the Congress in the district as a whole in a communalized election atmosphere. There is, therefore, a political *cum* communal rioting *cum* political sequence, from university politics to rival student communal confrontations to rioting in the city to the general election.

Reports on this riot by the press, and the commentary upon it by others afterwards that was reported in the press, are of great interest for what they do and do not reveal about the riot itself, the kinds of explanations that were generated about it, and the ways in which the riots were used in the process of blame displacement. With regard to the reporting in the *Times of India,* emphasis was placed on the conflict among the students on the AMU campus as the precipitant of the riot, from which the action in the city was seen almost as part of an inevitable and understandable sequence. Yet, there were two kinds of reactions from the city. One was the mobilization, massing, and movement of a crowd said to be "about 8,000 including some students," who "came from the city side and made an attempt to cross the railway line and rush towards Aligarh university," but were stopped by the police.[56] Here we have in this major Aligarh riot—the most serious in its history to this time— a situation exactly the reverse of that for which the U.P. government prepared in 1946–47, namely, the attempted crossing of the railway line by Hindu students seeking to reach and presumably to attack the AMU, rather than the reverse. The second response to the incidents on the AMU campus was the action within the city itself, notably in Manik Chauk, mentioned above. Yet, the names of none of the localities in which rioting occurred in the city, including Manik Chauk, were given in the press.

The meager factual reporting in the *Times of India* on the riot in Aligarh was confined to a single day, datelined October 4. However, commentary on the riot by the paper's editor and reports of the statements of politicians on it continued in the press almost daily for the rest of the month. In the commentaries, there were two frames: one placed it in the context of Hindu-Muslim relations, the unity of the country, and the place of the AMU in relation to both; the second placed it in the context of interparty conflicts. Within both these contexts, blame was partly focused, partly dispersed, but largely failed to identify the principal sources of riotous activity in the city.

Blame was to a considerable extent focused on the AMU and its authorities for failing "to postpone elections to the Students Union even after it became clear that the contestants were canvassing openly on communal lines."[57] To a considerable extent, the blame directed at the AMU also focused on the institution itself, its past and present. A Hindu journalist, Prem Bhatia, wrote an analytical article in the *Times of India* which began by stating that "Aligarh [referring to the riots] has posed the first serious challenge to the efforts for national integration." However, he averred, the riots that began at AMU and spread to other parts of the state, while they certainly reflected serious problems at the university, extended more broadly than that, reflecting as well a "disease which afflicts a large number of Muslims in this country."[58] Atal Bihar Vajpayee, then secretary of the Jan Sangh and leader of its parliamentary group, urged the government of India to appoint a committee "to investigate the state of affairs in Aligarh University" and to shed its belief "That the University can be allowed to retain its 'communal character' without jeopardising national interests and the principles of secularism."[59]

With regard to the second context, of interparty conflicts, the state's home minister, Charan Singh, "attributed the communal disturbances in the western districts of the State, to an 'organized' attempt by some political parties," whose intentions were deliberately to "disrupt communal harmony" for political advantage just before the general elections. His remarks were echoed by the chief minister of the state as well, Mr. C. B. Gupta.[60] Two days later, Charan Singh was more explicit in his charges, saying that the riots in Aligarh and those that followed it elsewhere were a deliberate attempt "to discredit the Congress among the Hindu and Muslim masses with a view to capturing political power."[61]

Blame was also partly dispersed as commentary upon it extended up to the highest levels of leadership in the country, including the president and prime minister. The president, Dr. Radhakrishnan, said that the events in Aligarh occurred just at the time when "a conference on national integration had been held" and that they "showed 'how distant the goal is.'"[62] Prime Minister Nehru adopted his usual schoolmaster's stance, maintaining an equable balance in his remarks, in which he was reported to have described "the communal disturbances in the State" as "unfortunate, but a happy sign was that the masses did not take any interest in such ugly happenings." He was reported to have strongly denounced the "communal incidents" and remarked that "it was most painful that students instead of pursuing their studies participated in disturbances." He placed no blame on Hindus or Muslims as such; on the contrary, he "said that Hindus and Muslims were sons of the same soil and there should be no hatred."[63]

It is noteworthy in all the commentary on these riots that the vast majority of statements took the riots out of their local context of a tussle between undisciplined students from the two communities at a university, almost completely ignored the very considerable militant Hindu mobilization that followed in the city itself and that was followed later in other towns in many districts in the state, and instead placed it within the framework of Hindu-Muslim relations in general, the unity of the country, and the loyalty to India of Muslims in particular. Further, in the face of the wide dispersion of charges in which virtually the only factual materials provided referred to the student disturbances, the authorities at the state and national levels decided against appointing an inquiry commission to fix responsibility for the criminal acts committed during these riots.[64] In so avoiding an impartial judicial inquiry, charges made by three ministers of the central government, which were utterly lost in the extralocal contextualization of the violence, could not be investigated. One of the ministers, after a visit to Aligarh on October 6, "expressed the opinion that 'most of the deaths and injuries' caused in the incidents had 'no direct connection with the communal trouble.'" On the contrary, he said, "advantage had been taken by certain elements of the 'tense situation in the town,' following trouble in the university, 'for wreaking private revenge' and in the course of these incidents eight persons had lost their lives and a large number received injuries." In contrast, the incidents in the university area led to "only three" deaths.[65]

We have here, in short, a clear example of the distorting effects of post hoc commentary on communal collective violence. The leading English-language newspaper of the country devoted many of its pages for an entire month to commentary by its own editors and journalists as well as the political leaders whom it quoted extensively, without providing more than a fragment of reporting on the incidents themselves. Further, it raised no serious questions concerning how such extensive mass mobilizations, most of them emanating from Hindu students at colleges and universities in several districts of the state, could have been organized so quickly. Finally, it ignored completely the main scene of riotous activities perpetrated in the center of Aligarh City itself. Instead, virtually all commentary followed an agenda, a text that emanated from the minds of the commentators and from a discourse of national unity that emphasized the threat to it posed by communal conflicts between Hindus and Muslims, which may not have yet infected the entire populations of the two communities, but had done so before and might yet do so once again.

### 1971 Riots

An even more deadly riot occurred in the midst of the polling for parliamentary elections on March 1, 1971.[66] The election in Aligarh was of great importance at this time because the years immediately preceding it had been marked by an upsurge in Muslim political activity centered on a list of grievances that included opposition to the central government's efforts to alter the character of the AMU and, as it was seen by Muslim political organizations, to undermine its character as a minority institution.[67]

The importance of the Aligarh parliamentary seat to Mrs. Gandhi's Congress, then known as Congress (R), was reflected in the choice of a candidate from this constituency, a Muslim member of the central government, Deputy Minister for Railways Mohammad Yunus Saleem. His opponent, Shiv Kumar Shastri, contested on the ticket of the BKD. Shastri was a militant Hindu supported by, though not a member of, the Jan Sangh/RSS, which was a component of a four-party alliance against the Congress (R). The election campaign had been marked by agitations at the AMU in favor of restoring its minority character and counterdemonstrations by students at the D.S. College organized by the RSS.

Violence broke out on March 2 that lasted for four hours, during which Congress (R) candidate Saleem alleged that "shops of Congress (R) supporters had been 'looted' and set on fire by an unruly mob of RSS workers." He also said that the Jan Sangh president, Shiv Hari Singhal, had been arrested in connection with these incidents. Saleem's opposing candidate, Shiv Kumar Shastri, gave a different explanation for the incidents, namely, that they followed upon a protest by student demonstrators against an attempt by a young supporter of his rival candidate, clad in a woman's *burqa,* to cast an illegal vote, which precipitated "an altercation between two groups."[68] Whatever the actual precipitant, considerable violence followed in several riot-prone localities of the old city, during which 17 persons were said to have been killed.[69] The district magistrate and the senior superintendent of police were suspended for failing to prevent and control the violence,[70] the chief minister of the state visited the town along with a former chief minister (both part of the four-party alliance), and an inquiry commission was appointed.

There was complete disagreement that has never been resolved among observers concerning every aspect of this riot. The Congress (R) candidate, Saleem, insisted that the incidents were political, not communal, whereas his opponent, Shastri, said they appeared "to be taking a communal colour."[71] The former chief minister, C. B. Gupta, who visited the scene after the riots, went further and declared that the riots were preplanned and that it was "the majority community," that is, Hindus, who had suffered from most of the violence that occurred. He also implied that the Congress (R) candidate himself was responsible for the violence.[72] The state government appointed Justice Mathur as a one-man commission of inquiry; his report conformed to the views of the government that appointed him, blaming the riots on the AMU and relieving the RSS and the Jan Sangh and several RSS/Jan Sangh leaders who had been accused of fomenting the riots of any responsibility for them, despite the report that students from the D.S. College and the Hiralal Barahseni Degree College had massed, taken out processions, and engaged in arson.[73]

The following features of this riot are especially relevant to the analyses that will be presented in the later chapters of this volume. First, complete disagreement on the origins and character of the incidents, not resolved even by the findings of an inquiry commission. Second, the direct relationship between the violent incidents and an election campaign in progress. Third, the existence of sharp political divisions not only in the local election contest, but between the central and state governments, which were reflected in their opposed explanations of the causes of the riots. Fourth, the salience at the time of the election of issues concerning the grievances of Muslims in Indian society and politics, including the status of the AMU. Fifth, the occurrence of agitations at the AMU on these issues followed by the mobilization of students from the local Hindu- and RSS-dominated degree colleges preceding the outbreak of violence. Finally, the identification and arrest by the local administration of a prominent leader of the Jan Sangh, Shiv Hari Singhal, for contributing to the outbreak of violence.

## 1972

During the general elections of 1962 in Aligarh, held in the aftermath of the October 1961 riots, leaders of the so-called communalist group in AMU politics joined with opposition political party leaders to administer a defeat to the Congress in the city from which it never recovered. Ten years later, the internal politics of the university once again spilled outside into the broader political arena, but this time embracing the entire country and merging its ideological differences with the national issues concerning the identity of the Indian nation, the place of secularism and Hindu values within that identity, and the place of Muslims in Indian society as a whole. At the center of this merged local/national debate was the former leader of the Communist/progressive group in AMU politics, Nurul Hasan, past head of the history department, a lifelong member of the Communist Party of India (CPI), at this time minister of education in the government of India led by Prime Minister Indira Gandhi.

Nurul Hasan undertook to restructure the internal governance of the AMU and to reorient its mission as well. The latter was to be redefined from "devoting special attention to the promotion of oriental and Islamic studies and the teaching of Muslim theology" to promoting "the study of the religions, civilisation and culture of India."[74] To ensure this reorientation of mission, the structure of the AMU's internal governance was also to be changed and it was to come more closely under the direct supervision of the central government, which provided most of its finances.[75] The vice-chancellor was now to be appointed, in effect, by the central government and was to be given enhanced powers.

The Aligarh Muslim University (Amendment) Bill was moved in the Lok Sabha on May 31, 1972, and passed after a day-long debate the next day. It was then quickly moved in the Rajya Sabha as well, where it passed the next day on a voice vote.[76] Three sharply opposed points of view were expressed in the debates on this long day, each reflecting one of the three main streams of Indian nationalist ideology. Members of the Muslim League[77] and some other Muslim MPs protested on the grounds that the minority character of the AMU would be destroyed by this legislation. They argued, in effect, that the Muslims of India were a minority with a distinct religion, culture, and civilization, that the AMU had been founded by the Muslim community, and that its separate existence as a minority-run institution ought to be maintained.

Minister of Education Nurul Hasan responded by saying that "the university should have [a] national and not minority and theocratic character and in the name of tradition progress should not be hampered."[78] Indeed, he averred that "the Bill would help the university to shed the 'dirt and filth of obscurantism.'"[79] In effect, the minister was presenting the secular progressive view of Indian nationalism and the proper place of Muslims within it.

The third position, of militant Hinduism, was articulated by both the Jan Sangh and by Shiv Kumar Shastri, the candidate elected to Parliament from Aligarh in 1971 by the anti-Congress (R) coalition, which had included the Jan Sangh. The Jan Sangh members took the occasion of the debate to attack the AMU, in one case criticizing the bill as inadequate for its failure to order an enquiry into "the snake pits and snakes"[80] in the university. Their position clearly was that the AMU was a source of anti-Indian sentiment that needed to be utterly extinguished before the Muslims of India could be integrated into the nation. Both the Jan Sangh members and Shiv Kumar Shastri also criticized the bill for its failure to affiliate the two Hindu- and RSS-dominated local degree colleges to the university, a measure which would more surely finish any pretension on the part of AMU to being a center for Islamic education and a minority institution. It would also have satisfied the long-standing demand of the administrators, staff, and students of these degree colleges to have access to the superior facilities, salaries, and emoluments available to the AMU faculty and students.

In response to the enactment of the AMU legislation, demonstrations were staged in Aligarh by persons from among both communities opposed to the bill for the reasons articulated by their representatives in Parliament. These demonstrations were not confined to the AMU campus, but involved processions in the communally sensitive Upar Kot area (see Map 2) of the old city by local Muslim leaders on one side and militant Hindu leaders and organizations on the other side. The local administration acted promptly to arrest some 63 processionists.[81] On the next day, a fortuitous incident occurred in which a child was hit by a scooter driver in Sabzi Mandi (the wholesale vegetable market)[82] just as a procession of Muslim activists reached the spot. Some stone throwing, looting, and arson followed. The administration again acted promptly, dispersed the crowd by firing in the air, and arrested an additional 20 persons.[83] It also imposed curfew in all affected areas or areas likely to be affected, in some cases for 65 hours at a stretch, and arrested other persons, bringing the reported total to 334.[84]

On June 9, it was reported that Aligarh was "quiet" and no further incidents had been reported.[85] No deaths were reported by the press in this riot.[86]

A follow-up article on this riot in the *Times of India* raised another, local explanation for the agitations that preceded it. It was suggested that they were as much concerned with local as with national politics, specifically the likelihood that municipal elections, which had not been held in the town for many years, would soon be scheduled in Aligarh. In this interpretation, local forces, particularly the Muslim Majlis and the Jan Sangh, were staking out positions in anticipation of those elections to win support, respectively, from Muslims and Hindus.[87]

The Aligarh demonstrations against the AMU Act were part of a broader movement throughout the state led by the Muslim Majlis-e-Mushawarat and several other Muslim organizations, including the Aligarh Old Boys' [Alumni] Association. In two other U.P. towns—Firozabad and Varanasi—the demonstrations were followed by extensive rioting, destruction, and deaths.[88] So, in comparison, on this occasion, rioting in Aligarh was far less severe than in other towns in the state and, apparently, much more effectively controlled.

Nevertheless, the focus of the demonstrations and counterdemonstrations as well as the reporting on these riots was on the AMU and the Act that had changed its governance. Further, the press and the Congress (R)—the ruling party at the Center and in the state capital in Lucknow—attacked the Muslim organizations in ways that implied that they were antinational. One report in the *Times of India* devoted several paragraphs to blaming the partition of India upon the AMU and its graduates, claiming that Mohammad Ali Jinnah, the leader of the Pakistan movement, had also been "closely associated with this university."[89] In an editorial, the *Times of India* characterized the leaders of the AMU agitation as "obscurantist" Muslims who were "playing with fire" since their actions would only lead to provoking "a similar ganging up by Hindu extremist bodies."[90]

Feeding militant Hindu concerns itself, the *Times of India* presented as its front page lead article the very next day a report on the results of the decennial Indian census by religion, showing that the minorities in India, including the Muslims, were proliferating at a faster rate than the Hindus, thus vindicating "the secular atmosphere in the country in which all communities can thrive." Far from demonstrating anything of the sort, such figures only provide further impetus to militant Hindu fears that, having vivisected India in 1947, the Muslims along with other minorities would one day take over India as well.

It would seem, therefore, that this riot belongs, in effect, to a series of incidents that began in 1966, of which this and the previous riot in March 1971 are the most prominent. Both are notable for the intermixing of local and national politics and issues, including issues concerning the very identity of the Indian nation-state. Both involved also an intermingling of university, local, and national politics. Both may have involved also some relationship to electoral politics, evident in the March 1971 incidents, suggested in the 1972 incidents.

There are similarities also that pertain to the problem of explanation, particularly concerning the issues of precipitants (a scooter accident or the processions) and of containment, that is, the effectiveness of administrative action. With regard to the latter, the administration appears to have acted promptly and effectively and to have learned from its failure to control the previous riot, but we cannot be sure. It is quite possible that the protagonists themselves were less interested in provoking a full-scale riot on this occasion, though there can be no doubt that some kind of confrontation was desired of the type that so frequently does result in murderous rioting; it is obvious that there was extensive organization of pre-riot activities. But was the riotous action that ensued after the scooter accident—even if it was not a result of it—spontaneous or deliberate, motivated by communal "frenzy" or by other, unknown motives? No matter how detailed the information available on such events as even this relatively small riot, the realm of the unknown that is open to competing interpretations remains always extensive. Those interpretations, as we have just seen, extend from the trivial—a scooter accident—to the deliberate designs of communalist leaders, particularly "obscurantist" Muslim leaders, to undermine the unity of the country.

### October–November–December 1978

This series of riots[91] began with a scuffle between the supporters of two wrestling *akharas* (one Hindu, the other Muslim) in Aligarh town. Attacks, including stabbing incidents between the two groups, then occurred over succeeding weeks.[92] One of the Hindu wrestlers, called Bhura (or Bhure Lal), who had been assaulted and wounded in a fight, finally died in the Civil Hospital on October 5, after which a large crowd carried his body through the Muslim localities demanding revenge. Rioting broke out "independently but simultaneously" both in Chauraha Abdul Karim (an important four-way crossing) when the procession arrived at that crossing and in the nearby Hindu-majority *mohalla* of Manik Chauk,[93] both in the old city (see Map 2). Altercations occurred between processionists and shopkeepers when the former demanded that the latter close their shops. It was reported that 12 persons were killed in this first phase of rioting.[94]

The wrestling *akhara* to which Bhure Lal belonged is located some distance from the city limits on the Khair road. It is situated within the precincts of a Shiva temple. (See Figures 3.2, 3.3, and 3.4.) According to Alter, this association between Hindu religiosity and gymnastics is embedded deeply in the minds of the wrestlers.[95] However, it is also the case that wrestlers in Aligarh and in places such as Hyderabad are often involved in criminal activities, including Hindu-Muslim riots.[96]

These riots occurred at a time of intense political division within the Janata governments in both New Delhi and Lucknow, which had replaced the Congress Emergency regime in the 1977 General Elections. The situation in Aligarh was immediately politicized at multiple levels by direct and contradictory comments from all political sides, that is, from the Congress (I), now in opposition, as well as from the disparate elements that had formed the Janata Party, which also included the former Jan Sangh. As a consequence, a series of individual and collective teams of state and national politicians and religious leaders descended on the city while the riots were still in progress and made partisan pronouncements concerning them.[97]

On October 10, a three-person team deputed by the national president of the Janata Party, Mr. Chandra Shekar, visited Aligarh.[98] The team called for a judicial inquiry into the riots, but the contents of its own report were disputed. According to Chandra Shekar, it absolved the RSS of all blame for instigating the communal riots. When asked specifically about the Aligarh leader, Krishna Kuman Navman, he acknowledged that allegations had been made against him, but claimed that "nobody had said that he had engineered the riots" and that the team deputed had "also found no evidence of his presence at any of the troubled spots."[99] Chandra Shekar's remarks were criticized the next day by the presidents of the AMU Staff Association and the Students Union, respectively, noting that they contradicted the views of most "prominent leaders of different parties" that the RSS had, in fact, "engineered the Aligarh riots." Members of the Congress (I) in Parliament, including its Congress Socialist Forum group, also declared their belief that the RSS was behind the Aligarh riots.[100]

Two RSS ministers in the U.P. government, including Kalyan Singh, also prepared a report for the state chief minister in which, predictably, they absolved the RSS of any blame. Further, they specifically absolved from blame Krishna Kumar Navman, despite the admitted fact that he had "an altercation with a policeman" on October 7 while "touring the affected areas with a valid pass." All blame was placed by state RSS leaders on the Congress (I) and the CPI for snatching the body of Bhure Lal and taking out the provocative procession.[101]

FIG. 3.2. Shiv temple at *akhara* site

It needs to be noted, however, that, as on most occasions of rioting in the old city, Mr. Krishna Kumar Navman's name is prominent and that it is clear that he and other RSS workers somehow manage to roam about freely in affected areas during riots, including, in the case of Navman, during curfew hours.

Several politicians blamed police inaction for the events leading up to the riots, particularly the snatching of Bhure Lal's body.[102] The state president of the Congress (I) blamed the state government for failing "to maintain law and order" and demanded the "dismissal" of the ministry.[103] There was also a noticeable tendency on the part of politicians and the press to disperse blame to no one in particular. One of the members of the Janata team, for example, bemoaned the fact that "even after 31 years of independence we have not been able to integrate ourselves and cultivate communal harmony."[104]

A report prepared on behalf of the Peoples Union for Civil Liberties (PUCL), however, was quite specific in assigning responsibility to particular persons, groups, and state agencies. It commented on the outbreak of the

FIG. 3.3. Wrestlers

riots on October 5 as follows: "Hindu communalists ran berserk against poor Muslims. The Provincial Armed Constabulary of Uttar Pradesh echoed the same Hindu communal sentiments by shooting down and killing innocent and unarmed Muslims."[105] As for the slain wrestler, Bhure Lal, the PUCL report remarked that "everyone with whom we talked agreed that he was a notorious anti-social element." Further, both sides involved in the fight that led to Bhure's death were, they were told, "comprised of mere gangsters and rough-necks drawn from both Hindus and Muslims." Moreover, the PUCL report emphasized that the wrestler's death was misreported in the press as "a sequel to the fight over a wrestling competition on September 12," but was in fact nothing but the "result of [an] inter-gang fight" and had nothing whatever to do with "communal feeling."[106] In fact, the stabbing of Bhure Lal had been preceded by weeks of intergang fighting in which several wrestlers had been attacked and stabbed, including one other person, also a Hindu, who was killed on September 18.[107]

The PUCL report argued that the actual buildup to the riot of October 5 was an agitation that had been led for several months previous to the killing of Bhure Lal by known Hindu communal persons on the issue of the AMU Bill concerning the status of the university, which was once again before

FIG. 3.4. Wrestling pit

Parliament at the time. The killing of Bhure Lal was, in effect, nothing but a pretext on the part of these Hindu communal persons in the town to instigate a riot for political reasons. The Hindu leaders mentioned were persons whose names will recur throughout this book: B. D. Gupta, lecturer in the psychology department of AMU; Manga Ram, lecturer in the Barahseni Degree College in the town; Shiv Hari Singhal, advocate and former president of the Jan Sangh; and Krishna Kumar Navman, businessman. Several if not all of these persons were also involved, according to the PUCL report, in the incident that precipitated the riot, in which Navman allegedly played a leading role, namely, the "snatching" of the dead body of Bhure Lal, which was then taken out in a procession through the predominantly Muslim areas of the old city accompanied by shouts from the processionists demanding "blood for blood" and "ten for one," that is, ten Muslims for one Hindu killed.[108]

Allegations were made that rich Varshney Hindu businessmen provided money for the criminal attacks on Muslims, that the RSS was behind it, and that Navman played a very important role. The PUCL report alleged that "RSS elements" in the Manik Chauk *mohalla* where Navman resided also used the riot in an attempt to force Muslims occupying ten or fifteen houses in the *mohalla* "to leave the houses or face serious consequences."[109] The PUCL team visited some houses in Manik Chauk and interviewed persons in the locality on the streets and in their homes. Witnesses provided them with names of persons who had murdered others in the riots, including one of Krishna Kumar Navman's sons, Satya, who was said to have been "seen with a gun supervising the murder" of two persons by others, who used a long spear to impale their Muslim victims. These and several other attacks upon Muslim houses in Manik Chauk were carried out during curfew hours between 5:30 P.M. and midnight, a short distance away from the Madar Gate police station.[110] In addition to Navman's son, Professor B. D. Gupta was also named "among the prominent personalities who led the attack" on Muslim houses in Manik Chauk.[111] The actual work of killing, burning, and looting, however, was said to have been carried out by "a handful of notorious characters— known hoodlums and criminals," none of whom were arrested before or after "the carnage of October 5."[112]

Political divisions at the national, state, and local levels also clearly played their part in the production of Hindu-Muslim-police violence in this riot. As noted above, the 1978 riots occurred at a time when the former Jan Sangh members had been incorporated within the Janata Party that came to power in the central government and in U.P. after the landmark 1977 General Elections.[113] In Aligarh, the former Jan Sangh members constituted the core of the Janata Party, whose candidate, a Muslim, won the Legislative Assembly seat.[114] Divisions within the Janata Party between the former Jan Sangh/RSS members and the other principal northern Indian party, the Bharatiya Lok Dal, existed at all levels. It was reported that internal divisions in the state cabinet were likely to produce a "cabinet crisis" and that "at least two cabinet ministers [had] threatened to resign, while a minister of state [had] openly blamed a Janata Party constituent [that is, the Jan Sangh] for fomenting communal trouble."[115] Consequently, neither the state government nor the central government were prepared to take decisive action to prevent rioting in Aligarh or to control it after it had broken out.[116]

These divisions in turn made it difficult for the district administration to act decisively to head off the riots and to control them after they had broken out. Their efforts to "arrest all the wrestlers of the town" on October 4 and their actual arrest of "five Hindu[s] and two Muslims the same evening" were vigorously opposed by Navman, whose supporters surrounded the central police station that night "demanding the release" of a friend of Bhure Lal's, "who had been arrested earlier." Navman himself was provided with police protection by two Provincial Armed Constabulary (PAC) *jawans* (police officers) posted at his house.[117]

AMU students did not get involved in these riots, but did help with relief activities.[118] However, the university was closed down on the grounds that the police could not ensure the safety of students attending classes.

The 1978 riots in Aligarh constitute a benchmark in the development of Aligarh's institutionalized system of riot production, containing all the major elements that will recur in many riots thereafter. These elements include intense inner party and interparty division. Not only was the Janata Party divided in Aligarh City at this time, but there was fierce interparty competition as well between that party and the Congress. These divisions in turn made forceful administrative and police action impossible. Not only that, the PAC revealed itself as a harsh anti-Muslim force. These prevailing conditions in turn made possible the staging of a riot for which the killing of Bhure Lal provided the pretext, though the buildup to the riot had been a several-months-long political campaign over the continuing issue of the status of the AMU. In the actual riots themselves, we witness the evident involvement also of several types of persons performing different roles: known political, business, professional, and university/college persons playing leadership roles in the organization of actions designed to provoke a confrontation between Hindus and Muslims, and known criminal and hoodlum elements recruited for the commission of the actual acts of violence. Little information is provided about the composition of the crowds, though it is likely that, as in the past, students were recruited from the local Hindu- and RSS-dominated degree colleges. There is also a specific form for riot-provoking activities, namely, the procession, in this case of the dead body of a Hindu wrestler, deliberately carried through Muslim-populated and communally sensitive areas with the accompaniment of inflammatory slogans designed to provoke Muslims to respond with brickbats, to justify the slaughter that is to take place thereafter. Finally, under the cover of the communal conflict and the political issue of the status of the AMU, local economic factors are also revealed in the efforts to displace Muslims from their homes in a Hindu-dominated locality in order to gain possession of their property.

Political parties and partisan newspapers continued to make political capital out of the Aligarh riots into November. Opposition parties accused the government of inept handling of the situation[119] and the CPI newspaper, the *Patriot,* continued with the theme that "the organised killing of Muslims at Aligarh was due to the 'conspiracy of RSS and police and PAC.' "[120] While charges, countercharges, and accusations were flying, further large-scale rioting broke out in the city on November 6.[121] By November 9, 1978, the *Times of India* reported that another 15 persons had been killed.[122]

The worst-hit localities were Sarai Sultani, Sarai Kaba, Turkman Gate, Jaiganj, and Babri Mandi (see Map 2).[123] It was also reported that most of the people killed in this new phase of rioting were shot by the police. Further visits by government and political party fact-finding teams and by the Shahi Imam of the Delhi Jama Masjid followed and the same charges and countercharges were made concerning party, police, administrative, and RSS culpability.[124] Specific names of RSS persons from the Hindu community were again mentioned in the press as bearing direct culpability for encouraging the rioting, namely, Professors B. D. Gupta and Manga Ram.[125] By November 15, the official death and injury tolls had increased to 16 and 54, respectively.[126] On November 20, it was reported that a warrant of arrest had been issued against Navman for involvement in the riots, but that he had absconded.[127] In the meantime, the district magistrate and the senior superintendent of police were replaced.[128] By November 26, it was reported that the official death toll from the beginning of the first phase of the riots on October 5 had risen to 28.[129]

Curfew continued in the town throughout the month of December, terminating on the last day of the month. Under the strict control of the new district civilian and police administration, no further deaths occurred. However, conditions in the old city remained disturbed and there were further outbreaks of violence during the month, including bomb explosions and stabbings.[130] The administration not only retained curfew throughout the month, but engaged in continuous house searches for arms, arrested "more than 1,000 persons," and engaged local persons in the *mohallas* to participate in peace committees.[131]

By the time the curfew was lifted, large parts of the city of Aligarh, particularly the old center, had been under varying curfew hours for 88 days continuously, that is, since its imposition after the second phase of rioting on October 6. The prolonged character of the disturbances in Aligarh, from the beginning of the first incident on September 12, that is, the brawl between the two wrestling groups, and the length of time the city was under curfew in both the first and second phases of rioting, suggest that the term *riot* is a misnomer for what occurred during these months. These events were of a different order from the riots that occurred before in Aligarh, which, like most events classed as riots, lasted only a few days. But it is not at all clear how to label it, what specific events should be included as part of the communal attacks involving Hindus and Muslims, and what should be considered mere crimes. We cannot label it urban civil war, for that would minimize the activities of known criminal elements for whom the disturbances provided an occasion to loot and plunder. It was certainly not an insurrection, since the violence was not directed against authority except insofar as the police intervened between Hindu and Muslim groups or attacked one side or the other. All that can be said with a measure of accuracy is that large parts of the city underwent disorder, anarchy, violence, and that state of potential war of all against all in which no person could feel safe from harm and sudden death and no one's property was secure, a state in which most people suffered while some also gained. The gains for some were loot, harming of one's rivals, stealing of the property of the weak and helpless, displacing of unwanted elements from one's neighborhood, and not least of all the political advantages gained by political persons in the city, state, and country through stentorian statements exclaiming sympathy for the victims while blaming others for the violence.

Indeed, the process of blame displacement continued throughout these long months of violence in Aligarh, in the press and in a full-scale debate in the Lok Sabha on December 4–5, 1978.[132] The string of outside visitors to Aligarh also continued.

The Minorities Commission heard an interpretation of the riots as arising out of economic rivalries. One view was that rivalries between Hindu and Muslim businessmen in the lock industry were "behind the tension." A second was that Hindu businessmen who coveted Muslim property contrived riots for the purpose. Similar reports appeared also in the press. One such report argued that, in this riot, as in the previous riots of 1961 and 1971, "rising property values in some poorer sections of the town could be a motive behind the destruction of the houses in the present riots as in previous ones.... In both these riots, separated by a decade, miserable hovels of poor people were obliterated and in their place has come up a prosperous commercial centre."[133] It was also reported that Muslim owners of houses that had not been destroyed were "receiving ... offers by potential buyers" at prices "lower than ever before."[134] Other reports referred to "business rivalries between Muslims and upper caste Hindus" as having "played their role in engendering feelings of hatred."[135]

Although the sequence of events in connection with the incidents involving the wrestling competition is generally accepted, it is not universally accepted that the wrestling competition was itself the "cause" of the riot. On the contrary, at least four interpretations have been put forth to explain the transformation of the scuffle, the stabbings, and the funeral procession of Bhure Lal into a major riot in which the passions aroused by the death of the Hindu wrestler are considered mere pretexts. Those interpretations were laid out for me in an interview with one respondent, a Muslim, who was president of the Aligarh Muslim University Students Union, a supporter of the

Janata Party, and a person actively involved in efforts to restore peace in the city at the time.

PRB: So, the '78 riots . . .

JH: Yes, actually, it was, uh, the theory was that, uh, some local persons, they want to purchase a particular piece of land, or a particular market. . . . Therefore, there were two theories. One theory was that it was an unplanned riot started just after a wrestling competition. That was one version.

PRB: That fellow Bhure . . .

JH: Yes, Bhure Lal, Bhure Lal and maybe any. . . . They said that it was just a sponta- neous thing, but it had become a communal riot and because the mind of the people is polluted always, therefore, it—and due to the lack of some policemen who were on duty that, uh, the dead body of the *pahalwan,* that Bhure Lal or . . . *pahalwan,* it was allowed to go in a procession like that. That was one version. The second version was that . . . Mr. Navman was behind the riot, and that he planned a riot to emerge as the leader of the Hindus, and that was the second. The third and very famous theory was that . . . some persons want to purchase a particular area of land for their commercial and economic purposes. Therefore, *they* [original empha- sis] created a situation of the riot in order to get the Muslim [persons in the] local- ity there migrated from that [area]. . . . These were three main theories. And there were many local things and all. . . . But, after three theories, the fourth element was added by Congress (I) at that time. And they said that it is RSS and Janata Party and Muslims must beware of that because Navman is . . . part of Jan Sangh and man of RSS, therefore, Janata Party means Jan Sangh and means RSS is respon- sible for that.[136]

Four theories, each one of a type that is repeated in virtually every account of the origins of Hindu-Muslim riots in India. Moreover, the realm of expla- nation has remained wide open concerning this riot, for a judicial inquiry commission appointed after the riot never completed its work and was ulti- mately discontinued by the succeeding state Congress government in August 1980, while the state was experiencing yet another round of rioting (see below). The same charges and countercharges were made in the U.P. Legislative Assembly when the chief minister, Mr. Vishwanath Pratap Singh, announced the termination of the inquiry committee. Opposition leaders who had been in power during the 1978 riots charged that the inquiry was being withdrawn because it had discovered the involvement of "some Congress (I) men" in it. BJP leaders implied that it was being withdrawn for the same reasons as well as because the commission found no RSS involvement in those riots, while a CPI member bemoaned the withdrawal of the inquiry because it would not reveal the truth "about the involvement of the RSS and a then cabinet minister in the Aligarh riot." He remarked further that, "if inquiries were scrapped like this, the people would never come to know who were the real culprits."[137]

## May 1979

In this riot, the issue of the status of the AMU was again at the forefront. The sequence of events began with the response of AMU students to the passage under the Janata Party government of a bill in the Lok Sabha meant to restore the status, powers, and governing institutions of the university to the position prevailing before the passage by the previous Congress governments in 1965 and 1971 of laws that were held to have undermined them. The bill was passed on May 3, 1979, but was criticized by many Muslim leaders, organizations, and the conservative group at the AMU for not explicitly restoring the "minority character" of the university by designating it as such under the terms of Article 30(1) of the Constitution of India.[138]

A protest meeting was arranged by AMU students in Delhi for August 9. Delhi being only a few hours' train journey from Aligarh, probably several hundred students boarded the train on the morning of the day of the rally, taking up four bogeys.[139] On the way, for a distance of some 24 kilometers between the Dadri Railway Station in Meerut District and Delhi, the students, according to initial reports, were soundly thrashed and many of them beaten bloody by groups of local men from the Gujjar caste, a predominantly rural agricultural caste. The thorough thrashing of the students immediately gave rise to conflicting explanations of the circumstances that led to it. The press cited prominently "sources" who attributed the incident to the misbehavior of the students, who sought to take up all the seats on the train, displacing or making them inaccessible to the Gujjars, including their women and children. The Gujjars responded by beating the students and calling for reinforcements from members of their own caste as the train passed through various stations en route. The students, however, many of whom arrived at the rally in Delhi with their clothes torn and some of them "soaked in blood," claimed that they had been peacefully travelling to Delhi, that they were "beaten up and looted by miscreants," and that the RSS was responsible for the attack.[140]

This incident proved quite useful to several political organization and their leaders. Dissidents in the Janata Party, who were then fighting an internal battle to remove RSS members from party membership, used it as an example to support the need to rid the party and the country as well of the RSS entirely.[141] Congress (I) members of Parliament, now in opposition, also found the incident useful to belabor the RSS and the Janata government together. The former Jan Sangh and RSS members in Parliament, of course, found wholly satisfying the explanation of the train beatings as having arisen out of an altercation among passengers. The authorities, however, including the home minister of the government of India and the local police and administration, insisted that they did not have adequate information to reach a conclusion, but that they had information that contradicted the student accounts.[142]

Upon their return to Aligarh the next day, many AMU students took out their resentment by first attempting to set fire to a state transport authority bus and by setting fire to a couple of dozen shops owned by non-Muslims in the Shamshad Market adjoining the campus. The authorities responded by imposing an indefinite curfew on the city and the AMU and by posting PAC and Central Reserve Police Force (CRPF) forces on the campus itself. Students protested against the police emplacement on campus and police-student clashes ensued, in which 5 persons were killed, whose identities—that is, whether they were students or not—were not given in the press reports.[143] The campus was closed down and the students evicted from their hostels and escorted by the police to departing trains to prevent further incidents.

In the meantime, the state government also took up the issue. The chief minister, also a member of the Janata Party, though not of the former Jan Sangh, gave an interpretation of the origins of the violence at Dadri differing from the original reports that it was a brawl between Gujjars and the students. He said that his intelligence reports indicated that it was a conflict "between two groups of student commuters." He also said that "intelligence reports showed that the AMU students going to New Delhi had molested a newly-married bride in the train."[144] He criticized those who were trying to give a "communal colour" to the incidents, but then proceeded to lay the blame for doing so upon "Muslim communalists," who had been "responsible for the partition of India."[145] Thus, once again do we see how a brawl of uncertain origin is immediately subject to a multiplicity of explanations that provide political benefits to political parties, groups, and leaders, while in the meantime expanding to encompass not only the relations between Hindus and Muslims, Muslims and police, but the very origins and identity of India.

It was pointed out in the press that the incidents of May 1979 were entirely different from those that had occurred the previous October, in that they had "engulfed the campus and students," whereas, in the previous riots, the campus had been unaffected and the AMU students had provided relief to riot victims in the city.[146] On this occasion, however, it was the city that was unaffected except by the imposition of preventive curfew. Yet there was some effort to involve the city in the disturbances. The two leading traders' organizations called for an "Aligarh *bandh,*" that is, a closure of shops "to protest against the violent incidents on AMU campus on May 10." The Vyapar Mandal, the larger of the two, and the one dominated by militant Hindu Varshney businessmen and RSS members, also adopted a resolution demanding "that the AMU should not be allowed to open unless sufficient security arrangements were made for non-Muslim students and teachers on the campus."[147] One can only wonder why a traders' association in the city should have taken up the issue of the protection of Hindu students and teachers on the campus. The other organization, also dominated by Hindu businessmen, was said to have "issued a pamphlet leveling false charges against Muslims."[148]

But why, then, did the AMU agitation not spread to the town on this occasion, as it had in March 1971 and in the 1972 demonstrations and counter-demonstrations over the passage of the AMU (Amendments) Act? In May 1979, there simply was no connection to electoral politics, the last election having been held in 1977 and no other election being in the offing at that time. Second, administrative failings were considered to have been a factor in the failure to prevent and contain the riots in 1971, though not in 1972. In May 1979, it was generally acknowledged that the district and university authorities moved immediately after the Dadri incident to prevent any incidents in the town, by imposing curfew, and to contain the violent student demonstrations on the AMU campus as well, through the use of force and by sending the students home. Once again, therefore, political and administrative factors appear on the face of it to make a critical difference in the development, prevention, and control of potentially riotous communal confrontations.

### Incidents of August to November 1980

In August 1980, one of the worst incidents of collective violence in the history of U.P. occurred in Moradabad City and District, near Aligarh, leading to a massacre of upwards of 115 persons, of whom nearly all were Muslims. Riots followed in several other U.P. towns across the state and elsewhere in India. The first violent incidents in Aligarh were reported on August 16; it was said that a "mob was protesting against the Moradabad incidents." Police had fired, 2 persons had been killed, and indefinite curfew had been imposed on the entire city, excepting the Civil Lines.[149] Two days later, it was reported that, "in all, two police constables" had been killed and "23 others including 19 policemen" had been injured.[150] It is not clear whether the two policemen killed were the same as the two persons reported killed earlier. A clash of this sort, in which policemen are killed and injured in the circumstances obtaining in Aligarh at the time, could only mean large-scale confrontation between police and Muslim crowds. Reports from Aligarh on this and succeeding days referred to relaxation of curfew, arrests of a large number of people,[151] and formation of peace committees to visit "the affected areas in a bid to reduce tension and restore communal harmony."[152]

Nevertheless, violence broke out again on August 24 in the old city during a period of curfew relaxation, though no further deaths were reported. The district administration was reported to be "handling the Aligarh situation with firmness" and "the authorities" were said to "have posted four columns of troops there besides units of the BSF, the PAC and the local police."[153] There then followed several more days of reports in the press from Aligarh that there had been no further incidents, curfew was being relaxed gradually in terms of the numbers of hours of the day as well as the areas affected, additional persons had been arrested to prevent further violence, and peace committees had again begun visiting the affected neighborhoods.[154] Meanwhile, the situation in Moradabad had been brought under control sufficiently to allow the beginning of army withdrawal from the town on September 2.[155]

As usual, a multiplicity of explanations for the outbreak of violence in Moradabad, Aligarh, and elsewhere in the state were offered instantly by politicians and the press. In contrast to the situation in 1978, when Janata governments were in power in Lucknow and New Delhi while the Congress (I) was in opposition, the situation was now reversed. A state Congress (I) minister, himself a Muslim, visited Aligarh and declared at a meeting at the AMU that "the current disturbances were not communal but seemed to be the work of certain lawless elements," but a central government minister of state for home affairs, Yogendra Makwana, blamed the RSS, Jan Sangh, and BJP.[156] Indira Gandhi, however, consistent with her views in general concerning the sources of the country's problems, suggested "that foreign forces could be behind the recent communal incidents in U.P. and other parts of the country."[157] The formulation that ultimately emerged as the central government's position on these riots was that "a neighbouring country," which, of course, meant Pakistan, as well as "some communal parties" were involved in promoting them. Union Minister Makwana noted, in support of this formulation, that "for the first time riots had broken out between two minority communities—Muslims and Harijans." Since these two "groups had always sided with the Congress," the aim was said to be "to weaken the ruling party."[158] Although the formulation contained considerable vagueness, especially on the particular communal parties involved, that is, whether they were Hindu or Muslim or both, one implication was that Pakistan, in collusion with Muslim communal parties, was responsible, and that, therefore, it was the Muslim minority and the Harijans, but not the upper-caste Hindus, whose members were doing most of the rioting.

Girilal Jain, editor of the *Times of India,* added his support for the plausibility of the central government's interpretations. He blamed "anti-social elements" among the Muslims for being "at least partly responsible for the riots in Moradabad and other U.P. towns" and Muslim leaders for not admitting the facts themselves, but instead blaming the RSS as usual. He absolved the RSS from any responsibility whatsoever and lent support to Mrs. Gandhi's contention that "foreign interference" was involved.[159] In a move that we have seen practiced earlier during the 1978 riots, the *Times of India* followed the next day with a news item listing the number of persons from Pakistan who had been visiting U.P. in the past few years and noted that there had been a considerable increase, particularly in towns such as Bareilly, Aligarh, and Moradabad, where extensive rioting was now taking place.[160]

There occurred at this time, in fact, a convergence of views among the Congress (I) leadership, the leading English-language newspaper, and the BJP leadership that must have appeared menacing to many Indian Muslims. For, at the same time, the BJP leader, L. K. Advani, while denying any attempt on his part to blame the Muslim community as a whole for this latest round of rioting in northern India, nevertheless thought that "the manner in which the riots spread to Meerut, Delhi, and other towns almost simultaneously and in an identical pattern did suggest to him some kind of planning." He was then quoted directly as follows: "It appears that some Muslim elements are trying to pit the community against the law and order machinery. In Srinagar [Kashmir] they clashed with the army; in Moradabad and some other towns, they attacked the police." He then directed his accusation specifically at Muslim organizations and leaders, namely, the Muslim League, the Jamaat-i-Islami, and the imam of the Delhi Jama Masjid.[161]

In the midst of reports that the rioting in Moradabad and Aligarh was being brought under control and the post-mortem speculations, further violence broke out in Moradabad and Aligarh. In this latest outburst, the killing was greater in Aligarh than in Moradabad. In Aligarh, nine people were reported to have been killed on September 8 in "clashes between groups of people," but none in police firing.[162] The reference to "groups of people" means that, on this occasion, the confrontation was not between Muslims and the police, but between Hindus and Muslims. The next day, it was announced that the district magistrate and the senior superintendent of police had been replaced. The new DM was Rajiv Ratan Shah, the SSP was Mr. B. P. Singh. B. P. Singh, especially, was said to have dealt with the Aligarh "underworld" quite effectively, that is, according to my sources, by gathering up more than forty known and alleged Muslim *goondas* and simply taking them outside the city limits and killing them.[163] From this point until 1990, Aligarh had no major riots.[164]

Although sporadic rioting continued in Moradabad over the next two months, it was contained in Aligarh by the new administration.[165]

During these months and for some time thereafter, there was a multiplicity of incidents that have not been given a clear focus in public documents, press reports, or my own interviews.[166] Responses to my questions concerning the riots during this period were quite diffuse. They suggest a general state of anarchy and local warfare that, as noted in other sources, included "pitched battles between Muslims and the Provincial Armed Constabulary."[167]

In 1983, I asked respondents, both Hindu and Muslim, to tell me about these riots. Some respondents, and others who have written about the riots, mostly without direct knowledge of them and not having heard of any particular reason for riots to have broken out in Aligarh in 1980, attributed the outbreaks to a spontaneous response on the part of Muslims to the police firing against Muslims in Moradabad at that time, which involved much loss of life amongst Muslims there. Others with more direct knowledge of the incidents in 1980 and in the preceding years gave more elaborate responses. According to one Muslim politician, these incidents were not riots, but a systematic attempt on the part of the Hindu Banias associated with the Jan Sangh in the locality of Manik Chauk to harass and intimidate Muslims in order to get them to flee so that they could obtain their valuable property cheaply. Eleven persons were killed in consequence, but the police, this respondent said, acted promptly and effectively to contain the effects to the *mohalla* of Manik Chauk.[168]

*Communal Incidents between 1980 and 1990*

Among the various incidents that occurred during this—for Aligarh—relatively peaceful period, those that occurred in October 1988 are of considerable interest because of the extent to which they reveal the dynamic processes of riot production and riot control as well as their close connection to political events.

*The Riots of October 1988.* The riots of October 1988 were underreported in the *Times of India* because they were overshadowed by the much larger disturbances in the nearby district of Muzaffarnagar, which had never before experienced communal rioting. Rioting occurred later in the month in other districts in U.P. as well. All the rioting in the state in that month was associated in press reports with the opposed Hindu and Muslim agitations in connection with the militant Hindu movement to bring down the Babri Masjid in Ayodhya, to replace it with a temple to Ram. The agitation and counteragitation began with the announcement of a planned march to Ayodhya by five hundred Muslim leaders sponsored by the Babri Masjid Action Committee to offer prayers at the contested site. The march was scheduled for March 14. VHP leaders promptly announced a countermove in opposition to the march, calling for a *bandh* (closure of shops) throughout the state on March 8 in protest against it. The call for a *bandh* in a context in which Hindus and Muslims have opposed interests is a highly provocative tactic that has many times in modern Indian history precipitated violence, both during the nationalist movement and since Independence. In most cases, the violence has followed attempts by Hindus to compel resisting Muslim shop owners to pull down their storefront shutters. Press reports on the events in October in the districts that experienced violence during and after the *bandh* call indicate clearly that this is precisely what happened.

However, riots were reported from only two of the 54 districts in the state: Aligarh and Muzaffarnagar. Riots also occurred later in the month in Faizabad (adjacent to Ayodhya), Hardoi, and Bahraich. In Aligarh and Muzaffarnagar, rioting was clearly associated with the March 8 *bandh* call.

Although the precipitating incidents were said to be similiar in Aligarh and Muzaffarnagar, the political context in the two districts was entirely different, and so were the results. Rioting was reported in the first *Times of India* dispatch from Aligarh and Muzaffarnagar on October 8, in which it was stated that two persons had been "stabbed to death in Aligarh, and eight seriously injured in Muzaffarnagar and Khatauli" (a town neighboring Muzaffarnagar).[169] The rioting was sufficiently serious in both places to warrant the sending of CRPF personnel to both Aligarh and Muzaffarnagar towns. The home secretary of the state government was given as the source for the information concerning the events in Aligarh, where "two groups clashed . . . around noon," "exchanged brickbats and resorted to arson resulting in the destruction of several shops. Stabbing incidents were also reported from some parts of the city." In these fracases, 27 people were said to have been injured, of whom two died of their wounds. In Muzaffarnagar, the outbreak of violence occurred "while members of a particular community [Hindu] were taking out a procession over the Ram Janmabhoomi issue," during which "some participants . . . asked shopkeepers to close their shops and this led to a clash."

Although curfew was imposed in both Aligarh and Muzaffarnagar throughout most of the rest of the month, it is noteworthy that the situation in Aligarh—despite its more violent history—was kept under control while that in Muzaffarnagar was not. No further deaths were reported from Aligarh after the initial stabbings, but the *Times of India* reported 13 killed in Muzaffarnagar and the neighboring town of Khatauli by October 11; the last report on the death toll there gave a figure of 22 killed.[170]

The contrast between the situations in Aligarh and Muzaffarnagar on this occasion throws additional light on the factors that promote and sustain communal violence in northern India. The *Times of India* itself raised the question of why the violence was contained in Aligarh while it spiraled out of control in Muzaffarnagar.[171] Its answers, based on its own reports from the district and state headquarters, were that the administrative and political situations in the two districts differed. In Muzaffarnagar, the district administrative officials were accused of outright negligence on the first day of the incidents, in contrast to Aligarh, where prompt and effective action was taken from the first outbreak of violence. The second reason was that the political situation in Muzaffarnagar was even more volatile at the time than in Aligarh because two ministers in the state Congress government, one a Hindu, the other a rising Muslim politician, both from Muzaffarnagar town, were hostile to each other and contesting for local political control. A prominent Hindu supporter of the Hindu minister, one Harish Chabra—not a BJP man, but a Congress man—went around "mobilising support for the October 8 bandh" that provoked the initial violence. Following upon the arrest of "scores of persons . . . in connection with the violence," this same Chabra led "a mob" that "surrounded the Kotwali police station" demanding their release.[172] Then, on October 11, there was a further clash between a procession led by Chabra and an interparty peace march, leading to further violence. The *Times of India* editorial suggested further that the administration's ability to control the rioting was hamstrung by the reported involvement of two powerful ministers in the state government and their supporters.

The differences between Aligarh and Muzaffarnagar at this time suggest the limitations of both the method of paired comparisons and the game theory approaches to explaining communal violence/peace. Muzaffarnagar had experienced no communal violence since 1947, but it suddenly faced a massive outburst comparable to the worst in Aligarh in previous years. Yet Muzaffarnagar, because of its demographic and economic similarities with the two most riot-prone districts in western U.P., had been included by the Centre for Research in Industrial Development for comparison with Aligarh and Meerut.

The study, though it selected mostly on the dependent variable of riot-proneness, identified several differences between Muzaffarnagar, on the one hand, and Aligarh and Meerut, on the other hand, that appeared to explain the former's freedom from violence. The differences included, especially, the sharp separation of predominantly Hindu and predominantly Muslim localities, the generally subordinate, noncompetitive economic and political position of the Muslims in relation to Hindus in the town of Muzaffarnagar, and a history of intercommunal relations in the surrounding area that included even some intermarriage and joint decisions on political action, as well as a secular attitude on the part of traders from both communities. Indeed, their study reported that many Muslims supported the BJP and that RSS volunteers were engaged in promoting Hindu-Muslim friendship. Finally, they reported that their survey research showed, in contrast to Aligarh and Meerut, that the two communities shared an appreciation for both Hindu and Muslim historical figures who are associated in Indian historical hagiography with secular attitudes.[173] The only ominous sign they saw in the future was the existence of "increasing competition" in a context of "locational confrontation" between two subgroups from the Muslim and Hindu communities, Qureshi Muslims and Scheduled Castes, in competition in the beef and meat business.[174]

However, the evidence available from the newspaper reports suggests that it was political competition between Hindu and Muslim leaders, rather than any change in the existing economic and social patterns, that produced the massive rioting in 1988. Further, it is evident that what occurred was a spiralling of conflict that is inconsistent with the Fearon/Laitin assumptions. Indeed, as noted above, there was even a peace march "taken out by various sections of the people" (meaning both intercommunal and interparty) during the riots, which was attacked by rioters.[175] Insofar as Aligarh is concerned, the limited evidence available on the riots there suggests just the opposite of the situation in Muzaffarnagar: a highly politicized, communalized political environment known for both the intensity of its interparty competition and the tendency for intercommunal incidents to spiral out of control was contained by the presence of firm, prompt administrative action and the absence of an immediate local political advantage. One of the variables, the political context, was to change within the year, while the administrative context remained the same.

*The riots of November 1989.* The context in which the reported incidents of November 1989 took place was framed by the dramatic events preceding the 1989 elections and the election itself. The announcement of elections and the scheduling of polls was made by Prime Minister Rajiv Gandhi on October 17. During the period before the elections, the VHP intensified its campaign to replace the Babri Masjid in Ayodhya with a newly constructed temple to the god Ram, through the famous *shilanyas* march of militant Hindu volunteers to Ayodhya, bringing bricks to be consecrated for the foundation of the new temple to be constructed there. The procession reached Ayodhya and laid the foundation for the Ram temple at a site adjacent to the mosque on November 9. On October 26, one of the worst communal riots in post-Independence India, including some incidents of a particularly atrocious character, began in the district of Bhagalpur in Bihar; the reports on these riots, which extended to other parts of Bihar and continued for weeks, with mounting death tolls, reverberated among Muslims throughout north India. Polling for the Lok Sabha and Vidhan Sabha elections was held between November 22 and 26 in different parts of the country.

A further issue that became prominent at this time concerned the granting to Urdu the status of a second official language in the western districts of U.P. Severe riots occurred between September 28 and October 2 in the district of Budaun, adjacent to Aligarh District, attributed to agitation over this issue.[176]

Aligarh City and the AMU both were affected by these events in the month of November. On November 7, a broadside was distributed in the city and on the AMU campus announcing a meeting of intellectuals to oppose the declaration of Urdu as the second state language of U.P.[177] Three Hindu students at the Engineering College of the AMU were noticed by two Muslim students with the broadside and possibly some other material in their possession, presumably to be distributed on the campus. The Muslim students apparently reported the matter to the university authorities, who immediately took the strong action of suspending the three students from the university and ordering them to vacate their hostel rooms for having "brought some objectionable/provocative material" to the Engineering College on November 7. On the following day, one of the students wrote to the dean of the engineering faculty proclaiming his innocence and stating that he was given the "printed cards" in question by another Hindu student. He wrote again to the District Magistrate, Aligarh, to protest his innocence. It appears from this letter that the grounds for his suspension included the allegation that "some pamphlets inciting communal hatred" were found in his room, of which he denied any knowledge.

In the midst of this argument over the distribution of the broadside calling for the anti-Urdu meeting, it appears that there was a much more serious matter involved, namely, the plastering on the walls of buildings on and near the university campus of scurrilous and indecent posters and banners attacking the Congress (I) and Rajiv Gandhi personally. It has never been revealed whether or not the three Hindu students had anything to do with these posters, which instead were attributed to Muslim students of the AMU angry over the *shilanyas* and the riots in Bhagalpur. These posters would be plastered at night, then removed the next day by the authorities, only to reappear the next night. The slogans plastered on the walls were considered so uncouth and indecent that their substance was not reported in the English-language press and only one or two of the least offensive of them were mentioned in the Hindi press. There were also reports of similarly offensive effigies of Rajiv Gandhi.[178]

In the midst of these provocative calls for meetings, plastering of slogans and placing of effigies, and the election campaign itself, the *Times of India* reported from Aligarh with a November 10 dateline on mob violence in "some Muslim localities in the old city." The citing of Muslim localities and the grounds given for the violence—anger over the news that the *shilanyas* in Ayodhya had been allowed to take place the previous day—implies that the rioting was done by Muslims. The story also referred to an attack by "an angry mob of slogan shouting students on the Vice-Chancellor's residence," the hoisting of a black flag there, shouting of "anti–Rajiv Gandhi slogans," a call by a Muslim student leader for a "war against the ruling party," and the burning of "half a dozen effigies of Mr Rajiv Gandhi."[179] A Hindi newspaper, datelined November 13, referred to the violence of November 10 as having involved firing, presumably police firing, and brickbatting in Upar Kot. There were no reports of deaths. Another report in a Hindi newspaper, datelined November 11, referred to the same violent incidents and named a number of *mohallas* in which they had occurred: four of them in the central Muslim areas and one, Shamshad Market, adjacent to the university.[180] The report went on to say that, although the city had gone back to normal, an atmosphere of communalism persisted at the AMU and in some other parts of the city because of the posters. There were also reports of processions and meetings on the campus and in the city: by the nonteaching staff of the university accusing the government of bowing down and giving support to Hindu communalism; meetings of people of "a religious community" (that is, Muslims) in some parts of the city to oppose the Congress (I); and tearing up of the offensive posters and banners around the university campus.

Both the district and the university administration were extremely alert to all these manifestations of anger and protest and took firm actions, some of which, however, backfired. For example, the district administration closed down all educational institutions in Aligarh City, both the AMU and the local degree colleges, from November 13 until November 27, that is, until after the elections. However, the closing of the university had the opposite of the effect intended. It was assumed, wrongly, that the students would take advantage of the vacation time to return to their homes, but instead, according to the Hindi press, the student organizations announced various actions such as the declaration of November 15 as a "black day" on which students would court arrest in protest against the *shilanyas*. Meanwhile, the poster campaign against the Congress (I) continued on the AMU campus. The Hindu students were also active, calling for the revocation of the suspension of the three Hindu students and naming the two Muslim students who reported their activities as "the real culprits." For their part, the Muslim AMU students announced their support for the Janata Dal candidate for Parliament, Mr. Satyapal Malik, a Hindu known for his secular attitudes, but said they would not necessarily support the Janata Dal in other constituencies because of its arrangement for adjustment of seats with the BJP in the Lok Sabha elections. Mainly, however, they announced that they would work for the defeat of the Congress, including the defeat of Congress Muslim candidates.

The last newspaper report from Aligarh, from the *Times of India,* datelined November 15, reported on the basis of a large number of interviews conducted on the AMU campus that there had been "a sharp change in the mood of the Muslim voters . . . in the last ten days," such that the Congress could not expect to get more than 25 percent of the Muslim vote in the state. Muslim disaffection was attributed particularly to Rajiv Gandhi's decision to launch his election campaign from Ayodhya and "the fallout of the shilanyas ceremony at Ayodhya."[181]

It appears from the newspaper reports of the violence in the inner city that, despite the fact that there were no deaths, the incidents constituted a riot under existing laws. At the same time, the violence was also evidently contained quickly and effectively. The news reports cited above all referred to quick police action, institution of day-and-night street patrolling, and the closure of all educational institutions. Further, in the midst of all the hubbub surrounding the *shilanyas,* election campaigning, poster plastering, and the anti-Urdu agitation, the district administration was faced with the movement of large crowds of Hindu devotees through the town on the way to the Ganga River to observe the Hindu bathing festival of Kartik Purnima (eighth-month full moon). Newspapers reported that, because of this festival, "the administration has kept special watch over persons, vehicles, and trains passing by or near the [AMU] campus."[182] It would appear, therefore, that the district administration had multiple reasons for acting effectively to contain this riot, and that they did so.

At the same time, we can learn from the course of events in this riot much about how riots begin in Aligarh and elsewhere and how they spread. This riot was marked by a sequence of provocative actions, of which the call for the anti-Urdu meeting was the least provocative and was certainly within the range of normal, legal, democratic action. The other two major events were also within the range of democratic participation in some societies, but pass the margin of democratic acceptability in India because of their association with or deliberate instigation of communal enmity, a violation of Indian laws. The *shilanyas,* while technically a legal act, was everywhere in India associated with provocative actions that aroused Muslim anger: processions through their neighborhoods, ringing of bells in the night, and many other demonstrative acts, ending in the ultimate provocation of laying the foundation stones for a temple designed to be built over an existing mosque in Ayodhya.

The indecent posters were clearly both provocative and illegal. They were attributed to Muslim students at AMU. If this is true,[183] then signals were being sent from elements in both communities for the start of riotous or potentially riotous activities. Further, these signals involved elements both in the city and at the AMU. Whereas Muslims were angry over the *shilanyas* and the implication of the Congress (I) and Prime Minister Rajiv Gandhi in allowing it to take place, Hindus were opposed to the imposition of Urdu as a second language. But, more important, militant Hindus in Aligarh remain always ready to pounce upon the AMU as the source of Muslim communalism, separatism, and anti-Hindu sentiments. Whenever communally sensitive or provocative events in the city and the university occur or are made to appear to occur simultaneously, the danger of large-scale Hindu-Muslim violence is extreme in Aligarh, as events in the following year (discussed in the next chapter) were to demonstrate.

There is, finally, the association of these events with the election campaign, another aspect of the situation that promoted simultaneous feelings of anger among Muslims in both the city and the AMU who shared resentment against the Congress for its behavior in relation to the *shilanyas* at Ayodhya. The results of this election, in fact, depended heavily on Muslim reactions throughout the state and did indeed contribute significantly to the defeat of the Congress in the state as well as in the country, leading to the installation of Janata Dal governments in New Delhi and Lucknow. The association of communal riots with election campaigns has been noted above and will be discussed further in detail in succeeding chapters.

*Summary*

Since the 1990 riots took place after a long gap from their most violent pre-cursors in 1980, and stand apart in other ways from their predecessors between 1956 and 1989, the main features of this long series of riots will be summarized here before discussing the new series of incidents and rioting that began in 1990. First, it should be noted that there is a shift, from the early to the later incidents in the decades between 1961 and 1989, in spatial origins. Among the earlier riots, several involved actions and reactions between town and university, with students playing major roles on both sides.[184] These include the 1956 disturbances involving the Muslim student protest on the AMU campus over the republication of a book alleged to contain "disrespectful references to the prophet," which was followed by the false reports that the AMU students had burned a copy of the *Bhagavad Gita*, providing a pretext for a student protest strike in the city's degree colleges. Also included is the 1961 riot, in which the precipitating incident was the scuffle over the AMU Students Union elections, which was then followed by action on the AMU campus, with news and rumors concerning it sent to the city, precipitating an action by the Hindu students in the city colleges. The third, in 1971, aris-ing out of the agitation on the university campus over the issue of restoring the minority character of the university, also began on the campus and was followed by riot in the city. The fourth, however, the riot in the aftermath of the train beating at Dadri, did not move to the city.

Second, although most of the Aligarh riots of this type do not arise directly out of quarrels between rivals from organized political parties, there is usu-ally a political connection of some type. The 1961 riot led to Muslim politi-cal action against and defeat of the Congress in the broader arena of district politics. The 1971 and 1989 riots were associated with the elections of those years. Other riots have been precipitated by the politicized issue of the sta-tus of AMU, which is highly charged symbolically and "represents" Hindu-Muslim relations in significant ways.

Many of the later riots, however, are clearly marked by incidents within the town and by the involvement of local politicians in them. There is also an allegation of profit motivations by greedy Hindu businessmen.

When we come to 1989, however, and then to 1990, there is a kind of merging of the two types of riots. The 1990 riots start in town, as we shall see, but move to AMU as well. In this respect, the 1989 riots constituted a kind of rehearsal for what was to take place the next year.

When we consider that several of the incidents that took place in the above years spread over weeks, months, and even years and that each of them involved the imposition of curfews, one could almost say that there was a kind of semiperpetual curfew in Aligarh marked also by the presence of armed forces at strategic crossings. At such times, they are mostly standing and sitting idly and uselessly by crossings and other sites where incidents have occurred in the past (see Figure 3.5). Similar situations exist in other towns in western U.P., such as Meerut.

Some of the riots display a kind of ritual of provocation of a type noted by Gaboricau, involving "codified procedures" that include the "selection of key symbols representing each community" and the "selection of the means by which such symbols may be most effectively desecrated," followed by the implementation of acts of violence against those symbols—mosques and temples—and extending, finally, to destruction of property belonging to persons from the other community and to killing.[185] That patterning of Hindu-Muslim riots has been present at times in this series of riots, for example, in those involving the throwing of colored water on Muslims during the Hindu festival of Holi, but it does not seem to be prominent in most of them, especially the later ones. Instead, there is a different kind of sequence or perhaps two different types of sequences, even more deadly and provocative. In one, people from the two communities are already massed in one way or another in either peaceful contestation (student union elections, a wrestling match, or a political demonstration) and a scuffle breaks out between individuals, after which the rumors spread, there may be further provocative actions, and larger mobs are brought into play. In the second type, an incident occurs between two individuals, one Hindu, the other Muslim, and conscious efforts are made to mobilize members of one community to avenge the harm caused to one of its members. Sometimes, the second sequence is required to bring into full play the first; the second sequence, however, is one that is in operation all the time. I will return later to the significance of the perpetual operation of this second sequence.

Insofar as the change in the dynamics of riot provocation and action are

FIG. 3.5. Police picket at Phul Chauraha

concerned, the Minorities Commission itself took note of it in its first report, quoting the prime minister at the time, Morarji Desai, who noted that "petty quarrels between two individuals are transformed into riots between two communities," in contrast to the traditional forms of provocation involving "music before mosques" or "taking out processions during festivals, etc."[186] Figures were given for the country as a whole for the year 1977 regarding how many of the 188 communal incidents of the year arose in each way: it was found that the large majority (113) arose out of "petty quarrels." The Commission expressed its inability to understand why this should be so, but offered three possible alternative explanations.

The first explanation proffered by the Commission was "that the feelings between the two communities are so strained that an attack on an individual is construed as an attack on the whole community." This explanation would seem to be consistent with the Gaborieau model. It also fits the spiral equilibrium pattern. The second construction offered by the Minorities Commission was "that there is a particular section in each community which has a design to take advantage of every opportunity to spark off a communal riot." A third explanation is that "communal riots are engineered by persons who have an avaricious eye on the property of the minority community and who succeed in acquiring such property on their own terms after each riot."[187]

The first two explanations could be consistent with each other, but it depends on how much organization and effort is implied in the second and what kinds of people are involved in the riots according to the second explanation. In fact, as will be shown later, none of these explanations can account satisfactorily for the dynamics of riots: their timing, the triggering incidents that allegedly set them off, and the course they follow. The first is wholly unsatisfactory. The second is unsatisfactory, among other reasons, because it does not define what constitutes an "opportunity" to set off a riot. The third, the property explanation, can be fit into a more general one, but the idea that large-scale riotous events are "engineered" by avaricious businessmen will not stand.

Communal riots are preeminently political events in which many other forces come into play once they are fomented. None of the explanations offered by public, political men present the preeminently political aspects of these events, because to do so would expose not only themselves, their political organizations, and their inability to control riots when they occur, but the overall functioning of a polity in which riot production is as much a routine aspect of politics as interest articulation, mass mobilization, and electoral competition. Indeed, it is embedded in these latter processes. Further, the very act of explanation is itself a part of these processes that contributes to the production and persistence of riots framed within a communal context.

# 4 / The Great Aligarh Riots
## of December 1990 and January 1991

I n the minds of most commentators, reporters, and my own interview respondents, the 1990–91 riots in Aligarh were dramatically different from all that preceded them in several respects. First, the scale surpassed all previous riots in the city, including those just before Partition in 1946, both in the extent of the areas touched by them and in the numbers of persons killed. The official figure for deaths in these riots given out by the district magistrate was 92, of whom "about 2/3 were Muslims." However, Muslim groups provided a figure of 100 for Muslims alone, with a documentary list of the victims. On the basis of their own inquiries, the Peoples Union for Civil Liberties (PUCL) placed "the number of persons killed at 125 to 150."[1]

Pertinent also to this matter of scale is the allegation made by Muslims and confirmed by some Hindu observers as well that the riots broke out simultaneously in a large number of places in the city. This pattern contrasts with previous riots, which began with an incident in a particular site and then spread to other parts of the city. This allegation also carries the presumption that these attacks were preplanned and coordinated. As one Muslim respondent, an AMU professor, put it, "they [the rioters] attacked the Muslim community from every corner."[2]

Second, this riot, in contrast to all the others discussed above, was associated with a mass movement that engulfed the entire state as well as other parts of northern and western India. This movement was inaugurated with the *rath yatra* of L. K. Advani, which began in Somnath in western Gujarat on September 25, 1990, and proceeded across central India to Bihar, where it was stopped by the arrest of L. K. Advani on October 23. The journey was originally planned to end at Ayodhya, where *kar seva* (voluntary work) was to begin for the construction of a new temple on part of the disputed site. Although the *rath yatra* itself was prevented from entering Uttar Pradesh on its way to Ayodhya, the movement of tens of thousands of Hindus from all over northern and western India and their convergence upon Ayodhya was not stopped. These crowds passed through many of the important cities and towns of U.P. in processions, raising slogans along the way, many of them deliberately directing insulting remarks towards Muslims, and bringing along with them additional persons from the sites through which they passed. During the movement, in most towns in U.P., including Aligarh, Hindu supporters of the movement "would start a cacophony" every evening at a pre-arranged time, involving ringing bells, beating *thalis* (stainless steel dinner plates) and blowing conch shells."[3]

In the town of Ayodhya, on October 30, the police, under orders authorized by the chief minister of the state himself, Mulayam Singh Yadav, stopped an assault upon the mosque with bullets that resulted in the deaths of 16 Hindus in the crowd. News of the killings in Ayodhya naturally spread quickly through the media, but also by word of mouth as devotees returned from Ayodhya and dispersed back into their home places. Processions of devotees also moved out of Ayodhya carrying the ashes of victims of the police firing, to be spread across the state, including in Aligarh. Serious rioting and killing began in Aligarh City on December 7 and continued with great intensity for several days thereafter. The rioting included an attack on December 8 by a large Hindu mob that stopped a passenger train, the well-known Gomti Express, killing as many Muslims as could be identified, in a manner that recalled the horrors of Partition and the great train massacres associated with that catastrophic event. Muslims in Aligarh expressed the view that the spreading of the violence in the aftermath of the October 30 police firing to places where there had been no rioting since Partition, and its intensity in Aligarh, were attributable to the "communal feeling which was being created by Vishwa Hindu Parishad, RSS, Bajrang Dal, and other elements of the same feeling." That feeling, it was said, included "taking revenge of the death of *kar sevaks*, who were shot dead in Ayodhya when *kar seva* started on 30th October and to November 2."[4]

It is common to attribute rioting that follows in the aftermath of mass movements such as the one that developed in connection with L. K. Advani's *rath yatra* to the spontaneous outbreak of communal hostilities in areas that have a history of Hindu Muslim tension and violence. When the rioting spreads to new areas or areas not well known for such a history, it is said that communal passions were inflamed or provoked by the mobilization and, in the case of Ayodhya, particularly by the police firing on the Hindu crowd. Such attributions are quite misleading insofar as they focus on alleged communal passions that break out spontaneously. On the contrary, these passions are fostered and kept alive in particular places through the actions of communal activists and deliberately stoked to inflammatory proportions in conjunction with such broad movements. Such was certainly the case in Aligarh in the months before the beginning of the 1990 riots on December 7. The Peoples Union for Civil Liberties report comments on the way in which such intense sentiments were stimulated in U.P. as a whole and in Aligarh in particular.

> With the Ramjanmabhumi/Babri Masjid controversy, and particularly the Rathyatra of BJP leader L. K. Advani, the divide between Hindus and Muslims had deepened. The divide became near complete after certain events took place—the karseva programme at Ayodhya on 30-10-90 [October 30, 1990] and 2-11-90 [November 2, 1990] accompanied by violence and police firing, playing of audio/video cassettes of provocative speeches by BJP/VHP/Bajrang Dal members against Muslims, holding of so called religious 'melas', circulation of highly objectionable leaflets by some Hindu organisations, kites with provocative slogans against Muslims released over Muslim areas of the city, almost total communalisation of the Hindu press in UP—all these had already built up a tense atmosphere.[5]

All these actions require a considerable degree of organization that varies from town to town in north India. In Aligarh, that organization is extensive, active, and ever ready for violence.[6]

### THE PATTERN OF RIOTING IN ALIGARH

It is also evident from the pattern of rioting in the city that considerable advance planning was undertaken. The rioting did not follow the usual sequence of a disturbance, a fracas, a killing, or some other violent act in one area mimicked in a so-called retaliatory act in another area, then spreading to the usual riot-prone areas. On the contrary, in this riot, there were virtually simultaneous outbreaks extending to many parts of the city and into the Civil Lines area as well, including especially the Aligarh Muslim University Medical College.[7] As we have seen, the AMU is not usually affected by rioting in the city, though it stands as a symbol for militant Hindus as the source of all communal problems and Muslim disloyalty not only in Aligarh, but in India as a whole.[8] Extending the attacks to the university campus added further emphasis to the fact that the Ayodhya movement itself was not only about a mosque allegedly destroyed by Muslim conquerors centuries ago, but was about the relative place of Hindus and Muslims in India.

Although, therefore, the extent of the rioting in Aligarh compared to other cities and towns in U.P. cannot be understood without an appreciation of the higher degree of mobilization and organization among militant Hindus, it is also generally accepted by most observers that there was much more mass support for this riot than for any other riot in Aligarh since 1946. Nor was this mass support confined to the lower classes. On the contrary, if anything, militant Hindu sentiment and the feeling that it was past time to give the Muslims their due in Aligarh as elsewhere in north India spread more widely among the middle and upper-middle classes.[9] The lower classes, particularly the Scheduled Castes, participated significantly in the violence, fighting with Muslims in various localities, not because they shared the militant Hindu nationalist ideology, but for purposes of "looting."[10]

Also noteworthy was the role played by the Hindi vernacular press in this riot, particularly by the newspaper *Aaj,* which had since the days of the nationalist movement a reputation as the leading Hindi newspaper of north India. This newspaper was responsible for the spreading of a vicious and false rumor on December 10 in "a full-page banner headline on the front page that 74 people including 28 patients in Jawaharlal Nehru Medical College Hospital of Aligarh Muslim University were killed."[11] It is generally accepted that rioting, particularly attacks by Hindu mobs on Muslim persons and property, intensified after this date. However, *Aaj* was by no means an exception. The Hindu populace of U.P. and Aligarh was fed with fantastic stories and lies from many of the prominent Hindi newspapers in north India throughout the *rath yatra.* These newspapers included *Amar Ujala* and *Swatantra Bharat.* The stories, obviously designed to instill "hatred for the minorities," included "highly exaggerated" accounts of the death toll in Ayodhya and elsewhere in the state, ranging in the thousands and tens of thousands. They also included mythological fabrications designed to imply divine intervention on behalf of Hindu activists and against the police who attacked the Hindu mob at Ayodhya, featured as front page news in the *Swatantra Bharat,* published in Lucknow.[12]

It was also alleged by some persons that the role of the PAC in these riots was different, much more extreme in its anti-Muslim behavior than in previous riots. One Muslim AMU professor whom I interviewed on January 3, 1991, commented in this respect that, in contrast to previous riots in Aligarh, in this one "the philosophy and the naked aggression of the PAC was very much marked."[13]

Although much is known about this riot, much is also in dispute. As is almost invariably the case, especially in large-scale riots such as this one, there are different versions of how the rioting began. Even the PUCL team that visited the city within a few weeks of the rioting, between January 4 and 6 and again on January 12, 1991, remarked in its report, "It is futile to try to find out the exact starting point of the riots in view of the conflicting versions given . . . both by Hindus and Muslims." I visited Aligarh myself on January 1–3, 1991, and heard similarly conflicting versions.

The PUCL report takes the position that the atmosphere had been so "polluted" by the mobilizing activities and techniques used in Aligarh, as elsewhere, to mobilize Hindus in connection with the *rath yatra* and the *kar seva* to be done at Ayodhya that it is not only "futile," but "pointless to ask the question: who started the riots and to find out the starting point." In other words, given the polluted atmosphere, a riot was bound to happen and it hardly matters exactly how it started. However, it matters greatly to those on opposite sides of the communal divide, who seek to convince themselves, their followers, and especially the rest of public opinion outside Aligarh that it was the other side that began the riots, which would not have occurred or would not have been so uncontrollable had it not been started in a particular way by the other side.

Despite the caveats expressed by the PUCL about the contradictory nature of different versions of the origins of the riots, there is some convergence in their summary of the two leading ones, which are quoted below.

> One version is that after Friday prayer at a Mosque at Upperkot on 7.12.90 [December 7, 1990] when provocative speeches (by way of sermons) were delivered, some Muslims attacked two PAC jawans near the Police Station. In retaliation PAC killed a number of Muslims and in some other areas Hindus attacked Muslims.
>
> The other version is that a bomb was hurled at a Mosque in Sarai Sultani on 7.12.90, and as a result fighting started between Muslims and Hindus at Sarai Sultani. The sound of the bomb blast was easily audible at Upperkot Mosque (Jama Masjid). Muslims gathered in front of Kotwali [police station] to protest, and there a section of the mob tried to snatch rifles from some PAC jawans. PAC then opened fire killing 3 Muslims and injuring many.

In the first, Hindu version, all blame is placed on Muslims: their religious leaders delivered provocative sermons, Muslims attacked the PAC, the PAC merely retaliated. In the second, Muslim version, Hindus are presumed to have started the riots by throwing a bomb at a mosque not far from the Jama Masjid itself, Muslims protested peacefully in front of the police station, some persons tried to grab the rifles from some PAC men, and the PAC then "opened fire." Although the precipitating event differs in these two accounts— provocative sermons in the mosque at Upar Kot or a bomb thrown at a mosque in Sarai Sultani—they converge in agreement that the critical event was the confrontation between a Muslim crowd and the PAC at the police station just opposite the principal mosque of Aligarh, where the PAC opened fire and killed several Muslims.[14] They also converge in agreeing that pro-vocative action on the Muslim side—the attempt to grab the rifles of PAC *jawans*—precipitated the first fatalities.

From this point on, there is no convergence between Hindu and Muslim versions. For Muslims, the riots then became a series of attacks launched by the PAC and Hindu mobs, sometimes in collusion, on Muslims and their prop-erty in many areas of the old city, extending out to the Civil Lines area near the university as well. For Hindus, the riots constituted spontaneous outrage over the news, generally believed by the Hindus of the town, that Hindu patients at the AMU hospital had been massacred, in effect a Hindu response to a classic blood libel charge against Muslims, comparable to the alleged effect in European history upon Christians who attacked Jews in countless pogroms, allegedly in response to blood libel charges against Jews.

The PUCL team, whose members included four Hindus and one Muslim, placed the weight of its report upon the aggressive behavior of both the PAC and the Hindu mobs, giving the following examples. In Sarai Sultani, a Muslim locality "surrounded by Hindu localities," as Muslims "gathered in the Mosque for Friday prayer," they "were alarmed when they saw hundreds of people on roof tops of Hindu houses throwing bombs at Muslims and their houses and at the Mosque." Although a PAC force was on the scene, its *jawans* not only failed "to control the rioters," they "provided a cover" for them, allow-ing them to continue their attacks while firing on any Muslims who dared to emerge from their houses. Some Muslims who, the PUCL report says, "here were fairly well organized," "threw bombs or similar articles at the PAC who then opened fire to kill."

In the adjacent Muslim locality of Jogipara (not on maps), the PUCL report states that "17 Muslims were killed" on December 8, 1990. An FIR (First Information Report) was filed by some person or persons concerning these deaths, reporting that the victims were burned to death. These 17 persons were not included in the official death toll because the police did not recover any dead bodies there. Six of these 17 persons, said to have been witnesses to the killing of the other 11, were thrown into a factory furnace "used for melting metal."

The PUCL team visited several other Muslim riot-affected areas, from which "more or less the same picture" emerged, "namely PAC resorting to firing to kill indiscriminately, Hindus being helped by PAC cover, Mosques attacked, houses destroyed." All the colonies so affected were "surrounded by Hindu areas." The team was also "given graphic accounts of how PAC entered some houses and shot people dead." Although the report places the heaviest responsibility upon the PAC and Hindu mobs, it also notes that, in some localities, Muslims attacked Hindus, notably in one with a large Scheduled Caste population, where Muslims attacked, burnt, and looted Harijan houses. As Hindu mobs, some of whom came "from nearby villages," extended the rioting to the Civil Lines localities adjacent to the university with large Muslim populations, "a Muslim mob" also attacked a number of "establishments . . . belonging to Hindus."

All the above events occurred on December 7 and 8, before the Gomti Express killings and the false *Aaj* report on the massacre of Hindus in the AMU hospital. After the latter two events, the PUCL report notes that rioting spread to many other areas of Aligarh, but provides no further details. Nor has any official report ever been published to document the events described by the PUCL and those that it could not cover. Despite the huge scale of this riot, no enquiry commission was appointed.

Insofar as the Gomti Express killings are concerned, a judicial enquiry was ordered, but its findings were never published. We must rely again, therefore, upon the PUCL account. According to the latter, "a Hindu mob of about 1000" at first tried but failed "to stop the Kalka Mail" in the morning, but "succeeded in stopping the Gomti Express (very near the Station) and killed several passengers." The PUCL report found definite evidence of "human failure," as well as grounds for suspecting the collusion of Hindu railway officials and workers at the scene in allowing the mob to stop the train and gain access to the passenger compartments to do their work of killing.

Insofar as the rioting in the city is concerned, the PUCL report was unequivocal in its condemnation of the actions of the PAC.

> There is no doubt that the PAC killed a large number of Muslims. On some occasions Muslims may have acted in a provocative manner by way of trying to snatch rifles, going out during curfew hours, etc. but the PAC retaliated with disproportionate brutality.

The part played by the PAC in the Aligarh riots is indeed reprehensible.

Almost every where [*sic*] Muslims told us that at least as many persons of their community were killed by the PAC as by Hindus. In several places we were shown the high terraces from which PAC personnel fired at fleeing Muslims. Even young Muslim children were thus killed by the PAC. At many places PAC fired at Muslims when neither they (the PAC) nor Hindus were attacked. The PAC acted as a highly communalised force.

It may be noted that PAC's bonhomie with Hindus made Muslims angry. For example Hindus fraternised with PAC personnel, offered them sweets, garlanded them; and if any of them declined to accept their offers Hindus raised slogans and exhorted them to listen to the call of Hindutva and Ram Bhakt [devotion to the god Ram]. It would indeed require tremendous self-control on the part of an average Muslim to tolerate such Hindu fraternisation with the police.[15]

Such charges have been made by Muslims against the PAC in numerous riots all over the state of U.P. for the past several decades. When official personnel are asked to comment on such accusations, they rarely support the charges against the PAC fully. Such was the case when the PUCL team spoke to the new district magistrate (DM) who arrived on the scene towards the end of the riots to replace the previous DM who failed to anticipate or control them. Such has been the case also in all my interviews with officials over the past decades. The PAC, it is said, is a tough, well-trained force that is brought out to handle the most difficult situations and often faces provocative behavior from crowds, such as the alleged rifle-snatching incident. Its responses are, therefore, either justifiable or understandable.

There are, however, at least two strong reasons for accepting the Muslim point of view that the PAC is, in effect, an anti-Muslim force as essentially accurate. The first is that these charges have been repeated so often in so many situations in so many different parts of the state, including countless eyewitness testimonies and reports of impartial teams such as that of the PUCL, that the weight of the evidence is too strong to discount. Second, the Muslim charges are not always directed against other armed forces, that is, the civil police, the CRPF, and the army. Muslims sometimes, and more frequently in recent years, also accuse the local police of partiality, but they never blame either the CRPF or the army. That was the case in Aligarh in 1990 91 as well. In fact, Muslim leaders beg for the intervention of the army to displace the PAC whenever and wherever the latter force is deployed in their localities to control major civil disturbances.

It is noteworthy also that the PUCL report found few credible witnesses among Hindus they interviewed "from various walks of life." They found that the only matter that concerned Hindus in Aligarh during and after the riots was "the alleged killing in the Medical College Hospital as reported in AAJ [*sic*] and other Hindi Dailies." When Hindus were asked to provide instances to support their claims that Hindu "properties had been "destroyed and burnt" and "that Muslims had acquired a lot of arms and weapons," nothing concrete or substantial emerged. The team found no "evidence of Hindu temples having been damaged or attacked except a slight touch on a small temple in Jamalpur." However, they "found ample evidence of Hindus having attacked Mosques. Also, [they] found ample evidence of Hindus using abusive language about Muslims and Islam. . . . The most foul and obscene language was used in slogans written on walls. We were sad to observe that communal hatred against Muslims has assumed pathological dimension." Finally, the team pursued several specific charges made by Hindus that patients whose names were provided to them had been "killed in the Hospital." After extensive inquiries, the team concluded that all the charges were false.

## THE FALSE RUMORS
## OF THE MEDICAL COLLEGE HOSPITAL MURDERS

Thanks to the work of the PUCL, there is ample documentation concerning the origins and consequences of the false reporting of murders at the AMU Medical College Hospital. False rumors are central in the spread of many riots everywhere in the world. They are usually attributed, like riots themselves, to the credulity of the masses, already inflamed by prejudices against another group and ready to gather in large crowds to take revenge for the actions falsely attributed to that group or for real, but trivial, actions enlarged upon in the rumor process. In other words, they are part of the myth of spontaneity that has for long provided the dominant explanation of riotous behavior. The origin and spread of this rumor in Aligarh suggests the opposite conclusion and provides further evidence of the existence of institutionalized riot networks in which rumormongering and rumormongers play important roles.

It deserves to be especially emphasized that these riot-provoking networks are not confined to the locality in which the riots occur. The outside vernacular press in particular, many of whose journalists and editors are themselves sympathetic to militant Hindu ideology, often play significant roles in spreading rumors and interpreting incidents in a manner whose effect is to inflame Hindu passions.[16]

As in most other aspects of research on riots, it is necessary to carefully distinguish self-evident truths from speculative linkages, cause from consequence. The first matter that has to be considered is the timing of the news report. The accepted date for the start of the rioting is December 7, 1990. On December 8, a mob of Hindus attacked the Gomti Express and butchered at least 4 and possibly 10 or 15 Muslim passengers. On December 10, the false news reports of the Medical College Hospital massacres appeared, completely overshadowing all other reporting in the Hindi press on the riots, especially the true report of the deliberate massacre of uninvolved Muslims targeted by a Hindu mob that set out deliberately for the train station to carry out its murderous acts. This sequence presents us with a speculative possibility that the false news reports were deliberately planted in the Hindi press to distract attention from the premeditated, obviously organized actions of the Hindu mob. We have no way of knowing that this was the case, but it was certainly the effect.

It is also certain that the Hindi-language press, its journalists and editors, took a deliberate decision to publish news that they either knew was false or that they took no trouble to verify, and that they knowingly published false or unverified reports with front-page headlines—in the case of *Aaj,* "a full-page banner headline on the front page that 74 people including 28 patients" had been killed, in the case of *Amar Ujala,* 50 persons killed, and in the case of *Dainik Jagaran,* 124 persons proclaimed dead. These "reports were filed on the basis of accounts of two witnesses, Mahesh and Satish Aggarwal [*sic*]" who allegedly reported to the district magistrate that they had escaped with their lives from the hospital with six other men.[17] If they did in fact go to the district magistrate with their false story, he did not believe it, for he contradicted the news reports after they were published.

The newspaper owners certainly knew the consequences of publishing such false reports. Their actions, therefore, raise the suspicion that these newspapers maliciously sought to throw wood on a burning fire. Moreover, the three leading newspapers that published these malicious fabrications were important newspapers. *Aaj* is a Hindi newspaper with a hallowed nationalist reputation going back to pre-Independence days. *Dainik Jagaran* and *Amar Ujala,* which also published the false news, are circulated widely throughout northern India. It is evident, therefore, that these three newspapers and their journalists and editors fed into the institutionalized riot systems that exist in north India. In short, they bear a large measure of responsibility for the additional rioting and deaths that followed in the wake of their reports.

One should also note those who took responsible actions in response to the newspaper reports. They included the district magistrate and senior superintendent of police, Aligarh, several Hindu members of the faculty of the Medical College, and the national media, including especially the English-language press and the official Hindi TV network, Doordarshan. The authorities and persons from the national press and broadcasting networks investigated the reports, found them baseless, and announced their falsity, while Hindu faculty members had the courage to deny publicly lies spread by and believed by many, if not most, other members of the Hindu community living in Aligarh.[18] Yet, the reports continued in *Aaj* and other papers even afterwards.[19]

It is also evident that the effect, if not the purpose, of the false news reports was to place the AMU, which had nothing to do with these riots, at the center of them. The RSS and other militant Hindu organizations have consistently argued over the years that the AMU is a great center of conspiratorial activity against the Hindu nation, a hotbed of Muslim communalist and anti-national activity, a place where Muslim criminals abide and are protected by the university authorities, and the like. This propaganda is widely believed by Hindus in the city. It is, therefore, not farfetched to accept the argument of the Medical College Hospital authorities, published in the midst of the turmoil occasioned by the riots and the false reports, as cited below.

> To escape from that reckoning [concerning the killings on the Gomti Express] the stories about the AMU Hospital were concocted. This was the plan to divert the attention of the nation, to hide the real massacre that was allowed to happen during the curfew, and to force the AMU to be on the defensive—first, aghast at the stupidity of the charges and, then, busy in giving denials and explanations. In all the resultant hue and cry and denial about the Medical College, nobody remembered the unfortunate Gomti Express. And, it was intended to be so.[20]

Once again, whatever the intent, the effect was such. The PUCL team found in their interviews with Hindus in the city that "almost all Hindus" whom they met "were only concerned with and agitated over the alleged killing in the Medical College Hospital." They blamed the AMU "and wanted action to be taken against the University."[21]

There is usually some kernel, if not of truth, at least of circumstance that gives occasion for the spreading of false rumors. In this case, there were two circumstances that fed the rumor. One was that injured riot victims were brought to the hospital on the 7th when the riot began and on the 8th in the aftermath of the Gomti Express killings. Most of the injured brought to the hospital were Muslims, but there were a few Hindus among them as well. Second, Muslim mobs, presumably agitated over the killing of Muslim passengers on the Gomti Express, did collect outside the hospital on those two days and riot; they engaged in stabbing, killing, and looting of Hindus and Hindu-owned shops. One of the persons stabbed was a Hindu, who was brought to the hospital for treatment and survived.[22]

However, these facts notwithstanding, the PUCL team noted that several Hindus associated with trade and professional associations in the city, teachers at the degree colleges, and businessmen and industrialists either themselves visited the hospital and the few Hindu patients who were being attended there or had access to reports from Hindus who had done so after the false news reports were published and were, therefore, in a position to know the truth. These included "representatives of Vyapar Mandal, faculty members of local colleges, members of the Bar, and senior citizens." The team also met with a respected "local industrialist," Promod [*sic*] Kumar, "who was one of the first to visit the hospital after the news was published."[23]

The first question that must be asked is why certain people belonging to particular organizations and associations either rushed to the hospital upon the publication of the false news reports or in other ways took a special interest in the situation there. The Vyapar Mandal is an association of traders dominated by persons of the Barahseni (Varshney) caste, among whom most are RSS members or sympathizers.[24] Why should a trade association in the city be preoccupied with the alleged murders of Hindus at a hospital in the Civil Lines area—across the tracks from their businesses in the city, where large-scale riotous activity was in progress? Not only did the Vyapar Mandal take an interest in the alleged happenings at the AMU Hospital, but it was their leadership who produced the "witnesses," the brothers Mahesh and Satish Agarwal, one a general merchant, the other a cloth merchant, and both "important members of Vyapar Mandal."[25] The fact that they were merchants could explain the interest of the leaders of the trade association in their story, but it does not explain why they materially assisted them in spreading the false stories.

The presence of the Agarwal brothers on the scene is adequately explained by the fact that their mother was admitted as a patient in the hospital on December 7 and they were concerned for her welfare, especially at a time when a riotous Muslim mob was active outside the hospital. After seeing to their mother's admission to the hospital, according to the account they gave to the

PUCL team, they set out for home, were attacked by a Muslim mob, and "returned to the Hospital," where "they saw injured people coming in the Hospital and students shouting slogans." They came again to the Hospital on December 8 and witnessed similar scenes. They also heard stories of people having being stabbed in the vicinity. Again, on the 9th, they came to the hospital, witnessed a "person being stabbed in front of the Emergency section," and "managed to get away from the Hospital . . . along with 6 others." The brothers now "spoke to leaders of the Vyapar Mandal" and went to meet the "District Magistrate and Police officials" in the company of "Shri Navman, BJP M.L.A. During their meetings with officials," according to the PUCL report, "there were angry exchanges between Shri Navman and Police officials." After this meeting, the brothers were taken to the hospital; their mother was removed from the hospital and "transported to their residence in [the] District Magistrate's car" on December 11.

While the concern of the brothers Agarwal for their mother and their anger over the riotous activity outside the hospital are understandable, especially if it is true that one of them was attacked by a Muslim mob, they personally observed that the situation inside the hospital was in no way a danger to the patients. The PUCL report sums up their account as follows.

> This account of these two important members of Vyapar Mandal make[s] it quite clear that they had witnessed no untoward happenings in wards. They saw none being killed in wards; they saw one person being stabbed outside the Emergency section; they heard but did not see themselves that 12/13 persons were stabbed outside the Hospital. [They say] that their brother was attacked by a Muslim mob but not injured; they have not reported [the matter] to the police. [They observed] that Hospital authorities did not allow anyone from the mob to enter the Hospital building.[26]

It is understandable that any Hindus of the city whose relatives were under treatment in the hospital would be fearful for the safety of their loved ones, given the circumstances outside the hospital, and would even want to have the persons removed to a safer setting. It might not have been sufficiently reassuring for such persons to have noted that many of the medical practitioners in the hospital were themselves Hindus. Furthermore, Hindus visiting their relatives in the hospital during those days endangered their own lives by doing so. The wife of one Hindu patient was murdered when she left the hospital to get some medicine for him. There were, however, no grounds for believing that patients in the hospital were being killed and that the AMU was somehow responsible for their deaths. It is evident that the PUCL team did not believe the account of the brothers Agarwal. The entry of the Vyapar Mandal onto the scene and, even more so, the presence of K. K. Navman, brought the RSS and the BJP centrally into the picture, politicizing it and communalizing it.

The brothers Agarwal were not the only "witnesses" to the hospital "murders." Two Hindu women were admitted to the hospital on December 7, each of whom died on the following two days. Their husbands were later produced by "Vyapar [M]andal leaders and faculty members of D.S. College, Aligarh" as false witnesses to the killing of their wives in the hospital. The names of the "faculty members of local colleges" with whom the team discussed the above situation and other circumstances surrounding the spreading of false rumors about the situation in the hospital are not given, but many of the faculty of the local degree colleges in Aligarh are also RSS members and sympathizers, among whom are several who are classed as riot-mongers by the district administration.

All in all, after extensive prodding of interested Hindu leaders from such organizations as the Vyapar Mandal, the local colleges, and others to provide the names of persons allegedly killed in the hospital, the PUCL team was given the names of four persons, two of whom were found to have died of "natural causes," while the other two were alive. Yet such people continued to talk about 28 patients who had been "killed in Medical College Hospital." The PUCL team concluded its report with the flat statement that, in fact, "there was *no* killing of patients in the Hospital" [emphasis in original]. Further, it provided testimony from Hindu patients that they were extremely well treated, that, in the account of one of them, there was "no discrimination between Muslims and Hindu patients," and that, during the riots, "the doctors and other staff members worked throughout nights because of the large number of patients coming to the Hospital from 7th December onwards." In short, the PUCL team discovered what any conscientious journalists themselves could have discovered had they been at all interested in the truth of the matter.

Two prominent Hindus, Promod Kumar, an "industrialist," and Ashok Chauhan, who visited the hospital to assess the situation there, are named and are characterized in the PUCL report as honest and truthful persons. Why, then, did they not publicly contradict the reports that had been published in the newspapers when they discovered their falsity, as indeed they did?

These two named persons came to the hospital certain that the news reports were true. The PUCL team members were present and asked them to provide the names of the persons they believed to have been killed. At first, they refused, saying it was up to "the Hospital authorities to prove that the news was baseless and that none was killed." After considerable persuasion, they did produce some names and also visited several hospital wards where they had been told that people had been killed. They found two of the allegedly killed patients alive in the hospital. Promod Kumar was then asked by the hospital doctors to immediately issue a statement contradicting the false stories of murder in the hospital. He replied that he "wanted to go about the matter in a detailed and thorough manner so that he could issue a comprehensive statement in order to allay public misgivings caused by the mischievous and baseless news." His refusal to issue a statement immediately led to an altercation with the doctors. No statement was ever issued. The PUCL team felt that the doctors had made a mistake, that if Promod Kumar and Ashok Chauhan had been allowed to do things their way, they might have been able to persuade "the press and Hindus of Aligarh . . . to tone down their misconceived reaction." However, it is equally plausible that they might never have issued the desired statement or have issued it too late to influence the course of the riots and save lives. We cannot know what might have happened in a counterfactual situation.[27]

What we can know is that Promod Kumar, by his own admission, felt constrained from issuing an immediate statement because, as he told the PUCL team later, "he had to face such formidable forces like the RSS (the Vyapar Mandal, as we could see, is controlled by RSS) and Bajrangdal." In other words, his statement either was not meant for the general public, but for those organizations in the city that keep Hindu animosities against the AMU alive and that are active on the Hindu side during riots, or, if it was meant for the general public, these same organizations would become angry with him. In a word, these organizations and/or many members of them are intertwined with the institutionalized riot system of Aligarh: they produce the rumors or spread them, if they do not themselves produce them; they either want to believe the rumors themselves or want the Hindu public to believe them; they want the public mobilized and they want revenge—if not for the acts of murder that never took place, then for the continued existence of the AMU and what it represents to them. The PUCL team expressed a similar view.

Moreover, once the riots had gained momentum and the Hindu slaughter of innocent Muslims on the Gomti Express had taken place, it clearly also suited the purposes of riot organizers to distract attention from those events and to focus blame upon the Muslims and the AMU for the entire riot. These remarks constitute my own interpretation of these events based upon what I have seen and heard over 38 years in Aligarh City. They are also consistent with the PUCL team report, as expressed in the statement below.

> Rumours spread, and baseless news items published in Hindu papers have dou-ble significance—they tarnish the image of the Hospital and AMU, and at the same time they are communal in character in that they are anti-Muslim.[28]

They do not, however, constitute evidence that would stand up in a court of law. On the basis of this interpretation, however, I do not believe that the two gentlemen, Promod Kumar and Ashok Chauhan, would ever have been allowed or been able to issue a mollifying public statement; they would have been castigated by the riot-mongers in their community.

It is also quite likely that, even if a mollifying statement had been issued by the two persons in question, it would not have been believed by the Hindu public. More important, the riot activists would not have been persuaded and would not have cared. It is, I believe, a mistake to think that a riot is pro-duced by rumors and stopped by falsification of them. This is a fallacy that is part of the myth that riots are produced by spontaneous mass action inflamed by such things as false rumors. These rumors are merely precipitants that may or may not lead to the activation of the riot network, depending upon other factors, usually political ones, as in this very case.

Moreover, the false news was publicly contradicted by "newspapers from Delhi" and by the government of U.P., which published an advertisement in one of the irresponsible newspapers, *Amar Ujala*, directly contradicting the false news reports. The advertisement was published in the December 18, 1990 issue.[29] The rioting continued throughout the rest of the month.

# 5 / The Control of Communal Conflict in Aligarh

WHY WERE THERE NO RIOTS IN ALIGARH IN THE
DECADE BETWEEN 1978–80 AND 1988–90?

For a decade there was relative peace in the town of Aligarh. No incidents classed as riots occurred during this period. Yet, during this same decade, in the nearby district of Meerut, two of the most vicious communal riots in this state since Independence occurred in 1982 and 1987, respectively. Why were there no riots in Aligarh in this period? Answers given to this question also lead naturally to answers to the obverse question: why did the worst riots in Aligarh's history break out in Aligarh in December 1990, after a decade of relative peace towards the end of which two much less severe riots occurred, in October 1988 and on November 10, 1989?

When I visited Aligarh in 1983, I did not feel that a peace that would last for several more years had returned to the town. In fact, I did not feel that there was peace, only a kind of hiatus enforced by heightened police vigilance, marked by the continuous presence of armed police forces at many major four-way street crossings, or *chaurahas*, as they are called in Hindi (see Figure 3.5). I passed through Aligarh several times between 1983 and 1990–91, before and after parliamentary elections. I was present in Aligarh the day the votes were counted in November 1984, when the Congress under Rajiv Gandhi won its greatest landslide victory since Independence, returning the Congress to a position of dominance in this district, as elsewhere, that it had not enjoyed in many years.

As an afterthought, in some of my interviews with people in January 1991 concerning the riots that had just occurred—indeed, that were still in progress—I asked some respondents how they explained the absence of large-scale riots in Aligarh between those of 1978–80 and the present ones. I heard four explanations for the relative peace of those years: economic, political, administrative, and relating to police action. I discussed these several explanations with an AMU professor, a Hindu, whose political sympathies were with the left and secular parties. Although he mentioned first the economic explanation, he gave primary importance to the political one, and some importance to the administrative one, but discounted police action except insofar as it came under the head of "good administration."[1]

The economic explanation was quite simple, though its implications are not: there had been no riots in the intervening years because the "business community" did not want further riots after the long series that disrupted the economic life of the city in 1978–79. I have heard similar statements made in other contexts after major riots, in response to questions from me concerning whether or not there would be further riots at a particular site; I have been told that, no, there would not be for a long time because people in business do not want them. What is not simple about this kind of statement is the implication that must lie behind it, that businesspeople play critical roles in riot production, either as instigators or as financers of them, and that riots cannot, therefore, be produced if they do not at least finance them.

It was clear that, for this respondent, the business role was necessary, but not primary. The primary factor in riot production was, for him, political. In the intervening years, he noted, the Congress was dominant and the "BJP was not a force here." Riots, he said, arose out of "political necessity." Only if political party leaders feel that a riot is necessary for their advancement, particularly for their electoral success, can a riot take place, "but if they think that there is no necessity for [a] riot, then there will be no riot." In the course of elaborating on this explanation, this respondent articulated a set of electoral calculations for each of the main political parties in competition for national, state, and local power at that time, which he used to illustrate why it was in the particular interest of the BJP, but not of other parties, that there be riots in Aligarh and elsewhere at this time.

The core of his arguments was that the Ayodhya movement had lifted the BJP both in Aligarh and in U.P. to a position from which it could hope to increase its gains in the elections anticipated after the resignation of the Janata Dal government of Prime Minister Vishwanath Pratap Singh in October 1991. The V. P. Singh government's resignation was precipitated by the withdrawal of the BJP's support to it in Parliament after the arrest of L. K. Advani in Bihar on October 23, 1990. The BJP, which had electoral adjustments with the Janata Dal in the 1989 elections, was now determined to fight the coming general elections on its own. The *rath yatra* of L. K. Advani was, clearly, a calculated move to begin the building of electoral support in anticipation of the fall of the central government, and to counter the advantage that the Janata Dal hoped to gain from the announcement in August 1990 of its intention to implement the Mandal Commission recommendations for reservation of 27 percent of all posts in the Union government sector for backward castes. The BJP, in effect, sought to counter the electoral advantage the Janata Dal hoped to gain through dividing Hindus, by seeking instead to consolidate Hindu sentiment and voting around the demand to remove the mosque at Ayodhya and build a new temple to Ram.

In Aligarh, the Congress had already lost support in the 1989 U.P. Legislative Assembly elections, in which Krishna Navman had won the city seat on the BJP ticket. (See Chapter 9.) Navman himself was accused of having played a major role in the instigation of the riots in Aligarh, along with his son, who was the chief of the Bajrang Dal in the city. Navman senior, himself a big businessman, had the support of the *vyaparis* (traders) of the town, who, my informant stated, were "united behind him." Because of Navman's support among the business community and also because, my informant alleged, some Muslim businessmen had been "coming up" in the city, challenging the dominance of Hindus in local trade, the (Hindu) business community was no longer opposed to riots, and the relative peace of a decade was broken.

After listening to this explanation, I said that I had heard an entirely different one, namely, that the senior superintendent of police who had brought an end to the rioting in Aligarh ten years earlier had accomplished his task by executing extrajudicially all the known Muslim criminals who had been responsible for so much of the killing and property destruction in those riots. This respondent acknowledged that such executions had taken place, but said that the SSP had not discriminated between Hindu and Muslim criminals and had killed both, though there may in fact have been more Muslim *goondas* in those days than Hindus. Nor did he deny the important role that *goondas* played in communal riots. However, he reiterated his emphasis on the political factors in relation to criminal participation even more than with business participation. Without any "political force" behind riots, he argued, *goondas* could not "make" a riot. The *goondas* might be in the forefront, they could certainly be purchased, but if "there is no political force behind them, they can't do [it]."

Having minimized the importance of criminals in producing riots, and by the same token, minimizing the police action that led to the elimination of a large number of them, this respondent then proceeded to eliminate police action entirely from his explanation of why there had been no riots in Aligarh for a decade. Instead, he added an alternative third factor, which he called "good administration." Good administration to him implied two things. The first was prompt and effective action in anticipation of riots at times of political turmoil and agitation, such as had occurred in Aligarh during the mobilizations and demonstrations that accompanied the *rath yatra* of L. K. Advani. This respondent and many others criticized the district magistrate for failing to take such action in Aligarh between August and December 1990. The second aspect of good administration, in his mind, was specific to Aligarh, namely, the establishment of cordial relations of cooperation between the city administration and the administration of the university. Such cooperation had existed during the decade of relative peace, but had broken down at the onset of the riots in December 1990.

The PUCL report, published after my inteview with this respondent, confirmed his views on the failings of the district administration both in preventing and in dealing effectively with the 1990–91 riots. That report commented on the ineffectiveness of the district administration as follows.

Riots in Aligarh did not start all of sudden. The seeds of riots had already been sown, not only in Aligarh, but throughout U.P.; only the District Administration did not take notice. And significantly enough a blue-print to meet riot situations was also circulated quite sometime [*sic*] ago and it was in the District Magistrate's office. It appears that the then District Magistrate was benignly ignorant about it. . . .

Given the background, the polluted and totally communalised atmosphere, near break-down of the law and order machinery, and increasingly scant respect for rule of law, communal riots were almost inevitable. The Administration knew, or ought to have known, that riots were in the offing. And yet killings went on unchecked during the period 7–10 Dec. 90. Hardly any administration existed in Aligarh during this period. The District Magistrate Mr. Verma and some other officials were transferred (this was the only punishment for erring officials); and a new District Magistrate Mr. Misra took over on 10-12-90 [December 10]. Many people we met said that given the debris left by his predecessor and the story that appeared in AAJ on the very day he took over charge, resulting in increased violence, the new District Magistrate did a fairly good job. Even though riots were widespread upto [*sic*] about 15-12-90 [December 15] and Muslims were at [the] receiving end, Mr. Misra was able to instil some confidence in the victims.

Two assumptions behind the PUCL report deserve to be especially noted. The first is that riots do not start spontaneously. "Seeds" must be sown. In the months preceding the first major outbreaks, those seeds were sown in the actions and demonstrations associated with the *rath yatra* and the *kar seva* to Ayodhya. The nature of those actions in Aligarh was such as to "pollute" and communalize the atmosphere. Second is the assumption that the local administration has the capacity to prevent riots or, at the very least, to prevent killings from going on "unchecked." This assumption is strong enough in the PUCL reports for its authors to imply that the officials transferred because of their ineffectiveness should have been punished more severely than by a mere transfer. The assumption is also evident in the mild commendation given to the new district magistrate, Mr. Misra, for having done his job of checking the spread of the riots under difficult conditions "fairly" well. Finally, the assumption is also evident in one of the final recommendations in the report for the prevention of such riots in the future: "Local administration must be instructed to act promptly and impartially at the very emergence of a communal riot situation."

The last statement, however, introduces a further question, namely, whether the district administration was ineffective because it, too, was communalized and acted partially. This charge has been made repeatedly in U.P. wherever riots have occurred. It has been made with increasing frequency in recent years. The PUCL report does not suggest that the district administration was anti-Muslim, though it does imply that the previous district magistrate, Mr. Varma, lacked the confidence of Muslims, since it commends the new district magistrate for having instilled confidence among them.

Before the publication of the PUCL report, I also asked our AMU professor about the role of the district administration in the Aligarh riots. In his view, the previous district magistrate and SSP had been unrealistic. They had known many days before the outbreak of rioting that "the situation [was] very dangerous." However, the DM assured people like the professor, who visited him and "presented a memorandum to him" to express their concerns, that the administration knew about it and would control it. This respondent said that the DM said there was no need for curfew, and that he held a news conference on December 1st in which he announced that, should there be any incidents in any *mohalla*, the miscreants would be immediately punished. However, the riots did not start with isolated incidents in one or two *mohallas*; "they started in ten places simultaneously, in all the Civil Lines and [the] whole city, [on the] 7th and 8th and 9th." However, this respondent did not consider that Mr. Verma was "a communalist" for failing to prevent such a large-scale outbreak, in which mostly Muslims were killed; he was only "unimaginative" and "incompetent."

However, Muslims in Aligarh did not accept this limited view of the former DM's failings. For example, the *mufti shahar* of Aligarh, who is not given to extreme statements, said in an interview that the "mentality of the [ex-] DM was very bad." He thought that the "mentality" of the senior superintendent of police was not so bad, he was merely incapable of handling the situation. However, he faulted both the former DM and the additional district magistrate (ADM), City, and gave the following example of their mentality as well as their incompetence. He said that rioting began in the Muslim locality of Shah Jamal (no. 69, Map 4) on the night of the very day on which he had spoken on the telephone to the DM, who had informed him that he was imposing curfew in Aligarh not because of "any danger," but as "a precautionary measure." Then, when Hindus attacked the Shah Jamal locality, the ADM informed him that four Muslims had attacked Hindus in that locality, which was false. The mufti also claimed that the DM and other officers had gone round the localities of Aligarh warning Muslims that they would "create another Maliana, another Hashimpura in Aligarh also, as the PAC had done in Meerut district."[2]

## THE CONTROL OF COMMUNAL CONFLICT
### IN ALIGARH IN THE 1990S

### *Control of Rioting in December 1992*

Rioting was reported from Aligarh in the aftermath of the destruction of the mosque at Ayodhya on December 6, 1992, but no details were given in the press reports, which focused more on the major riots in the state (Kanpur and Varanasi) and in other parts of the country, especially in Bombay. On this occasion, however, Aligarh remained for the most part under control. Aligarh was listed among thirteen towns in U.P. that were placed under curfew on December 7, the day after the destruction of the mosque.[3] On the following day, Aligarh was listed among cities and towns in U.P. where deaths had occurred, but no figures were given. It was also reported that more than nine hundred people had been arrested in cities and towns throughout the state, of which the largest number, "about 400," were in Aligarh.[4] It appears that, on this occasion, the large number of arrests in Aligarh reflected as much or more preventive measures, on the part of a district administration which wanted no repetition of the previous year's catastrophic violence, rather than the seriousness of the rioting in the city.

Why, then, were there no riots in Aligarh on this occasion, when numerous other cities and towns in U.P. and other parts of India, most notably Bombay, experienced severe rioting—indeed, a classic "wave" of riots comparable to those that have occurred at previous major junctures in modern Indian history, notably in 1946–47? A *Times of India* journalist appeared to be anticipating rioting in Aligarh in his report of December 12, in which he noted that "tension in this city was fast reaching a flashpoint." However, the tension, which this reporter detected "in the Muslim-dominated areas of the city," was "suddenly released" when the announcement came that the BJP government had been dismissed, President's Rule had been imposed on the state, and the prime minister had made an "impassioned appeal to the nation." But the prime minister's appeal had little noticeable effect elsewhere, where rioting continued through the month and into January as well. Moreover, though the tension was said to have been relieved in the Muslim areas of the city, there was considerable agitation on the AMU campus, where, "around midnight," "several thousand slogan-shouting, emotionally charged students had gathered . . . and were trying to take out a procession on the main streets." This dangerous situation was also "defused" by the appeals of "some student leaders and officials," but was repeated again "around noon the next day," when the "highly charged" president of the AMU Students Union remarked that "things have reached a boiling point" and that he did not know how he could "control the situation." Once again, the students were "persuaded to give vent to their feelings by courting arrest," a time-honored Gandhian political practice of expressing protest without provoking violence, of which "more than 300 students" took advantage. Then "several thousand students" gathered on the campus next day and passed a resolution, another peaceful form of protest, declaring that their "faith in the country's Constitution [had] been shattered."[5] The AMU staff association also convened to express peacefully "its deep sense of shock, indignation and anger" over the destruction of the mosque and called for "the resignation of the Central government," while the vice-chancellor wrote to the president of India to convey the "sense of insecurity, uncertainty and anger" that prevailed among Indian Muslims.[6]

Such meetings, courting of arrest, and protests emanating from the AMU campus continued throughout the month. The Students Union "demanded that action should be taken against all those responsible for demolishing the mosque under the terrorist act," failing which "'the culprits of the Ayodhya tragedy' will provoke and face the wrath of the Muslim community." Yet, at the same time, the Students Union president claimed that the union had "been working hard to ensure communal harmony in Aligarh and [had] seen to it that Hindu students do not feel afraid or persecuted in the Campus."[7] AMU students also travelled to Delhi for a protest rally in defiance of an order banning such assemblies, courted arrest, and were released without any reported violence.[8] In the midst of these mostly peaceful actions, a repetition of the May 1979 beatings of AMU students on the train to Delhi occurred, in which fifteen students of the university returning to their homes for vacation "were thrown out of the running train 'by *Kar sevaks*' returning from Ayodhya." Further, two students "had been hammered as well," one of whom died in hospital from his head injuries, while a second had "lost part of his memory."[9] Even in the face of this provocation, which had led to rioting by AMU students in May 1979, the Students Union responded only by complaining that the incident had "not been investigated."[10]

What were the factors, then, that prevented rioting in Aligarh in December 1992? Timely and firm administrative action has already been noted. The above summary of the actions on the AMU campus also suggests that great efforts were made by students, staff, and the vice-chancellor to maintain calm and confine actions to peaceful protests. A third explanation was provided by "Mr Gyan Chand Varshney, general secretary of the Udyog Vyapaar Mandal," who was reported to have said, "The people here were so traumatised by the 1990 riots that they were not willing to fall prey to senseless violence again. The economy of this city was almost completely shattered in 1990 and it had taken us nearly two years to limp back to normalcy." In other words, the people in general did not want riots again after the experience of 1990, and the business community, the mainstay of the BJP and RSS in Aligarh, did not want disruption of its business again. In the same article, a "local journalist" remarked that the people in general were "simply fed up with communal riots here." A further explanation for the lack of rioting in Aligarh at this time was that the BJP chief minister of the state, Kalyan Singh, who himself had played a critically important role in making possible the destruction of the mosque at Ayodhya, did not want riots in Aligarh and "issued clear directives to prevent communal riots in the district and they were implemented meticulously" after the destruction of the mosque. The *mufti shahar* of the city (Figure 5.1) also issued an appeal to the Muslims of the city for restraint.[11] Finally, it was also reported that "*mohallah* peace committees" had "been activated at Aligarh well in time."[12]

This welter of explanations for the absence of rioting provides a mirror

FIG. 5.1. *Mufti shahar,* Aligarh, Upar Kot, December 1984

image of those that are given to explain rioting when it does occur, and reveals the same assumptions. Those who say that "the people" were fed up with rioting must assume that "the people" are responsible when rioting does occur; similarly with regard to the business community. Those who say that appeals from political and religious leaders to the people to show restraint were effective must assume both that, absent such appeals, the people will act spontaneously to express their rage violently and that, in the past, the politicians and religious leaders have been remiss in not issuing them. Those who praise administrative action and political decision for preventing rioting must assume that rioting can be prevented when firm political directions from above are issued and followed with firm administrative action in the localities.

But all the explanations given above have left out of account the factors that I have argued have been critical to riot production in Aligarh in the past. The local BJP and RSS leaders did not seek to produce a riot there in December 1992. For one thing, their leaders were in Ayodhya participating in the destruction of the mosque or in cheering the demolition gangs. Further, in contrast to the situation in other cities and towns where Muslim protests turned violent, providing a pretext for massacres of Muslims by Hindu mobs later—notably in Bombay and in Kanpur[13]—Muslims in the city and at the AMU either were prevented from engaging in violent action by firm administrative action or were restrained by the appeals of the mufti. The AMU students also were similarly held back. Riots in Aligarh had been produced previously either by police-Muslim confrontations or by confrontations between Hindu and Muslim crowds; the latter have always been the more serious. Had Muslims in Aligarh not shown restraint on this occasion, it is likely—if not certain—that the BJP and RSS network would have been activated and further killings such as those that occurred in 1990–91 would have taken place.

### The Riot of March 1995

On March 10, 1995, the *Times of India* reported from Lucknow that "group clashes" (meaning Hindu-Muslim) had occurred in Aligarh during which 3 persons were killed and 13 injured. "Twenty companies of security forces" as well as the new Rapid Action Force (RAF) had been deployed to control the situation.[14] In another news item from Aligarh, datelined the same day, the newspaper reported that curfew had been imposed in the city and quoted "official sources" that the violence had broken out in the locality of Sarai Sultani, but they were not able to provide a clear statement of the reasons for, nor even the precipitants that led to, the outbreak:

> There are two versions of why the clashes took place. According to some people, the violence erupted following an incident of eve-teasing [harassment of a female], while others put it down to a quarrel between a shopkeeper and a customer.
>
> However, within minutes there was a heavy exchange of fire and brick-batting between members of the two communities.

This brief description suggests the working of the Fearon/Laitin spiral equilibrium in this instance. However, other events followed thereafter that do not conform to that pattern. One small but fatal incident occurred on the next day, March 11, when a married couple were returning from Aligarh to their home village and were attacked by a man with a knife. The wife later died from the injuries sustained during the attack. The same report referred to the recovery of three bodies of persons who were said to have been "killed in separate incidents," but the localities in which these incidents occurred were not mentioned. An additional twelve companies of "police and paramilitary forces" were deployed. "Indefinite curfew" already imposed "in the five police station areas of the old city would continue." The same report also referred to another incident in which a major catastrophe was averted through the courageous action of a lone woman.[15]

> Senior police officers said a major incident was averted yesterday evening, when a bus carrying a marriage party of the minority community was surrounded by rioters in the Achal Tank area. The members of the party, including women, were forced to come out from the bus and one of them was stabbed to death. A woman, Mrs Mithilesh Yadav, who was watching the scene from the window of her house, rushed to the rescue of the female members of the marriage party. Mrs Yadav and her husband Surendra Mohan Yadav, a local advocate, succeeded in turning away the rioters and gave shelter to the entire marriage party in their house.
>
> Other members of the locality maintained a night-long vigil and early this morning the police escorted the marriage party to safety. Prominent members belonging to both communities have praised the woman's courage.

There are two features of this report that especially deserve notice. The first, of course, is that we have here a documented case, for which I have no similar reports in the history of post-independence rioting in Aligarh, of civic action at the local level that prevented imminent death and destruction. The second is the reported site of this incident, Achal Tank (Achal Talab or Achal Sarowar in Hindi), an area not listed as among the riot-prone localities in the city, but one which is the center of Hindu religious activity in Aligarh as well as of militant Hindu presence (see Figure 2.1 and Map 2).

The last news report on this riot came on March 15, when it was said that "normalcy" was returning to the old city and day curfew was being removed. In the meantime, the brave woman received effusive praise, nomination for a presidential gallantry award, and for a state government award as well. Moreover, praise for the woman came from both sides of the communal divide: from the president of the AMU Students Union and from the state secretary (Gyan Chand Varshney) of the Uttar Pradesh Vyapar Mandal (Uttar Pradesh Traders' Association).[16]

In addition to the news reports on this riot, we have the firsthand observations in its aftermath of Asghar Ali Engineer. Engineer, as noted above, has been a leading proponent of the view that communal riots in India are most often planned, with the direct involvement of local politicians, and that economic rivalries also come into play. However, in this case and in a few other riots that occurred in other parts of India at this time, Engineer argued that they were not the same as previous riots. On the contrary, he argued that they were not "a result of either offensive propaganda or planning by the Hindutva forces," but were "a result of spontaneous outbursts of violence on the part of the people of these towns." At the same time, he attributed the very spontaneity of these riots to the "sustained communal propaganda at a very high pitch for close to a decade," which had "created a deep chasm between the majority and minority communities" such that "any trivial incident can lead to serious communal incidents."[17] Engineer was here referring, of course, to the decade-long Ram Janmabhoomi movement that culminated in the destruction of the Babri Masjid on December 6, 1992.

Engineer noted, as had the *Times of India,* that there were conflicting versions concerning the precipitating incident from which rioting ensued, but he was able to track its source to "a scuffle between a Hindu and a Muslim trader" in the Madar Gate area near Sarai Sultani (Map 2). Although he considered this riot to be spontaneous, he noted a different view held by Muslims living in Sarai Sultani, namely, that "communal riots are engineered to force them to sell their properties and go away."[18] Engineer also confirmed the newspaper reports that, "as soon as the trouble began . . . a big crowd from both the sides gathered and resorted to stone throwing. . . . Private fire-arms were used from both the sides." Although local people interviewed by him made the common charge that the local police did nothing to stop the rioting and instead allowed it to spread, all also said that "this riot was not planned nor was it provoked by the BJP."

With regard to the near-disaster visited upon the Muslim marriage party, Engineer reported that this incident took place near the D.S. College and that the attackers were thought "likely to be students" of that college.[19] The attackers used bicycle chains and iron rods, one of which was used to kill the bridegroom's brother.[20]

Except for the initial police failure to act promptly and decisively with the first outbreak of violence, administrative and police action thereafter was firm, decisive, and politically coordinated. The state chief minister, Mulayam Singh Yadav, the Samajwadi Party leader and the principal opponent of the BJP in this state, had adopted a policy to deal with communal violence that was imposed immediately in Aligarh. The DM and SSP, having failed to control the riots within 24 hours, were immediately replaced with a new team, substantial police, paramilitary, and military forces were deployed, and the rioting was effectively contained.[21]

I believe that Engineer is correct in distinguishing this riot from previous riots in Aligarh, but the distinction that he draws between planned and unplanned or spontaneous rioting is too sharp. Moreover, his explanation for the spontaneous character of this riot introduces the political context as a kind of background element, namely, the militant Hindu movement of the previous decade that created a Hindu-Muslim chasm. My argument differs from Engineer's in the following respects. First, the Hindu-Muslim chasm was not created by the movement of the past decade, only intensified by it. Second, the spontaneous aspects of this rioting were located in areas of the city in which the Hindutva elements, as well as elements in the Muslim community, are always alert and active and are always ready to rush to the scene of an incident to defend their brethren and to counter the actions of crowds from the other community. The areas in which this violence was centered are adjacent localities. One, Sarai Sultani, which will be discussed in detail below, is predominantly Muslim, surrounded by Hindu localities in which militant Hindu organizations are active. The second, Achal Talab, is located in the midst of Hindu and Jain religious and educational institutions. It is here that the local Hindu degree colleges are located and from which Hindu students have been mobilized in so many of the disturbances and major riots discussed in this and the preceding chapter, including the March 1995 incidents. We are here, therefore, at the center of Aligarh's institutionalized riot system.

Absent in this case was a political context into which riotous activity could be placed and that would justify its expansion. Rather than use the term *spontaneous* to describe this riot, it would be better to describe it as unanticipated. It was not preceded by mobilizations of crowds for local electoral purposes, or in mass meetings connected with statewide or national issues or on issues connected with the AMU, or even a wrestling match or a cricket match. What appear as spontaneity are, rather, conditions and practices that extend throughout both communities that allow for the instantaneous reaction of persons from both communities to an incident, a rumor, a provocation from the other side, to rush to the scene and to mobilize others for attack and defense. It is, therefore, appropriate to use the Fearon/Laitin term *spiral equilibrium* for this kind of riot, an unfortunately infelicitous term that nevertheless suggests not preplanning, but a predictable outcome in communities ever alert for provocations from the other side and ever ready to be mobilized.

Such riots are more easily contained than others that we have examined above because the political mechanisms for expansion that inhibit the local administration from acting against political persons who have influence with the state authorities are not brought into play. Absent also was divided political authority. Although there was a Congress government in New Delhi and an SP government in the state, the central government had no reason or authority to interfere in a situation where the state government had made it clear that it would not tolerate communal violence and would hold every DM and SSP accountable for any riotous activity that occurred on their watch. Thus, once again, we see clearly the elements of riot containment and control in situations where riots expand and where they do not. In broad terms, the elements are threefold: (1) presence or absence, activation or inactivation of a preexisting institutionalized riot system; (2) presence or absence of a context of electoral competition, political mobilization, or other context in which symbols of communal opposition are present; (3) presence or absence of political and administrative coordination of the forces available to the authorities for immediate suppression of violence.

### Riot Prevention in Dahi Wali Gali

During a visit to Aligarh in November 1997, I was informed that there was an ongoing dispute between Hindus and Muslims over a religious site in a locality in the old city known as Dahi Wali Gali. This locality, which derives its name from the production of *dahi,* or curd, that takes place along the *gali,* or alley, is as crowded a *qasbah* lane as one can possibly imagine. Here, as in many lanes and alleys in the old city, population has grown to such an extent—as well as the number of vehicles—that one cannot move on foot in a straight line in any direction. One has to weave and dodge constantly to avoid jostling others and to prevent oneself from being hit by vehicles of every description.

I was taken to this *gali* by an AMU professor, a Muslim, to visit the disputed site, where a *mandir* exists adjacent to a Muslim *mazar,* or saint's tomb, which Hindus claim is temple property and where they wish to install additional idols. There is also a mosque across the way from which the call to prayer could be heard as we were touring the *gali.* This dispute had been simmering for seventeen years (as of 1997), while a civil case concerning it had been in the courts. Throughout these seventeen years, the PAC had been posted here to prevent an outbreak of violence in connection with the dispute. In fact, I saw also posted here a huge Rapid Action Force truck. The Rapid Action Force is a relatively new force that has been brought into use in such riot-prone areas only in the 1990s. It is a "state-of-the-art" riot-prevention force. Its huge truck is said to be provided not just with men and arms but with medical facilities to care for the injured in case of bloodshed.[22]

I had a very clear sense, in my interviews in Dahi Wali Gali and with the district officials at the time, concerning two aspects of this situation. First, obviously, this situation is a generic type in India. Its counterpart exists in thousands of sites all over the subcontinent. It is a very dangerous situation that, by its very nature, could lead to local strife and even violence. It is also of the type that is easily susceptible to political manipulation. In the absence of political manipulation, or of the work of other larger forces, however, such potential conflict can be limited to the specific site. Second, my impression was that the district administration in Aligarh at the time was very much aware of the potential for an outbreak of violence at this site, was on top of the situation, and was determined to ensure that no significant violence did in fact break out. My impressions, therefore, are consistent with the analysis given above concerning the factors that promote and contain large-scale rioting. In the case of Dahi Wali Gali, however, we confirm those conclusions from an opposite direction. In the March 1995 riots, we saw a "spontaneous" or unanticipated riot, precipitated by a trivial, everyday quarrel, brought under control. In Dahi Wali Gali, we see a continuing local dispute in which the feelings of members of both communities are involved, in which both sides remain always alert for transgression by the other side, but in which the same mechanisms operate to prevent its expansion.

Much more will be said in the four chapters in Part IV concerning the relationship between riots and political competition. Before turning to that subject, however, I want to consider as well the extent to which other factors that have been cited in my interviews above play a part in the production of Hindu-Muslim violence in Aligarh. I will consider first the demography and geography of violence in Aligarh City, paying special attention to the spatial location and communal composition of the various *mohallas* of the city where riotous violence has often been centered. Second, I will consider the economic factors commonly cited as either primary or secondary causes in the production of violence. I will then return in some detail in Part IV to an analysis of the political and electoral context in which communal violence occurs in Aligarh.

# PART III

# Demographic, Social, and Economic Factors in the Production of Riots

# 6 / The Geography and Demography of Riots

INTRODUCTION

Collective violence such as riots rarely—indeed almost never—engulfs an entire town or city of any substantial size. Nor does it ever include all elements in the city's social organization, whether defined by class, caste, religion, or other cultural community. This obvious and elementary character of collective violence is usually ignored in studies that identify the sites of violence as the cities or towns in which they occur. The literature commonly refers to racial or religious riots as having occurred in Detroit or Chicago or Newark or, in our case, in Bombay or Hyderabad or Aligarh. Paired comparison and ecological studies almost invariably also take the social, economic, and demographic characteristics of the entire city or town as the bases for comparison. Rare is the study, Michael Keith again providing a stunning exception, that identifies precisely the site within the urban area in which violence occurs and within which nobody living within its boundaries could escape noticing, if not participating in, the action. Keith's study goes even further and takes us down to the street and the community centers in which the action occurs. He describes not just that action occurring when the violence breaks out, but the action that is continuous and that lays the basis for the explosive violence that follows.[1] Only in that way can the dynamics of riot production be uncovered.

In this chapter, I will first identify the broad areas of the city in which riotous violence is concentrated. I will then identify specific areas which have repeatedly been sites of violent outbreaks, and specify the types of demographic, social, and economic environments in which they occur. In the second chapter in this part, I will consider the economic bases for communal conflict and violence in Aligarh.

GEOGRAPHY AND DEMOGRAPHY

There are several geographical and demographic features of Aligarh City that are of great importance in understanding political change and communal relations there since Independence. The first is the fundamental division created during colonial rule between the Civil Lines area and the old city. The Civil Lines is a characteristic British creation that existed in most of the towns and cities where there was a significant presence of British administrators. These areas were cantonments for British armed forces and posh residential areas for its administrative officers, usually created out of rural space on the outskirts of existing towns. In Aligarh, in addition—and ultimately of greater importance—the Civil Lines provided the site for the establishment of the Aligarh Muslim University (AMU) and, with its expansion, for the residential bungalows of its faculty and staff.

Largely because of the presence of the AMU and its predominantly Muslim faculty in the Civil Lines, the population of the Civil Lines ward was more than 50 percent Muslim in 1951. Insofar as the university community itself is concerned, the vast majority of whom live in the Civil Lines, 86 to 88 percent are Muslim today.[2]

The division between the Civil Lines and the old city is sharply marked, physically, emotionally, demographically, culturally, and in lifestyle. Physically, the Civil Lines is separated from the old city by the railroad line and the Ramghat Road, which meet to form a triangle comprising the northeastern sections of the city, and by the flyover (viaduct) at Kathphula, over which one travels to reach the old city (see Map 1).[3] Most of the land lying to the northeast of the railway line, "except the Railway Colony and the Indian residential mohallas on the eastern side"[4] is included in the Civil Lines. Lelyveld, in his reconstruction of the life and times of Aligarh at the founding of the AMU, remarked on the contrast existing even then between the old city and Civil Lines with its newly founded college as follows: "Nothing could be greater than the contrast between the chaos of Koil's [Aligarh's] winding streets and the deliberate order of the Aligarh College."[5] Hirt described the Civil Lines area in 1955 as follows.

> It is characterized by large, widely spaced upper class residences and administrative and judicial buildings arranged along wide, predominantly straight streets. The Muslim University occupies a large tract of land in the northwestern part of the area.[6]

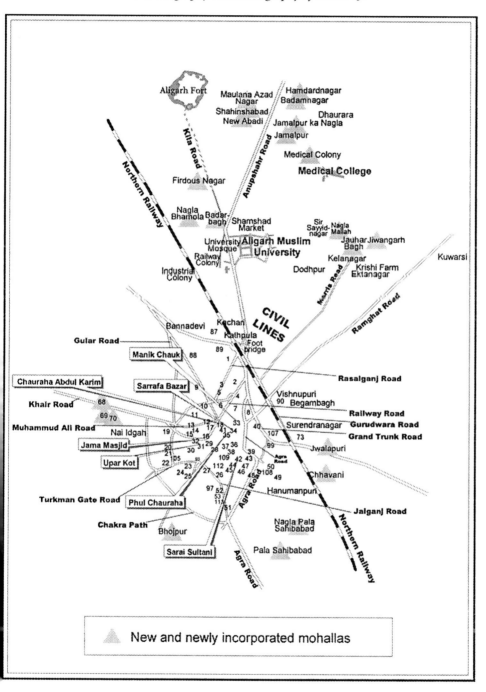

MAP 1. Aligarh City

In more recent times, especially in the last decade or so, new business money and old aristocratic money have been used in the Civil Lines to build fantastic houses—huge in their dimensions, with spacious lawns, sometimes grotesque in architecture and color—for members of former landlord families and businessmen from the old city who have amassed fortunes from their commercial and industrial activities. (See Figure 6.1.) Many of these houses are located on the relatively wide Marris Road.

The division is also an emotional one. Most people living in the Civil Lines never travel across to the other side, while most of those living in the old city would have no reason to do so. Some people do cross from the Civil Lines to the old city to shop and some people from the city side cross over to the Civil Lines to engage in meinial labor. Recently, also, as just noted, those who amass sufficient wealth may move out of the filthy slums on the city side to spacious new bungalows on the Civil Lines side.

A further emotional division arises out of the presence of the AMU in the Civil Lines and the attitudes towards it that exist on the other side. The importance of the AMU as a symbolic presence in the town—a living *lieu de mémoire*,[7] conveying a multiplicity of strong emotional meanings in the present—has already been noted and will be discussed further below. For the moment, it is sufficient to note that, despite its emotional significance, there is little actual contact between the AMU, its faculty and staff, and the population in the city. In fact, it was the original intention of the founder of the university to wall in the students, in the manner of an English cloistered university, to provide them with a peaceful, sequestered atmosphere to pursue their studies and to foster a communal life inside the campus walls separate from that of the outside world.[8]

However, as noted in Chapters 3 and 4, there have been dramatic occasions when crossovers have taken place in politics and in the enactment of communal violence. Faculty from the university have at times, most notably in 1962, entered the Legislative Assembly contest for Aligarh City. Hindu students in the university have sometimes gone to the city to recruit fellow Hindu youths to redress insults and grievances they have claimed to suffer in AMU student politics at the hands of Muslim students. Cadres from militant Hindu organizations, student crowds from the degree colleges in the city, and gangs of rowdies and criminals have for other reasons also from time to time crossed the boundary to create violent disturbances around the university. At times, the university hostels have became havens for criminals from the city. Partly for such reasons, the walls originally established to provide a communal, collegiate atmosphere have recently been raised to block off the university still

FIG. 6.1. Posh new house in the Civil Lines area, March 1999

further, but now in order to wall off the university grounds from unwanted intruders.

The second demographic feature of great importance in understanding politics and communal violence in Aligarh is the fact that the bulk of the population of the city and most of the Muslim population lives south-southwest of the railway line in enormously congested *mohallas*. Although the area occupied by the Civil Lines is larger than that of the rest of the city south of the railway line, the population distribution is highly skewed in the opposite direction. In 1951, only 12 percent of the population of Aligarh lived in the spacious Civil Lines area.

The major population concentration in Aligarh is in a section of the city known as Upar Kot (Upper Fort) (Map 2), although there is no ward or other census division designated by that name. At the highest site in Upar Kot stands the Jama Masjid (Friday Mosque; Maps 1 and 2 and Figure 6.2), the principal mosque for the Muslim population of the old city. In this respect, too, there is a distinct division between the old city and the Civil Lines, in this case among Muslims, for the AMU has its own Jama Masjid on the university campus (Figure 6.3), which makes it unnecessary for faculty, staff, and students ever to visit the other. In the old city itself, however, the more significant fact is that the mosque and the Muslim-majority *mohallas* around it are "located in the centre . . . and are surrounded by Hindu majority and mixed [Hindu-Muslim] localities."[9]

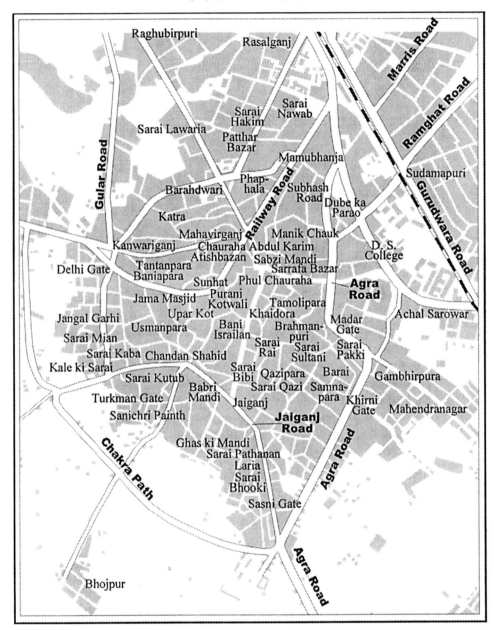

MAP 2. Upar Kot

FIG. 6.2. Mosque, Upar Kot

A third demographic feature of great political importance, especially in recent years, has been a substantial expansion of the population of the city into outlying areas on both sides of the railway line, including the Civil Lines areas. This expansion has included the incorporation of former villages and their transformation into urban *mohallas*, the creation of new "colonies" or *abadis* (as new urban settlements are often called in India), and the migration of persons from rural Aligarh into these areas. Many of these new *mohallas* are not included in the 1951 census nor are there any data on them in later censuses, which use artificial agglomerations rather than living neighborhoods as their units. In many cases, however, I have been able to count or estimate the proportion of Muslims and Hindus and others from recent voters' lists (Table 6.3) and to place them on the maps.

Many of the new *mohallas* (see Map 1) are populated entirely or predominantly by Muslims. They include areas to the north and northeast such as Jamalpur, Jamalpur Mafi (not on map), Jamalpur Nagla (village), Badamnagar/Hamdardnagar, and Jiwangarh (Map 1). On the southern outskirts of the city lies predominantly Muslim Bhojpur. To the west is Shah Jamal (no. 69, Map 1), for which no census information is available, but which is overwhelmingly Muslim, adjacent to a locally famous *dargah* (no. 70, Map 1) and to the Idgah (Muslim festival celebration site). To the northwest, between the railway line

FIG. 6.3. Mosque, Aligarh Muslim University campus, 1962

and the university, almost at the outer boundary of the city near the old Aligarh Fort, is another cluster of new *mohallas*, of which the largest is Firdous Nagar. Another *mohalla* in this cluster, attesting to its newness and its Muslim character, is Maulana Azad Nagar, named after the famous Congress nationalist Muslim leader; two others are Shahinshabad and New Abadi (New Settlement).

There are also several newly incorporated areas where the Hindu population has expanded, some of which are entirely populated by Hindus (including Scheduled Castes and others). These lie mostly to the east and southeast. One such area comprises Pala Sahibabad, Nagla Pala Sahibabad, and the older locality of Mahendranagar (number 49, Map 1). This grouping is populated entirely by Hindus and others. A second newly populated area, Chhavani, lies to the north of the previous grouping; its population consists entirely of Hindus, Scheduled Castes, and others, with no Muslims.

Several of these areas will feature prominently in the discussion to follow later in this chapter concerning the extension of riot sites in the great riots of 1990–91. They will also feature in the electoral analysis to follow in Part IV. To anticipate briefly, the political significance of these newly settled and incorporated areas lies in the fact that the predominantly Muslim areas have been included in the boundaries of the Aligarh City Legislative Assembly constituency, while several of both the older and newer overwhelmingly Hindu areas have been excluded, leading to a substantial increase in the percentage of Muslim voters in the constituency as a whole that has, in recent elections, been transformed as a result into a Muslim-majority constituency. However, in the municipality of Aligarh, and consequently in the corporation elections, the predominantly Hindu localities are included, with the result that Hindus (including Scheduled Castes and others) retain a majority therein.

## WARDS AND *MOHALLAS*

### *The Wards of Aligarh*

The 1951 census divided the city into eight wards and 241 *mohallas*. Since that census, however, the number of census wards has been increased several times while the *mohallas* have been replaced by "enumerator's blocks" as the primary census units. As far as I have been able to determine, there is no correspondence between these blocks, listed by serial number only, with the living neighborhoods of the city. Nor does there appear to be any correspondence between the political division of the city into wards and the census division. We are, therefore, compelled to use the 1951 census as the basic source for the information of most concern in this book, namely, the caste/communal composition of the population. The data from that census have, however, been checked against voters' lists in my possession for later periods, to detect any significant discrepancies in the proportions of persons in the wards and *mohallas* by religion, and to provide relevant information on the communal composition of new neighborhoods.

Table 6.1 below provides the distribution of the city population wardwise by religion and caste from the 1951 census. Three wards then had a Muslim majority: Civil Lines, Kanwariganj, and Turkman Gate. However, the bulk of the Muslim population (76 percent) in the city as a whole was concentrated in the more heavily and densely populated wards of Kanwariganj and Turkman Gate in the old city. The Hindu population, the majority in five of the eight wards, was more evenly distributed throughout the city.

Politically, as indicated in Chapter 2, the Aligarh municipality is now divided into 60 wards that encompass the original 241 *mohallas* as well as several newly incorporated areas. The correspondence between the old and new wards as well as the distribution of municipal corporators by new ward number are shown in Table 6.2. The table shows that the BJP in 1995 dominated completely all the wards in Achal Talab, which, in 1951, had a Hindu population above 80 percent. The BJP is also the predominant party in all the other Hindu-majority areas, namely, Raghubirpuri, Mamubhanja, Shahpara, and

TABLE 6.1. Population of Aligarh City wards, 1951

| No. | Name | Muslims | | Scheduled Castes | | Others | | Total Population | |
|---|---|---|---|---|---|---|---|---|---|
| | | No. | Percent | No. | Percent | No. | Percent | No. | Percent[a] |
| 1 | Civil Lines | 8,461 | 50.35 | 1,027 | 6.11 | 7,315 | 43.53 | 16,803 | 100.00 |
| 2 | Achal Talab | 540 | 3.52 | 2,401 | 15.67 | 12,381 | 80.81 | 15,322 | 100.00 |
| 3 | Raghubirpuri | 6,601 | 34.44 | 2,497 | 13.03 | 10,071 | 52.54 | 19,169 | 100.00 |
| 4 | Mamubhanja | 4,273 | 25.17 | 1,803 | 10.62 | 10,898 | 64.20 | 16,974 | 100.00 |
| 5 | Shahpara | 3,401 | 17.53 | 1,877 | 9.68 | 14,118 | 72.79 | 19,396 | 100.00 |
| 6 | Jaiganj | 4,462 | 29.54 | 2,340 | 15.49 | 8,303 | 54.97 | 15,105 | 100.00 |
| 7 | Kanwariganj | 14,030 | 60.22 | 644 | 2.76 | 8,622 | 37.01 | 23,296 | 100.00 |
| 8 | Turkman Gate | 7,128 | 52.05 | 1,562 | 11.41 | 5,004 | 36.54 | 13,694 | 100.00 |
| | TOTAL | 48,896 | 34.99 | 14,151 | 10.12 | 76,712 | 54.89 | 139,759 | 100.00 |

[a]All percentages rounded to 100.00.

TABLE 6.2. Correspondence between 1951 and 1995 wards and the distribution of corporators by new ward number

| Old Ward Name[a] | New Ward Numbers | BJP | BSP | SP | Ind. |
|---|---|---|---|---|---|
| Civil Lines | 9, 31, 39, 40, 43, 44, 47, 49, 51, 52, 57 | 9, 39, 40, 44, 51 | | 31, 43, 47, 49, 57 | 52 |
| Achal Talab | 1, 11, 15, 17, 22, 32, 33, 34, 42, 60 | 1, 11, 15, 17, 22, 32, 33, 34, 42, 60 | | | |
| Raghubirpuri | 12, 14, 16, 21, 27, 37, 39, 46, 50 | 12, 14, 16, 21, 39, 46 | | 50 | 27, 37 |
| Mamubhania | 1, 10, 27, 39, 58, 59 | 1, 39, 58, 59 | 10 | | 27 |
| Shahpara | 5, 6, 12, 13, 35, 45, 55 | 5, 6, 12, 13 | 55 | | 35, 45 |
| Jaiganj | 4, 5, 6, 19, 23, 24, 25, 55, 60 | 4, 5, 6, 25, 60 | 19, 23, 24, 55 | | |
| Kanwariganj | 20, 39, 54, 55, 56, 58, 59 | 20, 39, 58, 59 | 55, 56 | 54 | |
| Turkman Gate | 2, 3, 8, 9, 12, 14, 16, 19, 38, 54, 56 | 9, 12, 14, 16 | 2, 3, 19, 38, 56 | 54 | 8 |

[a]There is some overlap in the case of several wards that lie on the boundaries between the old wards.

Jaiganj. In contrast, in areas where the Muslim population is above 50 percent, namely in the old Civil Lines, Turkman Gate, and Kanwariganj wards, the SP, BSP, and independent corporators are well represented, though, even in Kanwariganj, the BJP has stronger representation than other political forces.

### The mohallas of Aligarh

Many of the *mohallas* of Aligarh have names that suggest their past historical function, their present function, or the dominance or prominence of particular castes or *baradaris* in their past or present. At the extremities of the inner part of the old city are a series of "gates" or, in Hindi, *darwazas*, which were probably at one time the entry ways into what must have been a walled city.[10] These gates are also the names of the *mohallas* around them. Most of them are situated on or near main roads that take one out of the city. Forty-four of the *mohallas* of Aligarh bear the name Sarai, reflecting the fact that they originated as caravanseries for travellers in earlier times.[11] Nine of the Aligarh *mohallas* carry the Urdu word *bazar*, which, of course, implies exactly what it says, namely, a market for the sale of goods. A few carry the Hindi word *mandi* in their name, which means the same thing, though it more commonly refers to a wholesale market. For example, the main vegetable market in Aligarh, as in every city in north India, is called Sabzi Mandi.

*Sensitive, Riot-Hit, and Crime-Prone* Mohallas. It was shown in Chapter 3 that there has been an increase in the intensity of riots in Aligarh since Independence by the measure of the number of deaths in those five-year periods in which there were riots with deaths. (Refer to Table 3.1 and Figure 3.1.) A further feature of Aligarh riots has been an increase in their locational spread. Figure 6.4 selects from Table 3.1 the seven riots in which there have been five deaths or more since 1961. It is immediately apparent from the figure that there is an extremely close relationship between the intensity of riots measured by deaths and their spatial spread. Indeed, the correlation coefficient between number of deaths and number of localities affected is .97, giving an $R^2$ of 94 percent. Further, although there have been fluctuations in the intensity and spread of riots, there has been a long-term trend towards spatial spread, notable first in 1978 and then dramatically so in 1990–91. Although the number of deaths in 1961 and in 1971 reached 15 and 17, respectively, by official count, most of the killing and other riotous activity occurred in four locations. In 1961, rioting began on the AMU campus and spread to the Shamshad Market (Map 1) on the main arterial, the Anupshahr Road, that adjoins it, after which rioting then occurred for utterly different reasons in two localities in the old city, namely,

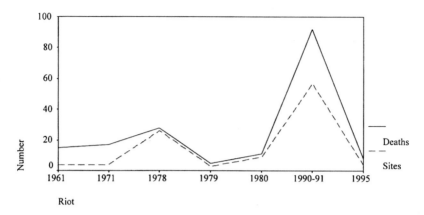

FIG. 6.4. Number of deaths and number of sites of riotous activity
in Aligarh riots in which there were five or more deaths

Manik Chauk and Mamubhanja (Map 2). In March 1971, although the rioting was associated in some accounts with the agitation at AMU concerning
the demand for restoration of its minority status, all rioting occurred in the
old city, particularly in the four localities of Achal Talab, Babri Mandi, Phul
Chauraha, and Sabzi Mandi. (See Appendix Table A.2 and Map 2.)

It is necessary to pause here for a moment to note particular features of
these localities in the old city. Manik Chauk and Mamubhanja are *mohallas*
dominated by the Varshney caste, centers of militant Hindu and anti-Muslim
hostilities. Achal Talab (Achal Sarowar on Map 2) contains the most important Hindu temple in Aligarh (Figure 2.1) as well as three degree colleges on
whose faculty are several leading RSS organizers and whose students are mobilized in all large-scale riots for processions and attacks against Muslims and
their property. Indeed, although Achal Talab is not mentioned as a site of
riotous activity, in 1961 and in most later riots, excluding 1995, it is primarily because Hindu rioters move out from this locality to march, protest, and
attack elsewhere in the old city. Babri Mandi (Map 2), in contrast, is a locality dominated by the Muslim *baradari* of Qureshi, the most numerous of
the Muslim *baradaris* of Aligarh. Phul Chauraha (Map 2) is at the epicenter
of many riots because it is a major crossing and market, situated between
Hindu and Muslim *mohallas*. Finally, Sabzi Mandi (Map 2) is another market situated at "the intersection of the major bazaar streets."[12] In short, the
latter two are focal points where streets, crossings, and bazaars converge,
toward which provocative processions generally proceed at times of Hindu-

Muslim confrontation, and where the heavy concentration of shops of all kinds provides targets.

The first great extension of riotous activity in Aligarh occurred in the riot months of 1978, when 28 deaths were officially recorded and some 27 *mohallas* were riot-hit. The intensity, duration, and spatial spread of this rioting in Aligarh was, as we have seen above (Chapter 3), widely commented upon in the press and by the politicians and led to official and nonofficial post-riot inquiries. By then, also, the local authorities had identified for their own purposes, presumably for establishing curfew and for determining deployment of forces, a list of riot-prone *mohallas*. At the same time, the Minorities Commission also published in its report a list of "disturbed areas" that it visited in the course of its inquiries. Finally, an unpublished report by the Centre for Research in Industrial Development, "Communal Violence," compiled a list of some 29 *mohallas* divided into five categories: (communally) sensitive; riot-hit, but not crime-prone; crime-prone, but not riot-hit; riot-hit and crime-prone; sensitive and crime-prone, but not riot-hit.[13]

Most of the riotous and other criminal activity of the city takes place in these 29 *mohallas*,[14] comprising 12 percent of the total number listed in the 1951 census. They are listed in Appendix Table A.1 with the available caste/communal data on their composition. Spatially, all 29 *mohallas* are located in the central area of the old city where the Muslim population is most heavily concentrated, especially in the broad area known as Upar Kot (see Maps 2 and 3). The term "Upar Kot" means, simply, "upper fort," referring to the high ground of the city once occupied by a fort, but now the site of the grand mosque of the city, the Jama Masjid (Friday mosque). Although the term "Upar Kot" is often used to refer to the site on which the mosque is located and the entire area surrounding it, it also refers to a specific *mohalla*; I will, therefore, use the term "Upar Kot" to refer to the broad area and the term "Upar Kot proper" to refer to the specific *mohalla* where the mosque is actually located. Upar Kot, as Mann has noted, "is almost entirely populated by Muslims, while encircling it are mostly Hindu *mohallas*, with some of mixed Hindu/Muslim populations."[15] This heavily congested area lies across both the railway line and the Gurudwara Road, which run parallel to each other and divide the new from the old city. It also lies to the west of the Grand Trunk Road that joins the Gurudwara Road and the railway line at Kathphula and the footbridge. One reaches the old city (see Map 1) from the Civil Lines area in which the university is located by ascending, at Kathphula, a steep hill that crosses over the railway line. The Railway Road that brings one up from the new city and down into the old city ascends again into the heart of the old city, up to Upar

Kot proper and the Jama Masjid, which occupies the highest ground. Side by side, to the east of the mosque, is the *kotwali* or police station (Map 2), which occupies a site approximately equal in size to that of the mosque. The two buildings are separated by a broad street. Both are adjacent to the Railway Road. The latter road is busy with all kinds of foot and vehicular traffic, but is fairly broad up to the mosque.

On either side of the Railway Road, lanes extend in every direction into the *qasbah* that is old Aligarh, a maze of alleys filled with human, animal, and vehicular traffic of every description through which one picks one's way, whether by foot, bicycle rickshaw, or car, with great difficulty and with constant risk of jostling others or being hit by bicycles or other wheeled vehicles. Most of these lanes are unsanitary in the extreme, with open sewage flowing in channels down the streets, and excreta, animal and human, dotting the lanes and alleys to such an extent that one must keep one's eyes firmly focused upon the ground and upon each step one takes, while simultaneously, through peripheral vision, attempting to avoid being struck by passing vehicles. It is in these filthy, choked lanes, which also contain subterranean passages, that most of the criminal and riotous activity and violence are perpetrated. The authors of the Centre for Research report on riots in Aligarh remarked that, in these *mohallas*, "the continuous tension permeating daily life is nearly tangible, as people go about their business, alert to detect the slightest disturbance."[16]

Let us move now to consider two clusters of *mohallas* that have been identified repeatedly as centers of riot production and victimization. Moving south on the Railway Road to where it forks, and following the fork through the locality of Mamubhanja (Map 2), we reach the famous four-way crossing known as Chauraha Abdul Karim. To the southeast of that crossing is another famous crossing known as Phul Chauraha (Flower Crossing; Figure 6.5). Police pickets are posted constantly at both these crossings. To the north of Phul Chauraha are Sarrafa Bazaar (Jeweller's Market) and Sabzi Mandi, and further to the north is the infamous *mohalla* of Manik Chauk. Manik Chauk is communally mixed, being 76 percent Hindu, 24 percent Muslim. It is the *mohalla* of Aligarh most identified with the Varshney community, which has always provided strong support for the RSS, the Jan Sangh, and the BJP. There is also a large concentration of Agarwals, the second prominent Hindu trading caste.[17] Manik Chauk is also the home and business site of Krishna Kumar Navman, the Varshney businessman and BJP politician considered by the authorities to be one of the principal instigators of communal riots.

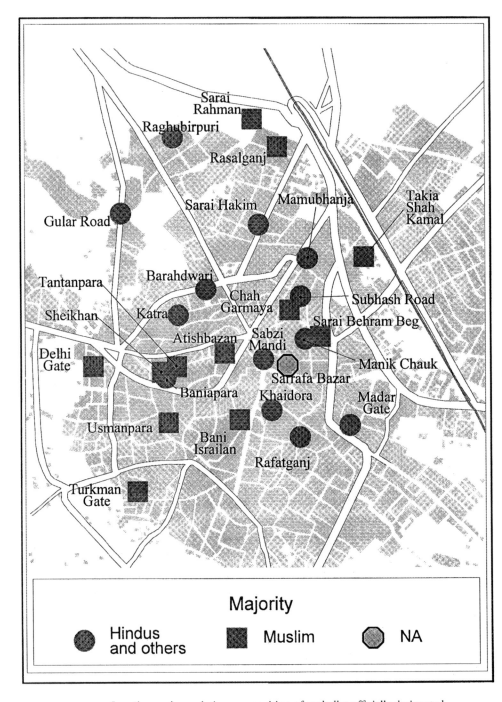

MAP 3. Location and population composition of *mohallas* officially designated as communally sensitive, riot-hit, and/or crime-prone

FIG. 6.3 Phul Chauraha

Manik Chauk figured prominently in the 1961 riots, as indicated in the account below.

> A major incident took place [during the 1961 riots] in the Manak Chowk [*sic*] locality which lies on the Agra-Aligarh road. There was some dispute regarding property between Lachhman Das, a well-to-do [Hindu] businessman, and Sharafuddin [a Muslim]. Litigation, so far, had been in favour of Sharafuddin. Taking advantage of the situation, [Lachhman] Das and his men accompanied by a mob of students raided the houses of Sharafuddin and other Muslim residents living in the area. One IAS Joint Magistrate who was posted in that district on training later told the case-writer that the police [were] present at this spot but did not make any effort to stop Lachhman Das and others from burning and looting the houses. . . . This alone accounted for seven killed and 21 injured, all Muslims.[18]

Even in 1974, when the sparking incident that precipitated riots occurred far from Manik Chauk and the old city, in the university area, there was violence in this *mohalla*.[19]

Both Manik Chauk and Phul Chauraha were at the center of the riotous activity of 1978, which began in Phul Chauraha when, after the death of the Hindu wrestler Bhura at the hands of an assassin, "a crowd of 30 or 40

Hindus . . . removed the body from the hospital" and "carried it provocatively through Muslim localities," shouting the Hindi slogan *khoon ka badla khoon se lenge* (blood for blood). Rioting predictably broke out "in certain areas of the town." In Phul Chauraha, "police opened fire in which one Muslim was killed." The report of the Minorities Commission continues as follows.

> The Commission found bullet marks on the walls of houses some of them situated deep inside the Muslim localities and also on the walls inside the mosque and on the wooden ceiling of the verandah of the mosque near Phool Chauraha, indicating that firing was done either from the entrance of the mosque or after entering the mosque. The Commission also found blood stains inside the houses of some Muslims which indicated that the Muslims were shot while they were inside their houses. On the same evening there was large scale arson and looting of Muslim houses at Manek Chowk [sic].[20]

The report of the Centre for Research also pinpoints Manik Chauk as a major flash point for the riots both in October 1978 and May–June 1981.

> With the phenomenal rise in the price of land in the Aligarh town, the tendency to force the Muslim artisans to vacate their houses and shops located in the business centres or more developed residential areas dominated by Hindu Banias has been steadily gaining strength. This tendency manifested itself prominently in the riots of October, 1978, and May–June, 1981. During these riots killings in Manik Chowk [sic] and Dahi Wali Gali are known to have been organized by the local roughs in league with the land hungry rich of these localities.[21]

These two accounts of the sources of riotous activity in Manik Chauk provide different perspectives. In that of the Minorities Commission, the emphasis is on the deliberate provocation of anti-Muslim feelings by Hindu crowds, who insisted upon carrying the body of Bhura in procession through Muslim localities, and on the anti-Muslim activities of the PAC, whose forces fired indiscriminately upon Muslim crowds, as well as inside their houses and mosques. The emphasis is clearly upon Hindu-Muslim animosities, upon Hindus and Muslims as collectivities. The Centre report, on the other hand, reduces the sources of conflict in Manik Chauk and similar areas to the greed of rich businessmen and to the activities of a specific segment of the Hindu community, namely, the Varshneys, who use hooligans to harass, intimidate, and kill Muslims to get rid of them in order to gain control of their land and property.

Violette Graff's account of the events at Phul Chauraha and the attack upon

Muslims in Manik Chauk in 1978 also emphasizes the role of Varshney business interests, the use of *goondas*, and the complicity of the PAC. However, she adds a further dimension, namely, the participation of known militant Hindu political figures.

> The worst carnage . . . took place in . . . Manak Chowk [sic], a *mohalla* where a small pocket of 10–15 Muslim houses was surrounded by Barahseni (Varshney) houses. . . . Two young men were burnt alive. And it was not done by *goondas*. Most conspicuous at the head of the assailants was K. K. Navman, the Janata Chief in Aligarh, and a host of persons "known to be members of the RSS." Among them, although he was later to demonstrate that there was no evidence against him, was Dr. B. D. Gupta, a lecturer from AMU who was in the forefront in the fight against the Minority Bill.[22]

Graff's observations on the riots of October 1978 extend the ring of complicity so that it now includes Hindu traders, specifically of the Varshney caste, local criminals in their employ, and local militant Hindu politicians, all protected by the police and all out to attack Muslim property and religious places and to kill Muslims.

Graff's account is supported in several respects by my own interviews conducted in 1983 and 1991. Specifically, for example, with regard to the roles played by known individuals, most especially Navman, the following remarks from one of my interviews are pertinent.

> And Navman, since very beginning, has been creating problem like last time, '78, I know about that incident, what happened in Manik Chauk. He was there, standing himself and trying to, and directing people to destroy the houses and to burn the houses of the Muslims. And, he has a group and he has a RSS cadre.[23]

Graff's report concerning the links between Hindu businessmen and the police is also supported by Zoya Hasan.[24]

Further observations on the origins of the 1978 riots and the centrality of Manik Chauk in them come from Elizabeth Mann, whose account is consistent with the others, but adds yet a further dimension, namely, the suspicion of a direct link between the militant Hindu organization, the RSS, and the local police. She describes a series of incidents that followed upon the initial tussle at the wrestling match, after which a Hindu was stabbed here, a Muslim there, with each side blaming the other. In the midst of these incidents, she notes as follows.

> There was a function held in mohalla Manak Chowk [*sic*] by the . . . RSS. . . . The RSS are strong patrons of many Aligarh *akharas* (though not all *akharas* are patronised by the RSS), where drills and organised fights (*sakhas*) are held. At this RSS function was a Senior Superintendent of Police (SSP), P. S. V. Prasad, who took part in the religious ritual. The SSP subsequently said he had attended at the invitation of personal contacts, a statement which gave Muslims little confidence in the unbiased attitude of the Aligarh police. Moreover, the mohalla of Manak Chowk [*sic*] is a sensitive one, bordering the area separating Hindu from Muslim localities. It had formerly been a largely Muslim mohalla, but concerted efforts of the Varshney and Aggarwal [*sic*] (Bania) castes had been made to purchase property there and transform it into a Hindu mohalla. Muslims claimed, and Hindus confirmed, that pressure, including intimidation and threats, had been put on Muslim householders to sell at concessional rates. A further aggravation to Muslims was that the Bania castes are strong supporters of militant Hindu groups such as the RSS and the Vishwa Hindu Parishad (VHP).[25]

With Mann's account, we enter a still broader ring of complicity, one suggesting the active participation of specific organizations in the events surrounding Hindu-Muslim riots that are so often attributed to Hindu-Muslim passions and animosities. The account also suggests that it is no accident that the police played a partial role in supporting Hindu violence and attacking Muslims, that the sympathies of the chief police officer of the district at the time were with the RSS and militant Hindus.

When, more than two weeks later, on October 3, the Hindu wrestler Bhura was stabbed and died in hospital on the following day, the nexus of *goondas*, politicians, criminals, and police facilitated the provocative actions of the Hindu crowd, itself composed primarily of *goondas* from a group of thugs known as the Golden Gang as well as "volunteers of the RSS," in carrying Bhura's body in procession to the areas of the old city where revenge and retaliation could best be enacted, namely, at the two crossroads of Abdul Karim and Phul.

> The violence grew once the procession reached the Muslim-populated area of Chauraha Abdul Karim, and the arson and looting reached a climax. Simultaneously, trouble flared up in Manak Chowk [*sic*]. . . . tension continued throughout October into the succeeding month. On 5 November, violence flared again in Manak Chowk, the main targets of attack being the poorer Muslims of that mohalla, most of whom were fruit-sellers, members of brass band teams, or mazdoori labourers. The trouble was sparked off by an unrelated incident in Phul Chauraha, an adjacent mohalla.[26]

The collusion between local Hindus in Manik Chauk and the police, suggested in several of the accounts given above, was also confirmed by "an outside team sent in by the Peoples Union for Civil Liberties to report on events" during the 1978 riots.

> The Provincial Armed Constabulary (PAC) resorted to firing . . . it fired deliberately at the Muslim houses. . . . According to Iqbal Ansari of AMU, a Hindu gentleman of the area was asked on October 5 by the PAC men to identify the Muslim houses so that they could shoot them from a vantage point. In Manak Chowk [*sic*], it was estimated that of 40 Muslim houses with about 200 residents, . . . 16 were burnt down and 20 residents remained after this incident, the rest having fled to Muslim mohallas.[27]

The complexity of the accounts given above of the incidents that took place in this one *mohalla* of Manik Chauk and nearby areas suggests two aspects of riot activity in Aligarh that deserve stress. One is the multiplicity of motivations attributed to the actors. Second is the evidence of considerable organizing activity by known individuals and organizations. Third is the existence of a network of relationships that comes into play before and during riots, involving specific individuals, organizations, economic interests, criminals, politicians, and the police, a network that is partially active at all times and in which many of the participants have distinctive roles to play. These roles include, among others, the organization of processions, the arousing of sentiments, the gathering of crowds, the recruitment of specialists in violence, the transmission of information between organizers and the authorities, particularly the police, to whom are assigned the ultimate work of killing Muslims, the principal victims in most riots.

Manik Chauk figured prominently yet again in the series of incidents between 1979 and 1981, especially those centering on the construction by a Hindu businessman of a new cinema hall exiting into a Muslim *mohalla*. Hindu and Muslim accounts in my interviews agree that violence was centered in Manik Chauk.[28]

Although a large number of people were killed in the 1979–80 violence, nearly all Muslims, the police were acknowledged even by Muslim respondents to have played a different role on this occasion, acting "properly," that is, impartially, to end the rioting rather than providing cover to Hindus to attack Muslims and killing Muslims themselves. It is also noteworthy that Manik Chauk is perceived in accounts of these riots as a storm center from which originate riots that will spread to other parts of the city unless such proper police action is undertaken. I was told, for example, that Varshney businessmen eager to gain control of Muslim property were responsible for violent attacks against Muslims in this *mohalla* in 1980 in which eleven persons were killed, but "the police acted properly, at once, so it was not spread all over [the] city.[29] There is, therefore, a double reduction in such accounts, from the elevated heights of general Hindu-Muslim animosities in Aligarh and beyond, to a specific *mohalla* where commercial greed appears as the primary motive rather than communalism, and where proper action taken by the police can confine and control violence at its source.

This tendency to localize the significance of riots in Aligarh also appears in many police accounts. For example, in 1983 the SSP, who appeared to me to be impartial on Hindu-Muslim matters, isolated Manik Chauk along with Upar Kot as the principal areas of riot activity from time to time and reduced the conflicts further to conflicts between segments of the two communities:

> Upar Kot and Manik Chauk are the two most riot-prone areas. Both have equal number of people from both the communities and generally the trouble starts with quarrels between Varshneys among the Hindus and Qasai among the Muslims.[30]

Leaving Manik Chauk now and moving south, following the broad road known as the Agra Road on the east, we soon reach another cluster of *mohallas* (Map 2), with Sarai Sultani just to the west of the Agra Road, surrounded by the localities of Brahmanpuri, Madar Gate, Sarai Rai, and Barai (Map 2). Sarai Sultani itself is overwhelmingly Muslim (89 percent according to the 1951 census, the remaining 11 percent being Hindu and others with no Scheduled Castes listed). However, the surrounding *mohallas* are either overwhelmingly Hindu-majority or mixed Hindu-majority *mohallas*. Strangely enough, none of these *mohallas* are classified as sensitive, riot-hit, or crime-prone, with the exception of Madar Gate, which is classified as communally sensitive. Yet, Sarai Sultani has been at the center of perhaps the most vicious killings in Aligarh since Independence and has been caught up in nearly all the post-Independence riots.

There is ample secondary documentation of the riotous activity in Sarai Sultani during both the 1978 and 1990 riots. Insofar as the 1978 riots are concerned, the report of the Minorities Commission on that riot noted that "on 8th November the situation worsened and the police again opened fire at Turkman Gate, Sarai Kaba and Sarai Sultani, during which five Muslims were killed in Sarai Kaba."[31] Hasan notes that when the curfew was, "rather unadvisedly, lifted" on November 9, "a number of Muslims were killed in police firing and violence spread like wildfire," the "worst affected areas" being "Manak Chowk [*sic*], Phul Chauraha, Turkman Gate, Sarai Kaba and Sarai Sultani."[32] Mann also lists Sarai Sultani as among the worst affected *mohallas* in the 1978 riot and notes as well the partiality of the police in these *mohallas* in searching Muslim houses, patronizing "known anti-Muslim organisations," firing indiscriminately at Muslim houses, and also firing with discrimination directly at Muslim houses identified by Hindus in the area.[33]

Sarai Sultani was also at the center of the great riot of 1990. In fact, the riots of 1990 began in Sarai Sultani and Upar Kot and only after the initial incidents there on December 7 did the rioting move to other areas of the city. According to hearsay and eyewitness accounts, discussed in Chapter 4, the initial precipitating incident occurred when a bomb was thrown at a mosque in Sarai Sultani, following which, in one account, "people from the mosque came rushing towards the kotwali to complain." Their movement towards the police station, interpreted by the PAC as an impending attack upon them, was greeted with police bullets. The crowd responded by "snatching" the rifle away from the "particular jawan [who] fired the first shot." Further police firing followed in which two persons were killed. According to some reports, "a Hindu mob joined the PAC in attacking the Muslims." The next morning, the PAC took revengeful action and "fanned out into the sensitive Muslim areas" near Sarai Sultani, where an additional nine persons, all Muslims, were killed.[34]

The Peoples Union for Civil Liberties (PUCL) team heard a similar account. Moreover, in their visit to the *mohalla* of Sarai Sultani, further information was provided suggesting that the Muslims were attacked by both Hindus and the PAC. Below are excerpts from the PUCL report on the 1990 riots in and around Sarai Sultani.

> The area of Sarai Sultani/Sarai Rai is largely composed of Muslims but is surrounded by Hindu localities. Muslims who gathered in the Mosque for Friday prayer on 7.12.90 [December 7, 1990] were alarmed when they saw hundreds of people on roof tops of Hindu houses throwing bombs at Muslims and their houses and at the Mosque. We saw impacts of bombs [they must be crude bombs] on the houses in the locality and many houses destroyed in PAC firing and rioting. We were also told that the . . . PAC provided a cover to the rioters by preventing the Muslims from approaching the Mosque to rescue their friends and relatives; that some Hindus with country-made pistols were mov-

ing along with PAC jawans; that Muslims were confined to their houses and
inside the Mosque. If any Muslim dared to come out the PAC is alleged to have
fired at them.

Further evidence of Hindu participation in the actions against Muslims in
this area was provided to the PUCL team in their visit to the surrounding
Hindu areas.

> In a Hindu area Jogipara, adjacent to Sarai Sultani, we met some Hindus, . . .
> but they were just not willing to speak to us. However, one elderly Hindu lady
> told us that a huge crowd had gathered on the 7th morning from the Hindu
> mohallas. Muslim neighbours were scared. Many of them came to her area;
> she and some of her neighbours helped 20/25 escape through the backdoor
> unhurt. She also told us that she too was scared because the mob was unruly
> and they were unkind to even those people like her who were helping
> Muslims.

In Sarai Sultani and other nearby areas visited by the PUCL team, its mem-
bers heard repeatedly "more or less the same picture, namely PAC resorting
to firing to kill indiscriminately, Hindus being helped by PAC cover, Mosques
attacked, houses destroyed, people subdued but angry."[35]
Several of my interview informants who had some contact with people in
Sarai Sultani had similar accounts to relate. According to one of them, a
Muslim professor at AMU who is involved in running a small school for
Muslims in Sarai Sultani, this *mohalla*—and several others in the city where
there were small pockets of Muslims, or *mohallas* such as Sarai Sultani that
are completely surrounded by predominantly Muslim *mohallas*—was deliberately selected for destruction. This informant referred specifically to Sarai
Sultani as an example of the manner in which deliberate, concerted attacks
were launched against Muslims in areas where they were in small numbers
surrounded by Hindu populations.

> The same pattern is in Sarai Sultani. Every night they are throwing bombs
> and this is an area surrounded on all sides, it is a small pocket. I go there, I used
> to go about twice in a month there. . . . Nobody can come out because . . . all
> around they are being surrounded. . . . Now, PAC also, sitting on the top,
> rooftops of the residents and then they attack. Pattern is they throw a bomb,
> the people will come out, they will think that some attack is being made, and
> then the PAC will start shooting them. Sometimes, a real attack, sometimes

they have gas [?]. They throw the gas [?] in such a way that the people think the *mohalla* is being attacked, they come out and the PAC start. This happened in Sarai Sultani.

This informant connected this general pattern of attack to the incident at the mosque that precipitated the first killings. However, he added an element to it that I heard nowhere else, namely, that there was some kind of dispute over this mosque, which had been repossessed by Muslims in Sarai Sultani after having been abandoned for some time. It was at this mosque that the bomb was thrown during Friday prayers, allegedly by people (presumed to be Hindus) who were trying "to get hold of this mosque."[36]

I heard another account at the residence of the mufti of Aligarh in Upar Kot proper at the very end of the 1990–91 riots when Muslims were walking up the hill to tell their tales of victimization in the days of rioting. The stories that were brought to the mufti concerning Sarai Sultani were that the area was attacked by Hindus, supported by the police, creating panic among the Muslims there. On December 7, the frightened residents of Sarai Sultani had been forewarned that there would be an attack on the mosque during the *jama namaz* (Friday prayers), so they went to the mosque to pray an hour before the proper time in order to avert the attack. Nevertheless, as they were returning home from the mosque, they were attacked. They found PAC men surrounding the roads. The crowd was fired upon and bombs were thrown.[37]

## THE SPATIAL ENLARGEMENT AND DISTRIBUTION OF RIOT SITES IN THE GREAT ALIGARH RIOTS OF 1990–91

The survey of riot-hit *mohallas* presented above covers only the localities in the old city that traditionally have been the centers of riotous activity. We must now refer again to Appendix Table A.2 and Figure 6.4 to consider once again the great riots of 1990–91. It is evident from the table and figure that there was a vast increase in the number of localities hit by these riots compared to all that preceded it: 55 compared to 27 in the 1978 riots, previously the most widespread in Aligarh's history.

But it is not just the increase in the number of sites that is of interest here, but their spatial location (see Map 4). A considerable number of riot-hit sites were never hit by riots before, including a large number for which we do not have census data comparable to that for the other *mohallas*, because they are areas newly populated or newly incorporated into the municipal limits and

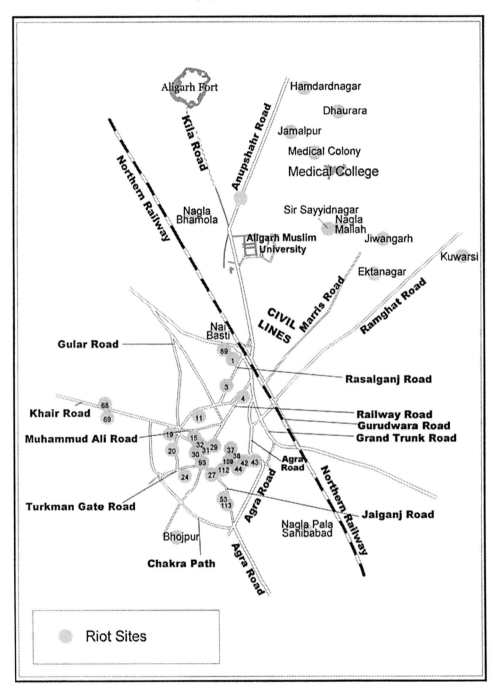

MAP 4. Riot sites, 1990–91

TABLE 6.3. Major Aligarh *mohallas* not included in the 1951 census

| Mohalla | Ward No. | P.S. Nos. (1989–91)[a] | Voters (1984/1995)[b] | Muslim voters (%)[c] |
|---------|----------|-----------------------|----------------------|---------------------|
| PREDOMINANTLY MUSLIM | | | | |
| Bhamola Mafi | | 46–49 | 3,632 | 73.13 |
| Bhojpur | 23 | 184–87 | 1,186 | 63.41 |
| Firdous Nagar, Kila Road, Shahinshahabad, Maulana Azad Nagar | 31 | Not included | 4,543 | 97.80 |
| Hamdardnagar | 36 | Not included | 3,193 | 100.00 |
| Hamdardnagar/ Badamnagar | 41 | Not included | 3,306 | 97.22 |
| Jamalpur, Jamalpur Mafi, Jamalpur Nagla | 30 | 40–45 | 8,190 | 87.34 |
| Jauhar Bagh | 43 | 17–20[d] | 7,132 | 100.00 |
| Jiwangarh | 43 | 22–27 | 3,230 | 93.22 |
| Jiwangarh | 47 | 22–27 | 7,036 | 100.00 |
| Nagla Mallah | 43 | 21 | 1,766 | 64.04 |
| PREDOMINANTLY HINDUS AND OTHERS (INCLUDING SCs) | | | | |
| Chhavani | 28 | Not included | 6,865 | 0 |
| Nagla Pala Sahibabad, Pala Sahibabad, and Nai Abadi | 29 | Not included | 3,441 | 0 |

[a]Polling station numbers, according to the 1989 and 1991 delimitation of the Aligarh City Legislative Assembly constituency.

[b]All figures in this column are from the 1995 voters' list except Bhojpur.

[c]Figures in this column are, in some cases, exact counts, in others estimates based on a 1 percent random number count.

[d]Includes Kela Nagar and Krishi Farm.

lie on the outskirts of the city, not in the center. They include areas whose newness is indicated by their names, that is, areas named after prominent polit-ical leaders of India since Independence, such as Indira Nagar (after Indira Gandhi) and Jagjivan Rampur (after the famous Scheduled Caste politician, Jagjivan Ram), areas that have received an influx of Muslims from the sur-rounding countryside, such as Hamdardnagar, and outlying villages as well, such as Bhojpur and Jamalpur (see Table 6.3 and Map 4). The AMU author-ities also released a cyclostyled sheet that listed some of the areas just men-tioned as well as others near the university and on the outskirts of the city that suffered disturbances, violence, and killings, based partly on reports that reached them from university employees living in those areas. The localities so listed were the Anupshahr Road, Badamnagar/Hamdardnagar, Bhamola, Dhaurara, Ektanagar, Jamalpur, Jiwangarh, Nagla Mallah, the Medical Col-lege Colony near the Medical College, and Sir Sayyidnagar (see Map 4). No census or other information is available with regard to Sir Sayyid Nagar or Ektanagar. Dhaurara was listed only in the 1951 census as a village in Koil *tahsil*, but is not included in either the Aligarh municipality or the Legislative Assembly constituency. Census and electoral data are, however, available for all other areas included in the AMU list.

Let us now examine the available evidence on these riot-hit areas and what was said to me concerning the happenings therein. Insofar as Nagla Mallah is concerned, there is no census information whatsoever on this village up to the present. It is located on the northeastern outskirts of the city (Maps 1 and 4) along a road by the same name to the east of the AMU campus. According to the voters' lists for 1995, the *mohalla* was communally mixed; out of 1,766 voters, 1,131 or 64 percent were Muslim (see Table 6.3), the rest Hindus and others. One of my informants referred to it as a small village inhabited, as the name would suggest, by "a community called Mallahs." Mallahs are a somewhat notorious caste in northern India, fishermen and boatmen by tra-ditional occupation, many of whom live on or near the banks of rivers, who are said to engage in numerous forms of criminal activity such as looting and smuggling, in addition to or instead of their traditional occupation. The same informant previously cited alleged that, from this village, Mallahs came out to attack Muslims in various places, such as Shah Jamal and Sarai Sultani, both areas some distance from Nagla Mallah. He alleged further that this was a deliberate, planned operation that was part of a general strategy to attack "the Muslim community from every corner."[38]

Shah Jamal (no. 69 in Maps 1 and 4), whence rioting began on November 1, was mentioned very frequently in my interviews. No census information is available on this site either. However, it can be precisely located and described. It lies to the south of the Khair Road leading westward out of the city from the Delhi Gate. It is close to one of the most important religious sites for Muslims in Aligarh City, the Ustad Sahib ka Dargah (no. 70 in Map 1), a shrine that "attracts a wide following from Aligarh District, among Hindus and Muslims."[39] In 1990–91, however, despite its intercommunal appeal— not at all uncommon for such shrines throughout northern India—the area in which it was located was, according to numerous accounts, a site for deliberate attack by Hindu rioters and the PAC. The informant just cited included this area among several others never attacked before to argue that there was "a plan, . . . a pre-plan because . . . in every corner of the city, even this area [AMU campus], behind Medical College, Jamalpur area, and then . . . around the whole city, Shah Jamal area, . . . all these small pockets, they were just burned and even Qazipara, . . . in the last forty-three years of Independence, they never attacked." Insofar as the Shah Jamal area is concerned, this informant alleged that a concerted attack was launched upon it by persons living in the new colony of Indira Nagar (no. 68 in Maps 1 and 4) just across the Khair Road from Shah Jamal, along with PAC personnel.

The *mufti shahar* also referred to the violence in Shah Jamal and noted that communal violence erupted in that area on the very night on which curfew was imposed in Aligarh.[40] Still another Muslim informant reported to me that "some element of [the] Hindu community attacked the Shah Jamal community and, in return, there was pelting [of] stones from both the communities. And when the police action was started, the police action was one-sided." The police even attacked and damaged some portions of a mosque in Shah Jamal.[41] Six persons, this informant claimed, including two women, were killed in police firing in this area.

Also of great interest is the fact that two new colonies in the northeastern outskirts of the city and just to the northeast of the AMU campus as well, Hamdardnagar and Jamalpur (Maps 1 and 4), came under heavy attack.[42] Hamdardnagar comprises all of ward no. 36 and had 3,193 voters in 1995, all of whom were Muslims; the adjacent ward, no. 41, comprises Badamnagar as well as Hamdardnagar, the two settlements being lumped together in the voters' list. The corporator for ward 36 was a Muslim, elected as an independent. The BJP had no candidate in this ward. The corporator for ward 41, also a Muslim, was elected on the SP ticket. The BJP polled a mere 59 votes out of 2,350 cast in this ward.

Two villages were listed in the 1951 census under the name Jamalpur: Jamalpur Muafi (Mafi) and Jamalpur Sia. The latter has remained in the rural *tahsil,* while Jamalpur Mafi has been incorporated in the municipality along with another village not listed in any census, called Jamalpur ka Nagla (Map 1). The population of Jamalpur Mafi in 1951 was recorded as 1,027, of whom 259 (25.22 percent) were Scheduled Castes. The two Jamalpur villages comprised all of ward number 30 in 1995. The total voting population in this ward in 1995 was 8,190 (Table 6.3). Seven candidates contested the 1995 corporation election, of whom five were Muslim. The winning candidate, a Muslim independent, gained 1,446 out of the total 4,737 valid votes cast (30.53 percent). The BJP candidate, a Hindu, polled second from last with a mere 148 votes. The second Hindu candidate polled better than the BJP, but still quite miserably, with only 323 votes. So, the vote for the two Hindu candidates combined accounted for less than 10 percent of the total valid votes polled (9.94 percent). The locality is overwhelmingly Muslim. It is also said to have a large population of Qureshis.[43]

In Jamalpur, I was told that 7 or 8 people were killed in police firings.[44] The PUCL report, cited earlier, also took note of the spreading of the riots in 1990–91 to areas in the Civil Lines near the university, including the Zakaria Market, Hamdardnagar, and Jamalpur. Hamdardnagar, the report noted, "is a purely Muslim area" that was attacked by a "Hindu mob from nearby villages." Here, also, "a number of Muslims were killed by PAC firing." Jamalpur was described in the same report as "a Muslim area with a small Hindu pocket—about 95% Muslims and 5% Hindus." In the rioting here, "one Hindu was stabbed to death and another injured" and, confirming my own interview just cited, "a number of Muslims were killed in PAC/Police firing."[45] The *Times of India* also remarked upon the incidents in these two localities as follows.

> Violence spread to the outskirts of the city today when members of two communities clashed at Hamdard Nagar and Jabalpur [Jamalpur], hardly half-a-km from Aligarh Muslim University (AMU). The Provincial Armed Constabulary (PAC) personnel opened fire to disperse the rioters, killing at least five persons. Officially, however, only three deaths were reported from these localities. . . .
>
> Contrary to official reports, bloody clashes took place on the city outskirts this morning. A mob of 2,000 people set afire many houses in Hamdard Nagar locality. Residents of the area narrated gory tales of PAC brutality. When this reporter visited the house of two brothers, who were shot by the PAC personnel in their residence, the victims' fresh blood stains were still visible. The widows said their husbands, both rickshaw-pullers, were at home when six PAC

jawans barged in and despite repeated pleas shot them from point blank range. "They were innocent. Please remove the PAC or they will kill all of us," one of them said, wailing uncontrollably. Their neighbours expressed the same apprehension. Scores of residents began to migrate to safer places after the firing, with their scanty belongings.

The scene at the AMU's Jawaharlal Nehru Medical College was heartrending. The bodies of the five killed in Hamdard Nagar were still lying in the hospital with those of victims from other localities.[46]

These incidents near the AMU occurred a day after the massacres of Muslims on the Gomti Express and a day before the circulation of the false newspaper stories concerning the killing of Hindus at the AMU Medical College Hospital.

These new areas are sites of an influx of Muslim migrants from the rural areas, whose presence has been particularly noted by Krishna Kumar Navman. Navman estimates Muslim migration to these new areas altogether, including other sites such as Jiwangarh, which lies just to the east of Nagla Mallah, and Bhojpur on the southern side of the city, has amounted to twenty to twenty-five thousand persons. Most important from Navman's point of view is his claim that, although some of these new areas lie outside the boundary of the Aligarh City Legislative Assembly constituency, the Muslims have succeeded in registering to vote illegally in the constituency and have voted against him.[47] It would stray too far from what is known to say that this information suggests preplanning on the part of Navman and the BJP to teach these Muslims a lesson or to encourage their out-migration. It can only be said for certain that these new areas of Muslim migration were hit hard in 1990–91, that they were hit for the first time in the history of Aligarh at that time, that their presence in the city limits is resented by militant Hindus, and that, therefore, they are sites of political contestation for control of the constituency that, as we will see in succeeding chapters, has been closely fought.

Jiwangarh in 1951 was an insignificant place with a small population. However, forty years later, it had become a huge *mohalla* with an electorate of 10,266, of whom 98 percent were Muslim (Table 6.3). It comprised six polling stations in the Legislative Assembly constituency and the bulk of two wards in the municipality. Navman polled a mere 84 votes out of 1,919 cast in 1989, and *zero* votes in the six polling stations in the 1991 elections. Of course, I cannot determine whether or not any of the votes cast in these polling stations were illegal, but they certainly posed a serious threat at that time to Navman's and the BJP's continued predominance in the constituency.

Let us consider now the locality of Bhojpur, also hit for the first time in the riots of 1990–91. It is located on the southern outskirts of the city below and to the southwest of the Sasni Gate (Maps 1, 2, and 4). In the 1951 census, it was listed as a village in Koil *tahsil* with a total population of 451, of whom 99 (21.9 percent) were Scheduled Castes, but there was no breakdown by religion. The voters' list for 1984 listed 1,186 voters, of whom I have been able to identify positively 752 Muslim names, giving a Muslim population percentage of 63.41 percent (Table 6.3).

Before 1967, Bhojpur was included within the Koil Rural Legislative Assembly constituency. Since 1967, it has been included within the Aligarh municipality and in the Aligarh City Legislative Assembly constituency. Because of its relatively small population, it was lumped together with other *mohallas* in the polling stations of which it was a part, with seven other *mohallas* in the 1996 and 1968 delimitations and with two other *mohallas* in the 1980 and 1985 delimitations. However, by 1989, its population and number of voters had grown sufficiently for Bhojpur alone to comprise four polling stations. I have the polling station results for two elections conducted after and based upon this delimitation, the 1989 and 1991 Legislative Assembly elections, which sandwiched the great riots of 1990–91. They are of great interest from several points of view. In 1989 and 1991, 1,443 and 1,604 votes, respectively, were cast in these polling stations. Of these votes, 75.26 and 78.05 percent, respectively, went to the Janata Dal candidates, who were, in both elections, Muslims, while 15.66 and 17.02 percent went to the BJP candidate, who was, in both elections, Krishna Kumar Navman.

However, there was a marked difference in the results among the four polling stations. In polling stations 184 and 195, the BJP polled 29.90 percent in 1989 and 35.19 percent in 1991, while the Janata Dal polled 58.67 percent and 59.24 percent, respectively. However, in polling stations 186 and 187, the BJP polled a mere 1.91 percent and 1.62 percent in the two elections, while the Janata Dal polled 91.28 percent and 94.01 percent. In these elections, the Janata Dal was seen by Muslims as their main protection against the militant Hindu onslaught against the Babri Masjid and as the party most likely to defeat the BJP and its candidate, considered by Muslims to be the leading riot-monger in the Hindu community; as will be shown in detail in later chapters, Muslims voted overwhelmingly for this party in nearly all *mohallas* of Aligarh City. It can be safely assumed that virtually all Muslims in these polling stations voted for the Janata Dal and that most Hindus voted for the BJP. In short, in the elections that preceded and followed the riots in Aligarh in which Bhojpur was badly hit, the electorate in this area was politically polarized.

In 1995, Bhojpur comprised approximately half of ward 23 in the municipal elections, which were won by the Samajwadi Party of Mulayam Singh Yadav with a Muslim candidate. In an election in which there were ten candidates, all but one of whom were Muslim, the winning candidate garnered 1,286 votes out of 4,066 votes cast (31.63 percent). The lone Hindu candidate, contesting on the ticket of the BJP, polled 518 votes (12.74 percent).

It is clear, therefore, from all the demographic data and the election results available that pinpoint this locality, that it is preponderantly Muslim, that its population has increased greatly since 1951, presumably by in-migration from the rural areas, that the BJP has little strength here and probably none from Muslims, and that the Hindu and Muslim populations in the locality are sharply divided politically.

There were two reports in the *Times of India* concerning rioting in Bhojpur. One referred to "a[n] . . . outbreak of violence in the Bhojpura [*sic*] locality" on the night of December 28. The news reports linked the violence here to two factors. The first was a visit to the city on December 25 by the chief minister, Mulayam Singh Yadav. "A senior police official" was reported to have said that, as a reaction to his visit, "there appeared to be a 'deliberate attempt' to engineer violence in certain parts of the city." The second "major factor" was said to be "the relationship between the Muslim community and the Provincial Armed Constabulary (PAC)" that had "now definitely reached 'boiling point.'" The disenchantment of Muslims with the PAC had led, it was said, to "militancy in a section of the Muslims, who are seeking 'desperate solutions.'" So, it went on, when violence broke out in Bhojpur on the night of December 28, "the PAC opened fire and, according to official figures, two persons were killed. But local residents claim that at least another three persons are missing and accuse the PAC of disposing of their bodies."[48]

A second report from the same newspaper stated that there was violence again in this locality on the night of January 1, when "police resorted to firing at Bhojpura [*sic*] locality when some miscreants set five houses on fire. Two of them received bullet injuries. They hurled bombs at policemen in retaliation. Two persons were stabbed to death in Bhojpura."[49]

I have comments in my interviews on the happenings in Bhojpur during these riots from the *mufti shahar* and from riot victims who were beaten and who lost relations. The mufti, who had stressed that most of the violence in these riots had been directed against Muslims on the outskirts of the city, noted also that such violence had occurred on the southern and western outskirts in areas such as Laria, Jangal Garhi, and Bhojpur (Map 2). I also heard

victim accounts of the happenings in Bhojpur from several residents, including two bearded Muslims, who said that the police entered their house, pulled
their beards, and "beat them mercilessly" on the night of December 31. I asked
if there was any reason for the police behavior and received the following reply.

> The police opened the door and asked us, "Where are your sons? They were
> firing from here." But none of us was firing and we don't have anything. So,
> just pretending about the firing, they said, "Beat them up."
> PRB: But there was no firing from the house at all, nor firing from the roof?
> INTERLOCUTOR: No.
> PRB: Nothing in the locality?
> INTERLOCUTOR: There was firing in the locality, but it was police firing and
>     one person was killed by the police, a boy of nine years.
> PRB: And it's not possible the police were making some mistake, only they were
>     doing this just to harass, not making some mistake?
> INTERLOCUTOR: No, no, they are harassing. They're doing it deliberately.
> PRB: And this is police or PAC?
> INTERLOCUTOR: He's saying—he's a very old man—[he's saying] I can't
>     differentiate. . . . He's saying they broke open the door. He's crying with pain.
> PRB: From being beaten?
> INTERLOCUTOR: Yah, yah. With the rifle butts. And these are the [people].
>     [Laughing sardonically.] According to them, according to police and the
>     PAC, these are the rioters. These people and that woman, these are the riot-
>     ers. [Laughs ironically again.] They can't walk, they can't stand up straight.
>     You see. [Again laughing ironically.] They can fire and they can make the
>     riots. What a fun.[50]

In reflecting on these events in Bhojpur, it should be noted that no connections
have been explicitly made to economic factors, caste-communal rivalries in
the *mohalla,* or any other factors by those who commented upon them in the
press and in my interviews. All we know for sure is that, like other localities
on the outskirts of the city that were hit for the first time during these riots,
Bhojpur has been a site of greatly increased in-migration of Muslims and a
site also of great political concern to the BJP for that very reason. If, however, it was the intention of anti-Muslim rioters, whoever they may have been,
to provide negative incentives to the Muslim residents of Bhojpur and other
such areas to move out of these areas and back to their villages, it failed. Indeed,
on the contrary, one of my respondents claimed that there had been a considerable further influx of Muslims from the rural areas into these localities

that turned the balance against the BJP in successive elections, leading to its ultimate defeat,[51] which will be analyzed in subsequent chapters. According to my estimates from the 1984 and 1995 voters' lists and the corporation election count of actual voters, the number of voters, most assuredly mostly Muslims, tripled in one decade in this locality, a matter of the greatest political concern to the BJP.

Two other areas close to the university were mentioned in the AMU list of affected sites, Anupshahr Road and Bhamola. Anupshahr Road was classed as a *mohalla* in the 1951 census. It had then a population of 1,105, of whom 930 (84.16 percent) were Muslim. In 1995, Anupshahr Road was included in ward 57, University, which comprised, as suggested by its name, other localities in the neighborhood of the AMU. The number of electors in this ward was 3,686 at that time, of whom 3,500 (94.95 percent were Muslim). The area also comprised six polling stations in the 1989 and 1991 elections. The Janata Dal was the favored party in both elections, winning 85.99 percent of the vote with Khwaja Halim as the candidate in 1989 and 80.85 percent with Mohammad Sufiyan as the candidate in 1991. The BJP was of little consequence in these polling stations, where Navman polled less than 4 percent in 1989 and less than 5 percent in 1991.

Bhamola, unlike Anupshahr Road, fits better in the category of the new and newly incorporated areas that have experienced an influx of Muslim residents and voters. In 1951, it was a village in Koil *tahsil* with a total population of 880, of whom 229 (26 percent) were Scheduled Castes. No information was provided on the Muslim population. In 1995, Bhamola comprised the largest portion of ward 53, along with another village called Nagla Munda. Bhamola was then predominantly Muslim. It comprised all of four polling stations and half of another shared with Nagla Munda. In the former four polling stations, the percentage of Muslim voters ranged between 55.57 and 88.89 percent, whereas Nagla Munda, on which incomplete information is available, appears to have been either completely or overwhelmingly Hindu and others. The ward, therefore, was divided in its communal composition, which was in turn reflected in the election results. The winning candidate, a Muslim independent, was elected with less than 40 percent of the vote.

In the 1989 and 1991 elections, Bhamola alone comprised all of four polling stations, numbers 46 to 49, in which, as in Anupshahr Road, the Janata Dal candidates polled higher both times, but with less strong majorities of 60.57 and 66.61 percent, respectively. Navman had some strength here, having polled 28.09 and 21.76 percent, respectively, in the two elections.

The addition of Anupshahr Road and Bhamola to the long list of areas that experienced unprecedented communal violence in the northern half of the city brings out another feature of the 1990–91 riots, namely, that the entire university area was encircled by riotous violence. It cannot be said that such violence was instigated entirely by Hindus or by RSS/BJP/Bajrang Dal activists. In fact, there was even a suggestion in the above-mentioned AMU list of disturbed sites that the safety of "non-Muslim teachers" was threatened in the Medical College colony. It was noted therein that these non-Muslim teachers "were extremely apprehensive of [their lives] and property particularly because of the infiltration of large number of refugees where it was felt that anti-social elements have also got mixed up." The AMU authorities, therefore, requested the DM to post a CRPF force therein, which was done on the night of December 9.

A further factor mentioned to me in interviews concerning these riots concerned the alleged participation of persons from Scheduled Castes, on the instigation of non–Scheduled Caste Hindus, in attacks on Muslims, as well as alleged Muslim attacks on Scheduled Castes. In particular, the locality of Qazipara (Map 2) was mentioned, which lies in the heart of the old city but, as noted above by one respondent, had never been hit by riots since Independence, until these riots. The same respondent alleged that Scheduled Castes, who had in previous riots sided with Muslims, had been instigated, incited, bribed, and provided with liquor by "RSS people" to attack Muslims in this and other localities. It was even alleged that some masked persons, presumably Hindus masquerading as Muslims, deliberately killed Scheduled Caste persons in order to incite them to attack Muslims in retaliation. It was said also that the attack on Qazipara was launched in this way from a new colony, on which I have no information, known as Jagjivan Rampur after the famous Scheduled Caste leader.[52]

While there is no way to prove or disprove these allegations, two localities adjacent to Qazipara—Sarai Qazi and Samnapara (Map 2)—are overwhelmingly populated by Scheduled Castes, their proportion in these localities in 1951 having been recorded as 93.16 percent and 88.50 percent, respectively. Moreover, similar accounts were provided in the PUCL report, which noted that Qazipara, like several other *mohalla*s in the old city that were attacked during these riots, was surrounded by predominantly Hindu areas and that "Kazipara [sic] was attacked by a mob from the nearby Harijan colony." The report also referred to instigation of Scheduled Castes by persons from the Hindu "trading community to attack Muslims" in another locality called Sarai Hakim Takia. It was also noted that the Harijan colony in this area had been attacked by Muslims and Harijan houses had been burnt and looted.[53]

The *Times of India* also reported that "a Harijan youth" had been killed on November 24 in Ghuria Bagh locality in the old city, another *mohalla* with a large population (above 20 percent) of Scheduled Castes, and that the incident "had led to renewed tension in some parts of the old city" on November 25.[54]

Finally, it also deserves to be noted that the participation of Scheduled Castes in attacks on Muslims—and on Sikhs in the 1984 riots in Delhi—was reported from other areas of the country as well during this period. In one case, in Kanpur City, of which I have personal and direct knowledge and information, these attacks were led by a Scheduled Caste leader who was at the time a member of the BJP and who was made into a hero by the RSS and Jan Sangh leaders in the city for his activities during the post-Ayodhya riots there in December 1992.[55]

All the evidence available, therefore, suggests that the enlargement of the spatial spread of disturbances in 1990–91 compared to all previous riots in the history of the city may have been related to two factors: first, the in-migration of Muslims to outlying areas of the city, which has been resented by militant Hindus and has posed obstacles to the maintenance of the recently ascendant BJP in the political life of the city; second, the recruitment of Scheduled Castes into the process of riot production, probably not for the first time, but in a much more significant way at this time. That evidence also suggests the possibility openly stated to me by respondents and reported by the PUCL and the press that these enlarged attacks on new areas of the city were deliberate and preplanned.[56] I cannot say that proof has been provided on these matters, for proof has been made impossible by the failure of the authorities to appoint an inquiry commission that might have explored these matters in Aligarh, as in most other parts of the country.[57]

Moreover, the circumstantial evidence that indicates selective targeting of *mohallas* is somewhat mixed. All the *mohallas* on the outskirts of the city that were attacked in 1990–91, except Hamdardnagar, were part of the Legislative Assembly constituency in the two elections of 1989 and 1991. But there are several other overwhelmingly Muslim *mohallas* located in ward no. 31, Firdous Nagar (Map 1), located to the northwest of the AMU and close to the very hard-hit area of Jamalpur. In addition to the *mohalla* by the same name, there are three other localities in this ward: Kila Road (part), Shahinshahabad, and Maulana Azad Nagar (Map 1). The total voting population of the ward in 1995 was 4,443, of whom the estimated proportion of Muslim voters was 98 percent.[58] The corporator elected in 1995 was a Muslim on the ticket of the SP, the nemesis of the BJP. However, this area did not suffer in the 1990–91 riots. While there may be other reasons for its having escaped attack, it deserves note that the area was *not* a part of the Legislative Assembly constituency. On the other hand, Hamdardnagar, which was part of the constituency, *was* attacked.

On the whole, however, it is clear enough that, though some areas of Muslim in-migration and population expansion did escape attack, all the outlying areas that suffered *were* areas of concentrated Muslim population and in-migration. Such evidence of deliberate targeting also further demonstrates the importance of going beyond ecological analysis of demographic factors in the search for the causes of rioting. It is not that an ecological analysis would ignore the differences in, say, the communal/caste/ethnic composition of different sites or the proportion of migrants—very common sources of explanation, indeed, for riots everywhere in the world—as explanations for their occurrence here and not there. Rather, it is that such analyses are useful only to describe the sites of disturbances, but cannot be used to explain why they have occurred here and not there. Social science research that stops at the statistical demonstration of an association, even when it asserts that the finding of an association does not demonstrate causality, provides raw material for uninformed speculation. Only through on-site observation at the micro level can we begin to grope towards the truth of things, towards the actualities of human agency, purposive activity, and active production of violence.

## A Visit to Sarai Sultani

In April 1999, I visited Sarai Sultani and interviewed persons in the locality concerning the history of communal violence there. My primary informant was a Qureshi Muslim bicycle lock manufacturer, nephew of the municipal corporator from that area. His lock business has a turnover of three million rupees annually and employs forty persons who produce twelve hundred locks per day. He sends all his production to the Delhi markets. He sells his locks for Rs. 14 each; they are sold on the retail market at around Rs. 32 each. A Muslim manufacturer, his locks are sold under the brand name "Krishna," the name of a Hindu deity.

I had actually not planned to interview this informant, but his uncle, the municipal corporator. It was only by chance, while waiting for his uncle, who never arrived, that in the course of conversation we discussed the communal situation in the area. I summarize below the gist of that very lengthy conversation.[59]

FIG. 6.6. Lock manufacturing, Sarai Sultani, Aligarh, 1999

He said that only Muslims live in this *mohalla* of Sarai Sultani. There are no Hindus living in the *mohalla*. However, there are Hindus living on all sides of Sarai Sultani and Hindu organizations as well, as the tongue is between all the teeth. Pointing in different directions, he said that is the side of the Bajrang Dal, that is the side of Vishwa Hindu Parishad, that is the side of the Hindu Mahasabha office, that is the side of the RSS, that is the main circuit of the riots.

Several Muslim *baradaris* live in Sarai Sultani, including Qureshis, Dhobis, Ansaris, and Kumhars, among whom the Qureshis constitute about 40 percent of the total population.

Conversation concerning riots in the area began in response to a general question that I put to him concerning whether or not there had been riots in this *mohalla*.

He began quite emphatically by referring to his personal experiences in 1979[60] when he himself was beaten by the police, as a consequence of which parts of his body had swelled and never returned to normal, including a knob on his head that he showed me as well as a knee injury. Further, his father, his brothers, his uncle, the whole family were beaten and jailed by the police. For two days, on the 19th and 20th in the month of June [invariably a month of hellish heat and humidity], they were held without being given water to drink. When they asked for water, they were told to piss and drink.[61]

I questioned him repeatedly concerning whether or not they had done anything, provoked the police in any way, given them any ground whatsoever for beating and jailing them.

> That night they were just sleeping and the police came and surrounded the whole area and they called him up, called up his neighbors also and they all, all the police force, took them away to the police station. There were five police stations in the area and they took them to one only 50 meters away from his house.

I asked again, "But they were sleeping, doing nothing?"

> Yes, nothing. They were doing nothing but sleeping that night. I asked then why the police came and called them out. He said that, because the riot was going on around the area and there was no other Muslim mohalla anywhere in this area, so they came to this mohalla.

One might question how the entire family could have been sleeping blissfully, doing nothing, in the midst of the turmoil of a riot in the area. However, the family was in no position to do anything else, unless they were deliberately seeking trouble, since curfew had been imposed two days earlier on the 17th of June.

> So, I asked again, what did he think, what was the reason the police came here? The main factor was communal feeling. They saw that here there are Muslims, so why not drive them away from here? They feel that there are two Muslim parts in this [broad] area. One is Upar Kot and the other is this place. So why not drive them away and kill those Upar Kot people also?

He repeated again that all his family members were beaten bitterly and their bones were broken.

I asked yet again, trying to find some justification for such police behavior: the Muslims in here did not come out and fight?

> They were just sleeping and when they got up, they found that the whole area is surrounded by the police, and particularly by PAC, and with them, there were people of Hindu organizations like Bajrang Dal, Hindu Mahasabha, and RSS.

I then said, "But, you know, if I talk to the police, they will say the Muslims come out, they come out in the street and we have to shoot to protect ourselves and that the Muslims are aggressors and so forth. [There was] no attack on the [police], they were not angry because Muslims had come out and attacked them anywhere?"

> No, no, no. Our total population is only 2,000, and that includes women and children, so how can Muslims, being such a small population, go and attack anywhere or attack anybody? It's difficult to defend ourselves, how can we be offenders? So, we defend, we always try to defend ourselves; never are we the aggressors.
>
> PRB: So the police came here and dragged you out, [and beat you] with *lathis*.
> RESPONDENT: Yes, yes. The police called all the young men from their houses and they collected them all. There were around fifty-five. The police gathered them near the main entrance [to the *mohalla*].
> PRB: And beat them there?
> RESPONDENT: While they were gathered there, there were two groups of police on different sides. One group was calling them [residents] to this side and the other was calling them to that side. While they [the residents] were going to one side, the other group [of police] was saying you are going to that side, you are trying to run away, and so they started picking on these people bitterly.
> INTERLOCUTOR: So, all the parts of their bodies were broken and their bodies started bleeding, including his body and his uncle's. He had seven stitches.

At this point, he again showed me his knee that had been cut with a bayonet and a big bump on his head from a *lathi* blow.

*The 1990 Riots.* This respondent had much to say also about the 1990 riots in Sarai Sultani. Recall that several secondary sources and my informants in 1991 had referred to the incidents in Sarai Sultani, precipitated by a bomb thrown at a mosque. The mosque is actually not in Sarai Sultani, but in the adjacent, mostly Hindu *mohalla* of Barai. Here is what he had to say about it.

> Nineteen-ninety was the biggest riot. Here the nearby masjid [mosque] was burned. The imam [prayer leader] was in the mosque at the time and was burned alive. One M. M. Jain had a furnace[62] nearby. Twenty-two Muslims were taken there and all of them were thrown in the furnace and burned alive. This was done in the presence of the Station Officer, one Sharma, from Sasni Gate police station. He is a very infamous person because of this incident.
>
> One person [whom I soon met] survived this incident, but all his family

members were killed. Since that time, he has become mad and a drunkard. One of the survivors of this incident also had a sister, who had just been married when the riots broke out and she was raped by the police for seven days, after which she was killed.

Once again, I asked: "And that time also there was no provocation on the part of the Muslims here? There was curfew. Muslims stayed in their houses or the Muslims had come out and the police came?"

No, there was no provocation on the part of the Muslims. They didn't provoke anybody. On this side, in Barai, there are only five houses of Muslims and there are 5,000 Hindus, so how can anybody imagine that people from these five houses go and provoke and challenge those 5,000? He also had his own personal story to tell about the 1990 riots.

At that time, his factory was being constructed. There were five Hindu laborers working in this factory, so, when the riots began, he called the police and handed over all the five workers to the police.

But at that time, his own brother [cousin-brother, that is, mother's sister's son], a ten-year-old boy at the time, was shot in his hands and a bomb was thrown at him and exploded on his stomach, as a consequence of which that part of his body was burned. [I later met the young man and saw the wounds; see Figure 6.7.] At the same time, two Muslim men, one of them a prominent district Congress officer, were also shot and injured. He himself was just sitting here at his factory when his brother was injured. The injuries to his brother occurred at the entrance to the mohalla, not far from the factory, quite near the police chowki. He went to the site and had a confrontation with the police and the district authorities who were there, including the District Magistrate and the SSP. He asked the police there how could it happen that the Hindus shot [sic] his brother while you were here, but they had no answer. He then had a heated exchanged with the SSP and the DM, but they also had no answer. He was just asking how come the whole administration is here and the Hindus are killing my brother? What are you doing here?

Yet again, trying to find some reasonable explanation for these incidents, I said to him, but there was curfew, what were your brother and you doing out during curfew? He replied that the curfew was off for two hours when his brother went out and was shot. In fact, he said he asked the administration, the DM and the SSP, "How come there was still a half-hour remaining

and you imposed curfew a half-hour early?" It appears that, while the curfew was off for those two hours, there was a big fight and the curfew had been
reimposed.

There was yet a further atrocious incident in Sarai Sultani in 1990 that this
respondent recounted, which occurred while he was at the AMU Medical
College, where he had taken his injured brother for treatment.

> According to his account, during the 1990 riots, there was curfew for 21 con-
> tinuous days. And there was no water, no electricity, no milk, and the children
> were weeping because they did not even have any milk to drink. [This seems
> to contradict his earlier statement that curfew was lifted for two hours each
> day.] And so, what happened was that two women entered the Hindu area
> and took their children, two children, aged four and five years, also with them,
> to the entrance point of the mohalla. At the entrance point, the PAC men asked
> them why they had come there. Then the women said that we have come for
> milk, we have to get milk. So these PAC men took the two children with them
> and the milk pot and went away while the two women were standing there wait
> ing for the milk, but what happened actually was that these PAC men burned
> those two children alive.
>
> PRB: Burned them alive!
> RESPONDENT: Yes.
> PRB: How did they know that they were Muslims?
> RESPONDENT: They were sure that, because they were coming from the side
> of Sarai Sultani, these women had masked themselves, but were actually
> Muslims. Besides, there were Bajrangi men sitting there and they knew that
> they must be Muslim women. This incident of the burning alive of the two
> children has been [officially] recorded.

*Other Riots in and around Sarai Sultani.* Having listened to this respondent's
accounts of riot activity in the two most severe riots in post-Independence
Aligarh, I inquired whether or not he had experienced any other difficulties
in the years between 1979 and 1990. He replied that he had many difficulties
during that long period. He said that there had been several disturbances in
the early 1980s. However, there was a period of relative calm in the mid-1980s,
which he attributed to the judicious administration of District Magistrate K. M.
Punia, a Scheduled Caste man from the Jatav caste, whom I knew personally
as well.[63] Punia, being a Jatav, was favorable to the Muslims, supported the
Muslims, and appointed several Muslims, including the respondent, to peace

committees of police and citizens. This respondent referred to Punia in English as "my best friend."

After Punia left, a new DM was appointed, one Gupta, during whose tenure a riot occurred in the nearby flower market. This respondent described this riot as being directly connected to economic competition between Hindu and Muslim flower sellers. The problem here was that there were some Hindus as well as Muslims in that market, in the flower business, and they sold flowers at Rs. 500 per [quantity not given] whereas Muslims sold the same quantity of flowers at only Rs. 200. So, that led to the tension and the entire Muslim market was burned by Ram Bhakts [devotees of Ram], Bajrang Dal people. When the Muslims went to see the district administration to ask what these Ram Bhakts were doing there and why were they allowed to burn the whole market, the DM said: "What can we do? We can't do anything." And, in that trouble, about Rs. 50 lakh [5 million] worth of property was destroyed.

I asked then whether there had been any problems in Sarai Sultani since the great 1990 riots. He said there had been disturbances in 1992 during the Babri Masjid movement, but that there had been no problems in Sarai Sultani thanks to the actions of the local police commanding officer, one Subhash Baghel, who, like Punia, was also a Scheduled Caste man. The respondent had a personal acquaintance with him, a good relationship with him.

He was sent to this area since this was a known trouble spot. Baghel sealed the entire area around Sarai Sultani and there was no incident of communal violence. Further, he told the population of the area that, if there is any disturbance, there will be great trouble for the whole population. And he told the policemen that, if even a single incident occurs, [they] will be responsible for that. So, no incident occurred at that time.

He went on to remark that, normally, whenever curfew is imposed in the city, it is only the Muslims who have to undergo all kind of troubles and suffering. But, if you go into any Hindu area at such times, you won't feel there is any kind of curfew. But, when this Subhash Baghel was in this area, then the Hindus for the first time realized what is curfew because he sealed the whole area.

At that time, there was only one small incident at Adda Hathras, where there is a small mosque and these Ram Bhakts attempted to burn the mosque. But, this Subhash Baghel put a stop to it and the masjid was not burned. And, in that incident, 25 people, Hindus, were arrested and they were beaten.

At the end of my interview with this respondent, he expressed his hopelessness and fear for the future if he continued to live in Sarai Sultani.

He's not very hopeful. He fears his future at this place. He says it's actually hopeless. He says that he will ultimately have to leave this place. He's not safe here, he does not feel safe here. Always, these days, these Bajrang Dal people and VHP people are increasing their activities, different kinds of activities, different kinds of programs. They sometimes start processions in all these areas, so these people feel very threatened. He gave one example that, during kite flying season, these people write very abusive things against the Muslims on their kites, saying Muslims go away from here, and they write abuses against mothers and sisters. There have also been incidents of some pamphlets issued by the Bajrang Dal and VHP people saying that you, the Muslims, leave this place, you have no right to live over here. When the Muslims here report these matters to the police, the police say what can we do? We cannot do anything. But the Muslims are hesitant to leave this place. They think that if they leave these places, their mosques will be deserted. Already, there are areas from which the Muslims are leaving: for example, they have vacated five or ten houses in Barai and in other places. And, in those areas, there are around 25 mosques and they are deserted, nobody goes there to offer prayer. In this area also, there are six mosques. They think that, if they leave the place and go somewhere else, these mosques will be desecrated. Nevertheless, they are thinking of leaving this place and going to the university area because they do not feel safe here.

What the Hindus want is to provoke the Muslims and kill them. They want some kind of pretext to kill them, so they try to provoke Muslims and kill Muslims. They try to make the Muslims react and then they kill. Suppose, for example, there is some small incident, somebody is beaten or somebody is killed, and the news spreads like wildfire all over an area. Suppose this incident occurs anywhere in the city, it will spread everywhere and the whole area will be disturbed and then the killing starts. Many people are killed. It can happen anywhere in the city. Any Muslim can be anywhere around here in this area or in the Hindu area mainly. While they are [walking], since this kind of news spreads so fast, they may be killed in any spot here or there. So, they do not feel safe in this area. There is no hope.

After this very long interview, I was taken through the *mohalla* to visit the sites where the several incidents occurred to which the respondent referred. I visited the mosque and met the survivor from the group of 22 people who had been thrown into the furnace in 1990, all of whose family members had been part of the number killed. I was shown newly constructed houses that had replaced the ones that had been burned.

I also visited the mosque in the adjacent *mohalla* of Jogipara where the imam had been burned to death in 1990. At this spot, I interviewed a Muslim man who had been taking care of the mosque and who formerly owned five houses adjacent to it. I was told that he had sold four of the houses to Hindus. The reason given was that the Hindus were trying to push him out by threatening him, so he had to sell these houses at low prices. He still maintained a small cloth shop there. I was told that this was the very person whose family members had been burned to death and whose daughter and sister had been raped and who had gone mad since then. I was told also that he had given many interviews of this type and had shown these places to other people, other intellectuals also.

I was shown also a small garden park that this Muslim man owned, which the Hindus are also pressuring him to sell. However, since it is just next to the mosque, he feels that it will be a threat to the mosque if he sells it to the Hindus, for it will come under their control and they will disrespect it. And, if the Hindus did so, nobody would come to the support of the Muslims, neither the administration nor the police nor anybody. I was taken to a shop owned by a Muslim man and shown a formerly Muslim house that had been purchased by Hindus for a very small amount. I was shown a small community hall that had been used by persons from the Muslim community for marriage ceremonies or other parties. I was shown a small platform and walls that had been damaged by Hindus. The place was occupied by buffaloes belonging to Hindus, who are trying to seize the property. I also met the younger cousin-brother of the respondent, who raised his shirt to show me the wounds he had suffered from the bomb blast when he was a youth. (See Figure 6.7.)

During the latter half of this tour, a young Hindu man appeared in an alleyway on a motorcycle. He idled his cycle and stopped to watch us as we moved about. In a brief exchange of words with him, he urged me to meet with the Hindu municipal corporator from the area. I made an appointment to do so and met the corporator the next morning, but he had virtually nothing to say to me.

*Summary.* How can we summarize the situation in Sarai Sultani? First, it is a context in which Muslims live in a locality in which they feel and are in fact surrounded by Hindu-majority localities. Second, it is not just an amorphous Hindu population that surrounds them, but a range of Hindu militant groups and organizations located at points all around their *mohalla*. Third,

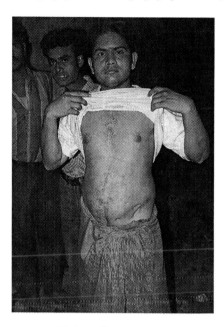

FIG. 6.7. Victim of bomb blast in 1990 riots

these groups are said to engage and I believe do engage in provocative actions directed against the Muslim population. Their very presence is a provocation since they are anti-Muslim organizations, promote a cult of violence, and have an organization, the Bajrang Dal, specifically devoted to the practice of violence against Muslims.[64] Fourth, it is not only the militant Hindu groups who are perceived as hostile to the Muslims, but other elements in the population. My interviews contain references to specific acts in "normal" times such as the alleged writing of nasty anti-Muslim curses on kites. Further, the interviews in Sarai Sultani and elsewhere point to the existence of other elements in the population who seek to take advantage of Muslim discomfiture to acquire their property at cheap prices and to compel them to move elsewhere. Fifth, the authorities, notably the police, are generally perceived to be anti-Muslim in normal times, extracting more than the usual share of graft from Muslim businessmen compared to that taken from Hindu businessmen.[65] In a word, the entire atmosphere in the area in usual times is permeated with provocation, threat, insult, and the fear of injury or sudden death in an outburst of violence. Finally, most important, it is simply not the case that riots occur only occasionally in such places as Sarai Sultani. It was not just in the years 1978–80 and in 1990–91, in the riots reported in

FIG. 6.8. Riot damage, Sarai Sultani, 1999

the newspapers, that violence occurred in this and adjacent *mohallas*. On the contrary, riotous violence has occurred on many other occasions before 1978, between 1978 and 1990, and after 1990, not all of which have been reported in the press.

What about the how part of the question? How does violence break out and how does it come to be directed against Muslims who are doing nothing but sleeping in their beds during curfew? How do such ghastly atrocities akin to Nazi violence occur in democratic India? First, the police are predominantly Hindu, many of them imbued with the same anti-Muslim feelings as the general population. Second, there is a special police force, the PAC, that is notoriously anti-Muslim. Third, repeated accounts in Sarai Sultani and elsewhere make it clear that the police and the PAC work hand in hand with members of the militant Hindu organizations in beating and killing Muslims.

But what about the atrocious character of some of these acts of violence? How can these be explained? It is idle to seek explanations of that type. They can no more be provided in a convincing manner than can explanations for equally atrocious acts committed in Nazi Germany and around the globe in today's world in Cambodia, Rwanda-Burundi, Sierra Leone, and Kosovo. The most one can say is that such acts in some cases take place within a context, a discourse, that isolates and demonizes a particular group of people—in this case Muslims, their religion, and their social practices—and characterizes them as a physical danger to Hindus and to the unity of the country. In such contexts, not only will "ordinary" injuries and killings by stabbing, bombing, and gunshot take place, but so also will major atrocities.

But there is something further to be said concerning how such atrocities and riotous behavior in general can be allowed to continue in places such as Sarai Sultani. What about the higher authorities in the district, leaving aside the state authorities for the moment? We have in this respondent's account a rather clear indication that social origins and the attitudes of the authorities matter a great deal. It is not the case that, if caste Hindus occupy the positions of DM and SSP or CO, violence against Muslims will be allowed, and that if Muslims are in those positions, violence against Muslims will not be allowed. Indeed, there have been occasions in which Muslims in authority have appeared as helpless to prevent violence against Muslims as their Hindu counterparts. It is, however, a matter of great interest that violence against Muslims was said to have been prevented on two occasions in the history of Sarai Sultani when Scheduled Caste men were in positions of administrative and police authority. What these men were said to have done, moreover, was what many caste Hindu officers can and will do when their own sense of propriety or orders from the state government lead them to it. They made it clear that they would not tolerate acts of violence, that they would use necessary force against Hindus as well as Muslims to prevent them, and that every police officer would be held responsible for preventing acts of violence or containing any that occurred under their eyes.

There is one other important question to be answered, namely, as to the timing of the larger, uncontrolled riots. The two largest events of this type, as we have seen, were the long series of incidents between 1978 and 1980, on the one hand, and 1990–91, on the other hand. The first took place during the period of turmoil between the elections of 1977 and 1980, when politics at the Center, in the state, and in the districts were undergoing major transformations that included the fall and return to power of Indira Gandhi and the Congress at the Center, Janata rule in the central and state governments in which former Jan Sangh members and RSS cadres were included, and corresponding changes in Aligarh City, in short, a period of intense interparty competition. The 1990–91 riots took place at another dramatic turning point in national, state, and local politics, namely, during the mass mobilizations around the issue of demolition of the Babri Masjid that the BJP used to further the downfall of the Congress and the defeat of its other set of rivals in the Janata Dal. These were times, also, when the local administrations in Aligarh and elsewhere in the state were not given clear instructions to prevent riots, or where the local authorities themselves were sympathetic to Hindu mobilization that had clear anti-Muslim aspects. So, two elements seem to be required to explain large-scale rioting: intense political competition in which Hindu-Muslim relations are involved and in which voting by community is expected or encouraged, on the one hand, and an administration that does not have instructions or its own will to act decisively to prevent or control rioting.

Before turning to a detailed analysis of the broader political context in which large-scale riots take place, however, I want to consider further the role of economic factors in the riots in Aligarh, which my informants and the documentary sources have repeatedly mentioned as among the important causes of rioting. I will show in the next chapter that economic factors must be included in any comprehensive account of the underpinnings of Hindu-Muslim violence in Aligarh, but that they, too, comprise only a part of the whole.

# 7 / The Economics of Riots

## Economic Competition and Victimization

### THE ECONOMY OF ALIGARH

Aligarh, like several other towns in western U.P. that are also riot-prone, has developed in the twentieth century from what is known in the Indian literature as a *qasbah* town dominated by a rentier class of rural landholders—from both the Hindu and Muslim communities—with an economy "based on small shopkeeping, service occupations, and cultivation of crops," to a semi-industrialized economy in which "manufacturing, processing, servicing and repair operations" now provide jobs for approximately a third of the workforce.[1] Modern industrial activity began in Aligarh during British rule when cotton cultivation expanded for the export trade in the nineteenth century in the rural areas of the district and ginning and pressing factories were established in the town by both British and local Hindu and Muslim entrepreneurs.[2] However, the cotton industries declined and mostly disappeared long ago. Aligarh has provided a site for a few other large industries, including "*dal* [lentil] and vegetable oil mills, an instrument factory, and the Government of India Press."[3] A Glaxo factory was also established on the outskirts of Aligarh in 1961.[4] The large-scale industrial sector is not, however, a major force in the economic life of the city either in its contribution to production or to the workforce. Nor are there any large-scale trade unions in the city.[5]

The predominant industry in the town now is lock manufacturing, for which Aligarh has long been famous.[6] This industry, which also began in the town in the late nineteenth century, has traditionally been dominated by Muslims, with its manufacturing units heavily clustered in the predominantly

Muslim center of the old city known as Upar Kot. Lock manufacturing has also been the principal industry in which Muslims have been involved: half of all Muslim-owned industries in Aligarh in the early 1980s were engaged in lock manufacturing.[7] Nowadays, however, Hindus participate in the industry as both workers and owners of manufacturing establishments.[8] Although small- and medium-scale factory production of locks has probably increased in recent years, the work traditionally has been done and is still largely done by "artisans at home."[9]

Insofar as "the marketing and supply of raw material" is concerned, however, this aspect of the business "is controlled mainly by Hindu Bania middlemen."[10] The metal scrap dealers who provide a good portion of the raw material for the lock industry have in the past all been Banias, from two castes in particular: Agarwals and Varshneys.[11] As noted above, these two castes have often been considered to be antagonistic to each other in social life, to have for some time followed different political paths, and also to have been in competition with each other in trade. Persons from the Varshney caste have, as we have seen above, provided the principal leadership for militant Hindu politics and anti-Muslim agitations. Recently, Mann noted that "two Muslim families" had entered the scrap trade, "hoping to break the Bania monopoly"[12] in that business.

Before the scrap metal reaches the lock manufacturers, it must pass through foundries, "which are operated by Kolis," a Hindu Scheduled Caste, and then through "rolling mills, owned by both Muslims and Hindus."[13] There is, therefore, in this most important industry in Aligarh, what Mann describes as "considerable interdependence . . . between Hindus and Muslims."[14] However, intercommunal relations among Hindus and Muslims involved in the lock trade in the town are virtually confined to commercial activities. Only when persons from these two communities have attained a level of prosperity and sophistication to move to the Civil Lines area of the town do their relationships extend beyond business to social ties.[15]

Also of relevance both to the lock industry and to other commercial and industrial enterprises in the city is the fact that "almost all" moneylenders are "Punjabi Hindus."[16] Punjabi Hindus, many of them refugees or descendants of refugees from Pakistan at the time of partition in 1947, are, along with Varshneys, the principal supporters of militant Hindu ideas and organizations.

A further—and often-cited—example of Hindu-Muslim economic rivalry and competition in Aligarh and one that has also been related to communal riots in some of my interviews concerns the "trade in meat and hides." The slaughter of animals—particularly, of course, of cows—is anathema to many

Hindus in India. Even where it is not religiously proscribed, as in the case of the slaughter of goats, whose meat is relished by many Hindu castes, the occupation of slaughtering is held in the lowest esteem. It is no surprise, therefore, that this occupation has been traditionally monopolized by Muslim butchers from the caste known as Qasais and by low castes, formerly called Untouchables. In Aligarh, hostility between these two communities arising out of competition to "control the lucrative trade in meat and hides"[17] has been often reported.[18] Further, there are some areas of the town that are riot-prone in which Qasais and low-caste Hindus live side by side. It appears that, at times of riotous violence, these two groups do come into conflict with each other.[19] In some riot-prone areas, Qasais also live in *mohallas* adjacent to large Varshney populations. Some interview respondents gave greater weight to Varshney-Qasai conflicts as riot-precipitants than to conflicts between Qasais and low castes.

Competition between Hindus and Muslims in several other trades and industries in Aligarh has been reported, but as often as not there is as much or more competition between sections of Muslims as there is between Hindus and Muslims. Nevertheless, in her interviews in Aligarh, Mann found that the rise of various Muslim *baradaris* and their entry into various parts of the growing urban economy of Aligarh have been considered to be among the main causes for Hindu-Muslim violence in the city.[20]

Beyond the lock industry, the two most important industries in Aligarh in which Muslims are involved are building fittings and brass casting and hardware.[21] Most of the Muslim-owned factories are located in the Upar Kot area (see Map 2),[22] notably in the *mohallas* of Turkman Gate, Tantanpara, Usmanpara, Delhi Gate, Bani Israilan, Sarai Mian, and Chauk Bundu Khan, all of which save the last two are classed as communally sensitive, riot-hit, and/or crime-prone (see Map 3) but there are many other *mohallas* in the old city as well as in the Civil Lines and the new Industrial Estate in which Muslim-owned factories are located. Muslims also have been increasing their share in small-scale industries and have a small share in the "handloom and weaving sector" as well.[23]

Like every other town of comparable size in India, Aligarh also has its share of bazaars of many types, some carrying a range of goods, others specializing in particular types of goods. In the former category is the extensive bazaar known as Rasalganj,[24] which begins on the southern side of the railway and extends up the Rasalganj Road into the Upar Kot area. In the more specialized category are included bazaars such as Bara Bazaar, specializing in cloth and shoes; Dube Ka Parao, the vegetable and grain market; Mahavirganj, with its grain and grocery shops; Sarrafa Bazaar, with its jewelry shops; Phul

FIG. 7.1. Muslim medical clinic in Sarai Hakim

Chauraha (Flower Crossing), the flower bazaar; Sabzi Mandi, as its name indicates, the wholesale vegetable market; Sarai Hakim, containing many Muslim medical clinics (see Figure 7.1 and Map 2); and Centre Point, a new market area where many different types of goods are sold and containing some relatively modern shops and restaurants. Some markets, such as Barahseni Bazaar, are named after particular castes.[25] Some of the bazaars are dominated by Hindu, others by Muslim shopkeepers. Most of the shops in Phul Chauraha and Sarai Hakim are owned by Muslims,[26] those in Dube Ka Parao, Sarrafa Bazaar and Mahavirganj by Hindus.[27]

Communal riots often begin in these extraordinarily crowded bazaars, which are also commonly the principal targets for arson and looting once riots begin. Among the worst-affected areas in the riot of 1978, for example, were Sarrafa Bazaar and Phul Chauraha.[28] Indeed, the first clear signal that a riot has begun or is about to begin is the sudden slamming down by shopkeepers of the iron shutters that enclose their shops at the end of the day.

## ECONOMIC FACTORS IN RIOT PRODUCTION IN ALIGARH

There have been many suggestions in the literature on riots in India in general and in Aligarh in particular, some of them noted in the previous chapter, that they have their main foundation in economic competition and rivalry between Hindu and Muslim businessmen, on the one hand, and in attempts by Hindu commercial interests and real estate developers to grab valuable urban land owned or occupied by Muslims. Thus, the Minorities Commission, in its report on the 1978 riots, noted that it had "been suggested that the economic rivalries between groups of businessmen of the two communities who thrive on the lock-making industry at Aligarh may be the reason behind the tension" that led to the riots.[29] The press also reported on the 1978 riots the view of "senior officials" in the district that "business rivalries between Muslims and upper caste Hindus have played their role in engendering feelings of hatred" that in part explained the spread of riots in previously unaffected areas of the city.[30]

Similarly, the Centre for Research study noted that "the most sensitive and intensely riot-hit areas are located in the CBD [Central Business District], where there is a preponderance of Muslim houses and where most of the trading and commercial activities are in the hands of the Hindus."[31] The Centre study also remarked that, owing to "the phenomenal rise in the price of land in the Aligarh town," Hindu Banias had been seeking to force "Muslim artisans to vacate their houses and shops located in the business centres or more developed residential areas" such as Manik Chauk and Dahi Wali Gali, where, as noted above, "killings are known to have been organised by the local roughs in league with the land hungry rich of these localities."[32] The Centre's information was based on its study of "the riots of October, 1978, and May–June, 1981."[33]

Many Muslims in Aligarh concur in the economic explanation for the recurrence of riots in Aligarh, seeing them as a form of minority persecution for the sake of Hindu profit. It is said, for example, that Banias from the business classes, many of whom are Jan Sanghis,[34] attack Muslims in order to expand their business in the city. They precipitate riots in order to try to force the Muslims to leave and sell their houses at low cost—or even at high cost— but mainly to get their property somehow. So, they create communal tension and then, during riots, attack Muslim houses.

It is said that Hindu big businessmen also have other economic motivations concerning Muslim laborers in their own establishments. They turn labor troubles into communal troubles so they can avoid giving proper pay and bonuses to their own workers.[35]

Perhaps the most common explanation of an economic type that I have heard repeatedly over the years concerns the AMU and the way it is perceived in the town, especially by teachers and students in the local colleges that are primarily Hindu-run and have mostly Hindu students. It has been said repeatedly that there is deep resentment in these local colleges among the teachers there over the advantages Muslim professors at the university have, particularly salaries that are much higher than those prevailing in the colleges.[36] Since most of the riots noted above involve teachers and students from the local colleges in one way or another, this explanation is quite satisfying to many observers of them.

The most bizarre explanation of this type concerned the vicious rumors circulated during the 1990–91 riots that Hindu patients were being slaughtered in the AMU Medical College Hospital. The rumors, as we have seen, were totally false, but the question remained as to why they were circulated in the first place. The economic explanation was that private medical clinics instigated these rumors about the AMU to make money by diverting business to them![37]

While not all these explanations can be discarded entirely, none of them constitute anything close to a reasonable explanation for riots of the scale that have been produced in Aligarh from time to time since 1961. At best, they suggest the operation of economic motivations that impel some participants to participate in such riots, to take advantage of them when they occur. While economic interests have been pursued in such a way in Aligarh as to precipitate riots, notably the incident of the cinema hall that constituted the starting event in the incidents that occurred in May–June 1979, such interests cannot account for most of the events that then follow.

### THE ECONOMICS OF RIOTING IN MANIK CHAUK *MOHALLA*

The names of one community in Aligarh, the Barahsenis (or Varshneys, as they are commonly known), and of one man from that community, Krishna Kumar Navman, recur repeatedly both in my interviews and in published accounts of the origin and course of riots in Aligarh since Independence. Varshneys are heavily concentrated in the locality of Manik Chauk, which we have seen is the locality most often mentioned as a center of riotous activity. Many Varshneys also live in the locality of Brahman Tola. It was noted above that they have their own market as well, called Barahseni Bazaar. The Varshneys and Navman are also associated in the minds of many with the RSS and with the Jan Sangh/BJP. Navman is himself a businessman, a publisher of commercial books and calendars,[38] whose large warehouse is located in Manik Chauk.

Varshneys and other business castes in Aligarh have often been economic and political rivals, competing with each other in similar business lines and supporting different political parties. Agarwals, in particular, have been business rivals of the Barahsenis. Many Agarwals, in the early years after Independence, supported the Congress. In the famous 1962 election for the Aligarh Legislative Assembly constituency, a Varshney candidate, Madan Lal Hiteshi, contested as an independent and placed third behind the Republican Party and the Congress, while Tota Ram Vidyarthi, a Marwari Bania, contested on the Jan Sangh ticket, coming in fourth place. From 1989 through 1996, Krishna Kumar Navman was the BJP candidate for the assembly constituency, while all his principal rival candidates were Muslims. By then, most Hindus from the business classes had become BJP supporters.[39] Navman was elected in three successive elections in 1989, 1991, and 1993 before he was finally defeated in 1996. (See below, Chapters 9–12.)

Muslim respondents single out the Varshneys among Hindu castes, including other business castes, as exploiters of poor Muslims, and always mention Navman when they discuss the activities of the members of this caste, as in the following quotation from one of my interviews with an AMU professor.

> There is a community called Barahseni, Banias. These people . . . all belongs to RSS . . . and that is also a special factor in this [communal/riot situation]. Agarwal Banias are not so bad, but in Aligarh these people [Barahsenis] are— this Navman comes from the same community—and they are actually very moneyed people. They have money, they use that money [implying their use in riots].[40]

The names of the Varshney community and of Navman are particularly prominent in accounts of the 1978 riots. Although its origins had nothing to do with the community, Navman, or the locality of Manik Chauk—having arisen out of the rivalry between two wrestling *akharas*—it has been reported that "the extremely communal minded section of the Hindus," that is, the Varshneys, "appeared to have planned attacks on Muslims" after the death of the Hindu wrestler, Bhure Lal. This same report records the allegation that "rich Varshney Hindus" provided the "money for this plan" and that Navman, then "president of the Aligarh City Janata Party and his close associates, by all accounts, seem to have played a very prominent role in these plans and their later execution."[41]

This report of the Minorities Commission does not, however, explain why the rich Varshney businessmen decided—made a "plan"—to attack Muslims in Manik Chauk. Other reports, however, do provide such an explanation, a quite specific one that has nothing to do with extreme communal-mindedness. It is said, rather, that as a consequence of a "phenomenal rise in the price of land" in Aligarh in the years preceding the 1978 riots, there developed a "tendency to force the Muslim artisans to vacate their houses and shops located in the business centres or more developed residential areas dominated by Hindu Banias."[42]

One of my own interview respondents gave an account of the origins of these incidents that fully supports the above documentary reports. These incidents that occurred between 1978 and 1981 were not actually riots, he said.

> There was a—actually—not a riot. A section of the—Manik Chauk, predominantly of the—Banias, yah, predominantly of the Jan Sangh community, business class community—in Manik Chauk—attacked . . . the Muslims.

When I asked why, this respondent continued as follows.

> Why? Just I will tell you. Because there is a very few Muslims in this *mohalla*, and they are dominating—Hindus [are]. And they want the Muslims [to leave] this place. Because—they—they, . . . for expansion of their business in city. City is very costly: lands, and houses. Particularly in this—in that area, in Manik Chauk. And they could not expand their business, their houses. [So] there is the costly lands. Very costly houses. They want to harass the Muslim so Muslim[s] will [leave] this area and sell their houses on—very low cost—yah, any cost, low or high cost; the—there is no problem of the money; they want to purchase their houses, they want to come—mm—set[tle] . . . —on this area, particularly. [So] this is the major. Then—when the communal tension [is] created, they attack . . . the Muslim houses.[43]

However, this attribution of specifically economic motives to the businessmen of Manik Chauk and Dahi Wali Gali localities is not a sufficient explanation, for it must be asked why only Muslim artisans were targeted, not Hindu artisans. Either there were none of the latter, which is unlikely, or we are back again to a communal explanation, at least in part. A wholly satisfying explanation for the 1978 attacks on Muslims is that the communal atmosphere and the opportunity to mobilize people for retaliation against Muslims because of the death of Bhure Lal provided a cover for and the opportunity to take possession of Muslim property. To do the same against small Hindu proprietors would expose "the land hungry rich" as merely that, and would arouse hostility against those "known" to have organized the attacks. In effect, therefore, the communal and the economic explanations for riotous activity here merge. The explanation is satisfying in the sense that it is complete and leaves no unexplained motivations; it is not, however, necessarily the truth, and certainly is not the whole truth for rioting that extended beyond Manik Chauk.

### RIOTING FOR PROFIT

There is no doubt that, in Aligarh as well as in many other cities and towns in India, including notably Bombay, urban land—even the smallest portion in the nastiest slum—commands a high premium.[44] Mann has noted that, in general, "the urban development of Aligarh has accelerated building activity, while growth of the urban population and subsequent pressure on existing housing and related facilities have created a high demand for residential and business premises."[45] This demand opens up many kinds of potential conflicts that are exacerbated whenever persons from one community are affected by the demand for such residential or business premises by persons from the other community. For example, the issue of control of scarce land in Aligarh also featured in the incidents that followed upon the opening of the Chandra Talkies cinema in June 1978, which was protested by local Muslims and by Muslim politicians, including Khwaja Halim "and a volatile young advocate, Sujatullah Khan, local President of the Muslim League."[46] In this case, however, the issue was not one of Hindu businessmen gaining control of Muslim property, but of a Hindu businessman opening a cinema hall in an alley that opened up into a Muslim locality, as a result of which, it was claimed, the privacy of the residents, particularly of the women, would be threatened by the exiting of large crowds into the alleys late at night.[47] Furthermore, in this case, it appears that the prime movers in enlarging the scope of the issue were Muslim politicians. This set of incidents, therefore, does not provide much support for the view that economic motivations are primary in Hindu-Muslim rioting.

The economic explanation for riots that focuses upon the land grabbing of the Varshneys and other rich Hindu businessmen falls into the category of the rich exploiting the poor and vulnerable, "the business classes against the poor Muslims," as one of my respondents put it. A variation on this theme was provided by the same respondent and by others, who alleged that "big business houses" took advantage of communal riots to solve their labor problems; they, in effect, turned their labor problems into communal problems, thereby making a profit by not giving their laborers "proper money, proper finance, proper bonus, et cetera," during times of "communal troubles."[48] Quite similar statements were made to me by a Hindu station officer at Sasni Gate, a major area of communal conflict. This officer also provided a list of other alleged advantages gained by businessmen during riots. He was responding not to a question concerning the causes of communal riots, but to the question of who benefits from persistent communal riots in Aligarh. Though the question was, therefore, loaded, insofar as it assumed that some people must benefit, I left the respondent free to choose the beneficiaries. He chose, first of all, businessmen.

> Sometimes during the riots certain people have good business. Laborers on daily wage have no job during curfew. They go to the industry bosses and ask for financial help, which is offered, but the bosses exploit the situation afterward. They may give a low wage, and the laborer has an obligation because he was helped during bad days, so it becomes almost like bonded labor. Also, the laborers prefer to work at factories that can still run during riot or curfew, so again they are forced to work for lower wages. So business owners benefit.
>
> Sometimes, during the riots, there are certain people who have good business; they may be Hindu and Muslims. What they do is that they have laborers on daily wages. And during curfew, these people go out of—er—they don't have any job or any work to do. So—and they go to their . . . [employees] . . . and promise financial help to them.
>
> And exploit the situation afterwards, because they may give them . . . not the proper wage, and afterwards—it also puts them under obligation because . . . they always tell them that, "We helped you during the bad days." So later on they also employ them on lower wages. So somehow they become bonded laborers. And the other thing is that there are certain people who manage to run their installations, and during that time because of the daily wages, he depended upon his wages, he prefers to work there. And again, because of the fact that he does—he doesn't work there, so then he might not get that job, because there are other people who are willing to work. So then again he is supposed to work on lower wages. So some—that way, the business owners—they benefit a lot in this kind of situation.[49]

## RIOTS AND ECONOMIC COMPETITION

Other economic explanations refer to more general competition between Hindus and Muslims in particular economic niches. There is, for example, the claim that some of the rioting in Aligarh is attributable to "increasing competition between [Muslim . . . butchers] and Harijans in the beef and meat business and, with their mohallas opening into each other, incidents are more and more frequent."[50]

As in the case of Hindu businessmen of different castes who are in competition with each other, so there is competition among Muslims from different segments of the Muslim community—lineages and *baradaris*—for leadership within the Muslim community as a whole. Success in "business and industry" for such Muslims provides them with an opportunity for recognition within their community.[51] However, Muslims of all *baradaris* in Aligarh in general have been far behind Hindu business castes in the economy of the city. In recent years—that is, since the 1970s and 1980s—Muslims have entered into direct competition with Hindu castes in particular economic niches dominated by Hindus.[52]

Even where there is "interdependence" rather than competition in business relations between Hindus and Muslims in Aligarh, it does not extend beyond "commercial expediency," at least in the old city.[53] Moreover, even in such situations of interdependence, let alone competition, the organization of business and the structuring of business relations tend to follow kinship, caste, and *baradari* lines.[54] The caste and *baradari*—not just the religious affiliation—of every business owner in Aligarh will certainly be known by everyone who deals with him. Further, once a member of a caste or *baradari* becomes established in a particular branch of business or industry, others of his community will soon follow,[55] among whom relations of cooperation are more likely to develop than with persons from other status groups. This does not mean, however, that only persons of the same caste, lineage, or *baradari* as the owner(s) will be employed. On the contrary, as will be shown momentarily, employees often come from members of the other community and from different subgroups within each community.

Whether or not economic competition between Hindus and Muslims is a contributory cause in the production of communal violence in Aligarh, communal violence and the tensions that have intensified between the two communities as a consequence have adversely affected "economic relations," even leading "in some cases to severance of long-established business links."[56] As early as the 1950s, Pars Ram, reporting on the results of interviews with fifty Hindus concerning their relations with Muslims in his famous *UNESCO Study* of communal tensions in Aligarh, done in collaboration with Gardner Murphy, remarked that 32 of the 50 met with Muslims "as business partners and as acquaintances, and some of them at meals, but they entertain an inward image of the Muslim as dirty, a cow killer and a cruel person."[57] Since then, as Varshney has noted,

> Religion has continually interfered with business. For some time, trade and business associations of the city tried to weather communal tensions and integrate businessmen from both communities, but the effort did not succeed. Trade associations were broken along political lines, rather than business lines.[58]

Furthermore, the fact that a proprietor employs or depends for his supplies or finished products upon artisans or traders from the other community does not necessarily mean that his prejudices against the other community are diminished. Here again the Varshney community enters the picture, at least in the mind of one of my Muslim respondents.

> Artisans are Muslims. They are making locks and they are supplying them and these Banias are getting richer and richer on the poor Muslim artisans. They [Barahsenis] do nothing. . . . They [Muslims] make locks for them, they [Barahsenis] take the locks, they collect the lock[s], . . . and then they sell [them]. But, they're all [the locks] done by Muslims.
>
> Now probably, now they are more afraid because now the educated Muslim boys are coming up and now they are trying to hold that business in their own hands and that is also agitating them. Now, the educated boys from Aligarh University, they have started businesses. Very few, but they are entering into this and they want to do business themselves, they don't want to go to the Banias and say, "Please give us five hundred rupees advance and we'll do," and then they become their, under their control for all the life to come. So, probably this is also maybe a slight cause in their mind, is now the business is going out of their hand.
>
> There was one businessman called _____ Kumar, he was a top businessman of locks and entire force, manufacturing force, was Muslim, and he was an RSS man. And the reason [for his RSS affiliation] I could not understand. He used to be in Marris Road, a very big man. Still he has a very big bungalow there. And he used to say to us, oh, I'm so secular, my entire business is because of them and whatever I am is because of Muslims and whatever money I have is because of them, but he was a man of RSS.

This respondent went on to contrast the situation in Moradabad, where Muslim competition with Hindus in traditional industries—in this case, brass utensils—was more intense as a consequence of the entry of educated Muslims into the sale of these utensils previously monopolized by Banias. He saw a similar process developing in Aligarh. Moreover, he also revealed how economic advancement of Muslims and their competition with entrenched Hindu business groups may spill over into politics. He mentioned the name of a former student of his in the AMU, who was now doing very well in the lock industry. Having become established in this industry, he and others thought the former student should now make his mark in Aligarh politics as well.

> We asked him [to] please contest for the mayorship or chairmanship of the municipal board and he gave a very tough fight because the money mattered, votes are bought. So, he was able to fight with a Bania, O. P. Agarwal, he is RSS man, and he [the Muslim] was only defeated by . . . one vote.[59]

In fact, there has been a dramatic increase of Muslim participation as owners in several industries during the past three decades. In the lock industry, traditionally dominated by Muslims, the number of registered units (that is, factories rather than small-scale shops) owned by Muslims increased from 4 in 1965–75 to 33 in 1976–80 and to 87 in 1981–85, a very substantial increase, indeed. The second most important industry into which Muslims have advanced as owners is building fittings (hardware). Muslim unit ownership increased in these three periods from 2 to 9 to 24, but nearly 90 percent of such units were Hindu-owned in 1982.[60] Such increases in Muslim ownership do not necessarily involve direct competition with Hindus, for the communal division of labor in the industry is more complementary than competitive. Muslims have traditionally produced the locks, either as artisans or, increasingly nowadays, as laborers in medium-size factories. Hindus have provided the raw materials through their dominance of the scrap trade and have purchased the finished locks for sale outside of Aligarh.[61] Even today, the trade in locks is mostly controlled by Muslims, while the manufacturing—artisanal or factory—is carried on by Muslims.[62]

In the 1996 Legislative Assembly elections, Navman was defeated by Abdul Khaliq, a second-generation Muslim lock manufacturer, graduate of the AMU, and owner of a factory employing about one hundred persons and producing a thousand locks per day. Abdul Khaliq gave an ambiguous response to questions concerning whether or not communal tensions in the city had affected business relations between Hindus and Muslims. At first, he claimed that Hindus and Muslims in the lock business had good relations, being "involved with each other," and denied that there was any business conflict between Hindus and Muslims as such in this regard. When I pressed him further, however, he said that not only in Aligarh, but in India as a whole, whenever Muslims "dominated" economically, the "BJP, or say RSS, want to disturb things."[63] In other words, in this man's mind, the cause of communal tension did not arise out of intercommunal business relations, but out of political action on the part of militant Hindu organizations.[64]

Muslim employment in the small-scale sector, outside the lock industry, is quite low, probably less than 3 percent.[65] Nevertheless, the labor force in some small and medium enterprises is communally mixed. Hindu owners employ Muslim artisans and workmen; so do Muslim owners employ Hindus. For example, a Muslim proprietor of a small building-fittings enterprise in Upar Kot employed 15 people. Of these, seven were Hindus, including by his own account his "main labor[er] who is guarding my factory and is [on] twenty-four-hour duty." The other six were employed in casting and molding his brass items. He was emphatic that he experienced no problems with either his Hindu employees or with Hindu competitors. His business relations in Aligarh were only with laborers and traders. He claimed that the question of competition with Hindu rivals in the city did not arise at all since he was supplying his goods only to exporters in Bombay. He acknowledged that some of the Hindus of U.P. are "communal-minded," but said that "outside of U.P., they are not [so] communal-minded."[66]

Our lock-manufacturing informant in Sarai Sultani who gave the extensive account cited in the previous chapter emphasized communal hostilities on the part of Hindus more than economic factors as an explanation for the recurrent rioting in Aligarh and in his *mohalla* in particular. At one point, however, I said, "All right, [you say] the Hindus feel why not throw the Muslims out of here? Maybe this was the reason. But was there any rivalry, jealousy, some Hindus here making locks like [you do], who want to take over [your] business, or some such reason?" He acknowledged that there certainly was competition between Hindu and Muslim lock makers in Aligarh and gave me a long explanation of its several aspects. However, there did not appear to be a direct connection in his explanation or in his mind between this economic competition and communal violence. At the same time, he gave examples of how the police victimized Muslim businesses, including his own, and helped his competitors.

He explained that there was significant price competition between Muslim and Hindu lock sellers, the former selling much more cheaply than the latter. He added that they were able to do so because their household expenses were less than those of the Hindus and they could, therefore, subsist on a smaller profit margin, and because the Muslim manufacturers did their own manufacturing while the Hindu sellers contract the manufacturing out to laborers. For the latter reason, the Hindu traders faced heavier capitalization costs for raw materials that had to be purchased, then contracted out, while the Muslim manufacturers used the same raw materials in a much shorter time period—two or three days compared to 15 or 16 days for the Hindus. All the raw materials come from Hindu suppliers, but the respondent did not complain of any discrimination from this quarter. Finally, the Muslim manufacturers sell to nearby Delhi, a market that they monopolize, while the Hindu sellers have huge transport costs to their more far-flung markets in south India.

Given this description of economic competition between Hindu and Muslim lock manufacturers and sellers, I asked if this respondent thought that the lock industry's Hindu owners were encouraging the police to beat them, or the police were beating them just because they don't like Muslims. He replied as follows.

> These Hindus bribe the police to oppress the Muslims. For example, a [Muslim] worker in his own factory had to pay Rs. 2,000 extortion money to the police only two or three months previously. He was just a worker, an ordinary worker, a laborer, earning Rs. 2,500 per month.

I asked how this could be and was given the following explanation.

> Suppose a Muslim worker is working in a Hindu factory. He works there for a month and gets paid for that. For some reason or other, he quits and then comes to his factory and works here. Then, the Hindu factory owner will come to know where his former worker is working, will come here, ask for that worker, and claim falsely that the worker owes him Rs. 5,000. Then, that Hindu manufacturer will go to the police station and he will return with the police and, in their presence, will demand the Rs. 5,000 from the worker. Then, to settle matters, the Muslim proprietor will have to pay Rs. 5,000 to the Hindu factory owner and the worker will have to pay the Muslim proprietor back monthly, off his wages. This was the case with the worker who had to pay Rs. 2,000, in fact, but such situations have occurred several times. The purpose of this harassment is to discourage the Muslim manufacturers, to get them out of the business.

Such extortion directed against Muslim manufacturers was said to be beyond the ordinary police extortion that both Hindu and Muslim businessmen have to pay. The police, he said, come sometimes two or three times a month for 50, 100, or even 500 rupees. During the year, he will have to pay out around Rs. 5,000 to 8,000 in this manner.

Here we have a businessman, a secular person, not involved in Muslim religious or fundamentalist organizations or causes, a person in fact who has been a Congress man all his life and remained so as of the date of the interview, long after the Congress had ceased to be a significant force in the politics of the city. As a Muslim businessman living in a predominantly Hindu country, he has no compunction—like so many Jewish businessmen in European history—in making compromises and adjustments to his environment in order to sell his products, which carry the name of the Hindu god Krishna. He, like other Muslim lock manufacturers, must buy his raw materials from Hindus. He does not mention any discrimination on the part of his Hindu raw materials suppliers, with whom, as Mann has pointed out, Muslim lock manufacturers exist in an interdependent economic relationship. There is also competition between him and Hindu lock sellers, though they both manage to survive by selling their locks to different markets in India.

Economic competition among lock sellers does not, however, appear to be a primary cause of the riotous activity and anti-Muslim killings that have occurred in Sarai Sultani and adjacent *mohallas*. A more relevant factor is the pressure on the part of local Hindus to gain control of Muslim-owned property, to put pressure on the Muslims, intimidated by the militant Hindu groups that surround them, to sell their property at cheap prices. However, I do not believe that this economic factor provides the motivation for the intimidation of Muslims that has existed in this area for decades. This is a matter of judgment on my part, but it is my perception that Hindu businessmen and real estate operators are taking advantage of a situation created for other reasons, rather than creating the situation in order to take advantage of it.

## CONCLUSION

What can we conclude, then, concerning the role of business and business relations—including dependency relations as well as interdependence, cooperation, and competition—between Hindus and Muslims in Aligarh as a factor in riot production? Modern business and industry were for long dominated by Hindus. Muslims for the most part occupied positions as artisan manufacturers and wage earners, producing and working for Hindu businessmen. The increasing entry of Muslims into trades, occupations, and industries previously dominated by Hindus has certainly been noted by Hindus and resented and feared by some of them. There is little evidence, however, that such competition has been a factor in the production of riots. Rather, there is more evidence that, in particular localities, competition between Hindus and Muslims in the same traditional trades—such as butchering—has been a factor providing recruits from particular castes and *baradaris* for riotous activity against each other. There is also substantial documentary evidence that rich Hindu businessmen have taken advantage of poor Muslim artisans at times of communal riots and, as we have seen, have allegedly deliberately planned their attacks upon the latter for economic advantage. There is the further allegation that both Hindu and Muslim businessmen take advantage of their laborers during riots to settle labor disputes, create dependencies upon the owners, and reduce wages and other benefits in exchange for secure employment. Finally, there is resentment as well as competition arising from the fact that some educated Muslims from the hated AMU have entered into direct competition with Hindus in the lock industry and in transportation, among other possible business lines.

However, none of these economic factors implicated in riot production stand by themselves as sufficient explanations. They occur in a communal discursive context and are almost always associated with political activities. The communal context predates Independence, feeds upon the presence in Aligarh of the AMU as a symbol of Muslim treachery to the projects of Indian and Hindu nationalism, and derives further sustenance from traditional prejudices instilled in Hindus and Muslims as part of their upbringing. This discursive context in turn sustains political movements that thrive upon the promotion of communal tensions even when they do not set out deliberately to produce riots. The series of riots that occurred between 1978 and 1980, the ones in which business interests have been most directly implicated, occurred at a time of dramatic political change in India, of turmoil and transformation in interparty relations and conflict in the state and in the country. That turmoil was reflected in Aligarh, where it took on a distinctive character nourished by the historical breeding of Hindu-Muslim communal tensions, in which both Hindu and Muslim politicians played roles. Navman and his Varshney supporters came into the limelight during the October 1978 and May–June 1979 riots, while Khwaja Halim and other local Muslim activists stood forth as the protectors of Muslim interests against the

Hindu owner of the Chandra Talkies cinema. These riots did not arise out of business conflicts per se. Rather, Hindu businessmen gained economic advantage and a Hindu politician-businessman gained political advantage under the cover of communal action for the alleged benefit and protection of the Hindu community, while Muslim politicians gained advantage by standing forth as the protectors of poor Muslims against avaricious Hindu businessmen.

# PART IV

# Riots and the Political Process

# 8 / Riots and Elections

## INTRODUCTION

Wilkinson has argued that the principal cause of Hindu-Muslim riots in India, indeed of ethnic riots in general, is a "close electoral race in which one party believes it can win by appealing to ethnic majority-group voters."[1] Although I have argued above that the search for causes of such large-scale and multiplex events as riots is problematic, I will nevertheless treat this argument seriously here, to discover what can be said precisely about the relationship between riots and party/electoral politics in Aligarh in general and the intensity of interparty competition in that city in particular. The opposite possibility will also be considered, namely, that riots produce intense interparty competition. I have already established the case for a close association between riots and politics in Aligarh in the preceding chapters and elsewhere in my previous work. The association will be further demonstrated here.

The analysis in succeeding chapters will focus on the Legislative Assembly constituency, comprising most of Aligarh City, and the city segment of the parliamentary constituency. A chapter will also be devoted to demonstrating the relationship between riots and the communalization and polarization of the electorate in particular *mohallas*. However, on the basis of the discussion in Chapter 6, it is not to be expected that there will necessarily be a direct relationship between riots and the intensity of electoral competition at the *mohalla* level, for it has already been demonstrated that riots may be produced from *mohallas* in which militant Hindu sentiment is predominant and where that predominance is reflected in voting for the BJP. It has also been shown that the *mohallas* targeted for riot production may be overwhelmingly Muslim or mixed, that there may be deliberate efforts to attack and intimidate Muslims in places where the demographic balance provides insurmountable obstacles to the BJP through the normal electoral mechanisms and where other-than-political calculations are also involved. To put the matter in a nutshell, riots are produced in specific *mohallas*, but the political context that matters most is citywide, where the stakes are greatest. Thus, riot production, whether concentrated in a few or spread in many *mohallas*, influences to lesser or greater extent, respectively, the political balance in the city as a whole, not just in the *mohallas* that experience violence.

The gist of my argument on the relationship between party politics and riots was stated in one of my earlier works as follows: "there is a continuum from political rivalry leading to communal riots to political rivalry feeding on communal riots."[2] The continuum may, however, start at either end, that is, from political rivalry to riots as well as from communal riots to intensified political rivalry. However, the sequence in Aligarh has been primarily in the latter direction, that is, communal riots have preceded and have led to intensification of interparty competition. The mechanisms that lead to this intensification arise from the tendencies that follow from riots to foster increased communal solidarity and polarization, which in turn are promoted by political parties and/or individual candidates who stand to benefit from such solidarity and polarization. The resultant communalization and polarization in turn reduce the electoral prospects of parties and candidates who stand for secular political practices, intercommunal cooperation, and class or caste/ *baradari* mobilization rather than communal mobilization.

The operation of these mechanisms is, of course, affected profoundly by the social composition of the electorate. Communalization and polarization obviously tend to offer greater political and electoral advantages where the numbers of any two potentially cohesive groups, in our case Hindus and Muslims, are of a sufficient size. We expect neither riots, nor electoral advantage to be gained from them, where there is an insufficiently large population of one of the communities. There is no precise ratio between Hindus and Muslims that can be stated to incline towards the production and political use of riots. It depends as well upon other factors, particularly the divisions within each community on the basis of caste or *baradari* and how deep-seated these are. But there is no doubt that numbers matter. Indeed, it will be demonstrated later that, in the given conditions of Aligarh—which have tended for decades to produce from time to time riotous violence, communalization and polarization of the electorate, and intense interparty competition—important alterations in the boundaries and in the communal composition of the electorate have recently changed dramatically the electoral contests and the party configuration, reducing the political value of riotous violence.

## THREE PERIODS IN THE PARTY/ELECTORAL HISTORY OF ALIGARH CITY

Table 8.1 gives the election results for 28 elections in Aligarh City held between 1952 and 1998 for which I have information, including Legislative Assembly, parliamentary, and mayoral contests. The mayoral and Legislative Assembly constituency boundaries are somewhat different, the former comprising the entire municipality of Aligarh, whereas the assembly constituency does not include some parts of the municipality, though it is entirely urban. The Aligarh parliamentary constituency comprises five segments, each of which is a separate Legislative Assembly constituency. Wherever possible in the table, I have reported the results of the election for Parliament for the Aligarh segment of the parliamentary constituency only, since the other four of the five segments that constitute the parliamentary constituency are rural. The Aligarh City segment of the parliamentary constituency and the Aligarh City Legislative Assembly constituency correspond exactly.

The Legislative Assembly elections have constituted the dynamic center of Aligarh politics for the most part since Independence, the mayoral elections having been held only sporadically. There were, however, citywide mayoral elections in 1991 and in 1995. Until recently, therefore, the Legislative Assembly constituency was the only arena that included most of the city. At times, also, the parliamentary contest in the Aligarh City segment has been as or more hotly contested than the Legislative Assembly contest, though the results for the parliamentary constituency are inevitably decided by the votes from the four predominantly rural segments. The results in the Aligarh segment are always quite different from those in the rural segments. They sometimes bring out even more clearly than in the assembly contest the communal and political identities of Hindus, Muslims, and Scheduled Castes.

The table provides at a glance a summary view of the development of party politics in the city over the past half century, which can be divided roughly into three periods. The first period is the first decade of electoral politics after Independence, marked by *Congress dominance in the city.* Although that dominance was destroyed by the Republican Party in 1962, the latter party faded away thereafter. (However, in the 1980s the Bahujan Samaj Party, also a party representing primarily the lower castes, emerged to capture the same support base of its predecessor party.) The second period,

TABLE 8.1. Winning party or independent candidate, Aligarh City Legislative
Assembly, Lok Sabha, and mayoral elections, 1951–98[a]

| Year | Election Type | Winning Party or Independent |
|---|---|---|
| | PHASE 1: Congress dominance | |
| 1952 | Assembly | Congress |
| 1952 | Lok Sabha | Congress |
| 1955 | Assembly (bye-election) | Socialist |
| 1957 | Assembly | Congress |
| 1957 | Lok Sabha | Congress |
| | PHASE 2: Congress dominance contested by two rival parties | |
| 1962 | Assembly | Republican Party |
| 1962 | Lok Sabha | Republican Party |
| 1967 | Lok Sabha | Independent |
| 1967 | Assembly | Jan Sangh |
| 1969 | Assembly | Congress |
| 1971 | Lok Sabha | BKD |
| 1974 | Assembly | Jan Sangh |
| 1977 | Lok Sabha | BLD |
| 1977 | Assembly | Janata Party |
| 1980 | Lok Sabha | Congress |
| 1980 | Assembly | Janata Party (SC) |
| 1984 | Lok Sabha | Congress[b] |
| 1985 | Assembly | Congress |

which followed immediately after the Congress defeat in 1962, lasted through
the 1985 election. It was marked primarily by *struggle between the Congress
and two other rival parties:* the militant Hindu Jan Sangh and the party led
by the peasant leader, Charan Singh, which took different names—BKD,
Janata Party (SC), Lok Dal, and BLD. In the table, Charan Singh's party is
shown as the winner in the 1971 Lok Sabha, 1977 Lok Sabha, and 1980
Legislative Assembly constituencies. The strength of militant Hinduism was
greater in this period than the table indicates because the Janata Party candidate in the 1977 assembly election was supported by the former Jan Sangh.
The Congress underwent a temporary resuscitation at the end of this period

TABLE 8.1. *(continued)*

| Year | Election Type | Winning Party or Independent |
|------|---------------|------------------------------|
| PHASE 3: Reconstitution of interparty struggle between the BJP and the JD/SP | | |
| 1989 | Assembly | BJP |
| 1989 | Lok Sabha | Janata Dal |
| 1991 | Assembly | BJP |
| 1991 | Lok Sabha | BJP |
| 1991 | Mayoral | BJP |
| 1993 | Assembly | BJP |
| 1995 | Mayoral | BJP |
| 1996 | Assembly | Samajwadi Party |
| 1996 | Lok Sabha | BJP |
| 1998 | Lok Sabha | Samajwadi Party[c] |

[a]Results in all Lok Sabha elections except those for 1952, 1957, 1971 and 1977 were for the Aligarh City segment of the parliamentary constituency only. Segment-wise results were not available in the other years. Since the parliamentary constituency consists of five nested segments corresponding to individual Legislative Assembly constituencies, the winner in the parliamentary constituency as a whole may or may not have won a plurality of votes in a particular segment, in this case the Aligarh segment.

[b]The constituency as a whole was won by the Janata Party (S).

[c]The constituency as a whole was won by the BJP.

after the assassination of Indira Gandhi and the rise to power of her son, Rajiv Gandhi, as prime minister of the country. The third period, from 1989 to 1998, is marked primarily by the *disappearance of the Congress as a serious contender in Aligarh politics and the reconstitution of interparty struggle as one primarily between the BJP and the SP,* the party of militant Hinduism and the party representing the interests of backward castes and Muslims, respectively.

Figure 8.1 shows the number of deaths in riots during the three political periods in Aligarh. Since the 1988 riots occurred in the time between political phase 2 and political phase 3, but closer to phase 3, they have been included in the latter period. Because the periods are of different length, no statistical assertions can be made from this figure concerning the relationship between the configuration of party competition and the number of riots. The figure merely illustrates the facts, namely, that (1) the lowest number of deaths in riots occurred during the nine-year period of Congress dominance from 1952

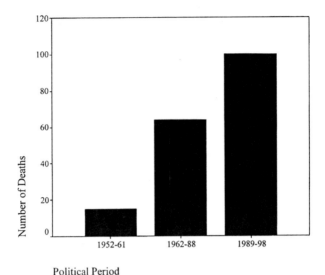

FIG. 8.1. Number of deaths in riots by political period

to 1961, when there were three riots, two with no fatalities and one, in 1961, with 15; (2) during the period of struggle between the Congress and rival parties in the 16 years between 1962 and 1985, the number of riots with deaths and the number of deaths both increased, to five and 62, respectively; (3) in the ten-year period between 1988 and 1998 marked by the disappearance of the Congress and the reconstitution of interparty struggle between the BJP and the SP, there were four riots with deaths, and the number of officially recorded deaths reached the maximum of 102.

## ELECTORAL TURNOUT, INTERPARTY COMPETITIVENESS, AND RIOTS

From the history of the electoral contests, we may learn much about the prominent political aspirants, their political and ideological affiliations, their caste and communal identifications, the intensity of popular political involvement and of party competition, and the relationship of all these, particularly the latter, to the history of communal riots in the city. Let us consider first the overall pattern of party competition and displacement in the 14 Legislative Assembly contests during the 45 years for which we have the results. The two principal contending forces over most of this long period have been the Congress and the militant Hindu parties. In the 14 elections, the Congress

TABLE 8.2. Winning party in 14 Legislative Assembly contests,
Aligarh constituency, 1952–96

| Year | Congress | Militant Hindu | Other |
|------|----------|----------------|-------|
| 1952 | X | | |
| 1955 | X | | |
| 1957 | X | | |
| 1962 | | | RPI |
| 1967 | | BJS | |
| 1969 | X | | |
| 1974 | | BJS | |
| 1977 | | JP | |
| 1980 | | | BKD |
| 1985 | X | | |
| 1989 | | BJP | |
| 1991 | | BJP | |
| 1993 | | BJP | |
| 1996 | | | JD |

has won five times, the militant Hindu party six times, and other parties three
times (see Table 8.2).

Figure 8.2 shows the history of the constituency for the two leading political forces from 1952 to 1996,[3] namely, the Congress and the militant Hindu
parties. The latter term includes the Bharatiya Jan Sangh (BJS) from 1952 to
1974, the Janata Party in 1977, and the BJP in succeeding years. It is evident
from the chart that the electoral contest between these two parties in the constituencies divides neatly for the Legislative Assembly contests into the same
three periods identified above: Congress dominance in 1952 and 1957, intense
competition between the two party forces from 1962 to 1985, and finally displacement of the Congress by the BJP as the stronger force after 1985. This
long-term dual contest for predominance between the Congress and the militant Hindu parties has, however, been interrupted from time to time by parties representing the lower and backward castes. In 1962, the seat was won by
the low-caste party, the Republican Party, and in 1980 and 1996 by parties
identified especially with the interests of the backward castes, the BKD in 1980
and the Janata Dal in 1996.

In order to consider more precisely the relationship between interparty
competition and riots, it is necessary to look more closely at the temporal

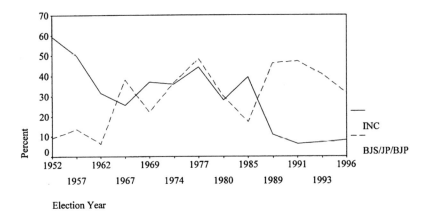

FIG. 8.2. Vote shares for Congress and militant Hindu parties,
Legislative Assembly elections, 1952–96

proximity of riots and elections, and at their juxtaposition—that is, whether
riots precede elections with intense interparty competition or follow them.
In other words, if a causal connection is to be established, we need to know
whether interparty competition is a factor in riot production or whether riot
production intensifies interparty competition. Two standard indicators of the
intensity of electoral competition are turnout and the interval between the
winning candidate and the runner-up. Each will be examined in turn below.
In addition to these, two others suited to the specific situation in Aligarh will
be considered, namely, the degree of communalization and polarization of
the electorate—that is to say, the extent to which voters vote as communal
blocs, and the extent to which, in particular elections, they vote as antagonistic, polarized communal blocs.

### Turnout

Electoral turnout has varied considerably between 1952 and 1996, as revealed
in the table and charts showing turnout rates in Aligarh compared with those
in the state as a whole. Looking first at the turnout figures for Aligarh City
alone in Table 8.3, it is evident that there has been a considerable range in
turnout rates, from a low of 45.08 percent in the 1985 election to a high figure of 71.15 percent in the 1974 midterm election. There have also been notable fluctuations in turnout, with two rising slopes and two declining slopes
(Figure 8.3).

TABLE 8.3. Comparison of turnout rates in Aligarh and Uttar Pradesh
Legislative Assembly elections, 1952–96[a]

| Year[b] | Aligarh turnout | State turnout |
|---|---|---|
| 1952 | 46.54 | 37.88 |
| 1957 | 57.89 | 44.92 |
| 1962 | 64.78 | 48.58 |
| 1967 | 62.39 | 50.96 |
| 1969 | 70.35 | 52.22 |
| 1974 | 71.15 | 55.17 |
| 1977 | 56.11 | 44.87 |
| 1980 | 45.99 | 44.00 |
| 1985 | 45.08 | 45.22 |
| 1989 | 55.14 | 48.49 |
| 1991 | 54.10 | 47.20 |
| 1993 | 62.08 | 55.83 |
| 1996 | 52.13 | 54.91 |

[a] Figures are valid votes turnout.
[b] The atypical 1955 by-election has been left out of this table.

Between 1952 and 1974, the overall trend in Aligarh turnout was upward, with only a slight downward deviation in 1967. The trend in Aligarh in those years corresponds for the most part with that for the state as a whole, with the significant difference that the turnout figures are very much higher for Aligarh City than for the whole state. The first concern, therefore, must be to explain why the increasing interest in electoral politics between 1952 and 1974 was so much greater in Aligarh than in the state as a whole[4] and what, if anything, the greater turnout in Aligarh had to do with riots.

The first declining slope in turnout rates occurs in the period between 1974 and 1985. The slope is downward in this period for both Aligarh City and the whole state. Moreover, the two lines converge in 1985. The convergence, however, is momentary; both lines move upward again between 1985 and 1993 while the Aligarh slope regains some distance between it and the line for the whole state. However, the distance between the two slopes is not so great as in the earlier period. Our second problem, therefore, is to explain Aligarh's divergence again—not from the general upward trend, but from the general average.

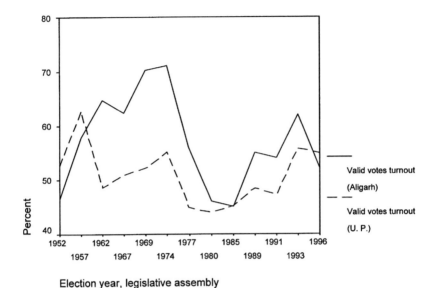

FIG. 8.3. Valid votes turnout in Aligarh City Legislative Assembly elections, 1952–96

The second declining slope occurs between the 1993 and 1996 elections, when the decline is much greater for Aligarh than the whole state. Further, turnout in Aligarh in the 1996 election crosses that for the whole state for the first time since 1962, but on this occasion moving below the state line. The third puzzle, then, is to explain the considerable decline in turnout between the two most recent elections, in this case a decline that is not really paralleled by the much more modest downward movement in the state slope.

The three divergences in turnout rates between Aligarh and the whole state cannot be explained solely with reference to the incidence of communal riots and a corresponding state of communal tension in the town. The assumption behind such an explanation would be that communal tension is mirrored in interparty conflicts as the different parties blame each other for it and the violence associated with it, thus increasing interest in the elections that occur after riots. That explanation is supported insofar as the first rising slope is concerned by the fact that there was a sequence of riots in the town during this period, beginning with the October riots of 1961 before the 1962 General Elections and including the 1971, 1972, and 1974 riots (Table 3.1). It is also supported by the rising slope between 1985 and 1993, for it was between these two dates that the buildup of communal tension associated with the Ayodhya movement occurred in the state as a whole, but probably to a greater extent in Aligarh than in most other cities and towns in the state. The great riot of 1990–91 in Aligarh provides evidence sufficient in itself for the latter statement. On the other hand, this explanation is not consistent with the plunge in turnout rates in Aligarh between 1974 and 1985, a period that witnessed the long series of riots and violent communal incidents over the three years between 1978 and 1980.

## Interparty Competitiveness

We must, therefore, look further into the election results to consider what kind of relationship exists, if any, between communal riots and party/ electoral politics. One possibility, already stated above, is that there may be a relationship between the intensity of interparty competition, on the one hand, and communal tension and riots, on the other hand—that is, that communal riots may contribute to an increase in interparty competitiveness or, vice versa, that increased electoral competitiveness may contribute to communal tension and riots. There does in fact appear to be a closer correspondence between interparty competitiveness—measured by the size of the interval between the two main parties, as shown in Figure 8.4[5]—and the incidence of riots. It appears especially close in the long period of intense interparty competition between 1974 and 1993, when six of the major riots in which there were deaths occurred.

Leaving aside the exceptional circumstances of the 1955 bye-election,[6] the period in Aligarh between 1952 and 1962 was, as we have seen, associated with the dominance of the Indian National Congress and with a huge interval between it and the second-place party. Interparty competitiveness then increases significantly in the first election held after the 1961 riots, remains at roughly that level during the next two elections, increases greatly once again during the 1974 elections (a year in which riotous violence occurred, but was contained), and remains high throughout the next decade. During the decade of the 1980s—free of large-scale rioting—competitiveness increased in 1985, but declined in 1989, then increased again in both the 1991 and 1993 elections during the period of rioting and extreme tension associated with the 1990 riots and the Ayodhya movement. Finally, in the absence of major rioting since 1991 and the decline of communal tensions generally in the years since the destruction of the mosque in 1992, interparty competitiveness declined in 1996 to its lowest level since 1957.

In effect, therefore, interparty competitiveness is more strongly associated on the whole with rioting and communal tensions than is turnout.

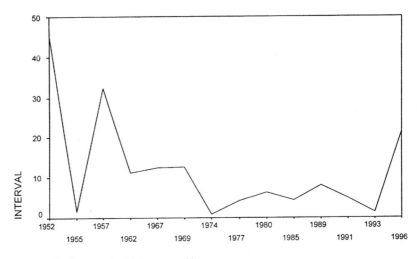

FIG. 8.4. Percent interval between winning and runner-up candidates,
Aligarh City Legislative Assembly elections, 1952–96

Moreover—and curiously—interparty competitiveness acts independently
of turnout, with which the correlation is negative(−.12). That is, the common
positive association in electoral systems generally between competitiveness
and high turnout does not hold in Aligarh. Evidently, therefore, considering
both these measures in relation to the incidence of riots, riots in general are
not necessarily followed by elections in which there is a high turnout.
However, riots or near-riotous mobilization have preceded elections in
which interparty competitiveness was intense, and interparty competitiveness has declined in the absence of riots.

Intense electoral competition is associated with riots in Aligarh and usually, though not always, precedes them. Moreover, riots have often occurred
in close temporal proximity to elections. The association is illustrated more
clearly in Table 8.4, which gives the dates of riots and elections in Aligarh from
1946 to 1998. Thus, the riots of March, 29, 1946, occurred just after the elections of February–March 1946. The February 1962 General Elections were preceded by the October 1961 riots, four months earlier. The series of riots in the
years 1978 to 1980 sandwiched the elections in January and May 1980. The
contained riots of November 10, 1989, occurred in the midst of the 1989 election campaign. The great riots of December 1990–January 1991 preceded by
four to five months the elections of May 1991.

If, however, one tries—as Wilkinson has done[7]—to make a precise calculation regarding the proximity in time and the precedence in sequence of riots and elections, the relationship is partly obscured. First, there is the problem of counting the number of riots, especially in the two long periods of rioting in 1978 and 1980, which extended sporadically over months in both cases. These riots could be counted as many riots or as one. I have listed these riots on the charts as two separate, ongoing disturbances. If we do so, the number of riots on the list is 24, of which 22 are dated. Using Wilkinson's criterion of six months on either side of an election as a proximity measure, 12 of these riots occurred beyond the six-month period before or after an election (coded NP for non-proximate), whereas 10 occurred within the proximity period, including 3 that occurred in the month of the election (coded S for simultaneous), thereby eliminating any obvious correlation between riots and elections. Further, of the 10 riots within Wilkinson's proximity period (including the 3 "simultaneous"), 5 occurred before and 5 after an election.

Even if we confine the analysis to the 12 most intense riots, those which produced deaths, there is a similarly ambiguous division. Six occurred beyond the proximity period and 6 within it, including 2 in the month of the election. Of the remaining 4 within the proximity period, 3 occurred before the elections, 1 afterward.

Although the statistical association, therefore, is indeterminate, there is no doubt that riots in Aligarh have been implicated deeply in the political process, including both electoral politics and the politics of mass mobilization, as in the Ayodhya movement that intensified and led to violence there just before the December 1990–January 1991 riots. Thus, in the case of the worst riots in Aligarh's history, they were preceded by a statewide mass mobilization of militant Hindus out to destroy the mosque in Ayodhya, creating havoc in Aligarh as well, and were followed by the elections the following May. This type of association supports more broadly the Clausewitzian argument I made 25 years ago in connection with the August 1967 Ranchi riots in Bihar, namely, that in India, riots are a continuation of politics by other means,[8] of routine by violent politics, but the political ends are the same. Those ends are what politics are so much about in so many places, plainly and simply the capture of power through scapegoating and intimidation of others, rather than persuasion of voters on issues of public policy. The means, whether routine or violent, are to consolidate the votes of one ethnic/religious group by portraying another as a dangerous threat and, as we will see in later chapters, by blaming the violence upon the victimized group.

TABLE 8.4. Riots and elections

| Riots | Elections | Proximity |
|---|---|---|
| | February 13–March 25, 1946[b] | |
| March 29, 1946[a] | | S[f] |
| March 4, 1950[a] | | NP |
| | January 3–25, 1952 (LA/LS)[c] | |
| June 6, 1954 | | NP |
| | Till July 31, 1955[d] | |
| September 14, 1956 | | 6B |
| | February 24, 1957 (LS) | |
| | March 12, 1957 (LA) | |
| October 1–3, 1961[a] | | 4B |
| | February 19, 21, and 25, 1962 (LS/LA) | |
| 1966 | | NA |
| | February 15–28, 1967 (LS) | |
| 1969 | February 9, 1969[e] | NA |
| | March 1, 1971 (LA/LS) | |
| March 2, 1971[a] | | S |
| June 1971 | | A3 |
| June 1972[a] | | NP |
| August 1972 | | NP |
| | February 24 or 26, 1974 (LA) | |
| October 3–5, 1974 | | NP |
| | March 20, 1977 (LS) | |
| | June 10, 12, or 14, 1977(LA) | |
| October–December 1978[a] | | NP |
| May 1979[a] | | NP |
| June 17, 1979 | | NP |

## Communalization and Electoral Polarization

A third variable to consider in the history of electoral contests in Aligarh City in relation to communal tension and riots may be called "communalization." To what extent has the electoral contest in the city itself become a contest between spokesmen for the Muslim and Hindu communities, respectively, in which other factors such as economic and other noncommunal issues, or even intercaste relations, have been of less significance? A fourth variable may be called "polarization." To what extent has the electoral contest eliminated

| Riots | Elections | Proximity |
|---|---|---|
| | January 6, 1980 (LS) | |
| | May 28 or 31, 1980 (LA) | |
| August–November 1980[a] | | A3 |
| March 1983 | | NP |
| | December 28, 1984 (LS) | |
| | March 6, 1985 (LA) | |
| June 1987 | | NP |
| October 1988[a] | | NP |
| November 10, 1989 | November 22, 1989 (LA/LS) | S |
| November 1990–January 1991[a] | | 4B |
| | May 20, 1991 (LA) | |
| December 1992[a] | | NP |
| | November 21, 1993 (LA) | |
| March 1994 | | A4 |
| December 1995[a] | | 5B |
| | May 7, 1996 (LS) | |
| | October 9, 1996 (LA) | |
| | March, 1998 (LS) | |

[a]Riots with deaths.

[b]Elections for different types of constituencies were held on different days throughout this period; P. D. Reeves et al., *A Handbook to Elections in Uttar Pradesh, 1920–1951* (Delhi: Manohar Book Service, 1975), p. 245.

[c]LA = Legislative Assembly; LS = Lok Sabha.

[d]I have not been able to find the date on which this midterm election was held, only that it was held before July 31, 1955.

[e]Uttar Pradesh, Office of the Chief Electoral Officer, *Results of Mid-Term General Elections (1969) to the Legislative Assembly of Uttar Pradesh* (Allahabad: Superintendent, Printing and Stationery, 1969), p. 75.

[f]S = riots occurring simultaneously with election; A = riots occurring after election; B = riots occurring before election. Numbers refer to months preceding or following the closest election: NP = non-proximate; NA = not available.

other factors than communal identity as predictors of voting behavior and concentrated the votes of the two communities in more or less total opposition to each other to such an extent that no other factors and no parties or candidates representing counter-tendencies of any sort could influence the outcome? Most important for our purposes, to what extent have the degrees of communalization and polarization in particular elections been influenced by previous or continuous intercommunal violence before or during the election campaign period itself?

In order to answer these questions, I have created an extensive dataset for

12 elections, including both the Aligarh City Legislative Assembly constituency and the parliamentary segments, by polling booth. This dataset
makes it possible to identify the specific polling booths and *mohallas* in which
each candidate polled his or her best and worst votes. Reaggregation of the
polling booths to conform to *mohalla* boundaries also made it possible to
run correlations and regressions to determine the precise association between
the religious and Scheduled Caste populations, on the one hand, and the
vote shares of every candidate by *mohalla* or groups of *mohallas*, on the other
hand. The data are too extensive to be presented easily within the compass
of this volume. Consequently, while the overall correlations will be reported
by community/caste and party for all the 12 elections for which I have the
data, the detailed results will be provided only for those elections that illustrate most clearly the relationship between riots and party electoral politics. I
have selected for the latter purpose the elections of 1962, held in the aftermath
of the October 1961 riots, and the sequence of elections in 1989, 1991, and 1993
which occurred after the great Aligarh riots of 1990–91 and the contained rioting that occurred after the destruction of the mosque in Ayodhya. The overall results for the 12 elections will be presented in the remainder of this chapter,
the detailed results on specific elections in the following chapters.

## THE SUPPORT BASES OF THE BJP
## AND THE CONGRESS FROM 1957 TO 1985

The major strength of the BJP, of its predecessor party, the Jan Sangh, and
of candidates seen as spokesmen for militant Hindu nationalism is the consistency of the support base that underlies it. Table 8.5 suggests that, at least
from 1957 until 1985, these candidates have been able to rely upon a stratum
of militant Hindu sentiment that has persisted through time. The size of the
support base has certainly fluctuated, but there can be no doubt about the
existence of a steadfast seam within the Hindu population of the city that
has been mined successfully to some degree in every election throughout
this period. Every election for which station-wise polling data are available,
whether for the Legislative Assembly or for Parliament, has produced high
correlation coefficients at significance levels of $p=.000$, with the range in the
correlations from a low of .47 in the 1980 Lok Sabha election to an extraordinary high of .96 in the 1962 Lok Sabha election. Even in 1980, the somewhat lower correlation between the Janata Party vote and Hindus and others
is misleading, since there were two militant Hindu candidates in this election. Krishna Kumar Navman ran as an independent at this time, dividing

the militant Hindu vote. Even so, the correlation coefficient between his vote and percent Hindus and others was .38 (p=.005).

In contrast to the relative consistency of the support base for militant Hinduism, that for the Congress in relation to Hindu and Muslim population concentrations has fluctuated drastically from election to election, as indicated in Table 8.6. It is evident also that the fluctuations depend heavily upon the religion of the Congress candidate. The strongest negative correlation coefficient with percent Hindus and others, as well as the strongest correlation with percent Muslims, occurred in 1969 when the Congress candidate was a Muslim, Ahmad Loot Khan. The second strongest set of negative/positive correlations occurred in the 1967 Legislative Assembly elections when, likewise, the Congress candidate was a Muslim. On three occasions when the Congress fielded Muslim candidates, namely, in the 1962 Lok Sabha and the 1980 and 1989 Legislative Assembly elections, the correlations with percent Hindus and others were positive, but the significance levels were low. Conversely, the four highest positive correlations with percent Hindus and others occurred when the Congress fielded Hindu candidates, in the 1962, 1985, and 1991 Legislative Assembly and the 1984 Lok Sabha elections. On all those occasions, the significance level of the Congress correlation with Hindus and others was above .002.

The contrast between the consistency of the militant Hindu support base and the fluctuating support base of the Congress is brought out in Figures 8.5, 8.6, and 8.7. Figure 8.5 graphs the results of the struggle between the Congress and militant Hindu candidates for the Hindu vote. Figure 8.6 demonstrates the relative stability of the militant Hindu vote shares among all three population categories, while Figure 8.7 reveals the instability of the Congress vote share among the same three categories. More specifically, while the militant Hindu candidates' correlation coefficients with percent Hindus and others remained above .47 throughout the entire period from 1957 to 1985 (Table 8.5 and Figure 8.5), those for the Congress took a very steep drop from the 1962 election onwards until 1984 and 1985. During the Rajiv Gandhi landslide in 1984, the Congress candidate was Usha Rani. In the Legislative Assembly election that followed, the Congress candidate was identified with Rajiv Gandhi. In these two successive elections, the correlations for the Congress returned to their highest points since the 1962 elections, nearly equalling those for the BJP. Then, of course, everything changed again with the rise of the Ayodhya movement in the four elections that followed, for only two of which we have the detailed polling station data. The Congress correlation with percent Hindus plummeted to .06 with a Muslim candi-

TABLE 8.5. Correlation between votes for militant Hindu candidates and local population composition across Aligarh *mohallas* in selected elections, 1957–91

| | Election Year and Type (Legislative Assembly [LA] or Lok Sabha [LS]), | | | | |
|---|---|---|---|---|---|
| | 1957 (LA) (N=39) | 1962 (LA) (N=44) | 1962 (LS) (N=44) | 1967 (LA) (N=41) | 1967 (LS) (N=41) |
| Community/ Caste | Jan Sangh | Jan Sangh | Shiv Kumar Shastri | Jan Sangh | Shiv Kumar Shastri |
| Hindus and others | .59** | .58** | .96** | .76** | .77** |
| Muslim | −.50** | −.44** | −.86** | −.65** | −.68** |
| Scheduled Castes | −.15 | −.30* | −.11 | −.22 | −.18 |

\* = .05 or less.
\*\*p = .01 or less.

TABLE 8.6. Correlations between votes for Congress and local population composition across Aligarh *mohallas* in selected elections, 1957–91

| | Election Year and Type (Legislative Assembly [LA] | | | | |
|---|---|---|---|---|---|
| | 1957 (LA) (N=39) | 1962 (LA) (N=44) | 1962 (LS) (N=44) | 1967 (LA) (N=41) | 1967 (LS) (N=41) |
| Community/ Caste | Anant Ram Verma | Anant Ram Verma | Jarrar Haider | Ravind Yusuf Rashid Khwaja | Netra Pal Singh |
| Hindus and others | −.00 | .73** | .22 | −.74** | −.66** |
| Muslims | −.04 | −.74** | −.31* | −.74** | .66** |
| Scheduled Castes | .05 | .12 | .29* | −.06 | −.05 |

\*p = .05 or less.
\*\*p = .01 or less.

| and Party or Name of Principal Militant Hindu Candidate | | | | | | |
|---|---|---|---|---|---|---|
| 1969 (LA) (N=41) | 1980 (LS) (N=53) | 1980 (LA) (N=53) | 1984 (LS) (N=65) | 1985 (LA) (N=66) | 1989 (LA) (N–70) | 1991 (LA) (N–70) |
| Jan Sangh | Janata Party | BJP | BJP | BJP | BJP | BJP |
| .57** | .47** | .68** | .59** | .63** | .76** | .73** |
| −.52** | −.53** | −.62** | −.48** | −.51** | −.75** | −.73** |
| −.12 | .22 | −.08 | −.26* | −.24 | .06 | .07 |

| or Lok Sabha [LS]), and Candidate | | | | | | |
|---|---|---|---|---|---|---|
| 1969 (LA) (N=41) | 1980 (LS) (N=53) | 1980 (LA) (N=53) | 1984 (LS) (N=65) | 1985 (LA) (N=66) | 1989 (LA) (N=70) | 1991 (LA) (N–70) |
| Ahmad Loot Khan | Ghanshyam Singh | Ahmad Loot Khan | Usha Rani | Baldev Singh | Mohammad Furkan | Bhanu Pratap |
| −.90** | −.42** | .23 | .51** | .59** | .06 | .36** |
| .91** | .45** | −.32* | −.49** | −.62** | −.09 | −.40** |
| −.01 | −.13 | .23 | −.00 | .13 | .09 | .14 |

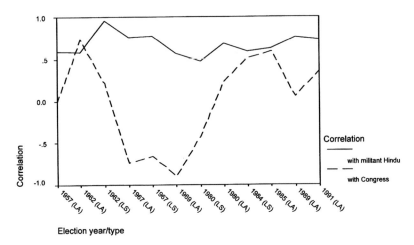

FIG. 8.5. Correlations for Congress and militant Hindu candidate vote shares
with percentage of Hindus and others, 1957–91

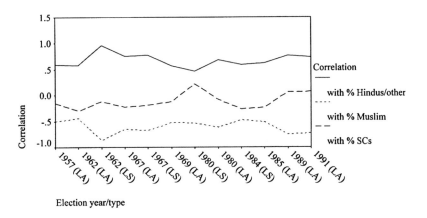

FIG. 8.6. Correlations for militant Hindu party vote shares
with percentage of religious/caste groups, 1957–91

date in 1989, then rose again to .36 with a Hindu candidate in 1991. In those
elections, its overall vote share also plunged, while the electoral contest
became polarized between the BJP candidate, Krishna Kumar Navman, and
his invariably Muslim opponent from either the Janata Dal, the BSP, or the
SP—which latter finally defeated him.

The evidence provided so far, therefore, is overwhelming and persuasive

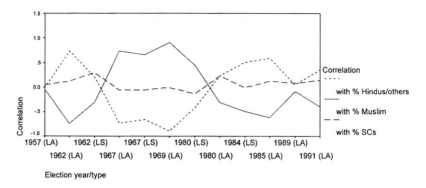

FIG. 8.7. Correlations for Congress vote shares with percentage
of religious/caste groups, 1957–91

on two points. The first is that *major riots before an election are followed
by—and most probably produce—intense interparty competition.* Second, *such
collective violence produces not only intensified party competition, but a communalized and polarized electoral result.* It will be shown in the next chapter
how the politicians in Aligarh contribute to the intensification and communalization of party competition through their involvement in several ways
in the production, exploitation, interpretation, and use of collective violence
for political advantage.

# 9 / The Practice of Communal Politics

Although I have argued that, insofar as Aligarh City is concerned, riots that precede elections intensify interparty competition and provide a basis for it through communalization and polarization of the electorate, Aligarh is also part of a broader framework of interparty competition at the state and national levels that must also be kept in mind in considering the overall relationship. In the case of the mass mobilization that accompanied the three successive communalized elections of 1989, 1991, and 1993 in Aligarh, interparty competition intensified only after the great riots of 1991. However, it was the intense struggle for power at the Center and in the state of U.P., accompanied by the Mandal agitation and the Ram Janmabhoomi movement, that initiated the process. As one of my respondents put it just after the 1990–91 riots, they were a consequence of the "particular game . . . going on in Delhi, how to win votes and how to become the prime minister. I think that was one of the important reasons of [the communal riots] in the whole U.P. state and Aligarh."[1]

Moreover, as this same respondent put it, "the riots did not occur in a day or so," but involved three years of continuous preparation and rehearsal on the part of the BJP, the VHP, and other parts of the *Sangh Parivar*, punctuated by the *shilanyas* of 1990 and the vast rioting that was associated with it in Aligarh, followed by the destruction of the mosque on December 1992 and the vast rioting associated with it throughout most of the country. Nor can there be any doubt that there was deliberate provocation of Hindus to attack and kill Muslims, available in the form of tape cassettes of the fiery speeches of the BJP female "*sannyasi,*" Sadhvi Rithambara. Although we do not have any recorded speeches of RSS-BJP-VHP leaders in Aligarh, it cannot be doubted from what they have said to me in polite encounters with a foreign scholar that they spoke even more directly to their followers and to their voters in the communalized Hindu *mohallas* of Aligarh than they did with me.

Furthermore, the militant Hindus have their own object of hatred in Aligarh, their own Babri Masjid, as it were, in the presence of the AMU, which has been used for the past half century "as a symbol that this is a Pakistani center, antinational center,"[2] and was used so effectively in the great rumor about the AMU Medical College Hospital killings in 1991. So, the AMU, like the Babri Masjid, was "very much a part of this whole game" of competition for votes.

Throughout this broader vote competition, Mulayam Singh Yadav and the Janata Dal appealed directly and successfully to the Muslim voters, standing forth as their protector and as the protector of the mosque. Although his police saved the mosque from destruction in 1990, they did not save the Muslims of Aligarh from the riots that descended upon them in its aftermath. Further, it was the BJP that emerged victorious, riding the electoral wave produced by the *shilanyas* and its riotous aftermath, in both Aligarh and in the state as a whole. Indeed, the May 1991 elections themselves were accompanied by additional waves of rioting in many constituencies in the state. Moreover, those elections brought the BJP to power in the state for the first time.[3] That government in turn created the conditions that made possible the destruction of the mosque in December 1992.

The respondent previously quoted remarked to me at the tail end of the 1990–91 riots in Aligarh, "This is a political riot, . . . a communal-cum-political riot."[4] Indeed, the whole period from the first stirrings of the VHP mobilization over the mosque in Ayodhya in 1984 until its dénouement in December 1992 was a deliberately provocative buildup of communal tension that intensified political competition. It also produced—predictably—waves of communal rioting that in turn built heightened communal solidarities in constituencies with large Muslim populations deliberately targeted by the BJP for special efforts; the rioting in turn fed back into the competition for votes, in a circle that ended only in the aftermath of the destruction of the mosque, when the returns from communalization of the electorate and the production of communal violence rapidly diminished.

## THE POLITICIZATION OF COMMUNALISM AND RIOTS AS A CONTINUATION OF COMMUNAL POLITICS BY OTHER MEANS

My interviews are replete with explanations that consider the political process central to the communalization of Hindu-Muslim relations in India. It also happens to be my own preferred contextualization, the one I have used and presented over many years in several of my writings. It is not, however, my own invention. One can find it articulated by persons at many levels in Indian society, particularly from those in the secular parties and factions associated with left and agrarian politics in north India, and especially the moderate and radical left parties that used to carry the words "socialist" or "people" somewhere in their title (such as Samyukta Socialist Party [United Socialist Party], or Lok Dal [People's Party]), and nowadays generally carry the word "*janata*" in their title (as in Janata Dal [People's Party]).[5]

My interviews also provide evidence to support the general point of view that riots are an integral part of the process of political/electoral competition. Politicians and political parties benefit directly from the politicization of communal affiliations, in which the fomenting of communal riots plays an important part. The responsibilities of particular groups and parties in promoting riots and the extent to which they are preplanned and organized in advance is often difficult to demonstrate, but it is equally often clear enough that there is a direct connection between the politicization of communal differences and the killing that takes place in the riots that result from them. Moreover, the politicians all know this very well.

It is in this sense, among others, that communal riots in India are a continuation and extension of communal politics by other means.[6] That does not mean that the murderers, arsonists, looters, and rapists are themselves political people. Sometimes politicians or political activists are found among the perpetrators, but most are not. Nevertheless, communal riots play upon preexisting communal antagonisms, many of which have in turn been created by previous political movements. One cannot say, therefore, that there is an independent bedrock of communal prejudices having nothing to do with politics that lies slumbering, waiting to explode. These antagonisms are partly created by political mobilizations, nurtured in apparently peaceful periods, and drawn upon by political leaders and parties when an emotional issue, such as the status of the Urdu language or the alleged existence of a mosque built upon a Hindu temple destroyed by Muslims in centuries past, becomes salient or is made salient and is presented in order to divide and polarize Hindus and Muslims politically, and to gain political/electoral advantage thereby.

The riots that often follow from such politicization of communal difference and mobilization of community support are then used by political parties to discredit one another, to gain the support of one community, and to consolidate a community's votes. The electoral strategies of political parties and groups may change dramatically after major riots in a district such as Aligarh or in the state as a whole. Such was the case in Aligarh District as early as 1962, when the Congress's virtual monopoly of power was broken by the alliance between newly mobilized Scheduled Caste voters, on the one hand, and Muslim leaders from the AMU angered by the riots of 1961, on the other hand. The latter, as will be described in detail in the following chapter, joined forces with the Republican Party, representing the Scheduled Castes, to defeat the Congress in the contest for the Aligarh parliamentary seat and in several of its component Legislative Assembly constituencies. Such was the case in the elections of 1991 in the entire state, when the combined issues of reservations for backward castes and Ayodhya, played upon by the BJP, created a consolidation of upper-caste Hindu voting, particularly in constituencies with large Muslim minorities, which the BJP specifically targeted for communal mobilization and Hindu consolidation.

## THE INSTIGATION AND JUSTIFICATION OF COMMUNAL VIOLENCE

At the center of the Aligarh organization of communal violence is the local network of the RSS family of organizations, and allegedly in its forefront are Krishna Kumar Navman and his son. Navman's name has appeared many times in the accounts above. It is time to pay closer attention to his role in these events, which became ever more important with the rise of the militant Hindu movement in the 1980s.

Mr. Navman was born and raised in Aligarh City. He was born in 1936 and joined the RSS as a young man, sometime in his teenage years. When asked why he joined the RSS, he said that it "build[s] up your character" and is "a nationalist organization." He was educated up to the Intermediate standard and graduated after taking the Hindi Visharat examination from the Hiralal Barahseni Inter College.

Navman, as noted earlier, is a big businessman engaged in the publication of commercial books. His factory, warehouse, and home are in the riot-prone *mohalla* of Manik Chauk. Two-thirds of the population of the *mohalla* are Varshneys by caste, to which Navman himself also belongs. He believes that "Aligarh politics are basically dependent on the relations between Hindus and Muslims" and that the Muslims are responsible for what he characterized in 1983 as a "virus" of communal violence that was "spreading all over,"

FIG. 9.1. Krishna Kumar Navman, November 1997

not only in Aligarh. From 1970 to 1974, Navman was secretary of the Jan Sangh. In 1974, he contested his first election in a rural constituency of Aligarh District, Barauli, as the Jan Sangh candidate, and came in third with 11.1 percent of the vote, not enough to retain his security deposit. When I first met Navman in 1983, he said he was a member neither of the Jan Sangh nor of the BJP, though he proudly acknowledged his association with the RSS. In fact, however, he had defied the discipline of the RSS in the 1980 parliamentary elections. The RSS supported the Janata Party in that election, but Navman chose to contest as well as an independent. He came in fourth in a field of 26 candidates, but polled only 7,039 votes, amounting to a vote percent of 2.12. Navman's vote share in the Aligarh segment of the constituency, though somewhat higher, was still not impressive; he polled 3,735 votes, which gave him a vote share of 5.74 percent. His candidacy had no effect on the election outcome and he again lost his security deposit. In 1983, Navman was "still angry with the RSS, and the RSS [was] still angry with him."[7]

Even the local police inspectors in riot-prone areas named Navman as "the main fellow among Hindus" instigating people to riot against Muslims.[8] Navman and his defenders, however, insist that he has never instigated any riots and that, on the contrary, he has been repeatedly victimized by a biased administration and falsely arrested and implicated in cases arising out of riots. For example, during the 1978 riots, at a time when the Janata government was in power in the state, and Kalyan Singh of the BJP, elected from another constituency in Aligarh District, was a minister in that government, Navman was "implicated" (allegedly falsely) in "eight to ten murder cases" as well as some arson cases.[9]

When I first met Mr. Navman in 1983 in a prearranged interview appointment, I found him waiting for me upstairs in an office in his business premises, a quite large business and warehouse complex. He was sitting with a folio-size copy of the Koran in front of him in a trilingual edition (Hindi, Urdu, and English), from which he quoted me several passages that to him clearly indicated the evil character of the Muslims and their religion, which he considered to be the root cause of the communal problem and of riots in Aligarh. Among the passages he found particularly relevant was one that he read to me in English: "Mohammedans should not make any non-Mohammedans their friends." The establishment of friendships between Muslims and non-Muslims is a danger to Islam because Muslims then may become *kafirs*. Therefore, he interpreted the Koran as saying that "such people must be found and killed." I tried repeatedly to interrupt his readings and the conclusions he drew from them, in order to get him to focus specifically on the causes of and circumstances surrounding riots in Aligarh, but he insisted that these passages and the Koran itself were "the source of all riots" in Aligarh and elsewhere in India. He was particularly offended by what he perceived as the Muslim condemnation of all *kafirs* and by the term itself.[10]

Navman felt personally aggrieved, also, that Muslims of Aligarh were out to get him, as indicated in my 1983 interview with him.

PRB: Why are these cases against you?

KKN: They want to denigrate the RSS through me. They say, Navman belongs to RSS, Navman started the riots, so the RSS started, or is the main cause of the riots.

PRB: Who started the cases?

KKN: Muslims at the instigation of AMU.

PRB: Who in AMU?

KKN: No one in particular.

PRB: What are the charges against you, specifically?

KKN: Murder, dacoity [gang robbery], robbery. They don't say I personally did it, but that at my direction others did these things.[11]

When I met Navman a third time in 1997, having interviewed him also in 1993, he greeted me as an old friend. I asked him how old he was. He said he was 61, to which I replied that we were exactly the same age. He then revealed to me a sense of weariness at the difficulties he has had to face in his life. He began by saying he had "faced lots of problems in [his] life."[12] By then, he had been to jail about 25 times by his rough reckoning, of which the last times were during the Ramjanmabhoomi movement in December 1990 and again in January 1991.

In December 1990, during the great riots, Mulayam Singh Yadav was the chief minister and, according to Navman, Mulayam Singh himself sent instructions to the district administration for Navman's arrest. He was actually arrested initially on October 12, presumably as a preventive measure at a time of growing tension in the city. A first "installment" of rioting took place between October 18 and November 6, during which time Navman was in jail. He was released a few days after the end of this first phase of rioting, so Navman was present in the city during the main phases of rioting in November and December.[13] When rioting again broke out and curfew was imposed, orders again went out for Navman's arrest. Although the city was under curfew, Navman was "roaming around this area" (that is, Manik Chauk) until the police came to arrest him at 4 A.M. one morning, but they could not do so because, he claims, "more than 20,000 persons" came out of their houses in the midst of the curfew, with the result that the police "could not get the courage to arrest him." He was not finally arrested until January 20, 1991, when he was on his way to give a speech at the Ram Lila fairgrounds. From there, he was taken straight to the Fatehgarh Central Jail and locked up for two months under the National Security Act, after which he was released without any proceedings being instituted against him.[14]

Navman's son also was said by one informant to have been quite active during these riots. His son is considered to be even more militant than he, said to be "a Bajrang Dal chief." Navman himself virtually acknowledged his son's activities, although at first, when I asked where his son was during these riots, he replied that "he was in his home." When I pressed further and remarked that people had said his son had also played a big role in these riots, going around mobilizing the people (that is, the Hindus) to attack Muslims and the like, and that he had become famous, he responded, "People believe that if they have any difficulty or if they are in a dire hour of crisis, then he would come and help them. So, maybe he was approached by a few people and went out to help them." Navman's son was arrested as a consequence of his helping activities in the first week of January 1991.[15]

Navman was present in Ayodhya at the time of the destruction of the mosque on December 6, 1992, and gave me his own eyewitness account of it. When he arrived in Ayodhya just after noon on December 6th, he said, "there was total confusion and a lot of hulla [*sic*] going on there" and people had already climbed up to the domes. He claims that L. K. Advani personally admonished the crowd and attempted to stop them from their work of destruction.

NAVMAN: But the people were in no mood to listen to him. . . . They scolded him back and they told him, *ki,* you go and give your speeches and let us do our work. Actually, the people were very tired, being called there again and again and being dispersed and called again and being told to go back and called again and told to put some sand somewhere or perform some *puja* somewhere and then go back. They were not willing to listen to anybody.

PRB: And how did you feel, at that time?

NAVMAN: I was happy to see it.

PRB: So you were on the side of the crowd, that wanted to take down that mosque right then and there and not follow Advani's advice?

NAVMAN: I felt every bit like the crowd. It is a headache and it is a national humiliation and an issue like this ought to be ended once and for all.[16]

In my second interview with Navman in 1993, I asked him to explain to me why there had been such a terrible riot in Aligarh in December 1990, but no riot at all in the city after the destruction of the Babri Masjid. He gave the following response.

Whenever there have been riots in this city, it has been because the Muslims have taken the initiative. In 1971, there was a fact-finding commission appointed and the decision which the commission gave was that the Muslims had started the riot which the commission was investigating. So, always in Aligarh City, it is the Muslims who begin the riot. Now this time, the Muslims were a little scared because they kept getting the feeling that previously when Mulayam Singh's government was in power and it was a government which was sympathetically inclined towards them, even then they had to put up with so many hardships and this time now that the BJP had been in power, they were sure that maybe they would be put to grief if they indulged in riots.

It is evident from these interviews with Navman over a period of fourteen years that he harbors strong resentment against Muslims, that he was happy to see the destruction of the mosque at Ayodhya, that he believes Muslims always start riots when they can, and that he believes one of the benefits of BJP rule is to make Muslims sufficiently aware and fearful that they will not even think of starting any riots. Navman, as we have seen, was elected to the

Legislative Assembly for the first time in 1989 on the rising wave of the Ayodhya movement. Behind Navman, himself "a very big businessman," as one of my respondents described him, is the organization of traders who support his election campaigns and communal activities.[17] But it is not only Navman and his coterie who provide leadership and organization to militant Hindu activities in Aligarh. Another RSS man, one in fact not friendly to Navman, was secretary of the Vishwa Hindu Parishad for the state as a whole at the time of the Ayodhya movement.[18]

It is, however, Navman whom the BJP chose to contest four consecutive elections in a constituency with a large—and lately a majority—Muslim population. How did it happen that the BJP chose to allow Mr. Navman to be its candidate in successive elections? Before the rise of the Ram Janmabhoomi movement, Navman had been an unsuccessful local politician. In his first election contest, in the 1974 election, as just noted, he ran as a Jan Sangh candidate and lost his deposit; in the 1980 Lok Sabha elections, he ran as an independent against the candidate supported by the BJP, polled miserably, even in the Aligarh segment, and lost his security deposit once again. It is clear that his relations with the local RSS were strained at that time. But Navman had assets that were valuable to the BJP, when the time came for increased militancy, that other RSS men did not have. He had a long history of activity in mobilizing Hindus during riots. He was a member of the VHP as well as the BJP and his son became the local Bajrang Dal chief. He has been a prosperous businessman of the Varshney caste, the solid core of BJP support in the city. Although there are many other Varshney RSS men, some of whom have aspired to the ticket that has gone to Navman in four successive elections, he has had an additional asset, namely, the support of the traders, who have been "united behind him."[19] Thus, when the time came for the mobilization of Hindu militancy, including the deliberate "playing of the Hindu card,"[20] the instigation of Hindu-Muslim confrontation, and the provocation of the Muslim population, Navman was the man in Aligarh City who had the right combination of personal and financial resources: a reputation for devotion to the militant Hindu cause, strong support from the leading Hindu caste in the city, considerable personal wealth, and the financial backing of the traders.

## THE POLITICAL CONTEXT OF COMMUNALISM

Although Mr. Navman and his supporters have been of central importance in the communalization of politics that has contributed to the production of riots in the city, he has been far from alone. Nor should one conclude that the politicians whose actions promote riots from which they then benefit politically are extraordinary. Once the political calculations are made and the game of politicization of communal identities begins, all politicians get caught up in it, either willfully or simply because it is the only available context in which they can appeal for votes. Muslim politicians are no different from Hindus in this respect. All that differs is the rhetoric used to justify their entry into the electoral process, the means they use to garner votes, and the ways in which they seek to benefit from riots. Consider the following nine statements made to me in various interviews by Hindu and Muslim politicians over the years.

The first is from an interview in 1983 with a person associated with a conservative and allegedly fundamentalist group in university politics. This group is in turn associated with the agitation to maintain the minority character of the AMU, and hostile to the Congress because of its policies, which are considered to have undermined that status. He later contested two Legislative Assembly elections and is cited again below.

> I supported BJP in Aligarh City in the last election [1980] and before that also with the intention to patch up the differences between Muslim community and Hindu community, to remove communalism from the minds of these two communities. . . . So we support Jan Sangh, BJP, so that they may come close to us, and we may *understand* what they want, with that intention to have a communal harmony in the city, we supported them. Frequently there are riots here, and political parties exploiting the situation. Not one party; we cannot blame Jan Sangh that Jan Sangh is the only party which is exploiting situation in Aligarh often now. But sometimes Congress (I) also exploits. When Congress (I) comes in power, Jan Sangh exploits, other parties exploit. If, say, Jan Sangh or BJP comes in power [or] Janata comes in power, then Congress (I) exploits the situation.[21]

These remarks, made in 1983, followed upon a discussion of university politics. I had not brought up the question of riots in the city. The respondent introduced the matter as well as his support for the BJP on his own. Though he was at that time among the discontented, anti-Congress Muslims who had either joined or supported the BJP, it is obvious that he did not do so out of sympathy with that party's ideology. He did so, he avers, for the sake of promoting communal harmony in a city with a history of riots.

The second statement is from an interview in 1983 with an advocate, and ex-president, BJP, Aligarh District.

PRB: Now you said you joined [politics and Jan Sangh] in 1966—especially in view of the communal conditions in . . . Aligarh.

RESPONDENT: Ah—communal conditions, circumstances and conditions then prevalent at Aligarh—

PRB: What were those conditions, exactly?

RESPONDENT: Is it very pertinent to ask me?

PRB: Yes!

RESPONDENT: The very fact has been that the policies and principles of the government, whosoever had been ruling, unfortunately the Congress (I) . . . has been divided in two. Unfortunately, as well, Aligarh has been not exactly predominant by Muslims, but had a substantial percentage of Muslims, including—*mane*—. . . coming to about 37 percent in 1966 and 1967.

PRB: In the city?

RESPONDENT: In the city. Unfortunately, . . . Aligarh Muslim University—I always thought to be a snake pois—a snake-pit of communalists. *All* communal riots, *all* communal hatreds, *all* communal bias, et cetera—and even all communal riots here perpetrated, plans organized, any start of a problem, the proceedings of the Aligarh Muslim University with the help—of innocent Muslims . . . —er— persons of the town.

PRB: I see.

RESPONDENT: That—that has been my firm conviction. And therefore I would in the same perspective and relevance—request you to kindly go through the finding[s] . . . of Aligarh Inquiry Commission, which was headed by his Lordship Justice . . . Mathur. You probably—you might not . . . be remembering that there was a major communal riot, at Aligarh, on the 2nd of March 1971, wherein Mr. Mohammed Sharif [*sic*; actually Mohammad Yunus Saleem], who was at the [time] Deputy Minister in the Railways, at Center, had contested here. . . . It has been a repeated history of Aligarh to have communal riots after five or ten years—every— every time. That has been unfortunate. And then, . . . the property of Hindus they are lost. I was also accused of instigating communal riots in Aligarh. It was alleged against me that I organized a big . . . procession, I collected a rally of the students, took the procession through the market, burnt the city—*mane*—houses and buildings of Muslims; I was also responsible for the murder of certain—Muslims, for looting of their property, burning of their shops, etc. For—in that, the Government of U.P. . . . was pleased in appointing a Commission, Aligarh Riot Commission, which was headed by his Lordship, Justice . . . Mathur . . . And he has—openly RSS and Jan Sangh, myself and Shri Inder Pal Singh and one Mr. Ranjan Pal Singh were accused. He has himself written that the riot was sponsored and arranged by Aligarh Muslim University, in order to get Mohammad [Saleem] arrested [*sic;* elected]. And the charges leveled against—against RSS or Jan Sangh are absolutely . . . fantastic.

PRB: Did you—did you organize any procession or anything of the sort?

RESPONDENT: Absolutely fantastic!

PRB: Nothing?

RESPONDENT: Absolutely fantastic!

PRB: Completely all [false]?

RESPONDENT: All—all [false]. All concocted version. And that is a judicial finding. Which has been published.

PRB: Hm. Hm! (Pause) So—this was the . . . 1971 riots?

RESPONDENT: Yes. . . . And I was also arrested in connection with everything.

PRB: *Achcha?*

RESPONDENT: *HaN.* On the spot. Because I had myself seen—Muslims firing from—from within the mosque upon innocent Hindus, burning their shops, etc. And the district administration was watching like—like a tomfool. Or a dumb fool organization. When I became very hot they had no other—And the Hindus also got agitated, on seeing that the Jewelry Market . . . was being burnt and looted. They had no other option excepting arresting me. So if that is—if *that* is communalism, I am opposed. . . .

PB: Hm.

RESPONDENT: If *that* is communalism—I am proud to be communalist. If that is Hinduism, I am proud to be a Hindu. That's my positive, concrete, pattern, principle. . . . [22]

This second, long set of remarks made by a former BJP district president is of great interest from several points of view. First, to the general question concerning why he entered politics in 1966 and specifically why he joined the Jan Sangh, he gave the single response that it was because of "the communal conditions" in the city. Second, there can be little doubt that his attitude towards Muslims is that of a rabid communalist. He cites precisely the population percentage of the Muslims in the city as a matter of concern. He speaks of the AMU as a snakepit of Muslim communalism, the source of "*all* communal riots" in Aligarh. Like Mr. Navman, he distinguishes between educated and "innocent Muslims," the latter being led astray by the educated elite among them. Third, he points to a direct connection between riots and elections, specifically the riot of March 2, 1971, that occurred on the day after polling for the Legislative Assembly and Lok Sabha elections of 1971, which he implies was related to the candidacy of Congress candidate Mohammad Saleem, supported by people at the AMU.

Fourth, he lists several charges against him of instigating a communal riot and participating in criminal activities during the riot, for which he was arrested "on the spot," but denies vehemently their accuracy. Here I want to say that I believe this respondent's denials on the specific points that he described as "absolutely fantastic." But then, he also reveals that his actions during this riot were far from innocent. Let us note that, by his own admission, he was out in the street in the midst of the turmoil in the riot-prone *mohalla* of Sarrafa Bazar [which he calls the Jewelry Market], far from his home or office. He admits that he "became very hot" and "the Hindus also got agitated," and finally that the police "had no other option excepting arresting me." Let us also keep in mind that this respondent was not then an ordinary citizen of Aligarh. He was president of the BJP at the time. He was a big lawyer in the town, whose clients included both Hindus and Muslims accused in riot cases. According to the administrative and police authorities of the district, he defended Muslim criminals involved in riot cases. While that fact would seem to suggest his lack of communal bias, my interviews with police suggest otherwise, namely, that these Muslim criminals were useful in starting riots desired by self-proclaimed, proud Hindu communalists such as this respondents.

All these facts and implications point to one conclusion. The respondent, an intelligent and educated lawyer, did not commit criminal acts. His role was different. He is a prime example of what I call a "conversion specialist," the person who plays the role of mobilizing people, including local criminals, leading them into potentially riotous confrontations, bringing them to the brink of criminal activity, and then, depending upon the specific circumstances, most notably a competitive political context, giving the signal for the riot to begin. That signal may be getting "hot" oneself, yelling out that the Muslims are burning and looting, or getting oneself arrested.

Shortly after my interview with this respondent, I interviewed two local police station officers, one of whom identified succinctly the political context for riot production and also named the three most active Hindu militants in producing them. Insofar as the political context is concerned, the inspector described the matter simply as follows.

> During and before the election, for sympathy and votes, some politicians may start a rumor or a small riot to gain support of one side, then that community goes largely on that basis for the politician.[23]

The inspector described the roles of the three militant Hindu communalists as follows.

Krishna Kumar Navman is the main fellow among the Hindus. Shiv Hari Singhal is the lawyer for most Muslim criminals. Manga Ram first looks at the situation, then goes to the colleges, instigates the students, and they go there. These three minds play the most important parts during riots.

We know enough about Navman so that further commentary is unnecessary at this point. Manga Ram, however, is another case, a professor at one of the local degree colleges, who openly declared to me the most extreme hostility to Muslims. Among his important roles during the production of riots is the specific task of instigation, collection, and mobilization of students to potential riot sites. Shiv Hari Singhal, a BJP leader and a "conversion specialist," allegedly has another task after the riots, of defending the criminals who engage in riotous activity. Whether or not the charge is true in his case, there is no doubt that this is a specific role in riot production that makes it possible for criminals to loot, kill, and burn during riots in the knowledge that they will escape prosecution for their criminal acts. The same role is performed by all the politicians of the city, who go to the police stations after the arrests of their supporters during and immediately after riots to demand their release.

The latter role is described in my second interview with a station officer in 1983. When I asked him about the part played by politicians in riots in a tape-recorded interview, I offered to shut off my tape recorder. He said it was not necessary because "everyone knows this."

These politicians . . . *do* matter, because whatever they say carries a lot of weight. But mostly the politicians are not around during these times [of riots]. And even if they are around, . . . they don't give . . . good advice. And . . . in case they had given good advice, the situation might not turn to—big riots.

[For example, a constable] met some Jatavs, who were all drunk. And they . . . had a small altercation among themselves. And the constable came back to the *thana* and reported the matter. So the S.O. went there himself, without the force. And as he entered the mohalla, . . . the rumor spread around that . . . the police has come to arrest the people. So they started throwing stones at him, and he got injured. So then there was a—small *jhagara* [fight or quarrel] between the people and the police. And then . . . a lot of politics got . . . in it and— [Interruption from outside].

PRB: Yes, yes, go on. What kind of politics?

SSY: And the people—then said that police has . . . been against the Jatavs, and they approached the officers and they approached the politicians.

PRB: Which politicians?

SSY: Local politicians of the mohalla. These leaders interfere in little, little things all the time. [ . . . ] The local politicians always interfere. And if you don't listen to them, then *they* get annoyed; in case you listen to them, then the other party gets annoyed. So the working of the policeman is a very tough job. And . . . the politicians are always eager to exploit the whole situation.[24]

The third statement is from an interview in 1983 with Krishna Kumar Navman, then considered by the civilian and police administration as the principal riot-monger among militant Hindus, but not yet the successful politician he was to become.

> Aligarh politics are basically dependent on the relations between Hindus and Muslims.[25]

Enough has been said about Mr. Navman so that his comments at the time need no interpretation. All that need be noted is that we have here an example of the self-fulfilling prophecy; anyone who might have then disputed Navman's contention has been proven mistaken in no small measure in consequence of his own efforts.

The fourth statement is from an interview in 1983 with a successful Muslim candidate on the Janata Party ticket (precursor of the BJP in Aligarh) for the Legislative Assembly in 1977.

> Now—my aim, when I had joined the Jan Sangh, was to see what happens when we make a new political experiment. *My* aim primarily was somehow or the other to put an end to the riots in Aligarh, *see* if this new political experiment . . . open[s] up some avenues where we can go further, hand in hand, the two sister communities. But this program could not be continued, because the Emergency came in [1975].[26]

The fifth statement is from an interview in 1983 with a professor of psychology, AMU, then vice-president of the BJP, Aligarh, and an RSS man.

> Dr. Manga Ram. Raj Puri Navman. These are the Hindu leaders who are responsible—for—er— . . . for *preparing* the people for retaliation. That also I can tell you. I am very clear, and very *clean* on this matter, that they get . . . political capital out of it. They get recognition by Hindus. Because otherwise Jan Sangh is a *dead* party. Madhok's Jan Sangh. They get recognition by Hindus only, only

for this reason, that they take the code [cause?] of Hindus at their—during communal riots—in their heads. And *they* prepare the people to attack Muslims, in case—er—more than six or seven Hindus—Hindus are killed by them and the patience is lost of Hindus. Hindus also go to them, for complaint, *ki,* "No, this our man is killed. See, our man is killed. While we are not able to do anything."

This is the situation of the politicians. They *want* that communal . . . tension should prevail. If one-hundred or two-hundred Hindus or Muslims are killed, they don't bother for that. Because they know that this situation is going to give them—Muslim votes. Because vote banks is with . . . Muslim—Muslims only. Hindus are divided, among different parties, because Hindus are intellectuals basically. And they—they know where to join according to their philosophy of life. Muslims have got no philosophy of life, frankly speaking, because they are backward, illiterate, and uncultured people, most—most of them. So they follow their leader. That suppose the leader says, "Oh, all right, you are—under—tension. You are—mm—mm—insecure. You should go for Congress (I)."[27]

This interview is of particular interest for several reasons. First, the respondent himself is what I call a "fire tender," someone who moves about the city uncovering incidents—such as the elopement of a Hindu girl with a Muslim boy, to be discussed below—ostensibly to prevent such incidents from turning into communal riots. However, the actual effects of his actions and those of others who play this role is to keep the embers of communal hostilities from dying out.

Yet, at this time, when the militant Hindus of Aligarh were divided organizationally, between the most extreme communalists who remained with the rump Jan Sangh, on the one hand, and the vast majority who joined the BJP, on the other hand, this AMU professor was with the more "moderate" BJP. Although he acknowledged that the two forces joined together when there were riots, he considered the rump Jan Sanghis he named—Manga Ram and Raj Puri Navman, Mr. K. K. Navman's son—as themselves guilty of riot instigation. These men, he said emphatically, prepare "the people for retaliation," prepare them "to attack Muslims." He himself, he stresses, is free from blame on the matter, he is "very clean," but they "get political capital out of it" in the form of "recognition by Hindus." So are the Hindus in general free from blame. They are so patient that, even after "six or seven Hindus" are killed by Muslims, they do not retaliate unless prodded to do so by the likes of Manga Ram and Raj Puri Navman. It is to the latter persons also that the Hindus go to report when a Hindu has been killed in a riot.

This professor, diligent fire tender though he is, extends blame further to all the politicians. He says outright that they want communal tension to prevail, whereas he sees himself as calming communal tensions. But the persons whom he calls politicians do not care how many persons from their own community are killed as a result of the riots that follow from their efforts. Hindu and Muslim politicians are both guilty, but the Congress politicians are most guilty, because the Muslims constitute an ignorant vote bank, easily deluded by the very politicians who are maintaining the communal tensions into voting for the Congress (I) as their protector.

The sixth statement is from an interview in 1997 with the Muslim candidate who defeated Mr. Navman in the 1996 elections.

PRB: How did you come into politics?
RESPONDENT: I was simply a businessman when I felt that the communal forces are disturbing the Aligarh peaceful city. Then I [was] feeling that I should join the politics and then I came to try MLA-ship with the BSP party.[28]

The seventh statement is from an interview in 1997 with an unsuccessful Muslim candidate for the Legislative Assembly on the BSP ticket in 1996.

PRB: And what is the communal situation now in Aligarh in the old city?
RESPONDENT: At present, it is all election gimmick, that Hindus are trying to exploit the Hindu sentiments and the Muslims are exploiting that, some political parties, Muslim political parties, and also the person in power is also just trying to consolidate Muslims.[29]

The eighth statement is from an interview in 1999 with a retired professor of education, Barahseni Degree College, Aligarh, a lifelong member of the RSS, former secretary of the VHP.

PRB: And what is the reason [for persisting riots in Dahi Wali Gali and various other *mohallas*]?
RESPONDENT: Efforts are being made even now, efforts are being made to create a riot in the town. This is also political. Because Kalyan Singh is supposed to be a RSS man and who is leader of Bajpa [BJP], is chief minister of U.P.[30]

The ninth statement is from an interview in 1999 with the unsuccessful Muslim Janata Dal candidate for the Legislative Assembly in 1993.

PRB: How did you come into politics?

RESPONDENT: In '90, in Aligarh, there was a communal riot. In that communal riot, in the whole city, there were around two hundred casualties, and this was how. I mean, I was very much affected, I was quite sensitized, and I got inspiration, I saw the atrocities committed by the police, their support to the other community, and I stood against that, my voice, and the people came behind me, people gave me support, supported my voice. That's how I entered the politics. People knew me and I thought to contest the election and enter into politics.

So that was the entry point for me and then I joined party, I formally entered into politics, I started some constructive program on the [part-time] basis, and I found that the Janata Dal, which was on rise at that time, is the better alternative of Congress. This was the party which was mainly concerned with the problems of the Muslims. It had genuine concern for the people. So, I thought it had also good programs for the people, so I thought to join this party and work from Aligarh, and this is how I entered in politics.[31]

It should be noted that in several of the interviews cited above, I had not yet broached the communal question at all. As in nearly all my interviews with active politicians, I began with general questions concerning the respondent's background, including always the question, "How did you come into politics?" When a respondent first mentioned that he had joined a particular political party at some point, I generally asked why he chose that party. In all such cases cited above, respondents began with the communal answer to a neutral question. The successful Muslim Janata Party candidate in 1983 declared that it was his intention, in the strange position of a Muslim joining with the former Jan Sangh, to do some good, to bring an end to communal riots in Aligarh. The winning Muslim candidate in 1996, himself considered by Hindus as a firebrand likely to appear with a large group of people at a disputed site, averred that he came into politics because "communal forces" were disrupting the peace of the city. The unsuccessful Muslim candidate in 1993, who does not have a reputation as a firebrand, and entered politics only after the great riots of 1990–91, also said that he did so because of his reactions to "the atrocities committed by the police" and the latter's partiality in favor of the Hindus in those riots. Further, he avers that he chose the Janata Dal because, of all the alternatives to the Congress, this was the party most sympathetic to Muslim concerns.

In the two cases, when I was first to broach the communal question or the reasons for rioting, the responses placed them promptly in a political context. The Muslim BSP candidate in 1996 characterized the communal question as nothing but an "election gimmick," exploited by persons from both communities. The RSS respondent in 1999 attributed the persistence of riots to political factors and maintained that efforts were being made even as we spoke "to create a riot in the town" to embarrass the then BJP government led by Kalyan Singh, himself a man of the RSS.

## ALIGARH'S INSTITUTIONALIZED RIOT SYSTEM

From several of the interviews cited and commented upon above, we have detected aspects of what I call an "institutionalized riot system," by which I mean a perpetually operative network of roles whose functions are to maintain communal hostilities, recruit persons to protest against or otherwise make public or bring to the notice of the authorities incidents presumed dangerous to the peace of the city, mobilize crowds to threaten or intimidate persons from the other community, recruit criminals for violent actions when it is desired to "retaliate" against persons from the other community, and, if the political context is right, to let loose widespread violent action. That network has been in existence for a very long time. In my own experience, it has been in existence from the time of my first visit to Aligarh just after the October riots in 1961. However, it extended vastly over the next thirty years, displaying its expanded powers in the great riots of 1990–91, which were marked by two features that distinguished them sharply from all earlier riots. The first was the ability of militant Hindus to produce violent anti-Muslim crowds at a multiplicity of sites in different parts of the city at roughly the same time. The second was the reported extensive participation of large crowds of ordinary people in the cheering, looting, and killing that went on.

Riot systems exist in both the Hindu and Muslim communities of Aligarh, but the militant Hindu riot system is a widespread, well organized, continuously functioning one that bears no comparison with the mostly local Muslim networks. As we have seen from the many quotations provided above from interviews, the entire system that produces Hindu-Muslim riots is sustained by the political framework in which nearly all successful politicians have operated since the destruction of the Congress organization in Aligarh City in the 1962 election. It is sustained, in other words, by a political discourse that legitimizes it, even while condemning it, as nothing but routine politics. The communal politics that provide the context are said to be mere "election gimmicks." The politicians who are playing the game may not even be "communal" persons, they may even be "decent" men, as one respondent put it,[32] but the game they are playing is the game of communal politics, which has often fatal consequences for many of its victims.

The inner workings of the organization of riot systems is not something that can be described in detail. To penetrate it thoroughly, one would have to be a Bill Buford, make friends with organization members and join in the action oneself, something quite beyond what a foreigner could do even if so inclined. What I have seen and tried to present here are but glimpses of a system that operates at many levels, from the high level of the communal discourse to the lowest level of the criminals deliberately recruited and paid to kill.

I want to conclude this discussion with two further such glimpses taken from interviews previously cited, with two respondents, the first being an example of the "conversion specialist," the second the "fire tender." The former described to me an incident that had occurred in 1961 in which he was personally involved: "There was one incident in 1961 when the son of a Punjabi Khatri was arrested for committing a theft in AMU. However, apparently, he was badly beaten at AMU before being arrested and we had to rush to the AMU to rescue him."[55]

A Hindu thief is arrested in the AMU. It is said he was badly beaten. This is clearly a matter for the police, but somehow the news reached this respondent and his associates, who then "had to rush to the AMU to rescue him." Revealed here is something that occurs repeatedly in Aligarh: the existence of a news and action network concerning all incidents that involve Hindus and Muslims. The news is transmitted instantly from the scene to persons in the RSS and in the Jan Sangh/Janata Party/BJP—whichever political formation represents the RSS ideology—who then decide whether or not it is worthy of their attention and action. If it is deemed so—that is, if the political context is such that "political capital" can be gained from it—then a group will be gathered to rush to the scene. They will not necessarily rush with the intent to begin a fracas, but they go to observe, to confront, and, if necessary, to decide whether or not further forces should be mobilized.

At times, it is possible to witness the operation of the communal discourse in practice as well as in speech, as illustrated by my observation of and interview with the AMU professor. I observed him first by chance in a visit to the office of the senior superintendent of police (SSP), where, when called upon by the SSP to state the reason for his presence, he said he had come to report the alleged kidnapping of a Hindu girl by a Muslim. The SSP immediately challenged the use of the term *kidnapping* and said, "You mean eloped." With this professor, who was neatly dressed in Western clothes, was a scruffy-looking bunch of dirty people whom he told me later were all citizens of

Aligarh, including another professor and some people from the local branches of the State Bank of India and the Bank of Baroda.[34]

When I asked him later in a formal interview why he had gone to the police station with these people to report the elopement, he said that he believes that, when such things happen, they should immediately come forward and seek police help in order to prevent a communal riot before rumors start to spread. When I asked what interest the people with him had in the matter, the reply was they were all Hindus, so they came for the Hindu girl. When I asked him how he himself had come to know about it, he said the girl's brother came to him and he immediately arranged for the people to go in the form of a delegation to the SSP.

This gentleman admitted on my pressing him that the girl was not kidnapped, she was "lured"; he used the word *kidnapping* to get the attention of the SSP. She came from a very poor family, he said, which did not have two meals a day, so she might have been lured for money. He revealed to my assistants before I interviewed him and to me during the interview that, if the girl was recovered, she was likely to be killed by the members of her family. He believed that was the proper thing to do in the circumstances because it would save hundreds of lives in Aligarh, preventing a riot that might otherwise occur; therefore, it was better that one person be sacrificed to save the lives of many. The girl was seventeen and a half years of age at the time. He stressed, however, that "the Hindus will do nothing with the Muslim man because that will lead to a communal riot. It is up to the Muslims what to do with him. There are some good-thinking Muslims in Aligarh and they should punish that boy."

My respondent also made the argument that, if the girl married the Muslim man, nobody would mind, but the man—or boy—was already married. However, he then went on to say that if she went to the family of a Muslim, she would produce only Muslim children and they (Hindus of Aligarh and India) don't want the Muslim population to increase because, once they are in majority, they will behave with their minorities as they do in Iraq and Iran. Thus does a trivial incident involving two youths become projected spatially and temporally to encompass the worlds of Hindu India and of an imagined Islamic universe, in a dire future in which the 85 percent majority of the second largest country in the world becomes a minority dominated by prolific Muslims.

While this man's speech is likely to seem to us the ravings of a lunatic, it would be a mistake to believe that he is unrepresentative of the views and sentiments of a large and increasingly outspoken segment of the Hindu population of north India. Equally important is the specific role he is playing in this context, one which I have seen repeatedly in different forms in other places in north India. He proclaims that he seeks to prevent a riot, whereas it would seem his actions are designed to promote one. In fact, I do not believe he sought either to prevent or to provoke a riot. He was, rather, performing a critical role in the perpetuation of the communal discourse and communal tensions in Aligarh, a role that is being performed in most cities and towns in northern and western India these days—namely, keeping the fires of communalism tended so that, when the opportunity arises, the fire may be stoked into a flame, into one of those apparently spontaneous conflagrations that we all hear about in connection with riots everywhere.

# 10 / Communalization and Polarization

## Selected Constituency-Wise Results for Aligarh Elections

T he effects of riots on the processes of communalization and polarization in Aligarh elections are dramatically illustrated by the elections that followed the communal riots in October 1961 and by the series of elections associated with the Ram Janmabhoomi movement and the riots that occurred along with it. The effects of a decline in communal violence on the electoral process in Aligarh are illustrated by the elections that followed after the ebbing of the great wave of violence in India and in Aligarh after the destruction of the mosque in December 1992; they will be discussed in Chapter 12.

### THE 1962 GENERAL ELECTIONS

#### Legislative Assembly

The entire pattern of electoral politics in Aligarh City changed dramatically in 1962, a major watershed in the political history of the city. As indicated in Figures 8.3 and 8.4, turnout and interparty competitiveness (leaving aside the 1955 bye-election) reached new highs. The elections of that year, fought in the aftermath of the October 1961 Hindu-Muslim riots, saw the merger of two discontented segments of the electorate—Muslims and low caste Chamars/Jatavs—in an alliance under the banner of the Republican Party of India (RPI). The leader of the low castes in Aligarh was B. P. Maurya, himself a Jatav and the RPI candidate for Parliament. His running mate in the Aligarh City Legislative Assembly constituency was Dr. Abdul Bashir Khan, professor of law in the Aligarh Muslim University and the leader of a group in university politics commonly dubbed as the "communalist" group, as opposed to the so-called Communist group. It would be less pejorative to say that Dr. Abdul Bashir was a conservative, attached to his identity as a

TABLE 10.1. Election results for Aligarh City Legislative
Assembly constituency, 1962

| Turnout No./% | Candidates | Caste/ Community | Party | Votes Polled | Percent of Total Valid Votes |
|---|---|---|---|---|---|
| 51,308 | | | | | |
| 68.25% | Abdul Bashir Khan | Muslim | RPI | 21,909 | 42.70 |
| | Anant Ram Verma | Kayastha | INC | 16,164 | 31.50 |
| | Madan Lal Hiteshi | Barahseni | IND | 5,584 | 10.88 |
| | Tota Ram Vidyarthi | Bania (Marwari) | BJS | 3,270 | 6.37 |
| | Bhoj Raj | NA | IND | 1,949 | 3.80 |
| | Kanhiya Lal | NA | PSP | 881 | 1.72 |
| | Deo Datt Kalanki | NA | IND | 844 | 1.64 |
| | Devki Nandan Sharma | NA | SWA | 316 | 0.62 |
| | K. K. Trivedi | Brahman | IND | 157 | 0.31 |
| | Tota Ram | NA | IND | 118 | 0.23 |
| | Hafisur Rehman Dausi | Muslim | IND | 116 | 0.23 |

SOURCE: Result sheets in the Aligarh District election office.

Muslim, who stood for the defense of Muslim interests that he saw endangered by the October riots, during which he was proctor of the university. While he was proctor, the Students Union elections had been communalized by the mobilization of Hindu and Muslim candidates behind candidates of their respective communities, leading to a clash that in turn was followed by anti-Muslim rioting of Hindu mobs from the city—both in the old city and in areas adjacent to the university—in which fourteen or fifteen Muslims were killed (see Chapter 3). Among Dr. Bashir's complaints at the time was that the police failed to provide adequate protection to Muslims and to university employees when these crowds attacked in the vicinity of the university.

In the election of 1962 in the city, most Muslim voters mobilized behind the candidacy of Dr. Bashir, who also was supported by Chamars. With this dual support base, Dr. Bashir won a decisive victory against the Congress candidate, Anant Ram Verma, who polled less than a third of the votes (Table 10.1). The Congress was also weakened by the continuing factional feuds within the organization that led some Congress men to sabotage the campaign of their ostensible candidate by remaining aloof or working against him. There was, therefore, a communal and caste mobilization behind the candidacy of Dr. Bashir as well as the beginnings of a polarization between Hindus and Muslims. The polarization was not, however, complete. The Congress candidate did not speak for Hindu interests. The Jan Sangh candidate, who did so, placed fourth and lost his deposit with only 6.37 percent of the vote. In fact, the Jan Sangh dropped to fourth place in this election, polling less than half the vote it secured in 1957. Third position in this election was occupied by another Hindu candidate, Madan Lal Hiteshi, a prominent Hindi journalist, Barahseni (Varshney) by caste, who drew considerable Hindu support away from the Jan Sangh.

A professor of political science at the Barahseni College in Aligarh remarked on the impact the latter two candidates had upon the election contest in 1962 in the following manner, in the notes from my interview with him.

> There are two business communities in Aligarh—Barahsenis and Agarwals—and there is a tug-of-war between these two communities; they don't see eye to eye in the public life of the city. The Barahsenis have their own market—Barahseni Bazaar. However, when the news went around that Dr. Bashir was going to win, all the Hindus united around Anant Ram Verma. The Jan Sangh candidate, Tota Ram Vidyarthi, is also a Bania (Marwari); he is a lawyer, manager of a school (Maheshwari Intercollege), and connected with a number of sectarian institutions. All those who would have voted for these two candidates voted for Anant Ram Verma.[1]

While the distribution of the votes for these four candidates by polling station, as well as the correlation coefficients between party vote shares and percent Hindu and Muslim, do support the view that the election was communalized, they do not support this respondent's assessment of the election as completely polarized between Muslims voting for Dr. Bashir and Hindus uniting behind Anant Ram Verma. Rather, they indicate that, in 1962, Hindus were not fully consolidated and remained at least partly divided along lines of caste antagonisms and party affiliation within the Hindu community.

The communalization of the electorate in 1962 is evident from both a comparison of the leading party and independent candidate votes in 1962, shown in Table 10.2, and from a comparison of the distribution of votes among the parties between 1957 and 1962. Table 10.2 shows starkly the concentration of RPI votes in the high Muslim population *mohallas* and the virtual irrelevance of this party in the high Hindu population *mohallas*. The difference between Dr. Abdul Bashir Khan's vote in his top five polling stations and his bottom

TABLE 10.2. Vote shares for party candidates in their top and bottom five polling stations, 1962 Legislative Assembly elections, and demographic data for the *mohallas* included in them, according to the 1951 census (all data in percentages)

| Best/Worst Polling Stations | Vote Share | Muslims | Scheduled Castes | Hindus/Others |
|---|---|---|---|---|
| RPI top 5 | 91.39 | 88.99 | 3.53 | 7.48 |
| RPI bottom 5 | 1.84 | 1.07 | 1.44 | 97.49 |
| INC top 5 | 67.18 | 4.94 | 2.08 | 92.99 |
| INC bottom 5 | 2.57 | 81.98 | 0.91 | 17.11 |
| IND top 5 | 44.35 | 11.98 | 3.93 | 80.07 |
| IND bottom 5 | 0.56 | 84.55 | 6.32 | 6.06 |
| BJS top 5 | 24.74 | 11.68 | 0.42 | 87.90 |
| BJS bottom 5 | 0.17 | 72.37 | 10.05 | 17.59 |

five is nearly 90 percent. The difference in the Muslim and Hindu populations in those polling stations is nearly 88 percent for the Muslim population and 90 percent for the Hindu. It is also noteworthy that five of the 14 *mohallas* contained within Dr. Bashir's five best polling stations were among those later classified as communally sensitive (see Chapter 6), of which three are considered both riot-hit and crime-prone. The latter included Turkman Gate, where there is a three-way division, demographically, among Muslims (38.70 percent), Scheduled Castes (29.08 percent), and Hindus and others (32.21 percent), the most explosive population mixture imaginable at times of rioting in Aligarh. It also included Sabzi Mandi, where there is a mixed Hindu-Muslim population ratio of 71–29 in favor of Hindus, and Bani Israilan, nearly 100 percent Muslim.[2]

The spread in the Congress vote share between its candidate's top and bottom polling stations and the Muslim and Hindu populations is also huge: there is a difference of nearly 65 percent in its vote share and a spread of above 77 percent in the size of the Muslim population and above 75 percent in the Hindu population. The case is similar with the Hindu independent candidate and with the BJP candidate as well; the vote share spread between the top and bottom polling stations is much smaller than in the case of the two leading candidates, but only because their total vote was also much smaller. However, the spread in the percentage of Hindus and Muslims between the top and bottom polling stations for these two candidates is also huge.

The damage done to the Congress candidate—the same person who contested in 1957—by the communalization of the electorate is also evident from a comparison of the distribution of his vote shares in his best and worst polling stations in the two elections. In 1957, the interval between Anant Ram Verma's vote shares (a spread of 43.67 percent vote share between his best and worst five) was very much less than in 1962 (spread of 64.61 percent between his top and bottom five polling stations), as was the spread in communal composition of those polling stations with respect to the proportions of Hindus and Muslims in them.[3] Further, the polarization of the vote between the two leading candidates in 1962 was very high, as indicated by the correlation coefficient for the votes of the RPI and the Congress in all 96 polling stations $(-.78, p = .000)$. There was, therefore, a polarization of votes but not of candidates representing the two communities. Muslims were clearly united behind Dr. Bashir, but Hindus were divided among three candidates: Congress, independent, and Jan Sangh.

Indeed, the outcome in this assembly election might well have been different had Hindus united behind a single candidate. The degree of communalization of the electorate as a whole, the division of the Hindu vote among three candidates, and the concentration of Muslim and Scheduled Caste votes are illustrated by examination of the results in particular polling stations. For this purpose, I have selected the polling stations in which the intensity of interparty competition was greatest on the interval measure, namely, polling stations 55 (men) and 56 (women). The interval between the first- and second-place candidates (Anant Ram Verma and Dr. Abdul Bashir, respectively) was 2.64 percent. The polling stations comprised six *mohallas* in which Hindus and Scheduled Castes were the two largest categories, with a population distribution as follows: Hindus and others 59.85 percent; Scheduled Castes 30.63 percent; Muslims 9.53 percent. The Congress candidate polled 38.65 percent of the vote, the RPI candidate 36.01 percent. However, the distribution of the vote for all the leading candidates mirrored very closely the population percentages, such that the vote for the three Hindu candidates was 59.46 percent (virtually identical to the population of Hindus and others), whereas the RPI vote was 40.16 percent (four percentage points above the combined population of Muslims and Scheduled Castes). Had the Hindu vote consolidated behind one of the Hindu candidates, the vote in these polling stations would have been nearly 23 percent above that for the RPI. In the constituency as a whole (Table 10.1), had the Hindu vote of the three leading Hindu candidates been combined around a single Hindu candidate, the margin of victory would have been around 6 percent.

## Lok Sabha

The 1962 elections for Parliament were held simultaneously with those for the Legislative Assembly. They were even more intensely fought in the Aligarh segment than those for the Legislative Assembly seat. In the dataset of 21 elections, this contest ranks fourth in interparty competitiveness in the history of assembly and parliamentary elections in Aligarh. The interval between the winning and runner-up candidates was only 2.44 percent.[4]

There are similarities, but also some differences between the results at the two levels because of the somewhat different caste and communal identifications of the candidates. As already noted, the successful RPI candidate for Parliament was Mr. B. P. Maurya, the most important Republican Party leader in the state of U.P. He led also in Aligarh City, polling only slightly more votes than his party's candidate for the assembly (see Table 10.3). Maurya was the true architect of the 1962 electoral transformation in the Aligarh parliamentary and Legislative Assembly constituencies. He had worked for the Jatavs since he began his political career in the 1940s. He had then joined the Scheduled Caste Federation of Dr. B. R. Ambedkar, the famous "Untouchable" leader and founder of the Republican Party, and had since led several agitations in Aligarh District and in other parts of the state for the satisfaction of Jatav demands and for the conversion of Jatavs to Buddhism.[5] He appealed specifically to caste antagonisms of lower-caste groups against the upper castes, particularly Brahmans.

The runner-up candidate in the constituency as a whole as well as in the parliamentary segment was Maurya's opposite in every way. A Hindu Rajput, he was the candidate of the Arya Samaj, the preeminent Hindu religious reform movement of northern India since the late nineteenth century. The Arya Samaj has always stood for unity of the Hindu community and unity of the country as well. At this time, it even favored the elimination of the federal system and the establishment of a unitary state, the adoption of Hindi as the sole official language of the country, and the combatting of both "parochial" attachments to any "particular part of India" and "extra-territorial" loyalties. The latter obviously referred primarily to Muslims allegedly attached by feelings of loyalty to Pakistan rather than India. Shiv Kumar Shastri's militant Hindu position won him the support of the Jan Sangh as well as broad support among Hindus in Aligarh City, enabling him to win 40.31 percent of the city's vote share, displacing the Congress, whose candidate came in second in the assembly contest, to third place in the Aligarh parliamentary segment (Table 10.3).

TABLE 10.3. Election results for Aligarh City segment
of Aligarh Lok Sabha constituency, 1962

| Turnout No./% | Candidates | Caste/ Community | Party | Votes Polled | Percent of Total Valid Votes |
|---|---|---|---|---|---|
| 51,907 | Buddha Priya Maurya | Jatav | RPI | 22,190 | 42.75 |
| NA | Shiv Kumar Shastri | Rajput | IND | 20,296 | 40.31 |
| | Jarrar Haider | Muslim | INC | 7,260 | 13.99 |
| | Nahar Singh | Jat | IND | 731 | 1.41 |
| | Vasant Rao Oak | NA | SWA | 568 | 1.09 |
| | Jaganath Prasad | NA | RRP | 232 | 0.45 |

SOURCE: For the data, as for table 10.1. For party affiliations, Government of Uttar Pradesh, Office of the Chief Electoral Officer, Uttar Pradesh, *Results of Third General Elections (1962) to the House of the People from Uttar Pradesh* (Allahabad: Superintendent, Printing and Stationery, 1962), p. 20. *Dates of poll*: February 19, 21, 25, 1962, are the dates given for phased polling for the whole Lok Sabha constituency.

The third-place Congress candidate, a Muslim, was an old Congressman who, however, had not been active in district politics in recent years. He was a lawyer in Aligarh town and, like both Dr. Abdul Bashir and B. P. Maurya, had close connections with the AMU, in his case as its legal advisor. He was a noncommunal, secular Muslim who had been opposed to the Pakistan movement and the partition of India. In AMU politics, he was identified with the group variously called secular, progressive, or Communist, and opposed to the policies of the group variously termed conservative, traditional, or communalist (that is, the group associated with Dr. Bashir). He claimed that Muslims who were angry about the October 1961 riots were opposed to his accepting the Congress nomination.[6] In short, Jarrar Haider was just the sort of candidate who fit Congress policies at the time, a man with a national, non-parochial, noncommunal outlook, whom the national leadership of the Congress would have welcomed in Parliament. He was Muslim in a predominantly non-Muslim constituency—that is, in the parliamentary constituency as a whole—a noncommunal Muslim in an environment where Hindu-Muslim relations were antagonistic, and a man unattached to local factions. However commendable his selection by the Congress under the circumstances, his qualities were a certain recipe for a severe defeat. He polled a mere 13.99 percent of the vote in the Aligarh City segment, compared to 31.50 percent for his "supporting" assembly candidate.[7]

The correlation coefficients for all important candidates in the two elections, assembly and parliamentary, for all 96 polling stations, are of extraordinary interest. First is the nearly perfect correspondence between the vote for the two RPI candidates, Dr. Bashir and B. P. Maurya, the correlation coefficient between their respective vote percentages being .9963, yielding an R Square of 99.26 percent. This correlation is most striking at a time in Indian political history when party loyalties were generally weak, the parties themselves were highly factionalized, and there was a relatively low correspondence between party vote shares in assembly and parliamentary contests held simultaneously, because of caste and communal cross-voting by ethnic rather than party identification. Also of great interest is the fact that there were no positive correlations between the vote share for the RPI for either Legislative Assembly or Parliament with any other party. In fact, all correlations with all other parties were not only negative (ranging from −.36 to −.94), but all were significant (at p−.000). These correlations suggest the following conclusions about caste/communal voting behavior in Aligarh City in 1962. There was extremely high solidarity between the Muslim and Scheduled Caste voters in this election and virtually total vote transfer across caste/communal lines, that is, virtually all Scheduled Castes who voted for B. P. Maurya for Parliament also voted for Dr. Bashir in the assembly contest. Further, virtually all Muslims who voted for Dr. Bashir in the assembly contest voted for B. P. Maurya for Parliament.

A further point of great interest for which the correlation coefficients provide evidence is the very high degree of polarization of voting that occurred in the Lok Sabha contest, much higher than that in the assembly contest where the Hindu votes were divided among three candidates. In the parliamentary contest, by contrast, the vast majority of the Hindu votes clearly were concentrated behind Shiv Kumar Shastri. The correlation coefficient between his vote share and that for B. P. Maurya is −.944; the correlation between his vote and that for Dr. Bashir is virtually identical at −.941. In contrast to the virtually total solidarity of Muslim and Scheduled Caste voting, however, the divisions in the Hindu vote at the assembly level were reflected in the correlation coefficient between Shiv Kumar Shastri's vote for Parliament and the combined vote for the Jan Sangh candidate and Madan Lal Hiteshi in the assembly contest, which stood at .70. At the same time, despite the divisions in the Hindu vote in the assembly contest, this correlation suggests the existence of a very considerable support base for politicized militant Hinduism in both electoral contests, one that displayed itself in cross-party voting. That is, most Hindus who voted for the Hindu Congress candidate, Anant Ram Verma, in the assembly contest did not vote for the Muslim Congress candidate for Parliament, Jarrar Haider.

Another set of data that throws further light on the communalization and polarization that took place in the 1962 elections and adds additional precision to it comprises correlations and regressions between party vote shares and the percent population Muslim, Hindus and others, and Scheduled Castes. A set of data for 44 electoral/census units in 1962 was generated by grouping polling stations and *mohallas* to correspond exactly, each one comprising one or two polling stations and several *mohallas*. Correlation coefficients were then run for all the leading parties and independents for both the assembly and Lok Sabha contests; they are presented below, arranged for each community in such a way that the highest positive correlations are shown on the left, the lowest on the right of Table 10.4.

Looking first at the party/independent vote share correlations with percent Muslims, there are several notable results. The first are the very high correlations between percent Muslim and the vote for the RPI. Second, confirming the findings above from our other data, the correlations for the RPI candidates for both Legislative Assembly and Parliament are very close. Third, the correlations for both Congress candidates are negative, bringing out clearly the loss of Muslim support for that party. Fourth, however, it should also be noted that the negative relationship for the Congress parliamentary candidate, Jarrar Haider, is much lower than that for the assembly candidate, Anant Ram Verma. This difference suggests the possibility that at least some Muslims, but certainly a very small minority among them, preferred to vote for a Muslim candidate, not the Jatav candidate, B. P. Maurya, on the RPI ticket. Fifth, the correlations with militant Hindu candidates are also of interest from several points of view. They demonstrate that the most disliked candidate in Muslim areas was the independent contestant for the Lok Sabha seat, Shiv Kumar Shastri. After Shiv Kumar Shastri, the least popular candidate in the Muslim *mohallas* was the Congress nominee, followed then by the independent, Madan Lal Hiteshi, and the Jan Sangh candidate, Tota Ram Vidyarthi.

Looking next at the correlations with Hindus and others, they are virtually a mirror image of the correlations with percent Muslim. The only important differences are the strikingly high correlations at both the positive and negative ends, with Shiv Kumar Shastri on the positive side and the RPI candidates on the negative. These correlations are, once again, extraordinary in social sci-

TABLE 10.4. Correlation coefficients of party vote shares with percent population Muslim, Hindus and others, and Scheduled Castes, 1962 Legislative Assembly (LA) and Lok Sabha (LS) elections (N = 44)

### MUSLIMS

| RPI (LA) | RPI (LS) | Congress (LS) | Jan Sangh (LA) | IND (LA) | Congress (LA) | IND (LS) |
|---|---|---|---|---|---|---|
| .90** | .88** | −.31* | −.44** | −.47** | −.74** | −.86** |

### HINDUS AND OTHERS

| IND (LS) | Congress (LA) | Jan Sangh (LA) | IND (LA) | Congress (LS) | RPI (LS) | RPI (LA) |
|---|---|---|---|---|---|---|
| .96** | .73** | .58** | .53** | .22 | −.95** | −.95** |

### SCHEDULED CASTES

| Congress (LS) | Congress (LA) | RPI (LS) | RPI (LA) | IND (LA) | IND (LS) | Jan Sangh (LA) |
|---|---|---|---|---|---|---|
| .29* | .12 | .04 | .01 | −.10 | −.12 | −.30* |

*p=.05 or less.

**p=.01 or less.

ence research. They explain approximately 92 percent of the variance in the vote for these candidates. It can be said with assurance that Shiv Kumar Shastri was the overwhelming favorite candidate for Hindus of Aligarh in the 1962 elections and that he received virtually all his votes from Hindus, especially militant Hindus whose dislike for the RPI candidate was intense.

Another striking result comes from stepwise regression equations run with the RPI assembly candidate's vote share as the dependent variable and percent Muslim and percent Scheduled Castes as the independent variables. The first equation gives a correlation with percent Muslim of .896, which translates to an R Square of 80 percent, leaving only 20 percent of the variance unexplained. In the second step, the addition of percent Scheduled Caste to the equation yields a Multiple R of .951 and an R Square of 90 percent. Thus, half the unexplained variance is accounted for by the addition of Scheduled Castes to the equation, leaving a mere 10 percent of the variance unexplained.

All the evidence available, therefore, indicates clearly and decisively the extraordinary high degree of communalization of the electorate in 1962, as well as a polarization between Hindus on the one side and Muslims and Scheduled Castes on the other side that was less than total only because there were two militant Hindu candidates in the assembly contest. The results in general also point without doubt to the connection between communal antagonisms and the communal riots of October 1961 and the results of the election. Muslims turned away from the Congress and towards the RPI out of resentment against the Congress because of the riots that occurred under Congress rule. The alliance with Scheduled Castes turned this resentment into a massive defeat for the Congress, from which it never fully recovered. For their part, Hindus turned in larger numbers than ever towards either the Jan Sangh or independent candidates who stood for militant Hindu feelings.

## THE LEGISLATIVE ASSEMBLY ELECTIONS OF 1989, 1991, AND 1993

A second illustration of the relationship between riots and elections comes from the three successive Legislative Assembly elections in 1989, 1991, and 1993, which were saturated with communal antagonisms. In all three Legislative Assembly elections, the BJP candidate was Krishna Kumar Navman. Navman's rise to prominence in Aligarh politics and the thoroughgoing communalization of the electoral contest occurred simultaneously with the intensification of the Ayodhya movement that took place in the years between 1989 and 1993. Furthermore, the intensity of the Legislative Assembly contest increased with each successive election in this triad, as reflected in the interval measure, which moved from 8.17 percent in 1989 to 4.87 percent in 1991 to 1.42 percent in 1993, the most closely contested Legislative Assembly election in the city's history.

The Ayodhya movement had its most serious consequences for Aligarh in the vicious communal riots of 1990–91 (see Chapter 4 ). In the midst of this highly charged and violent atmostphere, Navman won three consecutive elections, an unprecedented feat in the electoral history of the city. He won two of these elections, in 1989 and 1993, because of a division of the Muslim votes, but won the 1991 election even without such a division. Rather, in Aligarh as elsewhere in U.P. in 1991, the BJP benefited from the decline of the Congress as a serious competitor and its own capture of the bulk of the Congress's upper-caste Hindu vote base. That is, a thoroughgoing consolidation of the Hindu vote behind the BJP swept it to victory in 1991 despite a countervailing Muslim consolidation. Notwithstanding the division of the Muslim votes in two of these elections, all three elections were marked by a high degree not only of communalization but of polarization, with Muslims failing, however, to consolidate as effectively as did the Hindus behind the BJP.

## The Legislative Assembly Elections of 1989

In the 1989 election, Navman stood alone as the only strong Hindu candidate against three Muslims: Khwaja Halim, on the Janata Dal ticket, Mohammad Furkan, the Congress candidate, and Habibur Rahman, on the ticket of the BSP (Table 10.5), which entered the electoral contest for the first time in this election. Although the two other Muslim candidates besides Khwaja Halim lost their security deposits, they polled more than enough votes to deprive Khwaja Halim of victory. It is unlikely that the BSP candidate received any significant share of the Muslim vote, but it is probable that the Congress candidate did so.

Mohammad Furkan, who made his first and last appearance in a Legislative Assembly contest in Aligarh City in this election, was born in the town of Jalali in a former *zamindar* family of Aligarh District from the Qureshi *baradari*. He attended the Aligarh Muslim University, where his political career began when he took a prominent part in student union politics at the time of the mass student agitation directed against Professor Irfan Habib, over a newspaper article in which the latter was quoted as criticizing severely the decline in standards and student discipline at the university.[8] During that period, Furkan served as vice-president, then president, of the Aligarh Muslim University Students Union (AMUSU). He was, however, a moderate among the student militants in that agitation and ultimately worked to bring it to an end by supporting the vice-chancellor's efforts to restore the educational environment at the university. After his graduation from the AMU, Furkan joined the Congress and was appointed one of the joint secretaries of the U.P. Congress (I) in 1988. He was selected the very next year to contest the Aligarh City Legislative Assembly seat.

Furkan is a noncommunal person of the type commonly associated with the Congress in the past. In my interview with him, he emphasized that when he was a student at AMU, "he worked equally for the Muslims and the Hindus" and had no communal feelings. He claimed that it was because of his noncommunal outlook that he garnered as many as 12,000 votes in the 1989 election. However, his candidacy suffered from the communal atmosphere that pervaded the election of 1989, which occurred in the midst of the *shilanyas*,

TABLE 10.5. Election results for Aligarh City Legislative
Assembly constituency, 1989

| Turnout No./%[a] | Candidates | Caste/ Community | Party | Votes Polled | Percent of Total Valid Votes |
|---|---|---|---|---|---|
| 112,061 | Krishna Kumar Navman | Varshney | BJP | 51,982 | 46.39 |
| 55.14% | Khwaja Halim | Muslim | JD | 42,834 | 38.22 |
| | Mohammad Furkan | Muslim (Qureshi) | INC | 12,146 | 10.84 |
| | Habibur Rahman | Muslim | BSP | 2,182 | 1.95 |
| | Others (19) | | | 2,917 | 2.60 |

[a]Valid votes turnout. Total votes turnout was 56.70 percent (115,220 total votes in an electorate of 203,220).
SOURCE: U.P. Election Office, Lucknow.

the mass movement to bring consecrated bricks to Ayodhya for the building of a new temple to Ram on the site of the Babri mosque. The decline of the Congress in U.P. as a whole was already in progress and was further intensified by this movement, in which it was sidelined. During that time, also, the Shahi Imam of the Jama Masjid in Delhi issued a *fatwa* advising Muslims to vote against the Congress for its failure to defend the Muslim right to possession of the site. Finally, as noted above (Chapter 3), the election outcome was affected by the November 10 riots in the city and the turmoil over the poster campaign on and around the AMU campus, which contributed to the Muslim consolidation of its votes behind the Janata Dal candidates for both the Lok Sabha and the Legislative Assembly.

Table 10.6 shows the distribution of the vote for the three leading candidates in their five best and worst polling stations. The spread in the vote share for the BJP and the Janata Dal is among the highest ever witnessed in any post-Independence election in Aligarh City. As usual, the BJP's best and worst polling stations were in Hindu and Muslim *mohallas*, respectively, whereas the reverse was true for the Janata Dal candidate. It remains of interest to note once again also that the best and worst Congress polling stations were much more mixed than those for either the BJP or the Janata Dal. However low its vote share, the Congress has remained in Aligarh a party that has been able in most elections to remain in the political and demographic center on the communal issue.

Of equal interest in revealing the extent of communalization and polariza-

TABLE 10.6. Vote shares for party candidates in their top and bottom five polling stations, 1989 Legislative Assembly elections, and demographic data for the *mohalla*s included in them, according to the 1951 census (all data in percentages)

| Best/Worst Polling Stations | Vote Share | Muslims | Scheduled Castes | Hindus and Others |
|---|---|---|---|---|
| BJP top 5 | 93.68 | 9.36 | 4.62 | 86.02 |
| BJP bottom 5[a] | 0.15 | 75.62 | 11.40 | 12.98 |
| JD top 5[b] | 95.86 | 92.48 | 1.48 | 6.04 |
| JD bottom 5 | 1.38 | 21.00 | 5.56 | 73.44 |
| INC top 5 | 64.35 | 40.29 | 9.21 | 50.49 |
| INC bottom 5[c] | 0.15 | 67.71 | 0.94 | 31.36 |

[a]The demographic data are for the *mohalla*s of Tila, Sunet, and Sarai Rahman only. Census data for the *mohalla*s of Rorawar, Shah Jamal, and Qayyumnagar in polling station 139, Jauhar Bagh in polling station 18, and Jiwangarh in polling station 22 were not available. However, these are all predominantly Muslim areas. Rorawar was formerly a village included in rural Koil *tahsil* (*pargana* Koil), there were 88 registered voters here in 1984, of whom 55 (62.5 percent) were Muslim. Shah Jamal is the site of the oldest Muslim *dargah* in Aligarh District. The new Idgah (prayer ground for the celebration of the Muslim holy day of Id) also lies in this area. Jauhar Bagh and Jiwangarh, with a combined number of registered voters of 10,362 in 1995, were 100 percent Muslim. Assuming for purposes of a rough estimate only that the proportion of Muslim voters approximates the proportion of Muslims in the population and vice versa, then it is probable that the actual percentage of the Muslim population and voters in these polling stations was 91.69 percent, or closer to that figure than to the figure in the table of 75.62 percent.

[b]The demographic data are for the *mohalla*s of Tila, Sunet, Chowk Bundoo Khan, and Sheikhan only. Census data for the *mohalla*s of Rorawar, Shah Jamal, and Qayyumnagar in polling station 138 were not available. However, as indicated in the previous footnote, these are predominantly Muslim cultural areas.

[c]Census data for *mohalla*s in polling stations 138, 139, and 187 not available, that is, for *mohalla*s Rorawar, Shah Jamal, Qayyumnagar, Mullapara, and Bhojpur.

tion of the Hindu and Muslim electorate in this election is the presence or absence of communally sensitive, riot- and/or crime-prone *mohalla*s in the best and worst polling stations for the three main candidates. The top five BJP polling stations contained fourteen *mohalla*s, all but one with Hindu majorities, ranging from 54 to 100 percent, of which two were classed as communally sensitive (Madar Darwaza [Map 3] and Rafatganj [not on map]), and two riot-hit and crime-prone (Gular Road and Katra [Map 3]). These four *mohalla*s are also communally mixed: Katra is the least so, with a Muslim population of 9 percent but the others contain large Muslim populations: Gular Road with 37 percent, Madar Darwaza with 32 percent, and Rafgatanj with 21 percent. Only one small *mohalla*, Sarai Kalan, had a Muslim majority (above 98 percent). It also deserves note that four of these *mohallas* (Madar Darwaza, Tamolipara, Sarai Pakki, and Brahmanpuri) are in the group that forms a circle round Sarai Sultani, which, we have noted, has suffered greatly in most of the severe riots in Aligarh.

Although Khwaja Halim was said to have benefited also from communal sentiments in the aftermath of riots, the distribution of the sensitive and riot/crime-prone *mohallas* suggests that the BJP candidate was the prime beneficiary. Among the seven *mohallas* in Khwaja Halim's top five, one, Sheikhan, was classed as communally sensitive. Also in this candidate's top five, but in the BJP's bottom five, was the *mohalla* of Shah Jamal (no. 69 in Maps 1 and 4) that was to be attacked in the great riots of 1990–91. Among the ten *mohallas* in the Congress candidate's top five, one was classed as communally sensitive (Tantanpara, Maps 2 and 3), a second as riot- and crime-prone (Atishbazan, Maps 2 and 3). In this candidate's bottom five were included two of the *mohallas* that were targeted in the 1990–91 riots, Shah Jamal and Bhojpur (Maps 1, 2, and 4). It is, therefore, a matter of considerable interest to note the relative importance of these outlying *mohallas* in the top and bottom five polling stations for all the leading candidates. We cannot say that these Muslim-majority *mohallas*, whose very presence in the city limits has troubled Navman and the BJP, were targeted for revenge in the 1990–91 riots, but their importance in this election provides further evidence linking riotous activity with electoral competition in *mohallas* in which the results are perceived as critical to the electoral outcome. However, in this case, it is the electoral competition that precedes the targeting of a *mohalla* for later attack, rather than a riot in the locality that precedes intensified electoral competition.

The relatively small vote share for the Congress had little effect on the high degree of polarization between the BJP and Janata Dal candidates, displayed graphically in Figure 10.1. The huge white spaces on that chart, notably between polling stations 13 and 49, again between polling stations 97 and 133, and at several other places, indicate that, in large parts of the city, voters voted overwhelmingly for one or the other candidate. The contiguity of the polling stations in which such polarization occurred also reveals that the polarization is regional within the city.

The extent of two-party polarization is further demonstrated by the number and percent of polling stations in which one or the other of the two main parties polled above 75 percent of the vote. That was the case in 116 of 223 polling stations or 52 percent. In 96 polling stations or 43 percent of the total, one or the other party polled 80 percent or more. In 60 polling stations or 27 percent, the larger party polled 85 percent or more, and, in 28 or 12.56 per-

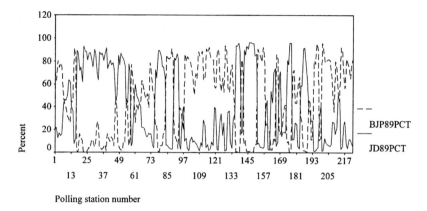

FIG. 10.1. Vote shares for two leading parties, 1989 Legislative Assembly election

cent, the larger party polled above 90 percent. The interparty correlation of
−.91 between the BJP and Janata Dal vote shares adds still further evidence
of the polarization between the two parties.

Finally, the correlation coefficients indicate that the polarization was
extraordinarily high between Hindus and Muslims, with Scheduled Castes
on the sidelines in this election (Table 10.7). The positive correlation of .82
between the Janata Dal and the Muslim vote percentage is the third highest
in any election since Independence, barring the watershed election of 1962
and the election of 1969. Similarly, the positive BJP correlation with percent
Hindus and others equals its previous high correlation in the 1967 election.
The sidelining of the Scheduled Castes is indicated by the unusually high correlation between the vote for all other parties combined and the Scheduled
Caste population (.43). By far the largest share of the other-party vote was
for the BSP candidate, Habibur Rahman, who polled 2,182 votes, 43 percent
of the total for other parties. His highest vote in a single polling station was
122 votes, garnered in a polling station containing the *mohalla* of Sarai
Lawaria (Map 2), with a Scheduled Caste population of 25 percent. His second highest vote in a single polling station was 120 votes, from a polling station containing a newly incorporated village known as Rasulpur, in which
the 1951 census showed a Scheduled Caste population of 64 percent.

Although, therefore, the two other Muslim candidates most likely drew
away the votes that would have defeated Navman and given the victory to
Khwaja Halim, the presence of the Congress candidate only partly softened
the high degree of polarization between the two leading candidates. The

TABLE 10.7. Correlation coefficients of party vote shares with percent
population Muslim, Hindus and others, and Scheduled Castes,
1989 Legislative Assembly elections (N = 70)

MUSLIMS

| Janata Dal | BJP | Congress (I) | Others |
|---|---|---|---|
| .83** | −.74** | −.09 | −.20 |

HINDUS AND OTHERS

| BJP | Congress | Others | Janata Dal |
|---|---|---|---|
| .76** | .06 | .03 | −.80** |

SCHEDULED CASTES

| Congress | BJP | Janata Dal | Others |
|---|---|---|---|
| .09 | .06 | −.16 | .43** |

**p=.01 or less.

Congress vote share correlated only at a very low level with Hindus, Muslims, and Scheduled Castes, indicating the likelihood that its candidate drew some votes from all three groups. The other Muslim candidate, contesting on the ticket of the BSP, most likely gained nearly all his votes from Scheduled Castes.

### The Legislative Assembly Elections of 1991

The General Election of 1991 is one of the most famous and important in post-Independence Indian history, another great watershed election for the country, the state of U.P., and Aligarh as well. It is the election known in popular and journalistic parlance as the "Mandal-*Mandir*" election because of its dual focus on the issues of backward castes reservations in public sector employment recommended in the Mandal Commission report and approved by the Janata Dal government before the election, on the one hand, and the militant Hindu demand to replace the mosque in Ayodhya with a Hindu temple (*mandir*). The conflicts engendered by the Mandal decision and by the *kar sevak* movement of volunteers journeying to Ayodhya to remove the mosque and build a temple to Ram on the same spot, and the fallout from the latter, namely, the actions of Mulayam Singh Yadav and the communal riots that occurred before, during, and after the *kar sevak* movement, provided the issues and determined the new alignment of political forces which dominated the parliamentary and Legislative Assembly elections in U.P. in May–June 1991.

So-called Hindu-Muslim communal riots were of extraordinary importance both before and during the election campaign. They provided both a general context in the state as a whole and a specific context within particular districts and cities that framed the interparty struggle. In Aligarh, riots occurred before the election. In this case, as in some others in the state, massive riots provided a background for the election campaign, helping to frame it in a way which worked to the advantage of the BJP. The Aligarh riots occurred during the *kar sevak* movement. They fed into the BJP propaganda theme of Muslim instigation, state police protection and pampering of Muslims, and Hindu martyrdom at the hands of "Muslim miscreants" despite the fact that here, as elsewhere, many more Muslims than Hindus were killed.

Although there were many districts in U.P. that remained relatively unaffected by communal rioting and somewhat less affected by the general atmosphere of communal hostility in the state, the communal atmosphere in U.P. as a whole and the widespread occurrence of Hindu-Muslim riots and confrontations affected profoundly the results of this election. This was not an ordinary election. The 1991 election in U.P. stands apart from all others held since Independence, constituting a serious deterioration in the quality of the democratic process.

The riots that occurred before and during the campaign had three consequences in the state as a whole, all of which worked to the advantage of the BJP: concentration of Hindu voting for the BJP, a high turnout among Hindus as well, and a communal polarization far greater than anything that has occurred since Independence, for which one has to look back to 1946 for a precedent. In Aligarh, the results paralleled those in the state as a whole insofar as communal and polarized voting are concerned. Where the Janata Dal and the Samajwadi Janata Party (SJP, predecessor of the SP) did not contest against each other, Muslims voted overwhelmingly for the Janata Dal. Where the two parties were divided, so was the Muslim vote. In the latter case, the high degree of polarization between caste Hindus and Muslims was partly diluted, though communalization was at a peak. Also mirroring results elsewhere in the state, caste Hindu mobilization overwhelmed Muslim solidarity and the combination of many backward caste and Scheduled Caste votes with the Muslims against the BJP.

In the 1991 election in Aligarh, the first after the great riots of December

TABLE 10.8. Election results for Aligarh Legislative
Assembly constituency, 1991

| Turnout No./%[a] | Candidates | Caste/ Community | Party | Votes Polled | Percent of Total Valid Votes |
|---|---|---|---|---|---|
| 111,353 | Krishna Kumar Navman | Varshney | BJP | 52,670 | 47.30 |
| 54.10% | Mohammad Sufiyan | Muslim (Qureshi) | JD | 47,249 | 42.43 |
| | Bhanu Pratap | NA | INC | 6,903 | 6.20 |
| | Hafiz Usman | Muslim | SJP | 2,445 | 2.20 |
| | Shamim Ahmad | Muslim | BSP | 728 | 0.65 |
| | Others (19) | | | 1,358 | 1.22 |

[a]Valid votes turnout. Total votes turnout (113,816) was 55.29 percent. Total electorate was 205,838.

1990–January 1991, Navman again was the only Hindu candidate with enough support not to lose his security deposit. He improved slightly his total votes and his vote share to 47.30 percent (Table 10.8). The runner-up candidate on the Janata Dal ticket, Mohammad Sufiyan, a Qureshi Muslim, polled 42.43 percent of the vote. Although the Congress candidate was this time a Hindu, the Congress decline that began all over U.P. in 1989 deepened and its candidate won only 6.2 percent of the vote. The fourth-place candidate from the SJP was also a Muslim, Hafiz Usman. Although he polled well in a few polling stations, his overall vote total and vote share were too small to influence the outcome in the constituency as a whole.

Navman gave the following analysis of the voting pattern in this election. He claimed that the Muslim candidate on the SJP ticket, the party of Mulayam Singh Yadav, got only the Ahir (Yadav) votes, that is, the votes of the community (defined by the Mandal Commission as a backward caste) that solidly supports that party throughout the state. He averred that his main opponent, Sufiyan, the Janata Dal candidate, got the votes of Scheduled Castes; however, because Sufiyan "himself was a Qureshi," a *baradari* of low status amongst Muslims, Navman claimed that some "upper-caste" Muslims as well as Shia Muslims voted for him (Navman).[9] This analysis, however, does not stand up against the large number of votes received by Mohammad Sufiyan. Although it is of interest that Navman takes a position consistent here with that of the BJP generally, that some Muslims support the party, it does not

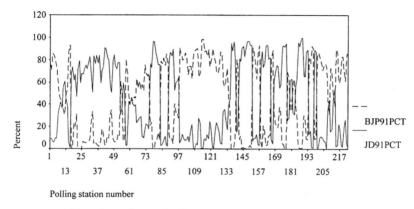

FIG. 10.2. Vote shares for two leading parties, 1991 Legislative Assembly election

appear likely that there was a significant division of the votes among the Muslim candidates. The election was, rather, an almost straight fight in a thoroughly communalized and polarized electoral contest—held in the aftermath of the first assault on the Babri mosque in November 1990—in which Navman emerged victorious once again, with a somewhat larger vote share, but a smaller margin between him and the runner-up.

However, it must be stressed that a straight fight in the constituency as a whole does not mean a straight fight in the *mohallas*. On the contrary, in Aligarh it means a regional, that is to say, locality-wise polarization of the votes. Polarization between the two leading candidates was even more extreme than in the previous election. The chart showing the dispersal of the BJP and Janata Dal vote shares of 1991 (Figure 10.2) again contains great white spaces, reflecting the huge spread in the vote between the two candidates, particularly in predominantly Hindu and predominantly Muslim polling stations. The number and percent of polling stations in which one or the other of the two leading candidates polled above 75 percent of the vote was also somewhat higher this time, 122 out of 223 polling stations, comprising 55 percent of the total. As in 1989, one or the other of the two candidates polled above 85 percent in 60 polling stations in 1991 as well. The correlation coefficient between the vote shares for the two parties was an extraordinarily high −.97 (N=223).

Polarization of the communal vote was also evident in the distribution of the votes for the leading candidates in their best and worst polling stations (Table 10.9). Especially notable in this election was the number of bottom polling stations in which the candidates polled zero votes or close to zero. The BJP candidate got no votes at all in nine polling stations, the Janata Dal

TABLE 10.9. Vote shares for party candidates in their top and bottom polling stations, 1991 elections, and demographic data for the *mohallas* included in them, according to the 1951 census or 1995 voters' lists[a] (all data in percentages)

| Best/Worst Polling Stations | Vote Share | Muslims | Scheduled Castes | Hindus and Others |
|---|---|---|---|---|
| BJP top 5 | 95.06 | 17.62 | 2.53 | 79.85 |
| BJP bottom 4[b] | 0.00 | 78.67 | 9.40 | 11.93 |
| JD top 5 | 97.58 | 79.24 | 9.03 | 11.73 |
| JD bottom 5 | 0.33 | 11.09 | 5.78 | 83.13 |
| INC top 5 | 30.25 | 12.23 | 6.11 | 81.66 |
| INC bottom 6[c] | 0.00 | 77.11 | 2.94 | 77.11 |
| JP top 5[d] | 26.11 | 98.79 | NA | NA |
| JP bottom 17[e] | 0.00 | 29.27 | 7.56 | 63.17 |

[a] All data are from the 1951 census except where otherwise noted.

[b] The BJP polled zero votes in nine polling stations, for which census *mohalla* data were available for only four.

[c] The Congress polled zero votes in seven polling stations, for which census *mohalla* data were available for only six.

[d] Muslim percent in this row is an estimate from a random number sampling of the 1995 voters' list.

[e] The Janata Party polled zero votes in 18 polling stations, for which census *mohalla* data were available for only 17.

candidate polled only 0.33 percent of the vote in his bottom five, the Congress candidate polled zero in his bottom seven, and the Janata Party candidate polled nought in eighteen. At the top end, the vote shares for the two leading candidates were extremely high: the BJP polled 95.06 percent of the vote in its top five polling stations dominated by Hindus while the Janata Dal candidate polled an even higher 97.58 percent in his top five polling stations dominated by Muslims. As for the third- and fourth- place candidates, the Congress Hindu candidate did relatively well only in Hindu-dominated polling stations. It is a matter of great interest to note that all the *mohallas* in the top five polling stations for the Muslim Janata party candidate are located in the northeastern corner of the city, center of in-migration of Muslims and the bane of the BJP and Krishna Kumar Navman for that reason.[10] The estimated percentage of Muslims in these areas is, moreover, nearly 90 percent. In contrast, this candidate's bottom seventeen polling stations, in which he got no votes at all, were in predominantly Hindu *mohallas*.

As usual, the BJP's best polling stations included a high proportion of communally sensitive and crime-prone *mohallas*: four out of eight, including Rafatganj, Manik Chauk (Navman's home *mohalla*), Gular Road, and Madar Darwaza. Also notable is the *mohalla*-wise distribution of the nine polling stations in which the BJP polled no votes. In addition to the four *mohallas* already mentioned for which we have the 1951 census data, there were four other *mohallas* located in the same northeastern corner of the city where the Muslim Janata Party candidate polled his best, namely, Jauhar Bagh, Jiwangarh, Kela Nagar, and Krishi Farm (Map 1). These *mohallas* are all located in two wards, numbers 43 and 47, which are SP strongholds and where the winning SP candidates in the 1995 corporation elections both were Muslims. In other words, the BJP was wiped out in precisely the same localities in which one of the Muslim candidates polled his best, in the area of Muslim in-migration. In contrast to the BJP, the Janata Dal candidate's top five polling stations contained only one riot-prone *mohalla* out of eight, while the Congress candidate's top five contained none.

### The Legislative Assembly Election of 1993

The 1993 election, held after the destruction of the Babri Masjid on December 6, 1992, was in some ways a repeat of the election of 1991, but in other ways foreshadowed the dramatic change that was to occur in 1996. As in 1991, there was a high degree of communalization of the election, but polarization was not as extreme because of a division of the Muslim vote between two Muslim major party candidates. This division, however, presaged the transformation of the constituency from a Hindu-dominated to a Muslim-dominated one, for the combined votes of the two leading Muslim candidates surpassed that of the victor, Krishna Kumar Navman. The vote shares for the four leading candidates are given in Table 10.10.

Although the Muslim vote was divided, Krishna Kumar Navman barely defeated his principal opponent, Abdul Khaliq, a Saifi businessman of Aligarh, owner of a lock factory, who contested on the ticket of the BSP. Mohammad Sufiyan, contesting again on the ticket of the Janata Dal, was displaced by Abdul Khaliq, but gained enough votes to ensure the latter's defeat and the victory of Navman. Here is how Mohammad Sufiyan himself described the voting pattern in this election.[11] He attributed his poor showing compared to 1991 to a division of the Muslim vote in 1993, which was not the case in the previous election. That division in turn was a consequence of what is generally described as strategic voting on the part of the Muslim community, in

TABLE 10.10. Election results for Aligarh City Legislative
Assembly constituency, 1993

| Turnout No./%[a] | Candidates | Caste/ Community | Party | Percent of Votes Polled | Total Valid Votes |
|---|---|---|---|---|---|
| 142,087/ 62.08 | Krishna Kumar Navman | Varshney | BJP | 58,027 | 40.84 |
| | Abdul Khaliq | Muslim (Saifi) | BSP | 56,005 | 39.42 |
| | Mohammad Sufiyan | Muslim (Qureshi) | JD | 15,338 | 10.79 |
| | Vivek Bansal | Agarwal | INC | 10,121 | 7.12 |
| | Others (54) | | | 2,596 | 1.83 |

[a]Valid votes turnout. Total votes turnout was 145,364 (63.51 percent).

SOURCE: Uttar Pradesh, Mukhya Nirvachan Adhikari, *Vidhan Sabha Samanya Nirvachan, Uttar Pradesh, 1993* (Allahabad: Government Press, 1996), pp. 507–08. *Date of poll:* November 21, 1993.

which Muslims vote as a bloc for the candidate perceived to be the most likely to defeat the BJP. Sufiyan did not use the term, but his account of what happened is consistent with that strategy. He remarked that in 1991 the Janata Dal "was emerging as the single largest party in India," whereas in 1993 it "was on decline and he was contesting from JD. So, in 1993, the Muslims thought that, if they all come together under the banner of BSP and vote against these BJP candidates, then they will get their candidate elected. That's why my share of the vote in 1993 declined." In other words, since the Janata Dal was on the decline, "there was a common perception that it's only the BSP that can give fight to the BJP. That's why Muslims all came together and they voted against the BJP candidate."

I asked Sufiyan then if he got any Muslim votes at all. He said that he got "some percentage of the Muslim vote," mostly "personal votes" that are in his "pocket," "based on his personal contacts." When I asked where he got his best votes, he listed the following *mohallas*: Delhi Gate, Sarai Mian, Khaidora, and Sarai Bibi. Three of these *mohallas*—Delhi Gate, Sarai Mian, and Khaidora—are predominantly Qureshi *mohallas*, two are classed as crime-prone *mohallas*—Delhi Gate and Khaidora—and all are predominantly Muslim *mohallas*. It is clear, however, that Sufiyan got his "pocket" votes primarily from the Muslim voters of his own *baradari*. Otherwise, he acknowledges that Muslims voted solidly for Abdul Khaliq.

Congress placed fourth in this election. Its candidate, Vivek Bansal, polled only slightly more votes than the Congress candidate in 1991, and, like his predecessor, lost his security deposit. Bansal, an Arya Samaji Hindu and an Agarwal Vaishya by caste, is a manufacturer of brass tacks and a manufacturer and exporter of brass art ware.[12] He is a young man, born and brought up in Aligarh, who has lived all his life in a mansion on the poshest road in Aligarh, the Marris Road. He is a completely noncommunal person, a graduate of AMU, who has personal relations with Muslims from both the former landed aristocracy of Aligarh and from the faculty of AMU. He employs 50–55 persons in his factory and claimed, in response to my question concerning the numbers of Hindus and Muslims in his workforce, never to have considered the matter.

Bansal gave the following explanation for his poor performance on the Congress ticket. First, he said that he was himself new to politics, a "greenhorn," as he put it. But second, the "[Congress] party's position was awful; this happens to be predominantly a Muslim constituency, . . . and minorities were very, very, very angry with the party on account of . . . the demolition of Babri Masjid in 1992."

Though he fared poorly, Bansal was hopeful of becoming a successful candidate on the Congress ticket for the Legislative Assembly or Parliament in future. In contrast to other candidates, who admitted the restricted caste/communal composition of their support bases, Bansal could not give any list of polling stations in which he fared well, saying that he did not think he had any particular strongholds, but got "votes from every booth irrespective of . . . how many I got." Further, he stressed that he believed in and had worked for Hindu-Muslim "communal amity" in the past, notably during the riots of March 1996 (*sic;* presumably March 1994) in the city, when he claims to have helped persons in the Sarai Sultani *mohalla*. When I questioned the ability of a Hindu to win in this communally polarized, predominantly Muslim constituency any longer, Bansal argued that Navman's tactics of mobilizing militant Hindus was an "easy solution" to winning the election, but that "people tend to vote for the person who is able to deliver the goods, in the long run." In short, Bansal was talking in the manner of the traditional, secular Congress politician of times past and elections past, but the contours of electoral politics remained communalized and, though the Muslim vote was divided, polarized between the leading Hindu and Muslim candidates.

# 11 / Communal Solidarity
# and Division at the Local Level

### SELECTED *MOHALLA*-WISE RESULTS
### FOR ALIGARH ELECTIONS, 1957 TO 1995

*Manik Chauk*

Let us now have a look at the available election results for the infamous *mohalla* of Manik Chauk, center of so many of the riots in Aligarh since Independence and home and business premises of Krishna Kumar Navman. Recall first the demographic characteristics of this *mohalla*. Even in 1951, it was a large *mohalla*, with a total population of 3,848 persons. It was also mixed in its communal composition, although the Hindu population was predominant with 75.55 percent of the total, Muslims comprising 24.01 percent and the Scheduled Castes having negligible representation. According to the 1984 voters' list, there were 2,485 voters in the *mohalla*, of whom, however, only 13.17 percent were Muslims. According to the 1995 voters list, the number of voters was somewhat less than in 1984; 2,375 voters were listed, of whom 345 or 14.53 percent were Muslim. It is not clear whether we can extrapolate from these figures to the total population of Muslims in the *mohalla* and assume that Hindu efforts to intimidate Muslims during riots here have succeeded in reducing their percentage in the population. It is, however, likely that something of the sort has happened. It is also quite possible that the number of Muslim voters in the *mohalla* has been deliberately undercounted. Let us recall also that Manik Chauk falls into the most severe category of riot-proneness, being both riot-prone and crime-hit. This is also a *mohalla* in which the predominant community is the Varshney caste. The *mohalla*, along with Sarai Barahseni and Patthar Bazaar, falls entirely in ward no. 58, where the successful BJP candidate in the 1995 municipal corporation elections was Krishna Gopal Varshney.

In 1957, the first election for which I have polling station data, Manik Chauk was included in polling station numbers 42 (men only) and 43 (women only), along with two other *mohallas*, known as Sarai Bairagi (not on map) and Sarai Nawab, both located some distance from Manik Chauk (see Map 2).[1] The total population of these two *mohallas* was 1,293 persons, thus comprising a quarter (25.15 percent) of the total population of the polling station. Sarai Bairagi was overwhelmingly comprised of Hindus and others (90.13 percent, while Sarai Nawab contained a mixed population, 60 percent Muslim, 28.91 percent Scheduled Castes, and 11.09 percent Hindus and others. In this election, no doubt because of the mixed character of the polling station, number 42 (men only) ranked first in the intensity of interparty competition by the interval measure, a mere two votes (0.28 percentage points) separating the first-place candidate from the second. In first place in polling station 42 was the Jan Sangh candidate, who polled 38.29 percent of the vote here in comparison with his showing of 13.53 percent in the constituency as a whole, whereas the Congress candidate polled 38.02 percent compared to his showing of 50.09 percent in the constituency as a whole. We know enough about these *mohallas*, especially Manik Chauk, by now to say with assurance that the Hindus in polling station 42 voted overwhelmingly for the BJP even at this early date in its history in the constituency. More interesting, however, from the perspective of hindsight in relation to the post-riot elections that followed this one, is that, despite the sharp division in Hindu and Muslim voting, Muslims clearly chose for the most part not to vote for the only Muslim candidate in this election, who polled only 31 votes in polling station 42. Instead, it is virtually certain that they cast their votes for the Congress candidate. So, in this first election in this polling station, we see the seeds of later Hindu consolidation in its militant Hindu epicenter of Manik Chauk, along with a communalized electorate in which Hindus and Muslims here—but not in the constituency as a whole—must have voted for different candidates. Further, the Muslims adhered to the Congress, then considered in principle and practice to be a secular political party.

From 1962 through 1991, the available polling station data are for the *mohalla* of Manik Chauk by itself. Figure 11.1 compares the vote share for the militant Hindu candidates in the Aligarh constituency as a whole with that for the Manik Chauk *mohalla* for the six Legislative Assembly elections in that period. There are three significant things to note from the chart. First, insofar as the line for the *mohalla* is concerned, there are two peaks, the first in 1962 following the October 1961 riot, the second in 1991 following the great riots of 1990–91. Second, the slopes of the two lines are, with the exception

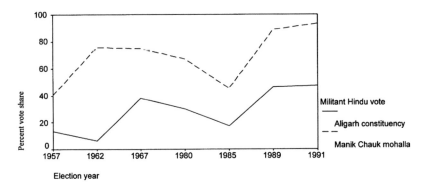

FIG. 11.1. Militant Hindu vote share in Aligarh Legislative Assembly
constituency and Manik Chauk *mohalla,* 1957–91

of 1962, virtually identical. Third, however, the line for the militant Hindu
vote share is consistently higher in Manik Chauk than that for the constituency
as a whole. Thus, in effect, insofar as the militant Hindu vote is concerned,
the results in Manik Chauk *mohalla* were exceptional in 1962 only. Thereafter,
the rest of the constituency followed the statistical and political lead emanating from this *mohalla,* but at a lower level of Hindu consolidation. Fourth,
the militant Hindu vote in this *mohalla* reached extraordinary heights in the
1989 and 1991 elections, the years in which the great militant Hindu mobilization took place on the issue of the Babri Masjid. The vote for Krishna
Kumar Navman, the BJP candidate in these two elections, reached 88.74 and
93.36 percent, respectively. These results, of course, are exactly what we should
expect from everything that we have learned about this *mohalla.*

Figure 11.2 compares the Congress vote share in the constituency as a whole
and in Manik Chauk *mohalla.* The results are partly a mirror image of the
results of the comparison of the militant Hindu vote in the constituency and
the *mohalla.* That is, the slopes are parallel, but that for the *mohalla* is for the
most part below that for the constituency as a whole, with one significant
exception, namely, the 1985 election. In the latter election, the Hindu vote
was divided between the BJP and the Congress. Although the BJP candidate
polled 45.19 percent of the vote in this *mohalla* compared to 42.92 percent
for the Congress candidate, the latter did better in the *mohalla* in 1985 than
in the constituency as a whole, where he polled only 39.49 percent. There are
two likely reasons for this result. First, the RSS at this time was divided and
many members were supporting the Congress, which, under Rajiv Gandhi's
leadership, was adopting stands similar to that of the BJP on both the issues

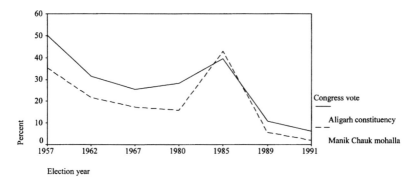

FIG. 11.2. Congress vote share in Aligarh Legislative Assembly
constituency and Manik Chauk *mohalla,* 1957–91

of national unity and the right of Hindus to worship at the Babri Masjid.
Second, it is quite likely that the Hindus in Manik Chauk as well as in other
parts of the city engaged in a form of strategic voting here, opting for the
Congress candidate as the one most likely to defeat Khwaja Halim, the Muslim
candidate of the Lok Dal.

Finally, a look at Figure 11.3, which gives the results for the militant Hindu
candidates and the Congress in all elections for which I have polling station
data, including the Lok Sabha elections, rounds out the picture of voting in
this *mohalla* over thirty-five years. The history of voting in the *mohalla* for
the time series for which I have data divides clearly into three periods. In the
1962 Legislative Assembly contest, the voters of Manik Chauk preferred a militant Hindu candidate to either the Congress or the Jan Sangh, namely, the
Hindi journalist Madan Lal Hiteshi, who polled 44.25 percent of the vote compared to only 15.86 percent for the Jan Sangh candidate and 21.62 percent for
the Congress. If, therefore, we combine the votes for the two militant Hindu
candidates, as has been done in Figure 11.3, the interval between their combined votes and that for the Congress is 38.49 percent. The gap in the 1962
Lok Sabha election is even greater, the voters of Manik Chauk having given
75.67 percent of their votes to the independent militant Hindu candidate, Shiv
Kumar Shastri, and only 8.60 percent to the Congress candidate.

This phase in the history of voting in Manik Chauk *mohalla* lasts from
1962 through the 1980 Legislative Assembly election. This is the period
framed by the riots of October 1961 and the beginning of the 1978–80 series
of riots. It is marked by a huge upsurge in voting for militant Hindu candidates and a vast gap between their vote share and that for the Congress. Krishna

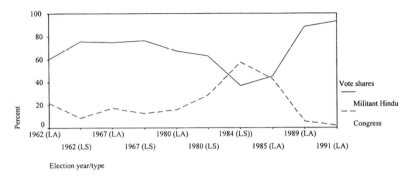

FIG. 11.3. Vote shares for all militant Hindu candidates and for the Congress,
Manik Chauk *mohalla,* 1957–91

Kumar Navman entered electoral politics for the first time as an independent candidate in the 1980 Lok Sabha election. Although he polled poorly in the city as a whole, where Hindu votes were divided between the Congress and the Janata Party candidates, he won a plurality of the vote in Manik Chauk (36.21 percent). If his votes and that of the Janata Party militant Hindu candidate are combined (as in Figure 11.3), then the gap between their combined votes and those for the Congress is above 33 percent.

In the second phase, which includes only the two elections of 1984 and 1985, the Congress vote share rises above that for the militant Hindu candidates for reasons indicated above. In the third period, the distance between the vote for the militant Hindu candidates and the Congress is enormous.

We have here in Manik Chauk a distilled and refined picture of the communalization of a segment of the Hindu electorate that has been the advance guard of militant Hindu nationalism and anti-Muslim sentiment in Aligarh since Independence. Not since 1962 has there been any significant deviation in the expression of that sentiment. The anomaly of the 1984 and 1985 elections itself confirms its persistence, since the militant Hindu voters of Manik Chauk divided only in their belief that the Congress had come closer to the RSS view of the Indian nation as a Hindu nation.

But these results raise a methodological issue. Till now, I have argued that there has been a relationship between riots and interparty competition (on the interval measure), such that pre-election riots produce an intensification of party competition. While that remains true for the city as a whole, it does not apply to each and every *mohalla* where the other variables previously introduced, namely, communalization and polarization, reveal their importance in the overall process. That is to say, communal riots have a dual effect in towns such as Aligarh where there are sizable populations of both Hindus and Muslims. In particular localities, where there is often a preponderance of members of one community, riots intensify communal solidarity (communalization), which translates in the context of the city as a whole into intensified interparty competition that, at its most intense, also involves a polarization in which religious and party identities merge. So, there is here a clear causal sequence as follows:

*communal riot > communal solidarity > intensified
interparty competition > communal polarization*

In particular localities, the entire sequence will reveal itself only if there is a communal balance within them, in which case an interval measure of interparty competition will correspond at the local level to that at the level above it. From a methodological point of view, the principal point here is that any kind of electoral analysis that concentrates on a single level to explain a phenomenon such as the relationship between riots (a societal occurrence)[2] and interparty competition (a political event) is flawed. I have demonstrated elsewhere that in a society as heterogeneous as India's, with multiple layerings of potential identities to kin, caste, clan, language, and religion, the level of ethnic/communal identification and competition will, in the normal course, depend upon the size of the political arena.[3]

The Legislative Assembly contest in Aligarh, or, for that matter, virtually all such constituencies in the state of U.P. and India as a whole, can be framed in a multiplicity of ways. The most common frame is a combination of intercaste and communal competition. There is in fact a predominant tendency towards a degree of fragmentation that corresponds in each constituency to the number of castes and communities of a size that provides a sufficient voter base to affect the result, usually in U.P. somewhere between three and five candidates from different castes and religions. To build a broader vote base, parties must either make intercaste or intercommunal deals or they must find an appeal that transcends the identities of particular castes and *baradaris*. In contemporary U.P. politics, there are three such transcendent appeals at work: to all backward castes, to all lower castes, or to religious community. It is because of the heterogeneity of castes and *baradaris*, each with its own particular interests and sense of separateness, that such broader appeals are so difficult to construct, so difficult in fact that only very dramatic events such as riots can provide an effective basis for them.

## Sarai Sultani

Let us now compare voting behavior in the Muslim-dominated *mohalla* of Sarai Sultani, which, as we have seen above, has experienced virtually the whole gamut of rioting in Aligarh since Independence. According to the 1951 census, the total population of this *mohalla* was 1,303, among whom there were 1,154 Muslims (88.56 percent) and 149 Hindus (11.44 percent); it contained no Scheduled Castes. According to the 1995 voters' list, there were 1,813 voters, of whom 281 were non-Muslim (15.51 percent). Once again, therefore, the figures suggest that the 1951 census data remain reliable indicators of caste/communal population proportions for most inner-city *mohallas*. They also suggest that, in the face of the alleged pressures from militant Hindu groups in the surrounding *mohallas* to intimidate the Muslim population to leave, the *mohalla* has remained predominantly Muslim. The predominant Muslim *baradari* in Sarai Sultani is Qureshi. Thus, in all the above respects, Sarai Sultani is the mirror image of Manik Chauk, that is, in its caste/communal population ratios and in the presence in each *mohalla* of the community alleged to be the most active during communal riots, Varshneys in Manik Chauk and Qureshis in Sarai Sultani.

Unfortunately, we cannot trace the electoral history of this *mohalla* as far back as for Manik Chauk since, until 1980, the polling stations that encompassed Sarai Sultani included several other *mohallas*, some predominantly Hindu, others predominantly Muslim; further, the *mohallas* joined with Sarai Sultani changed at each election. The results for the 1995 corporation elections also cannot be broken out for Sarai Sultani alone since it shared ward no. 35 with another *mohalla*. It is a matter of interest, however, that the corporator for this ward elected in 1995 was Abdul Rab, uncle of our principal informant concerning the riotous history of the *mohalla*. Abdul Rab won this election as an independent.

It is possible, however, to compare the election results for Sarai Sultani with Manik Chauk and Aligarh constituency as a whole for six elections between 1980 and 1991, of which four were Legislative Assembly elections and two (in 1980 and 1984) were for the Lok Sabha. Figure 11.4, showing the militant Hindu vote shares for these elections, gives as clean and clear a picture of these contrasts as one might expect from all that we have learned so far. The slopes of the three lines are virtually identical, but that for Manik Chauk is high above that for the constituency as a whole, while the one for Sarai Sultani runs considerably below.

There is much less clarity, however, when we compare the Congress vote

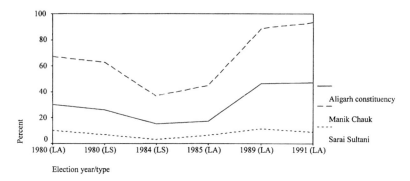

FIG. 11.4. Militant Hindu party vote shares in Aligarh constituency and Manik Chauk and Sarai Sultani *mohallas*, 1980–91

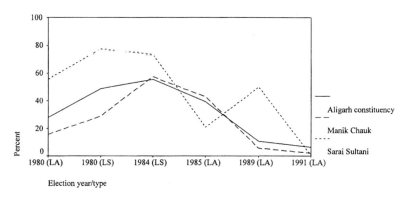

FIG. 11.5. Congress vote shares in Aligarh constituency and Manik Chauk and Sarai Sultani *mohallas*, 1980–91

shares in the three units under examination (Figure 11.5). The slopes all proceed in tandem for the first two elections, but that for Sarai Sultani crosses the other two steeply downward in 1985 (LA), steeply upward again in 1989 (LA), and close at near zero in 1991 (LA).

We have already explained the deviations from the mean for Manik Chauk; those for Sarai Sultani occurred partly for the same, partly for other reasons that are illustrated in the next figure. Figure 11.6 gives the party vote shares for the three principal political tendencies in Aligarh for Sarai Sultani alone. In the 1984 and 1985 elections, as we have seen, many militant Hindus in Manik Chauk found the Congress a party more suitable to their proclivities than even the BJP. However, the voters of Sarai Sultani remained loyal to

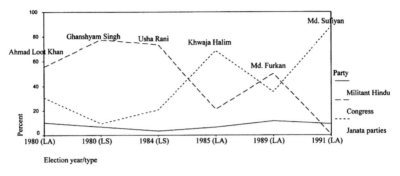

FIG. 11.6. Party vote shares in Sarai Sultani *mohalla,* 1980–91

the Congress through the 1984 Lok Sabha election, but then most deserted the Congress in favor of the Janata Party candidate, Khwaja Halim, in the 1985 Legislative Assembly election. In 1989, when the militant Hindu honeymoon with the Congress abruptly terminated, the voters of Sarai Sultani remained divided between Congress and the Janata Dal, but more this time preferred the Congress. Finally, in 1991, as the Congress vote in this *mohalla* plummeted to near zero, that for the Janata Dal candidate rose to 88.26 percent of the total.

Further factors influencing the voting in Sarai Sultani—aside from the disaffection with the Congress and the move towards the Janata parties experienced by Muslims in most parts of the state as well as in Aligarh during the Ram Janmabhoomi movement—were the community and *baradari* of the candidates of the Congress and the Janata parties. In the 1980 Legislative Assembly election, won by the Janata party (SC) candidate, Khwaja Halim, Sarai Sultani voters preferred another Muslim candidate running on the Congress ticket, Ahmad Loot Khan, who polled 55.80 percent of the vote in the *mohalla.* In the two Lok Sabha elections of 1980 and 1984, *mohalla* voters remained loyal to the Congress despite the absence of Muslim candidates. The Congress vote shares in Sarai Sultani were very high in these two elections: 77.54 percent for Ghanshyam Singh in 1980 and 73.63 percent in 1984 for Usha Rani. In 1985, however, *mohalla* voters deserted the Congress Hindu candidate in favor of Khwaja Halim, the Lok Dal candidate. In 1989, with the option to choose from two Muslim candidates, Khwaja Halim again on the Janata Dal ticket and Mohammad Furkan, the Congress nominee, Sarai Sultani voters divided between the two, but preferred the Congress Muslim candidate. Finally, in 1991, although there were two other Muslim candidates, one contesting on the SJP (SP), the other on the BSP ticket, *mohalla* voters concentrated their votes overwhelmingly behind Mohammad Sufiyan, a man of their community and also a man of the predominant Qureshi *baradari*.

It should be noted, therefore, that, though there is a general tendency throughout the period from 1980 to 1991 for the Muslim voters of Sarai Sultani to prefer—other things being equal—a Muslim candidate, they are less communalized than the Hindus of Manik Chauk. The latter have divided only when two Hindu candidates have been seen as ideologically militant Hindu or when the Congress itself came near the BJP ideology of nationhood. While Sarai Sultani voters, too, have divided when offered a choice between two strong Muslim candidates, their voting has also been influenced by party ties: initially to the Congress, then to the Janata parties. At the same time, it must also be recognized that the party loyalties of the Muslim voters of Sarai Sultani also reflect their communal interests to the extent—certainly considerable— that they perceive particular parties (initially the Congress, then the Janata parties) as the secular parties, seen at different times as the best protectors of their rights, safety, and security, and the parties most able to defeat the BJP.

So, while we see the tendencies in both *mohallas*, as in the city as a whole, towards communalization and, at times, polarization, there are evident countervailing tendencies as well. Amongst militant Hindus, however, the countervailing tendencies fall within a consistent ideological line of Hindu nationalism, while amongst Muslims, the countervailing tendencies are of party, community, and *baradari*. It is the pressure of militant Hindu mobilization and hostility to Muslims that feeds the tendency towards communal polarization. When that pressure recedes, other kinds of divisions appear and become politically important to Muslim voters and to Hindus as well, who divide according to caste as well as party.

# 12 / The Decline of Communal Violence
# and the Transformation of Electoral Competition

For a decade after the destruction of the Babri Masjid in December 1992 and the negative reaction to it in the country and around the world, there was a decline in communal violence in India as a whole and in the state of U.P. and Aligarh as well. This decline was in no small measure owing to the deliberate decision of the RSS and BJP leadership to move toward an accommodating stance in its drive to gain, maintain, and consolidate its power in particular states and in the country and the necessity for it to make alliances with noncommunal parties to do so. That strategy has, however, produced mixed results. Although the BJP was in power in 2000 at the Center and in several Indian states, it suffered a major defeat in the U.P. Lok Sabha elections of 1999. In Aligarh City, the BJP has been displaced in both the Legislative Assembly constituency and in the Aligarh segment of the parliamentary constituency. In this chapter, I will demonstrate its decline in the Legislative Assembly constituency and the reasons for it.

## THE LEGISLATIVE ASSEMBLY ELECTION OF 1996

In the past decade, a major demographic shift has been occurring in Aligarh City, the nightmare of all Hindu communalists, namely, a rise in the Muslim population of the city. Demographic shifts in the population of Aligarh City have combined with alterations in the delimitation of the boundaries of the constituency to affect significantly the communal composition of the voting population and the results of the last elections. These changes have involved the exclusion from the constituency of Hindu-majority areas and the alleged illegal voting of Muslims from another constituency in Muslim-majority areas.

Altogether, 16 *mohallas* from the old ward of Achal Talab, with a population of 10,792 in 1951, which can be estimated to have reached 36,584 by 1991,[1] were transferred out of Aligarh constituency after 1969 (after 1980 in the case of Madar Darwaza). These numbers constitute 70.43 percent of the total population of this predominantly Hindu ward, the ward with the highest proportion of Hindus (80.81 percent) in 1951. The proportion of Hindus in the 16 transferred *mohallas* was 88.02 percent (estimated total population of 27,782).

In the meantime, as noted earlier, there has been a very considerable increase in the Muslim population in outlying areas of the city, including many former villages and new *mohallas* that have grown in part as a consequence of migration from the rural hinterland. Table 6.3, discussed earlier, shows the voting population of those areas for which I have data from the latest voters' lists, categorized as Muslim or non-Muslim (Hindus, others, and Scheduled Castes), and as to whether or not they are included in the 1989/1991 delimination of the Legislative Assembly constituency, the latest delimination in my possession. Although some of the newly incorporated areas are predominantly Hindu, they are *not* included in the Legislative Assembly constituency, whereas many of the large predominantly Muslim *mohallas* are included. The proportion of Muslims in these included *mohallas* ranges from 63.41 to 100 percent. The total number of Muslim voters listed on the 1984 and 1995 voters' lists combined for those areas is 27,290, all added to the new Aligarh City Legislative Assembly boundaries.

It is, therefore, the case that the population balance in the Aligarh constituency has shifted in favor of the Muslims in consequence of successive deliminations of constituency boundaries and a substantial increase in the Muslim population in the outlying areas. It is evident also from the polling station-wise voting in the transferred *mohallas* discussed in the preceding chapters that the BJP has suffered in consequence of these shifts. Further evidence of the loss to the BJP comes from the results of the corporator elections. Seven of the eleven transferred Hindu-majority *mohallas* fall in wards 15 and 17 in the 1995 delimination.[2] The BJP won the 1995 elections in both these wards, polling 47.29 percent of the vote in ward 15 and 39.83 percent in ward 17. This and other differences between the boundaries of the assembly constituency and the municipality also explain why the BJP remains dominant in municipal politics, but has lost its dominance in the legislative constituency.

Navman had noted these trends with some concern in an interview in 1993, when he remarked to me that "one difficulty he faced in the 1991 election was that Muslims had been migrating to the city from the rural areas from time to time and that, as a consequence, the number of Muslim voters had increased." When I visited Aligarh in 1997, it was estimated that Muslims then comprised a majority of the voters in the city constituency, perhaps 60 percent of the total. As a consequence, by 1996, the Muslims could afford even to divide their votes to some extent, as they probably did in that election, and still provide the bulk of the support to the winning Muslim candidate on the ticket of the SP, defeating Navman by a wide majority (see Table 12.1). It was also reported that Navman had lost the consolidated support of the Hindu community as a consequence of his failure to take care of his constituency.

The man who succeeded in unseating Navman was Abdul Khaliq. He had joined the BSP in 1993 and, in his first attempt at the Aligarh assembly seat, nearly won it in a close contest against Navman. Abdul Khaliq's decision to fight on the ticket of the BSP had the effect of resurrecting the old alliance between the Muslims and the Scheduled Castes that unseated the Congress in the 1962 election, for Abdul Khaliq had the support of most Muslim voters, while the BSP was able to bring behind him the votes of most of the Scheduled Castes. He himself articulated his decision to join the BSP in those terms. When asked why he joined the BSP at that time, he said that he felt that "Scheduled Castes and Muslim votes will win the seat."

By 1996, however, he thought better of it, "joined Mulayam Singh Yadav," contested the seat on the SP ticket, and defeated Navman by a margin of more than 35,000 votes. Asked what the main issue in this campaign was, Abdul Khaliq replied that the "main issue was that Aligarh must be withdrawn from BJP." He described Navman as "a very communal person," which he noted that everyone knew "very well." He also attributed his victory in part to the alleged fact that "Navman did not do any work in the city."

In the 1996 election, the BSP again put up a Muslim candidate, pursuing the same strategy as in 1993. Their candidate this time was Kaisar Hayat, professor of law at the AMU. However, the BSP vote dropped by nearly 36,000 votes from the previous election. In 1993, the SP left this seat to the Janata Dal. Muslims preferred the BSP to the Janata Dal. Although the Janata Dal candidate lost his deposit, he won enough Muslim votes to deprive the BSP of its victory. In 1996, Kaisar Hayat won even more votes than the Janata Dal candidate in 1993, more than 20,000 votes, enough to retain his security deposit, but not enough to prevent the victory of Abdul Khaliq and the SP.

When I asked Abdul Khaliq if the Muslim vote had not been split in 1996, he said that it had not, that Kaisar Hayat received Muslim votes only from his own *baradari*, that is, the Qureshi community. Otherwise, Kaisar Hayat's votes came primarily from the Jatavs, who voted not for him as a person, but

TABLE 12.1. Election results for Aligarh City Legislative
Assembly constituency, 1996

| Turnout No./%[a] | Candidates | Caste/ Community | Party | Votes Polled | Percent of Total Valid Votes |
|---|---|---|---|---|---|
| 163,407/ 52.65 | Abdul Khaliq | Muslim (Saifi) | SP | 86,570 | 53.10 |
| | Krishna Kumar Navman | Varshney | BJP | 51,427 | 31.54 |
| | Kaisar Hayat | Muslim (Qureshi) | BSP | 20,294 | 12.45 |
| | Others (11) | | | 4,756 | 2.91 |

[a]Valid votes turnout. Total vote turnout was 53.24 percent.

SOURCE: India, Election Commission, *Statistical Report on General Elections, 1996, to the Legislative Assembly of Uttar Pradesh* (New Delhi: Election Commission of India, 1997), p. 561.

for the BSP as a party. He acknowledged that he had received a majority of the votes of the Qureshis and the Jatavs, but claimed he had votes from all castes and communities. As for the victory of Abdul Khaliq, Kaisar Hayat cited two factors in particular. First, he pointed to the fact that the Muslim vote had increased. Previously, the Muslim vote in the constituency had been between 46 and 48 percent, but now Muslims were in a majority. Second, as Abdul Khaliq himself had noted, "Hindus were not happy with the person who was elected thrice from the constituency, Navman."[3] Thus, in effect, Kaisar Hayat acknowledged that Abdul Khaliq won because he had garnered the votes of most Muslims in a Muslim-majority constituency while Navman had lost his previously strong support among Hindus.

Mr. Navman gave several reasons for his defeat, virtually all related to the faults of others. The most substantial reason he gave, however, was that the voters' list had been manipulated in such a way that some 20–25,000 people, Muslims from the Jamalpur and Hamdardnagar areas of the city, which are actually part of another constituency, voted in Aligarh instead, thus greatly increasing the Muslim vote against him. (Let us recall here again that these two localities were targeted for violent attacks for the first time during the 1990–91 riots.) Finally, he said that, in a constituency where "the voting pattern is based on religion," the Hindus had gotten too "confident about their victory" and had not come out to vote in large enough numbers while the

"Muslims got united on this basis that we have not been able to elect anybody since a long time, so let us unite." He went so far as to claim that even the "BSP candidate could not get Muslim votes," contrary to the statements of both Abdul Khaliq and Kaisar Hayat. Rather, Navman claimed that Kaisar Hayat got only the votes "from the BSP community," that is, the Scheduled Castes. He did not even get the votes of his own Qureshi community. The Muslims as a whole, he insisted, had decided not to divide their votes in order to ensure the victory of a Muslim candidate.

When I remarked to Mr. Navman that I had heard that the upper-caste Hindus did not vote for him this time, he acknowledged that this was true. However, he did not attribute it to his own failings, but to their "laziness."[4] They had become too confident of their victory, that is, of his victory as the representative of the Hindu community, and did not turn out to vote. "Otherwise," he said, "if they would have gone [to vote], then they had no option except to cast [their votes] for him."[5] In other words, if the Hindus wanted to defeat the Muslim candidates and retain the seat for the Hindu community, they would have had to vote for him.

In fact, there was indeed dissatisfaction with Navman among Hindu voters, as well as oppositon to his candidacy from within the BJP and the RSS. An older RSS worker had hoped to get the BJP ticket for this election, which had been awarded to him by the nominating committee in Lucknow, but then his name was dropped and that of Navman restored in the final selection by the party leadership in New Delhi on the grounds that he had won the seat in 1993 and should therefore be allowed to contest again in 1996.[6] The disappointed RSS leader attributed Navman's defeat to three factors. First, the Hindu community was dissatisfied with him, "with his character," including the BJP workers, who did not support him this time. So the Hindus did not turn out to vote in sufficient numbers. At the same time, the second reason was that the "Muslims were united." Third was the increased number of Muslims in the constituency. In short, the election contest was polarized between Hindus and Muslims, but allegedly because of Navman's bad character and his failures as a representative of the people, and because of the increased number of Muslim voters, the BJP could not retain this seat. Despite the latter factor, however, it is evident from many of the comments by the candidates themselves, including, especially, Navman's remarks about the "laziness" of the Hindu voters in this election and other evidences of dissatisfaction from within the ranks of the BJP and the RSS, that the intensity of interparty competition was thereby affected. Such "laziness" and disunity within the militant Hindu ranks does not occur when Hindus are being mobilized in the aftermath of riots.

The decline of communal violence since 1993 in Aligarh has been followed as well by a decline in the intensity of interparty competition by the interval measure used in Figure 8.4. The interval between the winning SP candidate's vote share in the 1996 election and the runner-up, Navman, was 21.60 percent, the fifth largest in the 20 elections for which I have interval data.[7]

It is evident in Aligarh, as elsewhere in the state, that the BJP has failed to attain the dominant position for which it has striven. It is also clear that, in the absence of powerful mobilizing issues that unite the upper-caste Hindu population and a major portion of the backward-caste population as well against the Muslims, the BJP cannot achieve a dominant position either in Aligarh or in the state as a whole, for that matter. Moreover, the demographic shift in the population of the Aligarh legislative constituency makes it impossible for the BJP to win an election there unless there is a significant division between the SP and the BSP and deviation in the voting behavior of Muslims and the Scheduled Castes. That being the case, there is no longer any incentive or use to the BJP and its allied organizations in the RSS family to foment riots in the city. That is even more the case since, in the municipality, where Hindus are in a strong majority, the BJP is the dominant party. Thus, with no need to make use of riots to retain its hold in municipal politics and no use in its doing so any longer in the city, it is likely that communal riots will not erupt on the scale and with the frequency as in the past. That does not mean, however, that communal tension and violence will disappear from Aligarh City, for it is endemic in certain parts of the town, as I have shown in previous chapters, and because it remains in the interest of the BJP, in order to retain its hold over the Hindu population, to maintain the institutionalized riot system that the RSS family of organizations has built.

We have here, therefore, discovered one of the principal precipitants of large-scale riots, namely, the political manipulation of local conflicts and their transformation into Hindu-Muslim confrontations whose function is to solidify communal identities, communalize the electorate, and polarize the electoral contest in order to achieve victory no matter the cost in human lives. Absent a political advantage for such political manipulation, the risk of large-scale riots is reduced. Other factors independent of party politics remain active, however, and other interests and sentiments continue to keep alive the potential for communal violence. Moreover, the history of Aligarh, of U.P., and of much of the rest of the country as well does not inspire confidence that there will be no occasion in future for the resuscitation of movements of mass mobilization, designed to mobilize Hindus, intimidate Muslims, and move India further in the direction of a militant Hindu national state.

# PART V

# The Process
# of Blame Displacement

A scathing denunciation of the recent happenings in Bombay and the conduct of those who had remained passive witnesses of the same constituted the core of Gandhiji's address after the evening prayer gathering at Rungta House today.

The news of these events, said Gandhiji, had filled him with shame and humiliation and he hoped that they too must have felt likewise. He hoped that none of those who attended the prayer had taken part in these disgraceful happenings. But that alone would not entitle them to congratulation. They had reached a stage when no one could afford to sit on the fence or take refuge in the ambiguous middle.

One had to speak out and stand up. Inaction at a time of conflagration was inexcusable. That might appear to them to be a difficult ideal to follow but that was the only course that would take them through the present difficult times.

It had become the fashion these days, continued Gandhiji, to ascribe all such ugly manifestations to the activities of hooligans. He deprecated the habit of taking refuge in that kind of moral alibi. Who were the hooligans after all? They were their own countrymen and so long as any countryman of theirs indulged in such acts they could not disown responsibility for it consistently with their claim of being one people and one nation. It mattered little whether those who were responsible for the happenings were denounced as goondas or praised as patriots. Praise and blame equally belonged to them. The only manly and becoming course for those who were aspiring to be free was to accept either.—*Free Press Journal,* March 12, 1946, reporting on Gandhi's reaction to the Bombay riots that accompanied the Royal Indian Navy employees strike.

# 13 / Riot Interpretation, Blame Displacement, and the Communal Discourse

The preceding parts of this book have focused on the first two stages in riot production: preparation/rehearsal and enactment. It has been demonstrated that preparation and rehearsal for the enactment of large-scale riots are ongoing activities in which known persons and groups are actively engaged and in which there is a specialized division of labor embedded within an institutionalized riot system. All the principal explanations for the outbreak of riots have been examined. It is not claimed here that there is a single causal explanation that will encompass the enactment of all communal riots. On the contrary, it has been shown that there are a multiplicity of factors that may precipitate riots and that there are a variety of factors and forces that come into play when the opportunity for producing a riot occurs. However, it is claimed that large-scale Hindu-Muslim riots are primarily political productions in which the precipitating incidents are pretexts and the enactment is in large part organized. Further, it has been shown that the intensity and scale of riot production in Aligarh has increased dramatically during the past half century, exceeding anything that occurred in the years before and during the partition of the subcontinent.

The fact that there remains a considerable diversity of motives and factors for participation in and production of communal riots leaves ample room for contestation in the third phase of riot production, that of post hoc explanation. In this part, therefore, we move once again from the "fact finding" realm of hard data to the nebulous realm of interpretation "after the fact." Once again, therefore, we review all the factors said to precipitate and produce riots by those who produce, participate, suppress, control, and seek to explain them. However, my approach to these "explanations" will be not quantitative nor merely analytical, but critical in two senses. Having established a factual basis for understanding the dynamics of riot production, including the roles played in them by specific persons and organizations, we are in a position to distinguish fact from fancy, justification from explanation, hypocrisy from truthfulness, and pathological fantasy from plausible reality. Second, we are in a position, now, also to appreciate the signal importance in a riot's production of the struggle for control of its meaning and interpretation in the aftermath. Like any dramatic production, the grisly play of communal rioting depends upon the ability of its perpetrators, abettors, and observers to provide an interpretation that justifies repeat performances. But there is a difference between the role of the critics upon whose judgment the success or failure of theatrical productions depends and the role of the interpreters of riots. In the former case, the play stands or falls on a favorable balance of praise over blame. In the case of riot production, the balance that ensures repeat performance is reversed: wide dispersal of blame masks responsibility and diverts the public gaze from the mechanisms that produce riots.

## TYPES OF EXPLANATIONS OF RIOT PRODUCTION

In my research extending over thirty-eight years in Aligarh, I have come across five or six distinct types of explanations for communal riots in response to my own questions concerning how and why such events in general as well as particular riots have occurred. Some of these explanations can be fit into broader discursive formations in the sense that they reflect fundamental understandings of human nature or of political society or of the relations between peoples as much as they do particular understandings of the events discussed. There is, for example, a discourse of profit that operates in Indian society, as elsewhere, that accounts for most human events in terms of the economic or otherwise self-interested calculations of individual actors. It is present in Aligarh as well, where several general and particular explanations of riots fit into this kind of context. I have summarized and analyzed those types of explanations in Chapter 7.

One primary function of such economic explanations is to displace blame from the authorities, politicians and political parties, the police, the general public, and the poor and disadvantaged onto the privileged and dominant classes. Sometimes, however, riots are seen to arise out of "understandable" grievances of particular classes or groups against others. Thus, the most com-

mon explanation I heard in 1961–62 for the October 1961 riots was the grievances of the faculty and students of the local degree colleges against the priv-
ileges and status of their counterparts at AMU. There is a third function served
by economic explanations as well, namely, to displace blame onto the basic
greed of human beings who are considered capable of any kind of evil action
for the sake of profit. Thus, the bizarre explanation of the rumors concerning the killings at the AMU Medical College Hospital that fed the riots of
December 1990–January 1991, that they were spread by private medical clinics to discredit the AMU Hospital and take business away from it that would
then come to them.

   In this and the following chapter, I will first consider the opportunities
provided by riots for blame displacement, then discuss several other types of
explanations—of which the most important are those that fit within the discourse of Hindu-Muslim communalism—that recur in my interviews and
which have not been analyzed fully above. Let us consider, first, the opportunities that riots provide for blame displacement, brought out very clearly
in an interview cited earlier concerning the 1978 riots, in which our respondent enumerated a multiplicity of interpretations that were given at that time
to explain the occurrence of the riots. Although he was actively involved in
monitoring the riot and in the relief activities afterwards, this respondent did
not make clear precisely which of the various interpretations he personally
considered most accurate. Moreover, although he is a Muslim, he did not
automatically accept the argument that it was the Jan Sangh and the RSS that
were mostly responsible for the riots. On the contrary, despite the fact that
he was an admirer of Indira Gandhi in several respects, he argued based on
the consequences, that the Congress (I) deserved the greater blame, reasoning as follows.

PRB: But, you know, to go back to the '78 [riots], you said there were three interpre-
    tations. One is that it just happened because of this, by accident, by—because of
    this Bhure Lal business.
JH: But, some person[s] was saying like that.
PRB: And another interpretation is the—Navman and his people. And the third is
    economic.
JH: Yes.
PRB: What is your own view?
JH: I could not say, but after the riots, who were the beneficiary? The Congress (I).
    My opinion is that.[1]

But how did the Congress benefit from these riots? It is clear that both the Congress at the local and national levels and Mrs. Gandhi personally did benefit from them, judging by the ways in which they used both the 1978 riots in Aligarh and several other riots and police-public confrontations to discredit the Janata government that came to power after the 1977 elections. The factions within the Janata Party at that time also indirectly helped Mrs. Gandhi, by making an issue of the presence of RSS members from the former Jan Sangh in the Janata government, and by themselves attributing blame for the riots to the local Jan Sangh/RSS cadre in Aligarh, particularly Mr. Navman. The demand was made for the suspension of Navman from membership in the party, which was done a month after the riots. In the meantime, however, Mrs. Gandhi integrated the Aligarh riots into her portfolio of charges against the government to the effect that Muslims and other disadvantaged groups in Indian society were being slaughtered under Janata rule—thereby emerging as their "protector" and making possible the return to the Congress in the 1980 elections of large numbers of Muslim voters who had deserted that party and Mrs. Gandhi in 1977. The 1978 riots were, therefore, taken out of their local context and merged into a national context, while a predominant section of the Janata government and the Congress organization as a whole accepted the explanation of the riots that most suited their political purposes.[2]

By so placing the riots of 1978 in a broad national context, blame is assigned, a particular explanation is accepted, and a particular party and leadership benefit from that resolution. One explanation is distilled from among all the various factors that contribute to a riot, the one that is most useful politically to the temporarily ascendant political party and political leader. All the other contributing factors can then be ignored. But the partial explanation does not satisfy, as my inconclusive interview on this point demonstrated when I pressed this respondent further to elaborate his implication that the Congress bore responsibility for the events in Aligarh in 1978.

PRB: But when you say, uh, Congress (I) benefited, implying that they must have had something to do with it . . .

JH: I'm not blaming, but I'm saying this, who was the beneficiary?

PRB: But you know, some people do say that, uh, there are Muslim Congress politicians in Aligarh who are as mischievous as Navman. I'm not sure it's true, you know, they mention nowadays Khwaja Halim.

JH: I don't, I cannot name any congressman of Hindus or Muslims, but I—who was beneficiary?

PRB: Yah, well that's a—that's—sometimes you can find the cause from the effect. From the consequences, yah.

JH: This much I can say.

But it is not clear that, as I suggested in the interview, one can find the cause from the effect. What is clear is that what is left from the process of distillation of factors into a satisfying and useful explanation is that all the factors, including the one identified as central, continue to operate. Those that are neglected continue to operate because they have not been brought more clearly into focus, whereas the political explanation that has come to the forefront is treated as just that—a political explanation that requires a political response. "No," say the RSS, the Jan Sangh, and later the BJP. "It is a lie that we are responsible for these riots. It is the Congress that is responsible. Moreover, whenever we have been in power, there have been no riots."

So the process of blame displacement continues without end, at the local and national levels. This respondent illustrated how the process worked in Aligarh in the immediate aftermath of the riots, at a meeting on the AMU campus called by the district magistrate, at which, the respondent claimed, university leaders and Hindu leaders from the town, including the president and professors of Barahseni College, were present. Asked to speak, he focused particularly on this very issue of blame displacement and the consequences as he saw them.

> Everybody's alleging everybody, another person [is at fault]. Either the allegations are correct—if the allegations are correct, therefore, every sinner is in this meeting—or the allegations are baseless. If it is so, then it is immoral for us that, at the time of crisis, we are blaming each other. . . . But really the dead bodies are there, wounded persons are there, and we can apply our humanity to solve this. My speech worked and really the atmosphere cooled down.

But then the solution adopted to cope with the dead bodies, this respondent himself acknowledged, is itself inhuman, as he later revealed.

JH: There are some things which . . . are the universal values and, uh, these are the human values. Now they are [assessing] the misery, now they count that Hindus, twenty, Muslims, thirty [have been killed]. It is such [an] inhuman act, really, even the dead bodies.

PRB: I know, this business of counting.

JH: Now, you see the misery of the conditions, whether Hindu widow or Muslim

widow.... Really, I—this Aligarh communal riot has changed my whole...
[ ... ] When I saw the misery of the people, the feeling of the people, the tragedy.
[ ... ] I cannot ignore that woman ..., I was ... when I was—because it is hor-
rifying memory for me that we were in town hall ... the district officials were
there and the university authorities were there, we were providing 20,000 rupees,
check of 10,000 rupees, check to the widows and the persons who have ... died. ...
I cannot say to you that—what was my emotional condition and everybody's
emotional condition, that one Hindu widow came with [her] ... father-in-law,
a young lady came, now the tears in the eyes of Hindu father-in-law and the
Hindu widow, that was a Hindu face. After that, we called a Muslim lady, she
came with ... her father. She was also young. I could not remember exactly, but
both are having one child ... with them, ... on their laps. Now what I suggest
is the same misery, same agony and pain in the eyes of—and we provided checks
[to] both of them. The feeling was the same and no power on earth can translate
a cry of human being in a misery. You cannot translate it.

In place of the impossibility of translation, the failure of language, the political process provides financial compensation and contextualization. The first
itself requires no act of speech. Although I have never witnessed these financial transactions, I have two comments to make about them. One is that it is
obvious that any act of speech—beyond those required for bureaucratic
accounting purposes—to a bereaved person from a government official hand-
ing over a check, who does not know the recipients in anything but his official
capacity, would be superfluous and meaningless. Another is that the whole
process of counting the bodies, identifying them by religion, assigning rightful payments to the bereaved, and paying them, is clearly dehumanizing.

For many years, at the end of each major communal riot, local officials
determined a count of the dead by methods that are not clear to me, and the
accuracy of whose results are always contested. The requisite compensation
payments to the bereaved were then made. Such counts were then cumulated
nationwide and ultimately published in a report or reports by the government of India, usually in tables of statistics as well, in which were noted that
in such and such a riot and in all cumulated riots for the period under review
so many Hindus were killed and so many Muslims. This kind of compensation and cumulation of data is dehumanizing not because it is in itself improper
but because of what is not and cannot be said and what is not done. The cry
of the bereaved cannot be recorded and published in a government document, but surely the government could publish the name, the occupation,
and a brief biography of *every single person killed in a riot*.[3] The government

could also report the circumstances of each killing and the measures taken to discover and prosecute the killers. By individualization of the statistics, people would at least come to know or be able to make some judgment concerning whether those persons killed were themselves rioters, or innocent people minding their own business, who suffered from the acts of violent mobs directed against them for reasons known or unknown. But the government, of course, cannot publish the circumstances of each killing and the measures taken against the killers because, in the majority of cases, the killers are the police, the agents of government, and in the overwhelming majority of cases absolutely nothing is done to apprehend and prosecute them. It is most probably for these reasons that the government of India has not published such statistics for the past eighteen years.

There is yet a further act of dehumanization that takes place in the aftermath of riots when the time for compensation to the bereaved arrives. This is the charge that many of the bereaved are bogus claimants. Their sons and husbands, officials say, have absconded so that the parents and wives can claim the compensation for themselves. It is more than likely true that such things happen in the aftermath of riots. But, once again, the blame is laid upon the people, not on governments under whose rule such events occur and whose leaders monetize the loss of life that occurs in them.

So, for the untranslatable cry of the bereaved, we have monetary compensation, but also contextualization, the removal of the cries of the bereaved from the reality of the tragedy of human lives lost, and of the sufferings of the bereaved to the political realm of explanation, where not only language, but rhetoric and symbols, fly and flourish. The factors that caused the riots are enumerated and assessed, charges are made against individuals and groups, some administrators are transferred, one or two policemen who misbehaved are temporarily sent to the lines, while all sides ready themselves for the next events.

## THE COMMUNAL DISCOURSE

By far the most common context into which explanations for riots are placed by local and extra-local observers is the communal discourse, which in turn has several variations. The most extreme form I encountered in my visits to Aligarh over the years came from persons in the rump Jan Sangh as well as the BJP, all of whom also have RSS backgrounds. Several of these respondents characterized riots as a form of Muslim jihad. Such explanations included generalizations about the nature of Islam and the so-called Semitic religions in general, in comparison with Hinduism, as well as specific statements concerning the organization of riots by Muslims in the local context of Aligarh and other places in India.

I will summarize here one example of the militant Hindu explanation, which may be described as a kind of essentialism applied to Muslims and Islam.

> Muslims are aggressive when they are dominant. Aggressiveness is built into Semitic religions, in contrast to Vedic, which believe in coexistence. Communal riots came to India only with the Muslims. Jews are small in number and Christians have become civilized, but the Muslims remain backward and barbarous. Moreover, their aggressiveness is built into their beliefs, into the Koran itself. Contrast this with the passivity of Hindus who, despite provocations such as the construction of mosques at or near Hindu places of worship in Mathura, Ayodhya, and Varanasi—still the Hindus do not cause communal riots even though the RSS is equally dominant in these three places. Muslims are so aggressive that they will even try to kill innocent Hindus who go into their *mohallas* for innocent purposes, such as a person who went to read an electricity meter or government house inspectors. Hindus need to learn from Muslims, especially concerning how they treat their minorities in Islamic countries, where minorities must live according to the wishes of the Islamic state.[4]

A second example of this type of explanation comes from a respondent who applied it to the specific context of Aligarh. This man remarked that, though Aligarh was not dominated by Muslims, it contained a substantial percentage, which he put accurately at 37 percent. The real root of the communal riots in Aligarh, he averred, was the Aligarh Muslim University. Riots, he said, were organized there and innocent Muslims of the town were brought into the fray afterwards. They are organized every five or ten years. Hindus lose property in these riots.

I asked this respondent specifically about the 1978 riot. He responded that it was planned and perpetrated by Muslims. Further, he remarked that the district administration—despite the fact that the Janata party, with its former Jan Sangh elements, was in power in the state—had supported the Muslims by lodging false reports against Hindus and falsely arresting them. He referred specifically to Mr. Krishna Kumar Navman.

More generally, he blamed Mrs. Indira Gandhi—who had been prime minister of the country throughout most of the years between 1966 and 1984—for communal riots on the grounds that her policies of "appeasement" towards the Muslims had emboldened them.

This respondent then went on to make stark essentialist comparisons between Hindus and Muslims, summarized below.

> Hindus, in contrast to Muslims, are meek and peace-loving, respect all religions, creeds, castes. Hindus retaliate only in extremity. However, Hindus never agitate, commit murder, loot, or arson. Riots are invariably started by Muslims. Nowadays, [riots] are started to preserve the minority character of AMU. Soon, they [Muslims] will demand the division of India. Before Independence, [riots] were started in order to get Pakistan. Already, there is a demand for reservation of places in government service for Muslims despite the fact that Muslims have all facilities.[5]

A third example of the articulation of the communal discourse in explaining Hindu-Muslim riots in Aligarh comes from the BJP's former three-term MLA, responding to questions concerning the causation of Hindu-Muslim riots in Aligarh. When I asked who killed whom in these riots, his reply did not support the view that mostly Muslims are killed. He said, "The first few killed are Hindus; after that, it's equal." When I asked if the wretched conditions in the *mohallas* in which riots occurred had anything to do with Hindu-Muslim riots, he replied that the "surroundings have nothing to do with it. It is a question of mentality." As for the police, considered by many people to be partial to Hindus and hostile to Muslims during riots, especially in western U.P., he responded to my question concerning their role that they were "mostly impartial," though he averred that "sometimes they overreact and people are forced to make complaints." It is clear from the context of this statement that this man meant that sometimes the police overreact and harm innocent Hindus. I believe also that he had himself in mind as someone against whom the police sometimes "overreacted."

This man's solution to the problem of Hindu-Muslim riots is also consistent with his explanation of their origins: "Muslims must change their mentality." He said that he had done his best "to claim them as brothers, but their interest [in such conciliation] is only superficial." He claims that he "even fought alongside Muslims in 1973 when the administration wanted to forbid the *tanzim* procession" during the annual Muharram holiday. Further, he noted that he had been chairman of a Save Urdu Committee in 1971.

Thus, it is clear in this man's mind that not only do Muslims instigate riots, but no sincere effort on the part of a well-intentioned person such as himself to cooperate with Muslims even in *their* struggle, and to work with them to maintain communal peace and provide relief to riot victims, is worthwhile. Muslims, at least those who are educated and literate, are virtually incorrigible because of their religious teachings and cannot be trusted or worked with for any good purpose.

This man's description of the behavior of Muslims, from their religious leaders down to ordinary believers, smacks of nothing so much as the blood libel charges against Jews in European history. The following paraphrased excerpt from my 1983 interview with him brings this out clearly.

PRB: What do you think are the causes of [the] 1978 [riots]?

RESPONDENT: The Koran. . . .

PRB: But Muslims read the Koran every day, and there isn't a riot every day. Why are there riots on certain days?

RESPONDENT: They can't kill every day. Situations are created where they can kill.

PRB: What are the situations?

RESPONDENT: One case—on 13 September 1978, at a wrestling contest, an altercation between Hindus and Muslims turned into a free-for-all. Then on 15 September a Hindu was murdered. On 17 September was Gyanchand's attempted murder, and then on 3 October Bhura Pahalwan was murdered. On 5 October, again two Hindus were murdered. After this the Hindus had to retaliate. They have tried to implicate me on communal charges, but my composing foreman, binding foreman and sales manager are all Muslim.

PRB: But they read the Koran. How do you know they won't try to kill you?

RESPONDENT: Ninety percent of Muslims don't know what's in the Koran.

PRB: So those doing the killing are actually the literate and educated, not the *goondas*?

RESPONDENT: These people give protection and financial help to *goondas*. On each level, town, district, up to central level, they have muftis who have the right to declare jihad on non-Muslims, and it is compulsory for Muslims to kill. If they don't they are also considered *kafir*.

PRB: So the muftis are responsible, they tell Muslims to kill Hindus?

RESPONDENT: They instigate people and consolidate support to attack non-Muslims.[6]

In this bizarre exchange, we confront the logic of the mad. For every question designed to suggest the idiocy of the reasoning, the respondent has a clear, quick, and logical answer. Moreover, the answers are irrefutable. They cannot be falsified for there is no evidence that can be provided to shake such fixed beliefs. We know that there is no such organization of Muslims, that not all Muslims are primed to kill non-Muslims by their holy book and the teachings and directions of their clerics, but how can we prove it? We doubt that Hindus only retaliate, never instigate. We doubt it especially in the case of the respondent himself.

But this BJP leader is not mad, nor are his views uncommon. They are views contained within a discourse, a pathological discourse of nationalism, fear, and resentment in which many Hindus in northern India are implicated and to which Muslims must also react.

This BJP leader is a central figure in the maintenance and perpetuation of Hindu-Muslim tensions and animosities in the town of Aligarh. His name— and in recent years that of his son as well—inevitably appears in the news during every riot in Aligarh. His name is kept on a list of communal trouble-makers in the town that is passed on to every new district magistrate and SSP posted to Aligarh. There are many others in the town, however, who make their own distinct contributions. Virtually all are members of the RSS and/or the BJP.

In Aligarh in 1983, there was a division among the militant Hindu nationalists, with some still maintaining allegiance to the original Jan Sangh. The first interview cited above in this section was with a gentleman who belonged to the Jan Sangh. I asked another man, then vice-president of the Aligarh City BJP and an RSS man, what the differences were between the BJP and the rump Jan Sangh, whose national leader was Balraj Madhok. He replied as follows:

> They come together on the same platform if there is a communal riot, but otherwise they are on a different platform. The BJP believes Muslims have got a right to stay in the country, to progress in the country, but they [Jan Sangh] believe that India should be a Hindu *rashtriya* [nation]. The BJP believes India should be a democratic country in which all cultures should progress, but not at the cost of other cultures. [According to the RSS ideology,] all Muslims in India are born from the Hindu womb. If they come to us, we will embrace them. They do not come from another country, they are Indian, they are Hindus, born from Hindu mothers and Hindu fathers. However, on a cultural level, we should have the same culture, just as Catholics and Protestants in Britain have the same culture, even Indians who migrate to Britain, so why shouldn't Muslims believe in Indian culture? They should believe in Indian culture, not Arab culture.[7]

This statement is fully consistent with the RSS ideology of Hindutva. It is one that, with only minor variations, can be cited by every RSS man. It carefully distinguishes the Hindutva ideology—which is proclaimed to be the only true "secular" ideology in India—from its perversion in the form of a racist ideology that would exclude Muslims rather than include them in the modern Indian nation-state as equal citizens—provided, of course, they accept the RSS definition of the Indian nation, which includes religious and mythological as well as historical figures. The fact that there are hardly any Muslims respected in their own community who are willing to accept these conditions for integration into the Hindu Indian nation matters not to the militant Hindu nationalists. Nor can it provide much comfort to Muslims to know that, whatever the ideological differences between them, the more extreme or racist and the more moderate or militant nationalist groups come together when there are communal riots.

Moreover, this ideology that accepts Muslims as part of the Indian nation is also consistent with an outlook that denigrates and disparages Islam and discredits and seeks to dismantle Muslim institutions. This outlook is reflected in statements by both this respondent and others concerning the role of the Aligarh Muslim University (AMU) in India as a whole as well as in Aligarh, where it is seen as involved in aiding and abetting communalism and communal riots. Indeed, the AMU, the leading educational institution of the Muslim in India, and its academic heads have been demonized not only as being responsible for communalism and communal riots, but for admitting thugs to the university to be used against Hindus in such riots. No fable concerning the AMU is too far-fetched for militant Hindus in Aligarh to believe, including one that the dead bodies of poor Hindu milkmen were buried inside the university's student accommodations during the 1980–81 riots.[8] Over and over again, we hear the "big lie" repeated that, insofar as Hindus are involved in such riots at all, it is only either as victims or while engaged in retaliation against Muslims for their instigation of riots and their attacks on Hindus.

This respondent also assigned blame for Hindu-Muslim tensions and violence to the political parties that appeal to voters as members of religious communities, that is, as Hindus, Muslims, and Sikhs, and to the government of India.

> The government itself is interested in creating or keeping communal tension in these cities; they know who are the people responsible for the mess here, both Hindus and Muslims; the Intelligence people know, but they don't take any action against them; they may occasionally arrest someone for a month or two, but then they are released; only on the local level can a good administrator encounter the leaders of the *goondas* in the university.

There are three features of this part of the interview that deserve note. The first is that the government itself wants to keep communal tensions alive for its own purposes, which are similar to those of the political parties, particularly—in this respondent's view—the then-ruling Congress. While this assignment of blame fits in with one of the general arguments of this book, that riots are functionally useful for both political parties and the Indian state, it partly goes beyond and partly says less than the functional utility argument. To say that communal tensions leading to riots are useful for governments is something different from saying that they create such tensions and riots. In the latter case, when such tensions do lead to riots, insofar as the government is implicated in them, then the term *pogrom* becomes more appropriate than *riots* to describe the carnage that follows. It is part of the argument of this book that, in fact, several of the riots of the 1980s and 1990s have been closer to pogroms or massacres of minorities than to riots, but it is not always the case.

This respondent's remarks also say somewhat less than the argument of this book in confining blame to the then-ruling Congress, by implication leaving the RSS and the BJP free of blame when, in fact, it is evident that most, if not all, political parties in India make use of riots in political contestation and that the fomenting of Hindu-Muslim riots in particular has been part of the routine of party competition in northern India for decades. The third feature to note is the respondent's reliance on the local administration and on encounter as the only way of eliminating communal tensions that lead to rioting at the local level. The term *encounter,* in the Indian context, means a deliberately staged, extrajudicial confrontation between the police and alleged criminals, terrorists, or riot-mongers in which the police have the advantage and use it to execute the latter.

For this man, then, the solution to the problem of communal rioting in cities and towns such as Aligarh was a purely administrative one, involving extrajudicial execution. The local administration, he said, should be supported "blindly." In this case, he was referring especially to what he described as "a good experience in this respect with the previous SSP, B. P. Singh," whose measures to prevent communal rioting in Aligarh were mentioned earlier (Chapter 3). This SSP is alleged—and I have heard the story from other independent commentators—to have resolved the communal prob lem in Aligarh for nearly a decade by rounding up more than 40 presumed criminals and riot-mongers, taking them outside the city limits, and executing them.

This respondent generalized this "good experience" into a paradigm for dealing with the danger of communalism and preventing communal riots.

Our party supported the SSP on one condition: if a Hindu kills a Muslim, you kill the Hindu immediately, if a Muslim kills a Hindu, you kill the Muslim immediately. Otherwise, if twenty-four hours pass, there will be a communal riot. We do not want to go to court; there should be immediate encounter. And Mr. B. P. Singh did that. In fact, however, there were no Hindu *goonda*s, because a Hindu never takes the lead, he only retaliates. Hindus never have started any communal riot anywhere in India. It is always the Muslims and only the *goonda* Muslims who are either starving for bread and butter or are creating trouble under the protection of people like Rahman Ali Khan [then a member of the law faculty of AMU]. So, in one year, the Muslim *goonda*s were killed by the administration and now we are living in a peaceful city. Before, this was a city of animals, but now everybody is peaceful. We go to Muslim areas, people know I am an RSS man, but no Muslim says anything to us because there are no *goonda*s there now. All the *goonda*s were taken by the government from Muslim areas, and they were encountered. There were no Hindu *goonda*s, and, if there were one or two Hindu *goonda*s, they were also encountered.

The communal situation would also be helped if the senior professors at AMU, who believe India is not their country and who communicate this in the classroom, who are *goonda*-mongers, who organize *goonda*s for communal riots in Aligarh or get *goonda*s from other cities for killing Hindus, if these people are stopped by the administration, the administration can encounter the *goonda*s very well. These *goonda*-mongers should be exposed, sent to jail, treated as spies by whatever method is appropriate for dealing with outsider spies, then there would be no communal riot in Aligarh. Of course, any Hindu leader who talks in a communal way also should be dealt with in the same way. These *goonda*s are fanatics and they are paid heavily by these supercommunal leaders and they are also told that they will get *shabaah* in the coming life if they kill these Hindu *kafirs*. And the mullahs, pandits and mullahs, who talk in communal terms—if you go to any mosque on Friday, you will hear communal talk only by the mullahs—they should be taught not to talk in communal terms.

Once again, it is necessary to point out that, though this respondent's remarks may sound extreme and far-fetched, they are neither unusual in relation to police work in India nor inconsistent with RSS ideology. False encounters have been a regular practice in Indian "police work" for three decades in many parts of the country and were used systematically for years in suppressing the Punjab insurrection. So there is nothing distinctive in the fact that an RSS man should favor such an approach in dealing with communal riots. At the same time, this respondent's remarks are unrefined. They would not be articulated to a foreign observer or in public at all by the senior leaders of the RSS or the BJP or any other party. It cannot be said, therefore, that this strategy of false encounters is part of the RSS ideology. What is consistent with that ideology, however—and brought out starkly in this fascistic account of how to deal with dangers to the peace of the state—is the thin veneer of evenhandedness that it projects. In this unsophisticated account—though it should be kept in mind that the respondent was a highly educated person and a lecturer in a social science department of the AMU at the time—the veneer of evenhandedness slips evidently as his phrases come tumbling out on tape.

The killings of riot-mongers should be done irrespective of whether the persons killed are Hindu or Muslim—but, of course, it is only the Muslims who are riot-mongers. There were, of course, no Hindu *goondas*, but maybe there were "one or two," and, if so, "they were also encountered." As for the Muslims, the entire community is not condemned, only the "starving" ones and those who are thugs under the protection of a Muslim professor of law at the AMU. Now that these dangerous elements have been eliminated and the Muslims cowed, an RSS man can walk with impunity through the Muslim localities. But there remains still a dangerous source of communal tension in one of the India's two national universities, the AMU. All the riot instigators have to be treated in an extrajudicial manner, if necessary, as foreign spies. Once again, of course, the same treatment should be meted out to "any Hindu leader" of a similar type, among whom in this case our respondent mentions the leaders of the rump Jan Sangh. In singling out these few extreme Hindu communal leaders, this respondent affirms his sincerity and his adherence to a policy of evenhandedness. But the veneer is too thin, as is the line which separates the former Jan Sanghis from the reasonable men of the RSS and the BJP.

One of the lines that has always separated the RSS and the BJP from the most extreme adherents of the militant Hindu nationalist ideology of the Hindu nation-state is their alleged openness to admitting Muslims into their ranks. There have often, in fact, been one or two Muslim members of the party at the national level and at the state and local levels, though I have yet to meet in 38 years of field research in India a Muslim RSS man. In Aligarh in 1983, there was one Muslim BJP member, also a member of the faculty of a social science department at the AMU and a former BJP member of the

U.P. Legislative Assembly. He described Aligarh as a sick society, in which the "Muslim mentality," as he put it, was as much at fault as the Hindu. In the Muslim mind, he remarked, "every Hindu is a Jan Sanghi," "the Jan Sanghi is the enemy of the Muslim," "therefore, every Hindu is the enemy of the Muslim." "In fact," he went on, "though RSS people, like anyone, may get involved in the riots on sentimental grounds, actually it is false that the RSS actually engineers the riots."

I pressed this respondent further on the charge that riots are instigated by organizations such as the RSS and the Jan Sangh or by other political parties. He responded with two rhetorical questions: "What purpose does it serve for them?" and "Are the RSS people so morally corrupt they would go for political gain at the cost of human lives?" He believed that riots served no useful purposes for the RSS and that they were not so morally corrupt.[9]

Most politically knowledgeable people in India, however, would give different answers to this man's two questions. To the first, most would respond by saying that Hindu-Muslim riots serve the purpose for the RSS and the BJP of consolidating Hindu sentiment behind the RSS and the BJP and providing votes to the latter in elections, since these two organizations are seen as the principal advocates of Hindu interests. A factual basis for this answer has been provided in the preceding part of this book. To the second question, concerning the moral character of the RSS, opinion would be divided, but most Hindus would certainly agree with the respondent. In fact, on the contrary, not only the RSS, but many of the most famous leaders of the Indian nationalist and Muslim separatist movements before Independence, as well as countless local leaders before and after Independence, have knowingly and willfully "sought political gain" by bringing tense situations involving Hindus and Muslims to the brink of violent conflict, knowing full well what the consequences were likely to be.

### A *"Sub-Discourse" of Conflict between Segments of Each Community*

In my interviews concerning the causes of Hindu-Muslim riots in Aligarh over the years, I heard frequently a specific explanation that displaced blame from the Hindu and Muslim communities as entities onto specific segments of each community. The groups named were the Hindu caste of Varshneys (Barahseni) and the Muslim caste of Qasais (also called Qureshis), whose traditional occupation, as noted earlier, is butchery, though most Qasais nowadays are not butchers at all. Having heard such comments for many years before engaging in a systematic study of communal riots in Aligarh, I specifically asked all my informants interviewed for this study to respond to this explanation even when they did not volunteer it themselves.

Let us begin first with the rather concise views of the SSP of Aligarh during my visit in 1983. Riots in Aligarh, the SSP said, were precipitated by "abnormal" Hindu white collar workers unreconciled to the idea and the fact of Pakistan's creation. They begin in riot-prone areas, of which he named two: Upar Kot and Manik Chauk. These two areas are riot-prone because the two communities are equal in number in them and there is a tendency for Varshneys and Qasais, who live side by side there, to quarrel.[10]

The SSP, a Hindu, displayed no communal prejudice in his laconic account. Indeed, he placed blame more on the pathological ideology of a particular class of Hindus. Otherwise, however, he distributes blame equally upon the two communities, but particularly the two segments of Varshneys and Qasais discussed above. Similar views were provided to me by a Yadav station officer at Sasni Gate.[11]

In contrast, those who spoke in the discourse of communalism rejected the idea that communal conflict in Aligarh was primarily a conflict between segments of the two communities rather than the whole. They adhere to an understanding of riots that starts from a general depiction of the essential character of Hindus and Muslims. Muslims are active, Hindus are passive. There cannot even be a generalized conflict between segments of the two communities, for Hindus do not engage in power struggles on communal lines. Since so many of the militant Hindu activists in Aligarh are from the Varshney community, my respondents were quick to defend the Varshneys, to refute the charge that the Varshneys are responsible for anything, least of all communalism, and to eliminate any differentiation within the Muslim community, which must be seen in the militant Hindu communalist mind as a unity.[12]

Mr. Navman also dismissed any alternative explanation of Hindu-Muslim riots in Aligarh, beyond the single cause that Muslims start riots to kill Hindus according to the injunctions of their holy book itself.[13] He insists that Hindu-Muslim riots are community-wide affairs instigated by Muslims and followed by Hindu acts of retaliation.

Muslims also tended to downplay the significance of the alleged conflicts between Varshneys and Qasais, as in one of my interviews with a politician from the Qureshi community, a member of the law faculty of the AMU. He denied that conflicts between Qureshis and Varshneys or the participation of Qureshis in communal riots in general were of any significance. While acknowledging that persons from among the Qureshi community were involved in riots and were frequently arrested by the police, he gave an explanation that absolved them from any responsibility for instigating or taking advantage of riots. He noted, rather, that it was a matter of chance, of the particular spatial distribution of the Qureshis. It just happens that Qureshis are living on the borders of *mohallas* with high Muslim population concentrations adjacent to Hindu localities. So, when riots start, persons from the adjacent, Hindu localities "come to the border, . . . play their part, and then run away." The Qureshis, being on the borders, therefore, get blamed for whatever happens at the borders of the Muslim localities. Further, when the police arrive on the scene, make raids, and "start arresting Muslims, Qureshis are arrested because they are living there, whether they are innocent or not innocent."[14] Thus do we find yet another kernel of truth in the mosaic of explanations that simultaneously implicate and free from blame categories of participants in Hindu-Muslim riots.

## THE ROLE OF THE ALIGARH MUSLIM UNIVERSITY

We have seen numerous references in the interviews cited above to the role of the AMU in riots in Aligarh. The range of views includes at one extreme those who argue that the presence of the AMU in Aligarh is a mere pretext for the organization of communal riots by Hindu chauvinists unreconciled to the creation of Pakistan, who also consider the Muslims of India a vast army of fifth columnists. At the other extreme are those who consider that the AMU has been very much involved in communal riots in Aligarh, not merely symbolically but in the provision of arms and shelter to criminals involved in riot activity.

### Criminals at the AMU

Although at the time I considered the charge far-fetched, I pursued this question of the direct involvement of the AMU in riots through support of criminal activity in many interviews conducted in 1983. I was, therefore, quite surprised to find that there was virtual unanimity among my respondents that the charges were at least partly true. The police and the civilian administration were emphatic that the charges were accurate. Moreover, not every policeman who accepted the truth of these charges appeared to be biased against the university as such.

For example, the SSP of the district, whose interview was previously cited, did not see the university as the source of the problems leading to riots, except, he noted, that criminals are sometimes sheltered there.[15] Riots as such, he said, began in the city, not in the university, and, insofar as they did affect the university, it was a consequence of a spillover effect from the city. Nevertheless, he remarked, it was true that criminals from the city got shelter in the AMU during riots as well as during normal times.

A second police officer in Aligarh, one whose own impartiality and honesty I came to doubt, but whose testimony on this matter is nevertheless relevant as reflecting a widespread police view in the district at the time, was emphatic on this matter. He said that it was "a thousand percent correct" that criminals are sheltered inside AMU itself. Those sheltered were not only ordinary criminals, but people who indulged in communal incidents, arson, and so forth, in order to get shelter there.[16]

Two lower-level policemen from the city also supported the same view. The Yadav station officer of Sasni Gate told me that, during and after riots, wanted criminals get protection at the AMU.[17]

The police inspector of Bannadevi remarked that criminals who had studied previously with AMU professors got protection at AMU.[18] After riots, all protection was provided by the AMU to these criminals. The inspector also noted in his remarks that people in Aligarh did not benefit from the AMU, reflecting thereby his identification with the antagonism of Hindus in the city towards the Muslim University. Nevertheless, he said, the cause of riots was not AMU as such. The cause, he said, was in the city.

The district magistrate, head of the civilian administration of the district, also responded that the charge that the AMU protected criminals was true. Even in normal times, he said, criminals take refuge there. He noted that the charges had been confirmed during a raid on one student hostel where many arms of all kinds were found.[19]

Even on the university campus, the police charges were not entirely dismissed. One noncommunal Muslim academic, himself a political scientist, gave the following response to the question concerning the AMU role in protecting criminals.

It is only twenty percent true that many criminals get refuge in the university campus during riots. However, it is not only Muslim criminals, but Hindu criminals also who get refuge there during riots. The attraction of AMU for criminals obviously is because the police are not allowed to enter easily. However, the issue has been blown up by the press, especially in the case of Muslim criminals. Nevertheless, it is true that the [university] administration definitely overlooked the problem of criminals on campus during [vice-chancellor] Khusro's times. However, since Syed Hamid's takeover [as vice-chancellor], most of the criminals were apprehended and the administration received active support from the students union. Anyway, singling out AMU is not helpful because the problem exists and is even worse at other universities.[20]

Overall, therefore, there is a very considerable consensus in my interviews that it is factually correct, on a scale somewhere between twenty percent and "a thousand percent," that the AMU did provide shelter and refuge to criminals, that arms were hidden on the campus as well, and that the problem had not yet been solved by the time of my interviews in 1983. It is at the same time noteworthy that the police and civilian administration treated this question as a police question and did not view the AMU as such as the source of the communal problem in the city. They argued instead that the source of the problems was in the city. The political science professor also insisted that the issue of criminal activity inside the AMU was not confined either to Muslims or to the AMU, but was a general problem. Both Hindu and Muslim criminals received protection at the AMU. Moreover, criminal activity in north Indian universities, he noted, was a commonplace at this time, as it has been in later years as well.[21]

### The Aligarh Muslim University as a Precipitating or Originating Factor in Communal Problems

A second rather broader issue concerning the role of the AMU in the communal situation in Aligarh concerned whether or not the university was a source in one way or another of communal problems in the city, including riots, rather than the reverse. The Hindu communalist view is clear enough on this matter. To persons of this persuasion, the AMU is the real root of the communal riots in Aligarh. It is charged that "AMU people" not only "inflame" the city population, they plan and organize riots in the city.[22]

Although several police officers interviewed agreed that shelter and some arms were provided to criminals at AMU and that some planning was done at the university, all insisted that riots start in the town and then may affect the univerity. But the militant Hindu argument goes much further and turns around completely the Muslim and secular intellectual charge that riots are preplanned and organized by militant Hindu groups such as the RSS. The militant Hindu argument rather is that everything is planned and organized at the AMU in order to achieve specific Muslim objectives, such as maintaining the minority character of the university, which, as we have seen above, had been a controversial issue in north Indian politics generally during the 1960s and 1970s. That the trauma of Partition lies behind everything in the Hindu communalist's mind is evident in the fantastic view that the Muslims are capable of demanding another "division of India." This can only be described as a pathology of the historical consciousness, a phenomenon that is endemic in India and in some other parts of the world today, a subject to which I will return below.

It is clear that the Hindu communalist view of the role of the AMU in riots differs substantially from the police views cited above. But the DSP, Intelligence presented an intermediate view. He did not take the position that people from the AMU planned and organized riots. Moreover, he said that there was "never any violence at AMU, except once in 1979, which was not a communal case."

Although the DSP was clear, therefore, that in his view the university was "not a contributing factor to the communal tension in Aligarh," it did constitute a symbolic presence that affected "the course of events." It had a "unique place in the Muslim world" and had "become a symbol of Muslim aspirations."[23] Although he did not say so, its very representation of Muslim aspirations distinct from those of the Hindus make it, in the words of the district magistrate at the time, an "eyesore for Hindus."[24]

How much of an eyesore the AMU is for militant Hindus, if not necessarily for all Hindus in Aligarh, was brought out forcefully to me once again as late as November 1997 in an interview with a lifelong RSS worker,[25] a man of 66 years of age, a retired chain factory foreman, born and brought up in Aligarh, and himself a graduate of AMU. He put the matter to me in a very long discourse as follows.

RESPONDENT: As a Hindu worker and as an experienced person of this university, I believe and I have written books on the subject that AMU was the root cause of the partition of this country. [ . . . ] We believe that this university is responsible for the partition of this country.

PRB: And you are old boy.

RESPONDENT: Old boy of university. And we Hindus are sorry that that mentality of this university has not changed even after the partition of this country. . . . So the basic question before the Hindus of Aligarh—and I think Hindus of the entire nation—is that the Muslims are again acting—and perhaps this time they will not demand partition, another partition of this country—and this is our honest opinion and I think I'm expressing the feelings of all the nationalist Hindus that this time they will not demand another partition of this country. Now, they are out to make this country *dar-ul-Islam.* The danger is not before Aligarh town, before the Hindus of this town, but the entire country is facing this danger: how

to, how to save this country from these terrorists. The conditions of Kashmir you
know very well.

PRB: Of course.

RESPONDENT: The same conditions are being created here. Aligarh University, whenever gentlemen like you come to this country to know certain things about the situation of this country, they don't allow the real Hindu workers to meet those
gentlemen. They will prefer secular socialist Hindus.

PRB: This is why I have come to see you.

RESPONDENT: And these secular socialist Hindus are more dangerous than Muslims,
so far [as] we Hindus are concerned. They are more dangerous. We cannot believe
them. We cannot [accept] them as our leaders. They are our hidden enemies. They
will never tell you the truth. They will abuse Hindus. They will defame Hindus. . . .
And this is the most unfortunate situation, that whenever outsiders or foreigners
come to this country and they try to meet citizens of Aligarh through this university, the university does not give them a chance to meet the real persons or the
nationalists of the town. I'm surprised that you are sitting in the office of the RSS
and talking to those people who believe that the country is facing perhaps a greater
danger than they faced in 1946 and '47. They are openly calling their community
for jihad. And nobody is taking action. Now, this is the situation in brief, which I
would like to put before you.

And here is what I would like to put before the readers of this volume.
The remarks of this gentleman are not exceptional. That should be to some
extent evident from several other statements quoted above. The beliefs contained in this statement are widely shared among Hindus in northern India.
They are presented in this respondent's remarks in a highly coherent and logical form. They are presented sincerely, they appear to be believed strongly
by the speaker, and they elicit a certain amount of sympathy in the listener—
not for their truth but for the feelings expressed. They are, nevertheless, nonsense. They display a package of sentiments that have been present in all kinds
of antidemocratic, paranoid, and fascist movements in the twentieth century: resentments against an "other" combined with gross ignorance of the
other's beliefs and sensibilities; fear of and magnification of the danger represented by the other, even though the other is manifestly weaker; identification of an internal enemy hated even more than the other, those who should
be of us, but have been corrupted by false ideologies; belief that the country,
the community, the nation, are all in danger and that no action is being taken
against the manifest presence and actions of hostile enemies operating openly
in our midst.

The resentment expressed is twofold. It is directed first against the Muslims of India, and against one of the leading symbols of their presence in India, in Aligarh itself, the AMU. But another kind of resentment also appears connected with the first, namely, that the voice this respondent represents, of aggrieved Hindus, is not heard by outsiders. His manifest pleasure at my presence and the opportunity that I represented in his mind, to be heard by the West, most likely prevented him from expressing that other resentment I have heard times without number in 20 or 25 visits to India over several decades: why have we (the United States) supported Pakistan, therefore the Muslims, therefore the enemy of the Hindus and of India?

Gross ignorance is displayed in the apparent belief, shared by so many millions upon millions of Hindus and Christians as well, that jihad presumes only violent conquest. That ignorance is compounded by exaggerated, paranoid fear that the Muslims, through jihad—whatever it means to the militant Hindu—and through "terrorist" actions, will be able to turn India into an abode of Islam. How can such a thing be imagined in a country where those people classed as Hindus comprise 85 percent of the population of their country and a sixth of the population of the globe? It can be imagined only by demonizing the other, by attributing to the other demonic powers that increase his strength, and, simultaneously, by attributing to oneself, that is, to the Hindus of India, internal weakness produced by disunity and the presence of enemies within one's own fold who are worse than the other. This, in a nutshell, is the essence of the ideology of militant Hindu nationalism shared by millions of RSS workers and many more sympathizers.

But we have come far from Aligarh in this analysis, without leaving it. We are clearly back here in the midst of the communal discourse, but not just there. We are in the larger world of not only Hindus and Muslims, but the conflict of ideologies in the country as a whole, the even larger world in which Hindus and India have not achieved their deserved place, are not heard by foreigners and not respected, because they have been displaced from their occupation of the rightful center of their own country by its partition. In this world, the riots that comprise my theme and subject are but specks in a much bigger frame.

# 14 / Police Views of Hindu-Muslim Violence

M ost of the persons killed in most riots in India and in all riots in
Aligarh since Independence have been Muslims; moreover, most
have been killed by the police. That fact alone would normally
arouse the suspicion that what are called riots in India and in Aligarh are actually pogroms, that is, the deliberate killing of Muslims by the agents of the
state. However, matters are more complicated than that and raise doubts about
the validity of the distinction between riots and pogroms. In fact, what has
been emerging from so much of the material presented so far is rather that
riots are political productions, in which, indeed, the police play a role—but
that role varies depending upon a number of factors, of which the most important for our purposes concerns administrative and political control of the
police. Neither the Indian state nor the province of U.P. are anti-Muslim institutions whose police are engaged in either systematic or sporadic slaughter
of Muslims. Rather, the police act against Muslims or do not act against
Muslims, when riots occur, depending primarily upon the inclinations of their
administrative and political superiors, which in turn depend upon which political party or coalition is in power. That does not mean that individual policemen do not act according to their own inclinations as well, but their range
of freedom to do so during communal riots depends critically upon the given
state of administrative and political control over them.

It is important also in this connection to make a distinction that further
complicates matters, between the ordinary armed police and the PAC. Police
constables are recruited from within their own district and are transferred
only within the district. Superior officers generally come from other districts.
The senior superintendent of police (SSP) will usually be an educated per-

son from another district who has been recruited by examination into the Indian Police Service. Transfers and postings of the senior officers are done by the state government, that is, by the party in power. They are done frequently and are influenced by political and patronage considerations. The state government wants men whom it can trust as SSPs in the districts that are communally sensitive. When the government changes hands from one party to another, there are usually wholesale transfers of SSPs. Within the district, transfers and postings are made by the SSP, who in turn may be influenced by the desires of locally powerful politicians, particularly the local MLAs.

The PAC, on the other hand, is an entirely different unit that operates under its own command hierarchy, but is ultimately beholden only to the state government. Very little is known about the organization of the PAC and about the effectiveness of state government control over it. The PAC *jawans* and their officers are not available to be interviewed by foreign scholars, nor have there been any scholarly studies of their functioning. It is commonly accepted, however, that the PAC is an anti-Muslim force.[1] Since, as I have said, it would be a simplification to consider the police as an anti-Muslim force, it is—given the fact that both the police and the PAC are under the ultimate control of the state government—an anomaly that the PAC appears to act consistently against Muslims whereas the police do not. I cannot explain this anomaly, but it is evident from it that it further confounds the distinction between riots and pogroms.

I want to present in this chapter two sets of perceptions: those of the public and the politicians about the police and the PAC, on the one hand, and the perceptions of the police concerning the role of the people and the politicians in riots.

## PUBLIC PERCEPTIONS OF THE POLICE

Public perceptions of the police do not always distinguish between the actions of the police and those of the PAC once the latter have been called out. While Muslims do distinguish the PAC from the police as separate forces, when they say there was a "police firing," it is not always clear whether it was the ordinary police who fire or the PAC. Insofar as the major riots in Aligarh are concerned, I have heard repeatedly from many respondents that the police in general engage in various actions that are considered either partial to the Hindus or outright and unprovoked assaults on Muslims with intent to kill. These accusations were especially prominent in my interviews after the 1990–91 riots. Indeed, the *mufti shahar* of Aligarh in January 1991 said to me that the violence that had occurred in the preceding months was not a riot, but a police action.[2]

I have already reported on the alleged behavior of the police in Sarai Sultani during that riot and previous riots. But Sarai Sultani has not been exceptional in this regard. Accounts I have heard again and again from Muslims contain the following elements.[3] If an attack breaks out between Hindus and Muslims, such as stone throwing by mobs from the two communities, the police act partially on the side of the Hindus, and shoot to kill Muslims. The police also engage in unprovoked actions, including the destruction of local mosques. The police kill and loot houses during riots, even in Muslim localities where there is no tension. Police fire upon crowds of Muslims returning from Friday prayers. Police enter Muslim houses without provocation or, alleging that shots have been fired from a particular residence, molest women and arrest them and their sons if they protest, or kill the sons. Police act during riots upon requests by local Hindus or Scheduled Castes who have had quarrels with Muslims, and shoot Muslims dead. Police deliberately kill even children, reportedly between the ages of six and twelve. In these cases, for all of which I have documentation from interviews, the respondents sometimes said that it was the police who committed the attack, sometimes the PAC, sometimes both combined, and sometimes that they could not differentiate the two.[4]

Other interviews suggest that a Muslim wounded in a riot, if he is lucky enough to make it to his home, cannot expect to receive any medical help. If the police are called, the likely response will be that the family is sheltering a rioter. Only if the family members have influential friends or if they are lucky enough to find a "kind and polite" police office can they expect their wounded relation to be taken to hospital.[5]

### SOME POLICE VIEWS ON RIOTS

The documented misbehavior of the police and the PAC in countless riots in India since Independence is said to be associated with a distinct police view of riots. That view has been expressed most clearly in an unofficial, unpublished, and undated report on "Communal Riots and Minorities," which provides an accounting of the numbers of Hindus, Muslims, "others," and police killed between 1968 and 1980, and concludes with a set of statements summarizing "the perception of the magistrates and senior police officers" in the country concerning riots. These perception constitute, in effect, in the judgment of the report's author(s), a police view of riots. I undertook in my own research numerous interviews with police to ascertain their views of riots, which I will compare with the conclusions in this document. I give below, first, a long quote, comprising the report's complete summarization of that police view.

(a) Riots take place in such districts where Muslims are either in a majority or they constitute a sizeable minority.

(b) Muslims are excitable and irrational people who are guided by their religious instincts. Hindus, on the other hand, are law abiding and cooperate with the police in controlling communal violence.

(c) Riots are started by the Muslims and they invariably take the first opportunity to strike at the other community and at the police.

(d) In all other previous riots in the country before the current riot, Muslims took the upperhand [*sic*] which resulted in huge loss to the Hindu community. Therefore, there is moral justification if in the current riot casualties on the Muslim side are heavier.

(e) State Government attaches a great deal of importance in ensuring quick control of rioting. Since Muslims are aggressive, therefore, in order to control violence, it is necessary that Muslim mobs must be taught a lesson through arrests, firing and third degree methods.

(f) Hindu casualties are as a result of Muslim mob action, whereas Muslim casualties are due to isolated stray incidents. Because of this difference in the nature of aggression by the two communities, more Muslims have to be arrested. Very little evidence is possible to collect regarding Hindu aggressions and this explains why the number of Hindus arrested for substantive offences is less.[6]

In short, despite the known evidence that more Muslims than Hindus are killed in most riots, the police view is said to be that Muslims start these riots in places where they have large enough numbers to do so and Hindus are for the most part victims of "Muslim mob action." The known facts that more Muslims are arrested and killed in most riots are not denied, but are explained away by placing the blame for them upon Muslims and freeing Hindus from all blame. In short, this alleged "police view" of riots is perfectly consistent with the militant Hindu communalist ideology discussed in the previous chapter.

The report cited above, published twenty years ago, also noted that the attitudes of the PAC, an armed police force even then notorious among and hated by all Muslims in the state of U.P., were even more negative than those of the local police—who actually come into contact with the people on a day-to-day basis, in contrast to the PAC *jawans*,[7] who remain in their

FIG. 14.1. PAC encampment, Aligarh, 1999

encampments (Figure 14.1) and are called out only for riot duty. Further, it was noted that Hindu district administrators and officers who acquire the confidence of the Muslims lose the confidence of the Hindus in the locality, with the result that "pressure is mounted to get them transferred," making it increasingly difficult "to have officers commanding the respect of both the communities."[8]

The police are widely condemned in India for their often partisan behavior during riots and particularly for the fact that mostly Muslims have been killed in most post-Independence riots in Aligarh, as elsewhere in the country. It is a matter of some interest, therefore, to discover in interviews with police officers at all levels that many of them present quite cogent interpretations of the causes of riots that depart significantly from the summary view given above and from the militant Hindu ideology. To the extent that there is a common police view of riots, it can be summarized as one that combines the idea that there is a pathology of ideology in Indian society and perhaps of personality as well with demographic and communal factors. That police view also includes the attribution of profit motivations to rioters. I will show below, however, that there are important differences in police views of the causes of riots between subordinate policemen such as station officers and police inspectors, on the one hand, and more senior officers, on the other hand. It is especially among the latter that Hindu-Muslim riots are attributed to fundamental differences between the two communities.

*Views from Below*

It was a matter of some surprise to me to find that local police inspectors and station officers in the *mohallas* of Aligarh in the riot-prone areas expressed their views on riots very coherently, fully, articulately, and sensitively, with many nuances.[9] For example, I asked the inspector of police, police station Bannadevi—very much a riot-prone area—what were the factors making the area near his police station riot-prone. I give below in compressed form, partly directly quoted and partly paraphrased, this inspector's response.[10]

> [The factors making this area riot-prone] are, first, high population density, such that "if there is even a small altercation people come out in huge numbers, and without knowing the issue they fight." Second, "criminals . . . exploit the situation." They stab someone and, if it is a Hindu, Hindus say a Muslim stabbed him; if is a Muslim, they say a Hindu stabbed him. Third, before and during elections also, politicians may start a rumor or even a small riot to gain the support of one side. They engage criminals to start a riot, then portray themselves as saviors of the people by distributing grain and cloth to the people during curfew. They collect money from different districts and distribute it among the criminals; they have formed committees for this.

Thus, this police inspector pointed to demography, criminality, and extreme political opportunism, cynicism, and hypocrisy as a triad of factors producing riots and making particular areas of the city riot-prone. He elaborated further, however, and added additional factors after giving an example of how riots began in Aligarh in 1980 in the aftermath of the terrible anti-Muslim riots in the nearby district of Moradabad in that year.

> In 1980, an AMU professor and another used money to form a group of criminals, held a meeting to organize, then spread through the area, first breaking the lights so there would be darkness, then stabbing people, with each criminal taking charge of a particular area. This was a repercussion from the Moradabad riot of 1980.

A fourth factor, therefore, now appears: the deliberate instigation of riotous activity by professors from the AMU, who use criminals in the task of paying back Hindus for their actions in another district. The involvement of AMU professors must, therefore, in the light of this inspector's account, be taken seriously, since the charge is made without evident rancor or prejudice, in contrast with the RSS respondents cited in the previous chapter. Yet another factor was mentioned by the police inspector, what he calls the "mentality of the people."

> Even ordinary people become susceptible to violence over even trivial incidents. For example, a child may fire a shotgun blast prematurely during Ramzan to confuse Muslims waiting for the blast to indicate their fast is over; this actually happened in 1982 and nearly caused a riot. People have also become inured to riots, expect them, and even have extra children because they feel they will lose some in riots.
>
> It's the mentality of the people, how they live. Most families have 12–14 children. Most children are uneducated, with nothing to do. In a riot, they will throw stones at the police jeeps. Rioting is the only form of entertainment available. Employment also is limited to the lock industry, with few jobs. The population must be reeducated. A new town must be constructed in which these narrow alleys are done away with, and the hygiene is improved.
>
> The nature of these areas also makes police work nearly hopeless. There are underground hiding places and numerous by-lanes through which criminals can reach the city outskirts. Moreover, in Muslim areas, the people support the criminals. Muslim women come and stand in front of the houses and say no one is inside and you cannot argue with them. Even if someone is caught, chances are that Muslims of the area will come out in support of him and throw stones at the police.

The number of factors continues to tumble out as this police inspector explains the conditions of the people in the *mohallas* in which riots occur. Rioting has become a routine aspect of the life of the people, arising out of how they live and how they think about how they live, and what they have come to expect. Consequently, riots can erupt spontaneously as a consequence of such trivial incidents as a child's prank. In an area with limited employment opportunities, hordes of children, no hygiene, little money for entertainment, and none available except for cinema halls that cost money, rioting becomes a "form of entertainment."[11]

This police inspector also believes, as would any Western urban planner or any casual Western visitor to these indescribably unhygienic and crowded areas, that these filthy slums must be torn down and "a new town must be constructed." This idea, as far as I know, has not occurred to any of India's planners, or, if it has, it has been kept a secret. Yet, within ten or fifteen kilometers of this *mohalla*—which, in the seventeen years since this interview was done, has become even more unhygienic and so crowded that one can barely move through it without coming into contact, often hard contact, with people, animals, scooters, cars, and assorted other mechanically and humanly powered vehicles—huge new buildings are being constructed in open areas, many of which would take up as much space as that occupied by hundreds of slum families, for the occupation of the newly rich (see Figure 6.1). The police inspector did not make any such comparison between his police station area and other, better-off areas of Aligarh. He was merely noting the obvious: if people have to live like animals, they will behave like them.

There is yet a further point in the police inspector's account that requires special notice. It is about police work, especially in the Muslim areas. The inspector was a Hindu, his area mixed Hindu and Muslim. He expressed no obvious hostility to Muslims, which does not mean that he did not harbor any that he might have expressed to persons other than a foreigner with a tape recorder. But I detected no tinge of it in his remarks. Therefore, we must take seriously his expressions of futility over the problems of police work during a riot in a *qasbah* town with "underground hiding places and numerous by-lanes" in which criminals are at work and where ordinary Muslims, including Muslim women, come out to protect the criminals and "throw stones at the police." In such circumstances, it is not difficult to imagine the police losing control, opening fire in frustration and rage, and killing many such "ordinary" people. Such actions, which have in fact occurred countless times in these kinds of situations, can in no way be excused. At the same time, it is easy to see also how the police in such situations become scapegoats for the intolerable conditions in which they must work, as a consequence of the failures of the politicians and so-called planners to give even a moment's thought to the conditions of these "ordinary" people of India, except to make use of them for their own political advantage. Police who must work day in and day out in such conditions also confront day in and day out not just the neglect of their masters, but their malevolent hypocrisy, as suggested by the police inspector himself in these additional comments in response to my question concerning who actually perpetrates the violence in communal riots.

The physical actions are done by persons from lower castes and classes, but persons from middle and upper classes give shelter and guidance: Big criminals [who become involved] are close to the top lawyers, who are paid by the politicians from the committee funds for the relief of the riot-affected. If the police take a criminal to court, even for section 362,[12] he is released, which sets a bad example. They also get the support of MLAs and people in Delhi, who pressure the government officials. The people responsible are known to the police. Navman is the main fellow among Hindus. Shiv Hari Singhal is the lawyer for most Muslim criminals. Manga Ram looks at a situation, then goes to the colleges, instigates the students, and they go there.

The inspector then proceeded to give a specific example of a "big criminal" responsible for riots in Aligarh who had "big connections" and was able to get a false passport, with the help of a central government minister, to go to Pakistan.

Although the inspector previously gave an account suggesting how riots may erupt spontaneously in crowded *mohallas*, in these remarks it is clear that there is in his mind a division of roles and responsibilities for the actions undertaken during riots. These include the actual rioters, who come from the lower castes and classes; leaders and protectors, who come from the middle and upper classes; and criminals, lawyers, politicians, and government officials tied together in a network of influence and mutual protection. These remarks were made in 1983 when the pervasiveness of the criminalization of politics in India was probably less than it has been in recent years, when a well-known mafia don of an eastern district of U.P. was made a minister in the state government run by the BJP (in 1999), and several other members of that government—as well as many in its predecessor governments run by other parties—have had criminal records.

This police view is remarkable in many ways. It contains a mixture of sense and nonsense, though more of the former than the latter. It focuses on particular behaviors and local factors rather than upon the history or the imagined future of Hindu-Muslim relations. It places blame generally on socioeconomic conditions, but also pinpoints particular individuals alleged to be fomenters of and organizers of riots, including one of the leading RSS persons in Aligarh, the lawyer Shiv Hari Singhal, who, the inspector is suggesting, is defending Muslim criminals. There is a clear implication that Muslim criminals are paid by Hindu communalist leaders to stab persons, including fellow Muslims, in order to set off a riot, and are then protected by them. The police inspector's statement also, of course—like virtually all explanations of communal and other riots—displaces blame, in this case from the police onto the criminals protected by the big lawyers and politicians.

It appears clear to me from the whole tenor of the police inspector's remarks that he did not have an anti-Muslim bias. I asked two further questions, the answers to which further bear out my impression. I asked, as I did with most respondents for this study, specifically about the roles placed in riots by Varshneys and Qasais. He responded that it is "true they play the most active part because they are the strongest of the communities" in Aligarh; "there are large numbers of both and they have the same mentality."

My second question was more direct: do Muslims always start the riots? His response was, "most of the time." However, he added that, "since 1981, Varshneys have taken to provoking Muslims." If my impression that the police inspector was not biased is correct, then how could he make the statement that most of the time Muslims do in fact start riots? He has himself pointed to the possibility that Muslims start riots, at least since 1981, because they are deliberately provoked by some anti-Muslim act to do so. Further, he has himself implied that Muslim criminals are paid and protected by the most extreme elements among the militant Hindu nationalists for their work in provoking riots. Here we come close to the heart of the matter of the labelling of such large, widespread, and multifarious events as riots. Who is a Hindu and who a Muslim in such affrays? Is a criminal, Muslim by faith, who is paid to precipitate a riot by an extremist Hindu politician/businessman and protected by an extremist Hindu lawyer, acting as a Muslim on behalf of his community? The constant repetition of the words "Hindu" and "Muslim" in these contexts, including by this writer, is both inescapable and misleading. How can a writer write about events already classified and embedded in a communal discourse without using such labels? I am here trying to sift and sort, but in the process of sifting and sorting, I too get caught in the mesh.

I have spent much time on this single interview with an inspector of police. A single in-depth interview does not count for much in contemporary social science, which rests so heavily on structured questionnaires. It will certainly not quell the doubts of social science practitioners to say that I have had many other such interviews.[13] But I am not attempting a scientific account of the causes of riots nor conducting a public opinion survey. I am seeking rather to discover, through repeated interviews asking the same simple questions over and over, whether or not there is a "police view" of riots that can be distinguished from other kinds of views of them. I can only demonstrate here—and could demonstrate further with other interviews from other districts that will not be covered in this book—that there was some consistency in the accounts given to me by policemen at the lower levels of the police hierarchy.

I will conclude this presentation of police views in Aligarh in 1983 with another set of responses to the same questions, from an interview with a Hindu station officer in another riot-prone locality, Sasni Gate. This interview, like the previous one, has been translated from Hindi, compressed and partly paraphrased, partly directly quoted.

PRB: How do riots get started?

SO: Riots occur because of mutual misunderstanding: certain elements exploit petty incidents of crime and give them a communal color for their own benefit. These elements are mostly white-collar people who try to convert every incident into a communal incident and exploit it. Then, they go into the background when it becomes a big issue. Small incidents are exploited, then rumors are spread, especially by telephone. Then there's a stampede as people come to believe something has happened. Then the market is closed, a crowd forms, and the situation goes out of control.

PRB: Who starts the riots?

SO: It is not always the Muslims. The RSS is no less strong than the Muslims and as disciplined and organized.

PRB: What about Varshney-Qasai conflicts?

SO: It is partly true. Varshneys are the biggest group in the RSS and Qasais are generally Muslim League or Jamaat-i-Islami.

PRB: What are the differences between Aligarh and other U.P. towns that do not have riots?

SO: In other cities, Hindus or Muslims may be in larger numbers [that is, one or the other predominates] or the organizations are not so organized and broadly based. Here, also, the intellectuals are Muslims with communal feelings. Moreover, Aligarh has always been divided on communal lines, with Hindus provoking other Hindus [to hostility against Muslims] by telling lies and Muslims doing the same.

PRB: Who benefits from riots?

SO: Businessmen, because laborers don't get paid during riots when there is curfew and then become dependent on the bosses for help and become almost like bonded labor; also, those industries which can keep people employed even during riots also benefit because they can pay the laborers at low wages. Professional criminals also benefit because they are well paid by vested interests for committing stabbings, et cetera. Otherwise, most groups suffer.

PRB: What about the politicians?

SO: Mostly, they are not around. When they are, they don't give good advice. If they did give good advice, these situations might not turn into big riots. Some politicians may exploit the situation by playing on the sentiments of the people to increase their popularity. Then, when the DM and the police have to pay attention to them, they become even more popular.

PRB: What about the general problems in these *mohallas*, of the alleyways and lack of education, et cetera?

SO: Naturally, because a child is born and grows up with communal riots, a riot psyche persists into adulthood.

Clearly, there is a close correspondence between the responses of the two lower-level policemen to my questions, though there are some interesting variations and emendations. One emendation is the idea that riots arise out of "mutual misunderstanding" through the manipulation of "petty incidents" that are turned into communal questions for the benefit of others. In this account, there are certain people from the "white-collar" classes who act, in effect, as what I call "conversion specialists" whose function is to "try to convert every incident into a communal incident": "rumors are spread, especially by telephone."

I have myself seen how the rumor network operates, from repeated occasions of sitting in interviews with BJP politicians who receive telephone calls or visits from persons alerting them to alleged incidents, such as that a cow has been "poisoned" or a Hindu girl has been raped by Muslims. These conversion specialists may or may not choose in each case to mobilize their forces to protest against the alleged insult, assault, or injury to Hindu sensibilities, but they remain always alert to that possibility and will do so if the political context justifies it. But others benefit from riots also, this station officer avers, particularly businessman and professional criminals.

The most striking aspect of the two statements by these lower-level officials is their debunking of the whole idea that riots arise out of "communal" differences between Hindus and Muslims. On the contrary, they say that what are called communal riots arise out of "trivial" or "petty" incidents, out of "misunderstandings" that are deliberately exploited by others who benefit from giving such incidents a "communal color" and fomenting riots, from which they derive concrete, material benefits in business, cash, or votes. Whether or not Muslims always or do not always start the riots is not important in their minds, because people are being provoked—and Muslims are being deliberately provoked by particular groups in Hindu society. In a word, the central feature of the police views cited above is that the incidents and the contexts in which riots occur are narrowed; they are decommunalized and decontextualized. In a sense, they are even "humanized," by which I mean that the factors they cite arise not out of prejudice and hatred between the two communities, but out of the general human or inhuman conditions in which both Muslims and Hindus in Aligarh live, and by human greed.

## Views from Above

Two further interviews with senior administrative/police officials of the district share features with those of the two policemen analyzed in the previous section, but differ in this one respect of contextualization. One was conducted with the district magistrate (DM), the senior civilian officer of the district, the other with the deputy superintendent of police, intelligence (DSP). I will summarize first the comments of the district magistrate in response to a general question concerning the "communal situation" in Aligarh.[14] He remarked first that the communal situation keeps him busy all the time because of the fact that any incident involving persons from the two communities could lead to a communal riot. He gave several examples of the type of situation he has had to face. But when asked for the "causes" of the communal situation, he began with the history of the city and of the AMU in the remarks summarized and paraphrased below.

> The DM pointed to the history of the city and noted that Muslims had always been very powerful here. There were riots here before Partition and many Hindus felt the Muslims should have gone to Pakistan at Partition. In addition, AMU is a major university of India and Muslims come from all over the world to study here. The Hindus see AMU as an eyesore, while the Muslims consider it a question of prestige. Everyone is concerned with their own prestige and dignity, and every small incident is considered to reflect upon them. A third cause is the Hindu-Muslim balance in the city, which is about 50–50. But basically it's because of Aligarh's history.

Thus, the DM begins by contextualizing "the communal situation" in relation to the history of the city and its relationship to the decisive moment in modern Indian history—not Independence, but Partition—and specifically to the place of the AMU in that history. Although our local policemen also mentioned the AMU, they talked about it in terms of their police work, as an alleged site for harboring criminals and instigators of riots, not as an originating source of the communal problem in the city. On the actual mechanics of riots, however, there was close agreement between the DM's view and that of the local police officers, as indicated in this summary of his remarks below.

> There are people here interested in creating problems, in engineering riots. It is not for economic benefit, but for prestige. So-called good people plan the riots, but criminals enact them. Criminals are on their payrolls. The main cul-

prits, he acknowledged, are Navman and Manga Ram. Shiv Hari Singhal is quiet now.

When I pressed the DM concerning whether or not there were similar persons engineering riots among the Muslims, he also gave the names of a couple of Muslims. However, it is clear that he attributed primary responsibility to the Hindus whose names were mentioned.

The DM, himself a man from a Scheduled Caste, concluded his analysis by referring to popular attitudes, to what he called the "communal mentality." "You can't find a 100 percent secular person in India; they are all Hindus or Muslims. And, in crises, every Hindu is a Hindu, every Muslim a Muslim." Although the DM, like the lower-level policemen, was, therefore, attributing responsibility for the communal situation and Hindu-Muslim riots to popular mentalities or the popular "psyche," there is a notable difference. By calling this popular mentality a "communal mentality," he was contextualizing it and generalizing it, placing it in the framework of a polarized population. He was, in effect, saying that the problem is not the conditions under which both communities live, but their identities as Hindus and Muslims. The problem in his mind is the Hindu-Muslim question.

A somewhat similar conceptualization of the communal situation in Aligarh was presented to me in an interview with the deputy superintendent of police, intelligence (DSP).[15] He, too, stressed what he called "the historical importance of the city" because of the presence in it of the "AMU and its minority character." He showed, as of course an intelligence officer would, knowledge of the internal politics of the university as well as of its relations with the people in the town.

> Muslims, he said, have a peculiar style of thinking. For them, AMU is an exclusive institution. A section thinks Muslim culture and style of education should be reflected in the curriculum, but a Marxist group is equally opposed to it. Under the present vice-chancellor, the atmosphere has changed considerably and become very secular.
>
> There is an emotional link between Muslims in India and Muslim countries. In AMU, 99 percent of the foreign students are from Muslim countries.

Although the then vice-chancellor received the praise of the DSP, there is no doubt that the DSP considered the AMU a central issue in the communal situation in Aligarh. Muslims have a "peculiar" way of thinking, an exclusive way of thinking, one that links them emotionally with Muslim countries.

Although he did not say it, this kind of statement is often followed by the further assertion—usually implied even when it is not stated—that Muslims lack sufficient emotional ties, loyalty, and patriotism to their own country. However, the DSP's further remarks on the "mentality of the people" generally in Aligarh suggest that he may not have felt that way.

> There is a tendency of the people of Aligarh to analyze all incidents from a communal angle. So, petty crimes like robbery and stabbing can take a communal turn. This leads to permanent hostility between Hindus and Muslims and an atmosphere of mistrust is built up. By and large, the Muslim intelligentsia is nationalist and secular, but the illiterate and semiliterate classes are totally communal. Respectable members of the two communities are not generally involved in communal troubles. However, a small section of the elite, a negligible percentage, enlists the support of criminals to gain a political foothold.

The DSP, again like the lower-level policemen, refers to the popular mentality, but is more like the DM in defining it as a communal mentality that has infected the entire Muslim lower class. This, of course, is quite the reverse of the RSS view articulated by Navman and others, that the trouble lies more with the intellectual Muslim classes than with the lower classes, who are, on the contrary, infected by their elites.

From history and popular mentality, the DSP turned to the specifics of Hindu-Muslim violence in Aligarh. When discussing the actual dynamics of how riots begin, he referred, like the lower-level policemen, to fabricated precipitating incidents. He, too, noted that there was "a formidable criminal content among Muslims." A riot might be started even by Muslim criminals fighting with each other. He remarked by way of example that, "in case a Muslim kills another Muslim, then a Hindu also is killed to distract the administration." In other words, a potential riot situation is created to occupy the district administration in order to distract them from focusing on a case of murder.

One further factor emphasized by the DSP, but not by other police officers, was his view that there was "a definite foreign hand involved." When Indians—police officers or ordinary citizens—make this remark, they are generally referring to either the CIA or the ISI (Inter Services Intelligence) of Pakistan, or to both. This officer's conspiratorial view of the malevolent force of foreign influence extended, however, to the foreign media. He blamed the "BBC and other foreign radios" for their "instant reporting of events in Aligarh," which "only help[ed] to turn the situation out of control."[16] While the DSP, intelligence, is supposed to know about such things as the involvement of "foreign hands" in internal disturbances in India, I believe his knowledge was little more than a reflection of the common exaggeration of such influences in Indian political life, a fantasy whose effect is to reduce Indian agency and responsibility for the country's own misfortunes. In other words, it is a further example of a particular aspect of the universal process of blame displacement that accompanies explanations of riots everywhere.

Insofar as the media are concerned, their role, discussed in the next chapter, in fact has often been to make matters worse. It is especially the case with the scurrilous vernacular press, but the DSP chose to emphasize the "foreign radios" instead.

It is noteworthy that in the case of all three senior police and administrative officers, including the SSP, the DM, and the DSP, rioting and "communal trouble" in Aligarh are placed in broader contexts than those provided by the inspector and station officers cited above. Although they mention some of the same factors, the senior officers stressed history, especially the Partition and attitudes of Hindus towards it, the importance of the AMU as a symbol of difference between the two communities, Indian Muslims' contacts with foreign countries, and foreign influences in general. In short, they conceptualize, contextualize, and communalize the relations between Hindus and Muslims in their very speech, even when they are striving to be or to appear to be impartial. In fact, the very process of contextualizing and communalizing is part of the striving to be or appear impartial: both sides are to blame. Although they say both sides are to blame, the police at all levels are also engaged in blame displacement. Muslim criminals, the politicians, and the media are all implicated. Left out of account, of course, are the police themselves.

# 15 / The Role of the Media

I n the months before Independence and Partition in 1947, the watchful British governor of the United Provinces, as Uttar Pradesh was then called, kept reassuring Mountbatten in his fortnightly reports to the Viceroy that the communal situation in the U.P. was manageable, if difficult. At the same time, he feared the effects on the communal situation in U.P. of news reporting of the developing catastrophe in the neighboring state of Punjab. He was concerned that another chain reaction might develop, such as had happened earlier after the Great Calcutta Killings of August 1946, which were followed by terrible riots in Noakhali, Bihar, and in western U.P. itself at Garhmukteswar, a site holy to Hindus where approximately five hundred Muslim men, women, and children were massacred. He blamed the Congress press for this chain of events: "Of one thing I am certain and that is that if the Congress Press had not been allowed to magnify Noakhali out of all reason, Bihar might never have happened and after Bihar, Garhmuktesar."[1]

While the governor's statement falls in the general category of blame displacement, in this case diverting blame from British governance at the end of its empire to the Congress press, it is certain that the press has also been deeply implicated in the dynamics of riot production in post-Independence India. The media, especially the newspapers, play important roles at all stages in the production of riots, including the planning and rehearsal stages, the instigation of riotous activity, and the interpretation phase. In recent years, TV reporting on riots has also come in for some share of blame both for inciting violence, however inadvertently, and for publication of false and damaging news in the midst of riots. The official national TV network, Doordashan, for example, has been severely criticized for several items of misreporting of the Aligarh riots of 1990–91.[2]

However, it is the considerably diverse array of newspapers in India that

are most directly and repeatedly implicated in the entire process of riot production. For analytical purposes, the press in India needs to be distinguished
by language, political orientation, sectarian identification, and locational
spread.[3] With regard to language, there is a marked difference between the
English-language press and the vernacular press, which, in north India, means
particularly the Hindi and Urdu newspapers. With regard to political orientation, several of the English-language papers as well as the vernacular newspapers are identified with and may even be owned or directed by particular
political parties. Each of the major political parties and organizations in India
also have their own newspapers, which will not be discussed here since they
are not addressed primarily to or read by the general public. Similarly, the
sectarian papers, such as the RSS organ, the *Organiser*, and the Jamaat-i-Islami
paper, *Radiance*, whose viewpoints are predictable, partial, and directed
towards an already committed audience, will not be discussed here. Only those
that are meant for a mass audience will be considered.

In general, the degree of partiality and the use of inflammatory material
that has the effect of provoking one side to retaliatory action against the other
is most extreme among papers that are local, vernacular, and sectarian.[4]
Indeed, at the height of the Ramjanmabhoomi/Babri Masjid movement and
at the time of the great Aligarh Riots of 1990–91, the PUCL report, in the midst
of its extensive comments on the role of the press in sustaining the riotous
momentum there, noted the "almost total communalisation of the Hindi press
in UP."[5] At the other end of the spectrum, more balanced, less partial, and
less deliberately inflammatory are the national English-language press as well
as the newspapers produced by the same publishers in Hindi or Urdu as virtual vernacular editions of their English counterparts. While there are
exceptions with regard to both the English-language and the independent
vernacular-language presses, it is generally the case that the English press presents a more moderate, balanced face in reporting on riots, whereas many of
the vernacular-language papers are partial to one or the other of the two religious communities (Hindus for the Hindi-language press and Muslims for
the Urdu press) and play a direct inflammatory role in the spread of riots.

Newspapers sometimes play a part in the opening phase of a riot by spreading "news" that originates in the institutionalized riot system network. Thus,
for example, Banerjee notes that "the Jabalpur riots of 1961 . . . were sparked
off by the news of a Hindu girl disappearing with a Muslim boy."[6] In most
societies, an event such as an elopement, which happens every day, would
not be considered "news" at all. In societies sharply divided ethnically or communally, it may become a matter of general interest, but it is obvious that

reporting of such an event in such societies is inflammatory and that information on it must be provided to the press by interested parties seeking to maintain and spread interethnic or intercommunal tension or even to deliberately provoke a riot. Any press reporting of such an incident, therefore, in the north Indian context, is grounds for suspicion concerning the motives of the press in publishing it.

But the "news" that appears in the press before and during riots is sometimes not only inappropriate but often completely false. In October 1974 in Aligarh, when the district administration and police were working assiduously to prevent the outbreak of violence in the aftermath of a quarrel between Hindu and Muslim students at the AMU, "all important dailies from Delhi, Agra and Lucknow carried a news item that Hindu girls inside the University were molested and attempts were made to rape them."[7] This news was utterly fictitious and could have easily been disconfirmed by any conscientious reporter. At this point in Aligarh, when the institutionalized riot network was in full operation, the press became a part of it.

The press also becomes complicit in the enactment phase of riot production by the attention it gives to statements of the riot's producers. In the midst of the long series of riots that began in Aligarh in October 1978, during which the principal militant Hindu figures were active—Navman, Shiv Hari Singhal, B. D. Gupta, and Manga Ram—Balraj Madhok, the most extreme of the national Jan Sangh leaders at the time, arrived in Aligarh to provide his assistance. He "addressed a press conference," after which "he was quoted saying that, since Hindus had been prevented from celebrating Diwali, Muslims must be taught a lesson, and should be prevented from celebrating Id."[8] Here again, we observe the local riot network in operation, assisted by the arrival on the scene of a national figure, whose presence draws the attention of the press, which then in effect carries out the purpose of the visit to Aligarh, namely, to keep the riotous activity going.

Most press reporting on riots begins after the initial outbreak and is almost always based upon "police hand outs"[9] or press releases issued by the state government. Most of the English-language newspapers will have access to the same information at this stage and will produce more or less the same accounts. Differences will arise only insofar as the particular newspaper has a stringer at the riot site or an informed person upon whom it relies for information. Lead reporters will go to the scene only in the case of larger riots. When there is a wave of riots at a number of different sites, naturally the lead reporters will concentrate at the largest city or the site of the most severe rioting. Even then, while the rioting and curfew are on, reporters remain highly dependent on police handouts, which in turn means, of course, dependence on the police view of the causes of the outbreak.

Two kinds of biases and misreporting may enter at this outbreak stage. The first concerns how it started, the second, who started it. Most press reports will refer to a specific incident, a quarrel between a Hindu and a Muslim over a trivial matter or a procession that ended in a communal mêlée. Bias enters at this stage because of the absence of investigative reporting on the events that preceded the precipitating incident, which, as I have demonstrated throughout this volume, involves continuous preparation and rehearsal. In Aligarh, the 1978 riots provide the clearest case in point. Those riots, precipitated during the funerary procession for the wrestler, Bhura, were preceded by weeks of intergang fighting, Hindu communal mobilization, and direct incitement to rioting by militant Hindu activists. Only after the rioting became savage and widespread did investigative teams enter the scene to provide background reporting. However, the best such reporting was not done by the press, but by civil liberties teams.

The second type of bias that occurs at this stage concerns who started the riots. In many cases, it has been reported in Aligarh and elsewhere that Muslims have begun riots by rushing out from their mosques to attack the police or by engaging in destruction of property and arson. It is, indeed, sometimes the case that the "first stone" is thrown by Muslims. Newspapers that report such facts, however, may fail to mention the provocations that preceded the disturbances. The best example here has also been mentioned earlier, namely, the confrontations between Muslim crowds and the police duly reported in the press, which followed upon the hourly presentation on BBC television of the destruction of the mosque at Ayodhya that brought Muslims all over South Asia into the streets and into such confrontations. The overall impression produced by such reporting in general confirms the prevailing beliefs that it is always the Muslims who start the riots and the Hindus who suffer the most from them.[10]

These two biases are also linked to the more general problem raised in the introduction to this volume, of establishing causality in the initiation and explanation of riots. The question of explanation will be discussed below. Here, however, it is important to note that there is a parallel between newspaper reporting on the causes of riots and social science analyses of them. Both types of analyses often use the term *cause* to refer to the precipitating incident. In most cases that do not receive extensive coverage, all that remains in the press, police, and government records is the precipitating incident, which stands as the cause for all time to come. In the larger riotous events, where investigative reporting or in-depth social science analysis may enter, the distinction may then be made between the precipitating incident—the proximate cause—and the "real" or underlying cause. It has been a central methodological argument of this entire volume to demonstrate that this kind of reporting and social science analysis is misguided[11] and fails to perceive that there is not merely a difference between proximate and underlying causes, but a dynamic process of riot production at work, and, in sites such as Aligarh, an institutionalized system and network of violence production.

Once the killing begins, a third type of bias may enter, namely, the reporting by religion of the principal victims of rioting, the numbers killed, the property destroyed, and the like. While the local and vernacular newspapers sometimes do give "lurid details and community-wise breakdown of casualties and loss of property,"[12] the national, English-language press generally does not do so. Circumlocutions are often used such as references to a "particular community" having engaged in a particular action. However, even so, it is usually evident which community is meant by such a reference. The English-language press, however, does not report deaths by community during riots.

Nevertheless, the English-language press has been by no means free of bias and has sometimes reported false or misleading news in the midst of rioting.[13] The savage 1980 riots in Moradabad, near Aligarh District, which had their repercussions in Aligarh as well, marked a turning point in press reporting and editorial commentary. Although, as usual in post-Independence India, it was Muslims who suffered most, press reporting, including that from national and English-language dailies, displayed bias against Muslims.[14]

Particular references were made several times in previous chapters to the reporting in the *Times of India* during the heyday of Girilal Jain, its editor for many years. The paper did not generally publish false news or misreport such matters as particular incidents at particular sites, the numbers killed, or other specific events that could be falsified by other accounts, although it did even go to that extent on some occasions.[15] More characteristic of Girilal Jain's leadership, however, was the frequent publication during riots and in their immediate aftermath of insinuating comments suggesting Muslim responsibility for riots, reports of the presence of persons from Pakistan at the riot site, reports on the more rapid increase of the Muslim than the Hindu population in the country, articles and editorials deploring the violence and its consequences for the Muslims while expressing understanding at the same time of Hindu resentments,[16] and the like. Virtually all newspapers in India today also make specific reference to the Pakistan ISI whenever Hindu-Muslim riots occur, implying its direct or indirect involvement in them. Among the vernacular and local newspapers, publication of obviously false and inflammatory items is common. The false rumor of the Medical College Hospital murders in Aligarh has been mentioned several times in this volume, but many similar kinds of reports have been published in such newspapers at other riot sites at other times.[17]

In general, the press in north India is directly involved in the spread of rumors during riots that aids their perpetrators in recruiting and mobilizing participants, playing "a critical role in exacerbating tensions between Hindu and Muslim communities"[18] and in prolonging riotous activities. Even though the national press does not usually resort to open partiality toward one side or the other, or seek deliberately to exacerbate a developing riot situation, it does not act as an adequate antidote against those local papers that do so. Thus, during the Meerut riots of 1982, the national press paid little attention, whereas "the local Hindi press acting as the mouthpiece of the RSS, of course, played havoc by publishing inflammatory materials against minorities."[19]

In fairness, however, at the same time it must be noted that some newspapers and many journalists have from time to time done investigative reporting that has defied popular beliefs and established utterly different and more fulsome and accurate accounts of how major riots have begun, in which responsibility has also been pinpointed. Such has been the case, for example, in the reports on the massacres of the Sikhs in Delhi in 1984 during the funeral of Indira Gandhi, which provided ample evidence of the direct complicity of "high officials of the Congress"[20] and described how they recruited the killers and provided them with transportation to the sites targeted. It remains the case, however, that such reporting is exceptional and has not been sufficient to overcome prevailing beliefs and stereotypes concerning the origins of Hindu-Muslim riots.

Coming now to the question of explanation and interpretation in the aftermath of riots, here is the decisive moment when the prevailing discourse of Hindu-Muslim relations and the connection of the latter to the unity of the country emerges full-throated. It is also the time for blame displacement and dispersion. The local vernacular and sectarian press will, of course, blame the other side and place the riot in the perspective of the hostility of the other and the other's threat to the country (perceived by militant Hindus) or to secularism (perceived by Muslims). The framing and blaming that comes from the national English-language press is quite different. It produces and reproduces the hegemonic elite discourse that is threatened both by Hindu-Muslim rioting and by the communal and venomous subterranean discourses of hatred.

The structure of the elite discourse is substantially as follows. There is indeed a problem of Hindu-Muslim relations that arises from the country's history since the arrival of the Muslims in South Asia, from the division of the country in 1947 preceded by the Muslim separatist movement, and from the animosities that have developed between the two communities in consequence thereof. This situation is, however, seen as deplorable and must be overcome by statesmanship, secularism, and responsible behavior on the part of the political parties. Not only in Aligarh, but in the country as a whole, the AMU occupies a central symbolic place in this discourse. As a symbol standing in for the Muslim community as a whole, therefore, it must disown its alleged separatist past and declare and practice secularism, failing which its governance must be restructured to ensure it does so. Muslims in general must integrate fully into the mainstream of the country by abandoning their attachment to their own Personal Law and accepting a uniform civil code.

If the leadership of the country, the political parties, the communal organizations such as the RSS and the Jamaat-i-Islami, and the students and faculty at the AMU are allowed to play upon the existing Hindu-Muslim prejudices, then it is inevitable—in the discourse of Hindu-Muslim difference—that these prejudices will erupt in a communal conflagration. The metaphor of fire is commonly used by the press, as well as by the politicians and by the press when choosing its quotes from the politicians.[21] Fires also may spread, leading to conflagrations in other towns and districts. Another metaphor used by the press is "the communal virus" that, of course, also may spread through "contagion" from one place to another. In the early years after Independence and during the decade-long attempt to transform the character of the AMU from a predominantly Muslim minority institution to a more "secular" one, elements in both the right and the left wing in the press and elsewhere saw it as a source of this virus. Once again, the *Times of India* offers the clearest example. Referring to the 1956 riots in Aligarh, that paper blamed the AMU students for the outbreak there and for its spread to other parts of the state. At the same time, it conflated the problems at the university with the attitudes of Muslims in the country as a whole; moving back and forth between the AMU and the alleged communalism of its students and teachers, it raised questions about Muslim loyalty to the country and Muslim sympathies for Pakistan.[22]

The second frame in the discourse of explanation for Hindu-Muslim riots is interparty competition, which has also been identified in this book as a central element in the production of such riots. However, the emphasis in the press is different from the one presented here. I have shown that there is a specific relationship between the production of riots and the communalization and polarization of the electorate and suggested that the targeting of particular sites in the town of Aligarh is designed both to produce that effect and to punish Muslims whose voting patterns either prevent the BJP from achieving dominance or endanger it. While the press sometimes provides evidence to support these statements, when the time comes for explanation in editorial and other commentary, it is usually the appeals of the parties to voters by caste or community that are condemned, rarely the deliberate involvement of specific political parties in riot production for their own advantage. By their appeals, it is implied, the parties contribute to the acting out on the part of the *public* of their animosities and hatreds.

Within both frames, therefore, that of the history of intercommunal relations and that of contemporary interparty conflict—which in turn are closely linked to each other in the discourse itself—blame is dispersed in press reporting and commentary. It lands on a general target, such as the communal prejudices of the population as a whole or the attitudes of Muslims in general, or it lands nowhere in particular.

PART VI

*Conclusion*

# 16 / The Persistence of Hindu-Muslim Violence

## The Dynamics of Riot Production

Riots persist in India and have become endemic at a multiplicity of sites in the subcontinent. They constitute, in effect, a normal, routine aspect of politics whose very normality and routine character are masked by both the sincere and hypocritical comments that follow in the aftermath of their most savage occurrences. So long as they are considered abnormal, exceptional, expressions of a disease that occasionally afflicts the polity, acts committed by the dregs of society drawn from the slums they inhabit, so long will their commonness remain hidden from view. So long, then, will the political elites, the educated, the upper-caste intellectuals, the editors of leading newspapers be able to reassure themselves that they live still in a basically peaceful land, in the world's largest democracy where such aberrations are bound to occur in the process of India's advance from backwardness to modernity.

On the more hypocritical side lie the simplistic explanations offered by the leaders of competing political parties, namely, that it was the other party that was responsible. Among some parties such as the BJP, the hypocrisy rises to an even greater height, where the national leaders of the party go to the extent of acknowledging that riots have been promoted at the local level by elements from their own party, and that, as L. K. Advani said to me years ago, "we know about" these people, implying that they would cleanse them from the lower levels of the party as soon as practicable. The height of that hypocrisy was, of course, reached at Ayodhya when the national leaders of the entire RSS family, its middle-level leaders from the districts, and many tens of thousands of their followers descended upon Ayodhya to destroy the mosque, after which some feigned surprise and blamed excessive zeal on some of their followers, when in fact the evidence of preplanning was overwhelming and the personal satisfaction of all those I saw and interviewed after the fact can only be described as joyous.

355

Riots, therefore, first and foremost persist because they are unacknowledged and illegitimate but well-known and accepted transgressions of routine political behavior in India. Moreover, the types of riots discussed in this book are only one form in the repertoire of collective violent enactments that exist widely in India, including the engagement of the Indian state in protracted civil warfare with insurrectionary groups, intracommunal sectarian violence, intercaste riots, the spread of mafia violence and criminality in the rural areas of north India, intergang killings, police-public confrontations of all sorts,[1] and the everyday violence everywhere in India of police against citizens. In one sense, therefore, Hindu-Muslim riots are but one form among many types of persisting violence in India. In another sense, however, such riots have a special status in that country because of the degree to which they go to the root of the identities of the two largest categories of its population and of that of the South Asian subcontinent as a whole, identities that are still being formed in the very crucible of violent conflicts. In this sense, they are linked with the two other much more violent forms of Hindu-Muslim confrontation in South Asia, namely, the war between Muslim separatists and the Indian state in Kashmir, and the perpetual hot-and-cold war between India and Pakistan. Indeed, in the minds of militant Hindus especially, all three of these sites of violence are marked upon a single grid of Hindu-Muslim confrontation for supremacy in the South Asian subcontinent. In their minds, the everyday riots in towns such as Aligarh and elsewhere are part of a single, much larger struggle.

But Hindu-Muslim riots have a distinct dynamic that shares some features with, but differs more substantially from, insurrectionary warfare between states and citizens or outright war between sovereign states. Those differences cannot be spelled out here, but they can be summarized in a nutshell as revolving around axes of unanticipated/anticipated, spontaneous/planned, illegitimate/legitimate. Riots, not entirely unlike insurrections and external wars, are said to break out either unexpectedly or as a consequence of a buildup of tensions that may or may not explode under fortuitous circumstances. Unlike most insurrections and wars, however, they are said to be primarily spontaneous rather than planned. They are also acknowledged by all, including the perpetrators, as illegitimate. All who justify the violence of their own side in riots allege that they acted only in retaliation, the aggressor's synonym for self-defense. The whole purpose of this book has been to demonstrate the falseness of these distinctions.

It is not my purpose to argue that there is a family resemblance between Hindu-Muslim riots and the civil war in Kashmir or the wars between India and Pakistan. Rather, these riots are another form of that conflict enacted and reenacted in minor fracases and disputes every day in the mixed *mohallas* of towns such as Aligarh. These riots have a form, a sequencing, and a dynamic of their own that must be masked in a self-proclaimed democracy in ways that are not required in civil and international wars. I have tried to penetrate the dynamic process in this book. I want to summarize here some aspects of that dynamic, to demonstrate the functional utility of riots, and to conclude by indicating the embeddedness of the justifications and explanations for Hindu-Muslim riots in the discourse of communalism, Hindu nationalism, and the different historical consciousnesses that reveal themselves in the attitudes of Hindu and Muslim protagonists.

## PREPARING THE GROUND FOR RIOTS

### Communal Tension

Most riots are *anticipated*. They are preceded by a period that is usually described as marked by *tension*. Everyone knows when tension is in the air, from ordinary citizens to the authorities of the district and, if the situation appears to be very threatening, to the state authorities as well. The term *tension* has both specific and vague connotations in the English language.[2] It implies tautness, as in a wire, strained to the utmost. It also refers specifically to "strained relations between persons or groups" and to "uneasy suspense."[3] In Aligarh, secondary accounts of the genesis of riots, and my respondents as well, often referred to the communal tension that preceded Hindu-Muslim riots. Such tension was sometimes said to have been precipitated by a specific incident, sometimes by a series of incidents that led to a building up of tension over a longer period.

Several perspectives emerge from documentary and interview sources on the relationship between communal tension and riots in Aligarh. At one extreme is the view that communal tension is a palpable and pervasive element in the life of the city. It is a kind of smoldering fire that can erupt into flames over any kind of incident, however trivial, in which actions are taken by members of one community that offend or harm a member or members of the other community. This perspective is embedded in the view commonly held throughout the world that riots arise out of spontaneous feelings of passion in societies where interethnic prejudices and hostilities are endemic and have a long history.

At the other extreme is the view that communal tension and the riots that follow in its aftermath are deliberate creations of avaricious businessmen and politicians, among other types of people sometimes mentioned—criminals and hooligans, for example. This view is often associated with the idea that riots are not spontaneous occurrences, but deliberately planned actions by individuals, groups, and organizations. The creation of communal tension is part of the process. Incidents are provoked, processions are taken out, mass mobilizations are organized deliberately to offend the sensibilities of the other community's members. Economic and political advantages are gained both from the tension and from the violence that sometimes follows such actions.

The perspective that seems most consistent with the results of my investigations over the years in Aligarh and elsewhere is that there are elements both of spontaneity and planning that contribute to the creation and persistence of communal tension and its development into riots. It is not that the two extreme views are completely wrong, but that they miss the action that takes place in intermediate space and time, between the prejudices that exist in Aligarh society and in every multiethnic, multicultural society in the world, on the one hand, and the undeniable element of purposive, planned action that accompanies every riot, on the other hand. Riots do not occur accidentally like fires from a smoldering flame nor are they meticulously planned and coordinated from beginning to end. Rather, they are dramatic productions, street theater performances that are meant to appear spontaneous, but that involve many people in a variety of roles and actions that include inciting the interest of the audience, the dramatization and enlargement of incidents into a fit subject for a performance, and, finally, the production of the event.

The people of Aligarh, like devotees of theater, are kept in a state of readiness for the next production through advertising of all kinds of trivial incidents that hold the promise of a great drama to follow. It is never certain whether or when the drama is going to be produced, because the production depends on propitious circumstances, especially political circumstances such as mass mobilizations and elections, anticipated or in progress. But the audience's interests and appetite must not be allowed to flag in the intermediate time between productions, for each production involves audience participation. There are many bit players who must be kept ready for action and myriad walk-on parts to be played.[4] The bit players are the criminals and hooligans brought in when the circumstances are propitious to start an action. The walk-on parts are played by those people in the *mohallas* who are always ready to come out for a fracas, to whom the word must be spread that an action, a production, is about to take place. All the events that take place in intermediate space and time to maintain a state of communal tension or to increase it when it flags are rehearsals for the production of riots.

## Rumors

Virtually everyone who has written about riots has given a central place to rumors. In fact, tensions and rumors go together.[5] Rumors keep tensions alive in areas where riots are endemic and are an integral part of the buildup of tension that takes place before a riot starts. During riots, rumors are used to sustain "the momentum of violence."[6] They keep "the crowds in an excited, potential mob state."[7]

In most accounts, rumors are seen as the "fuel" that sets aflame the combustible material of interethnic or intercommunal hostilities.[8] This association between rumor and riot is also critical to the predominant view of riots as events that arise spontaneously out of intergroup animosities.[9] Everyone seems to agree as well concerning the function of rumors in the fomenting of riots, namely, to communicate rapidly. Such rapid communication is especially effective when large crowds are gathered for recreational or other purposes,[10] but they can also "circulate at high velocity by word of mouth"[11] even without the availability of large, massed audiences. In fact, however, as with everything else about this approach, the association between rumors and riots gives a false impression. In this case, the false impression is that rumors somehow appear, spread like wildfire, arouse the passions of a community, move people into the streets into crowds that then join forces, massing into larger and larger groups as they assemble and march towards the quarters inhabited by other ethnic groups to retaliate for the atrocity or atrocities the news of which has been spread by the rumors.

Among writers on riots, few have challenged this simplistic notion. Keith is one who has done so. For one thing, he has noted, "rumours of imminent trouble abound" in local communities when news of a riot elsewhere is spread by the media, but, in fact, nothing at all happens in most communities, in which the rumors fly as fast as in the areas where violence does in fact take place.[12] Although he notes that "many parts of London . . . were . . . pump primed" during the 1981 disturbances by stories emanating from "the local gossipmongers and rumour-hawkers who constructed folk discussion in the metaphor of contagion," in most such areas there was no violence. In Keith's view, this nonresponse to rumors is "one of the most powerful arguments against the classification of collective violence as irrational."[13] If one agrees with Keith, as I do, then what are we to make of the universal presence of rumors that precede riots everywhere in the world and everywhere in history? If there was ever a case for a causal theory and a universal law, then surely it lies in the role of rumors as the fuel for riots.

In Aligarh, rumors have been present before, during, and after every riot in its history. Moreover, Pars Ram and Gardner Murphy's UNESCO study of communal tensions in Aligarh, for which the research was done shortly after Partition, noted that rumors abounded in the city as part of the daily life and fears of Muslims who had been transformed by Partition into "a very insecure minority group." The rumors that haunted them were that "their shops [would] be looted and disappear at night," that they would be attacked as "cow-killers," or that there would be "new killings" during the Hindu festival of Holi.[14] As in the case of the Russian pogroms of 1881, rumors in Aligarh in 1951 even assigned specific dates for the beginning of the next Hindu-Muslim rioting.[15]

However, rumors that reflect the fears of minority groups are not the kind that play a role in mobilization of crowds for violent action. These are the buzzing rumors of the marketplace. The more ominous rumors that signal the beginnings of mobilization and presage violence are those that report on an attack of some sort by a person of one community upon another, alleged to have taken place somewhere in the city. A rumor, after all, is "unverified information of uncertain origin."[16] Most such rumors in Aligarh and elsewhere arise out of actual or concocted incidents, often "minor incidents of a purely private character between two individuals or two groups (one Hindu and the other Muslim)" said to have occurred "in an out of the way place and at an unfrequented spot by a person whose identity had not been established by his victim."[17] But these types of rumors also often fly fast and loose and nothing at all happens in their aftermath.

Yet it is also the case that an increase in the density of rumors precedes and accompanies the start of violence. Such was the case before and during the long series of riots that began with the stabbing of the Hindu wrestler, Bhura, in 1978. This stabbing incident itself became the basis for a rumor that it was an act of retaliation by Muslims for the defeat of their group of wrestlers by the Hindu wrestlers. But other rumors soon followed, for example, that a Hindu sweet-seller in the Babri Mandi (market) had also been stabbed by a Muslim.[18] In such times, any private quarrel may be used to provide a kernel of fact to give credence to a rumor. Thus, a quarrel between two Muslims over a money debt in Phul Chauraha led to a stabbing in November 1978, but the rumor that was spread was that "members of different communities had been stabbed."[19]

But the rumor of rumors in the history of Hindu-Muslim riots in Aligarh was the totally false and concocted story of the AMU Medical Hospital murders. The PUCL report on this matter, cited in detail above, characterized this rumor as "motivated and orchestrated propaganda against the Medical College Hospital."[20] Let us recall also the salient features of this rumor, the persons and groups with whom it was associated, and the target towards which it was directed. It was deliberately and maliciously published in well-known and respected Hindi newspapers; it was spread further, locally, by known persons such as the Agarwal brothers, cloth merchants, and members of the RSS-dominated Vyapar Mandal; and it was directed at the central symbol of the Muslim community in India, the AMU. Moreover, it was accompanied by mobilization of crowds under the leadership of known persons and groups, including Krishna Kumar Navman and the RSS. Finally, it occurred in the midst of rioting that had already begun. It was, therefore, an instrument in the pursuit of violence used by known persons and groups and directed at a specific target.

There is, therefore, little or nothing that is either arbitrary or spontaneous about the occurrence of this rumor and others of its type. On the contrary, as exemplified especially in the case of the AMU, certain sites become perennial sources of rumors that have a specific purpose. Rumors serve the purpose of mobilizing members of a community for attack or defense. Rumors that affect the AMU generally serve the purpose of mobilizing Hindus in the city for attack upon that living *lieu de mémoire* of violence, confrontation, and the Partition that many Hindus refer to as the vivisection of India. Moreover, the rumors that revolve around AMU are repetitive: the same stories appear over and over at times of riot.

In order, therefore, to clarify the specific relationship between riots and rumors, I think it is necessary to distinguish between what Keith calls mere "gossipmongers," whose rumormongering may have no effect in the mobilization of crowds for violent action, and those who play a specialized role in the spreading of rumors,[21] whose activities are integral to the dynamic process of riot-production. The latter rumors are not randomly articulated from some general pool of blood libel accusations and are not directed randomly either. In local situations such as Aligarh, rumors that are designed to mobilize violent crowds will pinpoint a specific incident—which may be true, false, or exaggerated—in a specific *mohalla* or at the AMU to arouse crowds either to move to that place to retaliate or to take vengeance against those seen as the blood brothers of the perpetrators of a particular atrocity. They provide excuses for violent action that also is not random, that targets members of a particular group in particular areas or all the members of a particular group identified by lists provided to the crowds. Those screaming for blood and revenge in the crowd are making use of slogans provided to them as a justification for actions that serve either their interests or those of their political organizations, or for which they are paid, partly in cash and partly by the loot they gain—under the cover provided by the crowds so massed, by the justification given for the violence, and by the near certainty that they will escape prosecution.

If effective rumormongering is a specialized task in the process of riot production, so is the squelching of rumors an important task in the containment of riots. Suppression or denial of rumors may be undertaken by the authorities, the press, or responsible spokesmen from communities in potential conflict who deliberately take on this role.[22] But it would be a mistake to imagine that suppressive activities can be effective in situations where an institutionalized riot system is in operation, for in such situations, the rumors are a signal for action designed to bring out local party activists with their henchmen and gangs who are always ready to come out for pay and loot. It is not administrative or media action to suppress rumors that is critical, but swift administrative and police action to break up the crowds that form and to impose an impartial and effective curfew. If there is no such action, then the opportunities for loot and vengeance under the cover of rumors will encourage others to leave their homes and join the crowds. However, it is certainly the case that, in situations of high tension and the wild spreading of malicious rumors, most people are likely to prefer to close their shops, shut their windows, and seek to stay out of trouble. Those who participate in riots are not aroused merely by rumors, but by the organizational and mobilizing activities of practitioners skilled in the production of crowds and riots and by the opportunities made available for anonymous violent, destructive, and thieving actions in the crowds that are massed.

Rumors are a sign, a means of communication, a method of mobilizing an action and, sometimes, of stopping an anticipated action by the other side, as well as a tool used by politicians to gain support from a group that feels threatened by the possibility of violence. Rumors are first of all signs of the existence of a serious and potentially violent dispute. Members of opposed sides are attuned to the slightest move attributed to the other side toward a possible change in the status quo. Second, they warn one side of the possibility of an action by the other. Third, they serve to mobilize the side so warned. The function of this mobilization may be to attack or to demonstrate strength so as to prevent the rumored disruption of the status quo.

In areas where riots are endemic, rumors are routine and so are the mobilizations that follow them. The mobilizations that take place in such circumstances are of the type that give the impression of spontaneity, but it would be wiser to consider them routinization of a practice of confrontation for the sake of defense. Rumors sustain the tension that precipitates an unending stream of rumors that act not simply as the means of massing mindless crowds, but as the weapons of attack and defense in communities used to the perpetual threat and danger of violence to members who might be caught alone, isolated, and vulnerable to violence from members of the other community. Such massing may also be a form of defense against anticipated police action.[23]

What then are we to make of the statement by Veena Das that "there is no contradiction between the fact that, on the one hand, mob violence may be highly organized and crowds provided with such instruments as voters' lists or combustible powers, and on the other that crowds draw upon repositories of unconscious images" reflected in the fast-flying rumors "that crowds use to define themselves and their victims"?[24] Rumors certainly do have a function of arousal. They are most effective when they draw upon images, prejudices, and myths derived from family upbringing, socialization in community schools, or in school textbooks in government schools, that provide a distorted history, and political indoctrination. All these elements function within the discourse of Hindu-Muslim difference and antagonism that pervades contemporary Indian society, especially in northern and western India. But that discourse operates primarily as a source for explanation and blame displacement, for the maintenance of a set of power relations in Indian society that operates to the advantage of upper-caste Hindus and to the disadvantage of Muslims, many among the backward castes, and the lower castes. It justifies violent action against Muslims, explains how communal antagonisms persist, and suggests how the predominant groups and political organizations maintain or gain power, but it does not explain the specific actions of violent crowds.

Rumors may reflect deep psychological fears and animosities, but too much attention to that aspect of rumors can mislead us and has misled countless observers of riots concerning their function. Moreover, such an approach draws us too close to the type of explanation that focuses on mass hatred and animosities as an explanation for riots. Rumors decidedly have specific roles in riots and play a major role in mobilization for attack and defense. They are important instruments in the politics of violence to which the authorities must pay attention, but it is critical to distinguish the ordinary rumors that abound in daily life, which may provide source material for psychologists and psychoanalysts, from those that have specific functions that may or may not arouse persecutory and demonizing fantasies. It is the latter that are the material for the political and sociological analysis of riot production.

The actions of violent crowds and the explanations for their actions constitute separate, though interrelated, spheres. They depend on each other, but they constitute different arenas. How rumors have been treated in the literature on riots is an example of the confusion that may obfuscate the difference between the spheres. The psychological analysis of rumors belongs more in the sphere of explanation of riots by means of blame displacement, the functional analysis in the sphere of explanation of riot production as social action. When the differences are obfuscated and the two types of explanation become complementary, as they have been in contemporary India, they act together to perpetuate riotous violence. When they diverge, that is, when the explanations for riots reject the discursive framework into which they have been placed and which sustains them, and instead offer alternative explanations and ameliorative measures that replace the existing hegemonic discourse, in this case the discourse of Hindu-Muslim antagonism, then riotous violence may subside or take other forms.

### Provocation

It is common in causal analysis of riots to make a distinction between precipitating and underlying or "real" causes. The precipitating incidents, such as a police action against a Black citizen in an American city, are often considered to be fortuitous circumstances that may precipitate a riot because of the simmering rage that exists among Black people against police harassment, harm, and killing of Blacks in the past. The incident then acts as a trigger that sets off a spontaneous conflagration arising out of that rage, the root cause.

Often, however, riots are produced as a consequence of direct provocation, of which there are myriad forms in the Indian repertoire of riot production. Probably the most common is a universal form, the procession, which is enacted sometimes in a fashion that has clear parallels in other societies and cultures, sometimes with a distinctively Indian cultural flavor. Such processions have a long history in Indian demonstrations, both those that have been deliberately nonviolent and those that have been deliberately provocative and inciting towards violence.

The procession may or may not be a deliberate provocation. Sometimes it is an assertion of a right to use of public space, sometimes an assertion of the strength of the group whose members have taken it out, but there are certain types of processions that are deliberately designed to incite. In the latter category are processions of one community that deliberately pass through localities inhabited by another, that stop before religious places of the other community to play music or hurl insults, that in other ways interfere with the peace or even the property of the other community. Especially provocative and/or intimidating are processions that involve displays of arms, including in the Indian context *lathis* (bamboo sticks) and swords.

Among the distinctively Indian processions that have often provoked intercommunal violence are the Ram Lila processions that occur every year in most Hindu communities throughout north India in celebration of the god Ram, a celebration that is also associated with actual dramatic re-creations of Ram's life. Most such processions do not lead to Hindu-Muslim confrontations, but many of them have done so and many have been used deliberately to provoke Muslims by passing through their localities. Such religious processions and celebrations have for over a hundred years in northern and western India been susceptible to takeover by political leaders and groups for mobilization of Hindus for nationalist purposes, that is, against British rule, but also to provoke Muslims. In north India, the god Ram himself has become the political emblem of the RSS family of organizations and Ram Lila and Ram Navami processions are often led by or turned into provocative displays by militant Hindu organizations, including the VHP and the Bajrang Dal. On such occasions, competitive rallies of protest against or support for such processions and the particular routes they follow may also occur. The ultimate procession for Ram was the *rath yatra* of L. K. Advani that left many hundreds of Muslims dead in its wake.

Especially provocative are funerary processions in which the dead body of a member of one community allegedly killed by a person from the other community is carried through localities containing large concentrations of the other. This tactic also appears to be a recent addition to the repertoire of riot-provoking actions used by militant Hindu organizations. I have described one such in Kanpur in December 1992. The outstanding example from Aligarh was the funeral procession of the wrestler Bhura that precipitated the first in the very long series of riots that began in October 1978. The funeral processions in Kanpur and Aligarh shared the following features: forcible removal of the dead body from the hospital by a mob, which then formed a procession that moved through localities heavily populated by Muslims, the shouting of provocative slogans along the way,[25] leading finally to the signals and actions marking the beginning of a riot, namely, stone throwing, arson, the sound of gunshots, and the first killing(s). In both cases, also, RSS and BJP activists were present throughout.

We have seen yet other types of actions that are alleged to be part of the repertoire of riot provocations. The most grisly cited herein consists of the deliberate killing of a person of a particular community, his dismemberment, and the tossing of his body parts into a gutter to be found by persons from one of the communities in order to incite a so-called retaliatory action against the other community. I have no data that would indicate how often riots of any scale have been attributed to such actions. What needs to be noted about this type of action, however, is that it implies a deliberate action designed at least to maintain intercommunal animosities at a high level or to deliberately provoke a riot. Such an action, therefore, does contrast with other forms such as processions, which may be designed only to assert a right, demonstrate strength, and intimidate, but not necessarily and always to provoke a major confrontation.

### WHY DO RIOTS PERSIST?

Hindu-Muslim communal riots have been an integral part of the political process in modern India since the 1920s. Although, since then, there has never been an extended period of time when Hindu-Muslim riots have not occurred somewhere in India, there have been times when they have occurred in waves or chains that have covered large parts of the country, in the post-Independence period notably during Partition and before and after the great militant Hindu mobilization in the late 1980s that persisted until the destruction of the mosque at Ayodhya on December 6, 1992. The history of post-Independence riots in Aligarh has provided illustration at a single site of riots that have been confined to the city with no apparent connection to events elsewhere, those that have occurred more or less simultaneously with riots in adjacent areas under similar circumstances, and those that have occurred in the midst of a great wave. In effect, Aligarh can stand for India as whole in important respects. It is a site in which Hindu-Muslim riots may occur as a consequence of local quarrels, issues, and confrontations between members of the two communities; as a routine part of the political and electoral process framed within the local political context; or as a part of processes of wide political mobilization in the larger political context of the state or the country as a whole.

One answer, therefore, to the question why riots persist in Aligarh, U.P., and India is simply because, despite all protestations to the contrary, they are part of the general armory of weapons used by activists and interested parties within both communities for personal, local, and political advantage and by political activists and leaders to forge solidarity within their respective communities in order to defeat their opponents in elections. As such, therefore, there is in a sense nothing more to explain about riots than there is about why there are quarrels, conflicts, and violence in general in Aligarh or elsewhere in India, and in very large parts of the rest of the world, for that matter. Riots are simply there and they are there for as many reasons as there are for nonviolent conflicts. Moreover, there are other kinds of riots that occur regularly in India among Muslims and Hindus, notably Shia-Sunni riots among Muslims and intercaste riots among Hindus. Once one accepts that there are certain frameworks within which both violent and nonviolent contestation occurs within a particular country, the explanatory problem appears almost to dissolve. The issue then becomes *how,* not why, riots take place within a particular frame, that is, it becomes a processual issue bearing the forms just described, more than an issue requiring causal explanation.

Still, there is variation as well as persistence in the occurrence of riots in Aligarh, U.P., and India within the Hindu-Muslim framework. They do not occur with the same frequency as other events, particularly scheduled events such as elections, with which they are often associated. I have marshalled sufficient evidence, I hope, to demonstrate the latter association, particularly to show that large-scale communal riots are often staged events whose effect, if not their deliberate intention, is to produce communal solidarity to gain electoral advantage in a political context in which no other stratagem would work so well. I want to stress once again here that, for the most part, it is riots that produce solidarity, not electoral politics that produce riots. Those who argue that it is "democracy," electoral participation, the spontaneous enactment of "ancient hatreds," or the popular animosities of the masses that cause riots are undermining the foundations of competitive political processes. When one recognizes that it can work the other way and, on my evidence, works that way more often than not, it takes the burden off the masses, the electoral process, and "democracy," because authoritarian regimes also produce not only riots, but massacres and genocides directed at other ethnic, tribal, or religious groups when it is politically convenient to do so.

But I have also shown that there is variation in the temporal and spatial occurrence of rioting within Aligarh as well as in U.P. and India as a whole. I have examined all the causal factors that have been put forward in the literature on which I could provide evidence: personal, demographic, economic, and political. I have argued that particular personal, demographic, and economic factors play their parts in particular riots. I have also argued that all these factors come into play simultaneously in the larger riots. I have further established that the larger riots always occur within a context of political competition that they serve to intensify. Most important, I have argued that these latter riots, especially, are productions that involve constant rehearsal, careful timing, and specific targets of attack. From this perspective, most causal explanations of rioting of the type examined in this book, namely, interreligious or interracial or interethnic, appear to me to be flawed from the start. They have turned the independent variable into a dependent variable. They have sought to explain riots rather than to understand the purposes and effects of riots in interpersonal, economic, intercommunal, and political relations.

From this latter perspective, much that has appeared mysterious and elusive appears almost unproblematic. Is it surprising that, under the cover of large-scale rioting, individuals loot and rape and take vengeance on their enemies? Certainly not, but it is, on the other hand, ludicrous to consider that riots are caused by the desire for loot, rape, and vengeance. Is it surprising that Hindu-Muslim riots take place at sites where there are large Hindu and Muslim populations living side by side or in close proximity? Of course not, but tautological explanations for rioting have been common in the literature on Hindu-Muslim rioting in India and Black-white rioting in the U.S., presenting as causal findings statistical or impressionistic associations between the relative sizes of these two types of opposed groups living in juxtaposition to each other. Is it surprising that riots occur when authority is weak and vacillating and that they occur more rarely or not at all when authority is strong and determined to suppress them? Hardly, but such associations turned into causal explanations have provided justifications for authoritarian solutions to perceived social problems.

Is it surprising that riots occur in filthy slums in India and Black ghettos in the United States? Certainly not, but are the slums and the ghettos the causes of rioting? The answer in the literature is likely to be that they are, that the one produces economic distress that manifests itself in rioting, that the other arises from the discrimination that produces and polices the ghettos. But, of course, this does not work either, because not all slums and ghettos are centers of riot production. Yet, I have myself argued that slums and ghettos provide fertile grounds for riot production, not because of economic distress or discrimination in the abstract but for two other reasons: first, they provide a recruiting ground for specialists in crime and violence; second, communities within some slums and ghettos organize for attack and/or defense against the other community. The explanation may sound similar, but it is not; the reversal of terms is significant because it introduces agency, purpose, and practice.

The explanation provided for riots in this volume might bettter be described as purposive rather than causal. I say that *riots are dramatic productions, creations of specific persons, groups, and parties operating through institutionalized riot networks within a discursive framework of Hindu-Muslim communal opposition and antagonism that in turn produces specific forms of political practice that make riots integral to the political process*. Further, they generate post hoc interpretations, analyses, and explanations that are in no way scientific or adequate to yield satisfying causal statements, but rather themselves contribute to the persistence of riots. Just as drama cannot persist without drama critics who, through the media, provide audiences for some types of productions and not others, so Hindu-Muslim riots cannot persist without journalistic and academic interpretations and explanations of them that focus our gaze upon them and treat them as social problems rather than as intolerable violent productions. However, there is a difference here between the production of a dramatic play and the production of collective violence because, in the latter case, the violence is treated as evidence of a social problem for which there is no feasible solution since our gaze is directed away from the actors in the play to the nebulous realm of the causes of the existence of the drama.

It has proven difficult to answer the question, "What causes riots?" I have argued that, in effect, it is a misdirected question. It should rather be asked, who—individuals, organizations, groups—produces riots, how and when do they produce them, and how is our attention diverted from questions that could be answered to questions that cannot? But then, it is not sufficient to say that riots are produced by riot-mongers, even if we elaborate and provide details on the processual dynamics of riot production. That would be as if Robert Merton ended his analysis of machine politics by describing the ways in which the machines were built by the big party bosses and how they functioned. But Merton did not do that. In fact, the dynamics of machine politics were well known when he wrote, so he asked a further question, namely, how does one explain their persistence?

I want, therefore, now to present a set of more precise conclusions concerning the reasons for the persistence of Hindu-Muslim riots under conditions that obtain in India today. Those conclusions come under four headings: the functional utility of riots, the role of the state, the operations of institutionalized riot systems, and the role of contextualization.

*The Functional Utility of Riots*

Riots in Aligarh, as elsewhere in U.P., provide immediate material benefits for many persons. The beneficiaries mentioned over and over again in interviews include criminals, avaricious local businessmen and profiteers, and local politicians who gain political advantage by taking the role of protectors of the people of a particular community. Many explanations of the causes of riots in Aligarh have been provided in which one or more of these groups play critical roles. Marxists and other persons on the left, especially, argue that businessmen pay criminals to start riots from which both groups gain in precise ways.[26] Criminals get not only the money from businessmen, but the loot that becomes available during the course of a riot in which they may act with impunity and freedom from fear of arrest.[27] Businessmen gain advantage from the damage or destruction done to the property of their rivals. But virtually all persons interviewed, of whatever ideological persuasion, give a central place to politicians for fomenting riots in order to win the support of members of their own community by causing trouble for the other community and protecting or providing relief to their own.

One does not have to decide, however, whether such and such a riot or series of riots would have taken place had criminals been apprehended or eliminated, avaricious and dishonest businessmen arrested and prosecuted, communal politicians denied by a responsible party leadership the nominations of their parties to contest elections. It is sufficiently clear that all these forces are at work and that such measures would be beneficial. They cannot, however, all be undertaken at once and some cannot be undertaken at all.

Towards the end of the long series of riots between 1978 and 1980, a zealous police officer, in complete disregard of universal standards of proper police behavior, allegedly executed by extrajudicial means the most notorious, mostly Muslim criminals in Aligarh, after which no major riots occurred in the town for a decade. In some minds, the cause and the remedy are evident from these presumed facts. But then, the riots in 1990–91 were the worst ever seen in Aligarh, including the period 1946 to 1948. Those riots were associated with a broad Hindu mobilization in the state as a whole from which militant Hindus sought political advantage in the full knowledge that their actions were bound to lead to violence and bloodshed, much of which was directly fomented by their followers in districts such as Aligarh.

But then, what has happened to the explanation for riots in which criminals play such a central role? Did a new generation of criminals arise in Aligarh in the intervening decade or is it the political context that is decisive after all?

The evidence suggests it is the latter. Criminals can be found when needed, but they cannot produce riots on their own, as one of my informants put it. "Without [a] political force, you can't force [a] riot. *Goonda*[s are in the] forefront. You can purchase them, but if there is no politics, there is no political force behind them, they can't do [it]."[28] And what about the popular mentality of the people, their communal psyche, about which several respondents, especially in the police, spoke so clearly? In fact, all these aspects must be built into a full treatment of the production of riots, their dynamics, how they begin, and how they run their course.

We have learned enough from Aligarh to know that, while the causes of riots must inevitably remain contestable, consensus can be reached on who benefits from them. Our interview respondents in Aligarh disagreed fundamentally on their causes, but their explanations invariably involved displacement of blame. And through that process of blame displacement, we found a remarkable consensus concerning the identification of particular sets of beneficiaries. Of course, our party was not responsible, but the other was. Of course, our peace committee did not misuse funds for the relief of riot victims, theirs did. Yes, of course, criminals are active in riots and paid to instigate them, but it is done by the other side. One is led inexorably to the unsettling conclusion, therefore, that all persons involved are guilty, though some more than others. At one extreme, some are clearly responsible for direct physical acts or instigation of them. At the other extreme, some are responsible only to the extent that they refuse to see the ways in which their own talk and action or nonaction or that of their party or group may contribute to the persistence of communal hostility.

It is at this point that the whole political order in post-Independence north India and many, if not most, of its leading as well as local actors—more markedly so since the death of Nehru—become implicated in the persistence of Hindu-Muslim riots. These riots have had concrete benefits for particular political organizations as well as larger political uses. Under the first heading, it is evident that Hindu-Muslim opposition, tensions, and violence have provided the principal justification for and the primary source of strength for the political existence of some local political organizations in Aligarh and elsewhere in north India. While the Jan Sangh, the BJP, and all the organizations in the RSS family of organizations adhere to a broader ideology of Hindutva, of Hindu nationalism, that theoretically exists independently of Hindu-Muslim antagonisms, in practice that ideology has thrived only when that opposition is explicitly or implicitly present. In Aligarh, that opposition is always explicitly present because of the existence of the Aligarh Muslim

University, which stands in for the Muslims of India, for Partition and the creation of Pakistan, and for so many of the ills that afflict Indian society. Without the presence of the Aligarh Muslim University, the Jan Sangh, the BJP, and other local communal groups would have had greater difficulty in establishing a strong presence in the city.

But it is not just in riot-prone cities and towns such as Aligarh that political benefits are derived from Hindu-Muslim opposition. It has spread its benefits even further, to the most important north Indian and all-Indian political organizations as well as to organizations and movements within the Hindu and Muslim communities. Hindu-Muslim opposition has had such larger political uses since Independence. It has benefited organizations that claim to speak for the provincial victims of communal riots, the Muslims, by aiding them in the organization and consolidation of the Muslims of the country to gain political advantage, prevent the loss of special concessions such as the preservation of the Muslim Personal Law, and preserve their cultural institutions such as the Aligarh Muslim University itself. The fact that Muslim political consolidation has usually backfired in post-Independence India is another matter. The main point is that Muslim political leaders have hoped otherwise and have played upon the real sufferings of Muslims in towns such as Aligarh to build broader political movements. Does this then mean that these political leaders have wanted Hindu-Muslim riots? Usually not, but their focus has been on using them for purposes of political mobilization rather than on stopping them.

It is not so apparent, however, how useful the persistence of Hindu-Muslim riots has been for the secular nationalists who are supposedly their greatest opponents. Yet, from the very foundation of the Indian state, the Partition and the Hindu-Muslim violence that occurred during that time as well as the intermittent violence that continued thereafter for the next fifty years have been central to the secular nationalist justification of the need to create in India a composite nationalism, a united people, and a strong centralized state.[29] It has been argued that the very division of India into two hostile communities, created by the machinations of the separatist Muslim League, has made it necessary to strive ever harder to counter this hostility by recognizing their separate existence and their right to maintain separate cultural and religious and legal institutions *recognized by the state*. It is not, as in the United States, that the state is not allowed to interfere in the religious and cultural domains of the diverse religious communities, but that the state in India is called upon to enforce and patronize—supposedly equally, to be sure—the religious practices, laws, and institutions of these separate communities.[30]

But we have also seen in Aligarh that the secular parties use riots for purposes of political mobilization as do the Hindu communal parties, in their case to mobilize the Muslim community to vote for them on the grounds that only they can provide the necessary protection to the Muslims against their enemies. The Congress did so even during Nehru's tenure, and more especially during Mrs. Gandhi's tenure in office until she switched her strategy to pandering to the Hindu communal vote. The Janata Dal under V. P. Singh gathered the Muslims under its wing as the Congress turned away from them and appealed to Hindu sentiment by opening the gates of the Babri Masjid to Hindu worship. The Samajwadi Party of Mulayam Singh Yadav also built virtually solid support in the Muslim community in north India in the 1990s because Mulayam Singh stood forth in 1990 as the defender of the mosque at Ayodhya and, after its destruction under a BJP government, as the principal obstacle to the consolidation of the BJP's strength in U.P. No important party in U.P., however, has taken the stand of the Communist Party of India (Marxist) in West Bengal, namely, to avoid appealing on communal grounds to either Hindus or Muslims and to instead use the full powers of the state to ensure that communal riots simply do not happen.

There is yet another way in which Hindu-Muslim opposition and communal riots serve indirectly the grander purposes of the leaders of the Indian state. That is in the way these riots are explained, namely, as consequences of a communal mentality exploited by the Hindu communal parties. The cure, therefore, is, first, to change the mentality—a process that would take decades even if anyone had any serious intention of reformulating all the state educational curricula in India to do so—and, second, to rein in and occasionally ban the parties and organizations of militant Hindu nationalism. The first strategy is plainly meaningless and unworkable, the dream mostly of sincere but powerless Delhi intellectuals. The second strategy, to rein in or ban Hindu communal organizations, was for long itself part of the game of manipulating communal animosities and violence to the advantage of the secular parties.

But the banning of Hindu communal organizations is now out of the question, with the rise to power of the BJP as the dominant party in a ruling coalition at the Center and as the ruling party in several states of the Indian Union, including (in 2001) U.P. With its rise to power, there has been a downplaying of explicit attacks on Muslims and their leading institutions, as well as a decline in the production of large-scale Hindu-Muslim riots and anti-Muslim programs. No one should be deluded—although many are—into thinking that these changes reflect any modification of the Hindutva ideology and its fundamental goals of transforming India into a Hindu nation-state, a great military power, hegemon in its region, a member of the Security Council of the United Nations. It is militant nationalism that drives this government's policies. It expressed itself most clearly in the nuclear explosions carried out under the BJP government at Pokhran in 1998, the continuing hostile and exaggerated rhetoric directed against Pakistan, and India's defiance of the entire world in its refusal to sign the CTBT. In pursuit of its grand design to achieve Great Power status in the world, the Muslims of South Asia are a hindrance. They are seen as perpetual threats in Pakistan, in Kashmir, and in all the so-called mini-Pakistans in the cities and towns throughout India. They are seen as the major obstacle to the unity of the country—though in fact their presence is essential for the creation of Hindu unity in the first place. They must be molded into political Hindus or be disciplined, defeated, and otherwise put in their place.

## The Role of the State

How far is the Indian state as a whole or any of its federal units implicated in the persistence of Hindu-Muslim riots in India? It is obvious that both the central and state governments in India share responsibility for failing to prevent and control riots.[31] It is also evident that both the central and state governments have sometimes acted decisively in dealing with potential riot situations and have at other times not acted at all or have been ineffective. Finally, it is equally clear that some state governments with large Muslim populations, including some with a history of communal tensions, have acted more effectively than others. Governments in West Bengal, Tamil Nadu, and Kerala have demonstrated both the will and the capacity to prevent or control Hindu-Muslim riots.[32] In West Bengal, which experienced massive communal violence at the time of Partition and a major communal riot in Calcutta in 1964 under Congress rule, there have been no major communal riots in the past thirty years of Communist Party (Marxist) rule.

Insofar as the government of U.P. is concerned, there is ample evidence of its ineffectiveness and its dereliction of duty in preventing and controlling riots from time to time since Independence, as well as its noncooperativeness in post-riot inquiries. There is also evidence that some governments in U.P. have been able to act effectively when they have chosen to do so. This has been apparent in U.P. since the mid-1990s,[33] that is, since the last wave of riots that occurred in the aftermath of the destruction of the Babri Masjid in December 1992.

But no U.P. government has been willing since Independence to take any action whatsoever to reform and professionalize the police and to investigate the charges against the PAC of victimization of Muslims in riots. In 1978, when the long series of riots in Aligarh began, the representation of Muslims in the several state police forces ranged from zero to five percent. In the PAC forces, Muslim representation was "almost negligible." One oft-repeated proposal, therefore, has been to change the composition of the police forces and the civil administration through changed recruitment policies, to bring about "adequate representation of the minority community in the State and Central Government Police Forces and also in the Civil, District administration."[34]

A common Hindu objection to this proposal is that the communities are so divided that it will merely lead to the communalization of the police forces. It is not entirely clear what lies behind this objection, however. Communalization of the police forces might have one or two consequences. One is that the police would be divided against each other and become ineffective. The more likely fear, however, is that Muslim police might kill Hindus just as Hindu police have killed Muslims. And, indeed, when 16 Hindus were killed at Ayodhya by police forces that were still overwhelmingly Hindu, during the government of Mulayam Singh Yadav in 1990, the outcry and outrage in the Hindu population reverberated into the next election campaign and contributed to the defeat of Mulayam Singh's Samajwadi Party and the victory of the BJP.

But Mulayam Singh did not seek at that time to increase Muslim representation in the U.P. police forces. He sought instead to increase the representation of members of his own Yadav caste and other backward castes. In the years since then, recruitment into the police and civil administration in the state and their use by successive state governments have been the most divisive issues in interparty conflicts among the three principal contending parties in the state: the Samajwadi Party (SP) of Mulayam Singh, the BJP, and the BSP representing the interests of the Scheduled Castes. Both the SP and the BSP have sought to reduce upper-caste dominance in the civil and police administrations and have fought each other as well over the appointment of backward and Scheduled Caste persons. Although figures on the caste and communal composition of the current police and civil administrations are not available, it is probable that Muslim representation has not been increased significantly.[35]

In this context of contestation for control over the civil and police administrations, which is at the heart of a broader struggle for power in the districts and localities of this huge state, there are several matters that need to be noted that have a bearing on the issue of whether or not increased Muslim representation would make a difference in the prevention and control of riots. The first is that it is unlikely to do so by itself, when the police are seen as instruments of the party in power at the state and district levels. The assumption behind the demand for increased Muslim representation is that Muslim police will not vengefully kill innocent Muslims during riots and that, in an integrated force, Hindus, too, will be reluctant to do so when Muslim policemen on the force are there to observe them. But the police operate under the orders of those who control the government, who in turn use them to harass their political opponents, protect their supporters, and deny protection to the latter's local rivals. It is indeed quite likely that, in a society divided by caste and community in which the police are so used, those divisions will also affect police work. High-caste police officers may tip off their high-caste brethren when they have orders to arrest them for some offence against Scheduled Castes. Hindu police will look aside when Muslims are being attacked by Hindu crowds. Why should not Muslims do the same? In an integrated force, such discriminatory behavior might well lead to internal conflicts among the police themselves.

Two matters critical to the proper functioning of any police force are rarely mentioned in proposals to make the police somehow more impartial and more effective in preventing and controlling riots. One concerns professionalization, the creation of a police force trained to keep itself aloof from conflicts among groups within society and to act impartially. Such professionalization also, of course, requires internal incentives for proper behavior: adequate pay, respect in society and from political superiors, and opportunities for career advancement and promotion. Professionalization, of course, is no cure-all, as indicated by the behavior of supposedly professionalized police forces in industrial and postindustrial societies such as the United States from time to time, most recently demonstrated in Los Angeles. But as an option it is certainly superior to a force dominated by educated, upper-caste persons, deeply implicated in the everyday conflicts of society, operating with inadequate pay at the lower levels, heavily corrupted at all levels, and offering virtually no career incentives for any of the intermediate- and lower-level police to act differently.

But whether a professionalized force would be superior or not to the present situation is an academic question given the political framework in which the police operate. The politicians do not talk about professionalization of the police because control of the police is at the center of political conflict in a deeply and increasingly bitterly divided society. The proverbial spoils of office in India include not only control over the distribution of economic resources but control over the distribution of protection and safety. As the political struggle becomes more bitter, so does the struggle for safety for oneself and one's supporters. In the process, the dangers to all increase and so does the need for safety in a society in which politicians increasingly carry guns, have shadows (bodyguards) with them at all times, and, at higher levels, are surrounded by armed forces and convoys of vehicles on the roads.

Yet, when all is said and done, the evidence is overwhelming that, even with a nonprofessionalized police force, the control of which is itself a central prize in contemporary political conflict, riots can be prevented and controlled when the political will to do so exists. All political leaders in U.P. know which districts are riot-prone, who the principal riot-mongers are in such districts, and who are the civilian and police administrators who can be counted upon to maintain communal peace even under trying circumstances in difficult districts. The people in the districts who do not like riots also know these things. They do not condemn all the district officials and all the police. They say that one set of officers acted partially and/or ineffectively, another set impartially and effectively. But these police and administrative officers cannot act impartially and effectively unless they have a clear directive from the state administration to do so. Under the political circumstances of northern India for far too many years in the post-Independence period, especially since the late 1960s, that political will has as often as not been absent. On the contrary, riots have been too often treated as a normal and even a routine aspect of the political process. The advantages to be gained from allowing communal conflicts to occur or the disadvantages to be incurred from taking strong action have been too often apparent. In short, for many reasons and at all levels in Indian society, from the Center to the locality, riots have been functionally useful to far too many persons, groups, and parties.

### Institutionalized Riot Systems

I have argued throughout this book that an exclusive focus on a search for the "true" causes of riots is misdirected and itself is implicated in the persistence of riots. Its implication in riot persistence arises especially from the fact that the search for causes diverts our gaze from the dynamics of riots, from the critical issue of how riots are produced. My emphasis here has been on an alternative approach that focuses on the issue of persistence.

It must be stressed, first of all, that there is little spontaneous about Hindu-

Muslim riots. They are, on the contrary, dramatic productions in which what is spontaneous can occur only because the scene has been prepared with numerous rehearsals marked by tension, rumors, and provocations, in which the signals that an outbreak is about to occur and that the time for participation has arrived have been made clear.

Although elements of the riot ritual described by Gaborieau[36] have remained present in the riots in Aligarh, the idea behind his schemata of a direct connection between values and beliefs, on the one hand, and riots, on the other hand, has to be rejected. Missing in that analysis is a discussion of the role of intermediaries between the values of the people and the riot engineers. That is to say, we have to distinguish between the roles of those who mobilize latent hostilities and those who create the incidents that make it possible for those hostilities to be mobilized; we also have to consider more carefully who actually mobilizes. So, let us think of the following groups.

There are, first, the communalist mobilizers, including, especially, professionals like those associated with the former Jan Sangh, but including also many professional politicians and activists in today's BJP, RSS, and associated organizations. They also include rabble-rousing student mischief makers, including persons at both the local Hindu degree colleges and, at times, at the AMU as well. Also in this category are some local businessmen who want to take advantage of riot situations to cause harm to their enemies and rivals among Muslims.

A second category of intermediary, repeatedly mentioned in my interviews, whose members include both paid functionaries and unpaid participants, are criminals. The paid members are hired killers, who have two kinds of roles. One is to provide a signal for starting a riot by stabbing a victim. The religion of the killer as well as the victim may be either Muslim or Hindu. It has been said that even a Muslim criminal may be paid to kill another Muslim for the purpose of starting a riot. The unpaid participants are the countless numbers of criminals who are always ready for a riot to break out to make money by looting. Such people may be recruited into gangs by local politicians or they may act on their own. Shops owned by persons from the "targeted" community are obvious sources of enrichment, but sometimes it is necessary to storm the houses of rich men and kill all their occupants before one can steal their possessions.

Then there are the mobilized mobs, whose composition every analyst of riots and pogroms everywhere has faced the virtually impossible task of uncovering fully. It is certain, however, that the riffraff theory of riots is faulty insofar as Aligarh is concerned. It is not that criminals and *goonda*s of all sorts do not get involved, as well as the riffraff or "lumpenproletariat." Indeed, the latter are often recruited wholesale from particular categories of the population living in compact *mohallas*, who come out en masse when summoned to participate in a riot. There is no doubt either that students come out in large numbers during riots. My own interviews in Aligarh indicate clearly, in addition, that so-called ordinary people also come out during riots to lead gangs of killers and arsonists and to participate themselves in killing and burning. Besides my own interviews, there are countless affidavits in which high-caste and sometimes wealthy persons are mentioned by name by victims and their occupations and places of business noted. But the composition of any large-sized riotous mob can never be known fully, neither by arrest statistics nor by survey questionnaires or random sampling or any social science technique, not even by participant observation such as has been provided in the superb work of Bill Buford on England's football hooligans.[37] It is certain only that the very indefiniteness concerning the composition of riotous mobs will continue to provide materials for the authorities to displace blame upon riffraff, the mass of the people, the generic mob, scapegoats—even a decline in "family values"—and the like to mask their own incompetence, ineffectiveness, and culpability.

There is, finally, another category of persons involved in riots in Aligarh, namely, the ordinary constables and the PAC, who make it all worse. They do so in many ways. They show partiality: standing by while Hindus attack Muslims, as well as shooting down Muslims as soon as they leave their houses or mass in the streets. Insofar as the reports are true—and there are too many such reports to doubt that a great many of them must be authentic—the police are also riot participants; they knock down the doors of people's houses, beat up and even kill the male residents, molest the women, and even kill minor children. They themselves rampage in the streets, striking out wildly, responding in an undisciplined manner to provocations. One must never forget, also, when assigning responsibility for the prevention and control of riots, that the police are agents of the state. But one must also remind oneself of the even more unpleasant fact that the police are no different from the society from which they come. They have the same prejudices, the same lack of discipline, the same hierarchical attitudes, the same penchant to abuse power, the same tendency to corrupt behavior that exists broadly in Indian society, unleavened by any significant degree of professionalization that would serve—as it has for the Indian army until now, for the most part—to inculcate a different set of values while isolating them from society, and lack any pay, career, or other incentives to act differently.

*Contextualization*

There is yet a further large piece in the puzzle of riot persistence, which is the very way in which riots are explained and contextualized. I have argued above that large-scale riots—which provide the principal focus of this study—are too multifarious to be subjected to conventional causal analysis. Every large-scale riot brings out a multiplicity of persons, groups, and forces with a multiplicity of motives. Every effort to find a single cause, however broadly stated, will fail to encompass the whole. This search for causes becomes instead a means of blame displacement by relieving of responsibility all those left out of the causal explanation. But it does more than that. It provides also a license to many to loot, burn, and kill for revenge, profit, or pure fun under the cover of broader explanations provided by the authorities, journalists, and social scientists who attribute the criminal actions of rioters to feelings of rage against injustice, communal prejudices, class conflicts, and so forth.

It is at this point that the much-maligned police forces—who no doubt deserve the criticism they receive—do act differently from most of the rest of society. Insofar as they are doing their job—and even when they are not doing it or are misbehaving in this respect also—their task is to identify crimes as defined in the Indian code of criminal procedure. All policemen in India— in fact, virtually everyone in India—seem to know at least some of the vast number of clauses in this code by heart, so well that the foreign observer never knows what crime is being talked about unless he has memorized it as well, because the clauses are quoted by number. An offense is not defined as murder, but as a Section $x$ crime.[38]

Every person booked for a crime in India, including crimes committed during a riot, must be booked in an FIR (First Information Report) under a numbered clause of the criminal code. The police are also trained to investigate crimes by uncovering personal motives for them: greed, jealousy, revenge directed at particular persons. Although, in a large-scale riot, the mere apprehension of a person on the basis of police or other eyewitness testimony should be sufficient to book him, the police often think even in these situations of the personal motivations of the perpetrator of a criminal act. Why this act in this place at this time? The police especially pay attention to the criminal acts that become signals for a riot to begin. They will sometimes say that it was simply a criminal act of a certain type that was used as a pretext by others for starting a riot.

The police cannot escape this method of identifying and analyzing crimes even when they are behaving dishonestly. The police in north India frequently deliberately charge the wrong persons for crimes they suspect or know were committed by others. In doing so, they act in a characteristically corrupt manner. But they must still define the crime, however falsely, in relation to the specific clauses of the criminal code. There is no clause in the criminal code that justifies or explains away acts of looting, arson, and murder as expressions of spontaneous rage and, therefore, makes them understandable, excusable, or unpunishable. In fact, most such acts committed during riots go unidentified and unpunished, even when—as they almost always are—observed by eyewitnesses and, very often, reported in affidavits and FIRs by victims and witnesses. Nevertheless, the police have repeatedly said to me that riots are often precipitated by criminal acts, not by spontaneous rage, and that professional criminals roam freely during riots. The police, in my experience, are the least inclined to offer broader contextualizations for riots. When they do so, they do it on the basis of what they see before their eyes: filthy slums, unhygienic conditions, narrow alleyways through which criminals may escape, poverty, illiteracy, unemployment, and lack of other forms of "entertainment."

As I have already said, the police are in this case exceptional in Indian society—and probably nearly everywhere else in the world as well—in their focus on the specificities of incidents, in their desire to seek local and personalized explanations for them, and in their need to fit particular acts into state-defined definitions of what constitutes crimes. In the case of large-scale incidents such as riots or police-public confrontations, however, there is a societal tendency to seek to fit these incidents into broader contexts. Although the form of contextualization may differ at the local and extra-local levels, the linkage of both through modern systems of communication—even in India and many other developing countries—contributes to a propensity towards ever-broader forms of contextualization, especially in those cases where extra-local persons, agencies, and authorities become involved in them or interested in them for their own purposes. These broader forms of contextualization, even when they appear to be high-minded in directing attention to local incidents as examples of insidious forms of prejudice or racism or communalism, inevitably transform, distort, and sometimes condemn, but at other times justify criminal acts.

It is difficult to contest the argument that sometimes such contextualizations are necessary to rid a society of prevailing, widespread injustice, such as racism or discrimination against persons of a different religion, by providing special protections to particular social groups and even by defining new state crimes or magnifying ordinary crimes by placing them in a different category—not just killing, but killing from prejudice against a person's race or religion, for example. Thus, in the United States, the crime of murder may be treated as either an ordinary criminal act in local courts or as a civil wrong in federal courts, especially when it violates the rights of a person defined as being from a minority or disadvantaged or otherwise protected group. In India, there are ordinary crimes and crimes committed against Harijans, the only difference between the two being the identity of the victim. However, at the same time, it must be noted that this very process of broadening the framework of explanation into which criminal and civil wrongs are placed has many latent potential consequences that are undesirable for the peace and well-being of society and even for the pursuit of justice. They include distortions of justice that can lead to (or justify) the phenomenon of the "backlash" against former victims, now seen as privileged beneficiaries of a new form of discrimination against members of still-dominant social categories. In India, the backlash has taken the form of the highly distorted charge by militant Hindus that Muslims, protected by the Indian state, have become a privileged and pampered group in Indian society.

In discussing the phenomenon of Hindu-Muslim riots, we are clearly faced with this question of contextualization. I have been told over and over by police—before the mobilizations around the Ayodhya issue—that such riots have no "concrete" basis, that they arise out of local criminal acts, that they are placed wrongly in a broader Hindu-Muslim framework, and that all sorts of ordinary and extraordinary criminal acts are committed under the cover of these riots. This contextualization of Hindu-Muslim riots derives, as noted earlier, from a broader discourse of Hindu-Muslim communalism, which, however, is embedded in a divided historical consciousness. Militant Hindus and separatist Muslims have agreed on the "essential" differences between the two communities. At the same time, they have been divided not only in how they perceive those differences to have arisen and what needed to be done about it, but also in the very nature of their separate historical consciousnesses.

In India, as in Sri Lanka, the two communities that are seen to be at war or prone to intergroup violence are also associated with distinctive approaches to history, one that Daniel characterizes as "history," the other as "heritage."[39] In India, it is the Muslims who have a true historical consciousness, based upon their demarcation of their history as having begun at a certain time and place and having been announced by their prophet. From that date, a vast train of events were launched that are connected one to the other across the centuries, events that include wars, conquests, kingdoms, empires, and chronicles of them all, mosques and monuments whose dates and builders are known and recorded, and last but by no means least, histories of the development of their laws, punctuated from time to time by the interpretations and adaptations of them to different times and places by their greatest scholars and holy men.[40]

Most Hindus, by contrast, cannot and do not try to separate what others consider mythology from history. They point to great monuments and temples from the past, most of them dated by others. Their own dates for their origins, their books, their monuments tend to be fantastic, not credible, said to have arisen in eras that all schoolboys in the West know to have been pre-historic, even pre–Homo sapiens. Most persons educated in Indian universities emerge believing that the length of their history and culture surpasses that of all others, and having only contempt for countries like the United States, which they say has "only two hundred years of history."

Whatever the differences between Hindu and Muslim approaches to their past, it is evident that Hindus are far more absorbed in theirs than are Muslims. They live their imagined past in the present and perceive every imagined wrong, especially those imagined to have been done by Muslim conquerors, as if it happened only yesterday, not 500 years before by people differently defined and aligned in relation to each other. They blame Muslims for the loss of their past and of the monumental evidence of their former greatness in north India, which they believe was destroyed by Muslim generals and rulers. Further, they claim that, while *they* are prepared to recognize the history of Muslim rulers, along with the Indo-Muslim monuments, art, and literature, as part of Indian history, the Muslims refuse to identify with Indian history. Muslims, they say, see their history in India instead as part of an external, Islamic, physical and religious conquest of the subcontinent.

These conflicting historical consciousnesses and identifications culminated in a terrifyingly precise moment in modern Indian history, that is, the Partition, which stands for most educated Hindus—and, in northern India, most Hindus in general—as a historical scar that not only divided the subcontinent but defied the truth they had fought for as their rightful heritage: the unity of India. Muslims, for their part, fought for another truth invented out of their past in India, namely, that they constituted a separate civilization distinct from that of the Hindus, that they had always been separate, and would have to remain so in the future. Leaving aside the question of the causes of Partition, on which much ink has been spilt, it stands as the first catastrophe of the historical consciousness in modern South Asia. Partition certainly arose out of political struggles, but one of those struggles was over the past, combined with a fear of a future in which two cultures perceived as historically distinct would not be able to live together in peace. Sayyid Ahmad Khan, in

Aligarh, laid the Muslim foundation for separatism that Jinnah turned into a political weapon. And in Aligarh itself stands the very institution that Hindus deem to have constructed the ideology and the leadership that produced this moment of violence and chaos, the Aligarh Muslim University. Further, the militant Hindus claim to believe that the AMU and all the distinctive institutions of the Muslims in India, even their very religious beliefs, threaten Hindu India, India that is Hindu, with further partition, violence, and chaos.

For these Hindus, living in an imagined past, the path to the glorious future—which rightfully belongs to India because of the greatness of its ancient civilizations before the arrival of the Muslims and the British—is blocked. It is blocked, on the one hand, by the remnants of that more recent past of Muslim conquerors, empires, monuments, and mosques built upon the ruins, real and imagined, of Hindu monuments and temples. That past has to be rectified before Hindus can be released from its bonds to achieve the future greatness that belongs to them. A major step in this direction was the destruction of the mosque at Ayodhya, which, to countless Hindus, signified the beginnings of their release from "slavery."[41] For some, the destruction of at least two more mosques—those in Mathura and Varanasi—and perhaps many others may be necessary before the past can be finally rectified and Hindus achieve full freedom at last.

On the other hand, all militant Hindus and many who are not associated with the organizations of militant Hinduism also suffer from an obsessive concentration on that moment when Independence was achieved and sullied by Partition. They suffer from the presence in the very present of the evidences of Partition and the imagined dangers of future partitions. In Aligarh, the AMU stands for that presence. Elsewhere, in every major city and town in north India, there are further symbols of that presence wherever there are large concentrations of Muslim populations. These Muslim concentrations are called "mini-Pakistans." These "mini-Pakistans" in turn are seen as the centers of riot production designed to intimidate Hindus and generate more and more Partitions, more and more violence on the Hindu body. Until the process of historical rectification is completed and the "mini-Pakistans" are uprooted or their residents converted into political Hindus—free, of course, to practice their religion quietly—the concrete problems of the present cannot be satisfactorily dealt with and India cannot achieve its rightful place in the world. It is this mentality, inscribed in the minds of a large part of the Hindu population of the country, produced and reproduced over many decades, that sustains the beliefs that justify the practices that produce the dynamic productions called Hindu-Muslim riots.

# Postscript: Aligarh and Gujarat

## UTTAR PRADESH AND ALIGARH IN 2002

Uttar Pradesh (U.P.), and Aligarh as well, have experienced a reduction in the incidence of Hindu-Muslim violence during the past decade. Further, the February 2002 Legislative Assembly elections in Aligarh City produced a result that in itself reflects a decline both in riotous activity and in electoral communalization and polarization. Indeed, there has not been an election result in any way comparable to this one since the 1950s. Three features of this election result are notable.

First, the winning candidate was Vivek Bansal, contesting on the Congress ticket. As noted in chapter 10, Bansal—an Agarwal Hindu, a noncommunal person—fought the 1993 Legislative Assembly election and came in a poor fourth, losing his security deposit in a communalized electoral contest in which Krishna Kumar Navman, by defeating Abdul Khaliq, won this seat for the last time. Bansal did not contest at all in the 1996 elections, in which Abdul Khaliq finally defeated Navman. In the 2002 election, however, Bansal won an overwhelming plurality of the votes, 41.87 percent, compared to 20.46 percent for the runner-up BJP candidate.

Second, in this election at last, Navman was replaced as the BJP candidate by Deepak Mittal, an Agarwal Hindu who lives in a new colony, unaffected by previous communal violence, on the outskirts of the city. His vote percentage was the lowest polled by a BJP Legislative Assembly candidate since 1985. In third place was the only remaining communally oriented politician from the previous electoral contests, the sitting MLA, Abdul Khaliq, who did not contest as the candidate of either the SP or the BSP this time, but on the ticket of what the Election Commission of India classifies as a registered but unrecognized party, the National Loktantrik Party. He polled 18.04 percent.

All other Muslim candidates—including two on the tickets of the BSP and the SP, respectively, as well as others who polled only a tiny percentage of the votes—polled a total of 15.42 percent. Thus the total vote for all Muslim candidates, including Abdul Khaliq, was one-third of those polled (33.46 percent), still far below the vote for the winning candidate. Moreover, the total vote for all Hindu candidates, excluding Bansal, came to a mere 4.21 percent. It is clear, therefore, that Bansal won this election with support from both Hindu and Muslim voters and that the electoral results display neither a polarized nor even a communalized electorate.

Third and also significant, and consistent with the findings in this book, the turnout in this election was the lowest in the entire history of post-Independence Legislative Assembly elections in the city. There was no communal riot in Aligarh between 1995 and this election to intensify communal solidarity and, correspondingly, there was little interest in the election contest. Although high turnout is normally considered a favorable aspect of electoral politics in a democracy, for Aligarh it appears, on the contrary, to reflect the cleansing of an electoral process polluted for two decades by deliberate communal provocation and routinized violence.

### THE GUJARAT POGROM OF 2002

While communal violence in U.P. and in Aligarh have ebbed during the past decade, recent events in the Western Indian state of Gujarat have surpassed in ferocity, and probably in numbers killed, the post-Ayodhya killings that took place in the state of U.P. a decade earlier. This book has made several references to the images that emerge and prevail in the discourse of Hindu-Muslim violence, images that defy all reasoned analysis of the dynamics of such violence, how it begins, unfolds, and ends. Mention has also been made of two of the most murderously violent events in post-Independence India, where both the evidence of organizing and preplanning and the involvement of known political party figures and government ministers have been noted in the press and in official inquiries. In these two cases—the anti-Sikh violence in Delhi in 1984, and the murderous attacks on Muslims in the Bombay killings of 1992–93—the word "pogrom" and even, at times, the words "massacre" and "genocide" have vied with the term "riots" as a summary descriptive label for these events.

As I have noted in this book and elsewhere, the post hoc labelling of incidents of collective violence is an important aspect of the political struggle to gain control of their interpretation. The planners, organizers, and perpetrators of collective violence want all such events to be labelled riots, expressions of the spontaneous and justified feelings of people outraged by the actions of the victims who allegedly precipitated the violence. Critics of those alleged to have planned, organized, and perpetrated the violence seek to fix blame upon the latter by using the term "pogrom," which implies preplanning and organization by established political parties or other organizations, often aided by the police and ministers in the government. The term "massacre" is used by those who wish to demonstrate that an event of large-scale violence has either victimized poor, hapless, and defenseless people or involved the sudden indiscriminate killing of a large group of people irrespective of age or sex. Social science cannot settle such issues by precise definitions, since the whole project of production and criticism of collective violence of this type involves obfuscation by both sides of the differences just adumbrated. All that the social scientist can reasonably achieve in such situations is to expose to full view, as far as possible, the agents involved in the production of collective violence and the interests that are served by those who seek to capture its meaning. The social scientist must then make his or her own choice of labels.

Further, it has been noted that since the last great wave of riots that occurred after the destruction of the Babri Masjid, of which the Bombay violence was the most egregious instance, there was a decline—not a cessation, however—of communal violence in India, U.P., and Aligarh. For that decline, several reasons have been adduced, including the claim by the BJP that the relative reduction in violence in the past decade proved the argument that the BJP—and the RSS family of organizations *(Sangh Parivar)* of which the BJP is a part—has not been to blame for such riots because it is the BJP that has been in power during this past decade in the central government and in many states with previous records of large-scale violence.

These issues of images, labels, and responsibility emerged starkly once again in the months between February 27 and mid-June 2002, in the state of Gujarat, where widespread killings, mostly of Muslims, have been carried out on a scale and with a ferocity reminiscent of the genocidal massacres that occurred during the partition of the Punjab in 1947, and with the apparent involvement, according to several eyewitness accounts, of ministers in the government itself under the leadership of BJP Chief Minister Narendra Modi.[1] These events surpass, in these respects, all the riots in Aligarh described in this book, but all the elements of riot production outlined herein are echoed in Gujarat.

The common elements include, first, the obscurity and indeterminacy of the "causes" of the initial acts of violence: the horrific killing on February 27 of 58 militant Hindu volunteers (*kar sevaks*) returning from Ayodhya by train and burned alive in two bogeys of that train at the railway station in the town of Godhra, in Gujarat.[2] The process of blame displacement began before any credible facts at all had emerged about this incident. At a time when between a million and a million and a half troops of the armed forces of India and Pakistan were facing each other along the two countries' borders, in a standoff that seemed to be moving dangerously close to all-out war, one that might include the use of nuclear weapons, BJP leaders promptly blamed the ISI for the Godhra incidents. In the days that followed these BJP claims and accusations, however, news reports appeared—at first in the *Washington Post* and then in Indian newspapers and in the biweekly magazine *Frontline*—that cast doubt on them and pointed to several other circumstances, which opened up other interpretations. But the Godhra incidents were quickly overshadowed by what followed, namely, what all available evidence points to as a systematic pogrom, enacted with precision and extreme brutality, by persons and organizations in the institutionalized riot system of the RSS family of organizations, members of the BJP government, the police, and even members of the elite Indian Administrative Service.[3] This pogrom began on February 28, a day after the Godhra massacre, under the auspices of the VHP, which called for a *bandh* (closing down) to protest the killings in Godhra. The Gujarat pogrom continued until March 3, after which there was a hiatus that was followed in turn by "a new round of violence" from March 15.[4]

Within a week of the Godhra incidents, the press reported an official death toll of 677. By the end of the month, the figure quoted was 783. It is certain that these figures are too low, with the estimates of responsible observers, including the British High Commission, ranging as high as 1,500 to 2,000.[5] Some thirty cities and towns in the state were reported to be "still under curfew" on March 27.[6] Fifteen or sixteen districts were reported to have been affected by the riots,[7] though the rioting was most intense in five or six. Official figures provided by the Gujarat government and published in *Frontline* also show the characteristic predominance of Muslims in the numbers killed during rioting: more than 5 Muslims to 1 Hindu, including the 60 Hindus killed on the train at Godhra, but a ratio of 15 to 1 in the rioting that followed.[8] The number of displaced persons compelled to seek refuge in relief camps also speaks to the enormity of the cataclysm visited upon the Muslims of Gujarat: nearly 100,000 persons in 101 relief camps by March 27, 2002,[9] and nearly 150,000 in 104 relief camps two weeks later.[10]

Numerous features of these killings and this destruction of property sug-
gest the validity of the term "pogrom" and its systematic character.[11] Most
such features have been noted on a smaller scale in the Aligarh riots described
in this book. They include the destruction of "mosques and shrines" in
Ahmadabad, reportedly followed by the removal of the debris "by the
Ahmadabad Municipal Corporation" to remove any trace of the former
Muslim presence and even the replacement of such ruins, as in Ayodhya in
December 1992, by "makeshift" Hindu temples.[12] It has also been reported
that many if not most police either stood aside or coordinated or participated
in the violence against Muslims.[13] Moreover, the marauding mobs of killers
carried lists of voters with them and were thus able to identify the homes of
Muslims who were to be killed and whose property was to be destroyed. The
mobs also carried licensing documents "and other relevant papers" from the
offices of the municipal authorities and so were able to target Muslim properties for arson attacks.[14] The attacks were accompanied by the distribution
of leaflets "in different parts of the State," calling "for an economic boycott
of Muslims."[15] As in Aligarh in 1990–91, several of the vernacular media
agencies in Gujarat became, in effect, part of the institutionalized riot system of the *Sangh Parivar*.[16] Reports in the English-language press and in other
English-language sources noted that, months before the enactment of these
massacres, "a leading Gujarati newspaper published an article . . . naming the
restaurants in Ahmadabad owned by Muslims," which were then duly burnt
down during the pogrom.[17]

Also on the riot scenes, according to eyewitnesses, were prominent BJP
and VHP leaders who moved along with the mobs of Hindu rioters; sometimes they played the role of "conversion specialists," addressed the mobs,
and then discreetly left; after their departure, the mobs carried out their murderous attacks.[18] Other politicians or their relations and employees were seen
allegedly encouraging the police to fire on Muslim crowds, or were themselves observed "directing the mobs."[19] Similarly, as reported in Aligarh in
1990–91, when Scheduled Caste and other lower-caste persons fought with
Muslims or invaded and attacked Muslim *mohallas*, the BJP made use in
Gujarat of the poorest and most deprived segments of society, persons from
the tribal communities and backward castes, to carry out much of the killing
and destruction.[20] Again, as in the great Aligarh riots of 1990–91, when attacks
were made for the first time on predominantly Muslim *mohallas* at the outskirts of the city, so also in Gujarat "Muslims were attacked even in areas where
they constituted the majority."[21] Further, the killings extended to several villages in rural areas of the state. Finally, the involvement of real-estate land

grabbers and "mafia" elements with "well-known links with ruling-party politicians" was also reported.[22] These elements took advantage of the attacks on slum settlements to rid them of Muslim residents and property owners. They also exploited mob efforts to prevent residents from returning to their neighborhoods and homes.

It is necessary as well to underline not only the implication in this pogrom of the BJP state government, its members, and its agents but also that of the government of India, led by the BJP, which had the power and ultimate responsibility to stop this flagrant breakdown of law and order. Most significant was the failure of the government of India to dismiss the Gujarat government, under Article 356 of the Constitution of India, for its inability or unwillingness to maintain law and order. Indeed, the situation in Gujarat was by far the clearest case in post-Independence India for the rightful imposition of that article, which has been misused countless times during the past fifty years for inappropriate, partisan political reasons.[23]

But members of the government of India compromised themselves and the central government in many other ways, some blatant, some subtle. Although Prime Minister Vajpayee, under pressure from the non-BJP constituents in his governing coalition, addressed the country on television on the third day of rioting "to denounce the Gujarat riots,"[24] he did not visit Gujarat until thirty-six days after the Godhra massacre and the pogrom that followed it.[25] He was then reported to have remarked "that the carnage had shamed India." Aside from the fact that, once again, it was India's status in the world that was at stake, as much as or more than the plight of the victims of a state-supported pogrom, other features of his visit deserve note. Vajpayee visited Godhra first, thus expressing his solidarity with the Hindus who had been killed, the victims from the *Sangh Parivar*. Also, he took with him, on his tour of Gujarat, central minister Uma Bharati, member of the VHP, whose speeches, during the 1991 elections and prior to the destruction of the mosque at Ayodhya in 1992, were considered hostile to Muslims, and who was one of the most active proponents of the construction of a Hindu temple at that site.

In the meantime, violence continued sporadically day by day for several months, with reports of new killings coming from Ahmadabad, the state's metropolis, and several districts in the state. Not until May did the government of India undertake any significant action to bring a definitive end to the rioting. In May, the famous police chief K. P. S. Gill—no champion of human rights, but a firm believer in maintaining law and order evenhandedly, a man who had presided over the final suppression of the Punjab insurrection in the early 1990s and had a previous record of containing Hindu-Muslim violence in the northeastern state of Assam—was posted to Gujarat by Home Minister L. K. Advani as a "security adviser" to the Gujarat chief minister, who himself did not at all welcome the appointment.[26] Even Gill, however, who reportedly described the situation as late as May 9, 2000, as "exceedingly bad,"[27] was not provided with the quantum of force that he had requested to end the killings promptly and decisively. Nevertheless, in keeping with Gill's reputation for firmness and evenhandedness, it was reported that "more than 200 activists of the Hindu Right" had been arrested shortly after his arrival,[28] as well as 53 persons charged with "crimes such as rape, murder and arson at Naroda Patiya and Gulmarg Society" in Ahmadabad, among them some "local BJP leaders."[29]

In riot-prone India, whenever new great riots or waves of riots occur, leftist and secular writers, academics among them, commonly say that the latest wave of riots is the worst since the great Partition massacres of 1946–47. In some of the respects noted above, but especially if one takes account of all the features of this fierce outburst, it is fair enough to say as much about Gujarat in the year 2002. It is fair enough also to note that these riots, which took place under a majority BJP state government while the BJP was also the dominant party in the ruling coalition of the country, make a mockery of its claim to have freed India from riots.[30] Others, however, proclaim a different view, taking comfort from the fact that riots did not spread from Gujarat to other parts of India as they did in the last great wave of 1992.

But both types of statements, especially the latter type, are distractions that divert our gaze from the dynamics of riot production in present-day India. The first type of statement is useful only for the purpose of exposing to full view the dimensions of what actually happened and noting that yet further social and political boundaries have been transgressed. For Indians, the first image conjures up the retributive genocidal massacres of Partition in the Punjab in 1946–47 and seems to herald yet another monumental catastrophe that will include the further weakening or disintegration of India or the obliteration of its Muslim population. If the first view maximizes the implications of such events as Gujarat in 2002, the second minimizes them. Both views have the same focus: namely, the future of India, that is, its territorial integrity, societal peace, democratic functioning, and even its status in a world of nation-states. But what is truly important for India's present and future in all these respects is escape from the self-perpetuating traps of blame displacement and the complementary traps of maximizing and minimizing the significance of horrific violence. In short, it is necessary to fix responsibility and penetrate the clouds of deception, rhetoric, mystification, obscurity, and indeterminacy to uncover what can be uncovered, knowing full well that the whole truth can never be known, but that the evident actions and inaction of known persons, groups, organizations, political leaders, media, academics seeking causes, and patriots seeking comfort can be uncovered, exposed, and brought to book.

# APPENDICES

# APPENDIX A

## Supplementary Tables

TABLE A.1. Demographic data from 1951 census, by Muslim population per
centage (in descending order) for sensitive, riot-hit, and crime-prone *mohallas*

| Mohalla *name*[a] | *Percent Muslims* | *Percent Hindus and Others* | *Percent Scheduled Castes* |
|---|---|---|---|
| Usmanpara | 100.00 | .00 | .00 |
| Bani Israilan | 99.68 | .32 | .00 |
| Sarai Behram Beg | 86.89 | 13.11 | .00 |
| Turkman Gate | 86.33 | 11.75 | 1.92 |
| Atishbazan | 86.32 | 11.91 | 1.77 |
| Sheikhan | 84.17 | 12.47 | 3.36 |
| Rasalganj | 81.70 | 10.24 | 8.07 |
| Tantanpara | 72.65 | 27.35 | .00 |
| Shah Kamal | 63.79 | 31.38 | 4.83 |
| Delhi Darwaza | 63.60 | 25.00 | 11.40 |
| Sarai Rahman | 59.00 | 21.46 | 19.54 |
| Chah Garmaya | 55.43 | 44.57 | .00 |
| Madar Darwaza | 45.54 | 54.46 | .00 |
| Turkman Gate | 38.70 | 32.21 | 29.08 |
| Gular Road | 37.23 | 60.64 | 2.13 |
| Madar Darwaza | 31.56 | 53.91 | 14.53 |
| Sabzi Mandi | 29.41 | 70.59 | .00 |
| Manik Chauk | 24.01 | 75.55 | .44 |
| Madar Darwaza | 23.60 | 76.40 | .00 |
| Rafatganj | 21.26 | 78.74 | .00 |
| Mamubhanja | 15.42 | 74.40 | 10.17 |

TABLE A. 1. (continued)

| Mohalla name[a] | Percent Muslims | Percent Hindus and Others | Percent Scheduled Castes |
|---|---|---|---|
| Bara Dwari | 13.04 | 82.61 | 4.35 |
| Katra | 8.56 | 84.86 | 6.58 |
| Sarai Hakim | 1.91 | 83.96 | 14.13 |
| Baniapara | 1.35 | 98.49 | .16 |
| Raghubirpuri | .00 | 90.91 | 9.09 |
| Subhash Road | .00 | 100.00 | .00 |
| Khaidora | .00 | 100.00 | .00 |
| Sarrafa Bazar (Phul Chauraha) | NA | NA | NA |

[a]Turkman Gate and Madar Darwaza are divided among two and three separate wards, respectively, for which census data are provided separately.

TABLE A.2. *Mohallas* and other sites identified as riot-hit in major Aligarh riots, 1956–95

| Mohalla /Other Site[a] | 1956 | 1961 | 1971 | 1972 | 1978 | Centre Study[b] | 1979 | 1980 | 1989 | 1990–91 | 1995 |
|---|---|---|---|---|---|---|---|---|---|---|---|
| Achal Talab | | | X | | | | | | | | X |
| Agra Road/Chandra Talkies | | | | | X | | | | | X | |
| Aligarh–Atrauli Road (bypass linking Atrauli Road with GT Road) | | | | | | | X | | | | X |
| AMU | X | X | | | | | | | | | |
| Anupshahr Road | | | | | | | | | | X | |
| Atishbazan | | | | | | X | | | | | |
| Babri Mandi | | | X | | X | | | | | X | |
| Bani Israilan | | | | | X | X | | | | | |
| Baniapara | | | | | | | | | X | X | |
| Banna Devi/Thana Banna Devi | | | | X | | | | | | | |
| Bara Ganuhar Ali | | | | | | | | X | | X | |
| Barahdwari | X | | | | X | X | | | | | |
| Barain Gate (?) | | | | | | | | X | | | |
| Bazar Sarai Hakim | | | | | | | | | | X | |
| Bhamola | | | | | | | | | | X | |
| Bhojpur | | | | | | | | | | X | |
| Chah Basanta | | | | | | | | | | X | |

(continued)

TABLE A.2. (*continued*)

| Mohulla/Other Site[a] | 1956 | 1961 | 1971 | 1972 | 1978 | Centre Study[b] | 1979 | 1980 | 1989 | 1990–91 | 1995 |
|---|---|---|---|---|---|---|---|---|---|---|---|
| Chah Garmaya | | | | | | X | | | | | |
| Chandan Shaheed (Takia) | | | | | X | | | | | X | |
| Chauraha Abdul Karim | | | | X | X | | | | | | |
| Civil Lines | | | | X | | | X | | | X | |
| Delhi Darwaza (including Sarak | | | | | | | | | | | |
| Delhi Darwaza) | | | | | X | X | | | | X | |
| Dhaurara | | | | | | | | | | X | |
| Dodhpur Market | | | | | | | | | X | | |
| Ektanagar | | | | | | | | | | X | |
| Ghuria Bagh | | | | | | | | | | X | |
| Gular Road | | | | | | X | | | | | |
| Hamdardnagar | | | | | | | | | | X | |
| Hathi ka Puri | | | | | | | | | | X | |
| Indira Nagar | | | | | | | | | | X | |
| Jagjivan Rampur | | | | | | | | | | X | |
| Jaiganj | | | | | X | | | | | | |
| Jama Masjid | | | | | | | | | | X | |
| Jamalpur Tola | | | | | | | | | | X | |
| Jangal Garhi | | | | | | | | | | X | |

| Place | | | | | | | |
|---|---|---|---|---|---|---|---|
| Jiwangarh | | | | | | X | |
| Jogipara | | | | | | X | |
| Kab Beg | | | X | | | | |
| Kameshwar Mahadev | | | X | | | X | |
| Kanwariganj | | | X | | | | |
| Katra | | | | X | | X | |
| Khaidora | | | | X | | X | |
| Kotwali Road | X | | | | | | |
| Kuwarsi | | | | | | X | |
| Laria | | | | | | X | |
| Madar Darwaza (near Sarai Sultani) | | | X | X | X | | X |
| Mahavirganj | | | X | | | | |
| Mamubhanja | | X | X | | | X | |
| Manik Chauk | | X | X | X | X | | |
| Masjid Halwaian | | | X | | | | |
| Medical College Colony | | | X | | | X | |
| Mohammad Ali Road | | | X | | | | |
| Nagla Mallah | | | | | | X | |
| Nai Basti | | | | | | X | |
| Naurangabad Road | X | | | | | | |
| Pathwan Gate (?) | | | | | | X | |
| Phapala | X | | | | | | |
| Phul Chauraha/Sarrafa Bazar | X | | X | X | X | | X |

(continued)

TABLE A.2. (continued)

| Mohalla/Other Site[a] | 1956 | 1961 | 1971 | 1972 | 1978 | Centre Study[b] | 1979 | 1980 | 1989 | 1990–91 | 1995 |
|---|---|---|---|---|---|---|---|---|---|---|---|
| Purani Kotwali | | | | X | X | | | X | X | X | |
| Qazipara | | | | | | | | | | X | |
| Rafatganj | | | | | X | | | | | | |
| Railway Road | | | | | | | | X | | | |
| Rasalganj | | | | | | X | | | | X | |
| Rasalganj Bazar | | | | | | | | | | X | |
| Reori Talab (?) | | | | | | | | | | X | |
| Sabzi Mandi | X | | X | X | X | | | | | | |
| Saifi Colony | | | | | | | | | | X | |
| Sarai Behram Beg[c] | | | | | X | X | | X | | X | |
| Sarai Bhooki | | | | | | | | | | X | |
| Sarai Bibi | | | | | | | | | | X | |
| Sarai Hakim | | | | | X | | | | | X | |
| Sarai Khirni | | | | | | | | | | X | |
| Sarai Mian | | | | | X | | | | | | |
| Sarai Pakki | | | | | | | | | | X | |
| Sarai Rahman | | | | | | X | | | | X | |
| Sarai Rai | | | | | | | | | | X | |
| Sarai Sultani | | | | | X | | X | | | X | X |

| Site | | | | | | | | | | | |
|---|---|---|---|---|---|---|---|---|---|---|---|
| Sasni Gate | | | | | | | | X | | X | |
| Shah Jamal | | | | | | | | | | X | |
| Shamshad Market | X | | | | | | | | X | | |
| Sheikhan | | | | | X | | | | | | |
| Sir Sayyidnagar | | | | | | | | | | X | |
| Tila | | | | | | | | | | X | |
| Turkman Gate | | | | | | X | | | | X | |
| Upar Kot | | | | | X | | | | X | X | |
| Usmanpara | | | | | | | | | | X | |
| Zakaria Market | | | | | | | X | | | X | |
| TOTAL SITES | 7 | 4 | 4 | 5 | 27 | 15 | 4 | 9 | 6 | 55 | 4 |

[a] Sites identified either in press reports, in my interviews, or in published and unpublished documents. In a few cases indicated with question marks, where I could not identify the correct name, the sites are marked as printed in the original source.

[b] Designated as such in Centre for Research in Rural and Industrial Development (CRRID), Chandigarh, "Communal Violence and Its Impact on Development and National Integration," unpublished, undated; provided to me by Rashpal Mehrotra in 1983.

[c] Includes Dah. Wali Gali.

TABLE A.3. Vote shares for party candidates in their top and bottom polling stations, 1957 Legislative Assembly elections, and demographic data for the *mohallas* included in them, according to the 1951 census (all data in percentages)

| Best/Worst Polling Stations | Vote Share | Muslims | Scheduled Castes | Hindus and Others |
|---|---|---|---|---|
| INC top 5 | 71.98 | 28.39 | 6.54 | 65.06 |
| INC bottom 5 | 28.31 | 15.33 | 11.94 | 72.73 |
| BJS top 5 | 36.91 | 26.12 | 3.47 | 70.41 |
| BJS bottom 5 | 1.22 | 65.34 | 7.49 | 27.18 |
| PSP top 5 | 30.69 | 92.16 | 0.79 | 7.06 |
| PSP bottom 5 | 0.91 | 16.05 | 1.69 | 82.27 |

TABLE A.4. The twentieth-century decline in Muslim representation in the U.P. police

| | 1935–1936 | | | 1981 | | |
|---|---|---|---|---|---|---|
| | Total Police | Muslim Police | Muslim % | Total Police | Muslim Police | Muslim % |
| Senior (gazetted) officers | 188 | 34 | 18 | 230 | 6 | 3 |
| Inspectors | 159 | 65 | 41 | 789 | 14 | 2 |
| Sub-inspectors | 1,941 | 864 | 45 | 8,099 | 348 | 4 |
| Sergeants and assistant sub-inspectors | 35 | nil | nil | 290 | 22 | 8 |
| Head constables, corporals, and constables | 31,249 | 15,058 | 48 | 88,082 | 6,563 | 7 |
| TOTAL | 33,572 | 16,021 | 48 | 97,260 | 6,953 | 7 |

SOURCE: Steven I. Wilkinson, "The Electoral Origins of Ethnic Violence: Hindu-Muslim Riots in India," unpublished Ph.D. dissertation, Harvard University, ch. 3, p. 31.

# APPENDIX B

## *Key to Maps*

| | | | |
|---|---|---|---|
| Kelanagar | 82 | Sara Mian | 21 |
| Khaidora | 37 | Sarai Nawab | 2 |
| Khirni Gate | 48 | Sarai Pakki | 43 |
| Krishi Farm | 102 | Sarai Pathanan | 52 |
| Kuwarsi | 83 | Sarai Qazi | 45 |
| Laria | 53 | Sarai Rahman | 89 |
| Madar Gate | 39 | Sarai Rai | 109 |
| Mahavirganj | 12 | Sarai Sultani | 42 |
| Mahendranagar | 49 | Sarrafa Bazar | 34 |
| Mamubhanja | 4 | Sasni Gate | 51 |
| Manik Chauk | 33 | Shah Jamal | 69 |
| Maulana Azad Nagar | 57 | Shahinshabad | 67 |
| Medical College | 61 | Shamshad Market | 63 |
| Medical Colony | 103 | Shri Varshneya College | 73 |
| Nagla Bhamola | 65 | Sir Sayyidnagar | 104 |
| Nagla Mallah | 62 | Subhash Road | 7 |
| Nagla Pala Sahibabad | 95 | Sudamapuri | 90 |
| Nai Basti | 87 | Sunhat | 16 |
| Nai Idgah | 71 | Surendranagar | 72 |
| New Abadi | 58 | Tamolipara | 36 |
| Pala Sahibabad | 96 | Tantanpara | 14 |
| Patthar Bazar | 5 | Turkman Gate | 24 |
| Phaphala | 6 | University Mosque | 77 |
| Phul Chauraha | 35 | Upar Kot | 31 |
| Purani Kotwali | 29 | Usmanpara | 30 |
| Qazipara | 44 | Ustad Sahib ka Dargah | 70 |
| Raghubirpuri | 88 | Vishnupuri | 91 |
| Railway Colony | 110 | Women's College | 111 |
| Ram Lila Ground | 107 | | |
| Rasalganj | 1 | *Numerical Order* | |
| Sabzi Mandi | 41 | | |
| Samna Para | 46 | Rasalganj | 1 |
| Sanichri Painth | 25 | Sarai Nawab | 2 |
| Sara Bibi | 112 | Sarai Hakim | 3 |
| Sarai Bhooki | 113 | Mamubhanja | 4 |
| Sarai Hakim | 3 | Patthar Bazar | 5 |
| Sarai Kaba | 105 | Phaphala | 6 |
| Sarai Kutub | 23 | Subhash Road | 7 |
| Sarai Lawaria | 9 | Dube ka Parao | 8 |
| | | Sarai Lawaria | 9 |

| | | | |
|---|---|---|---|
| Barahdwari | 10 | Mahendranagar | 49 |
| Katra | 11 | Gambhirpura | 50 |
| Mahavirganj | 12 | Sasni Gate | 51 |
| Kanwariganj | 13 | Sarai Pathanan | 52 |
| Tantanpara | 14 | Laria | 53 |
| Baniapara | 15 | Bhojpur | 54 |
| Sunhat | 16 | Hamdardnagar | 55 |
| Atishbazan | 17 | Badamnagar | 56 |
| Chauraha Abdul Karim | 18 | Maulana Azad Nagar | 57 |
| Delhi Gate | 19 | New Abadi | 58 |
| Jangal Garhi | 20 | Jamalpur | 59 |
| Sarai Mian | 21 | Jamalpur ka Nagla | 60 |
| Kale ki Sarai | 22 | Medical College | 61 |
| Sarai Kutub | 23 | Nagla Mallah | 62 |
| Turkman Gate | 24 | Shamshad Market | 63 |
| Sanichri Painth | 25 | Firdous Nagar | 64 |
| Jaiganj | 26 | Nagla Bhamola | 65 |
| Babri Mandi | 27 | Badarbagh | 66 |
| Bani Israilan | 28 | Shahinshabad | 67 |
| Purani Kotwali | 29 | Indira Nagar | 68 |
| Usmanpara | 30 | Shah Jamal | 69 |
| Upar Kot | 31 | Ustad Sahib ka Dargah | 70 |
| Jama Masjid | 32 | Nai Idgah | 71 |
| Manik Chauk | 33 | Surendranagar | 72 |
| Sarrafa Bazar | 34 | Shri Varshneya College | 73 |
| Phul Chauraha | 35 | Jwalapuri | 74 |
| Tamolipara | 36 | Chhavani | 75 |
| Khaidora | 37 | Industrial Colony | 76 |
| Brahmanpuri | 38 | University Mosque | 77 |
| Madar Gate | 39 | Aligarh Muslim University | 78 |
| D. S. College | 40 | Dodhpur | 79 |
| Sabzi Mandi | 41 | Jauhar Bagh | 80 |
| Sarai Sultani | 42 | Jiwangarh | 81 |
| Sarai Pakki | 43 | Kelanagar | 82 |
| Qazipara | 44 | Kuwarsi | 83 |
| Sarai Qazi | 45 | Kachari | 84 |
| Samna Para | 46 | Kathpula | 85 |
| Barai | 47 | Bannadevi | 86 |
| Khirni Gate | 48 | Nai Basti | 87 |

# APPENDIX C

## Riots and Interparty Competition in the Corporation Elections: An Example from Ward No. 26

The most hotly contested ward in the city in the 1955 corporation elections was ward no. 26. The interval between the winning candidate and the runner-up in the ward was a mere 0.27 percent, a difference of only 7 votes. In fact, the contest was even keener than indicated by this figure, since there were four candidates who polled within three percentage points of each other with vote totals ranging from 501 to 570 out of a total of 2,547 votes cast. The seat was won by the BJP candidate from the backward caste of Saini. The runner-up, a Muslim, contested on the ticket of the BSP. In third place was the SP with another Muslim candidate. The fourth-place candidate, also a Muslim, ran as an independent.

The ward contains parts of three *mohallas*: Sanichri Painth, Sarai Kutub, and Turkman Gate (Map 2). The bulk of the voters in the ward come from the latter *mohalla*. Turkman Gate, classed as both riot-hit and crime-prone, has been a notorious center of riot production for many years. It was at the epicenter of the rioting in 1990–91. It also figured importantly in the famous 1962 elections that took place in the aftermath of the 1961 riots. In those elections, the Turkman Gate area fell among the top five polling stations in votes polled by the Republican Party candidate for the Aligarh City Legislative Assembly seat, Dr. Bashir. It is clear, therefore, that this locality has been at different times a center of high communal mobilization, riot production, and intense interparty competition. It is also socially and politically fragmented, containing a three-way caste-communal division among Hindus, Muslims, and Scheduled Castes, and, in 1995, as just noted, a closely contested four-way party division.

The three *mohallas* in ward 26 lie on the southwestern edge of the old city, with the Turkman Gate deriving its name from its location at a point where several roads lead out of the city in different directions (Map 1). The demographic mixture in these *mohallas* is uncommon in the city as a whole, but is characteristic of this section of it, in containing such a large concentration of Scheduled Castes. Unfortunately, how-

TABLE C.1. Community and caste composition of three *mohallas*, 1951 census

| Mohalla *name* | Hindus and Others | | Muslims | |
|---|---|---|---|---|
| | *Number* | *Percent* | *Number* | *Percent* |
| Sanichri Painth | 616 | 91.53 | 51 | 7.58 |
| Turkman Gate | 288 | 32.21 | 346 | 38.70 |
| Kutab ki Sarai | 765 | 50.50 | 84 | 5.54 |
| TOTAL | 1,669 | 54.15 | 481 | 15.61 |

ever, it is not possible to be precise about the number of Scheduled Castes in the ward. Insofar as the three *mohallas* are concerned, figures are available from the 1951 census, but they are for the *mohallas* in their entirety, whereas ward 26 contains only parts of them. The figures are, nevertheless, indicative (Table C.1).

The following features of the caste/communal composition of these *mohallas* are most relevant to the analysis of the political configuration of the ward. Hindus and others in 1951 were in the majority in the ward as a whole and in two of the *mohallas*, and an overwhelming majority in one of them. Muslims were a relatively small minority in two of the *mohallas*, but constituted a plurality of the population of Turkman Gate. Scheduled Castes were an insignificant minority in one *mohalla*, but a very substantial minority in the remaining two.

In 1951, the population of these three *mohallas* in their entirety numbered 3,082 persons. By 1995, the number of electors from the voters' list for those portions of these *mohallas* contained within ward no. 26 was 4,418 (Table C.2). Moreover, in 1995, Muslims constituted a majority in the ward as a whole, largely because their numbers had increased vastly in Turkman Gate. The ward was divided in 1995 into five parts, three of which were for Turkman Gate exclusively. In those wards, the Muslim percentage of registered voters ranged from 57.58 to 98.07. Non-Muslims, including both Hindus and others and Scheduled Castes, comprised 41.81 percent of the registered voters.

Given the majority Muslim population advantage in this ward in 1995, how can we explain both the intensity of interparty competition and the victory of the Hindu BJP candidate here? The segment-wise distribution of the vote in this ward provides the basis for answers to both questions. The BJP candidate, the only strong Hindu candidate in this ward, won most of his votes in the two segments (158 and 159) in which non-Muslims were in a majority (Table C.3). The other strong candidates, all Muslims, polled most of their votes in the *mohallas* (Sarai Kutub and Turkman Gate) where Muslims were concentrated, thereby dividing the Muslim majority and paving the way for the victory of the BJP. In addition, the BSP candidate, though a Muslim,

| Scheduled Castes | | Total | |
|---|---|---|---|
| Number | Percent | Number | Percent |
| 6 | 0.89 | 673 | 100.00 |
| 260 | 29.08 | 894 | 100.00 |
| 666 | 43.96 | 1,515 | 100.00 |
| 932 | 30.24 | 3,082 | 100.00 |

running on the ticket of the party of the Scheduled Castes, polled his highest vote share (30.62 percent) in the segment containing Sarai Kutub, which had, in 1951, a Scheduled Caste population of 43.96 percent. Thus, there was a division in this ward both between the Scheduled Castes and the Muslims and within the Muslim community as well. Those divisions were so great that the BJP candidate was able to win the seat even though he polled a majority vote in only one of the five segments, in contrast to the BSP, which won a plurality in two segments, the SP, which did so in one, and the strong independent candidate, also in one.

What can these results tell us about the relationship between riots and interparty competition? These elections were held in November 1995. The most proximate riot occurred in the city a month later, but did not affect directly the *mohallas* in ward no. 26. So the intensity of interparty competition here bears no relation to a proximate riot. What is most significant about interparty competition here is the degree of fragmentation of the electorate, both among the three census categories and within the Muslim category as well. Severe riots that precede elections have, as we have seen, the effect of intensifying interparty competition in the city as a whole, but we cannot expect to see that effect in particular *mohallas*, for the effect in particular localities will rather be communalization and polarization of the electorate. Since no major riot preceded these elections, there was in this ward, on the contrary, a fragmentation of the non-Hindu vote in general and the Muslim vote in particular that made possible a BJP victory.

The paradox is that the militant Hindu party, which in the past gained strength from communalization and polarization of the vote in the city as a whole, required precisely the opposite to win in a socially heterogeneous ward such as this. Moreover, that situation now exists in the constituency as a whole. Since Muslims now constitute a majority of the voters in the city Legislative Assembly constituency as a whole, the BJP also now requires division of the Muslim vote rather than, or as much as, consolidation of the Hindu vote to win the seat. That being the case, the prediction must be that riots of the type witnessed in earlier periods in the city are not to be expected in future under the existing electoral/political arrangements.

TABLE C.2. Number and percentage of registered voters by community in Ward 26, 1995

| Part Number of Ward | Mohalla Names(s) | Number of Registered Voters |
|---|---|---|
| 158 | Sanichri Painth/Turkman Gate | 858 |
| 159 | Sarai Kutub/Turkman Gate | 882 |
| 160 | Turkman Gate | 886 |
| 161 | Turkman Gate | 882 |
| 162 | Turkman Gate | 910 |
| TOTAL | Whole ward | 4,418 |

TABLE C.3. Party vote shares in Ward 26, 1995 corporation elections

| Segment Number | Mohalla Name(s) | Vote for BJP | | Vote for BSP | |
|---|---|---|---|---|---|
| | | Number | Percent | Number | Percent |
| 158 | Sanichri Painth/Turkman Gate | 350 | 66.79 | 59 | 11.26 |
| 159 | Sari Kutub/Turkman Gate | 138 | 30.40 | 139 | 30.62 |
| 160 | Turkman Gate | 46 | 9.60 | 86 | 17.95 |
| 161 | Turkman Gate | 6 | 1.17 | 147 | 28.54 |
| 162 | Turkman Gate | 38 | 6.61 | 140 | 24.35 |
| WARD TOTAL | | 578 | 22.69 | 571 | 22.41 |

| Number of Registered Muslim Voters | Percent Muslim Voters | Number of Registered Non-Muslim Voters | Percent Non-Muslim Voters |
|---|---|---|---|
| 174 | 20.28 | 684 | 79.72 |
| 420 | 47.62 | 462 | 52.38 |
| 583 | 65.80 | 298 | 33.63 |
| 865 | 98.07 | 17 | 1.93 |
| 524 | 57.58 | 386 | 42.42 |
| 2,566 | 58.08 | 1,847 | 41.81 |

| Vote of SP | | Vote for Independent no. 1 | | First-Place Party in Segment/Ward | Community of First-Place Candidate in Segment |
|---|---|---|---|---|---|
| Number | Percent | Number | Percent | | |
| 46 | 8.78 | 16 | 3.05 | BJP | Hindu |
| 84 | 18.50 | 65 | 14.32 | BSP | Muslim |
| 68 | 14.20 | 209 | 43.63 | IND | Muslim |
| 144 | 27.96 | 74 | 14.37 | BSP | Muslim |
| 191 | 33.22 | 137 | 23.83 | SP | Muslim |
| 533 | 20.93 | 501 | 19.67 | BJP | Hindu |

# NOTES

## 1 / EXPLAINING COMMUNAL VIOLENCE

1. On the distinction between riots and pogroms in relation to Hindu-Muslim violence in India, and on the more accurate description of many incidents of Hindu-Muslim violence since Independence as anti-Muslim pogroms, see Paul R. Brass, *Theft of an Idol: Text and Context in the Representation of Collective Violence.* (Princeton, N. J.: Princeton University Press, 1997), pp. 1ff. and passim; cf. also, among others, Amrita Basu, "Why Local Riots are Not Simply Local: Collective Violence and the State in Bijnor, India 1988–1993," *Theory and Society* 24 (1995): 35, and Gyanendra Pandey, "In Defense of the Fragment: Writing about Hindu-Muslim Riots in India Today," in *Economic and Political Weekly* [hereafter referred to as *EPW*] 36, nos. 11 & 12 (March 1991): 559–72.

2. A point emphasized at several places in the recent, extraordinarily fine study by Thomas Blom Hansen, *The Saffron Wave: Democracy and Hindu Nationalism in Modern India* (Princeton, N.J.: Princeton University Press, 1999).

3. The term *Center* is generally used in India to refer to the central (Union) Government of India, just as, in the United States, one refers to the government in Washington, D.C., as the federal government.

4. On these two movements and their relationship to the political calculations of and consequences for the parties and groups associated with militant Hindu nationalism, see Christophe Jaffrelot, *The Hindu Nationalist Movement and Indian Politics: 1925 to the 1990s* (London: Hurst, 1996), especially chapters 5 and 12.

5. The most notorious and vicious of these killings occurred in the town of Bhagalpur in Bihar, where not just a riot occurred but massacres of many hundreds of Muslims; see especially Indu Bharti, "Bhagalpur Riots and Bihar Government," *EPW* 34, no. 48 (December 2, 1989): 2643–44.

6. Paul R. Brass, "General Elections, 1996 in Uttar Pradesh: Divisive Struggles Influence Outcome," *EPW* 32, no. 38 (September 20, 1997): 2403–23.

7. Ashutosh Varshney and Steven I. Wilkinson, *Hindu-Muslim Riots 1960–93: New Findings, Possible Remedies* (New Delhi: Rajiv Gandhi Institute for Contemporary Studies, 1996), pp. 26–27. Their definition of riot-proneness is a town that has "had at least three communal riots, spread over at least two five-year periods in which a minimum of 15 deaths occurred."

8. Paul R. Brass, "Introduction: Discourses of Ethnicity, Communalism, and Violence," in Paul R. Brass (ed.), *Riots and Pogroms* (New York: NYU Press, 1996).

9. On the uses of the master narrative of Hindu-Muslim communalism and violence as an all-purpose explanation for disturbances of the public order in India during British rule, see Gyanendra Pandey, *The Construction of Communalism in Colonial North India* (Delhi: Oxford University Press, 1990).

10. See especially Doug McAdam, *Political Process and the Development of Black Insurgency, 1930–1970* (Chicago: University of Chicago Press, 1982); Charles Tilly, "Contentious Repertoires in Great Britain, 1758–1834," *Social Science History* 17, no. 2 (Summer 1993): 253–79; and Sidney Tarrow, *Power in Movement: Social Movements, Collective Action and Politics* (Cambridge: Cambridge University Press, 1994).

11. Brass, *Theft of an Idol*, pp. 9–20.

12. Journey by chariot, in this case placed on top of a Toyota.

13. Jayati Chaturvedi and Gyaneshwar Chaturvedi, "*Dharma Yudh*: Communal Violence, Riots and Public Space in Ayodhya and Agra City: 1990 and 1992," in Brass, *Riots and Pogroms,* p. 182.

14. Tilly and Tarrow have noted that, in every historical period of widespread protest activity, new forms of collective action appear that are considered illegitimate, but later become accepted and integrated into a new repertoire of accepted and legitimate forms. Their leading example is the industrial strike; see, for example, Sidney Tarrow, "Cycles of Collective Action: Between Moments of Madness and the Repertoire of Contention," *Social Science History* 17, no. 2 (Summer 1993): 289. As far as I know, however, no society, even Nazi Germany or fascist Italy, however much it has practiced violence—including in the form of pogroms—has integrated violent riots into a repertoire of accepted and legitimate forms of collective action.

15. Bill Buford, *Among the Thugs* (New York: W. W. Norton, 1992).

16. See Asghar Ali Engineer, "The Causes of Communal Riots in the Post-Partition Period in India," in Asghar Ali Engineer (ed.), *Communal Riots in Post-Independence India* (Hyderabad: Sangam Books, 1984), pp. 33–41; Hussain Shaheen, "Communal Riots in the Post-Partition Period in India: A Study of Some Causes and Remedial Measures," in Engineer, *Communal Riots,* pp. 165–74; Seymour Spilerman, "The Causes of Racial Disturbances: A Comparison of Alternative Explanations," *American Sociological Review* 35, no. 4 (August 1970): 627–49.

17. Raymond J. Murphy and James M. Watson, "Ghetto Social Structure and Riot Support: The Role of White Contact, Social Distance, and Discrimination," in Allen D. Grimshaw (ed.), *Racial Violence in the United States* (Chicago: Aldine, 1969), p. 236. According to these authors, "research findings from the riots of the 1960's" which found their "most obvious causes of unrest" in "the problems of poverty and discrimination," did "not exhaust our understanding of the motivations of rioters, nor do many of the findings 'make sense' in a purely economic or discrimination framework."

18. These and many other problems in causal analysis are not effectively handled in what has become the hegemonic statement of proper procedures for doing such analysis in political science, namely, Gary King, Robert O. Keohane, and Sidney Verba, *Designing Social Inquiry: Scientific Inference in Qualitative Research* (Princeton, N.J.: Princeton University Press, 1994). These authors say, "We must not ask for motivations, but rather for facts." While I agree that it is futile to attempt to verify or falsify individual motivations in the process of causal inference, it is nevertheless essential to "ask for motivations." Not to ask for motivations assumes we do not want to know anything about the framework that produces specific answers and the ability to produce them, including so-called factual answers concerning events. Although, in the next sentence, they qualify their statement about never asking for motivations, it is only to say that one may ask why someone did something only if the purpose is to generate hypotheses, not to penetrate the framework of meaning, the discourse that produces the statement.

19. See, for example, Ashish Banerjee, "'Comparative Curfew': Changing Dimensions of Communal Politics in India," in Veena Das (ed.), *Mirrors of Violence: Communities, Riots, and Survivors in South Asia* (Delhi: Oxford University Press, 1990), p. 54.

20. Spilerman, "The Causes of Racial Disturbances," p. 628.

21. Stanley Lieberson and Arnold R. Silverman, "The Precipitants and Underlying Conditions of Race Riots," in Grimshaw, *Racial Violence in the United States*, p. 362.

22. Ashutosh Varshney, *Ethnic Conflict and Civic Life: Hindus and Muslims in India* (New Haven: Yale University Press, 2002).

23. James D. Fearon and David D. Laitin, "Explaining Interethnic Cooperation," in *American Political Science Review* 90, no. 4 (December 1996), 715–35.

24. Keith notes in connection with the Brixton riots of July 1981 that "most political accounts or explanations of the riots were demonstrably, often openly, value-laden"; Michael Keith, *Race, Riots and Policing: Lore and Disorder in a Multi-Racist Society* (London: UCL Press, 1993), p. 72. A cursory reading of the press in the after math of the most recent great riots in America, in 1991 in Los Angeles, reveals the same in the statements of politicians during the presidential election campaign.

25. National Advisory Commission on Civil Disorders, *Report of the National*

*Advisory Commission on Civil Disorders* (Washington, D.C.: Government Printing Office, 1968); also known as the Kerner Commission Report.

26. Keith (*Race, Riots and Policing,* p. 81) argues that the association of cause with guilt goes back to the original Greek term *aitea,* "from which the term aetiology is derived." The Latin term *causa,* however, does not derive from the Greek and does not comprehend both meanings. It is, nevertheless, clear enough that, in everyday English, cause often implies guilt or blame, which leaves the question Keith means to raise, as to whether or not the scientific use of "the concept of causality" in the social sciences can escape its association "in common cultural understandings" with guilt and blame. I believe it cannot.

27. As in the work of Neil J. Smelser, *Theory of Collective Behavior* (New York: Free Press, 1962).

28. Keith, *Race, Riots and Policing,* p. 82. Here again, King, Keohane, and Verba, *Designing Social Inquiry,* provide inadequate guidance. Thus, on the question of meaning (p. 40), they acknowledge the necessity for qualitative research that is attuned to cultural meanings, using Geertz's famous example of distinguishing between a "wink" and an involuntary "twitch" of the eye. They fail to see, however, that, since actors know the meaning of such messages, they will alter them when they want to deceive. Further, the very methods of systematic observation that they propose for the discovery of cultural meanings will nullify their meanings or universalize them, requiring new codes for subterfuge or, in the issue discussed here, for blame displacement.

29. That being the case, to the extent that intentionality—actual rather than objectified human agency—becomes built into "causal analysis," it might be more suitable to characterize this form as "purposive analysis."

30. This is exemplified in the new research on the Russian pogroms in John D. Klier and Shlomo Lambroza (eds.), *Pogroms: Anti-Jewish Violence in Modern Russian History* (Cambridge: Cambridge University Press, 1992), and in books and articles published elsewhere by the contributors to that volume. So determined are many of them to debunk the causal theory that the Russian state was responsible for the pogroms that they avoid the more useful task of delineating clearly the multiplicity of actors and the roles played by them in producing the Russian pogroms in the nineteenth century, and also end up by going too far in minimizing the role of the state authorities. A frustrating example is I. Michael Aronson, *Troubled Waters: The Origins of the 1881 Anti-Jewish Pogroms in Russia* (Pittsburgh: University of Pittsburgh Press, 1990), which is full of archival and other documentation on the mechanics of pogrom production in Russia that is used overwhelmingly to batter to death the theory of Russian government involvement in the pogrom instead of constructing a coherent account of how the pogroms were carried out.

31. See Jorge Luis Borges, *Labyrinths: Selected Stories and Other Writings* (New York:

New Directions, 1964), where the theme of endless, precise repetition as a form of search for true knowledge recurs in several of the stories.

32. Robert K. Merton, "Manifest and Latent Functions," in *Social Theory and Social Structure,* rev. ed. (Glencoe, Ill.: Free Press, 1957), p. 71.

33. Ian Litton and Jonathan Potter, "Social Representations in the Ordinary Explanation of a 'Riot,'" *European Journal of Social Psychology* 15, no. 4 (October–December 1985), p. 372.

34. The leading historians and works in this group are Pandey, *Construction of Communalism;* Sandria Freitag, *Collective Action and Community: Public Arenas and the Emergence of Communalism in North India* (Berkeley: University of California Press, 1989); and Ayesha Jalal, *The Sole Spokesman: Jinnah, the Muslim League and the Demand for Pakistan* (Cambridge: Cambridge University Press, 1985). Each author has a distinctive perspective within the general framework of constructivism.

35. See, especially, studies of the origins of communal consciousness and communal riots in Bengal politics in the twentieth century, before and up to Partition, particularly Joya Chatterji, *Bengal Divided: Hindu Communalism and Partition, 1932–1947* (Cambridge: Cambridge University Press, 1994), and, specifically with regard to Hindu-Muslim riots in Bengal, Suranjan Das, *Communal Riots in Bengal 1905–1947* (Delhi: Oxford University Press, 1991), p. 170. Especially relevant to this study is that Das ultimately emphasizes the extent of preplanning in the Great Calcutta Killings of August 1946 and in others that followed it in Noakhali and Tiperra, and the direct and indirect involvement of politicians, parties, and government ministers in fomenting them.

36. In this group, C. A. Bayly is most prominent; see his "The Pre-History of 'Communalism'? Religious Conflict in India, 1700–1860," *Modern Asian Studies* 19, no. 2 (1985), pp. 177–203. Marc Gaborieau, an anthropologist, argues for an even earlier origin of communal identity and interreligious conflict; "From Al-Beruni to Jinnah: Idiom, Ritual and Ideology of the Hindu-Muslim Confrontation in South Asia," *Anthropology Today* 1, no. 3 (1985), pp. 7–14.

37. Most notable in this connection has been the intervention of a group of Marxist and other historians against the movement that led to the destruction of the mosque in Ayodhya, in which they took the position that it was a distortion of the historical facts to claim that the mosque was built upon the ruins of a Hindu temple on the site of the god Ram's birth or that Hindus have since ancient times believed that this very site was Ram's birthplace. See R. S. Sharma et al., *Ramjanmabhumi Baburi Masjid: A Historian's Report to the Nation,* undated [1991?], mimeographed paper, and the issue of *Seminar* (364 [December 1989]), titled "Mythifying History"; also relevant is an article by the lawyer and journalist A. G. Noorani, "The Babri Masjid–Ram Janmabhoomi Question," *EPW* 34, no. 45 (November 4–11, 1989), pp. 2461–66.

38. He heads the Centre for the Study of Society and Secularism, in Bombay (Mumbai), from which his publications emanate. The Centre for Research in Rural and Industrial Development (CRRID), Chandigarh, formerly headed by Rashpal Malhotra, but now by Pramod Kumar, has also sponsored ongoing studies of communal riots in India. The major publication by this organization in this connection is Pramod Kumar (ed.), *Towards Understanding Communalism* (Chandigarh: CRRID, 1992). This organization was also responsible a decade earlier for the most detailed demographic study yet done in India of the distribution of riot sites by *mohallas* in three western U.P. towns, including Aligarh. I make use of their study ("Communal Violence and its Impact on Development and National Integration," unpublished, undated) at several places below. Many other brief, but often valuable and insightful accounts written by others of particular riots in India have been published over the years in the pages of the *EPW*.

39. Asghar Ali Engineer, "An Analytical Study of the Meerut Riot," in Engineer, *Communal Riots,* p. 280.

40. Asghar Ali Engineer, "Bhagalpur Riot Inquiry Commission Report—A Comment," in *Progressive Prospective* 7, vol. 4 (July 1995), p. 1.

41. Beth Roy, *Some Trouble with Cows: Making Sense of Social Conflict* (Berkeley: University of California Press, 1994).

42. Varshney and Wilkinson, *Hindu-Muslim Riots.*

43. Varshney and Wilkinson, *Hindu-Muslim Riots,* p. 1.

44. Aside from the issue of the utility of the paired comparison method, Varshney's work suffers from a host of methodological problems that are revealed in a recent article (Ashutosh Varshney, "Ethnic Conflict and Civil Society: India and Beyond," *World Politics* 53, no. 3 [April 2001], pp. 362–98) heralding the imminent publication of his book, *Ethnic Conflict and Civic Life.* Although he draws upon Robert Putnam's ideas concerning the importance of civic engagement for democratic life, arguing that interethnic civic engagement prevents interethnic violence, in Varshney's hands it is pretty much a throwback to Arthur Bentley's arguments (though he does not refer to Bentley) about the importance of cross-cutting cleavages and the dangers of congruent cleavages between groups. In Varshney's hands, the argument becomes tautological. Where there is extensive civic engagement between Hindus and Muslims, there is peace, which amounts to saying that where there is peace, there is peace. Other methodological problems include the following: (1) a dataset that is inherently flawed, in which further errors were introduced in coding (a huge error was introduced, for example, into the Aligarh data, to which I alerted him and which was corrected in this article without acknowledgment); (2) an insistence that entire towns and cities are appropriate units of analysis; (3) the use of his independent variable, civic engagement, as in effect a pre-chosen cause rather than a genuine hypothesis to

be tested, with the selection of paired sites already proving the case in advance; (4) use of the misguided distinction between remote and proximate causes; (5) a basically primordialist perspective on how riots are generated through rumors and minor clashes that somehow "escalate," introducing a few new metaphors into this tired approach, such as "ethnic earthquakes," among others; (6) a complete failure to understand the workings of institutionalized riot systems, though he (inaccurately) cites my work on the subject; (7) turning the causal chain around so that violence itself, the dependent variable, suddenly at one point becomes the independent variable; (8) a virtual freeing of the BJP and the RSS (the latter not even mentioned in his article) from responsibility for the production of riots; (9) a complete freeing of the police, the principal killers in most riots in India, from responsibility; and (10) running through all this, an extraordinary faith in causal explanation and the ability of this kind of social science research to generate full-fledged causal statements. It is truly regrettable that such retrograde work is being brought forth at this stage in our knowledge of Indian politics and society, sanctified by the (mis)use of currently fashionable methodologies in the social sciences. In a word, Varshney's work constitutes a near-perfect example of the project of blame displacement applied to collective violence in the social sciences.

45. The case that seems to have come closest to involving an entire metropolitan area in the United States was the New York City draft riots in July 1863, on which see Iver Bernstein, *The New York City Draft Riots: Their Significance for American Society and Politics in the Age of the Civil War* (New York: Oxford University Press, 1990), and, for a graphic description, J. T. Headley, *Pen and Pencil Sketches of the Great Riots: An Illustrated History of the Railroad and Other Great American Riots. Including all the Riots in the Early History of the Country* (New York: E. B. Treat, 1882). In Europe, in the nineteenth century, such an event would have been called a revolution, except that in the New York case, it turned into a massacre of blacks by Irish.

46. Sudhir Kakar, "Some Unconscious Aspects of Ethnic Violence in India," in Veena Das (ed.), *Mirrors of Violence: Communities, Riots and Survivors in South Asia* (Delhi: Oxford University Press, 1990), pp. 134–45, and Sudhir Kakar, *The Colors of Violence: Cultural Identities, Religion, and Conflict* (Chicago: University of Chicago Press, 1996).

47. Kakar, *Colors of Violence*, pp. 12–13.

48. Kakar, *Colors of Violence*, p. 16.

49. Kakar, *Colors of Violence*, p. 22.

50. Kakar, *Colors of Violence*, pp. 40–41.

51. Kakar, *Colors of Violence*, p. 42.

52. On the Ranchi riots of 1967, see Paul R. Brass, *Language, Religion, and Politics in North India* (Cambridge: Cambridge University Press, 1974), p. 265. My analysis of

those riots formed the beginning of my own entirely different approach to the study of riots in India.

53. See S. D. Reicher's discussion of G. Le Bon, *The Crowd: A Study of the Popular Mind* (London: Ernest Benn, 1947), in "The St. Paul's Riot: An Explanation of the Limits of Crowd Action in Terms of a Social Identity Model," *European Journal of Social Psychology* 14 (1984), pp. 1–2; also, Stephen Reicher and Jonathan Potter, "Psychological Theory as Intergroup Perspective: A Comparative Analysis of 'Scientific' and 'Lay' Accounts of Crowd Events," *Human Relations* 38, no. 2 (1985), pp. 171–72 and 179.

54. Buford, *Among the Thugs.*

55. Kakar, *Colors of Violence,* p. 189 (emphasis in original).

56. Stanley J. Tambiah, *Leveling Crowds: Ethnonationalist Conflicts and Collective Violence in South Asia* (Berkeley: University of California Press, 1996).

57. Brass, *Riots and Progroms,* pp. 12–16, and Brass, *Theft of an Idol,* pp. 11–20.

58. Partha, Chatterjee, *The Nation and Its Fragments: Colonial and Postcolonial Histories* (Princeton, N.J.: Princeton University Press, 1993), p. 74.

59. Chatterjee, *The Nation and Its Fragments,* pp. 95–97.

60. Chatterjee, *The Nation and Its Fragments,* p. 98.

61. Chatterjee, *The Nation and Its Fragments,* p. 99.

62. Chatterjee, *The Nation and Its Fragments,* pp. 101–2.

63. Chatterjee, *The Nation and Its Fragments,* p. 102.

64. Pierre Nora, "From *Lieux de Mémoire* to *Realms of Memory,*" in Pierre Nora (ed.), *Realms of Memory: Rethinking the French Past,* vol. 1: *Conflicts and Divisions,* trans. by Arthur Goldhammer (New York: Columbia University Press, 1992), p. xvii: "A *lieu de mémoire* is any significant entity, whether material or nonmaterial in nature, which by dint of human will or the work of time has become a symbolic element of the memorial heritage of any community."

65. On which, see especially Paul R. Brass, *Language, Religion, and Politics in North India;* Francis Robinson, *Separatism Among Indian Muslims: The Politics of the United Provinces' Muslims, 1860–1923* (London: Cambridge University Press, 1974); and Mushirul Hasan, "Negotiating with Its Past and Present: The Changing Profile of the Aligarh Muslim University," in Mushirul Hasan (ed.), *Inventing Boundaries: Gender, Politics, and the Partition of India* (New Delhi: Oxford University Press, 2000), pp. 135–56.

66. Brass, *Theft of an Idol,* ch. 7.

## 2 / ALIGARH

1. The census data in the next several paragraphs and in Tables 2.1 and 2.2 are derived from the following sources: *Census of India, 1951, District Population Statistics, Uttar*

*Pradesh, 6–Aligarh District* (Allahabad: Superintendent, Printing and Stationery, 1953), pp. 10–13; *Census of India, 1951, District Census Handbook, Uttar Pradesh, 6–Aligarh District* (Allahabad: Superintendent, Printing and Stationery, 1954), pp. 182–83; *Census 1961, District Census Handbook, Uttar Pradesh, 20–Aligarh District* (Lucknow: Superintendent, Printing and Stationery, 1965), pp. 5, 10, xlviii–lv; *Census 1971, Series-21, Uttar Pradesh, District Census Handbook, Pt. X-A: Town & Village Directory, Aligarh District,* p. 10, and *Pt. X-B, Primary Census Abstract, Aligarh District,* pp. 64–97; *Census 1981, Series-22, Uttar Pradesh, District Census Handbook, Pt. XIII-A: Village & Town Directory, District Aligarh,* pp. 324–25, and *Pt. XIII-B, Primary Census Abstract, District Aligarh,* pp. 120–41; *Census of India, 1991, Series-1: India, Pt. IV-B (ii): Religion* (Table C-9) (Delhi: Controller of Publications, 1996), pp. 176–79, and *Series-25: Pt. II-A: General Population Tables* (Delhi: Controller of Publications, 1997), pp. 100, 453–54.

2. I have incomplete voters' lists for 1975, 1984, and 1995 by *mohalla,* but they are not aggregated by census categories. I have used these lists both to check the validity of the much older 1951 census data as a source for the Hindu-Muslim population proportions and to garner figures on the Hindu-Muslim population proportions in *mohallas* not included in the 1951 census.

3. Interview with head of the Political Science Department, Aligarh Muslim University, on December 27, 1961.

4. E. A. Mann, *Boundaries and Identities: Muslims, Work and Status in Aligarh* (New Delhi: Sage, 1992), p. 34.

5. S. A. H. Haqqi, *Urban Political Behavior (A Case Study of the Parliamentary Constituency, Aligarh)* (Aligarh: Aligarh Muslim University, 1978), p. 8, and Violette Graff, "Religious Identities and Indian Politics: Elections in Aligarh, 1971–1985," in André Wink (ed.), *Islam, Politics and Society in South Asia* (New Delhi: Manohar, 1991), p. 145.

6. Ashutosh Varshney, "Civic Life and Ethnic Conflict: Hindus and Muslims in India," unpublished draft manuscript, February 1998, p. 168 fn.

7. Haqqi, *Urban Political Behavior,* p. 9.

8. Zoya Hasan, *Dominance and Mobilisation: Rural Politics in Western Uttar Pradesh, 1930–1980* (New Delhi: Sage, 1989), p. 81.

9. Graff, "Religious Identities and Indian Politics," p. 145; Haqqi, *Urban Political Behaviour,* p. 9.

10. Interview with Tota ram Vidyarthi, municipal commissioner, Aligarh, defeated Jan Sangh candidate in 1962 election, in Aligarh City, on September 16, 1962.

11. For example, the mayor of the Aligarh municipal board in 1991, an Agarwal, was said to be a member of the RSS; interview, January 3, 1991.

12. Cf. Varshney, "Civic Life and Ethnic Conflict," p. 98. Also interview on July 19, 1983: "Jan Sangh is based on the business class, Banias. . . . All the shopkeepers and

business men . . . are . . . Jan Sangh. . . . there is a solid vote [of the business class for] the Jan Sangh." Many people in Aligarh continued to use the term *Jan Sangh* even after the creation of the BJP primarily by former Jan Sangh members.

13. For example, in 1997, the state vice-president of the Akhil Bharatiya Vidyarthi Parishad [All India Students Association] was an Aligarh man, Rajiv Agarwal; interview with RSS members, in Aligarh, on November 21, 1997.

14. For an example of Agarwal hostility to the AMU, see Mann, *Boundaries and Identities,* pp. 178–79. See also the book-length tirade against the AMU by an Agarwal writer, Shanti S. Gupta, *A.M.U.: The National Context* (Aligarh: Viveka Publications, 1980). Agarwal cloth merchants also allegedly played the roles of false witnesses during the 1991 riots (see Chapter 5), spreading malicious rumors that Muslim patients were being killed in the AMU Medical College Hospital; People's Union for Civil Liberties, "Communal Riots in Aligarh, Dec. 1990–Jan. 1991," *PUCL Bulletin* (March 1991).

15. Interviews, July 22, 1983 and November 20, 1997.

16. On the 1993 elections, see Chapter 10. Bansal ultimately won the seat for the Congress in 2002; see postscript.

17. Haqqi, *Urban Political Behaviour,* p. 8.

18. Interviews with Shri Niwas Sharma, MLA and President, Aligarh District Congress Committee, on December 27, 1961, in Aligarh: April 19, 1962, in Lucknow; and again in Aligarh on July 16, 1983.

19. E.g., on the 1996 Legislative Assembly election, see interview in Aligarh on November 21, 1997.

20. Interview, January 3, 1991.

21. Indeed, they claim that their ancestors came from Mithila and settled in Aligarh, though they no longer have any connection with the Maithil Brahmans of Bihar; interview in Aligarh, on April 2, 1999. Some of the Maithels in Aligarh also take the common Maithil Brahman surname of Jha. In order to distinguish the two herein, I have adopted the local English spelling of Maithels for those living in Aligarh.

22. Haqqi, *Urban Political Behaviour,* p. 8.

23. Interview, July 19, 1983.

24. Estimated from Haqqi, *Urban Political Behaviour,* p. 9.

25. Graff, "Religious Identities and Indian Politics," p. 146.

26. Interview with B. P. Maurya on June 28, 1963, in Chicago. Maurya claimed that 80,000 Jatavs converted to Buddhism in 1957, presumably from the whole district, but these numbers are not reflected in any census figures for the city or the district as a whole.

The term *Achal Talab,* though of Persian derivation, is commonly used to refer to this site, also called Achal Sarowar in Hindi (derived from Sanskrit), and Achal Tank (meaning lake or pool) in English.

27. Haqqi, *Urban Political Behaviour*, p. 11.

28. See also Hasan, *Dominance and Mobilisation*, p. 163, on the fluctuation in the vote of these two categories of voters in Aligarh in comparison to their support for the Congress in the rest of the state.

29. Interview in Aligarh on November 21, 1997.

30. Interview with Hashim Kidwai, faculty member, Department of Political Science, AMU, September 13, 1962.

31. Interview, November 21, 1997.

32. Haqqi, *Urban Political Behaviour*, p. 12.

33. Mann, *Boundaries and Identities*, p. 82.

34. Balmikis especially are said to support the BJP; interview, November 21, 1997.

35. Interview, January 3, 1991.

36. Interview, January 3, 1991.

37. Interview, January 3, 1991.

38. Interviews (including riot victims), in Upar Kot, Aligarh, on January 3, 1991.

39. Mann, *Boundaries and Identities*, pp. 43–44.

40. Mann, *Boundaries and Identities*, p. 135.

41. Haqqi, *Urban Political Behaviour*, pp. 39–40; Mann, *Boundaries and Identities*, p. 133, has also noted "that the baradari has become increasingly politicised as a voting block."

42. Mann, *Boundaries and Identities*, pp. 43–44.

43. Mann, *Boundaries and Identities*, p. 11. Indeed, contra Ernest Gellner, she argues (p. 75) that grand concepts of Islamic "renewal" and homogenization under an Islamic identity "have little relevance for Muslims in Aligarh."

44. Mann, *Boundaries and Identities*, pp. 16–17.

45. Mann discusses also the distinction between Ashraf (high status) and Ajlaf (lower status) groups, on the one hand, and *zat*, another kind of status ordering, on the other hand, both of which encompass multiple *baradaris*; *Boundaries and Identities*, pp. 38, 47, 51, 59.

46. Mann, *Boundaries and Identities*, pp. 48–49.

47. Mann, *Boundaries and Identities*, p. 34.

48. Mann, *Boundaries and Identities*, p. 51.

49. Thus, Qureshis were formerly known as Qasais (butchers), Ansaris as Julahas (weavers), and Saifis as Lohars (ironworkers); Mann *Boundaries and Identities*, pp. 65–66, 136–37. The Saifis formerly monopolized metalworking as "skilled craftsmen in the lock industry" of Aligarh (p. 81).

50. Interview, November 21, 1997.

51. Mann, *Boundaries and Identities*, p. 126.

52. Haqqi, *Urban Political Behaviour*, p. 10.

53. Designated as such in Centre for Research in Rural and Industrial Development (CRRID), Chandigarh, "Communal Violence and Its Impact on Development and National Integration," unpublished, undated (provided to me by Rashpal Mehrotra in 1983).

54. However, there are two *baradari*s of Ansaris, one of traditional high status, the other deriving from the Julaha group, so it is not certain, for example, that Ansaris at AMU and in other high-status occupations come from the Momin Ansars. More likely, they come from the traditionally high-status Ansari *baradari.*

55. E. A. Mann, "Religion, Money and Status: Competition for Resources at the Shrine of Shah Jamal, Aligarh," in Christian W. Troll (ed.), *Muslim Shrines in India: Their Character, History and Significance* (Delhi: Oxford University Press, 1989), p. 155.

56. Mann, "Religion, Money and Status," p. 159.

57. Mann, *Boundaries and Identities,* p. 158.

58. Mann, *Boundaries and Identities,* p. 184.

59. Mann, "Religion, Money and Status," p. 157.

60. Ashutosh Varshney, "Civic Life and Ethnic Conflict: Hindus and Muslims in India," unpublished manuscript (February 1998), p. 168.

## 3 / HINDU-MUSLIM VIOLENCE IN INDIA AND ALIGARH

1. Ashutosh Varshney and Steven I. Wilkinson, *Hindu-Muslim Riots 1960–93: New Findings, Possible Remedies* (New Delhi: Rajiv Gandhi Institute for Contemporary Studies, 1996), pp. 5–6.

2. Paul R. Brass, *The Politics of India since Independence,* 2nd ed. (Cambridge: Cambridge University Press, 1994), p. 240. The percentage-wise distribution of deaths in this period by religion, for Hindus and Muslims only, is 75 percent Muslim, 25 percent Hindu. Wilkinson has calculated the percentage of Muslims killed in four periods, including one pre-Independence period, as follows: 1924–27, 46 percent; 1961–70, 75 percent; 1971–80, 65 percent; 1985–87, 60 percent. For some reason, the percentage of Muslims injured is lower than for Hindus in all these periods, markedly so in all the post-Independence riots. The explanation for this discrepancy that comes to mind is that more Hindus than Muslims are injured in intercommunal crowd violence, but that more Muslims are killed by police firing. Figures from Steven I. Wilkinson, "The Electoral Origins of Ethnic Violence: Hindu-Muslim Riots in India" (unpublished Ph.D. dissertion, Harvard University), ch. 2, p. 24, citing various sources.

3. Anonymous, "Communal Riots and Minorities," confidential mimeographed memorandum, undated [1983?].

4. For example, in the Bhiwandi riots of May 1970, 17 Hindus, 59 Muslims, and 2 unidentified persons died. None of the Hindus, but 9 Muslims, were killed by police

firing. Muslims were fired upon on 26 occasions compared to only 4 occasions for Hindus. The evidence, therefore, indicates clearly that Muslims were killed in disproportionate numbers both by Hindu rioters and by the police. Figures from Anonymous, "Communal Riots and Minorities"; this report and the official commission reports from which the data were drawn provide ample further evidence from most other riots in the period between 1968 and 1980 of the disproportion in police assaults and killings of Muslims. Nor has the situation changed in the years since, as will be discussed further below.

5. Varshney and Wilkinson, *Hindu-Muslim Riots,* p. 12.

6. Asghar Ali Engineer, the most important chronicler of such riots, publishes reports on all major riots from his institute in Bombay, Centre for the Study of Society and Secularism, which also maintains a regular journal called *Secular Perspective.* His own articles, including year-end reviews, are also published frequently in the *EPW.* His most recent year-end review, titled "Communal Riots, 2000," appeared in *EPW* 26, no. 4 (January 27 – February 2, 2001), pp. 275–79.

7. Varshney and Wilkinson, *Hindu-Muslim Riots,* p. 19.

8. Wilkinson, "The Electoral Origins of Ethnic Violence," chapter 2, p. 6. It must be noted, however, that there are huge differences in the number of riots counted depending upon the sources and the methods used. For example, the inspector-general (IG) of police, U.P., released state government figures in 1971 that showed 924 communal riots in the twenty-three years from 1948 to 1971, many times more than the number shown by Wilkinson for the entire period from 1950 to 1993; *Times of India,* January 21, 1971. The Wilkinson/Varshney figures are based on reporting in the *Times of India,* which is incomplete and which often collapses many discrete incidents into one extensive "riot." The Wilkinson/Varhsney figures, in effect, do the same.

9. Ashutosh Varshney, "Civic Life and Ethnic Conflict: Hindus and Muslims in India," unpublished draft manuscript, February 1998, p. 115.

10. Wilkinson dissertation, ch. 2, p. 17. Ashutosh Varshney's manuscript, "Civic Life and Ethnic Conflict: Hindus and Muslims in India," using the same dataset as Wilkinson, updated to 1995, lists one additional death in riots, bringing the estimated total to 389.

Varshney also ranks all the riot-prone cities of India by the absolute numbers of deaths. In this ranking, Bombay (1,137) stands first, Ahmadabad (1,119) second, and Aligarh (389) third, but I have noted in the text that the Aligarh figure is inaccurate and far too high. Nevertheless, Bombay and Ahmadabad being many times larger than Aligarh in population, a death-per-person ranking would certainly put Aligarh, with 176 deaths, still very high in the whole of India. Citation to table from page 121 of Varshney manuscript. Although their Aligarh data have been corrected in response to my notification to Wilkinson of the problem, such errors are inevitable in large datasets of this type and cast considerable doubt on their utility, especially since, as in this case, an overcount here indicates undercounts in other parts of the database.

11. The figures are probably not accurate since the errors occurred in coding newspaper reports that lumped together deaths from several sites for riots that occurred during the same time period. Wilkinson and Varshney were informed of the inaccuracies and Wilkinson advised me that they were undertaking to correct their dataset; personal communication from Steve Wilkinson. However, in his latest publication, Varshney now gives a figure that is too low, rather than too high; he records 160 deaths for 1950–95, whereas my figures are 184 plus an unknown number of deaths in the riot of December 1992; Ashutosh Varshney, "Ethnic Conflict and Civil Society: India and Beyond," *World Politics,* 53, no. 3 (April 2001), p. 372.

12. Wilkinson, "The Electoral Origins of Ethnic Violence," ch. 2, p. 17.

13. Varshney, "Ethnic Conflict and Civil Society," p. 372. The population of Greater Bombay in 1991 was 9,925,891; Ahmadabad was 3,312,216, Hyderabad 4,344,437, Meerut 849,799, and Aligarh 480,520. Figures from *Census of India, 1991, Series-1, India,* Part IV-B (ii): *Religion* (Table C-9), pp. 60, 108, 176, and 356.

14. On the multiple (mis)uses of all types of commissions in India, see Upendra Baxi, *Mambrino's Helmet?: Human Rights for a Changing World* (New Delhi: Har-Anand, 1994), ch. 9 ("Sins of Commission(s)").

15. Ratanlal Ranchhoddas, Dhirajlal Keshavlal Thakore, and Manharlal Ratanlal Vakil, *The Law of Crimes,* 22nd ed. (Bombay: Bombay Law Reporter, 1971), p. 332.

16. For comparison, see the charts in Varshney and Wilkinson, *Hindu-Muslim Riots,* pp. 13 and 21, which are, however, not entirely comparable, being drawn on a yearly basis.

17. Indian Statutory Commission (hereafter referred to as ISC), volume IX, *Memorandum Submitted by the Government of the United Provinces to the Indian Statutory Commission* (London: HMSO, 1930), p. 66.

18. ISC, vol. IV, *Memoranda Submitted by The Government of India and The India Office to the Indian Statutory Commission,* Pt. I (London: HMSO, 1930), memorandum on "Communal Disorders," p. 100. I am grateful to Steven Wilkinson for referring me to this report.

19. *Times* (London), September 25 and 26, 1925.

20. ISC, "Communal Disorders," p. 111.

21. *Times of India,* April 12, 13, and 14, 1927.

22. Since the U.P. Legislative Assembly was in session at this time, these riots provided an occasion for a full-scale debate in the legislature, which occurred between March 8 and 22 in response to a statement by the premier (Pandit Govind Ballabh Pant) and an adjournment motion. The Congress was then in power with the Muslim League as the principal opposition. The debate degenerated into an exercise in blame

displacement in which the Muslim League leaders, including Nawabzada Liaquat Ali Khan, who was later to become Pakistan's first prime minister, blamed the Congress government, while the latter blamed the Muslim League and the Urdu press; *U.P. Assembly Debates,* vol. IV (1–23 March 1938), pp. 460, 732–33, 800, 844–45, 965, 967–68, 1016–26, 1036–39.

23. These citations come from the Home (Police) Box 378 File # 5004/1046 Aligarh—Riot Scheme) from the U.P. State Archives, kindly provided to me by Steven Wilkinson.

24. United Provinces, Governor's Report, dated April 1, 1946.

25. Government of the United Provinces, Confidential Department, Fortnightly Report for the Second Half of March 1946, dated Lucknow, April 5, 1946.

26. Government of the United Provinces, Confidential Department, Fortnightly Report for the First Half of April 1946, dated Lucknow, April 22, 1946.

27. United Provinces, Governor's Letter dated June 19, 1946.

28. United Provinces, Governor's Report to Lord Wavell from F. V. Wylie, April 30, 1946.

29. The main continuing sites of communal violence at this time were the cities of Allahabad and Kanpur, while the most vicious and atrocious violence occurred in the town of Garhmuktesar in Meerut District in November 1946, where several hundred men, women, and children, nearly all Muslim, were massacred.

30. Government of the United Provinces, Confidential Department, Fortnightly Report for the First Half of June 1946, dated June 24, 1946, and Fortnightly Report for the Second Half of June 1946, dated July 12, 1946.

31. Government of the United Provinces, Confidential Department, Fortnightly Report for the Second Half of September 1946, dated Lucknow, October 7, 1946.

32. Governor F. V. Wylie, fortnightly letter to Lord Wavell, dated October 19, 1946.

33. Government of the United Provinces, Confidential Department, Fortnightly Report for the First Half of November 1946, dated Lucknow, November 25, 1946.

34. Government of the United Provinces, Confidential Department, Fortnightly Report for the Second Half of November 1946, dated Lucknow, December 10, 1946.

35. Government of the United Provinces, Confidential Department, Fortnightly Report for the First Half of January 1947, dated Lucknow, January 29, 1947.

36. See Appendix Table A.4.

37. Wilkinson's code sheets. However, the *Free Press Journal,* March 6, 1950, reported four killed.

38. *Free Press Journal,* March 9, 1950.

39. Pars Ram, *A UNESCO Study of Social Tensions in Aligarh, 1950–51,* ed. with an introduction by Gardner Murphy (Ahmedabad: New Order Book Co., 1955), p. 173.

40. Wilkinson code sheets.

41. This riot appears in the Wilkinson/*Times of India* code sheets as one riot. The state government, however, classed it as five discrete riots; *Times of India,* January 21, 1971. A brief summary of this riot may be found also in Centre for Research in Rural and Industrial Development, "Communal Violence and its Impact on Development and National Integration," unpublished (Chandigarh: n.d. [1983?]), p. 35.

42. This does not translate well into English, but it refers to a central government-funded organization engaged in the production of knowledge through book publication.

43. *Times of India* (Bombay), September 22, 1956.

44. *Times of India* (Bombay), September 7, 1956.

45. *Times of India* (Bombay), September 12, 1956.

46. *Times of India* (Bombay), September 8, 9, 10, 14, 15, 16, 18, 19, 20, and 26, 1956. A later retrospective survey of riots in U.P. reported that rioting occurred in 12 districts of U.P.; *Times of India,* January 21, 1971.

47. *Times of India* (Bombay), September 14, 1956.

48. *Times of India* (Bombay), September 10, 1956.

49. *Times of India* (Bombay), September 15, 1956.

50. *Times of India* (Bombay), September 19, 1956.

51. *Times of India* (Bombay), September 24, 1956.

52. *Times of India* (Bombay), September 17, 1956.

53. *Times of India* (Bombay), September 18, 1956.

54. *Times of India* (Bombay), September 20, 1956.

55. My information on these riots is derived principally from personal interviews in 1961–62 in Aligarh, originally written up in Paul R. Brass, *Factional Politics in an Indian State: The Congress Party in Uttar Pradesh* (Berkeley: University of California Press, 1965), pp. 100–101. An account giving the same details as mine was prepared years later as an official, confidential document on Aligarh riots in Anonymous, "Riots in Aligarh," mimeographed, 7 pages (n.d., but possibly 1983).

56. *Times of India,* October 5, 1961.

57. *Times of India,* October 5, 1961.

58. *Times of India,* October 10, 1961.

59. *Times of India,* October 14, 1961.

60. *Times of India,* October 9, 1961.

61. *Times of India,* October 17, 1961.

62. *Times of India,* October 7, 1961.

63. *Times of India,* October 14, 1961.

64. *Times of India,* October 23 and 30, 1961.

65. *Times of India,* October 7, 1961.

66. These incidents are mentioned also in Graff, "Religious Identities and Indian

Politics: Elections in Aligarh, 1971–1985," in André Wink (ed.), *Islam, Politics and Society in South Asia* (New Delhi: Manohar, 1991), p. 153. Varshney also refers to a riot in March 1971, whose "reported cause" was the "arrest of a Hindu Nationalist student leader at the time of elections"; Varshney, "Civic Life and Ethnic Conflict," p. 185.

67. For further details on these issues, see Paul R. Brass, *Language, Religion, and Politics in North India* (London: Cambridge University Press, 1974), pp. 223–27.

68. *Times of India,* March 3, 1971.

69. *Times of India,* March 31, 1971.

70. *Times of India,* March 9, 1971

71. *Times of India,* March 3, 1971.

72. *Times of India,* March 5, 1971.

73. The report of the Mathur Commission was not submitted to government until 1975 and was never officially released; Mukundan C. Menon and Sumanta Banerjee, *Report to the People's Union for Civil Liberties & Democratic Rights (Delhi State) on Aligarh Riot (October 5, 1978),* p. 11. Although never officially released, the report has been published and some people have had direct or indirect access to it. Although I have the reference for this report, I have never been able to get hold of a copy of it. The citation is Mathur Commission Report, UP Government, 1975, *Uttar Pradesh Rajya ke Aligarh Nagar Mein 2 March 1971,* and *Uske Baad Huey Sampradayik UpadravoN ke Sambandh Mein Jaanch Ayoj ki Report* (Report of the Commission for Inquiry into Communal Disturbances of Aligarh, U.P., on March 2, 1971, and After) (Allahabad: Superintendent of Printing and Publishing, 1975).

74. *Times of India,* June 1, 1972.

75. Ninety-nine percent, according to one estimate; *Times of India,* June 20, 1972.

76. *Times of India,* June 3, 1972.

77. The Muslim League in post-Independence India is but a remnant of the pre-Independence organization. Its political strength is confined to the state of Kerala, where it is considered a legitimate party, not an antinational, pro-Pakistan organization.

78. *Times of India,* June 2, 1972.

79. *Times of India,* June 3, 1972. Later in the month, Nurul Hasan stated emphatically, at a Congress meeting on the status of the AMU, "We are not going to accept the minority character [of the AMU]"; *Times of India,* June 15, 1972.

80. *Times of India,* June 3, 1972.

81. *Times of India,* June 5, 1972.

82. Varshney gives the "reported cause" of this riot as "Hindu seven year old child knocked down by a Muslim scooter driver by accident"; (Varshney, "Civic Life and Ethnic Conflict," p. 185). Like most of his other "reported causes," this is obviously a gross misreading of the source of the rioting that trivializes it and casts doubt on the entire enterprise of counting riots by casual newspaper-reading.

83. *Times of India*, June 6, 1972.

84. *Times of India*, June 6 and 8, 1972.

85. *Times of India*, June 10, 1972.

86. However, one death is reported in Anonymous, "Riots in Aligarh." Since the account of this riot contains other erroneous information and no details are given concerning the death, it is possible that this information is also incorrect. This riot nevertheless has qualified for detailed discussion above because of the extent of injuries and the number of sites (five) from which violence was reported.

87. *Times of India*, June 11, 1972.

88. The riots in Firozabad and Varanasi and in two other towns in U.P. were reported in *Times of India*, June 17–21, 24, and 30, 1972.

89. *Times of India*, June 13, 1972. In fact, Jinnah did not have a close association with the AMU. He was not educated there. He visited the campus to make political contacts and speeches as he did in countless places throughout the country in the late 1930s and 1940s. He did, however, have considerable success in mobilizing faculty and students at the AMU, on which see Mushirul Hasan, "Negotiating with Its Past and Present: The Changing Profile of the Aligarh Muslim University," in Mushirul Hasan (ed.), *Inventing Boundaries: Gender, Politics, and the Partition of India* (New Delhi: Oxford University Press, 2000), pp. 135–56.

90. *Times of India*, June 20, 1972.

91. Varshney lists this sequence as three riots with their reported causes: (1) October, "clash between a Hindu and a Muslim wrestler," (2) November, "retribution for previous violence," (3) December, "retribution for previous violence"; "Civic Life and Ethnic Conflict," p. 185. Once again, such simplistic categorization and the use of the term *cause* are both utterly misleading.

92. *Hindustan Times*, October 17, 1978; *Times of India*, October 7, 1978.

93. Bhure Lal's house was located in the communally sensitive locality of Delhi Darwaza. The *Times of India*, October 19, 1978, report and that of *Radiance* (a Muslim paper owned by the Jamaat-ul Ulama), October 22, 1978, both allege that the processionists chose deliberately to pass through the extremely communally sensitive crossing of Chauraha Abdul Karim on their way, even though it was not on the direct route to Bhure Lal's house. The October 29, 1978, issue of *Radiance* also referred to the simultaneous breaking out of violence at Manik Chauk and Chauraha Abdul Karim. It is possible, even probable, that these newspapers are feeding off each other's reports, rather than obtaining information independently, or that they are all feeding from the same pool of informants.

In addition to Manik Chauk, three other areas were reported to have been "the worst-affected": Upar Kot, Rafatganj, and Phul Chauraha; *Times of India*, October 11, 1978.

94. *Times of India,* October 17, 1978.

95. See Joseph S. Alter, *The Wrestler's Body: Identity and Ideology in North India* (Berkeley: University of California Press, 1992).

96. Kakar notes that, even in popular parlance, the vernacular term for wrestler, *pahalwan,* also may connote *goonda* or hooligan. He has also noted that "Hindu-Muslim tensions [in Hyderabad] have led the police to ban wrestling matches in the city, since a bout between a Hindu and Muslim wrestler can easily ignite a riot between the two communities" (p. 56). During riots, these men may meet with other wrestlers and hooligans "on a daily basis and decide . . . where the killings have to take place and where they need to be stopped" (p. 80). Further, he remarks that the Muslim and Hindu wrestlers have also become, in effect, icons of each "community's physical power and martial prowess" and that they have also been "used by the politician, employing religious violence for his own purposes" (p. 85); Sudhir Kakar, *The Colors of Violence: Cultural Identities, Religion, and Conflict* (Chicago: University of Chicago Press, 1996).

97. *Times of India,* October 9 and 14, 1978.

98. *Times of India,* October 11, 1978.

99. *Times of India,* October 15, 1978.

100. *Times of India,* October 16, 1978.

101. *Times of India,* October 16, 1978.

102. *Times of India,* October 16, 1978.

103. *Times of India,* October 14, 1978.

104. *Times of India,* October 11, 1978.

105. Menon and Banerjee, *Report,* p. 1.

106. Menon and Banerjee, *Report,* pp. 1–2.

107. Menon and Banerjee, *Report,* p. 4.

108. Menon and Banerjee, *Report,* p. 5. For a similar incident of "body snatching" by BJP/RSS politicians of a Hindu killed in Kanpur City, who had previously been implicated in many murders of Muslims in the riots in that city in December 1992, see Paul R. Brass, *Theft of an Idol: Text and Context in the Representation of Collective Violence* (Princeton, N.J.: Princeton University Press), pp. 240ff.

109. Menon and Banerjee, *Report,* p. 4. The Communist (CPI) newspaper, the *Patriot,* used the same terms to describe the situation in Manik Chauk. Again, it is likely these reports come from a common source or are copied from one another.

110. Menon and Banerjee, *Report,* pp. 8–9.

111. Menon and Banerjee, *Report,* p. 9.

112. Menon and Banerjee, *Report,* p. 13.

113. These were the elections that followed the relaxation of the authoritarian Emergency regime imposed by Indira Gandhi between 1975 and 1977 and that led to

the election of the first non-Congress government in India's post-Independence history.

114. The rather anomalous and highly conflicted position of this man will be discussed later (see below, Chapter 13).

115. *Times of India,* October 20, 1978.

116. On the local divisions, see Menon and Banerjee, *Report,* p. 10.

117. Menon and Banerjee, *Report,* p. 12.

118. *Times of India,* October 10, 1978.

119. *Times of India,* November 7, 1978.

120. *Patriot,* November 9, 1978.

121. *Times of India,* November 21, 1978; this report said that the November 6th riot began close to Manik Chauk, but that it affected more severely the *mohalla*s of "Sarai Kaba and Sarai Miya [Mian], two adjacent areas with a mixed population of Hindus and Muslims."

122. *Times of India,* November 10, 1978.

123. *Hindustan Times,* November 10, 1978, and *Times of India,* November 21, 1978.

124. *Hindustan Times,* November 11, 1978.

125. *Times of India,* November 12, 1978.

126. *Times of India,* November 16, 1978.

127. Inder Malhotra reported on this matter of the failure to arrest Navman promptly during these riots a couple of years later as follows: "During the particularly nasty riots at Aligarh in 1978, when the university town was under continuous curfew for more than two months, there was no dearth of intelligence advice to the authorities that a certain Mr. Navman must be arrested. But he was an important local leader of the then ruling party, the Janata, and no one dared touch him for weeks. Eventually, however, he was taken into custody but only after a visiting American journalist had taunted the Chief Minister: 'Who is this Mr. 'no-man' you are so afraid of?'" *Times of India,* August 24, 1980. (There is a play on the pronunciation of Navman's name here, which can be pronounced either as Nuvmaan or as Naumaan.)

128. *Hindustan Times,* November 20, 1978, and *Times of India,* November 22, 1978.

129. *Patriot,* November 26, 1978.

130. *Times of India,* December 16, 1978.

131. *Times of India,* December 31, 1978.

132. *Lok Sabha Debates,* Vol. 20, Nos. 12–17 (6th Series), Dec. 5–13, 1978, *Motion Re: Situation Arising out of Recent Communal Riots in Different Parts of the Country* (New Delhi: Lok Sabha Secretariat, 1978).

133. *Times of India,* November 20, 1978. The specific area mentioned in this connection was Mamubhanja, but it is not clear whether it is the *mohalla* or the entire ward to which reference was made.

134. *Times of India,* November 21, 1978.

135. *Times of India,* November 22, 1978.

136. Interview in New Delhi on June 20, 1991; taped in English.

137. *Times of India,* August 30, 1980.

138. *Times of India,* May 4 and 15, 1979.

139. *Times of India,* May 11, 1979, reported the number as "about 1,000."

140. *Times of India,* May 10, 1979.

141. *Times of India,* May 10, 1979.

142. *Times of India,* May 11, 1979.

143. *Times of India,* May 11 and 12, 1979.

144. In fact, this alleged aspect of the Dadri affair, which was mentioned only once or twice in one-line statements in the press at the time, became the official explanation. In my interview with the DSP, intelligence, in 1983, he made the following comments without my having mentioned Dadri at all. "The university, which is a predominantly Muslim area, never witnesses any violence except once in 1979, which was not a communal case. A group of AMU students going to Delhi was beaten up at Dadri for alleged misbehavior with a Hindu girl. The students came back and, to express their resentment at what had happened at Dadri, burnt down some shops at Shamshad Market." Interview in Aligarh, July 30, 1983.

145. *Times of India,* May 13, 1979.

146. *Times of India,* May 16, 1979.

147. *Times of India,* May 21, 1979.

148. *Times of India,* May 22, 1979.

149. *Times of India,* August 17, 1980.

150. *Times of India,* August 19, 1980. Graff, in an earlier, mimeographed version of the article previously cited, titled "Religious Identities and Indian Politics, a Case-Study: Aligarh (1971–1981)" (Paris: Fondation Nationale des Sciences Politiques et Centre d'Etudes de l'Inde et de l'Asie du Sud [EHESS], n.d. [1982–83]), p. 73, reports that the two constables were beheaded.

151. *Times of India,* August 21, 1980.

152. *Times of India,* August 24, 1980.

153. *Times of India,* August 25, 1980.

154. *Times of India,* August 27–30, 1980.

155. *Times of India,* September 3, 1980.

156. *Times of India,* August 26, 1980.

157. *Times of India,* August 29, 1980.

158. *Times of India,* August 31, 1980.

159. *Times of India,* September 3, 1980. Girilal Jain was one of the most influential journalists in India, as editor of the *Times of India,* from 1978 to 1988. The piece

from which these quotations come is a fine example of his sophistical mode of argumentation. Many examples could be provided from this one piece alone, but perhaps the most telling was his convoluted argument that a farfetched conspiratorial theory such as Mrs. Gandhi's interpretation could not be proven wrong; therefore, it must be given some credence.

160. *Times of India,* September 4, 1980.

161. *Times of India,* August 24, 1980.

162. *Times of India,* September 9, 1980; the official death toll was increased to ten the next day when another person died of his injuries; *Times of India,* September 10, 1980. For the follow-up reports on Moradabad, see *Times of India,* September 9–12, 1980.

163. Reported to me from two sources: Graff, personal communication, and interview in Aligarh, July 30, 1983. Both sources confirm the killings, but I am uncertain about the number; the figures given to me orally, but not included in my written notes, were 41 or 49. Further information on the behavior of this SSP, including a reference to his alleged extrajudicial mode of execution, may be found in the *Indian Express,* December 6, 9, and 19, 1981.

164. Centre for Research, "Communal Violence," pp. 34–35. However, there were major disturbances on the campus of the AMU in May and June 1981 concerning internal disputes that did not involve Hindu-Muslim relations, which were also handled firmly by the new district administration.

165. *Times of India,* September 11 and 12, October 17, 20, and 31, November 2, 1980.

166. Varshney's list ("Civic Life and Ethnic Conflict," p. 185), which is quite inadequate for these events, runs as follows. In 1980: August, "Police fires [*sic*] at a Muslim protest. Rioting three times in two weeks"; September, "Arrest of two local journalists"; October, "Random stabbing"; November, "Muslims attack the Provincial Armed Constabulary." In 1982: July, "Cause insufficiently reported."

167. Varshney, "Civic Life and Ethnic Conflict," p. 174.

168. Interview in Aligarh on July 19, 1983; taped.

169. *Times of India,* October 9, 1988.

170. *Times of India,* October 12 and 15, 1988.

171. *Times of India,* editorial, October 15, 1988.

172. These quotes come from a signed *Times of India* report by two correspondents reporting from Muzaffarnagar, October 13, 1988. The newspaper's editorial followed this report two days later.

173. Centre for Research, "Communal Violence," passim.

174. Centre for Research, "Communal Violence," p. 46.

175. *Times of India,* October 13, 1988.

176. Atul Kohli, "From Majority to Minority Rule: Making Sense of the 'New'

Indian Politics," in Marshall M. Bouton and Philip Oldenburg (eds.), *India Briefing, 1990* (Boulder: Westview Press, 1990), p. 27. Dates for these riots are from *Muslim India* 83 (November 1989), pp. 525–26.

177. The broadside was distributed under the auspices of the *Dwitiya Rajbhasa Urdu Virodhi Sangarsh Samiti* (Action Committee against Urdu as Second State Language).

178. Here is a sample of some of the slogans, taken from a broadside listing 52 of them, distributed on November 20 by one Dr. Vedram Vidyarthi under the anti-AMU title, *Vishvavidyalaya ya Vishvraksh?* (University or Poison Tree?) ("a tree yielding poisonous fruit," according to McGregor's Hindi-English dictionary). Under the category of anti–Rajiv Gandhi, there appeared such slogans (rhymed in Hindi) as the following: (1) *Ham hain Muslim bis karor. Panje ko denge maror.* (We are two hundred million Muslims. We will bring you down.) (2) *Rajiv tune prajatantra ki hatya ki. Tujhe bhi yad kareNga musalman.* (Rajiv, you killed democracy. Muslims will think of you also [or, will certainly remember it].) This latter slogan makes use of the very derogatory form of the second person pronoun, used normally only for animals and little children. The slogan also implies a death threat against Rajiv. (3) *Aligarh se uthi hai anghi. Ur jayega Rajiv Gandhi.* (A storm has risen from Aligarh. It will carry off Rajiv Gandhi.) (4) *Rajiv Gandhi—R.S.S. tumhari.* (Rajiv Gandhi—you are R.S.S.) Under the category of anti-Hindu slogans, here is one example. *Sikh Muslim Isai— apas meN sab bhai-bhai.* (Sikh, Muslim, Christian—all are brothers in harmony.) Given the existence at this time of intense and violent insurrectionary movements amongst Sikhs in Punjab, Muslims in Kashmir, and Christian tribals in the northeastern part of the country, this slogan would naturally antagonize the Hindu population and would be considered an attack on the unity of the country, which was adopted as one of the central campaign themes of Rajiv Gandhi and the Congress in this campaign. The broadside also classified some slogans as traitorous, for example, the following: (1) Prepare for *jihad.* Donate your blood. (In English.) (2) No Islam—no India. (In English.) (3) *Naye rashtra ki nayi rajdhani—Ayodhya.* (The new capital of the new nation—Ayodhya.) The latter is an obvious sarcastic attack on the militant Hindu movement centered around the Ram Janmabhoomi movement in Ayodhya. (4) We want Babari Masjid. (In English.) Effigies were also seen, among which four were described in the broadside, including one of Rajiv Gandhi hanging from a noose. All translations mine.

179. *Times of India,* November 11, 1989.

180. I have only the clippings for these articles without the names of the newspapers or the dates.

181. *Times of India,* November 16, 1989.

182. My translation from the Hindi newspaper datelined November 13, 1989.

183. It is conceivable that these posters were plastered by Hindus deliberately to incite feelings against the Muslims and the AMU. There are several reasons for thinking of this possibility: (1) the inference that the three Hindu students suspended from the AMU may have been involved with it; (2) the crudeness of the slogans themselves, so crude that those who plastered them must have known that they would incite rage among Hindus that might lead to violence against Muslims and the AMU; (3) the use of these slogans in a printed broadside for the evident purpose of inciting rage, if not violence.

184. Centre for Research, "Communal Violence," p. 35.

185. Marc Gaborieau, "From Al-Beruni to Jinnah: Idiom, Ritual and Ideology of the Hindu-Muslim Confrontation in South Asia," *Anthropology Today* 1, no. 3 (1985), p. 8.

186. Government of India, Minorities Commission, *First Annual Report for the Year Ending 31st December, 1978* (New Delhi: Government of India Press, 1979), p. 91.

187. Minorities Commission, *First Annual Report*, p. 92.

## 4 / THE GREAT ALIGARH RIOTS OF DECEMBER 1990 AND JANUARY 1991

1. People's Union for Civil Liberties (PUCL), "Communal Riots in Aligarh, Dec. 1990–Jan. 1991," *PUCL Bulletin* (March 1991), p. 14.

2. Interview in Aligarh on January 3, 1991.

3. Debasish Mukerji, "The Dance of Death: Provincial Armed Constabulary Fuels the Communal Cauldron in Aligarh," *The Week* (December 23, 1990), pp. 35–37 (cover story).

4. Interview on January 3, 1991; also interviews (including riot victims) in Upar Kot, Aligarh, on January 3, 1991.

5. *PUCL Bulletin* (March 1991), pp. 14–15.

6. Ashutosh Varshney, "Ethnic Conflict and Civil Society: India and Beyond," *World Politics* 53, no. 3 (April 2001), p. 381, describes the situation in an obverse way: "Blinded by a Hindu nationalist fervor, . . . the city of Aligarh plunged into horrendous violence. . . . As in the past, Aligarh's local mechanisms of peace were remarkably inadequate to the task of dealing with an exogenous shock." His point is that Aligarh lacks a peace system. My point is that the Hindu residents of Aligarh are not so much "blinded" as stimulated by a locally well-established network of mobilizers, agitators, and killers, part of an institutionalized riot network or system. Furthermore, it shows an utter lack of knowledge of the Aligarh situation to imagine that the city is merely responding to "an exogenous shock."

7. Interview on January 3, 1991.

8. As one leftist Hindu AMU professor put it to me in connection with this riot, "Aligarh is very much a part of this whole game because here is . . . one thing, Aligarh Muslim University, so you can use it as a symbol that this is a Pakistani center, anti-national center"; interview, January 3, 1991.

9. My same informant, whom I interviewed after the 1961 riots and again after the 1990–91 riots, pointing to this aspect of mass participation in the latter, said that this was the "first time" that there was such an identification of the middle and upper-middle classes with violent, riotous attacks upon Muslims; interview, January 3, 1991.

10. Interview, January 3, 1991.

11. *PUCL Bulletin* (March 1991), p. 14.

12. These included a story concerning the dematerialization of a Hindu *mahant* (temple priest) after his arrest by the police, on the one hand, and the melting of "the pupil of a senior police officer's right eye" after he "had ordered firing on the karse-vaks in Ayodhya"; *PUCL Bulletin* (March 1991), p. 26.

13. Interview, January 3, 1991.

14. The first *Times of India* report on these riots was datelined December 7 in the December 8, 1990, edition, but it did not mention the confrontation between Muslim youths and the police at the police picket opposite the Jama Masjid. The first specific reference to that confrontation as the beginning of the riot came in an article in the paper in its December 16 issue. Such dating is artificial, assuming a precise beginning as well as a precise ending of a riot, whereas, in fact, there were many other incidents that preceded the one on December 7, which to others signified a different beginning for this riot.

15. *PUCL Bulletin* (March 1991), pp. 14–15.

16. Many of these journalists, a few of whom I have had occasion to meet over the past few decades, are persons without professional integrity or any concern for the discovery of truth or the exposure of falsehood. Many instances of their lack of professional behavior could be provided from my personal experiences as well those of others. See for, example, Ashutosh Varshney, "Civic Life and Ethnic Conflict: Hindus and Muslims in India," unpublished draft manuscript, February 1998, p. 123. My own experiences have been such that I always seek to avoid any contact with them while in India.

17. *PUCL Bulletin* (March 1991), p. 27.

18. *PUCL Bulletin* (March 1991), pp. 20–24, and the following publications and documents issued by the AMU, through its Public Relations Office. "Villification Compaign [*sic*] Against Aligarh Muslim University [December 1990 Communal Riots at Aligarh]," printed pamphlet issued by Aligarh Muslim University; "Why the Medical College was selected"; "A Victim of Rumours"; and an untitled chronology of riot incidents that especially affected the AMU from December 7 through December

16, 1990 (all typewritten or mimeographed sheets provided to me by the AMU authorities and the Public Relations Office in January 1991).

19. "Why the Medical College."

20. "Why the Medical College."

21. *PUCL Bulletin* (March 1991), p. 19.

22. *PUCL Bulletin* (March 1991), p. 20.

23. *PUCL Bulletin* (March 1991), p. 20.

24. According to Varshney, there are "two traders associations" in Aligarh, of which one, the Vyapar Sangh, is "BJP-supported." He notes that the Vyapar Mandal is smaller than the Vyapar Sangh and "has more than 20 percent Muslim members," compared to "only 4 per cent" Muslim members of the Vyapar Sangh; Varshney ms., "Civic Life and Ethnic Conflict," p. 164fn. To my knowledge, the only trader organization of any consequence in Aligarh is the Vyapar Mandal, which I believe is dominated by Hindus with militant Hindu sympathies, including many RSS members and BJP supporters.

25. *PUCL Bulletin* (March 1991), p. 23.

26. *PUCL Bulletin* (March 1991), p. 23.

27. Although it does not constitute the formal statement for which the PUCL team apparently hoped, the *Times of India* (December 16, 1990) referred to Ashok Chauhan and Pramod Kumar as "a two-member fact-finding team to look into the incident," describing the former as "general secretary of the district Congress committee" and the latter as an "industrialist." They were reported as saying: "Not only was this news item [reporting the murders in the hospital] totally false but it symbolised the threat which irresponsible journalism can cause the country's unity."

28. *PUCL Bulletin* (1991), p. 24.

29. *PUCL Bulletin* (1991), p. 24.

## 5 / THE CONTROL OF COMMUNAL CONFLICT IN ALIGARH

1. Interview, Aligarh, January 3, 1991.

2. Interview, Aligarh, on January 3, 1991; also interviews (including riot victims) in Upar Kot, Aligarh, on January 3, 1991. The reference is to the massacres of Muslims in the 1987 riots in Meerut.

3. *Times of India,* December 8, 1992.

4. *Times of India,* December 9, 1992.

5. *Times of India,* December 12, 1992.

6. *Times of India,* December 14, 1992.

7. *Times of India,* December 18, 1992.

8. *Times of India,* December 23, 1992.

9. *Times of India,* December 12, 1992.

10. *Times of India,* December 18, 1992. In this case, moreover, in contrast to May 1979, there were no contradictory reports denying that *kar sevaks* had committed these violently abusive actions upon AMU students.

11. *Times of India,* December 19, 1992.

12. *Times of India,* December 23, 1992.

13. On the post-Ayodhya Kanpur riots, see Paul R. Brass, *Theft of an Idol: Text and Context in the Representation of Collective Violence* (Princeton, N.J.: Princeton University Press, 1997), ch. 7.

14. *Times of India,* March 11, 1995.

15. *Times of India,* March 12, 1995.

16. *Times of India,* March 16, 1995.

17. Asghar Ali Engineer, "Aligarh Riots—An Unplanned Outburst," in *Towards Secular India* 1, no. 2 (April–June 1995), p. 87.

18. Engineer, "Aligarh Riots," p. 90.

19. Engineer, "Aligarh Riots," pp. 90–91.

20. Engineer, "Aligarh Riots," pp. 91–92. Engineer's account here differs from that of the *Times of India,* noted above, that attributed this death to a stabbing.

21. Engineer, "Aligarh Riots," pp. 92–93.

22. I would have liked to go inside the RAF truck, but it would have been impolitic for me to ask, and it was anyway desirable for me and my companions to leave the area as quickly as possible.

### 6 / THE GEOGRAPHY AND DEMOGRAPHY OF RIOTS

1. Michael Keith, *Race, Riots and Policing: Lore and Disorder in a Multi-Racist Society* (London: UCL Press, 1993), p. 167.

2. The current (1997) local telephone directory for the Aligarh Muslim University community, consisting primarily of university faculty and some alumni, contains approximately 1,075 names, among which I was able to identify only 130 names of Hindus and others and six uncertain: *Blessing Telephone Directory* (Aligarh: Blessing Enterprise, 1997).

3. Map locations are identified either by the name or by number, when necessary to avoid crowding on the maps. The names of all numbered locations on the maps are listed in alphabetical and numerical order in the Key to Maps in Appendix B.

4. Howard F. Hirt, *Aligarh, U.P., India: A Geographic Study of Urban Growth* (unpublished Ph.D. dissertation, Syracuse University, 1955), p. 160.

5. David Lelyveld, *Aligarh's First Generation: Muslim Solidarity in British India* (Princeton, N.J.: Princeton University Press, 1978), p. 156.

6. Hirt, *Aligarh,* p. 160.

7. Pierre Nora, "From *Lieux de mémoire* to *Realms of Memory,*" in Pierre Nora (ed.), *Realms of Memory: Rethinking the French Past,* vol. I: *Conflicts and Divisions,* trans. by Arthur Goldhammer (New York: Columbia University Press, 1992), p. xvii; for the definition of *"lieu de mémoire,"* see the previous citation, in Chapter 1, n. 64.

8. Lelyveld, *Aligarh's First Generation,* pp. 273–74.

9. Centre for Research in Rural and Industrial Development, "Communal Violence and its Impact on Development and National Integration," unpublished (Chandigarh: n.d. [1983?]), p. 54.

10. Hirt, *Aligarh,* p. 70.

11. Hirt, *Aligarh,* p. 70; E. A. Mann, *Boundaries and Identities: Muslims, Work and Status in Aligarh* (New Delhi: Sage, 1992), pp. 27–28.

12. Hirt, *Aligarh,* p. 225.

13. I have seen a map showing these *mohallas* posted on the walls of the office of the DM in Aligarh, but could not obtain a copy. Government of India, Minorities Commission, *First Annual Report for the Year Ending 31st December, 1978* (New Delhi: Government of India Press, 1979), listed 12 sites as "disturbance-affected areas" that its members visited in the aftermath of the 1978 riots.

14. This characterization of the *mohallas* of Aligarh comes from the report of the Centre for Research, "Communal Violence," done after the riots of 1978–79. Of the 29, one was listed as unpopulated in 1951. This *mohalla* is really a four-way crossing known as Phul Chauraha and is actually one of the most sensitive localities. Police pickets have been stationed there continuously 24 hours a day for many, many years. The census divides the *mohallas* of Turkman Gate and Madar Gate into two and three separate units, respectively. They have been consolidated (and the population composition for the separate census units recalculated accordingly) on Map 4 so that the number of *mohallas* shown thereon is thereby reduced to 25.

15. Mann, *Boundaries and Identities,* p. 33.

16. Centre for Research, "Communal Violence," pp. 22–23.

17. Mann, *Boundaries and Identities,* p. 34.

18. Anonymous, "Riots in Aligarh," undated mimeographed study of 7 pages, given to me in 1983 (it is obviously the confidential report of a former district magistrate of Aligarh); citation from pp. 3–4.

19. Interview on July 20, 1983.

20. Government of India, Minorities Commission, *First Annual Report for the Year Ending 31st December, 1978* (New Delhi: Government of India Press, 1979), pp. 74–77.

21. Centre for Research, "Communal Violence," pp. 34–35.

22. Graff, "Religious Identities and Indian Politics," mimeographed version,

pp. 67–69. The reference to the Minority Bill is to a bill in Parliament to maintain the minority character of the AMU.

23. Interview on January 3, 1991.

24. Zoya Hasan, *Dominance and Mobilisation: Rural Politics in Western Uttar Pradesh, 1930–1980* (New Delhi: Sage, 1989), pp. 160–61.

25. Mann, *Boundaries and Identities*, pp. 175–76.

26. Mann, *Boundaries and Identities*, pp. 176–77.

27. Cited in Mann, *Boundaries and Identities*, pp. 177–78.

28. Interview in New Delhi on January 2, 1991; interviews in Aligarh on July 20 and 24, 1983.

29. Interview, July 20, 1983.

30. Interview with senior superintendent of police on July 21, 1983. The SSP's remark about equality of numbers is, however, imprecise and not accurate for Manik Chauk, where Muslims are in a minority.

31. Government of India, Minorities Commission, *First Annual Report*, p. 77.

32. Hasan, *Dominance and Mobilisation*, p. 159.

33. Mann, *Boundaries and Identities*, pp. 177–78.

34. *The Week*, December 23, 1990.

35. *PUCL Bulletin* (March 1991).

36. Interview, January 3, 1991.

37. Interviews in Upar Kot, January 3, 1991.

38. Interview, January 3, 1991.

39. E. A. Mann, "Religion, Money and Status: Competition for Resources at the Shrine of Shah Jamal, Aligarh," in Christian W. Troll (ed.), *Muslim Shrines in India: Their Character, History and Significance* (Delhi: Oxford University Press, 1989), p. 145.

40. Interview, January 3, 1991.

41. Interview with riot victims, 1991.

42. Interview with riot victims, 1991, and interview on November 21, 1997.

43. Interview, November 21, 1997.

44. Interview with riot victims, 1991.

45. *PUCL Bulletin*, March 1991, p. 16.

46. *Times of India*, December 10, 1990.

47. Interview, November 21, 1997.

48. *Times of India*, January 20, 1991.

49. *Times of India*, January 2, 1991.

50. Interview with riot victims, 1991.

51. Interview in Aligarh on November 21, 1997.

52. Interview, January 3, 1991.

53. *PUCL Bulletin,* (March 1991), p. 16.

54. *Times of India,* November 27 and December 16, 1990.

55. Paul R. Brass, *Theft of an Idol: Text and Context in the Representation of Collective Violence* (Princeton, N.J.: Princeton University Press, 1997), ch. 7.

56. Similar situations have been reported from Bhiwandi (a Bombay suburb) in 1984 and Biharsharif (in Bihar) in 1981. In the former case, the population balance was transformed by an "influx of migrant U.P. workers" to the outskirts of the city in such a way that Muslims came to comprise 60–65 percent of the population of the town. Although the Shiv Sena was responsible for most of the violence in Bhiwandi, the BJP also had a stake in it, though behind the scenes. Rioters were recruited from outlying Hindu villages where the BJP was strong to attack Muslim *basti*s (rough-and-tumble settlements of poor people) in Bhiwandi. Similarly, in Biharsharif, rioters came from villages where "the RSS had been expanding its activities." In both cases, the evidence of preplanning and organization is substantial. Attempts were also made in Bhiwandi to recruit low castes to attack Muslims, but they were not generally successful on this occasion. See Asghar Ali Engineer, *Bhiwandi-Bombay Riots: Analysis and Documentation* (Bombay: Institute of Islamic Studies, 1984), pp. 13–14; on Biharsharif, see Asghar Ali Engineer, "Case Studies of Five Major Riots from Biharsharif to Pune," in Asghar Ali Engineer (ed.), *Communal Riots in Post-Independence India* (Hyderabad: Sangam Books, 1984), pp. 238–46.

57. With the notable exception of Bombay.

58. In some cases, because of the enormous labor involved in counting the Muslim names exactly, I have had to use a random number sampling method to arrive at an estimate of the number of Muslim names in the voters' list.

59. Interview with lock manufacturer in Sarai Sultani, Aligarh, on April 2, 1999; taped in Hindi-Urdu; running translation provided by Aftab Ahmad.

60. This was the time of the Chandra Talkies riot that began outside the cinema located in Mamubhanja, about a half kilometer from Sarai Sultani.

61. This is standard police practice in north Indian police stations, namely, denial of requests for water from prisoners whom the police particularly dislike, followed by the standard response to drink their own urine.

62. The term actually used in Hindi was *batti,* which means simply a light, but when I questioned the translation, I was told the term was being used here for a furnace. At one point, in fact, the term "blast furnace" was used. So I am not entirely sure what kind of furnace was used here.

63. The exact dates of Mr. Punia's stay as district magistrate in Aligarh are from May 29, 1982, to May 20, 1985. Three years as district magistrate is considered a relatively long term, especially in a riot-prone district such as Aligarh. Throughout his tenure, there was a Congress government in the state capital in Lucknow. The

Congress at that time, still dependent on the Muslim vote in U.P., did not want further rioting in Aligarh after the years of rioting that had plagued the city. It was clear to me during my visit to Aligarh during Punia's tenure that both he and the then SSP were alert to any possibility of a communal disturbance and had the will and ability to prevent any large-scale rioting.

64. And lately Christians elsewhere in India.

65. This point will be illustrated in the next chapter.

## 7 / THE ECONOMICS OF RIOTS

1. E. A. Mann, *Boundaries and Identities: Muslims, Work and Status in Aligarh* (New Delhi: Sage, 1992), p. 77.

2. H. R. Nevill, *Aligarh: A Gazetteer, Being Volume VI of the District Gazetteers of the United Provinces of Agra and Oudh* (Lucknow: Govt. Branch Press, 1926), pp. 59–60; David Lelyveld, *Aligarh's First Generation: Muslim Solidarity in British India* (Princeton, N.J.: Princeton University Press, 1978), p. 149.

3. Howard F. Hirt, *Aligarh, U.P., India: A Geographic Study of Urban Growth* (unpublished Ph.D. dissertation, Syracuse University, 1955), p. 150.

4. Interview with productivity services manager, Glaxo factory, Aligarh, on July 26, 1983.

5. Ashutosh Varshney, "Civic Life and Ethnic Conflict: Hindus and Muslims in India" (unpublished draft manuscript, February 1998), p. 133.

6. H. R. Nevill, in the 1926 *Aligarh Gazetteer,* noted the importance of the "industry of lock-making, for which Aligarh is famous throughout India"; p. 204.

7. Centre for Research in Rural and Industrial Development, "Communal Violence and Its Impact on Development and National Integration" (unpublished, Chandigarh, [1983?]), p. 28.

8. Mann, *Boundaries and Identities,* p. 84.

9. Interview with professor and head of the Department of Political Science, Barahseni College, on September 12, 1962.

10. Mann, *Boundaries and Identities,* p. 84. The term *Bania* refers to a specific caste category; it is also used as a generic term for castes that engage in business.

11. Both are Hindu castes, a great many of whose members are traders and businessmen.

12. Mann, *Boundaries and Identities,* p. 85.

13. Mann, *Boundaries and Identities,* p. 85.

14. Mann, *Boundaries and Identities,* p. 86. The Centre for Research report, "Communal Violence," pp. 46–47, describes this interdependence in considerable detail, noting that "Kohlis [*sic*] are mainly involved in casting activities, Muslims are

more or less exclusively doing polishing work and in the intermediate stage," "the assembling of the final products is done by Muslim Saifis, Maithel Brahmans, and Jatavs," and the "suppliers are mainly . . . Varshneys."

15. Mann, *Boundaries and Identities*, p. 86.

16. Mann, *Boundaries and Identities*, p. 103.

17. Mann, *Boundaries and Identities*, p. 124.

18. See also Centre for Research, "Communal Violence," p. 46, and Violette Graff, "Religious Identities and Indian Politics: Elections in Aligarh, 1971–1985," in André Wink (ed.), *Islam, Politics and Society in South Asia* (New Delhi: Manohar, 1991), p. 168, fn. 3.

19. For example, Mann reports that, in the 1978 rioting, "in Sarai Kaba and Sarai Miyan (both dominated by Muslim Qureshis), . . . the Kolis, a poor and low Hindu caste, were attacked"; *Boundaries and Identities*, p. 178.

20. Mann, *Boundaries and Identities*, pp. 130–31.

21. Mann, *Boundaries and Identities*, p. 79.

22. One hundred and fifteen out of 171 registered factories, according to Mann, *Boundaries and Identities*, p. 80.

23. Graff, "Religious Identities and Indian Politics," p. 148.

24. This bazaar, named Russellganj (hence Rasalganj in Hindi) after a former British collector (district magistrate), was characterized in the *Gazetteer* as "the principal bazar" of the city; Nevill, *Aligarh Gazetteer*, p. 200. It remains so today.

25. Interview, September 12, 1962.

26. S. K. Ghosh, *Communal Riots in India: Meet the Challenge Unitedly* (New Delhi: Ashish, 1987), p. 214.

27. Mann, *Boundaries and Identities*, p. 177.

28. *Times of India*, November 21, 1978: Ghosh, *Communal Riots in India*, p. 214; Mann, *Boundaries and Identities*, p. 177.

29. Government of India, Minorities Commission, *First Annual Report for the Year Ending 31st December, 1978* (New Delhi: Government of India Press, 1979), pp. 82–83.

30. *Times of India*, November 22, 1978.

31. Centre for Research, "Communal Violence," pp. 22–23.

32. Centre for Research, "Communal Violence," pp. 34–35.

33. Centre for Research, "Communal Violence," p. 53.

34. The Jan Sangh is the predecessor party of the BJP, which is now the party of militant Hindu nationalism, in power at the Center (2001) and in several Indian states. There is also a rump Jan Sangh, consisting of persons who objected to the loss of its identity that occurred when the original Jan Sangh joined with the Janata Party in 1975 and then reorganized as the BJP when the latter party collapsed. The term *Jan Sanghi* also continues to be used today as a term for Hindu communalists in politics by older persons who remember the original Jan Sangh.

35. Interview, Aligarh, July 19, 1983.

36. Interview with Colonel Zaidi, Vice-Chancellor, AMU, January 20, 1962, and interview, July 19, 1983. Colonel Zaidi put the matter as follows: "The [pay] grades of teachers in the colleges are lower than in the AMU. The amenities, buildings, etc. are much better. Whereas the local colleges are shabby and squalid, the AMU looks like a green oasis"; from notes.

37. "Why the Medical College was selected" (typewritten sheet provided by the Public Relations Office, AMU, January 1991).

38. Interview in Aligarh, July 24, 1983.

39. See also Varshney, "Civic Life and Ethnic Conflict," p. 168fn.: "There are two large business *(vaishya)* castes: the Barehsenis [*sic*] (12 percent), and the Agarwals (6 percent of the population). It is also believed that the latter traditionally supported the Congress but in all probability have switched to the BJP by now. The former have been big supporters of Hindu nationalism for a long time."

40. Interview in Aligarh, January 3, 1991.

41. Government of India, Minorities Commission, *First Annual Report,* p. 79.

42. Centre for Research, "Communal Violence," pp. 34–35.

43. Interview, July 19, 1983.

44. See Jim Masselos, "The Bombay Riots of January 1993: The Politics of Urban Conflagration," *South Asia* 17 (Special Issue, 1994), 79–86, where this type of explanation, among others, is discussed in connection with these riots.

45. E. A. Mann, "Religion, Money and Status: Competition for Resources at the Shrine of Shah Jamal, Aligarh," in Christian W. Troll (ed.), *Muslim Shrines in India: Their Character, History and Significance* (Delhi: Oxford University Press, 1989), p. 156.

46. Graff, "Religious Identities and Indian Politics," mimeographed version, pp. 72–74.

47. This issue of privacy, particularly for women, arises especially because of the fact that, during summer months, many people in such neighborhoods sleep in cots out in the open.

48. Interview, July 19, 1983.

49. Interview with station officer, Sasni Gate, Aligarh, July 24, 1983.

50. Graff, "Religious Identities and Indian Politics," published version, p. 168, fn. 3.

51. Mann, *Boundaries and Identities,* p. 57.

52. Mann, *Boundaries and Identities,* p. 85.

53. The situation changes, however, if a Muslim businessman moves to the Civil Lines area where intercommunal relations are not charged with the same level of suspicion and hostility as in the old city and where, in fact, "social relations" may develop between Hindus and Muslims in the same social stratum; Mann, *Boundaries and Identities,* p. 86.

54. Mann, *Boundaries and Identities,* p. 107.

55. Thus, for example, Mann notes that many Qureshis, traditionally butchers, have moved into the business of "inter-state transportation," that is, into trucking; Mann, *Boundaries and Identities,* p. 127.

56. Mann, *Boundaries and Identities,* p. 180.

57. Pars Ram, *A UNESCO Study of Social Tensions in Aligarh, 1950–1951,* edited and with an introduction by Gardner Murphy (Ahmedabad: New Order Book Co., 1955), p. 188.

58. Varshney, "Civic Life and Ethnic Conflict," p. 164.

59. Interview, January 3, 1991.

60. Mann, *Boundaries and Identities,* p. 81; Mohd. Izhar Ahmad, "An Over All [*sic*] View of Muslim's [*sic*] Participation in Small Scale Industries of Aligarh District," mimeographed, Aligarh Muslim University (1982–83).

61. Mann, *Boundaries and Identities,* pp. 84–85.

62. Interview in Aligarh on November 20, 1997 (taped in English).

63. Interview, November 20, 1997.

64. I am not sure that this man's responses concerning the absence of economic strains in Hindu-Muslim relations were honest. He seemed to want to assure me as an American that there was no conflict in India, a kind of response that I sometimes get when I have not established sufficient rapport with someone I have not met before.

65. Ahmad, "Small Scale Industries."

66. Interview in Upar Kot, January 3, 1991 (taped in English).

### 8 / RIOTS AND ELECTIONS

1. Steven I. Wilkinson, "The Electoral Origins of Ethnic Violence: Hindu-Muslim Riots in India" (unpublished Ph.D. dissertation, Harvard University, 1997), chapter 1, figure I-3. Wilkinson believes that the causal chain is from intense electoral competition to riots and discounts the counterargument "that riots cause close electoral contests"; personal communication. Leaving out the word "cause," the evidence from Aligarh to be presented below suggests that the sequence is often the reverse, namely, that riots precede close electoral contests.

2. Paul R. Brass, *Language, Religion, and Politics in North India* (London: Cambridge University Press, 1974), p. 265.

3. The atypical 1955 bye-election has been left out of this chart.

4. The correlation coefficient between the valid votes turnout for Aligarh and the state as a whole is a rather low .396 (N=13, p=.180).

5. Note that the larger the interval, the lower the degree of competitiveness, and

vice versa, so that a declining slope on the chart registers an increase in interparty competitiveness.

6. It should be noted also that a communal riot did precede this election—held sometime before July 31, 1955, the exact date not having been published—but by more than a year, in June 1954.

7. Wilkinson, "The Electoral Origins of Ethnic Violence," figure I-6.

8. Brass, *Language, Religion, and Politics in North India*, p. 265.

### 9 / THE PRACTICE OF COMMUNAL POLITICS

1. Interview in Aligarh on January 3, 1991 (taped in English).

2. Interview, January 3, 1991.

3. The Jan Sangh, however, had been in power in coalition governments in the period of governmental instability in the state between 1967 and 1971.

4. Interview, January 3, 1991.

5. *Lok* and *janata* in Hindi are synonyms for "people."

6. Paul R. Brass, *Language, Religion, and Politics in North India* (Cambridge: Cambridge University Press, 1974), p. 265.

7. Interview in Aligarh on July 24, 1983 (in Hindi, from notes in English).

8. Interview with inspector of police, Bannadevi Police Station, Aligarh, on July 23, 1983 (in Hindi, from notes).

9. Interview in Aligarh on July 22, 1983 [taped in English].

10. Which can be rendered nonpejoratively as *non-Muslim,* but literally carries a pejorative meaning in English as an unbeliever or infidel. The latter term in English, especially, has acquired a strongly pejorative meaning in relation to non-Muslims, even stronger than its literal meaning of infidelity or unfaithfulness to God.

11. Interview, July 24, 1983.

12. *Lekin maiNne jivan parishani bahut hoti haiN;* interview, Aligarh, November 21, 1997 (taped in Hindi with running translation by Professor Mathur).

13. Interview, Manik Chauk, June 14, 1993 (taped in Hindi with running translation by Jayati Chaturvedi).

14. Interview, November 21, 1997.

15. References to Navman's son's activities during riots and as "a Bajrang Dal chief" from interview, January 3, 1991; other citations from interview, June 14, 1993.

16. Interview, June 14, 1993.

17. Interview, January 3, 1991.

18. Interview with retired professor of education, Barahseni College, Aligarh, and RSS member, in Aligarh on November 21, 1997 [taped in English].

19. Interview, January 3, 1991.

20. This term was used at the time openly by the top national leadership of the BJP, including L. K. Advani in an interview with me on December 20, 1989, in New Delhi.

21. Interview, Aligarh, July 20, 1983 (taped in English).

22. Interview, July 22, 1983; all emphases in original.

23. Police inspector, Bannadevi, interview, 1983.

24. Interview with station officer, Sasni Gate, at the Sasni Gate Police Station, Aligarh, July 24, 1983; taped in Hindi with running translation by Pallav Kumar.

25. Interview, July 24, 1983.

26. Interview on July 26, 1983.

27. Interview, Aligarh, July 30, 1983; taped in English.

28. Interview, Aligarh, November 20, 1997; taped in English.

29. Interview, November 21, 1997; taped in English.

30. Interview with RSS members, November 21, 1997; this section taped in English.

31. Interview, March 30, 1999; taped in Urdu, with running translation by Aftab Ahmad.

32. Interview, January 3, 1991.

33. Interview, July 22, 1983.

34. I also observed from their dress that they were all Hindus.

10 / COMMUNALIZATION AND POLARIZATION

1. Interview with professor and head of the Department of Political Science, Barahseni College, Aligarh, on September 12, 1962.

2. The *mohallas* are as follows: Ghas ki Mandi, Rangrezan, and Turkman Gate in the old Jaiganj ward; Sabzi Mandi, Sarai Tahsil, Chauk Bundu Khan, Sunhat, Pir Ataullah, Tila, Sheikhan, Purani Kachehri, Ghosian, and Bani Israilan in the old Kanwariganj ward; and Turkman Gate in the Turkman Gate ward. Of these, five can be located precisely on the available maps in the broad Upar Kot area (Map 2). In contrast, Dr. Bashir's bottom five polling stations comprised the six *mohallas* of Sarai Raja Ram, Sudamapuri, Begambagh, Jaiganj, Baikunthnagar, and Vishnupuri, of which all that can be located precisely on Maps 1 and 3 are in the heart of the predominantly Hindu area, near the several Hindu-dominated colleges whose students contributed to the crowds mobilized in the October riots.

3. See Appendix Table A.3.

4. Rae's index of fractionalization (Fe) for this election was .63 for the constituency as a whole, but the mean for all 96 polling stations was .50, which, in Rae's index, signifies perfect two-party competition.

5. Part of the material in this paragraph was taken directly from Paul R. Brass, "Caste, Caste Alliances, and Hierarchy of Values in Aligarh District," in Paul R. Brass, *Caste, Faction and Party in Indian Politics,* vol. 2: *Election Studies* (Delhi: Chanakya, 1985), p. 228.

6. Interview with Jarrar Haider, lawyer, Congress candidate for Parliament from Aligarh constituency, at his residence, Dodhpur, September 17, 1962.

7. Much of this paragraph was taken from Brass, "Caste, Caste Alliances, and Hierarchy of Values in Aligarh District," pp. 228–29.

8. Interview on March 31, 1991; taped.

9. Interview, Manik Chauk, June 14, 1993; taped in Hindi with running translation by Jayati Chaturvedi.

10. The problems posed for BJP dominance in this constituency by the voting pattern in these *mohallas* are, however, somewhat complex. Had even all the votes of the SJP candidate gone to Mohammad Sufiyan, Navman would still have won the seat. The fact that Muslim votes were divided, moreover, increased Navman's margin of victory. On the other hand, if these *mohallas* were eliminated from the constituency altogether, Navman's margin of victory would have been even larger; he would have polled 48.40 percent and Sufiyan would have polled 41.78 percent, thus increasing Navman's margin of victory by 1.75 percent.

11. Interview on March 30, 1999; taped.

12. Interview on March 31, 1999; taped in English.

## 11 / COMMUNAL SOLIDARITY AND DIVISION
### AT THE LOCAL LEVEL

1. Sarai Bairagi is not listed on this map. It is located between the railway line and the old city; Howard F. Hirt, *Aligarh, U. P., India: A Geographic Study of Urban Growth* (unpublished Ph.D. dissertation, Syracuse University, 1955), p. 105.

2. I have, of course, been arguing throughout this volume that large-scale riots are often themselves political events, though they are generally treated as if they were societal, implying a clear separation between society and politics. The relationship is, therefore, often in fact one between rioting, as a societal/political event, and inter-party competition, an electoral/political event.

3. Paul R. Brass, "Caste, Caste Alliances, and Hierarchy of Values in Aligarh District," in Paul R. Brass, *Caste, Faction and Party in Indian Politics,* vol. 2: *Election Studies* (Delhi: Chanakya, 1985), pp. 207–79. Further evidence on these points is provided in Appendix C in this volume, which takes the electoral analysis down to the even lower level of *mohallas* within a city ward.

## 12 / THE DECLINE OF COMMUNAL VIOLENCE AND THE TRANSFORMATION OF ELECTORAL COMPETITION

1. Extrapolating from the change in the total population of the city, which multiplied by 3.39 in this period.

2. They include Gambhirpuri (part), Gandhinagar, Adda Hathras, Madar Gate, Dwarkapuri, Achal Road (but not Achal Talab), and Mahendranagar (part) in ward 15 and Gambhirpuri (part), Hanumanpuri, and Mahendranagar (part) in ward 17.

3. Interview on November 21, 1997; taped in English.

4. "*Ne, vote dale nahiN, log sosti rahe,* laziness"; interview, Aligarh, November 21, 1997 [taped in Hindi with running translation by Professor Mathur].

5. Interview, November 21, 1997.

6. Interview with RSS members, in Aligarh, on November 21, 1997.

7. However, it was not until 1998 that the intensity of interparty competition declined in the Aligarh segment of the Lok Sabha constituency. In 1996, the contest was among the closest in the dataset, only 3.98 percentage points separating the winning candidate from the runner-up, making this contest the fifth most competitive among the 21 elections. Then, in 1998, the interval increased substantially to 13.76 percent.

## 13 / RIOT INTERPRETATION, BLAME DISPLACEMENT, AND THE COMMUNAL DISCOURSE

1. Interview in New Delhi, June 20, 1991.

2. For the uses of the rhetoric of blame for communal and other riots in India, with specific reference to charges and countercharges before the election of 1980, see Paul R. Brass, *Theft of an Idol: Text and Context in the Representation of Collective Violence* (Princeton, N.J.: Princeton University Press, 1997), pp. 131–32.

3. The events of September 11, 2001, in New York occurred after this was written. Ever since, as the bodies of the victims of the attack on the World Trade Center have been identified, the *New York Times* has, day by day, for every person killed, done exactly what I have proposed here: included a photograph of each person and a summary characterization of the person in the words of one of the bereaved. The effect of such portrayals clearly is to humanize an enormous tragedy, as opposed to dehumanizing it by reducing it to a body count. Such portrayals, personal experiences, and eyewitness testimonies have sometimes been provided in films and books produced in India, notably concerning the anti-Sikh pogrom of November 1984, in Delhi, on which see Uma Chakravarti and Nandita Haksar, *The Delhi Riots: Three Days in the Life of a Nation* (New Delhi: Lancer International, 1987).

4. Excerpts and paraphrases from interview on July 20, 1983; taped in English.

5. Interview on July 22, 1983; taped in English.

6. Interview in Aligarh on July 24, 1983; in Hindi, from notes in English.

7. Interview on July 30, 1983; taped in English.

8. Interview, July 30, 1983.

9. Interview on July 26, 1983; taped in English.

10. Interview with senior superintendent of police, Aligarh, on July 21, 1983; in English, from notes.

11. Interview with station officer, Sasni Gate, at the Sasni Gate Police Station, Aligarh, July 24, 1983; taped in Hindi with running translation by Pallav Kumar.

12. Interview on July 22, 1983; taped in English.

13. Navman interview, 1983.

14. Interview, July 20, 1983.

15. SSP interview, 1983.

16. Interview with station officer, Civil Lines, on July 25, 1983; taped in English.

17. Sasni Gate station officer interview, 1983.

18. Interview with inspector of police, Bannadevi Police Station, Aligarh, on July 23, 1983 [in Hindi, from notes].

19. Interview with district magistrate, Aligarh, at his residence, Aligarh, July 30, 1983; in English, from notes.

20. Conversation in Aligarh, July 26, 1983; in English, from notes.

21. However, the AMUSU (AMU Students Union) president, cited earlier, challenged the militant Hindus of the town during the 1978 riots to make a surprise visit to any hostel or hostels of their choice in which they claimed that bombs were being made and arms kept. They did so on one occasion, but found neither. However, he did not claim to know about the situation in the hostels during the later riots. Interview in New Delhi on June 20, 1991; taped in English.

22. Interview, July 22, 1983.

23. Interview with DSP, intelligence, at his office, Aligarh, July 30, 1983; in English, from notes.

24. Interview with district magistrate, Aligarh, at his residence, Aligarh, July 30, 1983.

25. Interview with RSS members, Aligarh, November 21, 1997.

## 14 / POLICE VIEWS OF HINDU-MUSLIM VIOLENCE

1. Commonly, but not universally. For a defense of the PAC as an honest, well-trained, and highly competent force that ends up with the blame for actions ordered by others, see the article by K. S. Sastry, "A Much Maligned Force," *Times of India*, May 7, 1979. Sastry points out that the commands to the PAC forces to fire on rioting crowds are actually given by police officers or the civilian administration.

2. *Kya nam de diya gaya bana? Yah police action tha jo MusalmanoN ke khilaf am tor par [kiya jata hai].* (Loose translation: What name has been given to this? This was a police action, which is generally directed against Muslims.) Interview in Aligarh on January 2, 1991.

3. What follows are generalizations from specific incidents that have been reported to me in my interviews.

4. All these particular incidents and several others come from my interviews (including of riot victims) in Upar Kot, Aligarh, on January 3, 1991.

5. From an incident reported in interview in New Delhi, June 20, 1991.

6. Anonymous, "Communal Riots and Minorities," unpublished, n.d. [1980?], p. 11.

7. Literally, youths, but meaning the lowest rank of police and armed forces recruits.

8. Anonymous, "Communal Riots and Minorities," p. 12.

9. The reader should note that the police discussed in this section are the district and station police officers and men, not the PAC *jawans*, who are not accessible to interviews from foreigners. For that matter, I have never seen any reports from Indian scholars or newsmen of the attitudes of the PAC recruits and officers.

10. Interview with inspector of police, Bannadevi, Aligarh, on July 23, 1983.

11. It is certain that this police inspector has not read the literature on rioting for fun and profit.

12. That is, section 362 of the Indian criminal code, which refers to abduction.

13. For another specific example of what I am calling here "the police view" from my interviews in Kanpur City, see Paul R. Brass, *Theft of an Idol: Text and Context in the Representation of Collective Violence* (Princeton, N.J.: Princeton University Press, 1997), pp. 248–50, and the same volume, passim, for numerous accounts of police behavior and practice in riots in five districts of north India, including Aligarh.

14. Interview with district magistrate, Aligarh, at his residence, Aligarh, July 30, 1983.

15. Interview with DSP, intelligence, at his office, Aligarh, July 30, 1983.

16. This charge is not without merit. The great Bombay riots many years later in December 1992 were referred to by some as the "BBC riots," because of its broadcast on TV every hour on the hour of the scene of the mosque at Ayodhya being demolished, which was said to have inflamed Muslims and brought them onto the streets in cities and towns throughout the country.

## 15 / THE ROLE OF THE MEDIA

1. From Governor's fortnightly report to Mountbatten, dated June 9, 1947; India Office Library records L/P&J/5/276.

2. Anonymous, "Aligarh Muslim University, A Victim of Rumours" (mimeographed sheet provided to me in January 1991).

3. Subrata Banerjee, "Communalism as a Commodity in Media Industry," in Pramod Kumar (ed.), *Towards Understanding Communalism* (Chandigarh: Centre for Research in Rural and Industrial Development, 1992), p. 385.

4. Cf. Banerjee, "Communalism as a Commodity," pp. 386–88.

5. People's Union for Civil Liberties, "Communal Riots in Aligarh, Dec. 1990–Jan. 1991," *PUCL Bulletin* (March 1991), pp. 13–27.

6. Ashish Banerjee, "'Comparative Curfew': Changing Dimensions of Communal Politics in India," in Veena Das (ed.), *Mirrors of Violence: Communities, Riots and Survivors in South Asia* (Delhi: Oxford University Press, 1990), p. 53. On the "inflammatory role" of "the Hindi press" in the Jabalpur riot of 1961, see also Asghar Ali Engineer, *Lifting the Veil: Communal Violence and Communal Harmony in Contemporary India* (Hyderabad: Sanaam, 1995), p. 31.

7. Anonymous, "Riots in Aligarh," undated mimeographed study of 7 pages given to me in 1983 by a former Aligarh district magistrate, p. 6.

8. Violette Graff, "Religious Identities and Indian Politics, a Case-Study: Aligarh (1971–1981)," mimeographed paper (Paris: Fondation Nationale des Sciences Politiques et Centre d'Etudes de l'Inde et de l'Asie du Sud [EHESS, n.d.]), pp. 69–71.

9. Iqbal A. Ansari, "Introduction," in Iqbal A. Ansari (ed.), *Communal Riots: The State and Law in India* (New Delhi: Institute of Objective Studies, 1997), p. xv.

10. Ansari, *Communal Riots,* p. xv, and Rafiq Khan and Satyaprakash Mittal, "The Hindu-Muslim Riot in Varanasi and the Role of the Police," in Asghar Ali Engineer (ed.), *Communal Riots in Post-Independence India* (Hyderabad: Sangam Books, 1984), pp. 311–12.

11. Regrettably, the work of Varshney and Wilkinson has transferred to the study of collective violence in India this methodologically unsound form of organizing data on riots; see Ashutosh Varshney and Steven I. Wilkinson, *Hindu-Muslim Riots 1960–93: New Findings, Possible Remedies* (New Delhi: Frank Bros. for Rajiv Gandhi Institute for Contemporary Studies, 1996), pp. 8–9, 55, and at many other places in their joint and separate works.

12. Subrata Banerjee, "Communalism as a Commodity," pp. 387–88.

13. People's Union for Democratic Rights, *Walled City Riots: A Report on the Police and Communal Violence in Delhi, 19–24 May, 1987* (Delhi: PUDR, 1987), pp. 33–34.

14. Satish Saberwal and Mushirul Hasan, "Moradabad Riots, 1980: Causes and Meanings," in Engineer, *Communal Riots,* p. 226.

15. Subrata Banerjee, "Communalism as a Commodity," pp. 388–89.

16. Subrata Banerjee, "Communalism as a Commodity," p. 392, refers to a specific article by the respected free-lance journalist and writer, Prem Shankar Jha, writing in

the aftermath of the Moradabad riots, in which he expressed "great sympathy for the Muslims" along with anticipation of a "Hindu backlash" and a statement that "Hindus of all shades and castes" felt like a "beleaguered majority in their homeland."

17. Subrata Banerjee, "Communalism as a Commodity," pp. 388 and 394–95, provides several examples.

18. Amrita Basu, "Why Local Riots Are Not Simply Local: Collective Violence and the State in Bijnor, India, 1988–1993," *Theory and Society* 24 (1995), 57–58; see also Asghar Ali Engineer, "The Causes of Communal Riots in Post-Independence India," in Engineer, *Communal Riots,* p. 36, and Khan and Mittal, "The Hindu-Muslim Riot in Varanasi," p. 310.

19. Asghar Ali Engineer, "An Analytical Study of the Meerut Riot," in Engineer, *Communal Riots,* p. 280.

20. Madhu Kishwar, "Gangster Rule: The Massacre of the Sikhs," in *Religion at the Service of Nationalism and Other Essays* (Delhi: Oxford University Press, 1998), p. 21.

21. Thus, in the aftermath of the 1956 Aligarh riots, the *Times of India,* October 6, 1961, citing the remarks of the then Home Minister of U.P., Charan Singh, remarked upon how the actions of "thoughtless young men" at the AMU had set "the fire of communal frenzy. . . . ablaze."

22. *Times of India,* October 10, 1961. The *Times of India* editors revealed their true feelings even more clearly by their selection for publication, in their letters column a couple of weeks later, of the following: "Before partition Aligarh University was notorious for the encouragement it gave to separatist tendencies among the Muslims. In fact a substantial part of the credit for the creation of Pakistan must go to the activities of this university. Aligarh will remain a trouble spot as long as its basic character does not undergo a sea-change." Signed by one J. M. Kochar in *Times of India,* October 23, 1961.

## 16 / THE PERSISTENCE OF HINDU-MUSLIM VIOLENCE

1. Several incidents of the latter type are discussed in Paul R. Brass, *Theft of an Idol: Text and Context in the Representation of Collective Violence* (Princeton, N.J.: Princeton University Press, 1997).

2. Most secondary sources and many of my interview respondents use the English word. The word for tension in Hindi is *tanav,* but it did not appear often in my interviews. However, my informants frequently translated other expressions from Hindi that did not contain the word *tanav* into the English word "tension." For example, one of my respondents remarked that, in the town of Khurja before a riot took place, *Wahan abhi tak koi Hindu-Muslim baNdh nahiN hua* (There, until then, there was

no Hindu-Muslim [hindrance, difficulty, distress, etc.]). My informant translated the sentence as follows: "[Khurja] never had any communal tension." I sometimes introduced the word "tension" into an interview myself by declaring that I was "interested in the causes of communal tension in the city of Aligarh, and why these riots take place."

3. *The American Heritage Dictionary of the English Language.*

4. The metaphor here is similar to that generated by Tilly and his colleagues, who liken "the repertoire of collective action to a game that involves a set of basic rules around which a considerable degree of extemporization is not only permitted but required"; Mark Traugott, "Barricades as Repertoire: Continuities and Discontinuities in the History of French Contention," *Social Science History* 17, no. 2 (Summer 1993), p. 309.

5. *Vide* I. Michael Aronson, "The Anti-Jewish Pogroms in Russia in 1991," in John D. Klier and Shlomo Lambroza (eds.), *Pogroms: Anti-Jewish Violence in Modern Russian History* (Cambridge: Cambridge University Press, 1992), p. 45, who remarks in connection with the 1881 Easter pogrom in Elisavetgrad: "The start of Easter had been greeted with tensions and rumors."

6. Suranjan Das, *Communal Riots in Bengal 1905–1947* (Delhi: Oxford University Press, 1991), p. 57.

7. The Chicago Commission on Race Relations, "The Negro in Chicago: A Study of Race Relations and a Race Riot," in Allen D. Grimshaw (ed.), *Racial Violence in the United States* (Chicago: Aldine, 1969), p. 104.

8. Sudhir Kakar, *The Colors of Violence: Cultural Identities, Religion, and Conflict* (Chicago: University of Chicago Press, 1996), p. 35.

9. The association is quite pronounced in the revisionist history of the Russian pogroms of 1881, on which see especially I. Michael Aronson, *Troubled Waters: The Origins of the 1881 Anti-Jewish Pogroms in Russia* (Pittsburgh: Pittsburgh University Press, 1990), and "The Anti-Jewish Pogroms in Russia in 1881," in Klier and Lambroza (eds.), *Pogroms*. All the contributions on the 1881 pogroms in the latter volume share this view. This revisionist school has set out to debunk the idea that the 1881 pogroms were the result of a government-sponsored conspiracy. However, it has substituted one simplistic view for another, the theory of uncoordinated, unplanned, spontaneous action of the ignorant masses fed on rumors that floated naturally among them all the time, for a theory resting on the coordinated, detailed, centralized planning of the Tsarist state.

10. Neil J. Smelser, *Theory of Collective Behavior* (New York: Free Press, 1962), p. 240.

11. Stanley J. Tambiah, "Presidential Address: Reflections on Communal Violence in South Asia," *Journal of Asian Studies* 49, no. 4 (November 1990), p. 757.

12. Michael Keith, *Race, Riots and Policing: Lore and Disorder in a Multi-Racist Society* (London: UCL Press, 1993), p. 63.

13. Keith, *Race, Riots and Policing,* p. 71.

14. Pars Ram, *A UNESCO Study of Social Tensions in Aligarh, 1950–1951,* ed. with an introduction by Gardner Murphy (Ahmedabad: New Order Book Co., 1955), p. 15.

15. Aronson, *Troubled Waters,* pp. 95ff, and Ram, *UNESCO Study,* p. 83.

16. *American Heritage Dictionary.*

17. Ram, *UNESCO Study,* pp. 100–101.

18. *Radiance,* October 22, 1978.

19. *Hindustan Times,* November 10, 1978, and *Times of India,* November 21, 1978.

20. People's Union for Civil Liberties (PUCL), "Communal Riots in Aligarh, Dec. 1990–Jan. 1991," *PUCL Bulletin* (March 1991).

21. Tambiah, "Presidential Address," pp. 746–47.

22. Ashutosh Varshney and Steven I. Wilkinson, *Hindu-Muslim Riots 1960–93: New Findings, Possible Remedies* (New Delhi: Frank Bros. for Rajiv Gandhi Institute for Contemporary Studies, 1996), pp. 39–40. During the 1919 Chicago riots, it was noted that "the press was responsible for giving wide dissemination to much of the inflammatory matter in spoken rumors, though editorials calculated to allay race hatred and help the forces of order were factors in the restoration of peace"; Chicago Commission, "The Negro in Chicago," in Grimshaw, *Racial Violence,* p. 104.

23. The station officer, Sasni Gate, used an example of crowd action directed against him to illustrate how rumor leads to massing and attack. He noted how one of his constables encountered "some Jatavs, who were all drunk and . . . had a small altercation among themselves." The constable reported the matter back to him, the station officer went to the scene without a supporting force, and, "as he entered the mohalla, the rumor spread around that the police has come to arrest the people. So they started throwing stones at him, and he got injured." There was then a "small fight *(jhagara)* between the people and the police"; the SO referred to the massing of people that occurred under these circumstances as a stampede *(bhaggi).* This scene, of course, could literally come out of countless police-populace confrontations in black neighborhoods in the United States as well. Is it a stampede or is it rational action of communal defense of its members on the part of communities used to police harassment?

24. Veena Das, "Introduction: Communities, Riots, Survivors—The South Asian Experience," in Veena Das (ed.), *Mirrors of Violence: Communities, Riots and Survivors in South Asia* (Delhi: Oxford University Press, 1990), p. 28.

25. The shouting of political slogans in India is a virtual popular art form, which itself involves a specialized role, though everybody knows how to do it. Persons move in the middle or at the head of processions or stand on the hoods of cars, bellowing

out the opening line of a statement-response sequence, to which the crowd yells its response in unison. The person who gives the opening statement also is likely to throw his whole body into his performance, gesticulating pronouncedly and moving his legs in a dancelike manner. A simple example of such a statement-response slogan would be the bellowing of a hated person's name or the name of the opposite community itself, to which the crowd then responds, "Murdabad" (Death to). There are other standard violence-inciting slogans, such as "Khoon Ka Badla Khoon Se Lenge" (Blood for Blood), a direct call for violent revenge, assault, and death. This slogan was certainly used during the Bhura procession. Although some of the slogans are standard, there is a fair amount of variation and imagination in them to fit each occasion.

26. As in so many instances, there is a precise parallel here also with Russian pogroms. Writing about the 1881 riots in Russia, Aronson remarks as follows: "The Jews' well-to-do business competitors—merchants, industrialists, and professional people —while not participating actively in the riots themselves, may have contributed by spreading rumors, reading antisemitic newspaper articles aloud, and even assisting in the impromptu organizing of rioters on the spot, by dividing them up into groups and sending them to different parts of town." See Aronson, "The Anti-Jewish Pogroms in Russia in 1881," in Klier and Lambroza (eds.), *Pogroms,* p. 49.

27. The station officer, Sasni Gate, put it this way: "The professional criminal also benefits from this, because—people with vested interests give . . . the professional criminals good amount . . . for killing and stabbing at these times. So they stand to—Because their life is dependent upon crime, this offers them ample opportunity of indulging in crime, and making more money"; interview, July 24, 1983.

28. Interview, Aligarh, January 3, 1991.

29. See Paul R. Brass, "The Strong State and the Fear of Disorder," in Francine R. Frankel et al., *Transforming India: Social and Political Dynamics of Democracy* (New Delhi: Oxford University Press, 2000), pp. 60–88.

30. See Donald E. Smith, *India as a Secular State* (Princeton, N.J.: Princeton University Press, 1963); Donald E. Smith (ed.), *South Asian Politics and Religion* (Princeton, N.J.: Princeton University Press, 1966); Ved Prakash Luthera, *The Concept of the Secular State and India* (Calcutta: Oxford University Press, 1964); and T. N. Madan, *Modern Myths, Locked Minds: Secularism and Fundamentalism in India* (Delhi: Oxford University Press, 1997), for this and other differences between the secular state in theory and practice in the United States and India.

31. For a thorough, comprehensive summary treatment of all the proposals and measures recommended to governments over the years for riot prevention and control, virtually all unheeded, see Iqbal A. Ansari, *Report on Communal Riots: Prevention and Control* (New Delhi: Minorities Council, 1999).

32. On Tamil Nadu and Kerala, see Steven I. Wilkinson, "The Electoral Origins

of Ethnic Violence: Hindu-Muslim Riots in India" (unpublished Ph.D. dissertation, Harvard University, 1997), ch. 1, p. 2. Under the leadership of Laloo Yadav, Bihar, which has had a savage history of Hindu-Muslim violence, has also entered the list of states that refuse to countenance Hindu-Muslim riots.

33. Lance Brennan has described the changes in the attitudes and willingness of the state governments in U.P. to prevent and control Hindu-Muslim riots since Independence, and has argued that the will to do so declined after Independence until Mulayam Singh Yadav came to power in 1990, though he has also noted that the will to do so is not in itself sufficient given the communalization of the "lower echelons of the state apparatus" that has been taking place at the same time; "The State and Communal Violence in UP: 1947–1992," in John McGuire, et al. (eds.), *Political Violence from Ayodhya to Behrampada* (New Delhi: Sage, 1996), pp. 127–42. See also Wilkinson, "The Electoral Origins of Ethnic Violence," ch. 1, p. 32, on the change in the willingness to act effectively to prevent and control riots in U.P. in the mid-1990s.

34. Government of India, Minorities Commission, *First Annual Report for the Year Ending 31st December, 1978* (New Delhi: Government of India Press, 1979), p. 94.

35. Wilkinson's figures on the change in the composition of the U.P. police force indicate the dimensions of the problem; see Appendix Table A.4. His figures go up to 1981 only, but they would not be significantly different today.

36. Marc Gaborieau, "From Al-Beruni to Jinnah: Idiom, Ritual and Ideology of the Hindu-Muslim Confrontation in South Asia," *Anthropology Today* 1, no. 3 (1985), pp. 7–14. In contrast to Gaborieau, who sees riots as arising from the separate identities of Hindus and Muslims, van der Veer sees them as integral to the construction of opposed identities; Peter van der Veer, "Riots and Rituals: The Construction of Violence and Public Space in Hindu Nationalism," in Paul R. Brass (ed.), *Riots and Pogroms* (New York: NYU Press, 1982), pp. 154–77.

37. Bill Buford, *Among the Thugs* (New York: W. W. Norton, 1992).

38. Even ordinary behavior in India is sometimes defined by reference to a clause in the Indian Penal Code. Most famous in this regard, a clause known by everyone, including any foreigner with any serious knowledge of India, is clause 420, which refers to cheating. Persons and acts in everyday life—from overcharging on a taxi ride to every form of duplicity—are referred to as *char sau bis* (four hundred and twenty, spoken in English as "four-twenty").

39. E. Valentine Daniel, *Charred Lullabies: Chapters in an Anthropography of Violence* (Princeton, N.J.: Princeton University Press, 1996), pp. 28–60.

40. On the importance of the latter in Islamic history, see Francis Robinson, "Islamic History as the History of Learned and Holy Men," paper presented at the University of Washington in 1985 and as a lecture at the Centre d'Études de l'Inde et de l'Asie du Sud, "Lettre d'information, no. 5, Avril 1986."

41. In my first visit to India after the destruction of the mosque, I asked many people the same question over and over concerning that event: "Where were you when you first heard the news, what did you feel in your heart, and what did you do?" Several militant Hindus—BJP and RSS—replied in words to the effect that they felt that they had at last been released from slavery.

### POSTSCRIPT

1. *Frontline*, 19: 8 (April 13–26, 2002) points the finger directly at Chief Minister Narendra Modi, referring to him as "apparently, the alleged mastermind of the pogrom."

2. *Frontline* 19, no. 6 (March 16–29, 2002).

3. Asghar Ali Engineer, "Role of Police in Gujrat [*sic*] Carnage," *Secular Perspective*, June 16–30, 2002.

4. *Frontline* 19, no. 8 (April 13–26, 2002).

5. "Upwards of 1,500 Dead," *Frontline* 19, no. 6 (March 16–29, 2002). The figure of 2,000 was attributed to the British High Commission and announced over National Public Radio in the U.S. and the BBC World Service during the riots.

6. *Times of India*, March 27, 2002.

7. The number was given as fifteen in *Frontline* 19, no. 8 (April 13–26, 2002) and as sixteen in *Frontline* 19, no. 12 (June 8–21, 2002).

8. *Frontline* 19, no. 11 (May 25–June 7, 2002).

9. *Times of India,* March 27, 2002.

10. *Frontline* 19, no. 8 (April 13–26, 2002).

11. "An independent fact finding commission of eminent citizens"—professors from the Jawaharlal Nehru University and the Jamia Millia in New Delhi, and former senior bureaucrats in the government, including the police, none of them Muslims—described the Gujarat carnage as "a 'systematic and planned' pogrom against Muslims, carried out by the state government at the instigation of the Sangh Parivar" (*Deccan Herald*, April 11, 2002). All other fact-finding missions and commissions that visited Gujarat during the riots, including the National Human Rights Commission (NHRC) and the National Commission of Minorities, both statutory bodies of the government of India, have provided evidence that supports such charges; see *Frontline* 19, no. 8 (April 13–26, 2002). It also deserves note that the NHRC chairman is former Supreme Court Justice J. S. Verma, whose decisions in some cases affecting the RSS family of organizations have been considered favorable to those organizations and to the *Hindutva* ideology; see Gary Jeffrey Jacobsohn, *The Wheel of Law: India's Secularism in Comparative Perspective* (Princeton University Press, forthcoming), ch. 7. Several other independent organizations, such as the People's Union

for Civil Liberties, whose reports on Aligarh have also been cited in this book, all "indicted sever[e]ly the Gujarat government, the State police and outfits such as the Bajrang Dal and the Vishwa Hindu Parishad"; see *Frontline* 19, no. 12 (June 8–21, 2002).

12. *Frontline* 19, no. 6 (March 16–29, 2002).

13. *Sify News* (www.sify.com), March 7, 2002.

14. New Delhi Television (www.ndtv.com), March 12, 2002.

15. *The Hindu*, March 24, 2002; see also Asghar Ali Engineer, "Gujrat [*sic*]—An Area of Darkness," *Secular Perspective*, April 16–30, 2002.

16. *Frontline* 19, no. 7 (March 30–April 12, 2002); see also *Frontline* 19, no. 12 (June 8–21, 2002), where the papers singled out for special mention were *Sandesh* and *Gujarat Samachar*, along with "some local cable television channels."

17. "Report of a Delegation of the Communist Party of India (Marxist) and the All India Democratic Women's Association (AIDWA)," *The Hindu*, March 24, 2002, identifies the newspaper as *Sandesh*. I received this report via an e-mail message from Subhashini Ali that was forwarded to me by Clea Finkle. In subsequent notes, the Communist Party of India (Marxist) will be abbreviated "CPI(M)," and the document cited here will be abbreviated as the "CPI(M)-AIDWA report."

18. The names mentioned included Gujarat Home Minister Zadaphia [Jhadapiya] and Revenue Minister Harin Pandya (CPI(M)-AIDWA report), VHP leader Pravin Togadia, MLA Mayaben Kodnani, and VHP General Secretary Jaideep Patel; see *Frontline* 19, no. 8 (April 13–16, 2002).

19. This report names, for example, Bapu Jhadapiya, brother of Gujarat Home Minister Goverdhan Jhadapiya.

20. Asghar Ali Engineer, "BJP's Riot-Free India," *Secular Perspective*, March 16–31, and "Gujrat [*sic*]—An Area of Darkness."

21. *Frontline* 19, no. 8 (April 13–26, 2002).

22. *Frontline* 19, no. 11 (May 25–June 7, 2002).

23. A comment in *Frontline* 19, no. 11 (May 25–June 7, 2002) is noteworthy here, supporting the argument in this volume concerning the reasons why the central and state governments in India often do not act to control riots when they occur: "No one believes that the Union government will do the sensible thing and impose Central rule in Gujarat: it quite simply, has no reason to do so." In other words, from the point of view of functional-political utility, there was no advantage for the government to act. In fact, it would not be politically sensible. There were also political reasons for it not to act, the most important being that any action would have amounted to accepting the charges against its own party government in the state and would also have eliminated its last state bastion in the country after a series of electoral defeats for the BJP in other states.

24. *Frontline* 19, no. 6 (March 16–29, 2002).

25. *Frontline* 19, no. 8 (April 13–26, 2002).

26. The reasons are obvious, as reported in *Frontline* 19, no. 12 (June 8–21, 2002): "In the NHRC's view, the appointment of K. P. S. Gill as Security Adviser to the Chief Minister of Gujarat, Narendra Modi, implicitly confirmed that the State had failed to bring under control the persisting violation of the rights to life, liberty, equality and dignity of the people." The VHP, of course, openly criticized the appointment of Gill, calling it "objectionable"; see *Hindustan Times* (www.HindustanTimes.Com), May 9, 2002.

27. See *Hindustan Times* (www.HindustanTimes.com), May 8, 2002; and *Sify News* (www.sify.com), May 9, 2002.

28. *Frontline* 19, no. 11 (May 25–June 7, 2002).

29. *Frontline* 19, no. 13 (June 22–July 5, 2002).

30. Engineer, "BJP's Riot-Free India."

# INDEX

# INDEX OF *MOHALLAS*